HANDBOOK OF
THE ECONOMICS OF FINANCE
VOLUME 1A

HANDBOOKS
IN
ECONOMICS

21

Series Editors

KENNETH J. ARROW

MICHAEL D. INTRILIGATOR

ELSEVIER
NORTH
HOLLAND

Amsterdam • Boston • Heidelberg • London • New York • Oxford
Paris • San Diego • San Francisco • Singapore • Sydney • Tokyo

HANDBOOK OF THE ECONOMICS OF FINANCE

VOLUME 1A
CORPORATE FINANCE

Edited by

GEORGE M. CONSTANTINIDES
University of Chicago

MILTON HARRIS
University of Chicago

and

RENÉ M. STULZ
Ohio State University

2003

ELSEVIER
NORTH
HOLLAND

Amsterdam • Boston • Heidelberg • London • New York • Oxford
Paris • San Diego • San Francisco • Singapore • Sydney • Tokyo

ELSEVIER B.V.
Sara Burgerhartstraat 25
P.O. Box 211, 1000 AE Amsterdam, The Netherlands

First edition 2003

Library of Congress Cataloging-in-Publication Data
A catalog record from the Library of Congress has been applied for.

British Library Cataloguing in Publication Data
A catalogue record from the British Library has been applied for.

ISBN: 0-444-50298-X (set, comprising vols. 1A & 1B)
ISBN: 0-444-51362-0 (vol. 1A)
ISBN: 0-444-51363-9 (vol. 1B)
ISSN: 0169-7218 (Handbooks in Economics Series)

⊗ The paper used in this publication meets the requirements of ANSI/NISO Z39.48-1992 (Permanence of Paper).
Printed in The Netherlands.

INTRODUCTION TO THE SERIES

The aim of the *Handbooks in Economics* series is to produce Handbooks for various branches of economics, each of which is a definitive source, reference, and teaching supplement for use by professional researchers and advanced graduate students. Each Handbook provides self-contained surveys of the current state of a branch of economics in the form of chapters prepared by leading specialists on various aspects of this branch of economics. These surveys summarize not only received results but also newer developments, from recent journal articles and discussion papers. Some original material is also included, but the main goal is to provide comprehensive and accessible surveys. The Handbooks are intended to provide not only useful reference volumes for professional collections but also possible supplementary readings for advanced courses for graduate students in economics.

KENNETH J. ARROW and MICHAEL D. INTRILIGATOR

PUBLISHER'S NOTE

For a complete overview of the Handbooks in Economics Series, please refer to the listing at the end of this volume.

CONTENTS OF THE HANDBOOK

VOLUME 1B

FINANCIAL MARKETS AND ASSET PRICING

PREFACE

Financial economics applies the techniques of economic analysis to understand the savings and investment decisions by individuals, the investment, financing and payout decisions by firms, the level and properties of interest rates and prices of financial assets and derivatives, and the economic role of financial intermediaries. Until the 1950s, finance was viewed primarily as the study of financial institutional detail and was hardly accorded the status of a mainstream field of economics. This perception was epitomized by the difficulty Harry Markowitz had in receiving a PhD degree in the economics department at the University of Chicago for work that eventually would earn him a Nobel prize in economic science. This state of affairs changed in the second half of the 20th century with a revolution that took place from the 1950s to the early 1970s. At that time, key progress was made in understanding the financial decisions of individuals and firms and their implications for the pricing of common stocks, debt, and interest rates.

Harry Markowitz, William Sharpe, James Tobin, and others showed how individuals concerned about their expected future wealth and its variance make investment decisions. Their key results showing the benefits of diversification, that wealth is optimally allocated across funds that are common across individuals, and that investors are rewarded for bearing risks that are not diversifiable, are now the basis for much of the investment industry. Merton Miller and Franco Modigliani showed that the concept of arbitrage is a powerful tool to understand the implications of firm capital structures for firm value. In a world without frictions, they showed that a firm's value is unrelated to its capital structure. Eugene Fama put forth the efficient markets hypothesis and led the way in its empirical investigation. Finally, Fischer Black, Robert Merton and Myron Scholes provided one of the most elegant theories in all of economics: the theory of how to price financial derivatives in markets without frictions.

Following the revolution brought about by these fathers of modern finance, the field of finance has experienced tremendous progress. Along the way, it influenced public policy throughout the world in a major way, played a crucial role in the growth of a new $100 trillion dollar derivatives industry, and affected how firms are managed everywhere. However, finance also evolved from being at best a junior partner in economics to being often a leader. Key concepts and theories first developed in finance led to progress in other fields of economics. It is now common among economists to use theories of arbitrage, rational expectations, equilibrium, agency relations, and information asymmetries that were first developed in finance. The committee for the

Alfred Nobel Memorial Prize in economic science eventually recognized this state of affairs. Markowitz, Merton, Miller, Modigliani, Scholes, Sharpe, and Tobin received Nobel prizes for contributions in financial economics.

This Handbook presents the state of the field of finance fifty years after this revolution in modern finance started. The surveys are written by leaders in financial economics. They provide a comprehensive report on developments in both theory and empirical testing in finance at a level that, while rigorous, is nevertheless accessible to researchers not intimate with the field and doctoral students in economics, finance and related fields. By summarizing the state of the art and pointing out as-yet unresolved questions, this Handbook should prove an invaluable resource to researchers planning to contribute to the field and an excellent pedagogical tool for teaching doctoral students. The book is divided into two Volumes, corresponding to the traditional taxonomy of finance: corporate finance (1A) and financial markets and asset pricing (1B).

1. Corporate finance

Corporate finance is concerned with how businesses work, in particular, how they allocate capital (traditionally, "the capital budgeting decision") and how they obtain capital ("the financing decision"). Though managers play no independent role in the work of Miller and Modigliani, major contributions in finance since then have shown that managers maximize their own objectives. To understand the firm's decisions, it is therefore necessary to understand the forces that lead managers to maximize the wealth of shareholders. For example, a number of researchers have emphasized the positive and negative roles of large shareholders in aligning incentives of managers and shareholders. The part of the Handbook devoted to corporate finance starts with an overview, entitled *Corporate Governance and Control,* by Marco Becht, Patrick Bolton, and Ailsa Röell (Chapter 1) of the framework in which managerial activities take place. Their broad survey covers everything about corporate governance, from its history and importance to theories and empirical evidence to cross-country comparisons.

Following the survey of corporate governance in Chapter 1, two complementary essays discuss the investment decision. In *Agency, Information and Corporate Investment,* Jeremy Stein (Chapter 2) focuses on the effects of agency problems and asymmetric information on the allocation of capital, both across firms and within firms. This survey does not address the issue of how to value a proposed investment project, given information about the project. That topic is considered in *Corporate Investment Policy* by Michael Brennan in Chapter 3. Brennan draws out the implications of recent developments in asset pricing, including option pricing techniques and tax considerations, for evaluating investment projects.

In Chapter 4, *Financing of Corporations,* the focus moves to the financing decision. Stewart Myers provides an overview of the research that seeks to explain firms' capital structure, that is, the types and proportions of securities firms use to finance their investments. Myers covers the traditional theories that attempt to explain proportions of debt and equity financing as well as more recent theories that attempt to explain the characteristics of the securities issued. In assessing the different capital structure theories, he concludes that he does not expect that there will ever be "one" capital structure theory that applies to all firms. Rather, he believes that we will always use different theories to explain the behavior of different types of firms. In Chapter 5, *Investment Banking and Security Issuance,* Jay Ritter is concerned with how firms raise equity and the role of investment banks in that process. He examines both initial public offerings and seasoned equity offerings. A striking result discovered first by Ritter is that firms that issue equity experience poor long-term stock returns afterwards. This result has led to a number of vigorous controversies that Ritter reviews in this chapter.

Firms may also obtain capital by issuing securities other than equity and debt. A hallmark of the last thirty years has been the tremendous amount of financial innovation that has taken place. Though some of the innovations fizzled and others provided fodder to crooks, financial innovation can enable firms to undertake profitable projects that otherwise they would not be able to undertake. In Chapter 6, *Financial Innovation,* Peter Tufano delves deeper into the issues of security design and financial innovation. He reviews the process of financial innovation and explanations of the quantity of innovation.

Investors do not purchase equity without expecting a return from their investment. In one of their classic papers, Miller and Modigliani show that, in the absence of frictions, dividend policy is irrelevant for firm value. Since then, a large literature has developed that identifies when dividend policy matters and when it does not. Franklin Allen and Roni Michaely (Chapter 7) survey this literature in their essay entitled *Payout Policy.* Allen and Michaely consider the roles of taxes, asymmetric information, incomplete contracting and transaction costs in determining payouts to equity holders, both dividends and share repurchases.

Chapter 8, *Financial Intermediation,* focuses more directly on the role financial intermediaries play. Although some investment is funded directly through capital markets, according to Gary Gorton and Andrew Winton, the vast majority of external investment flows through financial intermediaries. In Chapter 8, Gorton and Winton survey the literature on financial intermediation with emphasis on banking. They explore why intermediaries exist, discuss banking crises, and examine why and how they are regulated. Exchanges on which securities are traded play a crucial role in intermediating between individuals who want to buy securities and others who want to sell them. In many ways, they are special types of corporations whose workings affect the value of financial securities as well as the size of financial markets.

The Handbook contains two chapters that deal with the issues of how securities are traded. *Market Microstructure,* by Hans Stoll (Chapter 9), focuses on how exchanges perform their functions as financial intermediaries and therefore is included in this part. Stoll examines explanations of the bid-ask spread, the empirical evidence for these explanations, and the implications for market design. *Microstructure and Asset Pricing,* by Maureen O'Hara and David Easley (Chapter 17), examines the implications of how securities trade for the properties of securities returns and is included in Volume 1B on *Financial Markets and Asset Pricing.*

2. Financial markets and asset pricing

A central theme in finance and economics is the pursuit of an understanding of how the prices of financial securities are determined in financial markets. Currently, there is immense interest among academics, policy makers, and practitioners in whether these markets get prices right, fueled in part by the large daily volatility in prices and by the large increase in stock prices over most of the 1990s, followed by the sharp decrease in prices at the turn of the century. Our understanding of how securities are priced is far from complete. In the early 1960s, Eugene Fama from the University of Chicago established the foundations for the "efficient markets" view that financial markets are highly effective in incorporating information into asset prices. This view led to a large body of empirical and theoretical work. Some of the chapters in this part of the Handbook review that body of work, but the "efficient markets" view has been challenged by the emergence of a new, controversial field, behavioral finance, which seeks to show that psychological biases of individuals affect the pricing of securities. There is therefore divergence of opinion and critical reexamination of given doctrine. This is fertile ground for creative thinking and innovation.

In Volume 1B of the Handbook, we invite the reader to partake in this intellectual odyssey. We present eleven original essays on the economics of financial markets. The divergence of opinion and puzzles presented in these essays belies the incredible progress made by financial economists over the second half of the 20th century that lay the foundations for future research.

The modern quantitative approach to finance has its origins in neoclassical economics. In the opening essay titled *Arbitrage, State Prices and Portfolio Theory* (Chapter 10), Philip Dybvig and Stephen Ross illustrate a surprisingly large amount of the intuition and intellectual content of modern finance in the context of a single-period, perfect-markets neoclassical model. They discuss the fundamental theorems of asset pricing – the consequences of the absence of arbitrage, optimal portfolio choice, the properties of efficient portfolios, aggregation, the capital asset-pricing model (CAPM), mutual fund separation, and the arbitrage pricing theory (APT). A number of these notions may be traced to the original contributions of Stephen Ross.

In his essay titled *Intertemporal Asset Pricing Theory* (Chapter 11), Darrell Duffie provides a systematic development of the theory of intertemporal asset pricing, first in a discrete-time setting and then in a continuous-time setting. As applications of the basic theory, Duffie also presents comprehensive treatments of the term structure of interest rates and fixed-income pricing, derivative pricing, and the pricing of corporate securities with default modeled both as an endogenous and an exogenous process.

These applications are discussed in further detail in some of the subsequent essays. Duffie's essay is comprehensive and authoritative and may serve as the basis of an entire 2nd-year PhD-level course on asset pricing.

Historically, the empirically testable implications of asset-pricing theory have been couched in terms of the mean-variance efficiency of a given portfolio, the validity of a multifactor pricing model with given factors, or the validity of a given stochastic discount factor. Furthermore, different methodologies have been developed and applied in the testing of these implications. In *Tests of Multi-Factor Pricing Models, Volatility, and Portfolio Performance* (Chapter 12), Wayne Ferson discusses the empirical methodologies applied in testing asset-pricing models. He points out that these three statements of the empirically testable implications are essentially equivalent *and* that the seemingly different empirical methodologies are equivalent as well.

In his essay titled *Consumption-Based Asset Pricing* (Chapter 13), John Campbell begins by reviewing the salient features of the joint behavior of equity returns, aggregate dividends, the interest rate, and aggregate consumption in the USA. Features that challenge existing asset-pricing theory include, but are not limited to, the "equity premium puzzle": the finding that the low covariance of the growth rate of aggregate consumption with equity returns is a major stumbling block in explaining the mean aggregate equity premium and the cross-section of asset returns, in the context of the representative-consumer, time-separable-preferences models examined by Grossman and Shiller (1981), Hansen and Singleton (1983), and Mehra and Prescott (1985). Campbell also examines data from other countries to see which features of the USA data are pervasive. He then proceeds to relate these findings to recent developments in asset-pricing theory that relax various assumptions of the standard asset-pricing model.

In a closely related essay titled *The Equity Premium in Retrospect* (Chapter 14), Rajnish Mehra and Edward Prescott – the researchers who coined the term – critically reexamine the data sources used to document the equity premium puzzle in the USA and other major industrial countries. They then proceed to relate these findings to recent developments in asset-pricing theory by employing the methodological tool of calibration, as opposed to the standard empirical estimation of model parameters and the testing of over-identifying restrictions. Mehra and Prescott have different views than Campbell as to which assumptions of the standard asset-pricing model need to be relaxed in order to address the stylized empirical findings.

Why are these questions important? First and foremost, financial markets play a central role in the allocation of investment capital and in the sharing of risk. Failure to answer these questions suggests that our understanding of the fundamental process of capital allocation is highly imperfect. Second, the basic economic paradigm employed in analyzing financial markets is closely related to the paradigm employed in the study of business cycles and growth. Failure to explain the stylized facts of financial markets calls into question the appropriateness of the related paradigms for the study of macro-economic issues. The above two essays convey correctly the *status quo* that the puzzle is at the forefront of academic interest and that views regarding its resolution are divergent.

Several goals are accomplished in William Schwert's comprehensive and incisive essay titled *Anomalies and Market Efficiency* (Chapter 15). First, Schwert discusses cross-sectional and time-series regularities in asset returns, both at the aggregate and disaggregate level. These include the size, book-to-market, momentum, and dividend yield effects. Second, Schwert discusses differences in returns realized by different types of investors, including individual and institutional investors. Third, he evaluates the role of measurement issues in many of the papers that study anomalies, including the difficult issues associated with long-horizon return performance. Finally, Schwert discusses the implications of the anomalies literature for asset-pricing and corporate finance theories. In discussing the informational efficiency of the market, Schwert points out that tests of market efficiency are also joint tests of market efficiency and a particular equilibrium asset-pricing model.

In the essay titled *Are Financial Assets Priced Locally or Globally?* (Chapter 16), Andrew Karolyi and René Stulz discuss the theoretical implications of and empirical evidence concerning asset-pricing theory as it applies to international equities markets. They explain that country-risk premia are determined internationally, but the evidence is weak on whether international factors affect the cross-section of expected returns. A long-standing puzzle in international finance is that investors invest more heavily in domestic equities than predicted by the theory. Karolyi and Stulz argue that barriers to international investment only partly resolve the home-bias puzzle. They conclude that contagion – the linkage of international markets – may be far less prevalent than commonly assumed.

At frequencies lower than the daily frequency, asset-pricing theory generally ignores the role of the microstructure of financial markets. In their essay titled *Microstructure and Asset Pricing* (Chapter 17), David Easley and Maureen O'Hara survey the theoretical and empirical literature linking microstructure factors to long-run returns, and focus on why stock prices might be expected to reflect premia related to liquidity or informational asymmetries. They show that asset-pricing dynamics may be better understood by recognizing the role played by microstructure factors and the linkages of microstructure and fundamental economic variables.

All the models that are discussed in the essays by Campbell, Mehra and Prescott, Schwert, Karolyi and Stulz, and Easley and O'Hara are variations of the neoclassical asset-pricing model. The model is *rational,* in that investors process information rationally and have unambiguously defined preferences over consumption. Naturally, the model allows for market incompleteness, market imperfections, informational asymmetries, and learning. The model also allows for differences among assets for liquidity, transaction costs, tax status, and other institutional factors. Many of these variations are explored in the above essays.

In their essay titled *A Survey of Behavioral Finance* (Chapter 18), Nicholas Barberis and Richard Thaler provide a counterpoint to the rational model by providing explanations of the cross-sectional and time-series regularities in asset returns by relying on economic models that are less than fully rational. These include cultural and psychological factors and tap into the rich and burgeoning literature on behavioral economics and finance. Robert Shiller, who is, along with Richard Thaler, one of the founders of behavioral finance, provides his personal perspective on behavioral finance in his statement titled *Finance, Optimization and the Irreducibly Irrational Component of Human Behavior.*

One of the towering achievements in finance in the second half of the 20th century is the celebrated option-pricing theory of Black and Scholes (1973) and Merton (1973). The model has had a profound influence on the course of economic thought. In his essay titled *Derivatives* (Chapter 19), Robert Whaley provides comprehensive coverage of the topic. Following a historical overview of futures and options, he proceeds to derive the implications of the law of one price and then the Black–Scholes–Merton theory. He concludes with a systematic coverage of the empirical evidence and a discussion of the social costs and benefits associated with the introduction of derivatives. Whaley's thorough and insightful essay provides an easy entry to an important topic that many economists find intimidating.

In their essay titled *Fixed-Income Pricing* (Chapter 20), Qiang Dai and Ken Singleton survey the literature on fixed-income pricing models, including term structure models, fixed-income derivatives, and models of defaultable securities. They point out that this literature is vast, with both the academic and practitioner communities having proposed a wide variety of models. In guiding the reader through these models, they explain that different applications call for different models based on the trade-offs of complexity, flexibility, tractability, and data availability – the "art" of modeling. The Dai and Singleton essay, combined with Duffie's earlier essay, provides an insightful and authoritative introduction to the world of fixed-income pricing models at the advanced MBA and PhD levels.

We hope that the contributions represented by these essays communicate the excitement of financial economics to beginners and specialists alike and stimulate further research.

We thank Rodolfo Martell for his help in processing the papers for publication.

GEORGE M. CONSTANTINIDES
University of Chicago, Chicago

MILTON HARRIS
University of Chicago, Chicago

RENÉ STULZ
Ohio State University, Columbus

References

Black, F., and M.S. Scholes (1973), "The pricing of options and corporate liabilities", Journal of Political Economy 81:637–654.

Grossman, S.J., and R.J. Shiller (1981), "The determinants of the variability of stock market prices", American Economic Review Papers and Proceedings 71:222–227.

Hansen, L.P., and K.J. Singleton (1982), "Generalized instrumental variables estimation of nonlinear rational expectations models", Econometrica 50:1269–1288.

Mehra, R., and E.C. Prescott (1985), "The equity premium: a puzzle", Journal of Monetary Economics 15:145–161.

Merton, R.C. (1973), "Theory of rational option pricing", Bell Journal of Economics and Management Science 4:141–183.

CONTENTS OF VOLUME 1A

Chapter 1

CORPORATE GOVERNANCE AND CONTROL

MARCO BECHT*

ECARES, Université Libre de Bruxelles and European Corporate Governance Institute (ECGI)

PATRICK BOLTON*

Bendheim Center for Finance at Princeton University, NBER, CEPR and ECGI

AILSA RÖELL*

Bendheim Center for Finance at Princeton University, CEPR and ECGI

Contents

* We are grateful to Bernardo Bortolotti, Mathias Dewatripont, Richard Frederick, Stu Gillan, Peter Gourevitch, Milton Harris, Gerard Hertig, Takeo Hoshi, Steve Kaplan, Roberta Romano, Christian Rydqvist and Scott Verges for helpful input and comments.

Handbook of the Economics of Finance, Edited by G.M. Constantinides, M. Harris and R. Stulz

Abstract

Corporate governance is concerned with the resolution of collective action problems among dispersed investors and the reconciliation of conflicts of interest between various corporate claimholders. In this survey we review the theoretical and empirical research on the main mechanisms of corporate control, discuss the main legal and regulatory institutions in different countries, and examine the comparative corporate governance literature. A fundamental dilemma of corporate governance emerges from this overview: regulation of large shareholder intervention may provide better protection to small shareholders; but such regulations may increase managerial discretion and scope for abuse.

Keywords

corporate governance, ownership, takeovers, block holders, boards

JEL classification: G32, G34

1. Introduction

At the most basic level a corporate governance problem arises whenever an outside investor wishes to exercise control differently from the manager in charge of the firm. Dispersed ownership magnifies the problem by giving rise to conflicts of interest between the various corporate claimholders and by creating a collective action problem among investors. [1]

Most research on corporate governance has been concerned with the resolution of this collective action problem. Five alternative mechanisms may mitigate it: i) partial concentration of ownership and control in the hands of one or a few large investors; ii) hostile takeovers and proxy voting contests, which concentrate ownership and/or voting power temporarily when needed; iii) delegation and concentration of control in the board of directors; iv) alignment of managerial interests with investors through executive compensation contracts; and v) clearly defined fiduciary duties for CEOs together with class-action suits that either block corporate decisions that go against investors' interests, or seek compensation for past actions that have harmed their interests.

In this survey we review the theoretical and empirical research on these five main mechanisms and discuss the main legal and regulatory institutions of corporate governance in different countries. We discuss how different classes of investors and other constituencies can or ought to participate in corporate governance. We also review the comparative corporate governance literature. [2]

The favored mechanism for resolving collective action problems among shareholders in most countries appears to be partial ownership and control concentration in the hands of large shareholders. [3] Two important costs of this form of governance have been emphasized: i) the potential collusion of large shareholders with management against smaller investors; and ii) the reduced liquidity of secondary markets. In an attempt to boost stock market liquidity and limit the potential abuse of minority shareholders some countries' corporate law drastically curbs the power of large shareholders. [4] These countries rely on the board of directors as the main mechanism for co-ordinating shareholder actions. But boards are widely perceived to be ineffective. [5] Thus, while minority shareholders get better protection in these countries, managers may also have greater discretion.

---

[1] See Zingales (1998) for a similar definition.

[2] We do not cover the extensive strategy and management literature; see Pettigrew, Thomas and Whittington (2002) for an overview, in particular Davis and Useem (2002).

[3] See ECGN (1997), La Porta et al. (1999), Claessens et al. (2000) and Barca and Becht (2001) for evidence on control concentration in different countries.

[4] Black (1990) provides a detailed description of the various legal and regulatory limits on the exercise of power by large shareholders in the USA. Wymeersch (2003) discusses legal impediments to large shareholder actions outside the USA.

[5] Gilson and Kraakman (1991) provide analysis and an agenda for board reform in the USA against the background of a declining market for corporate control and scattered institutional investor votes.

In a nutshell, the fundamental issue concerning governance by shareholders today seems to be how to regulate large or active shareholders so as to obtain the right balance between managerial discretion and small shareholder protection. Before exploring in greater detail the different facets of this issue and the five basic mechanisms described above, it is instructive to begin with a brief overview of historical origins and early writings on the subject.

2. Historical origins: a brief sketch

The term "corporate governance" derives from an analogy between the government of cities, nations or states and the governance of corporations.[6] The early corporate finance textbooks saw "representative government" [Mead (1928, p. 31)] as an important advantage of the corporation over partnerships but there has been and still is little agreement on how representative corporate governance really is, or whom it should represent.

2.1. How representative is corporate government?

The institutional arrangements surrounding corporate elections and the role and fiduciary duties of the board have been the central themes in the corporate governance literature from its inception. The dilemma of how to balance limits on managerial discretion and small investor protection is ever present. Should one limit the power of corporate plutocrats (large shareholders or voting trusts) or should one tolerate concentrated voting power as a way of limiting managerial discretion?

The concern of early writers of corporate charters was the establishment of "corporate suffrage", where each member (shareholder) had one vote [Dunlavy (1998)]. The aim was to establish "democracy" by eliminating special privileges of some members and by limiting the number of votes each shareholder could cast, irrespective of the number of shares held.[7] However, just as "corporate democracy" was being established it was already being transformed into "plutocracy" by moving towards "one-share–one-vote" and thus allowing for concentrated ownership and control [Dunlavy (1998)].[8]

In the USA this was followed by two distinct systems of "corporate feudalism":

---

[6] The analogy between corporate and political voting was explicit in early corporate charters and writings, dating back to the revolutionary origins of the American corporation and the first railway corporations in Germany [Dunlavy (1998)]. The precise term "corporate governance" itself seems to have been used first by [Richard Eells (1960, p. 108)], to denote "the structure and functioning of the corporate polity".

[7] Frequently voting scales were used to achieve this aim. For example, under the voting scale imposed by a Virginia law of 1836 shareholders of manufacturing corporations cast "one vote for each share up to 15, one vote for every five shares from 15 to 100, and one vote for each increment of 20 shares above 100 shares" [Dunlavy (1998, p. 18)].

[8] Voting right restrictions survived until very recently in Germany [Franks and Mayer (2001)]. They are still in use in Denmark, France, Spain and other European countries [Becht and Mayer (2001)].

first, to the voting trusts[9] and holding companies[10] [Cushing (1915), Mead (1903), Liefmann (1909, 1920] originating in the "Gilded Age" [Twain and Warner (1873)][11] and later to the managerial corporation.[12] The "captains of industry" in the trusts and hierarchical groups controlled the majority of votes in vast corporate empires with relatively small(er) amounts of capital, allowing them to exert product market power and leaving ample room for self-dealing.[13] In contrast, the later managerial corporations were controlled mainly by professional managers and most of their shareholders were too small and numerous to have a say. In these firms control was effectively separated from ownership.[14]

Today corporate feudalism of the managerial variety in the USA and the "captain of industry" kind elsewhere is challenged by calls for more "shareholder democracy", a global movement that finds its roots with the "corporate Jacksonians" of the 1960s in the USA.[15]

---

[9] Under a typical voting trust agreement shareholders transfer their shares to a trust and receive certificates in return. The certificate holders elect a group of trustees who vote the deposited shares. Voting trusts were an improvement over pooling agreements and designed to restrict product market competition. They offered two principal advantages: putting the stock of several companies into the voting trust ensured that the trustees had permanent control over the management of the various operating companies, allowing them to enforce a common policy on output and prices; the certificates issued by the voting trust could be widely placed and traded on a stock exchange.

[10] Holding companies have the purpose of owning and voting shares in other companies. After the passage of the Sherman Antitrust Act in 1890 many of the voting trusts converted themselves into New Jersey registered holding companies ("industrial combinations") that were identical in function, but escaped the initial round of antitrust legislation, for example the Sugar Trust in 1891 [Mead (1903, p. 44)] and Rockefeller's Standard Oil in 1892 [Mead (1903, p. 35)].

[11] The "captains of industry" of this era, also referred to as the "Robber Barons" [Josephson (1934), DeLong (1998)], were the target of an early anti-trust movement that culminated in the election of Woodrow Wilson as USA President in 1912. Standard Oil was broken up even before (in 1911) under the Sherman Act of 1890 and converted from a corporation that was tightly controlled by the Rockefeller clan to a managerial corporation. Trust finance disappeared from the early corporate finance textbooks [for example Mead (1912) vs. Mead (1928)]. In 1929 Rockefeller Jr. (14.9%) ousted the scandal ridden Chairman of Standard Oil of Indiana, who enjoyed the full support of his board, only by small margin, an example that was widely used for illustrating how much the balance of power had swung from the "Robber Barons" to management [Berle and Means (1932, pp. 82–83), cited in Galbraith (1967)], another type of feudal lord.

[12] For Berle and Means (1930): "[the] "publicly owned" stock corporation in America ... constitutes an institution analogous to the feudal system in the Middle Ages".

[13] They also laid the foundations for some of the World's finest arts collections, philanthropic foundations and university endowments.

[14] This "separation of ownership and control" triggered a huge public and academic debate of "the corporate problem"; see, for example, the Berle and Means symposia in the *Columbia Law Review* (1964) and the *Journal of Law and Economics* (1983). Before Means (1931a,b) and Berle and Means (1930, 1932) the point was argued in Lippmann (1914), Veblen (1923), Carver (1925), Ripley (1927) and Wormser (1931); see Hessen (1983).

[15] Non-Americans often consider shareholder activism as a free-market movement and associated calls for more small shareholder power as a part of the conservative agenda. They are puzzled when they

As an alternative to shareholder activism some commentators in the 1960s proposed for the first time that hostile takeovers might be a more effective way of disciplining management. Thus, Rostow (1959, p. 47) argued, "the raider persuades the stockholders for once to act as if they really were stockholders, in the black-letter sense of the term, each with the voice of partial ownership and a partial owner's responsibility for the election of directors". Similarly, Manne (1964, p. 1445) wrote, "vote selling [. . .] negatives many of the criticisms often levelled at the public corporation". As we shall see, the abstract "market for corporate control" has remained a central theme in the corporate governance literature.

2.2. *Whom should corporate government represent?*

The debate on whether management should run the corporation solely in the interests of shareholders or whether it should take account of other constituencies is almost as old as the first writings on corporate governance. Berle (1931) held the view that corporate powers are powers in trust for shareholders and nobody else.[16] But, Dodd (1932, p. 1162) argued that: "[business] is private property only in the qualified sense, and society may properly demand that it be carried on in such a way as to safeguard the interests of those who deal with it either as employees or consumers even if the proprietary rights of its owners are thereby curtailed". Berle (1932) disagreed on the grounds that responsibility to multiple parties would exacerbate the separation of ownership and control and make management even less accountable to shareholders.[17]

There is nowadays a voluminous literature on corporate governance. On many key issues our understanding has improved enormously since the 1930s. Remarkably though, some of the main issues over which the early writers have been debating remain central today.

3. Why corporate governance is currently such a prominent issue

Why has corporate governance become such a prominent topic in the past two decades or so and not before? We have identified, in no particular order, the following reasons:

---

learn that shareholder activism today has its roots in part of the anti-Vietnam War, anti-apartheid and anti-tobacco movements and has close links with the unions. In terms of government (of corporations) there is no contradiction. The "corporate Jacksonians", as a prominent critic called them [Manning (1958, p. 1489)], are named after the 7th President of the USA (1829–37) who introduced universal male suffrage and organised the Democratic Party that has historically represented minorities, labour and progressive reformers (*Encyclopaedia Britannica:* Jackson, Andrew; Democratic Party).

[16] Consequently "all powers granted to a corporation or to the management of a corporation, or to any group within the corporation, whether derived from statute or charter or both, are necessarily and at all times exercisable only for the ratable benefit of all the shareholders as their interest appears", Berle (1931).

[17] He seems to have changed his mind some twenty years later as he wrote that he was "squarely in favour of Professor Dodd's contention"[Berle (1954)]. For a comprehensive account of the Berle–Dodd dialogue see Weiner (1964) and for additional papers arguing both points of view Mason (1959). Galbraith (1967) in his influential *The New Industrial State* took Dodd's position.

i) the world-wide wave of privatization of the past two decades; ii) pension fund reform and the growth of private savings; iii) the takeover wave of the 1980s; iv) deregulation and the integration of capital markets; v) the 1998 East Asia crisis, which has put the spotlight on corporate governance in emerging markets; vi) a series of recent USA scandals and corporate failures that built up but did not surface during the bull market of the late 1990s.

3.1. The world-wide privatization wave

Privatization has been an important phenomenon in Latin America, Western Europe, Asia and (obviously) the former Soviet block, but not in the USA where state ownership of enterprises has always been very small (see Figure 1). On average, since 1990 OECD privatization programmes have generated proceeds equivalent to 2.7% of total GDP, and in some cases up to 27% of country GDP. The privatization wave started in the UK, which was responsible for 58% of OECD and 90% of European Community privatization proceeds in 1991. Since 1995 Australia, Italy, France, Japan and Spain alone have generated 60% of total privatization revenues.

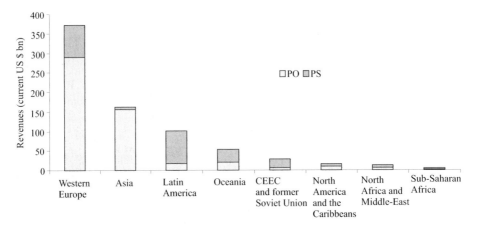

Fig. 1. Privatization revenues by region 1977–97. Source: Bortolotti, Fantini and Siniscalco (2000). PO, public offerings; PS, private sales.

Inevitably, the privatization wave has raized the issue of how the newly privatized corporations should be owned and controlled. In some countries, most notably the UK, part of the agenda behind the massive privatization program was to attempt to recreate a form of "shareholder democracy" [18] [see Biais and Perotti (2002)]. In other countries

---

[18] A state-owned and -controlled company is indirectly owned by the citizens via the state, which has a say in the affairs of the company. In a "shareholder democracy" each citizen holds a small share in the widely held company, having a direct interest and – theoretically – say in the affairs of the company.

great care was given to ensure the transfer of control to large shareholders. The issues surrounding the choice of privatization method rekindled interest in governance issues; indeed Shinn (2001) finds that the state's new role as a public shareholder in privatized corporations has been an important source of impetus for changes in corporate governance practices worldwide. In general, privatizations have boosted the role of stock markets as most OECD sales have been conducted via public offerings, and this has also focused attention on the protection of small shareholders.

3.2. Pension funds and active investors

The growth in defined contribution pension plans has channelled an increasing fraction of household savings through mutual and pension funds and has created a constituency of investors that is large and powerful enough to be able to influence corporate governance. Table 1 illustrates how the share of financial assets controlled by institutional investors has steadily grown over the 1990s in OECD countries. It also highlights the disproportionately large institutional holdings in small countries with large financial centres, like Switzerland, the Netherlands and Luxembourg. Institutional investors in the USA alone command slightly more than 50% of the total assets under management and 59.7% of total equity investment in the OECD, rising to 60.1% and 76.3%, respectively, when UK institutions are added. A significant proportion is held by pension funds (for USA and UK based funds, 35.1% and 40.1% of total assets, respectively). These funds are playing an increasingly active role in global corporate governance. In the USA ERISA [19] regulations oblige pension funds to cast the votes in their portfolio responsibly. This has led to the emergence of a service industry that makes voting recommendations and exercises votes for clients. The largest providers now offer global services.

Japanese institutional investors command 13.7% of total institutional investor assets in the OECD but just 8.3% of the equities. These investors are becoming more demanding and they are one of the forces behind the rapid transformation of the Japanese corporate governance system. As a percentage of GDP, the holdings of Italian and German institutional investors are small (39.9% and 49.9% in 1996) and well below the OECD average of 83.8%. The ongoing reform of the pension systems in both countries and changing savings patterns, however, are likely to change this picture in the near future. [20]

---

[19] ERISA stands for the Employee Retirement Income Security Act of 1974.

[20] One note of caution. The figures for Luxemburg and Switzerland illustrate that figures are compiled on the basis of the geographical location of the fund managers, not the origin of the funds under management. Judging from the GDP figures, it is very likely that a substantial proportion of the funds administered in the UK, the USA, Switzerland and the Netherlands belong to citizens of other countries. For governance the location of the fund managers matters. They make the investment decisions and have the power to vote the equity in their portfolios and the sheer size of the numbers suggests that fund governance is a topic in its own right.

Table 1
Financial assets of institutional investors in OECD countries[a]

	Value assets (billion US $)		Asset growth 1990–96	% Total OECD assets	Assets as % GDP		Pension funds 1996 (%)	Insurance comp. 1996 (%)	Invest. comp. 1996 (%)	Assets in equity 1996 (%)	OECD equity 1996 (%)
	1990	1996			1990	1996					
Australia	145.6	331.1	127.4	1.3	49.3	83.8	36.3	46.0	14.1	52	1.9
Austria	38.8	90.1	132.2	0.3	24.3	39.4	3.0	53.3	43.7	8	0.1
Belgium	87.0	169.1	94.4	0.7	44.4	63	6.5	49.0	41.0	23	0.4
Canada	332.8	560.5	68.4	2.2	58.1	94.6	43.0	31.4	25.7	9	0.6
Czech Republic	–	7.3[b]	–	–	–	–	–	–	–	–	<0.1
Denmark	74.2	123.5	66.4	0.5	55.6	67.1	25.2	67.2	7.6	31	0.4
Finland	44.7	71.2	59.3	0.3	33.2	57	–	24.6	3.4	23	0.2
France	655.7	1,278.1	94.9	4.9	54.8	83.1	5.5	55.2	44.8	26	3.7
Germany	599.0	1,167.9	95.0	4.5	36.5	49.9	5.5	59.2	35.3	14	1.8
Greece	5.4	35.1	550.0	0.1	6.5	28.5	41.6	12.3	46.2	6	<0.1
Hungary	–	2.6	–	<0.1	–	5.7	–	65.4	26.9	6	<0.1
Iceland	2.9	5.8	100.0	<0.1	45.7	78.7	79.3	12.1	8.6	6	<0.1
Italy	146.6	484.6	230.6	1.9	13.4	39.9	8.1	30.1	26.6	12	0.6
Japan	2427.9	3563.6	46.8	13.7	81.7	77.6	–	48.9	12.6	21	8.3
Korea	121.9	277.8	127.9	1.1	48	57.3	4.9	43.4	51.7	12	0.4
Luxembourg	95.9	392.1	308.9	1.5	926.8	2139.1	0.8	–	99.2		<0.1
Mexico	23.1	14.9	−35.5	0.1	8.8	4.5		32.9	67.1	17	<0.1
Netherlands	378.3	671.2	77.4	2.6	133.4	169.1	55.2	33.5	9.9	28	2.1
New Zealand	–	24.9	–	0.1	–	38.1	–	31.7	17.3	37	0.1
Norway	41.5	68.6	65.3	0.3	36	43.4	14.9	70.1	15.0	20	0.2

continued on next page

Table 1, *continued*

	Value assets (billion US $)		Asset growth 1990–96	% Total OECD assets	Assets as % GDP		Pension funds 1996 (%)	Insurance comp. 1996 (%)	Invest. comp. 1996 (%)	Assets in equity 1996 (%)	OECD equity 1996 (%)
	1990	1996			1990	1996					
Poland	–	2.7	–	<0.1	–	2	–	81.5	18.5	23	<0.1
Portugal	6.2	37.5	504.8	0.1	9	34.4	26.4	27.2	45.1	9	<0.1
Spain	78.9	264.5	235.2	1.0	16	45.4	4.5	41.0	54.5	6	0.2
Sweden	196.8	302.9	53.9	1.2	85.7	120.3	2.0	47.3	19.8	40	1.4
Switzerland	271.7	449.8	65.6	1.7	119	77.3	49.3	40.2	10.5	24	1.2
Turkey	0.9	2.3	155.6	<0.1	0.6	1.3	–	47.8	52.2	8	<0.1
UK	1116.8	2226.9	99.4	8.6	114.5	193.1	40.1	45.9	14.0	67	16.6
USA	6875.7	13382.1	94.6	51.5	123.8	181.1	35.6	22.6	25.2	40	59.7
Total OECD	15758.3	26001.4									
Mean OECD			94.6		49.3	83.8	26.3	33.6	24.9	22	

a Source: OECD (1999), *Institutional Investors Statistical Yearbook 1998*, Tables S.1., S.2., S.3., S.4., S.6., S.11, and own calculations.
b Value in 1994.

3.3. Mergers and takeovers

The hostile takeover wave in the USA in the 1980s and in Europe in the 1990s, together with the recent merger wave, has also fuelled the public debate on corporate governance. The successful $199 billion cross-border hostile bid of Vodafone for Mannesmann in 2000 was the largest ever to take place in Europe. The recent hostile takeovers in Italy (Olivetti for Telecom Italia; Generali for INA) and in France (BNP-Paribas; Elf Aquitaine for Total Fina) have spectacularly shaken up the sleepy corporate world of continental Europe. Interestingly, these deals involve newly privatized giants. It is also remarkable that they have not been opposed by the social democratic administrations in place at the time. Understandably, these high profile cases have moved takeover regulation of domestic and cross-border deals in the European Union to the top of the political agenda.

3.4. Deregulation and capital market integration

Corporate governance rules have been promoted in part as a way of protecting and encouraging foreign investment in Eastern Europe, Asia and other emerging markets. The greater integration of world capital markets (in particular in the European Union following the introduction of the Euro) and the growth in equity capital throughout the 1990s have also been a significant factor in rekindling interest in corporate governance issues. Increasingly fast growing corporations in Europe have been raising capital from different sources by cross listing on multiple exchanges [Pagano, Röell and Zechner (2002)]. In the process they have had to contend more with USA and UK pension funds. This has inevitably contributed to the spread of an 'equity culture' outside the USA and UK.

3.5. The 1998 Russia/East Asia/Brazil crisis

The East Asia crisis has highlighted the flimsy protections investors in emerging markets have and put the spotlight on the weak corporate governance practices in these markets. The crisis has also led to a reassessment of the Asian model of industrial organisation and finance around highly centralized and hierarchical industrial groups controlled by management and large investors. There has been a similar reassessment of mass insider privatization and its concomitant weak protection of small investors in Russia and other transition economies.

The crisis has led international policy makers to conclude that macro-management is not sufficient to prevent crises and their contagion in an integrated global economy. Thus, in South Korea, the International Monetary Fund has imposed detailed structural conditions that go far beyond the usual Fund policy. It is no coincidence that corporate governance reform in Russia, Asia and Brazil has been a top priority for the OECD, the World Bank and institutional investor activists.

3.6. Scandals and failures at major USA corporations

As we are writing, a series of scandals and corporate failures is surfacing in the United States, a market where the other factors we highlighted played a less important role. [21] Many of these cases concern accounting irregularities that enabled firms to vastly overstate their earnings. Such scandals often emerge during economic downturns: as John Kenneth Galbraith once remarked, recessions catch what the auditors miss.

4. Conceptual framework

4.1. Agency and contracting

At a general level corporate governance can be described as a problem involving an agent – the CEO of the corporation – and multiple principals – the shareholders, creditors, suppliers, clients, employees, and other parties with whom the CEO engages in business on behalf of the corporation. Boards and external auditors act as intermediaries or representatives of these different constituencies. This view dates back to at least Jensen and Meckling (1976), who describe a firm in abstract terms as "a nexus of contracting relationships". Using more modern language the corporate governance problem can also be described as a "common agency problem", that is an agency problem involving one agent (the CEO) and multiple principals (shareholders, creditors, employees, clients [see Bernheim and Whinston (1985, 1986a,b)]. [22]

Corporate governance rules can be seen as the outcome of the contracting process between the various principals or constituencies and the CEO. Thus, the central issue in corporate governance is to understand what the outcome of this contracting process is likely to be, and how corporate governance deviates in practice from the efficient contracting benchmark.

4.2. Ex-ante and ex-post efficiency

Economists determine efficiency by two closely related criteria. The first is ex-ante efficiency: a corporate charter is ex-ante efficient if it generates the highest possible

---

[21] Recent failures include undetected off-balance sheet loans to a controlling family (Adelphia) combined with alleged self-dealing by CEOs and other company employees (Computer Associates, Dynegy, Enron, Global Crossing, Qwest, Tyco), deliberate misleading of investors (Kmart, Lucent Technologies, WorldCom), insider trading (ImClone Systems) and/or fraud (Rite Aid) ("Accounting Scandals Spread Across Wall Street", *Financial Times,* 26 June 2002).

[22] A slightly different, sometimes broader perspective, is to describe corporate governance as a multi-principal–multi-agent problem, where both managers and employees are seen as agents for multiple classes of investors. The labelling of employees as 'agent' or 'principal' is not just a matter of definition. If they are defined as 'principal' they are implicitly seen as participants in corporate governance. When and how employees should participate in corporate governance is a delicate and politically sensitive question. We discuss this issue at length in Section 5.6 below. For now, we shall simply take the view that employees are partly 'principal' when they have made firm specific investments, which require protection.

joint payoff for all the parties involved, shareholders, creditors, employees, clients, tax authorities, and other third parties that may be affected by the corporation's actions. The second criterion is Pareto efficiency: a corporate charter is Pareto efficient if no other charter exists that all parties prefer. The two criteria are closely related when the parties can undertake compensating transfers among themselves: a Pareto efficient charter is also a surplus maximizing charter when the parties can make unrestricted side transfers. As closely related as these two notions are it is still important to distinguish between them, since in practice side transfers are often constrained by wealth or borrowing constraints.

4.3. Shareholder value

An efficiency criterion that is often advocated in finance and legal writings on corporate governance is "shareholder value", or the stock market valuation of the corporation. An important basic question is how this notion is related to Pareto efficiency or surplus maximization. Is maximization of shareholder value synonymous with either or both notions of efficiency?

One influential view on this question [articulated by Jensen and Meckling (1976)] is the following. If a) the firm is viewed as a nexus of complete contracts with creditors, employees, clients, suppliers, third and other relevant parties, b) only contracts with shareholders are open-ended; that is, only shareholders have a claim on residual returns after all other contractual obligations have been met, and c) there are no agency problems, then maximization of (residual) shareholder value is tantamount to economic efficiency. Under this scenario, corporate governance rules should be designed to protect and promote the interests of shareholders exclusively.[23]

As Jensen and Meckling point out, however, managerial agency problems produce inefficiencies when CEOs act only in the interest of shareholders. There may be excess risk-taking when the firm is highly levered, or, as Myers (1977) has shown, debt overhang may induce underinvestment. Either form of investment inefficiency can be mitigated if managers do not exclusively pursue shareholder value maximization.

4.4. Incomplete contracts and multiple constituencies

Contracts engaging the corporation with parties other than shareholders are generally incomplete, so that there is no guarantee that corporate governance rules designed to maximize shareholder value are efficient. To guarantee efficiency it is then necessary to take into account explicitly the interests of other constituencies besides shareholders. Whether to take into account other constituencies, and how, is a central issue

---

[23] Jensen and Meckling's argument updates an older observation formally articulated by Arrow and Debreu [see Debreu (1959)], that in a competitive economy with complete markets the objective of the firm – unanimously espoused by all claimholders – is profit (or value) maximization.

in corporate governance. Some commentators have argued that shareholder value maximization is the relevant objective even if contracts with other constituencies are incomplete. Others maintain that board representation should extend beyond shareholders and include other constituencies. There are major differences across countries on this issue, with at one extreme UK and USA rules designed mainly to promote shareholder value, and at the other German rules designed to balance the interests of shareholders and employees.

One line of argument in favor of shareholder value maximization in a world of incomplete contracts, first articulated by Oliver Williamson (1984, 1985b), is that shareholders are relatively less well protected than other constituencies. He argues that most workers are not locked into a firm specific relation and can quit at reasonably low cost. Similarly, creditors can get greater protection by taking collateral or by shortening the maturity of the debt. Shareholders, on the other hand, have an open-ended contract without specific protection. They need protection the most. Therefore, corporate governance rules should primarily be designed to protect shareholders' interests.

In addition, Hansmann (1996) has argued that one advantage of involving only one constituency in corporate governance is that both corporate decision-making costs and managerial discretion will be reduced. Although Hansmann argues in favor of a governance system by a single constituency he allows for the possibility that other constituencies besides shareholders may control the firm. In some situations a labor-managed firm, a customer co-operative, or possibly a supplier co-operative may be a more efficient corporate governance arrangement. In his view, determining which constituency should govern the firm comes down to identifying which has the lowest decision making costs and which has the greatest need of protection.

An obvious question raized by Williamson's argument is that if it is possible to get better protection by signing debt contracts, why not encourage all investors in the firm to take out debt contracts. Why worry about protecting shareholders when investors can find better protection by writing a debt contract? Jensen (1986, 1989) has been a leading advocate of this position, arguing that the best way to resolve the agency problem between the CEO and investors is to have the firm take on as much debt as possible. This would limit managerial discretion by minimizing the "free cash-flow" available to managers and, thus, would provide the best possible protection to investors.

The main difficulty with Jensen's logic is that highly levered firms may incur substantial costs of financial distress. They may face direct bankruptcy costs or indirect costs in the form of debt-overhang [see Myers (1977) or Hart and Moore (1995) and Hennessy and Levy (2002)]. To reduce the risk of financial distress it may be desirable to have the firm rely partly on equity financing. And to reduce the cost of equity capital it is clearly desirable to provide protections to shareholders through suitably designed corporate governance rules.

Arguably it is in the interest of corporations and their CEOs to design efficient corporate governance rules, since this would minimize their cost of capital, labor and other inputs. It would also maximize the value of their products or services to their clients. Firms may want to acquire a reputation for treating shareholders or creditors well, as Kreps (1990) and Diamond (1989) have suggested.[24] If reputation building is effective then mandatory regulatory intervention seems unnecessary.

4.5. Why do we need regulation?

A natural question to ask then is why regulations imposing particular governance rules (required by stock exchanges, legislatures, courts or supervisory authorities) are necessary.[25] If it is in the interest of firms to provide adequate protection to shareholders, why mandate rules, which may be counterproductive? Even with the best intentions regulators may not have all the information available to design efficient rules.[26] Worse still, regulators can be captured by a given constituency and impose rules favoring one group over another.

There are at least two reasons for regulatory intervention. The main argument in support of mandatory rules is that even if the founder of the firm or the shareholders can design and implement any corporate charter they like, they will tend to write inefficient rules since they cannot feasibly involve all the parties concerned in a comprehensive bargain. By pursuing their interests over those of parties missing from the bargaining table they are likely to write inefficient rules. For example, the founder of the firm or shareholders will want to put in place anti-takeover defenses in an attempt to improve the terms of takeovers and they will thereby tend to limit hostile takeover activity excessively.[27] Alternatively, shareholders may favor takeovers that increase the value of their shares even if they involve greater losses for unprotected creditors or employees.[28]

Another argument in support of mandatory rules is that, even if firms initially have the right incentives to design efficient rules, they may want to break or alter them

[24] Interestingly, although reputation building is an obvious way to establish investor protection, this type of strategy has been somewhat under-emphasized in the corporate governance literature. In particular, there appears to be no systematic empirical study on reputation building, even if there are many examples of large corporations that attempt to build a reputation by committing to regular dividend payments, disclosing information, and communicating with analysts (see however Carleton, Nelson and Weisbach (1998) for evidence on voluntary communications between large USA corporations and institutional investors). For a recent survey of the disclosure literature, including voluntary disclosure by management, see Healy and Palepu (2001).
[25] Compliance with corporate governance "codes" is mostly voluntary.
[26] On the other hand, if the identification and formulation of efficient corporate governance rules is a costly process it makes sense to rely on courts and corporate law to formulate default rules, which corporations could adopt or opt out of [see Ayres and Gertner (1989)].
[27] We shall return to this observation, articulated in Grossman and Hart (1980) and Scharfstein (1988), at greater length in Section 5.
[28] Shleifer and Summers (1988) discuss several hostile takeover cases where the value for target and bidding shareholders came apparently at the expense of employees and creditors.

later. A problem then arises when firms do not have the power to commit not to change (or break) the rules down the road. When shareholders are dispersed and do not take an active interest in the firm it is possible, indeed straightforward, for management to change the rules to their advantage *ex post*. Dispersed shareholders, with small interests in the corporation, are unlikely to incur the large monitoring costs that are sometimes required to keep management at bay. They are more likely to make management their proxy, or to abstain.[29] Similarly, firms may not be able to build credible reputations for treating shareholders well if dispersed shareholders do not take an active interest in the firm and if important decisions such as mergers or replacements of CEOs are infrequent. Shareholder protection may then require some form of concentrated ownership or a regulatory intervention to overcome the collective action problem among dispersed shareholders.

4.6. Dispersed ownership

Since dispersed ownership is such an important source of corporate governance problems it is important to inquire what causes dispersion in the first place. There are at least three reasons why share ownership may be dispersed in reality. First, and perhaps most importantly, individual investors' wealth may be small relative to the size of some investments. Second, even if a shareholder can take a large stake in a firm, he may want to diversify risk by investing less. A related third reason is investors' concern for liquidity: a large stake may be harder to sell in the secondary market.[30] For these reasons it is not realistic or desirable to expect to resolve the collective action problem among dispersed shareholders by simply getting rid of dispersion.

4.7. Summary and conclusion

In sum, mandatory governance rules (as required by stock exchanges, legislatures, courts or supervisory authorities) are necessary for two main reasons: first, to overcome the collective action problem resulting from the dispersion among shareholders, and second, to ensure that the interests of all relevant constituencies are represented. Indeed, other constituencies besides shareholders face the same basic collective action problem. Corporate bondholders are also dispersed and their collective action problems are only imperfectly resolved through trust agreements or consortia or in bankruptcy courts. In large corporations employees and clients may face similar collective action

---

[29] Alternatively, limiting managerial discretion ex ante and making it harder to change the rules by introducing supermajority requirements into the corporate charter would introduce similar types of inefficiency as with debt.

[30] A fourth reason for the observed dispersion in shareholdings may be securities regulation designed to protect minority shareholders, which raises the cost of holding large blocks. This regulatory bias in USA corporate law has been highlighted by Black (1990), Roe (1990, 1991, 1994) and Bhide (1993).

problems, which again are imperfectly resolved by unions or consumer protection organizations.

Most of the finance and corporate law literature on corporate governance focuses only on collective action problems of shareholders. Accordingly, we will emphasize those problems in this survey. As the literature on representation of other constituencies is much less developed we shall only touch on this issue in Sections 5 to 7.

We distinguish five main ways to mitigate shareholders' collective action problems:

(1) Election of a board of directors representing shareholders' interests, to which the CEO is accountable.

(2) When the need arises, a takeover or proxy fight launched by a corporate raider who temporarily concentrates voting power (and/or ownership) in his hands to resolve a crisis, reach an important decision or remove an inefficient manager.

(3) Active and continuous monitoring by a large blockholder, who could be a wealthy investor or a financial intermediary, such as a bank, a holding company or a pension fund.

(4) Alignment of managerial interests with investors through executive compensation contracts.

(5) Clearly defined fiduciary duties for CEOs and the threat of class-action suits that either block corporate decisions that go against investors' interests, or seek compensation for past actions that have harmed their interests.

As we shall explain, a potential difficulty with the first three approaches is the old problem of who monitors the monitor and the risk of collusion between management (the agent) and the delegated monitor (director, raider, blockholder). If dispersed shareholders have no incentive to supervise management and take an active interest in the management of the corporation why should directors – who generally have equally small stakes – have much better incentives to oversee management? The same point applies to pension fund managers. Even if they are required to vote, why should they spend the resources to make informed decisions when the main beneficiaries of those decisions are their own principals, the dispersed investors in the pension fund? Finally, it might appear that corporate raiders, who concentrate ownership directly in their hands, are not susceptible to this delegated monitoring problem. This is only partially true since the raiders themselves have to raise funds to finance the takeover. Typically, firms that are taken over through a hostile bid end up being substantially more highly levered. They may have resolved the shareholder collective action problem, but at the cost of significantly increasing the expected cost of financial distress.

Enforcement of fiduciary duties through the courts has its own shortcomings. First, management can shield itself against shareholder suits by taking out appropriate insurance contracts at the expense of shareholders.[31] Second, the "business judgement" rule (and similar provisions in other countries) severely limits shareholders' ability

---

[31] Most large USA corporations have taken out director and officer liability (D&O) insurance policies

to prevail in court[32] Finally, plaintiffs' attorneys do not always have the right incentives to monitor management. Managers and investment bankers often complain that contingency fee awards (which are typically a percentage of damages awarded in the event that the plaintiff prevails) can encourage them to engage in frivolous suits, a problem that is likely to be exacerbated by the widespread use of director and officer (D&O) liability insurance. This is most likely to be the case in the USA. In other countries fee awards (which mainly reflect costs incurred) tend to increase the risk of lawsuits for small shareholders and the absence of D&O insurance makes it harder to recover damages.[33]

5. Models

5.1. Takeover models

One of the most radical and spectacular mechanisms for disciplining and replacing managers is a hostile takeover. This mechanism is highly disruptive and costly. Even in the USA and the UK it is relatively rarely used. In most other countries it is almost non-existent. Yet, hostile takeovers have received a great deal of attention from academic researchers. In a hostile takeover the raider makes an offer to buy all or a fraction of outstanding shares at a stated tender price. The takeover is successful if the raider gains more than 50% of the voting shares and thereby obtains effective control of the company. With more than 50% of the voting shares, in due course he will be able to gain majority representation on the board and thus be able to appoint the CEO.

Much research has been devoted to the mechanics of the takeover process, the analysis of potentially complex strategies for the raider and individual shareholders, and to the question of ex-post efficiency of the outcome. Much less research has been concerned with the ex-ante efficiency of hostile takeovers: the extent to which takeovers are an effective disciplining device on managers.

On this latter issue, the formal analysis by Scharfstein (1988) stands out. Building on the insights of Grossman and Hart (1980), he considers the ex-ante financial contracting problem between a financier and a manager. This contract specifies a state contingent compensation scheme for the manager to induce optimal effort provision. In addition the contract allows for ex-post takeovers, which can be efficiency enhancing if

---

[see Danielson and Karpoff (1998)]. See Gutiérrez (2000, 2003) for an analysis of fiduciary duties, liability and D&O insurance.

[32] The "directors' business judgement cannot be attacked unless their judgement was arrived at in a negligent manner, or was tainted by fraud, conflict of interest, or illegality" [Clark (1986, p. 124)]. The business judgement rule gives little protection to directors for breaches of form (e.g., for directors who fail to attend meetings or read documents) but can extend to conflict of interest situations, provided that a self-interested decision is approved by disinterested directors [Clark (1986, pp. 123, 138)].

[33] See Fischel and Bradley (1986), Romano (1991) and Kraakman, Park and Shavell (1994) for an analysis of distortions of litigation incentives in shareholder suits.

either the raider has information about the state of nature not available to the financier or if the raider is a better manager. In other words, takeovers are useful both because they reduce the informational monopoly of the incumbent manager about the state of the firm and because they allow for the replacement of inefficient managers. The important observation made by Scharfstein is that even if the firm can commit to an ex-ante optimal contract, this contract is generally inefficient. The reason is that the financier and manager partly design the contract to try and extract the efficiency rents of future raiders. Like a non-discriminating monopolist, they will design the contract so as to "price" the acquisition above the efficient competitive price. As a result, the contract will induce too few hostile takeovers on average.

Scharfstein's observation provides an important justification for regulatory intervention limiting anti-takeover defenses, such as super-majority amendments,[34] staggered boards,[35] fair price amendments (ruling out two-tier tender offers),[36] and poison pills[37] (see Section 7.1.4 for a more detailed discussion). These defenses are seen by many to be against shareholders' interests and to be put in place by managers of companies with weak corporate governance structures [see, for example, Gilson (1981) and Easterbrook and Fischel (1981)]. Others, however, see them as an important weapon enabling the target firm to extract better terms from a raider [see Baron (1983), Macey and McChesney (1985), Shleifer and Vishny (1986), Hirshleifer and Titman (1990), Hirshleifer and Thakor (1994), Hirshleifer (1995)]. Even if one takes the latter perspective, however, Scharfstein's argument suggests that some of these defenses should be regulated or banned.

A much larger literature exists on the issue of ex-post efficiency of hostile takeovers. The first formal model of a tender offer game is due to Grossman and Hart (1980). They consider the following basic game. A raider can raise the value per share from $v=0$ under current management to $v=1$. He needs 50% of the voting shares and makes a conditional tender offer of p per share.[38] Share ownership is completely dispersed;

---

[34] These amendments raise the majority rule above 50% in the event of a hostile takeover.

[35] Staggered boards are a common defence designed to postpone the time at which the raider can gain full control of the board after a takeover. With only a fraction y of the board renewable every x years, the raider would have to wait up to $x/2y$ years before gaining over 50% of the seats.

[36] Two-tier offers specify a higher price for the first n shares tendered than for the remaining ones. They tend to induce shareholders to tender and, hence, facilitate the takeover. Such offers are generally illegal in the USA, but when they are not companies can ban them by writing an amendment into the corporate charter.

[37] Most poison pills give the right to management to issue more voting shares at a low price to existing shareholders in the event that one shareholder owns more than a fraction x of outstanding shares. Such clauses, when enforced, make it virtually impossible for a takeover to succeed. When such a defence is in place the raider has to oust the incumbent board in a proxy fight and remove the pill. When the pill is combined with defenses that limit the raider's ability to fight a proxy fight – for example a staggered board – the raider effectively has to bribe the incumbent board.

[38] A conditional offer is one that binds only if the raider gains control by having more than a specified percentage of the shares tendered.

indeed to simplify the analysis they consider an idealized situation with an infinite number of shareholders. It is not difficult to see that a dominant strategy for each shareholder is to tender if $p = 1$ and to hold on to their shares if $p < 1$. Therefore the lowest price at which the raider is able to take over the firm is $p = 1$, the post-takeover value per share. In other words, the raider has to give up all the value he can generate to existing shareholders. If he incurs costs in making the offer or in undertaking the management changes that produce the higher value per share he may well be discouraged from attempting a takeover. In other words, there may be too few takeover attempts ex-post.

Grossman and Hart (1980) suggest several ways of improving the efficiency of the hostile takeover mechanism. All involve some dilution of minority shareholder rights. Consistent with their proposals for example is the idea that raiders be allowed to "squeeze (freeze) out" minority shareholders that have not tendered their shares,[39] or to allow raiders to build up a larger "toehold" before they are required to disclose their stake.[40]

Following the publication of the Grossman and Hart article a large literature has developed analyzing different variants of the takeover game, with non-atomistic share ownership [e.g., Kovenock (1984), Bagnoli and Lipman (1988), Holmstrom and Nalebuff (1992)], with multiple bidders [e.g., Fishman (1988), Burkart (1995), Bulow, Huang and Klemperer (1999)], with multiple rounds of bidding [Dewatripont (1993)], with arbitrageurs [e.g., Cornelli and Li (1998)], asymmetric information [e.g., Hirshleifer and Titman (1990), Yilmaz (2000)], etc. Much of this literature has found Grossman and Hart's result that most of the gains of a takeover go to target shareholders (because of "free riding" by small shareholders) to be non-robust when there is only one bidder. With either non-atomistic shareholders or asymmetric information their extreme "free-riding" result breaks down. In contrast, empirical studies have found again and again that on average all the gains from hostile takeovers go to target shareholders [see Jensen and Ruback (1983) for a survey of the early literature]. While this is consistent with Grossman and Hart's result, other explanations have been suggested, such as (potential) competition by multiple bidders, or raiders' hubris leading to over-eagerness to close the deal [Roll (1986)].

More generally, the theoretical literature following Grossman and Hart (1980) is concerned more with explaining bidding patterns and equilibrium bids given existing regulations than with determining which regulatory rules are efficient. A survey of

---

[39] A squeeze or freeze out forces minority shareholders to sell their shares to the raider at (or below) the tender offer price. When the raider has this right it is no longer a dominant strategy to hold on to one's shares when $p < 1$.

[40] A toehold is the stake owned by the raider before he makes a tender offer. In the USA a shareholder owning more than 5% of outstanding shares must disclose his stake to the SEC. The raider can always make a profit on his toehold by taking over the firm. Thus, the larger his toehold the more likely he is to make a takeover attempt [see Shleifer and Vishny (1986) and Kyle and Vila (1991)].

most of this literature can be found in Hirshleifer (1995). For an extensive discussion of empirical research on takeovers see also the survey by Burkart (1999).

Formal analyses of optimal takeover regulation have focused on four issues: 1) whether deviations from a "one-share–one vote" rule result in inefficient takeover outcomes; 2) whether raiders should be required to buy out minority shareholders; 3) whether takeovers may result in the partial expropriation of other inadequately protected claims on the corporation, and if so, whether some anti-takeover amendments may be justified as basic protections against expropriation; and 4) whether proxy contests should be favored over tender offers.

From 1926 to 1986 one of the requirements for a new listing on the New York Stock Exchange was that companies issue a single class of voting stock [Seligman (1986)].[41] That is, companies could only issue shares with the same number (effectively one) of votes each. Does this regulation induce efficient corporate control contests? The analysis of Grossman and Hart (1988) and Harris and Raviv (1988a,b) suggests that the answer is a qualified "yes". They point out that under a "one-share–one-vote" rule inefficient raiders must pay the highest possible price to acquire control. In other words, they face the greatest deterrent to taking over a firm under this rule. In addition, they point out that a simple majority rule is most likely to achieve efficiency by treating incumbent management and the raider symmetrically.

Deviations from "one-share–one-vote" may, however, allow initial shareholders to extract a greater share of the efficiency gain of the raider in a value-increasing takeover. Indeed, Harris and Raviv (1988a), Zingales (1995) and Gromb (1993) show that maximum extraction of the raider's efficiency rent can be obtained by issuing two extreme classes of shares, votes-only shares and non-voting shares. Under such a share ownership structure the raider only purchases votes-only shares. He can easily gain control, but all the benefits he brings go to the non-voting shareholders. Under their share allocation scheme all non-voting shareholders have no choice but to "free-ride" and thus appropriate most of the gains from the takeover.

Another potential benefit of deviations from "one-share–one-vote" is that they may induce more listings by firms whose owners value retaining control of the company. Family-owned firms are often reluctant to go public if they risk losing control in the process. These firms might go public if they could retain control through a dual-class share structure. As Hart (1988) argues, deviations from one-share–one-vote would benefit both the firm and the exchange in this case. They are also unlikely to hurt minority shareholders, as they presumably price in the lack of control rights attached to their shares at the IPO stage.

Burkart, Gromb and Panunzi (1998) extend this analysis by introducing a post-takeover agency problem. Such a problem arises when the raider does not own 100%

---

[41] A well-known exception to this listing rule was the Ford Motor Company, listed with a dual class stock capitalization in 1956, allowing the Ford family to exert 40% of the voting rights with 5.1% of the capital [Seligman (1986)].

of the shares ex post, and is potentially worse, the lower the raider's post-takeover stake. They show that in such a model initial shareholders extract the raider's whole efficiency rent under a "one-share–one-vote" rule. As a result, some costly takeovers may be deterred. To reduce this inefficiency they argue that some deviations from "one-share–one-vote" may be desirable.

The analysis of mandatory bid rules is similar to that of deviations from "one-share–one-vote". By forcing a raider to acquire all outstanding shares, such a rule maximizes the price an inefficient raider must pay to acquire control. On the other hand, such a rule may also discourage some value increasing takeovers [see Bergstrom, Hogfeldt and Molin (1997)].

In an influential article Shleifer and Summers (1988) have argued that some takeovers may be undesirable if they result in a "breach of trust" between management and employees. If employees (or clients, creditors and suppliers) anticipate that informal relations with current management may be broken by a new managerial team that has taken over the firm they may be reluctant to invest in such relations and to acquire firm specific human capital. They argue that some anti-takeover protections may be justified at least for firms where specific (human and physical) capital is important. A small formal literature has developed around this theme [see e.g., Knoeber (1986), Schnitzer (1995), Chemla (1998)]. One lesson emerging from this research is that efficiency depends critically on which type of anti-takeover protection is put in place. For example, Schnitzer (1995) shows that only a specific combination of a poison pill with a golden parachute would provide adequate protection for the manager's (or employees') specific investments. The main difficulty from a regulatory perspective, however, is that protection of specific human capital is just too easy an excuse to justify managerial entrenchment. Little or no work to date has been devoted to the question of identifying which actions or investments constitute "entrenchment behavior" and which do not. It is therefore impossible to say conclusively whether current regulations permitting anti-takeover amendments, which both facilitate managerial entrenchment and provide protections supporting informal agreements, are beneficial overall.

Another justification for poison pills that has recently been proposed by Bebchuk and Hart (2001) is that poison pills make it impossible to remove an incumbent manager through a hostile takeover unless the tender offer is accompanied by a proxy fight over the redemption of the poison pill.[42] In other words, Bebchuk and Hart argue

---

[42] Bebchuk and Hart's conclusions rest critically on their view of why straight proxy fights are likely to be ineffective in practice in removing incumbent management. Alternative reasons have been given why proxy fights have so often failed, which would lead to different conclusions. For example, it has often been argued that management has an unfair advantage in campaigning for shareholder votes as they have access to shareholder lists as well as the company coffers (for example, Hewlett-Packard spent over $100 mn to convince shareholders to approve its merger with Compaq). In addition they can pressure institutional investors to vote for them (in the case of Hewlett-Packard, it was alleged that the prospect of future corporate finance business was implicitly used to entice Deutsche Bank to vote for

that the presence of a poison pill requires a mechanism for removing incumbent managers that combines both a tender offer and a proxy contest. In their model such a mechanism dominates both straight proxy contests and straight tender offers. The reason why straight proxy contests are dominated is that shareholders tend to be (rationally) sceptical of challengers. Challengers may be worse than incumbents and only seek control to gain access to large private benefits of control. A tender offer accompanying a proxy fight mollifies shareholder scepticism by demonstrating that the challenger is ready to "put his money where his mouth is". In general terms, the reason why straight tender offers are dominated is that a tender offer puts the decision in the hands of the marginal shareholder while majority voting effectively puts the control decision in the hands of the average shareholder (or median voter). The average shareholder always votes in favor of a value increasing control change, while the marginal shareholder in a tender offer only decides to tender if she is better off tendering than holding on to her shares assuming that the takeover will succeed. Such behavior can result in excessive free-riding and inefficient control allocations.

5.2. Blockholder models

An alternative approach to mitigating the collective action problem of shareholders is to have a semi-concentrated ownership structure with at least one large shareholder, who has an interest in monitoring management and the power to implement management changes. Although this solution is less common in the USA and UK – because of regulatory restrictions on blockholder actions – some form of concentration of ownership or control is the dominant form of corporate governance arrangement in continental Europe and other OECD countries.

The first formal analyses of corporate governance with large shareholders point to the benefits of large shareholders in facilitating takeovers [see Grossman and Hart (1980) and Shleifer and Vishny (1986)]. A related theme is the classic tradeoff underlying the standard agency problem with moral hazard: the tradeoff between optimal risk diversification, which is obtained under a fully dispersed ownership structure, and optimal monitoring incentives, which require concentrated ownership.

---

the merger). If it is the case that institutional and other affiliated shareholders are likely to vote for the incumbent for these reasons then it is imperative to ban poison pills to make way for a possible hostile takeover as Shleifer and Vishny (1986), Harris and Raviv (1988a), Gilson (2000, 2002) and Gilson and Schwartz (2001) have argued among others. Lipton and Rowe (2001) take yet another perspective. They question the premise in most formal analyses of takeovers that financial markets are efficient. They point to the recent bubble and crash on NASDAQ and other financial markets as evidence that stock valuations are as likely to reflect fundamental value as not. They argue that when stock valuations deviate in this way from fundamental value they can no longer be taken as a reliable guide for the efficient allocation of control or for that matter as a reliable mechanism to discipline management. In such inefficient financial markets poison pills are necessary to protect management from the vagaries of the market and from opportunistic bids. They maintain that this is the doctrine underlying Delaware law on takeover defenses.

Thus, Leland and Pyle (1977) have shown that it may be in the interest of a risk-averse entrepreneur going public to retain a large stake in the firm as a signal of quality, or as a commitment to manage the firm well. Later, Admati, Pfleiderer and Zechner (1994) and Huddart (1993) have considered the monitoring incentives of a large risk-averse shareholder. They show that in equilibrium the large shareholder has too small a stake and under-invests in monitoring, because the large shareholder prefers to diversify his holdings somewhat even if this reduces his incentives to monitor. They also point out that ownership structures with one large block may be unstable if the blockholder can gradually erode his stake by selling small quantities of shares in the secondary market. The main regulating implication of these analyses is that corporate governance might be improved if blockholders could be subsidized to hold larger blocks. Indeed, the main problem in these models is to give greater incentives to monitor to the blockholder. [43]

A related set of models further pursues the issue of monitoring incentives of firms with liquid secondary markets. An influential view generally attributed to Hirschman (1970) is that when monitors can easily 'exit' the firm they tend not to exercise their 'voice'. In other words, blockholders cannot be relied upon to monitor management actively if they have the option to sell their stake instead. [44] Indeed, some commentators [most notably Mayer (1988), Black (1990), Coffee (1991), Roe (1994) and Bhide (1993)] have argued that it is precisely the highly liquid nature of USA secondary markets that makes it difficult to provide incentives to large shareholders to monitor management.

This issue has been analyzed by Kahn and Winton (1998) and Maug (1998) among others. Kahn and Winton show how market liquidity can undermine large shareholders' incentives to monitor by giving them incentives to trade on private information rather than intervene. They argue, however, that incentives to speculate may be small for blue-chip companies, where the large shareholder is unlikely to have a significant informational advantage over other market participants. Similarly, Maug points out that in liquid markets it is also easier to build a block. This gives large shareholders an added incentive to invest in information gathering.

To summarize, this literature emphasizes the idea that if the limited size of a block is mainly due to the large shareholder's desire to diversify risk then under-monitoring by the large shareholder is generally to be expected.

An entirely different perspective is that the large investor may want to limit his stake to ensure minimum secondary market liquidity. This is the perspective taken by Holmstrom and Tirole (1993). They argue that share prices in the secondary market provide valuable information about the firm's performance. To obtain accurate valuations, however, the secondary market must be sufficiently liquid. Indeed,

---

[43] Demsetz (1986) points out that insider trading makes it easier for a shareholder to build a toehold and thus facilitates monitoring.

[44] The idea that blockholders would rather sell their stake in mismanaged firms than try to fix the management problem is known as the "Wall Street rule" [see Black (1990)].

liquidity raises speculators' return to acquiring information and thus improves the informativeness of the secondary market price. The more informative stock price can then be included in compensation packages to provide better incentives to managers. According to this view it is the market that does the monitoring and the large shareholder may only be necessary to act on the information produced by the market.[45]

In other words, there may be a natural complementarity between speculation in secondary markets and monitoring by large shareholders. This idea is pursued further in Faure-Grimaud and Gromb (1999) and Aghion, Bolton and Tirole (2000). These models show how large shareholders' monitoring costs can be reduced through better pricing of shares in the secondary market. The basic idea is that more accurate pricing provides not only greater liquidity to the large shareholder, but also enhances his incentives to monitor by reflecting the added value of his monitoring activities in the stock price. The latter paper also determines the optimal degree of liquidity of the large shareholder's stake to maximize his incentives to monitor. This theory finds its most natural application for corporate governance in start-ups financed with venture capital. It is well known that venture capitalists not only invest large stakes in individual start-ups but also participate in running the firm before it goes public. Typical venture capital contracts can be seen as incentive contracts aimed in part at regulating the venture capitalist's exit options so as to provide the best incentives for monitoring.[46, 47]

Just as with takeovers, there are obvious benefits from large shareholder monitoring but there may also be costs. We pointed out earlier that hostile takeovers might be undesirable if their main purpose is to expropriate employees or minority shareholders. Similarly, large shareholder monitoring can be too much of a good thing. If the large shareholder uses his power to hold up employees or managers, the latter may be discouraged from making costly firm specific investments. This point has been emphasized in a number of theoretical studies, most notably in Aghion and Tirole (1997), Burkart, Gromb and Panunzi (1997), and Pagano and Röell (1998). Thus,

---

[45] Strictly speaking, in their model the large shareholder is only there by default, because in selling to the secondary market he has to accept a discount reflecting the information-related trading costs that investors anticipate incurring. Thus, the large shareholder can achieve the desired amount of information acquisition in the market by adjusting the size of his stake.

[46] See Bartlett (1994), Gompers and Lerner (1999), Levin (1995) and Kaplan and Strömberg (2003) for discussions of contractual provisions governing the venture capitalist's 'exit'. See also Berglöf (1994) and Hellman (1997) for models of corporate governance of venture capital financed firms.

[47] Another form of complementarity is considered in a recent paper by Chidambaran and John (1998). They argue that large shareholder monitoring can be facilitated by managerial cooperation. However, to achieve such cooperation managers must be given an equity stake in the firm. With sufficient equity participation, the authors show that managers have an incentive to disclose information that brings market valuations closer to fundamental values of the business. They argue that this explains why greater institutional holdings are associated with larger stock option awards but lower compensation levels for CEOs [see Hartzell and Starks (2002)].

another reason for limiting a large shareholder's stake may be to prevent over-monitoring and ex-post opportunism. As privately held firms tend to have concentrated ownership structures they are more prone to over-monitoring. Pagano and Röell argue that one important motive for going public is that the manager may want to free himself from an overbearing owner or venture capitalist.[48]

It is only a short step from over-monitoring to downright expropriation, self-dealing or collusion with management at the expense of minority shareholders. Indeed, an important concern of many commentators is the conflict of interest among shareholders inherent in blockholder ownership structures. This conflict is exacerbated when in addition there is separation between voting rights and cash-flow rights, as is common in continental Europe. Many commentators have argued that such an arrangement is particularly vulnerable to self-dealing by the controlling shareholder [see e.g. Zingales (1994), Bianco et al. (1997), Burkart, Gromb and Panunzi (1997), La Porta et al. (1998), Wolfenzon (1999), Bebchuk (1999), Bebchuk, Kraakman and Trianis (2000)].[49] Most of these commentators go as far as arguing that existing blockholder structures in continental Europe are in fact likely to be inefficient and that USA-style regulations restricting blockholder rights should be phased in.

The analyses of Aghion and Tirole (1997), Burkart, Gromb and Panunzi (1997), and Pagano and Röell (1998), however, suggest that if there is a risk of over-monitoring or self-dealing it is often possible to design the corporate ownership structure or charter to limit the power of the blockholder. But Bebchuk (1999) and Bebchuk and Roe (1999) retort that although it is theoretically possible to design corporate charters that restrain self-dealing, in practice the Coase theorem is likely to break down and therefore regulations limiting blockholder rights are called for. Bebchuk (1999) develops a model where dispersed ownership is unstable when large shareholders can obtain rents through self-dealing since there is always an incentive to grab and protect control rents. If a large shareholder does not grab the control rents then management will. Bebchuk's extreme conclusion, however, is based on the assumption that a self-dealing manager

---

[48] Most of the theoretical literature on large shareholders only considers ownership structures where all but one shareholder are small. Zwiebel (1995) is a recent exception. He considers ownership structures where there may be more than one large shareholder and also allows for alliances among small blockholders. In such a setting he shows that one of the roles of a large blockholding is to fend off alliances of smaller blockholders that might compete for control [see also Gomes and Novaes (2000) and Bloch and Hege (2000) for two other recent formal analyses of ownership structures with multiple large shareholders]. An entirely different perspective on the role of large outside shareholders is given in Muller and Warneryd (2001) who argue that outside owners can reduce inefficient rent seeking of insiders and managers by inducing them to join forces to fight the outsider's own rent seeking activities. This story fits well the situation of many second-generation family-owned firms, who decide to open up their ownership to outsiders in an attempt to stop feuding among family members.

[49] Most commentators point to self-dealing and "private benefits" of control of the large shareholder. Perhaps equally worrying, however, is collusion between management and the blockholder. This aspect of the problem has not received much attention. For two noteworthy exceptions see Tirole (1986) and Burkart and Panunzi (2000).

cannot be disciplined by a takeover threat.[50] His general conclusion – that if self-dealing is possible under a lax corporate law it will inevitably lead to concentrated ownership – is a particular version of the general argument outlined in the introduction that under dispersed ownership management may not be able to commit to an ex-ante efficient corporate governance rule. Bebchuk and Roe (1999) make a complementary point, arguing that inefficiencies can persist if there is a collective action problem in introducing better corporate governance arrangements.

So far we have discussed the costs and benefits of takeovers and large shareholder monitoring, respectively. But what are the relative advantages of each approach? One comparative analysis of this question is proposed by Bolton and von Thadden (1998a,b). They argue that one potential benefit of blockholder structures is that monitoring will take place on an ongoing basis. In contrast, a system with dispersed shareholders can provide monitoring and intervention only in crisis situations (if at all), through a hostile takeover. The benefit of dispersed ownership, on the other hand is enhanced liquidity in secondary markets. They show that depending on the value of monitoring, the need for intervention and the demand for liquidity either system can dominate the other. The comparison between the two systems obviously also depends on the regulatory structure in place. If, as Black (1990) has forcefully argued, regulations substantially increase the costs of holding blocks[51] (as is the case in both the USA and the UK) then a system with dispersed shareholders relying on hostile takeovers might be best. On the other hand, if regulations which mainly increase the costs of hostile takeovers but do not otherwise substantially restrict blockholder rights (as in continental Europe) are in place then a system based on blockholder monitoring may arise.

Another comparative analysis is proposed by John and Kedia (2000). They draw the distinction between 'self-binding' mechanisms (like bank or large shareholder monitoring) and 'intervention' mechanisms (like hostile takeovers). They let underlying conditions vary according to two parameters: the costs of bank monitoring and the effectiveness of hostile takeovers. Depending on the values of these parameters the optimal governance mechanism is either: i) concentrated ownership (when bank monitoring is costly and takeovers are not a threat); ii) bank monitoring (when monitoring costs are low and takeovers are ineffective); or iii) dispersed ownership

---

[50] The issue of competition for control rents between a large shareholder and the CEO is analysed in Burkart and Panunzi (2000). They argue that access to control rents has positive incentive effects on the CEO. It also has positive effects on the blockholder's incentive to monitor. However, competition for these rents between the CEO and the blockholder may undermine the incentives of either party.

[51] Among USA rules discouraging shareholder action are disclosure requirements, prohibitions on insider trading and short-swing trading, rules imposing liability on 'controlling shareholders', limits on institutional shareholdings in a single company and fiduciary duty rules; a detailed account is given by Black (1990). One of the most striking restrictions is the rule governing shareholder proposals (Rule 14a-8): a shareholder "can offer only one proposal per year, ... must submit the proposal ... 5 months before the next annual meeting... A proposal cannot relate to ordinary business operations or the election of directors ... and not conflict with a manager proposal" [Black (1990, p. 541)].

and hostile takeovers (when anti-takeover defenses are low and monitoring is costly). One implication of their analysis is that corporate governance in Europe and Japan may not converge to USA practice simply by introducing the same takeover regulations. If banks are able to maintain a comparative advantage in monitoring these countries may continue to see a predominance of bank monitoring.[52]

5.3. Delegated monitoring and large creditors

One increasingly important issue relating to large shareholders or investor monitoring concerns the role of institutional shareholder activism by pension funds and other financial intermediaries. Pension funds, mutual funds and insurance companies (and banks outside the USA) often buy large stakes in corporations and could take an active role in monitoring management. Generally, however, because of regulatory constraints or lack of incentives they tend to be passive [see Black (1990), Coffee (1991), Black and Coffee (1994)]. One advantage of greater activism by large institutional investors is that fund managers are less likely to engage in self-dealing and can therefore be seen as almost ideal monitors of management. But a major problem with institutional monitoring is that fund managers themselves have no direct financial stake in the companies they invest in and therefore have no direct or adequate incentives for monitoring.[53]

The issue of institutional investor incentives to monitor has been analyzed mainly in the context of bank monitoring. The first formal analysis of the issue of who monitors the monitor (in the context of bank finance) is due to Diamond (1984). He shows that, as a means of avoiding duplication of monitoring by small investors, delegated monitoring by a banker may be efficient.[54] He resolves the issue of 'who monitors the monitor' and the potential duplication of monitoring costs for depositors, by showing that if the bank is sufficiently well diversified then it can almost perfectly guarantee a fixed return to its depositors. As a result of this (almost safe) debt-like contract that the bank offers to its depositors, the latter do not need to monitor the bank's management continuously.[55] They only need to inspect the bank's books when it is in financial distress, an event that is extremely unlikely when the bank is well diversified. As Calomiris and Kahn (1991) and Diamond and Rajan (2001) have emphasized more

---

[52] Yet another comparative analysis is given in Ayres and Cramton (1994). They emphasise two benefits of large shareholder structures. First, better monitoring and second less myopic market pressure to perform or fend off a hostile takeover [see also Narayanan (1985), Shleifer and Vishny (1989), and Stein (1988, 1989) for a formal analysis of myopic behaviour induced by hostile takeovers]. It is debatable, however, whether less market pressure is truly a benefit [see Romano (1998) for a discussion of this point].

[53] As Romano (2001) has argued and as the empirical evidence to date suggests [see Karpoff (1998)], USA institutional activism can be ineffective or misplaced.

[54] More generally, banks are not just delegated monitors but also delegated renegotiators; that is they offer a lending relationship; see Bolton and Freixas (2000) and Petersen and Rajan (1994).

[55] See also Krasa and Villamil (1992) and Hellwig (2000a) for generalizations of Diamond's result.

recently, however, preservation of the banker's incentives to monitor also requires a careful specification of deposit contracts. In particular, banks' incentives are preserved in their model only if there is no deposit insurance and the first-come first-served feature of bank deposit contracts is maintained. In other words, bankers' incentives to monitor are preserved only if banks are disciplined by the threat of a bank run by depositors. [56]

One implication of these latter models is that under a regime of deposit insurance banks will not adequately monitor firms and will engage in reckless lending. The greater incidence of banking crises in the past 20 years is sometimes cited as corroborating evidence for this perspective. Whether the origin of these crises is to be found in deposit insurance and inadequate bank governance is a debated issue. Other commentators argue that the recent banking crises are just as (or more) likely to have resulted from exchange rate crises and/or a speculative bubble. Many commentators put little faith in depositors' abilities (let alone incentives) to monitor banks and see bank regulators as better placed to monitor banks in the interest of depositors [see Dewatripont and Tirole (1994)]. Consistent with this perspective is the idea that deposit insurance creates adequate incentives for bank regulators to monitor banks, as it makes them residual claimants on banks' losses. However, these incentives can be outweighed by a lack of commitment to close down insolvent banks and by regulatory forbearance. It is often argued that bank bailouts and the expectation of future bailouts create a 'moral hazard' problem in the allocation of credit (see Chapter 8 in this Volume by Gorton and Winton for an extended survey of these issues). [57]

To summarize, the theoretical literature on bank monitoring shows that delegated monitoring by banks or other financial intermediaries can be an efficient form of corporate governance. It offers one way of resolving collective action problems among multiple investors. However, the effectiveness of bank monitoring depends on bank managers' incentives to monitor. These incentives, in turn, are driven by bank regulation. The existing evidence on bank regulation and banking crises suggests that bank regulation can at least be designed to work when the entire banking system is healthy, but it is often seen to fail when there is a system-wide crisis [see Gorton and Winton (1998)]. Thus, the effectiveness of bank monitoring can vary with the aggregate state of the banking industry. This can explain the perception that Japanese banks have played a broadly positive role in the 1970s and 1980s, while in the 1990s they

---

[56] Pension fund managers' incentives to monitor are not backed with a similar disciplining threat. Despite mandatory requirements for activism (at least in the USA) pension fund managers do not appear to have strong incentives to monitor managers [see Black (1990) for a discussion of USA regulations governing pension funds' monitoring activities and their effects].

[57] The moral hazard problem is exacerbated by bank managers' incentives to hide loan losses as Mitchell (2000) and Aghion, Bolton and Fries (1999) have pointed out. A related problem, which may also exacerbate moral hazard, is banks' inability to commit ex ante to terminate inefficient projects [see Dewatripont and Maskin (1995)]. On the other hand, as senior (secured) debtholders banks also have a bias towards liquidation of distressed lenders [see Zender (1991) and Dewatripont and Tirole (1994)].

appear to have been more concerned with covering up loan losses than with effectively monitoring the corporations they lend to.

5.4. Board models

The third alternative for solving the collective action problem among dispersed shareholders is monitoring of the CEO by a board of directors. Most corporate charters require that shareholders elect a board of directors, whose mission is to select the CEO, monitor management, and vote on important decisions such as mergers and acquisitions, changes in remuneration of the CEO, changes in the firm's capital structure like stock repurchases or new debt issues, etc. In spirit most charters are meant to operate like a 'shareholder democracy', with the CEO as the executive branch of government and the board as the legislative branch. But, as many commentators have argued, in firms with dispersed share ownership the board is more of a 'rubber-stamp assembly' than a truly independent legislature checking and balancing the power of the CEO. One important reason why boards are often 'captured' by management is that CEOs have considerable influence over the choice of directors. CEOs also have superior information. Even when boards have achieved independence from management they are often not as effective as they could be because directors prefer to play a less confrontational 'advisory' role than a more critical monitoring role. Finally, directors generally only have a very limited financial stake in the corporation. Most regulatory efforts have concentrated on the issue of independence of the board. In an attempt to reduce the CEO's influence over the board many countries have introduced requirements that a minimum fraction of the board be composed of so-called 'independent' directors.[58] The rationale behind these regulations is that if directors are not otherwise dependent on the CEO they are more likely to defend shareholders' interests. It is not difficult to find flaws in this logic. For one thing, directors who are unrelated to the firm may lack the knowledge or information to be effective monitors. For another, independent directors are still dependent on the CEO for reappointment. Perhaps the biggest flaw in this perspective is that it does not apply well to concentrated ownership structures. When a large controlling shareholder is in place what may be called for is not only independence from the CEO, but also independence from the controlling shareholder. In corporations with concentrated ownership independent directors must protect the interests of minority shareholders against both the CEO's and the blockholder's actions.

Many commentators view these regulations with much scepticism. To date, most research on boards and the impact of independent directors is empirical, and the findings concerning the effects of independent directors are mixed. Some evidence

---

[58] A director is defined as 'independent' if he or she is not otherwise employed by the corporation, is not engaged in business with the corporation, and is not a family member. Even if the director is a personal friend of the CEO, (s)he will be considered independent if (s)he meets the above criteria.

supporting the hypothesis that independent directors improve board performance is available, such as the higher likelihood that an independent board will dismiss the CEO following poor performance [Weisbach (1988)], or the positive stock price reaction to news of the appointment of an outside director [Rosenstein and Wyatt (1990)]. But other evidence suggests that there is no significant relation between firm performance and board composition [e.g., Hermalin and Weisbach (1991), Byrd and Hickman (1992); Mehran (1995); see Romano (1996), John and Senbet (1998), Hermalin and Weisbach (2003) for surveys of the empirical literature on boards].

In contrast to the large empirical literature on the composition of boards, formal analysis of the role of boards of directors and how they should be regulated is almost non-existent. An important contribution in this area is by Hermalin and Weisbach (1998). They consider a model where the firm's performance together with monitoring by the board reveals information over time about the ability of the CEO. The extent of monitoring by the board is a function of the board's 'independence' as measured by directors' financial incentives as well as their distaste for confronting management. Board independence is thus an endogenous variable. Board appointments in their model are determined through negotiations between the existing board and the CEO. The latter's bargaining power derives entirely from his perceived superior ability relative to alternative managers that might be available. Thus, as the firm does better the CEO's power grows and the independence of the board tends to diminish. As a result CEOs tend to be less closely monitored the longer they have been on the job. Their model highlights an important insight: the gradual erosion of the effectiveness of boards over time. It suggests that regulatory responses should be targeted more directly at the selection process of directors and their financial incentives to monitor management.

The model by Hermalin and Weisbach is an important first step in analyzing how directors get selected and how their incentives to monitor management are linked to the selection process. Other formal analyses of boards do not explicitly model the selection process of directors. Warther (1998) allows for the dismissal of minority directors who oppose management, but newly selected members are assumed to act in the interest of shareholders.[59] Since directors prefer to stay on the board than be dismissed, his model predicts that directors will be reluctant to vote against management unless the evidence of mismanagement is so strong that they can be confident enough that a majority against management will form. His model thus predicts that boards are active only in crisis situations. One implication of his analysis is that limiting dismissal and/or introducing fixed term limits tends to improve the vigilance of the board.

Raheja (2002) does not model the selection process of directors either. He takes the proportion of independent directors as a control variable. A critical assumption in his model is that independent directors are not as well informed as the CEO and inside directors. He considers two types of board decisions: project choice and CEO succession. Competition for succession is used to induce insiders to reveal the

---

[59] See also Noe and Rebello (1996) for a similar model of the functioning of boards.

private information they share about project characteristics. Raheja derives the board composition and size that best elicits insider information and shows how it may vary with underlying firm characteristics.

Hirshleifer and Thakor (1994) consider the interaction between inside monitoring by boards and external monitoring by corporate raiders. Takeover threats have a disciplining effect on both management and boards. They show that sometimes even boards acting in the interest of shareholders may attempt to block a hostile takeover. [60]

Adams (2001) focuses on the conflict between the monitoring and advisory functions of the board: the board's monitoring role can restrict its ability to extract information from management that is needed for its advisory role. Thus the model gives insight into the possible benefits of instituting a dual board system, as in Germany.

In sum, the formal literature on boards is surprisingly thin given the importance of the board of directors in policy debates. This literature mainly highlights the complexity of the issues. There is also surprisingly little common ground between the models. Clearly, much remains to be explored. The literature has mainly focused on issues relating to board composition and the selection of directors. Equally important, however, are issues relating to the functioning of the board and how board meetings can be structured to ensure more effective monitoring of management. This seems to be a particularly fruitful area for future research.

5.5. Executive compensation models

Besides monitoring and control of CEO actions another way of improving shareholder protection is to structure the CEO's rewards so as to align his objectives with those of shareholders. This is what executive compensation is supposed to achieve.

Most compensation packages in publicly traded firms comprise a basic salary component, a bonus related to short run performance (e.g., accounting profits), and a stock participation plan (most of the time in the form of stock options). The package also includes various other benefits, such as pension rights and severance pay (often described as "golden parachutes").

Executive compensation in the USA has skyrocketed in the past decade, in part as a result of the unexpectedly strong bull market, and in part because of the process of determining compensation packages for CEOs. In most USA corporations a compensation committee of the board is responsible for setting executive pay. These committees generally rely on 'market standards' for determining the level and structure of pay. [61] This process tends to result in an upward creep in pay standards. USA corporations set by far the highest levels of CEO compensation in the world. Although

---

[60] See also Maug (1997) for an analysis of the relative strengths and weaknesses of board supervision, takeovers and leverage in disciplining management.

[61] Compensation committees often rely on the advice of outside experts who make recommendations based on observed average pay, the going rate for the latest hires, and/or their estimate of the pay expected by potential candidates.

USA executives were already the highest paid executives in the world by a wide margin at the beginning of the past decade – even correcting for firm size – the gap in CEO pay has continued to widen significantly over the past decade – largely due to the growing importance of stock options in executive compensation packages [see Murphy (1999) for an extensive survey of empirical and theoretical work on executive compensation and Hallock and Murphy (1999) for a reader].

There has always been the concern that although stock options may improve CEOs' incentives to raise share value they are also a simple and direct way for CEOs to enrich themselves and expropriate shareholders. Indeed, practitioners see a grant of an unusually large compensation package as a signal of poor corporate governance [Minow (2000)].

Despite this frequently voiced concern, however, there has been no attempt to analyze the determination of executive pay along the lines of Hermalin and Weisbach (1998), by explicitly modelling the bargaining process between the CEO, the remuneration committee and the Board, as well as the process of selection of committee and board members. Instead, most existing formal analyses have relied on the general theory of contracting under moral hazard of Mirrlees (1976, 1999), Holmstrom (1979) and Grossman and Hart (1983) to draw general conclusions about the structure of executive pay, such as the trade-off between risk-sharing and incentives and the desirability of basing compensation on all performance measures that are informative about the CEO's actions.

The agency model of Holmstrom and Tirole (1993), which introduces stock trading in a secondary market, can rationalize the three main components of executive compensation packages (salary, profit related bonus, and stock participation), but that does not mean that in practice executive compensation consultants base the design of compensation contracts on fine considerations such as the relative informativeness of different performance measures. On the contrary, all existing evidence suggests that these are not the main considerations for determining the structure of the pay package [see again the extensive survey by Murphy (1999)].

Another complicating factor is that CEOs are driven by both implicit and explicit incentives. They are concerned about performance not only because their pay is linked to performance but also because their future career opportunities are affected. The formal analysis of Gibbons and Murphy (1992) allows for both types of incentives. [62] It suggests that explicit incentives should be rising with age and tenure, as the longer the CEO has been on the job the lower are his implicit incentives.

Finally, much of the agency theory that justifies executive compensation schemes unrealistically assumes that earnings and stock prices cannot be manipulated. This

---

[62] See also Holmstrom and Ricart i Costa (1986) and Zwiebel (1995) for an analysis of managerial compensation with implicit incentives. These papers focus on the issue of how career concerns can distort managers' incentives to invest efficiently. In particular they can induce a form of conservatism in the choice of investment projects.

is a major weakness of the theory as brought to light in recent accounting scandals involving Enron, Global Crossing, WorldCom and others. To quote corporate governance expert Nell Minow: "Options are very motivational. We just have to be a little more thoughtful about what it is we're asking them to motivate".[63]

All in all, while the extensive literature on agency theory provides a useful framework for analyzing optimal incentive contracts it is generally too far removed from the specifics of executive compensation. Moreover, the important link between executive compensation and corporate governance, as well as the process of determination of executive pay remain open problems to be explored at a formal level.

5.6. Multi-constituency models

The formal literature on boards and executive compensation takes the view that the board exclusively represents the interests of shareholders. In practice, however, this is not always the case. When a firm has a long-term relation with a bank it is not uncommon that a bank representative sits on the board [see Bacon and Brown (1975)]. Similarly, it is not unusual for CEOs of firms in related businesses to sit on the board. In some countries, most notably Germany, firms are even required to have representatives of employees on the board. The extent to which boards should be mandated to have representatives of other constituencies besides shareholders is a hotly debated issue. In the European Union in particular the issue of board representation of employees is a major stumbling block for the adoption of the European Company Statute (ECS).[64]

As important as this issue is there is only a small formal literature on the subject. What is worse, this literature mostly considers highly stylized models of multiple constituencies. Perhaps the biggest gap is the absence of a model that considers the functioning of a board with representatives of multiple constituencies. Existing models mainly focus on the issue of when and whether it is desirable for the firm to share control among multiple constituencies. These models are too stylized to address the issue of board representation.

5.6.1. Sharing control with creditors

A number of studies have considered the question of dividing control between managers, shareholders and creditors and how different control allocations affect future liquidation or restructuring decisions. A critical factor in these studies is whether share ownership is concentrated or not.

Aghion and Bolton (1992) consider a situation where ownership is concentrated and argue that family-owned firms want to limit control by outside investors because

---

[63] *New York Times,* 17 February 2002.

[64] Either the ECS would allow German companies to opt out of mandatory codetermination or it would impose mandatory codetermination on all companies adopting the ECS.

they value the option of being able to pursue actions in the future which may not be profit maximizing. They may value family control so much that they may want to turn down acquisition bids even if they are worth more than the net present value of the current business. Or, they may prefer to keep the business small and under family control even if it is more profitable to expand the business. In some situations, however, they may have no choice but to relinquish some if not all control to the outside investor if they want to secure capital at reasonable cost. Aghion and Bolton show that under some conditions the efficient contractual arrangement is to have a state-contingent control allocation, as under debt financing or under standard venture capital arrangements.[65] Although their model only considers a situation of bilateral contracting with incomplete contracts it captures some basic elements of a multi-constituency situation and provides a rationale for extending control to other constituencies than shareholders.

Another rationale for dividing control with creditors (or more generally fixed claim holders) is given in Zender (1991), Diamond (1991, 1993), Dewatripont and Tirole (1994), Berglöf and von Thadden (1994), Aoki (1990) and Aoki et al. (1994). All these studies propose that the threat of termination (or liquidation) if performance is poor may be an effective incentive scheme for management. But, in order to credibly commit to liquidate the firm if performance is poor, control must be transferred to fixed claimholders. As these investors get a disproportionate share of the liquidation value and only a fraction of the potential continuation value, they are more inclined to liquidate the firm than shareholders, who as the most junior claimholders often prefer to 'gamble for resurrection'. The commitment to liquidate is all the stronger the more dispersed debt is, as that makes debt restructuring in the event of financial distress more difficult [see Hart and Moore (1995), Dewatripont and Maskin (1995), Bolton and Scharfstein (1996)].

Interestingly, Berkovitch and Israel (1996) have argued that when it comes to replacing managers, shareholders may be more inclined to be tough than creditors. The reason why a large shareholder is more likely to fire a poorly performing manager is that the shareholder effectively exercises a valuable option when replacing the manager, while the creditor does not. Sometimes the large shareholder may be too eager to replace management, in which case it may be desirable to let creditors have veto rights over management replacement decisions (or to have them sit on the board).

Another way of limiting shareholders' power to dismiss management is, of course, to have a diffuse ownership structure. This is the situation considered by Chang (1992). In his model the firm can only rely on creditors to dismiss management, since share ownership is dispersed. Chang shows that creditors are more likely to dismiss a poorly

---

[65] The analysis of venture capital contracts in terms of contingent control allocations has been pursued and extended by Berglöf (1994), Hellman (1997) and Neher (1999). More recently, Kaplan and Strömberg (2003) have provided a detailed analysis of control allocation in 100 venture capital contracts. Their analysis highlights the prevalence of contingent control allocations in venture capital contracts.

performing manager the higher the firm's leverage. Since a large shareholder would tend to dismiss poorly performing managers too easily, Chang shows that there is an efficient level of leverage, implementing a particular division of control rights.

5.6.2. Sharing control with employees

Models of corporate governance showing that some form of shared control between creditors and shareholders may be optimal can sometimes also be reinterpreted as models of shared control between employees and the providers of capital. This is the case of Chang's model, where the role of employee representatives on the board can be justified as a way of dampening shareholders' excessive urge to dismiss employees.

But for a systematic analysis of shared governance arrangements one has to turn to the general theory of property rights recently formulated by Grossman, Hart and Moore [see Grossman and Hart (1986), Hart and Moore (1990), Hart (1995)]. The central issue in their theory is the so-called 'holdup' problem,[66] which refers to the potential ex-post expropriation of unprotected returns from *ex ante* (specific)[67] human capital investment. Much of the property-rights theory is concerned with the protection of physical capital [as in Grossman and Hart (1986)], but it also deals with human capital investments. An extreme example of 'holdup' problem for human capital investments is the case of a researcher or inventor, who cannot specify terms of trade for his invention before its creation. Once his machine or product is invented, however, the inventor can only extract a fraction of the total value of the invention to his clients (assuming there is limited competition among clients). What is worse, the ex-post terms of trade will not take into account the research and development costs, which are 'sunk' at the time of negotiation. The terms of trade the inventor will be able to negotiate, however, will be greater if he owns the assets that are required to produce the invention, or if he sits on the board of directors of the client company.

As this example highlights, a general prediction of the theory of property rights is that some form of shared control with employees is efficient, whenever employees (like the inventor) make valuable firm-specific human-capital investments.[68]

Building on this property-rights theory, Roberts and Van den Steen (2000) and

---

[66] See Goldberg (1976) and Klein, Crawford and Alchian (1978) for an early informal definition and discussion of the holdup concept. See also Williamson (1971, 1975, 1979, 1985a) for a discussion of the closely related concept of opportunism.

[67] It is only when investment is specific to a relation, or a task, that concerns of ex-post expropriation arise. If investment is of a general purpose, then competition ex-post for the investment provides adequate protection to the investor.

[68] The property-rights theory also provides a useful analytical framework to assess the costs and benefits of privatization of state-owned firms. Thus, Hart, Shleifer and Vishny (1997) have argued that privatized firms have a better incentive to minimize costs, but the systematic pursuit of profits may also lead to the provision of poorer quality service. They apply their analysis to the case of privatization of prisons. Perhaps a more apt application might have been to the privatization of railways in the UK and the Netherlands, where quality of service has visibly deteriorated following privatization. Schmidt (1996) and Shapiro and Willig (1990) emphasize a different trade-off. They argue that under state ownership the government has better information about the firm's management (that is the benefit), but the government

Bolton and Xu (2001) provide a related justification for employee representation on the board to Chang's. They consider firms in professional service or R&D intensive industries, where firm-specific human capital investment by employees adds significant value. As in Hart and Moore (1990), say, an important issue in these firms is how to protect employees against the risk of ex-post expropriation or hold-up by management or the providers of financial capital. More concretely, the issue is how to guarantee sufficient job security to induce employees to invest in the firm. Indeed, as with any provider of capital (financial or human), employees will tend to under-invest in firm-specific human capital if they do not have adequate protection against ex-post hold ups and expropriation threats. They show that in firms where (firm-specific) human capital is valuable it may be in the interest of the providers of capital to share control with employees, although generally the providers of financial capital will relinquish less control to employees than is efficient. Indeed, the providers of financial capital are concerned as much with extracting the highest possible share of profits as with inducing the highest possible creation of profits through human capital investments.[69]

Sharing control with employees can be achieved by letting employees participate in share ownership of the company, by giving them board representation, or by strengthening their bargaining power through, say, increased unionization. An important remark made by Holmstrom (1999) and echoed by Roberts and Van den Steen (2000) is that when employees cannot participate in corporate decision-making a likely response may be unionization and/or strikes. There are many examples in corporate history where this form of employee protection has proved to be highly inefficient, often resulting in extremely costly conflict resolutions.

Thus, in practice an important effect of employee representation on boards may be that employees' human capital investments are better protected and that shareholders' excessive urge to dismiss employees is dampened. Interestingly, there appears to be some empirical evidence of this effect of employee representation in the study of co-determination in German corporations by Gorton and Schmid (2000a). However, their study also suggests that shareholders in Germany do not passively accept board representation by employees. In an effort to counteract employees' influence they tend to encourage the firm to be more highly levered [as Perotti and Spier (1993) have explained, creditors are likely to be tougher in liquidation decisions than shareholders]. Also, in some cases, shareholder representatives have gone as far as holding informal meetings on their own to avoid disclosing sensitive information or discussing delicate decisions with representatives of employees.

---

also tends to interfere too much (that is the cost). Bolton (1995) looks at yet another angle. He argues that state ownership is actually a form of governance with extreme dispersion of ownership (all the citizens are owners). This structure tends to exacerbate problems of self-dealing. These problems, however, are not always best dealt with through privatization, which may also involve shareholder dispersion. Pointing to the example of Chinese Township and Village enterprises, Bolton argues instead that state ownership at the community level may be another way of mitigating the inefficiencies of state-owned firms.

[69] Again, see Aghion and Bolton (1987) for a formal elaboration of this point.

An extreme result highlighted by Roberts and Van den Steen (2000) is that it may even be efficient to have employee-dominated boards when only human capital investment matters. Examples of such governance structures are not uncommon in practice, especially in the professional services industry. Most accounting, consulting or law partnerships effectively have employee-dominated boards. Another example is universities, where academics not only have full job security (when they have tenure) but also substantial control rights.[70]

Hansmann (1996) and Hart and Moore (1996, 1998) are concerned with another aspect of governance by employees. They ask when it is best to have 'inside' ownership and control in the form of an employee cooperative or partnership, or when 'outside' ownership in the form of a limited liability company is better. A central prediction of the property rights theory is that ownership and control rights should be given to the parties that make ex-ante specific investments. In other words, it should be given mainly to 'insiders'. Yet, as Hansmann and Hart and Moore observe, the dominant form of governance structure is 'outside' ownership. Hansmann resolves this apparent paradox by arguing that often shareholders are the most homogenous constituency in a firm and therefore are generally the best placed group to minimize decision-making costs. He also accepts Williamson's argument that shareholders are the constituency in most need of protection due to the open-ended nature of their contracts. Hart and Moore (1996, 1998) also focus on distortions in decision-making that can arise in a member cooperative, where members have very diverse interests.[71] They compare these distortions to those that can arise under outside ownership. However, they only consider outside ownership by a single large shareholder and assume away all the governance issues related to dispersed ownership. Like Aghion and Tirole (1997), Burkart, Gromb and Panunzi (1997), and Pagano and Röell (1998), they argue that a large shareholder will introduce distortions in his attempt to extract a larger share of the firm's value. At the margin he will do this even at the expense of greater value creation. The central observations of their analysis are that employee cooperatives are relatively worse governance structures the more heterogeneous employees are as a group, and outside ownership is relatively better the more the firm faces competition limiting the outside owner's ability to extract rents. They apply their analytical framework to explain why greater worldwide financial integration, which has resulted in increased competition among stock exchanges, has led to a move towards the incorporation of exchanges.

---

[70] Bolton and Xu (2001) extend this analysis by considering how internal and external competition among employees can provide alternative or complementary protections to employee control [see also Zingales (1998) for a discussion of corporate governance as a mechanism to mitigate ex-post hold-up problems, and Rajan and Zingales (2000) for an analysis of when a shareholder-controlled firm wants to create internal competition among employees as an incentive scheme].

[71] It has often been highlighted that an important source of conflict in member cooperatives is the conflict between old and young members. The former want to milk past investments, while the younger members want to invest more in the firm [see Mitchell (1990)].

To summarize, the property rights theory of Grossman, Hart and Moore provides one basic rationale for sharing corporate control with employees and for employee representation on the board: protection of employees' firm-specific investments. But there may be others, like potentially better monitoring of management by employees. Indeed, the latter are likely to be better informed than shareholders about the management's actions, and they may be in a better position to monitor the management of, say, company pension plans. As persuasive as these reasons may be, however, it does not follow that rules mandating employee representation on the board, as in Germany, are necessarily desirable. As we have argued above, such rules can only be justified by appealing to a contractual failure of some kind. As we have already mentioned, one important potential source of contractual failure under sequential contracting, may arise when the providers of capital and the entrepreneur design the corporate charter partly as a means of extracting future potential rents from employees [see Aghion and Bolton (1987), Scharfstein (1988)]. Another possible failure, as Aghion and Bolton (1987), Aghion and Hermalin (1990), Spier (1992) and Freeman and Lazear (1995) have argued, may be due to the firm's founders' concern that allowing for employee representation may send a bad signal to potential investors.

But, even if contractual failures exist, they must be weighed against other potential inefficiencies that may arise as a result of multi-constituency representation on the board, such as shareholder responses to weaken employee influence, greater board passivity or less disclosure of valuable but divisive information by management. One argument against multiple constituencies that is sometimes voiced is that when the firm's management is required to trade off the interests of different constituencies one important 'side effect' is that management gains too much discretion. When the stock tanks management can always claim that it was acting in the interest of employees [see, for example, Macey (1992), Tirole (2001), Hart (1995), Jensen (2002)]. This argument is particularly relevant when defining the CEO's fiduciary duties (or 'mission'). If these duties are too broadly defined to include the interests of multiple constituencies they are in danger of becoming toothless. The current narrow definition of fiduciary duties in the USA is already balanced by the 'business judgement rule', which makes it difficult for plaintiffs to prevail. If one were to add a 'protection of other constituencies rule' it is likely that winning a suit would be even harder.

However, note that as relevant as this argument is when applied to the definition of the fiduciary duties of the CEO, it is less so when applied to board representation. Having representatives of creditors, employees or related firms on the board does not *per se* increase the manager's discretion. The manager is still monitored by the board and will still have to deal with the majority of directors that control the board, just as in any democracy the power of the executive branch of government is held in check by the majority in control of the legislature, no matter how diverse the representation of the legislature is. Unfortunately, a systematic analysis of these issues remains to be done, as there are no formal models of the functioning of boards with representation of multiple constituencies. Nor are there comparative empirical studies analyzing the differences in managerial accountability and discretion in Germany and other countries.

Finally, as the introduction of mandatory employee representation has both efficiency and distributive effects there must be a sufficiently strong political constituency supporting such rules. Although the link between politics and corporate governance regulation is clearly relevant there has been virtually no formal modelling of this link. A recent exception is Pagano and Volpin (1999) who derive the degree of investor protection endogenously from a political equilibrium between 'rentier', management and employees. [72] They show that depending on the relative political power of these constituencies, different laws on shareholder protection will be enacted. Thus, if the employee constituency is large and powerful as, say in Italy, then laws will be less protective of shareholder interests. [73]

6. Comparative perspectives and debates

Sections 4 and 5 illustrate the core issues of corporate governance: how to decide who should participate in corporate governance, how to solve the collective action problem of supervising management, how to regulate takeovers and the actions of large investors, how boards should be structured, how managers' fiduciary duties should be defined, what are appropriate legal actions against managerial abuses, all these issues have no unique simple answer. Corporations have multiple constituencies and there are multiple and interlocking tradeoffs. Different solutions may be needed depending on the type of activity to be financed. Human capital-intensive projects may require different governance arrangements than capital-intensive projects; [74] projects with long implementation periods may require different solutions than projects with short horizons. [75] It is not possible to conclude on the basis of economic analysis alone that there is a unique set of optimal rules that are universally applicable to all corporations and economies, just as there is no single political constitution that is universally best for all nations.

The practical reality of corporate governance is one of great diversity across countries and corporations. An alternative line of research that complements the formal analyses described in the previous section exploits the great diversity of corporate governance rules across countries and firms, attempting to uncover statistical relations between corporate governance practice and performance or to gain insights from a comparative institutional analysis. A whole sub-field of research has developed

---

[72] A second paper by Pagano and Volpin (2002) shifts the focus to the internal politics of the firm, arguing that there is a natural alliance between management and employees in staving off hostile bids.

[73] As we discuss below, there has been substantially more systematic historical analysis of the link between politics and corporate governance, most notably by Roe (1994), who argues that weak minority shareholder protection is the expected outcome in social democracies.

[74] See, for example, Allen and Gale (2000), Maher and Andersson (2000), Rajan and Zingales (2000) and Roberts and Van den Steen (2000) for discussions of how corporate governance may vary with underlying business characteristics.

[75] See Maher and Andersson (2000) and Carlin and Mayer (2003) for a discussion of corporate governance responses in firms with different investment horizons.

comparing the strengths and weaknesses of corporate governance rules in different
countries. In this section we review the main comparative perspectives on governance
systems proposed in the literature.[76]

6.1. Comparative systems

Broadly speaking and at the risk of oversimplifying, two systems of corporate
governance have been pitted against each other: the Anglo-American market-based
system and the long-term large investor models of, say, Germany and Japan. Which
of these systems has been most favored by commentators has varied over time as
a function of the relative success of each country's underlying economy, with two
broad phases: the 1980s – when the Japanese and German long-term investor corporate
governance perspective were seen as strengths relative to the Anglo-American market-
based short-termist perspective – and the 1990s – when greater minority shareholder
protections and the greater reliance on equity financing in the Anglo-American systems
were seen as major advantages.[77]

Japanese and German corporate governance looked good in the 1980s when Japan
and Germany were growing faster than the USA. In contrast, in the late 1990s,
following nearly a decade of economic recession in Japan, a decade of costly post-
unification economic adjustments in Germany, and an unprecedented economic and
stock market boom in the USA, the American corporate governance model has been
hailed as the model for all to follow [see Hansmann and Kraakman (2001)]. As
we are writing sentiment is turning again in light of the stock market excesses on
Nasdaq and the *Neuer Markt,* which have resulted in massive overinvestment in the
technology sector, leading to some of the largest bankruptcies in corporate history,
often accompanied by corporate governance scandals.[78]

---

[76] For recent surveys of the comparative corporate governance literature see Roe (1996), Bratton and
McCahery (1999) and Allen and Gale (2000); see also the collections edited by Hopt et al. (1998),
McCahery et al. (2002) and Hopt and Wymeersch (2003).

[77] The comparative classifications proposed in the literature broadly fit this (over)simplification.
Commentators have distinguished between "bank oriented" and "market oriented" systems [e.g., Berglöf
(1990)] and "insider" versus "outsider" systems [e.g., Franks and Mayer (1995)]. These distinctions are
based on a range of characteristics of governance and financial systems, such as the importance of long-
term bank lending relations, share ownership concentration, stock market capitalization and regulatory
restrictions on shareholder power. More recently, commentators such as La Porta et al. (1998) attempt
no such distinction and introduce a single ranking of countries' corporate governance systems according
to the extent of minority shareholder protections as measured by an "anti-director rights index" based on
six elements of corporate law. As we shall see, all attempts at objectively classifying country corporate
governance systems have been criticized for overemphasizing, leaving out or misunderstanding elements
of each country's system. Thus, for example, the declining importance of the market for corporate
control in the USA has generally been overlooked, as well as the lower anti-director rights in Delaware
[see Kraakman et al. (2003)]. Similarly, bank influence in Germany has often been exaggerated [see
Edwards and Fischer (1994), Hellwig (2000b)], or the importance of stock markets in Japan [La Porta
et al. (2000b)].

[78] Enron is the landmark case, but there have been many smaller cases on *Neuer Markt* that have these
characteristics.

Critics of USA governance in the 1980s have argued that Germany and Japan had a lower cost of capital because corporations maintained close relationships with banks and other long-term debt and equity holders. As a result Japan had a low cost of equity,[79] Germany a low cost of bank debt and both could avoid the equity premium by sustaining high levels of leverage [see e.g., Fukao (1995)]. Despite a convergence of the real cost of debt and equity during the 1980s [McCauley and Zimmer (1994)], they have enjoyed a lower cost of capital than the USA and the UK. As a result, Japanese corporations had higher investment rates than their USA counterparts [Prowse (1990)]. Interestingly, a revisionist perspective gained prominence in the early 1990s according to which the low cost of capital in Japan was a sign of excesses leading to overinvestment [Kang and Stulz (2000)].

Following the stock market crash of 1990, Japan lost its relatively low cost of equity capital, while the USA gradually gained a lower cost of equity capital as the unprecedented bull market gained steam. This lower cost of equity capital in the USA has been seen by many commentators as resulting from superior minority shareholder protections [see e.g., La Porta et al. (1998)], and was often the stated reason why foreign firms increasingly chose to issue shares on Nasdaq and other USA exchanges and why the *Neuer Markt* was booming [see Coffee (2002), La Porta et al. (2000b)]. Similarly the Asian crisis has been attributed to poor investor protections (see Johnson (2000) and Claessens, Djankov, Fan and Lang (2002); and Shinn and Gourevitch (2002) for the implications for USA policy to promote better governance worldwide). Exchanges that adopted NASDAQ-style IPO strategies and investor protections, like the *Neuer Market* in Germany, have witnessed a similar boom (and bust) cycle. With the benefit of hindsight, however, it appears that the low cost of equity capital on these exchanges during the late 1990s had more to do with the technology bubble than with minority shareholder protection, just as the low cost of capital in Japan in the late 1980s had more to do with the real estate bubble than with Japanese corporate governance.

Another aspect of Japanese corporate governance that has been praised in the 1980s is the long-run nature of relationships between the multiple constituencies in the corporation, which made greater involvement by employees and suppliers possible. It has been argued that this greater participation by employees and suppliers has facilitated the introduction of 'just in time' or 'lean production' methods in Japanese manufacturing firms [see Womack et al. (1991)]. The benefits of these long-term relations have been contrasted with the costs of potential 'breaches of trust' following hostile takeovers in the USA [Shleifer and Summers (1988)].[80]

One of the main criticisms of Anglo-American market-based corporate governance has been that managers tend to be obsessed with quarterly performance measures and

---

[79] The cost of equity was significantly lower in Japan in the 1980s. This advantage has of course disappeared following the stock market crash.

[80] As 'lean production' methods have successfully been implemented in the USA, however, it has become clear that these methods do not depend fundamentally on the implementation of Japanese-style corporate governance [Sabel (1996)].

have an excessively short-termist perspective. Thus, Narayanan (1985), Shleifer and Vishny (1989), Porter (1992a,b) and Stein (1988, 1989), among others, have argued that USA managers are myopically 'short-termist' and pay too much attention to potential takeover threats. Porter, in particular, contrasts USA corporate governance with the governance in German and Japanese corporations, where the long-term involvement of investors, especially banks, allowed managers to invest for the long run while, at the same time, monitoring their performance. Japanese *keiretsu* have also been praised for their superior ability to resolve financial distress or achieve corporate diversification [see e.g., Aoki (1990), Hoshi, Kashyap and Scharfstein (1990)]. This view has also been backed by critics in the USA, who have argued that populist political pressures at the beginning of the last century have led to the introduction of financial regulations which excessively limit effective monitoring by USA financial institutions and other large investors, leading these authors to call for larger and more active owners [see Roe (1990, 1991, 1994), Black (1990)].[81]

In the 1990s the positive sides of Anglo-American corporate governance have gradually gained greater prominence. Hostile takeovers were no longer criticized for bringing about short-termist behavior. They were instead hailed as an effective way to break up inefficient conglomerates [Shleifer and Vishny (1997b)].[82] Most commentators praising the Anglo-American model of corporate governance single out hostile takeovers as a key feature of this model. Yet, starting in the early 1990s the market for corporate control in the USA has essentially collapsed.[83] Indeed, following the wave of anti-takeover laws and charter amendments introduced at the end of the 1980s, most USA corporations are now extremely well protected against hostile takeovers.[84] Their control is generally no longer contestable.[85] In contrast, in the UK

---

[81] Interestingly, even the former chairman of the Securities and Exchange Commission argued against 'over-regulation' and 'short-termism' [Grundfest (1993)] and for "investors' ability to monitor corporate performance and to control assets that they ultimately own", an ability that the USA regulatory systems has "subordinated to the interests of other constituencies, most notable corporate management" [Grundfest (1990, pp. 89–90)]. The call for more active (and larger) owners is also typical of USA shareholder activists [see Monks and Minow (2001)].

[82] See Chapter 2 in this Handbook for a survey of the conglomerate literature.

[83] See Comment and Schwert (1995) for the early 1990s and Bebchuk, Coates and Subramanian (2002) for 1996–2000.

[84] See Danielson and Karpoff (1998) for a detailed analysis of takeover defences in the USA. Grundfest (1993) observed: "The takeover wars are over. Management won [...] As a result, corporate America is now governed by directors who are largely impervious to capital market electoral challenges".

[85] The introduction of the anti-takeover laws has also shifted perceptions on state corporate law competition. This competition is not depicted as a "race to the bottom" anymore as in Cary (1974) or Bebchuk (1992). Instead Romano (1993) has argued in her influential book, *The Genius of American Law,* that competition between states in the production of corporate law leads to better laws. She goes as far as recommending the extension of such competition to securities regulation [Romano (1998)]. On the other hand, Bebchuk and Ferrell (1999, 2001) have argued that it is hard to justify the race to pass anti-takeover laws as a race to the top. Supporting their view, Kamar (1998) has pointed out that network effects can create regulatory monopolies and that limited state competition may therefore be

the City Code prevents post-bid action that might frustrate the bid and few companies have put in place pre-bid defenses, thus making the UK the only OECD country with an active and open market for corporate control. [86]

An influential recent classification of corporate governance systems has been provided by La Porta et al. (1997, 1998). The authors show that indices designed to capture the degree of investor protection in different countries correlate very strongly with a classification of legal systems based on the notion of "legal origin" [inspired by David and Brierley (1985)]. [87] In a series of papers the authors go on to show that legal origin correlates with the size of stock markets, [88] ownership concentration, the level of dividend payments, [89] corporate valuation and other measures of the financial system across a large cross-section of countries [La Porta et al. (1997, 1999, 2000a, 2002)]. [90] Other authors have applied the legal origin view to issues like cross-border mergers and the home bias. [91] Stulz and Williamson (2003) add language and religion (culture) as possible explanatory variables.

In the same vein the regulatory constraints in the USA that hamper intervention by large shareholders, previously criticized for giving too much discretion to management [e.g., by Roe (1990, 1991, 1994), Black (1990), Grundfest (1990)], have been painted

---

consistent with the existence of inferior standards that are hard to remove. He goes on to argue that the break up of the monopoly of the SEC over securities regulation could lead to convergence to the standards of the dominant producer of corporate law, Delaware.

[86] In the UK institutional investors have larger holdings and regulation allows them to jointly force companies to dismantle their pre-bid defenses. For example, in the mid-1970s Lloyds Bank wanted to cap votes at 500 votes per shareholder, which would have left the largest twenty shareholders commanding 16% of the voting rights with 0.01% each. Institutional investors threatened to boycott Lloyd's issues and the plan was dropped [Black and Coffee (1994)]. In 2001 institutional investors "encouraged" British Telecom to rescind a 15% ownership and voting power ceiling, a powerful pre-bid defence dating back to BT's privatization.

[87] The La Porta et al. (1997, 1998) indices do not cover securities regulation and have been widely criticized, both conceptually and because the numbers are wrong for certain countries. Of course the direct correlation between "legal origin" and other variables is not affected by such criticism. Pistor (2000) broadens and improves the basic index design for a cross-section of transition countries. She shows that improvements in the index levels were larger in countries that implemented voucher privatizations (opted for ownership dispersion), concluding that corporate finance drives changes in the index levels, not legal origin.

[88] Rajan and Zingales (2001) show that the correlation of legal origin and the size of stock markets did not hold at the beginning of the century.

[89] On corporate governance and payout policies see Chapter 7 in this Handbook.

[90] La Porta et al. (2000b) provide a summary of this view.

[91] The "legal origin" view's prediction that bidders from common law countries increase the value of civil law targets, because the post-bid entity has (value-enhancing) common law level investor protection is supported by recent studies of cross-border mergers [Bris and Cabolis (2002), Rossi and Volpin (2003)]. At the same time, recent acquisitions by U.S. (common law) firms were generally poor, producing very large losses in bidder value [Moeller, Schlingemann and Stulz (2003a,b)]. Dahlquist, Pinkowitz, Stulz and Williamson (2003) relate investor protection to the size of free float in different countries and the "home bias".

in a positive light as providing valuable protections to minority shareholders against expropriation or self-dealing by large shareholders, reversing the causality of the argument [see La Porta et al. (2000b), Bebchuk (1999, 2000)].[92] In a recent reply, Roe (2002) argues that this argument is misconceived because it is based on a misunderstanding of corporate law. Law imposes very few limits on managerial discretion and agency costs, particularly in the United States, suggesting that the correlation between classifications of corporate law and ownership concentration is spurious or captures the influence of missing variables, for example the degree of product market competition. More damagingly, recent historical evidence shows that investor protection in the United Kingdom was not very strong before World War II [Cheffins (2002)], but ownership has already dispersed very quickly [Franks, Mayer and Rossi (2003)].

Recently, some commentators have gone as far as predicting a world-wide convergence of corporate governance practice to the USA model [see e.g., Hansmann and Kraakman (2001)].[93] In a variant of this view, world-wide competition to attract corporate headquarters and investment is seen like the corporate law competition between USA states portrayed by Romano (1993). Such competition is predicted to eventually bring about a single standard resembling the current law in Delaware or, at least, securities regulation standards as set by the USA SEC [see Coffee (1999)].[94]

Although few advocates of the Anglo-American model look back at the 1980s and the perceived strengths of the Japanese and German models at the time, there have been some attempts to reconcile these contradictions. Thus, some commentators have argued that poison pill amendments and other anti-takeover devices are actually an improvement because they eliminate partial bids "of a coercive character" [Hansmann and Kraakman (2001)]. Others have also argued that the market for corporate control in the USA is more active than elsewhere, suggesting that U.S. anti-takeover rules are less effective than anti-takeover measures elsewhere [La Porta et al. (1999)]. Finally, Holmstrom and Kaplan (2001) have argued that the hostile takeovers and leveraged

---

[92] This reversal of causality is particularly important in the context of emerging markets because it provides and alternative "ex-post" rationalisation of the voucher privatization experiment in the Czech Republic.

[93] Hansmann and Kraakman (2001) call the U.S. model the "standard shareholder-oriented model". In the shareholder model "ultimate control over the corporation should be in the hands of the shareholder class; [...] managers [...] should be charged with the obligation to manage the corporation in the interests of its shareholders; [...] other corporate constituencies, such as creditors, employees, suppliers, and customers should have their interests protected by contractual and regulatory means rather than through participation in corporate governance; [...] non-controlling shareholders should receive strong protection from exploitation at the hands of controlling shareholders; [...] the principal measure of the interests of the public corporation's shareholders is the market value of their shares in their firm". They contrast this "standard model" with the "manager-oriented model", the "labour-oriented model", the "state-oriented model" and the "stakeholder model".

[94] In Europe, The Netherlands now seems to be taking on Delaware's role. Andenas, Hopt and Wymeersch (2003) survey the legal mobility of companies within the European Union.

buyouts of the 1980s are no longer needed as USA governance "has reinvented itself, and the rest of the world seems to be following the same path".[95]

As we write, dissatisfaction with U.S. corporate governance is on the rise again. There is little doubt that the Enron collapse, the largest corporate bankruptcy in USA history to date, was caused by corporate governance problems. Yet Enron had all the characteristics of an exemplary "Anglo-American" corporation. As stock prices are falling executive remuneration (compensation) at U.S. corporations looks increasingly out of line with corporate reality. At the same time the global corporate governance reform movement is pressing ahead, but not necessarily by imitating the U.S. model.[96] The most visible manifestations are corporate governance codes that have been adopted in most markets, except the USA.[97]

6.2. Views expressed in corporate governance principles and codes

Following the publication of the Cadbury Report and Recommendations (1992) in the UK, there has been a proliferation of proposals by various committees and interest groups on corporate governance principles and codes.[98] These policy documents have

---

[95] Holmstrom and Kaplan (2001) emphasize that the lucrative stock option plans of the 1990s have replaced the disciplinary role of hostile takeovers and debt (see Section 7.5). They also stress the role of activist boards and investors (*op. cit.,* p. 140).

[96] Indeed, on takeover regulation many countries are explicitly rejecting the USA model adopting mandatory bid rules and not the Delaware rules. At the same time pension funds are lobbying corporations to take into account the interests of multiple constituencies, under the banner of "corporate social responsibility".

[97] There are indications that, as a result of the Enron collapse, the USA too will join in this global development originating from other shores.

[98] The Cadbury Report and Recommendations (1992) is the benchmark for corporate governance codes. Cadbury also set the agenda on issues and provided an example of "soft regulation" the business community in other countries was quick to endorse and emulate, for example the "comply or explain" principle of enforcement via moral suasion and implicit contracts. However, Cadbury did not invent the governance wheel. The subject was already receiving attention in Commonwealth countries like Hong Kong (1989) and Australia (1991).

Internationally, the OECD (1999) "Principles of Corporate Governance" have been the main catalyst for the development of further codes and a driver of law reform (see www.oecd.org). The OECD Principles were a direct response to the Asia/Russia/Brazil crisis (see Section 3.5).

In the UK, Cadbury was followed by the Greenbury Committee (1995), the Hampel Committee (1998) and the "Combined Code". Other Commonwealth countries followed suit: Canada [Dey Committee (1994)], South Africa [King Committee (1994)], Thailand [Stock Exchange of Thailand (SET) (1998)], India [Confederation of Indian Industry (1998)], Singapore [Stock Exchange of Singapore (1998)], Malaysia [High Level Finance Committee on Corporate Governance (1999)] and the Commonwealth Association (1999).

In Continental Europe, corporate governance principles, recommendations and "codes of best practice" are also numerous. France has seen two Viénot Reports (1995, updated in 1999), the Netherlands the Peters Report (1997), Spain the Olivencia Report (1998) and Belgium the Cardon Report (1998). Greece, Italy and Portugal followed in 1999, Finland and Germany in 2000, Denmark in 2001, and Austria

been issued by institutional investors and their advisors, companies, stock exchanges, securities markets regulators, international organizations and lawmakers.[99] We briefly take stock of these views here and contrast them with the general economic principles discussed in the models section (Section 5) as well as the available empirical evidence (Section 7).[100]

Codes provide recommendations on a variety of issues such as executive compensation, the role of auditors, the role of non-shareholder constituencies and their relation with the company, disclosure, shareholder voting and capital structure, the role of large shareholders and anti-takeover devices. But a quick reading of these codes quickly reveals their dominant focus on boards and board-related issues.[101] Topics covered by codes include: board membership criteria, separation of the role of chairman of the board and CEO, board size, the frequency of board meetings, the proportion of inside versus outside (and independent) directors, the appointment of former executives as directors, age and other term limits, evaluation of board performance, the existence, number and structure of board committees, meeting length and agenda, and assignment and rotation of members.[102] Interestingly, many of the most prominent concerns articulated in codes are not echoed or supported in current

in 2002. The European Association of Securities Dealers was first to issue European Principles and Recommendations (2000), followed by Euroshareholders (2000). From the investor side, there have been statements from France (AFG-ASFFI 1998), Ireland (IAIM 1992), Germany (DSW 1998), the UK (PIRC 1993, 1996, 1999; Hermes 1999).

In Asia, guidelines have been written for Japan (1998) and Korea (1999), in addition to the Commonwealth countries already mentioned. In Latin America, Brazil (1999), Mexico (1999) and Peru (2002) have their own guidelines. Undoubtedly, other countries are sure to follow.

In the USA, there is no "Code" as such but corporations have been issuing corporate governance statements [e.g. General Motors' guidelines (1994), the National Association of Corporate Directors (NACD 1996) and the Business Roundtable (BRT 1997)]. Pension funds also issue their own corporate governance principles, policies, positions and voting guidelines (TIAA-CREF 1997; AFL-CIO 1997; CalPERS 1998; CII 1998, revised 1999). The American Bar Association published a "Directors Guidebook" (1994). The American Law Institute (1994) adopted and promulgated its "Principles of Corporate Governance" in 1992. Although not binding in nature, these principles are widely cited in USA case law.

[99] The codes have triggered an avalanche of corporate governance statements from companies often leading to the creation of new jobs, job titles ("Head of Corporate Governance"), competence centres and task-forces within companies. From the investors' side, countries and companies are starting to be ranked and rated according to corporate governance benchmarks. The proposals tabled at shareholder meetings are scrutinised and compared "best practice".

[100] Not all policy documents mentioned here are included in the list of references. An extensive list, full text copies and international comparisons [in particular Gregory (2000, 2001a,b, 2002)] can be found on the codes pages of the European Corporate Governance Institute (www.ecgi.org).

[101] Gregory (2001a) compares 33 codes from 13 member states of the European Union and two pan-European codes to the OECD Principles. All the international and 28 national codes provide a board job-description and all the codes cover at least one board-related issue. In contrast, only about 15 national codes cover anti-takeover devices. A similar picture emerges from comparisons of codes from outside the EU [Gregory (2000, 2001b)].

[102] Again, see Gregory (2000, 2001a,b) for an extensive listing and comparisons.

empirical research, as we will discuss in Section 7. The striking schism between firmly held beliefs of business people and academic research calls for an explanation. For instance, why do independent directors feature so prominently in codes but appear to add so little in event studies and regressions? Equally, why do institutional investors attach so much importance to the separation of the roles of chairman of the board and CEO, while the empirical evidence suggests that this separation hardly matters?

6.3. Other views

Some commentators of comparative corporate governance systems attempt to go beyond a simple comparison of one system to another. Thus, although Black (1990, 1998) criticizes USA corporate governance rules for excessively raising the costs of large shareholder intervention, he is also critical of other countries' corporate governance standards. He argues that all countries fall short of what he would like USA governance to look like [Black (2000a)].[103] Taking a radically different and far more optimistic perspective Easterbrook (1997) has argued that no global standards of corporate governance are needed because "international differences in corporate governance are attributable more to differences in markets than to differences in law" [see also Easterbrook and Fischel (1991)]. Since markets are unlikely to converge, neither will the law. Although some fine-tuning might be required locally, market forces will automatically create the regulatory underpinnings national systems need.

7. Empirical evidence and practice

The empirical literature on corporate governance is so extensive that it is a daunting task to provide a comprehensive survey in a single article. Fortunately, a number of surveys of specific issues have appeared recently.[104] We shall to a large extent rely on these surveys and only cover the salient points in this section. In the introduction we have defined five different approaches to resolving collective action problems among dispersed shareholders: (i) hostile takeovers; (ii) large investors; (iii) boards of directors; (iv) CEO incentive schemes; and (v) fiduciary duties and shareholder suits. Each of these approaches has been examined extensively and recent surveys have appeared on takeovers [Burkart (1999)],[105] the role of boards [Romano (1996), Hermalin and Weisbach (2003)], shareholder activism [Black (1998), Gillan and Starks (1998), Karpoff (1998), Romano (2001)], CEO compensation [Core, Guay and Larcker (2003), Bebchuk, Fried and Walker (2002), Gugler (2001), Perry and Zenner

---

[103] See Avilov et al. (1999), Black et al. (1996) and Black (2000b) in the context of emerging markets.
[104] An earlier general survey taking an agency perspective is Shleifer and Vishny (1997a).
[105] Andrade, Mitchell and Stafford (2001) survey the stylised facts on takeovers and mergers in the USA, 1973–1998.

(2000), Loewenstein (2000), Abowd and Kaplan (1999), Murphy (1999)] and large shareholders [Short (1994), Gugler (2001),[106] Holderness (2003)]. Not even these surveys cover everything. In particular, research on the role of large investors is not fully surveyed – partly because research in this area has been rapidly evolving in recent years. The literature on fiduciary duties and shareholder suits is very limited.

7.1. Takeovers

Hostile takeovers are a powerful governance mechanism because they offer the possibility of bypassing the management to take permanent control of the company, by concentrating voting and cash-flow rights.[107] Corporate governance codes endorse hostile takeovers and the voting guidelines issued by investor groups come out very strongly against anti-takeover devices and for the mandatory disclosure of price sensitive information and toeholds.[108] Paradoxically disclosure and insider trading laws may actually make hostile takeovers harder, as Grossman and Hart (1983) have noted. Indeed, the market for corporate control should work better in regulatory environments with low shareholder protection and lax disclosure standards, so bidder incentives are not eroded by the free-riding problem. On the other hand, low shareholder protection can also give rise to excessive takeover activity by empire builders. Anti-takeover protections reduce the threat of hostile takeovers but both theory and empirical evidence suggest that they also strengthen the bargaining position of the target for the benefit of target shareholders. Finally, it is important to keep in mind that hostile takeovers are difficult to finance even in the most liquid capital markets. Despite their alleged importance, hostile takeovers are isolated instances and their study has been largely confined to the USA and the UK.

7.1.1. Incidence of hostile takeovers

Takeovers are well publicized, but in sheer numbers they are relatively rare events. Even at the peak of the USA takeover wave in the 1980s, takeover rates (the number of bids as a percentage of the number of listed companies) rarely exceeded 1.5% and

---

[106] Gugler (2001) surveys the English-language literature and draws on national experts to survey the local language literatures in Austria, Belgium, Germany, France, Italy, Japan, The Netherlands, Spain and Turkey.

[107] In the USA control changes often require board approval. In countries like the UK the bidder bypasses the management *and* the board; the change of control decision is the sovereign right of the target shareholders.

[108] For example, the OECD (1999) Principle I.E states that the "markets for corporate control should be allowed to function in an efficient and transparent manner". The Euro-Shareholder Guidelines (2000) state that "anti-takeover defences or other measures which restrict the influence of shareholders should be avoided" (Recommendation 3) and that "companies should immediately disclose information which can influence the share price, as well as information about those shareholders who pass (upwards or downwards) 5% thresholds" (Recommendation 5).

declined steeply afterwards [Comment and Schwert (1995)].[109] Hostile takeovers, the events that are of interest here, are even more elusive. Under standard definitions, even at their pre-1990 peak hostile bids never represented more than 30% of all USA deals [Schwert (2000)].[110] Between 1990 and 1998 only 4% of all USA deals were hostile at some stage and hostile bidders acquired 2.6% of the targets [Andrade, Mitchell and Stafford (2001)].[111] The paucity of hostile deals is also evident outside the USA; however, there is an unusually high amount of hostile activity in Europe in 1999 (Table 2).

If hostile takeovers are a disciplining device for management they should predominantly affect poorly performing firms. This prediction is not borne out by the available empirical evidence. Successful USA takeover targets are smaller than other companies, but otherwise they do not differ significantly from their peers [Comment and Schwert (1995)].[112] The targets of hostile bids are likely to be larger than other targets.[113] Indicators of poor target management contribute little or are not significant [Schwert (2000)].[114] The available evidence for the UK also fails to show that the targets of successful hostile bids had poorer pre-bid performance than other targets Franks and Mayer (1996)].[115]

---

[109] The causes of such cycles in takeover activity are many, and their relative importance is an open issue. The 1980s USA takeover boom has been attributed to, *inter alia,* the 1986 Tax Reform Act and to the 1978 Bankruptcy Act; see Kaplan (1994b) for a discussion of the latter point.

[110] Other characteristics of USA hostile deals are that they are more likely to involve cash offers and multiple bidders. Also, hostile bids are less likely to succeed than uncontested bids [Schwert (2000)].

[111] For 1973–79 8.4% of all deals were hostile at some stage, between 1980–89 14.3%; hostile acquisitions were 4.1% and 7.1%, respectively [Andrade, Mitchell and Stafford (2001)]. The full merger sample covers 4300 completed deals on the CRSP tapes, covering all USA firms on the NYSE, AMEX and Nasdaq between 1973–1998.

[112] Comment and Schwert (1995) estimate the probability of a successful takeover as a function of anti-takeover devices, abnormal returns, sales growth, the ration of net-liquid assets to total assets, debt/equity ratios, market/book ratios, price/earnings ratios and total assets (size) for 1977–91. They report that the results for hostile takeovers do not differ significantly (p. 34). We discuss the anti-takeover device evidence in Section 7.1.4 below.

[113] This is consistent with the view that bids in the USA are classified as hostile when the target boards have a lot of bargaining power. The boards of larger companies are more likely to reject a bid, at least initially, to obtain a higher premium.

[114] Schwert (2000) covers the period 1975–1996 and considers four definitions of "hostile bid". He concludes that "the variables [...] that might reflect poor management, market to book ratios and return on assets, contribute little. The variables [...] that probably reflect the bargaining power of the target firm, such as firm size and the secular dummy variables, contribute most explanatory power" (p. 2624).

[115] Franks and Mayer (1996) cover the period 1980 to 1986 and consider the pre-bid evolution of share prices (abnormal returns), dividend payouts, cash-flows and Tobin's Q. They find a 14 point difference in abnormal returns between successful hostile bids and accepted bids that is not statistically significant, a significant difference in Tobin's Q but no difference in dividend payouts or cash-flows. On Tobin's Q they observe that all values are larger than one, suggesting poor relative rather than absolute performance. Finally, companies with control changes have higher pre-bid stock returns that companies without control changes, the opposite of what the poor management hypothesis predicts.

Table 2
Number of takeovers by region[a]

	Australia	Canada	USA	EU15			Other
				Total	UK	ex-UK	
Number of announced uncontested takeovers[b]							
1989	81	184	1188	550	316	234	114
1990	69	193	834	597	290	307	188
1991	107	269	790	817	252	565	363
1992	46	194	746	824	181	643	296
1993	100	215	789	803	196	607	456
1994	124	224	1015	816	221	595	614
1995	162	296	1106	806	219	587	753
1996	142	277	1115	676	195	481	745
1997	107	258	1150	574	201	373	726
1998	103	231	1203	653	234	419	893
1999	100	289	1236	801	271	530	1180
Number of announced contested takeovers[c]							
1989	3	6	45	36	32	4	10
1990	2		12	24	22	2	5
1991	8	1	7	34	31	3	2
1992	10	2	7	20	15	5	4
1993	10	1	11	15	11	4	5
1994	8	11	33	11	8	3	4
1995	18	19	59	22	14	8	7
1996	22	8	45	20	13	7	11
1997	12	17	27	23	11	12	5
1998	12	14	19	14	12	2	5
1999	15	6	19	42	21	21	6

[a] Source: Thomson Financial Services Data (TFSD) and own calculations.
[b] Under the TFSD definition a tender offer that was recommended by the board of the target company to its shareholders.
[c] Under the TFSD definition a tender offer that was initially rejected by the board of the target company.

Hostile takeover activity in the USA sharply declined after 1989. Most observers agree that managers effectively lobbied for protection from the market for corporate control. The tightening of insider trading laws in the second half of the 1980s, a series of landmark cases in Delaware in 1985 and a new wave of anti-takeover laws made it virtually impossible to take over USA corporations without target board consent (see

Section 7.1.4 below). As a result, few hostile takeover attempts were made and less than 25% of the bidders succeeded in taking control of the target [Bebchuk, Coates and Subramanian (2002)]. Another explanation attributes the decline in takeover activity to the demise of the junk bond market, the business cycle and the credit crunch associated with the Savings and Loans crisis [Comment and Schwert (1995)]. Takeover activity has recently emerged in continental Europe in a number of spectacular cases where there were none before. Although there is no conclusive evidence in support it is possible that this change has brought about more managerial discipline. It is also a sign of the waning protection of national champions by European governments.

7.1.2. Correction of inefficiencies

If hostile takeovers correct managerial failure and enhance efficiency the value of the bidder and the target under joint control (V_{AB}) should be larger than the value of the bidder (V_A) and the target (V_B) separately, or $\Delta V \equiv [V_{AB} - V_A - V_B] > 0$. Generally, the change in value (ΔV) is taken to be the difference between the stand-alone pre-bid and the combined post-bid values in event studies. Other measures are based on changes in accounting data, such as cash flows or plant level productivity. Event studies find sizeable average premia (~24%) going to target shareholders in all USA acquisitions [Andrade et al. (2001)] and higher premia for hostile takeovers [Schwert (2000), Franks and Mayer (1996)].[116] In all USA acquisitions the gain for bidder shareholders[117] and the overall gain are indistinguishable from zero [Andrade et al. (2001)].[118] Although suggestive, the event study evidence cannot conclusively determine whether these premia arose from the correction of an inefficiency or from synergies between bidders and targets,[119] or whether they simply constitute transfers away from bidding shareholders or other constituencies [see Burkart (1999) for an extensive discussion of this issue].[120]

---

[116] Schwert (2000) reports that the total premia under the *Wall Street Journal* and TFSD definitions of "hostile deal" are 11.5% and 6.7% higher than for all deals, in line with the previous findings of Franks and Harris (1989) who report total premia of 42% for hostile and 28% for uncontested and unrevised bids in the USA. Franks and Mayer (1996) report premia of 30% for successful hostile and 18% for accepted bids in the UK.

[117] Most USA bidders are not individuals, or tightly controlled bidding vehicles, but widely held companies under management control [Shleifer and Vishny (1988)].

[118] The result holds for all subperiods 1973–98 for cumulative abnormal returns from twenty days before the bid to the close. During the announcement period the overall gains are slightly positive (1.8%), especially for large targets (3.0%) and no-stock transactions (3.6%).

[119] See Bradley (1980), and for evidence that this was the case in the 1980s, Bradley, Desai and Kim (1983, 1988).

[120] Positive takeover premia could also result from the correction of market inefficiencies caused by short-term myopia or undervalued targets. The most influential surveys of the evidence of the 1980s rejected these explanations on the grounds that there is evidence that stock markets are efficient and that the stock price of targets that defeat a hostile bid often returns to close to the pre-bid level [Jensen and Ruback (1983), Jarrell, Brickley and Netter (1988)].

7.1.3. Redistribution

How can one disentangle redistributive gains from overall efficiency improvements? A number of studies have identified and sometimes quantified the amount of redistribution away from other corporate constituencies resulting from a takeover. The constituencies in the target firm that may be on the losing side include bondholders [Higgins and Schall (1975), Kim and McConnell (1977), Asquith and Kim (1982), Warga and Welch (1993)], employees [Shleifer and Summers (1988), Williamson (1988), Schnitzer (1995)] and corporate pension plans [Pontiff, Shleifer and Weisbach (1990), Petersen (1992)]. But there may also be outside losers like the bidding shareholders and unprotected debtholders as well as the tax authorities.

An alternative strategy attempts to pinpoint the sources of efficiency gains through clinical studies, but no general pattern has emerged from a wealth of facts [Kaplan (2000)]. The source of gain for target shareholders, when overall gains are small or non-existent, has not been identified yet with precision.

7.1.4. Takeover defenses [121]

As we have seen there are theoretical arguments for and against takeover defenses. They reduce the disciplining role of hostile takeovers by reducing the average number of bids but they can also help the board extract higher premia from bidders. A large empirical literature has tried to estimate the (relative) size of these effects in the USA. Before turning to this evidence, we review the availability, mechanics and incidence of different defence mechanisms.

Numerous pre-bid and post-bid defenses are at the disposal of target companies in most jurisdictions. Pre-bid defenses include capital structure, classified boards, supermajority requirements, cross-shareholdings, enhanced voting rights, voting right restrictions, subjection of share transfers to board approval and change of control clauses in major contracts. [122] The most potent pre-bid defenses require shareholder approval. However, some important defenses which can be introduced without shareholder approval include control clauses and cross-shareholdings in Europe, poison pills in the USA [123] and, until recently, block acquisitions larger than 10% in Korea [Black et al. (2000), Chung and Kim (1999)]. The incidence of anti-takeover provisions is well documented in the USA [Danielson and Karpoff (1998), Rosenbaum (2000)] but less systematically in Europe and Asia. [124] In the USA, firms protected by

---

[121] For a recent, critical survey of takeover defences see Coates (1999).

[122] The list of possible post-bid defenses is much longer and includes litigation, white knights, greenmail and the pac-man defence.

[123] European Counsel M&A Handbook 2000, pp. 26–43. See Weston, Siu and Johnson (2001) for a detailed explanation of USA anti-takeover measures.

[124] Danielson and Karpoff (1998) provide a detailed analysis of the adoption of anti-takeover measures in a sample that roughly corresponds to the S&P 500 during 1984–89. Some form of anti-takeover

poison pills have relatively high institutional ownership, fewer blockholders and low managerial ownership, consistent with the view that institutional ownership presents a threat in a hostile takeover situation and that blockholders can prevent the adoption of poison pills [Danielson and Karpoff (1998)].

The evidence on the consequences of takeover defence adoption is mixed. Mikkelson and Partch (1997) show that CEOs are more likely to be replaced when hostile takeover activity is high, which is consistent with disciplining and entrenchment, i.e., when CEOs are able to protect themselves better they are less likely to be replaced. The wealth effects of pre-bid defence adoption has been measured in numerous event studies that generally find small negative abnormal returns. On balance, the results support the view that managerial entrenchment dominates the enhanced bargaining effect. However, contradictory evidence comes from Comment and Schwert (1995) who find that anti-takeover measures have increased bid premia, supporting the view that the enhanced bargaining effect dominates. Here the board literature provides an intriguing piece of evidence. Shareholders of target firms with independent boards (see Section 7.4) receive premia that are 23% higher than for targets with more captive boards [Cotter, Shivdasani and Zenner (1997)], even when controlling for the presence of anti-takeover devices. This suggests that independent boards are more ready to use anti-takeover devices to the advantage of target shareholders than other boards.

The latest panel data evidence suggests that anti-takeover provisions in the USA have had a negative impact on firm value [Gompers, Ishii and Metrick (2001)]. The same study finds that from 1990 to 1998 investors who would have taken long positions in companies with "strong shareholder protections" (as measured by an index they construct) and short positions in companies with "weak shareholder protections" would have earned abnormal returns of 8.5% per year. [125] As striking as these numbers are, however, the authors acknowledge that it is not possible to interpret this finding as measuring the market value of "good governance". The difficulty is that such abnormal returns can represent at best unanticipated benefits from good governance and may reflect changes in the business environment not directly related to governance.

7.1.5. One-share–one-vote

Deviations from one-share–one-vote are often associated with the issuance of dual

measure covers most of their sample firms and the median firm is protected by six measures. In Europe the most potent defence against a hostile takeover is a blockholder holding more than 50% of the voting rights; in continental Europe most companies with small (or no) blocks have statutory pre-bid defenses similar to USA companies, for example voting right and transfer restrictions or special shares with the sole right to nominate directors for election to the board [Becht and Mayer (2001)]; see Section 7.2.

[125] Using data on 24 different "corporate governance provisions" from the IRRC (the data we report in Tables 3A and 3B) the authors compare the returns on two portfolios and relate the provisions to Tobin's Q.

Table 3A
Corporate takeover defenses in the USA [a,b]

	% of companies				
	Fall 1999	Fall 1997	Mid-1995	Mid-1993	Mid-1990
Number of companies	1900	1922	1500	1483	1487
External control provisions					
Blank check preferred stock	89.1	87.6	85.0	n/a	n/a
Poison pill	56.0	51.9	53.3	53.6	51.0
Consider non-financial effects of merger	7.3	6.6	7.2	7.5	6.5
Internal control provisions					
Advance notice requirement	61.4	49.2	43.8	n/a	n/a
Classified board	58.7	58.4	59.7	58.1	57.2
Limit right to call special meeting	36.7	33.6	31.1	28.6	23.9
Limit action by written consent	34.6	32.2	31.1	28.1	23.7
Fair price	24.8	26.4	32.5	33.2	31.9
Supermajority vote to approve merger	15.3	14.8	17.8	18.1	16.9
Dual class stock	11.5	10.7	8.3	8.2	7.5
Eliminate cumulative voting	8.8	8.4	10.4	10.1	8.8
Unequal voting rights	1.6	1.6	2.0	2.1	2.3
Miscellaneous provisions					
Golden parachutes	64.9	55.8	53.3	n/a	n/a
Confidential voting	10.2	9.2	11.7	9.4	3.2
Cumulative voting	10.2	11.4	14.4	15.7	17.7
Antigreenmail	4.1	4.6	6.0	6.3	5.6

[a] Sources: Rosenbaum (2000), IRRC (2000a).
[b] Classification taken from Danielson and Karpoff (1998).

class stock and have been the source of considerable controversy.[126] Shares with different voting rights often trade at different prices and the resulting premia (discounts) have been related to takeover models (see Section 5) and interpreted as a measure of the value of corporate control and "private benefits" [Levy (1983), Rydqvist (1992), Zingales (1995), Nicodano (1998)].

Theory predicts that dual class premia vary with the relative size of dual class issues, the inequality of voting power, the value of the assets under control, the probability of a takeover (which itself depends on the regulatory environment), and the likelihood

---

[126] See Seligman (1986) for a comprehensive history of the one-share–one-vote controversy in the USA. In early corporations statutory voting right restrictions were the norm.

Table 3B
Corporate takeover defenses in the USA[a,b]

	Mid-1999	
	Number	% of states
States with anti-takeover laws	42	82.4
State anti-takeover laws featuring:		
Control share acquisition laws	27	52.9
Fair price laws	27	52.9
2–5 Year freeze-out laws	33	64.7
Cash-out laws	3	5.9
Profit recapture	2	3.9
Severance/pay labor contract provisions	5	9.8
Greenmail restrictions	6	11.8
Compensation restrictions	2	3.9
Poison pill endorsement	25	49.0
Directors' duties	31	60.8
States with no takeover provisions (8 + DC)	9	17.6

[a] Sources: Rosenbaum (2000), IRRC (2000a).
[b] Classification taken from Danielson and Karpoff (1998).

of a small shareholder being pivotal.[127] In addition, relative prices are affected by differences in taxation, index inclusion, dividend rights and/or stock market liquidity.

Empirical estimates of voting premia range from 5.4 to 82% and, taken at face value, suggest that the value of corporate control is large in Italy and relatively small in Korea, Sweden and the USA.[128] In practice the studies at best imperfectly control for all the factors affecting the price differential, making it an unreliable measure of "the value of corporate control". Time-series evidence also suggests that dual class premia should be

[127] Takeover regulation can prevent block transfers, require the bidder to offer the same price to all voting stockholders or force the inclusion of non-voting stockholders. Company statutes can have a similar effect, for example fair-price amendments in the USA. Nenova (2000) attempts to control for these factors across countries using quantitative measures of the legal environment, takeover regulation, takeover defenses and the cost of holding a control block in a cross-section regression, treating the control variables as exogenous.

[128] Canada, 8–13% [Jog and Riding (1986), Robinson, Rumsey and White (1996), Smith and Amoako-Adu (1995)]; France, mean 1986–1996 51.4% [Muus (1998)]; Germany, mean 1988–1997 26.3%, in 2000 50% [Hoffmann-Burchardi (1999, 2000)]; Israel, 45.5% [Levy (1982)]; Italy 82% [Zingales (1994)]; Korea, 10% [Chung and Kim (1999)]; Norway, −3.2–6.4% [Odegaard (2002)]; Sweden, 12% [Rydqvist (1996)]; Switzerland, 18% [Kunz and Angel (1996)]; UK, 13.3% [Megginson (1990)]; USA, 5.4% [Lease et al. (1983)], mean 1984–90 10.5%, median 3% [Zingales (1995), see also DeAngelo and DeAngelo (1985) for the USA]. Lease et al. (1984) analyse the value of control in closely held corporations with dual class shares.

interpreted with caution. While premia have been rising from 20% in mid-1998 to 54% in December 1999 in Germany [Hoffmann-Burchardi (2000)], in Finland they have dropped from 100% in the 1980s to less than 5% today. Similarly in Sweden premia have declined from 12% in the late 1980s to less than 1% today,[129] and in Denmark from 30% to 2% [Bechmann and Raaballe (2000)]. In Norway the differential was actually negative in 1990–1993, but has risen to 6.4% in 1997 [Odegaard (2002)]. It is, of course, possible that changes in the value of control explain these changes in premia but further research is required before one can conclude with any confidence that this is the case.

7.1.6. Hostile stakes and block sales

Takeover bids for widely held companies are, of course, not the only way corporate control can be contested and sold. In blockholder systems, hostility can take the form of "hostile stakes" [Jenkinson and Ljungqvist (2001)] and control is completely or partially transferred through block sales [Holderness and Sheehan (1988) for the USA; Nicodano and Sembenelli (2000) for Italy; Böhmer (2000) for Germany; Dyck and Zingales (2003) for 412 control transactions in 39 countries].[130] Control premia vary between −4% and 65% [Dyck and Zingales (2003)].[131]

7.1.7. Conclusion and unresolved issues

Hostile takeovers are associated with large premia for target shareholders, but so far the empirical literature has not fully identified the source of the premia. It is difficult to disentangle the opposing entrenchment and bargaining effects associated with hostile takeover defenses. The net effect of the adoption of takeover defenses on target stock market value is slightly negative, suggesting that the entrenchment effect is somewhat larger than the bargaining effect.[132] Recent evidence from the board literature suggests that independent boards implement defences to increase the bargaining position of target shareholders while captured boards tend to implement defences that increase entrenchment [Cotter, Shivdasani and Zenner (1997)].

---

[129] Personal communication from Kristian Rydqvist.

[130] Like dual-class premia, block premia can be interpreted as an indirect measure of "private benefits". However, block premia have the advantage that they are based on actual control transactions, not the marginal value of a vote in a potential transaction.

[131] In countries with a mandatory bid rule control transfers must be partial. A control block cannot be sold without making an offer to the minority shareholders. In such countries only block sales below the mandatory bid threshold are considered. This imposes serious limits on the comparability of the results across countries.

[132] This is corroborated by comparisons of announcement effects of anti-takeover amendments with a larger bargaining component relative to devices where entrenchment is likely to be prominent, e.g., Jarrell and Poulsen (1987).

Despite the widespread interest in hostile takeovers, the available empirical evidence is surprisingly sketchy. Although hostile takeovers are no longer confined to the USA and the UK, there appears to be no recent study of hostile takeovers in other countries.

7.2. *Large investors*

Shareholder rights can differ significantly across OECD countries and even across firms within the same country. These institutional differences make it difficult to compare the actions and effects of large shareholders across countries or firms.

Most of the time large shareholder action is channelled through the board of directors. Large shareholders are in principle able to appoint board members representing their interests. When they have majority control of the board they can hire (or fire) management. Large shareholders can also exercise power by blocking ratification of unfavorable decisions, or possibly by initiating decisions.

In practice corporate law, corporate charters and securities regulations impose limits on these powers, which vary significantly across countries. Even a basic right like corporate voting and appointments to the board varies considerably across governance systems and corporate charters. For example, some countries' corporate law prescribes discrete control thresholds that give a blocking minority veto power over major decisions. [133] In Germany employees appoint 50% of the board members in large corporations [Prigge (1998)]. In the UK the listing requirements of the London Stock Exchange require large shareholders to keep an arm's length relationship with companies, limiting the right of blockholders to appoint directors to the board. [134] Under the Dutch "structural regime" the corporate boards of larger companies must appoint themselves and their successors, with a consequent negative impact on corporate valuations [De Jong et al. (2001)]. In some Anglo-Dutch corporations special classes of shares have the sole right to nominate directors for election to the boards or to veto their removal [Becht and Mayer (2001)].

Initiation rights also vary considerably across jurisdictions. Thus, to remove a director, shareholders might have to show "cause", wait for three years, vote separately by share-class, pass a supermajority resolution or simply pass an ordinary resolution by majority vote. [135] In the USA shareholders cannot initiate fundamental transactions

---

[133] For example, corporate law in the Netherlands, Germany and Austria prescribes supermajorities for major decisions. Often the threshold can be increased via the statutes, but not decreased.

[134] A 30%+ blockholder cannot appoint more than 5 out of 12 directors [Wymeersch (2003)]. In the UK the distribution of blockholdings in listed companies tapers off abruptly at 30% [Goergen and Renneboog (2001)].

[135] Initiation rights differ across the USA, depending on the state and, within any one state, the company bylaws [Clark (1986, p. 105)]. Initiation rights are always strong in the UK, where directors can be removed at any time by an ordinary resolution brought by a 20%+ blockholder or coalition and a majority vote (Section 303 of the Companies Act 1985). The same is true in Belgium, where Article 518 of the company law explicitly states that the board cannot resist such a shareholder resolution. Obviously, removal rights are closely related to the anti-takeover devices we discussed previously.

like mergers, and boards are broadly shielded from direct shareholder influence [Kraakman et al. (2003)]. In contrast, shareholder proposals can force mergers or charter amendments if they receive a majority in the UK, Japan or France.[136] Ratification rights, on the other hand, are strikingly similar in most jurisdictions. The law prescribes a list of decisions that require shareholder approval, which can be extended in the charter.

Most empirical work on large investors has focused on simple hypotheses which are not always grounded in rigorous theoretical analysis. Much of the early work on large shareholders has been concerned with the implications of the trend towards shareholder dispersion and the effects of the decline of shareholder influence. We begin this section by tracing the available evidence on ownership and control patterns across countries and through time. We then address the empirical evidence on the causes and effects of ownership dispersion. In particular, we shall address the following questions: Does the presence of large investors or "relationship investing" improve corporate performance? Do large shareholders abuse their voting power? Do alternative forms of shareholder intervention (activism) improve company performance? Is there an empirical link between share blocks and stock market liquidity?

7.2.1. Ownership dispersion and voting control

As we pointed out in Section 5, with the exception of the USA some form of concentration of ownership and/or voting control is the most common corporate governance arrangement in OECD and developing countries.[137] The full impact and scope of this observation has only emerged very recently after a long period of confusion originally caused by Berle and Means (1932) with their assertions and empirical methodology.

The hypothesis that risk diversification leads to growing shareholder dispersion was first tested in 1924 by Warshow (1924). His study records an astonishing 250% increase in the number of shareholders between 1900 and 1923.[138] The test of the consequences for voting control followed. Means (1930) proposed that the new owners of the "modern corporation" no longer appointed the majority of directors on the board and, therefore, no longer controlled it. For 44% of the largest 200 USA corporations in 1929

---

[136] In some unlisted companies shareholders exert direct control of the company through voting, for example in Germany and France [Hansmann and Kraakman (2001)].

[137] For supporting evidence see La Porta et al. (1999), Claessens et al. (2000) and Faccio and Lang (2002) and voting block statistics based on modern disclosure standards [ECGN (1997), Barca and Becht (2001)].

[138] Warshow (1924) could not determine the exact number of shareholders because they were masked by custodians (nominee accounts, banks) or, in modern parlance, "street names". There are no comparative early studies for other countries because his method relied on the existence of registered shares and in many countries corporations have always issued bearer shares. Warshow's study was updated by Means (1930) and additional evidence is reported in Berle and Means (1932). See TNEC (1940, p. 198) for a survey of these and other classic studies using the Warshow method.

no large investors were found, leading to the conclusion that "control is maintained in large measure separate from ownership" [Means (1931b), Berle and Means (1932)]. [139] This hypothesis has become received wisdom for corporations in the USA [Larner (1966, 1970), [140] Herman (1981), La Porta et al. (1999)], but also for the UK [Florence (1947, 1953, 1961), Cubbin and Leech (1983), Leech and Leahy (1991), La Porta et al. (1999)], although other studies found that blockholders had never disappeared entirely in the USA [Temporary National Economic Committee (1940), [141] Eisenberg (1976), Demsetz and Lehn (1985), Holderness and Sheehan (1988)] and the UK. [142] The latest research confirms that blocks are indeed rare in the USA [Edwards and Hubbard (2000), Becht (2001)], but in the UK a coalition of the largest 1–5 blockholders – usually institutional investors – can wield a substantial amount of voting power in most listed companies [Goergen and Renneboog (2001)]. [143]

Means's method (see Footnote 139) for measuring shareholder concentration has been criticized and extended by numerous authors, for example by Gordon (1945), [144] Florence (1947) [145] and Eisenberg (1976). One particular source of measurement error is due to disclosure rules. [146] Depending on how disclosed holdings are treated one can

---

[139] A corporation was classified as management controlled if it had no known shareholder holding at least 5% of voting stock. Cases falling between 5 and 20% were classified as jointly management and minority controlled and "$\frac{1}{2}$ a company" was assigned to each category. Berle and Means (1932) used the same definition.

[140] Larner (1966) reduced the "management control" threshold to 10% and found that the fraction of management-controlled firms had increased from 44% to 84.5%. Eisenberg (1976) argues that Larner's study was biased towards finding "management control".

[141] The Temporary National Economic Committee (1940) (TNEC) relied on the SEC to collect this data for the 200 non-financial corporations in 1937.

[142] Florence (1961) reported that the median holding of the largest 20 holders in large UK companies fell from 35% in 1936 to 22% in 1951, a finding that was widely cited by Marris (1964) and other British managerial economists. However, Chandler (1976) argues that personal capitalism lasted longer than these numbers suggest and that British firms only adopted managerial capitalism in the 1970s. Consistent with Chandler's view is Hannah's (1974, 1976) observation that it was possible for bidders to bypass family-controlled boards only as late as the 1950s. See Cheffins (2002) for a survey.

[143] Goergen and Renneboog (2003) explore the determinants of post-IPO diffusion rates in the UK and Germany.

[144] Gordon (1945) argued that we should "speak [...] of the separation of ownership and active leadership. Ordinarily the problem is stated in terms of the divorce between ownership and "control". This last word is badly overused, and it needs to be precisely defined [...]. Our procedure [...] will be to study the ownership of officers and directors and then to ascertain the extent to which non-management stockholdings are sufficiently concentrated to permit through ownership the wielding of considerable power and influence (control?) over management by an individual, group or another corporation" [Gordon (1945, p. 24, footnote 20)].

[145] Florence (1947) proposed a measure of "oligarchic" minority control based on the full distribution of the largest 20 blocks and actual board representation.

[146] Statistics based on shareholder lists underestimate concentration unless the cash-flow and voting rights that are ultimately held by the same person or entity are consolidated. At the first level, it has been common practice to add the holdings using surnames, addresses and other obvious linkages; see

obtain significantly different measures of concentration. Thus, La Porta et al. (1999) and Claessens et al. (2000) – using the Means method – find very little ownership concentration in Japan. However, adding the ten largest holders on record in Japan in 1997 gives a concentration ratio, defined as the percentage of shares held by these shareholders, of 48.5% (51.1% in 1975; Hoshi and Kashyap (2001, p. 252). Inevitably, much research has been undertaken on the USA and the UK because the information about shareholdings in these countries is relatively easy to obtain. In contrast, in countries where corporations issue bearer shares information about shareholdings is generally not available. [147] Fortunately for researchers, modern securities regulation has begun to overcome this problem, at least in Europe. [148]

From a theoretical point of view static measures of concentration are not always satisfactory. What matters is not whether ownership and/or voting power are more or less concentrated on a permanent basis but the ability of shareholders to intervene and exercise control over management when required [see Manne (1965) and Bolton and von Thadden (1998b)]. If there is a well functioning market for corporate control (takeovers or proxy fights) managerial discretion is limited even when companies are widely held. On the other hand, when anti-takeover rules and amendments are in place shareholder intervention is severely limited, whether a large investor is present or not. In the Netherlands, relatively few corporations are widely held, yet the ability of shareholders to intervene is very limited. [149] Dynamic measures of concentration based on power indices can address some of these issues [150] but they have been considered in only a few studies [Leech (1987b,c), [151] Holderness and Sheehan (1988), Nicodano and Sembenelli (2000)]. [152]

for example Leech and Leahy (1991, p. 1421). First level blocks held through intermediate companies are consolidated by tracing control (or ownership) chains and adding those that are ultimately controlled by the same entity. Means (1930) applied a discrete variant of this method and classified a closely-held corporation controlled by a widely-held corporation as widely held.

[147] Obviously, when companies issue bearer shares there is no shareholder list.

[148] In the USA voting blocks are disclosed under Section 13 of the 1934 Act that was introduced with the Williams Act in the 1960s. The standard provides for the disclosure of ultimate voting power of individual investors or groups, irrespective of the "distance" to the company, the control device used or the amount of cash-flow rights owned. A similar standard exists in the European Union (Directive 88/627/EEC). It is also spreading to Eastern Europe via the Union's accession process.

[149] Under the structural regime corporate boards operate like the board of the Catholic Church and its chairman: the bishops appoint the Pope and the Pope the bishops; Means (1930) illustration of what he meant by management control.

[150] They do not take into account statutory anti-takeover devices.

[151] Leech (1987a) proposed a set of power indices that are related to the size and distribution of blocks for a given probability of winning a board election and applied it to Berle and Means original data [Leech (1987b)], the TNEC data [Leech (1987c)] and 470 UK listed companies between 1983–85 [Leech and Leahy (1991)].

[152] The exception is the "value of corporate votes" literature that uses Shapley values and other power indices to measure the value of corporate control, for example Zingales (1995).

7.2.2. Ownership, voting control and corporate performance

We distinguish four generations of empirical studies that have tested the proposition that there is a link between ownership dispersion, voting control and corporate performance (value).

The first generation has tested the hypothesis that free-riding among dispersed shareholders leads to inferior company performance. Starting with Monsen et al. (1968) and Kamerschen (1968) numerous authors have regressed performance measures like profit rates and returns on assets on a Means–Larner type or Gordon type corporate control dummy. [153] In most regressions the dummy was not significant and the authors have rejected the hypothesis that greater dispersion results in lower performance [see the surveys by Short (1994) and Gugler (2001)].

The method was also applied in other countries, finding the owner-controlled firms significantly outperform manager-controlled firms in the UK [Radice (1971), Steer and Cable (1978), Cosh and Hughes (1989), Leech and Leahy (1991)], [154] profitability is higher with family control in France [Jacquemin and de Ghellinck (1980)]. [155]

Demsetz and Lehn (1985) explain that ownership concentration is endogenous. Some firms require large shareholder control while others don't. They argue that without accounting for this endogeneity it is to be expected that a regression of firm performance on a control dummy in a cross-section of heterogeneous firms should produce no statistically significant relation if the observed ownership-performance combinations are efficient.

Following Stulz (1988) a second generation of studies focuses on inside ownership by managers and considers the effects of takeover threats. The hypothesis is a hump-shaped relationship between concentrated ownership and market capitalization. [156] Outside ownership merely shifts the locus. Morck, Shleifer and Vishny (1988) find some evidence of such a relationship. Similarly, McConnell and Servaes (1990) find a maximum at 40–50% insider ownership (controlling for ownership by institutional investors and blockholders). Short and Keasey (1999) find similar results for the UK. [157]

The third generation continues to test the Stulz hypothesis but vastly improves the econometrics, showing reverse causation. [158] Using instrumental variable and panel

---

[153] See footnotes 139 and 144 above.

[154] Holl (1975) found no significant difference between owner and manager-controlled firms.

[155] See Gugler (2001) for further details.

[156] Corporate value first increases as more concentrated insider ownership aligns incentives, but eventually decreases as the probability of hostile takeovers declines.

[157] They find a maximum at 15.6% insider ownership and a minimum at 41.9%.

[158] Typical econometric shortcomings of first- and second-generation ownership-performance studies are reverse causality (endogeneity), sample selection, missing variables and measurement in variables. For example, Anderson and Lee (1997) show that many second-generation studies used data from unreliable commercial sources and correcting for these measurement errors can flip the results. See Börsch-Supan and Köke (2002) for a survey of econometric issues.

techniques the studies find corporate performance causing managerial ownership [Kole (1995), Cho (1998)], or both determined by similar variables [Himmelberg, Hubbard and Palia (1999)], or no relationship between ownership and performance [Demsetz and Villalonga (2001)]. The impact of corporate performance on managerial ownership is not significant. An alternative approach looks for instruments in institutions where ownership concentration is not endogenous, for example in co-operatives with many members. However, these studies are likely to suffer from other biases, in particular sample selection (by definition) and missing variables. [159]

The fourth generation returns to the first generation specification and econometrics, but adds two missing variables, the legal system and voting rights held in excess of cash-flow rights. [160] They find no effects for European countries [Faccio and Lang (2002)] and a negative effect of large investors in Asia [Claessens et al. (2000)]. [161] La Porta et al. (1999b) run a Q-regression for 27 countries but neither the cash-flow rights of controlling blockholders nor the legal system have a significant effect on corporate valuation. [162] It seems inevitable that a fifth generation study will emerge that addresses the econometric problems of the fourth generation.

7.2.3. Share blocks and stock market liquidity

The empirical link between secondary market liquidity and shareholder dispersion is well documented. Starting with Demsetz's (1968) classic study, measures of liquidity such as trading volume and bid-ask spreads have been shown to depend on the number of shareholders, even when controlling for other factors [Demsetz (1968), Tinic (1972), Benston and Hagerman (1974)]. Equally, increases in the number of shareholders, for example after stock splits [Mukherji, Kim and Walker (1997)] or decreases in the minimum trading unit [Amihud, Mendelson and Uno (1999)] lead to higher secondary market liquidity. The inverse relationship also holds. An increase in ownership concentration, or a decrease in the 'free float', depresses

---

[159] Gorton and Schmid (1999) study Austrian cooperative banks where equity is only exchangeable with the bank itself and one member has one vote, hence the separation of ownership and control is proportional to the number of members. They find that the log ratio of the average wages paid by banks, relative to the reservation wage is positively related to the (log) of the number of co-operative members, controlling for other bank characteristics, period and regional effects. They conclude that agency costs, as measured by efficiency wages, are increasing in the degree of separation between ownership and control.

[160] However, the hypothesis is reversed. The authors do not expect to find that firms without a block perform worse than firms with a block, but expropriation of minority shareholders by the blockholders.

[161] The studies regress "excess-value" [the natural logarithm of the ratio of a firm's actual and its imputed value, as defined by Berger and Ofek (1995)] on Means–Larner control dummies and other control variables.

[162] La Porta et al. (1999) perform a number of bivariate comparisons of Means–Larner control groups for a larger set of variables.

liquidity [Becht (1999) for Belgium and Germany; Sarin et al. (1999) for the USA].

The positive effect of stock market liquidity is also well documented. More liquid stocks command a price premium and offer a concomitantly lower risk adjusted return, reducing the cost of capital for the company [Stoll and Whaley (1983), Amihud and Mendelson (1986)]. Hence, companies have a measurable incentive to increase the number of shareholders, providing further evidence on the existence of a monitoring–liquidity tradeoff.

To our knowledge the role of liquidity in spurring monitoring has not been explored empirically. Instead the literature has focused on asymmetric information problems and informed investors as a source of illiquidity. Empirically, higher insider ownership reduces liquidity because it increases the probability of trading with an insider [Sarin, Shastri and Shastri (1999), Heflin and Shaw (2000)].

7.2.4. Banks [163]

Traditionally the empirical corporate governance literature has taken a narrow view of delegated monitoring by banks and sought to measure bank involvement through the intensity of bank–industry links such as equity holdings, cross-holdings and/or (blank) proxies, board representation and interlocking directorates. [164]

Within this narrow view there is an empirical consensus that bank–industry ties in the USA were strong at the beginning of the century but became weak through anti-trust regulation and the Glass–Steagall Act, [165] were never strong in the UK, but always strong in Germany [166] and Japan [Hoshi and Kashyap (2001)]. A popular explanation for these patterns has been the different regulatory history in these countries [Roe (1994)]. [167]

---

[163] For a more general review of banks and financial intermediation see Chapter 8 in this Volume by Gorton and Winton.

[164] This approach has a long tradition, for example Jeidels (1905) for Germany and the Pujo Committee (1913) for the USA.

[165] See, for example, Carosso (1970, 1973, 1985), Chernow (1990), Tallman (1991), Tabarrok (1998), Calomiris (2000), Ramirez and DeLong (2001). The relative performance of J.P. Morgan-controlled and other corporations has been investigated by DeLong (1991) and Ramirez (1995). Kroszner and Rajan (1997) investigate the impact of commercial banks on corporate performance before Glass–Steagall, Kroszner and Rajan (1994) and Ramirez (1995) the impact of the Act itself.

[166] Edwards and Fischer (1994), Edwards and Ogilvie (1996) and Guinnane (2001) argue that bank influence and involvement in Germany is, and has been, very limited.

[167] The regulatory explanation of (low) bank involvement in industry is convincing for the USA, but less so for other countries. In the UK no restrictions apply and banks have always kept an arm's length relationship to industry. In Japan the Allied occupation forces sought to impose Glass–Steagall type restrictions, yet the *keiretsu* found other ways of maintaining strong ties.

The empirical literature has documented that equity holdings by banks are not very common,[168] but the presence of bankers on boards and their involvement in interlocking directorates is common.[169] Based on these empirical measures the literature has compared the performance of companies under "bank influence" to other companies, with mixed results.[170] Also, the influence of banks has been identified as an important driver of economic growth and for overcoming economic backwardness [Tilly (1989), Gerschenkron (1962), Schumpeter (1934, 1939)],[171] a view that has been challenged recently.[172]

Relationship banking[173] is a broader concept that emphasizes the special nature of the business relationship between banks and industrial clients. Relationship banking, broadly defined is "the connection between a bank and customer that goes beyond the execution of simple, anonymous, financial transactions" [Ongena and Smith (1998)].[174] The ability of banks to collect information about customers and their role in renegotiating loans gives them a role in corporate governance even if they hold no equity and have no board links.

The empirical literature documents that banking relations last from 7 to 30 years on

---

[168] In Germany banks hold many but not the largest blocks [Becht and Böhmer (2003)]. However, they exert considerable voting power through blank proxies for absent blockholders [Baums and Fraune (1995)]. There is also indirect evidence that banks' holdings of equity in non-financial firms were small at the end of the 19th century [Fohlin (1997)].

[169] Interlocking directorates started to become common in Germany towards the end of the 19th century [Fohlin (1999b)]. At the beginning of the 1990s only 12.8% of companies were not connected to another by some personal link and 71% had a supervisory board interlock [Pfannschmidt (1993); see Prigge (1998, p. 959) for further references]. Most of the links were created by representatives of banks and insurance companies [Pfannschmidt (1993)]. The same was true for about half of the companies in Japan, also when the bank has extended a loan to the company [Kroszner and Strahan (2001)]. In the USA 31.6% of the Forbes 500 companies in 1992 had a banker on board, but only 5.8% of the main bank lenders had board seats. Lenders are discouraged from appointing directors because of concerns about conflicts of interest and liability during financial distress [Kroszner and Strahan (2001)]. Banks also drive board seat accumulation and overlap in Switzerland [Loderer and Peyer (2002)].

[170] For surveys of this evidence, see Prigge (1998, p. 1020) for Germany, Gugler (2001) and Section 7.2 for a review of the econometric problems. In addition to the usual endogeneity problems blocks held by banks can arise from debt-to-equity conversion. The classic study for Germany is Cable (1985), the most recent study Gorton and Schmid (2000b).

[171] Banks collected capital, lent it to able entrepreneurs, advised and monitored them, helping their companies along "from the cradle to the grave" [Jeidels (1905)].

[172] Within the traditional view Fohlin (1999a) shows that the contribution of Italian and German banks to mobilising capital was limited. Da Rin and Hellmann (2002) argue that banks helped to overcome coordination failures and played the role of "catalysts" in industrial development.

[173] For a recent survey with emphasis on the empirical literature see Ongena and Smith (1998), with emphasis on the theoretical literature see Boot (2000).

[174] "Relationship banking" might involve board and equity links, but not necessarily. The labels "*Hausbank* system" for Germany and "Main Bank System" for Japan [Allen and Gale (2000)] are often associated with exclusive debt links cemented by equity control rights, but exclusive bank–firm relationships are also found in countries where banks hold little or no industrial equity, for example the USA.

average,[175] depending on the country and sample.[176] Relationships last longer when they are exclusive [Ongena and Smith (2000)], depending on interest rates and the range of services provided by the bank to the firm [DeGryse and Van Cayseele (2000)]. Most firms have multiple banking relationships.[177]

Event study evidence suggests that changes in banking relationships have an impact on stock prices. The announcement of a bank loan agreement (new or renewal) is associated with positive abnormal returns, while private placements or public issues have no or a negative effect [James (1987)], a finding that has been consistently confirmed for renewals [Lummer and McConnell (1989), Best and Zhang (1993), Billett, Flannery and Garfinkel (1995)].[178] The stock price reaction to loan commitments is also positive, in particular with usage fees [Shockley and Thakor (1997)]. Acquisitions financed by bank loans are associated with positive bidder announcement returns, in particular when information asymmetries are important [Bharadwaj and Shivdasani (2003)]. Equally, Kang, Shivdasani and Yamada (2000) show that Japanese acquirers linked to banks make more valuable acquisitions than acquirers with more autonomous management.

7.3. Minority shareholder action

7.3.1. Proxy fights

Corporate voting and proxy fights received considerable attention in the early theoretical literature, drawing on the analogy between political and corporate voting [Manne (1965)]. In the USA today, proxy fights are potentially very important because they allow dissident shareholders to remove corporate boards protected by a poison pill (see Section 5.1). Proxy fights are however not very common; occurring on average 17 times a year in the period 1979–94, with 37 contests in 1989, at the peak of the hostile takeover boom [Mulherin and Poulsen (1998, p. 287)].[179] This timing is no

---

[175] At the beginning of the 1990s the average relationship in Italy lasted 14 years [Angelini et al. (1998)], 22 in Germany [Elsas and Krahnen (1998)], 30 years in Japan [Horiuchi et al. (1988)], 15–21 years in Norway [Ongena and Smith (1998)], but only 7.8 years in Belgium [DeGryse and Van Cayseele (1998)] and 7 years in the USA [Cole (1998)]. In a German sample that is more comparable to the USA samples the mean duration is only 12 years [Harhoff and Korting (1998)]; see Ongena and Smith (2000, Table 2) for further references.

[176] The cross-country and cross-study comparison must be treated with some caution because the studies suffer from the usual econometric problems that are typical for duration analysis to different degrees: right and left-censoring, stock sampling and other sampling biases.

[177] For large firms, the median number of bank relationships is 13.9–16.4 in Italy, 6–8 in Germany, 7.7 in Japan, and 5.2 in the USA; see Ongena and Smith (2000, Table 3) for further details and references.

[178] The evidence is mixed for new loans; see Ongena and Smith (2000, Table 1).

[179] Mulherin and Poulsen (1998) is the most complete study of proxy contests in the United States to date. Previous studies for smaller samples and/or shorter time periods include Dodd and Warner (1983), Pound (1988), DeAngelo and DeAngelo (1989), Borstadt and Zwirlein (1992) and Ikenberry and Lakonishok (1993). An interesting case study is Van-Nuys (1993).

coincidence; 43% of these proxy fights were accompanied by a hostile takeover bid [Mulherin and Poulsen (1998, p. 289)].[180] Proxy fights are usually brought by minority shareholders with substantial holdings (median stake 9.1%).[181] In other countries with dispersed shareholdings (see Section 7.2.1), such as the UK, proxy fights are very rare.[182] The latest evidence suggests that proxy fights provide a degree of managerial disciplining and enhance shareholder value. Gains in shareholder wealth are associated with contest-related acquisitions and restructuring under new management [Mulherin and Poulsen (1998)].[183]

7.3.2. Shareholder activism

After the decline in hostile takeovers in the USA at the beginning of the 1990s, shareholder activism has been identified as a promising new avenue for overcoming the problems of dispersed holdings and a lack of major shareholders [Black (1992)].[184] Typical forms of activism are shareholder proposals, "focus lists" of poor performers, letter writing and other types of private negotiations. Typical activist issues are calls for board reforms (see Section 7.4), the adoption of confidential voting and limits on excessive executive compensation (see Section 7.5). There is anecdotal evidence that activism is also on the rise in other countries, focusing on similar issues.[185]

In the USA, the filing of ordinary shareholder proposals[186] is much easier than a full proxy solicitation but these proposals are not binding for the board or management, making such proposals the preferred tool of USA activists. In Europe most countries

---

[180] In the full sample 23% of the firms involved in contest were acquired.

[181] Furthermore, most proxy contests (68%) aim to appoint the majority of directors, just more than half are successful (52%), and most result in management turnover (61%) [Mulherin and Poulsen (1998, p. 289)].

[182] There are notable exceptions, for example the small shareholder action at Rio Tinto PLC (in the United Kingdom) and Rio Tinto Ltd (in Australia) in May 2000 (http://www.rio-tinto-shareholders.com/).

[183] Mulherin and Poulsen (1998) sought to resolve the inconclusive findings of previous research. In agreement with theory, event studies had shown that proxy fights occur at underperforming firms and that they increase shareholder wealth when the contest is announced and over the full contest period. However, some studies found that targets did not underperform prior to the contests, and that shareholder wealth declines after the announcement, in particular after the contest has been resolved – and relatively more when the challenger is successful in placing directors on the board of the target [Ikenberry and Lakonishok (1993)].

[184] As we reported in Section 3.2, this development is closely related to the size of pension funds in the USA, the largest in the OECD.

[185] Shareholder activism is the logical next step from the adoption of corporate governance codes and principles, pressing companies to implement the recommendations put forward in these documents (see http://www.ecgi.org for a listing and full-text copies of corporate governance codes).

[186] In the USA shareholder proposals are filed under Rule 14a-8 of the SEC's proxy rule. They are precatory in nature, i.e., even if a majority of the shares outstanding vote in favor of the proposal the board is not oblidged to implement the resolution.

allow shareholders to file proposals that are put to a vote at shareholder meetings [Baums (1998), Deutsche Schutzvereinigung für Wertpapierbesitz (2000)].

The empirical literature on shareholder activism in the USA is surprisingly large and there are no less than four literature surveys [Black (1998), Gillan and Starks (1998), Karpoff (1998), Romano (2001)]. They concur that shareholder activism, irrespective of form or aim, has a negligible impact on corporate performance. However, authors disagree on the cause and interpretation of this result.

Black (1998) concludes that institutional investors spend "a trivial amount of money" on overt activism and that their ability to conduct proxy fights and appoint directors is hindered by regulation[187] and other factors.[188] In contrast, Romano (2001) argues that shareholder activism in the USA has a limited impact because it focuses mainly on issues that are known to matter very little for company performance and value. Fund managers and/or trustees engage in this type of activism because they derive private benefits from it, such as promoting a political career.

The two explanations are, in fact, linked. Pension funds are subject to the same agency problems as corporations and pension fund regulation is concerned with minimizing investment and management risk for beneficiaries. Institutional activism pushes the corporate governance problem to a higher level, with even higher dispersion this time of policy holders (often with no voting right or "one-holder–one-vote" rules), no market for pension fund control and boards with poorly paid and/or trained trustees.[189] In the USA, trustees of 401(k) plans are appointed by the corporation, raising conflict of interest issues laid bare in the recent collapse of Enron.[190]

7.3.3. Shareholder suits

Shareholder suits can complement corporate voting and potentially provide a substitute for other governance mechanisms. Once again the institutional details differ across countries.[191] In the USA shareholder litigation can take the form of derivative suits,

---

[187] Initially Black (1992) argued that shareholder activism could overcome (regulation induced) shareholder passivity in the USA.

[188] In the UK there are fewer regulatory barriers than in the USA, but there are other reasons why institutional investors are reluctant to exercise voice, for example "imperfect information, limited institutional capabilities, substantial coordination costs, the misaligned incentives of money managers, a preference for liquidity, and uncertain benefits of intervention" [Black and Coffee (1994)].

[189] See Myners (2001) for a recent policy report on pension-fund management and governance in the UK. His survey of UK pension-fund trustees revealed that they received one day of training prior to taking up their job. Leech (2003) analyses the incentives for activism in the UK. Stapledon (1996) compares institutional shareholder involvement in Australia and the UK.

[190] Conflicts of interest and outright looting of pension-fund assets were at the bottom of the collapse of the Maxwell media empire in the UK in 1992; Bower (1995) and Greenslade (1992).

[191] In most countries shareholders can appeal to the courts to uphold their basic rights, for example their voting and cash-flow rights. However, the extent and incidence of shareholder litigation differs substantially. Here we only deal with suits brought against managers or directors.

where at least one shareholder brings the suit on behalf of the corporation, and direct litigation, which can be individual or class-action.[192] The incidence of shareholder suits in the USA is low. Between 1960–1987 a random sample of NYSE firms received a suit once every 42 years and including the OTC market, 29% of the sample firms attracted about half of the suits [Romano (1991)].[193] In Europe enforcing basic shareholder rights usually falls upon public prosecutors but direct shareholder litigation is also possible on some matters.

Three main hypotheses have been tested: who benefits more from shareholder suits, shareholders or lawyers; is there any evidence that managers are disciplined by shareholder litigation; and does shareholder litigation boost or replace other forms of monitoring?

The most comprehensive empirical study for the USA covers the period 1960–1987 [Romano (1991)].[194] She finds that shareholders do not gain much from litigation, but their lawyers do. Most suits settle out of court, only half of them entail a recovery for shareholders and when they do the amount recovered per share is small.[195] In contrast, in 90% of the settled suits the lawyers are awarded a fee. There are some structural settlements but they are mostly cosmetic. The market is indifferent to the filing of a derivative suit but exhibits a negative abnormal return of -3.2% for class action.[196] There is little evidence that managers are disciplined by litigation. Executive turnover in sued firms is slightly higher, but managers almost never face financial losses.[197] Suits both help and hinder other types of monitoring. For example, blockholders are likely to get sued[198] but they also use the threat of a suit to force change or reinforce their voting power. There seems to be no comparable empirical evidence for other countries.

---

[192] The details of procedure and financial incentive differ for the two types of action [Clark (1986)]. For derivative suits the recovery usually goes to the corporation, but it must reimburse a plaintiff's legal expenses, reducing the problem of shareholders at large free-riding on the shareholders bringing the suit. In practice lawyers have an incentive to seek out shareholders and offer to bear the cost if the suit is unsuccessful and take a large fee if it is successful. This provides lawyers with an incentive to settle for a low recovery fee and a high lawyer's fee [Klein and Coffee (2000, p. 196)].

[193] For more recent descriptive statistics on class action, see Bajaj et al. (2000).

[194] Unfortunately the study has not been updated (Romano, personal communication).

[195] The recovery in derivative suits is only half as large as in direct (class) action.

[196] This could be related to the fact that the recovery in derivative suits is only half as large as in direct (class) action and that the class action recovery goes to shareholders, not the company itself. Indeed, the latter might be selling shareholders, i.e., no longer hold any shares in the company [Romano (1991, p. 67)].

[197] Compensation packages are unchanged and settlement fees are met by special insurance policies taken out by the company.

[198] As we pointed out elsewhere this is consistent with the view that shareholder suits limit self-dealing, but also with the view that they generally discourage block holding [Black (1990)].

7.4. Boards[199]

7.4.1. Institutional differences

In practice the structure, composition and exact role of boards varies greatly between individual corporations (charters) and governance systems. The same is true for the rules governing the appointment and removal of a board member and their duties.[200] In formal terms, boards can have one or two tiers. One-tier boards are usually composed of executive directors and non-executive directors. In theory the executives manage and the non-executives monitor, but in practice one-tier boards are often close to management.[201] In a two-tier board system there is a separate management board that is overseen by a supervisory board. Supervisory board members are barred from performing management functions.[202] Informally, both types of board can be more or less "captured" by management or dominated by blockholders.[203] To avoid the problem of capture by such interests, corporate governance recommendations emphasize the role of "independent directors", non-executive directors who have no links with the company other than their directorship and no links with management or blockholders.[204]

The role of the board in approving corporate decisions also varies. In one system a decision that can be ratified by the board requires shareholder approval in another. Major decisions, like mergers and acquisitions, almost always require shareholder approval. In most systems the shareholders appoint and remove the board, but the rules vary substantially (see Section 7.2). The board appoints the managers. In some countries boards have a formal duty vis-à-vis the employees of the company or, as in Germany, employees have the right to appoint directors. In the USA statutes that require boards to take into account the interests of non-shareholder constituencies are commonly portrayed as "anti-takeover rules" [Romano (1993)].[205]

---

[199] Recent surveys on the role of boards include Romano (1996), Bhagat and Black (1999) and Hermalin and Weisbach (2003).

[200] Despite these differences, the OECD Principles (1999) contain a long list of board responsibilities and prescribes basic elements of board structure and working required to fulfil its objectives.

[201] For example, it is (or used to be) common that the chairman of the board and the chief executive officer are the same person and in some countries they must be by law.

[202] Most countries have either one or the other system, but in France companies can choose.

[203] For example, it is common that the supervisory board is staffed with former members of the executive board, friends of the CEO or the blockholder.

[204] Not surprisingly the exact definition of "independent" also varies a great deal and is the subject of constant debate. See the ECGN codes page (www.ecgn.org) for full text copies of such recommendations and definitions.

[205] See Kraakman et al. (2003) for a comprehensive discussion of the role of boards in a comparative perspective.

7.4.2. Board independence

There are few formal models of boards (see Section 5) and the empirical work has focused on loose hypotheses based on policy or practical insights and recommendations. The bulk of this work has investigated whether board composition and/or independence are related to corporate performance and typically rejects the existence of such a relationship.

In order to measure the degree of board independence, several criteria have been proposed.[206] Is the chief executive officer the chairman of the board? What is the proportion of independent directors on the board? Are there any board committees and how are they staffed? Coded into variables, the answers are related to performance measures like abnormal returns, Tobin's Q and/or the usual accounting measures with simple regression analysis. The evidence from the USA suggests that board composition and corporate performance are "not related" [Hermalin and Weisbach (2003)], the relationship is "uncertain" [Bhagat and Black (1999)], or is "at best ambiguous" [Romano (1996)].

7.4.3. Board composition

Most of these studies are subject to the econometric criticisms we highlighted in Section 7.2. In the model of Hermalin and Weisbach (1998) board composition is endogenous and what we observe in a cross-section might be efficient. Hence, we would not expect to see a significant relationship between board structure and general performance. Does board composition affect performance or do the needs of companies affect their board composition? The empirical analysis of boards is also in need of third generation studies.

Warther's (1998) model predicts that boards only play a role in crisis situations and there is some evidence that this is true for independent boards. In the takeover context bidder shareholders protected by outsider-dominated boards suffer less from overbidding (get smaller negative abnormal returns) than when boards are management-dominated [Byrd and Hickman (1992)]. Also, outside boards are more likely to remove CEOs as a result of poor company performance [Byrd and Hickman (1992)].

7.4.4. Working of boards

Recommendations of "best practice" [e.g., EASD (2000)] advance the practical hypothesis that the working as well as the composition of boards matters for performance. This proposition has been tested indirectly since it is virtually impossible

---

[206] Motivated by casual observation some studies have also investigated whether board size is related to performance.

to devise a quantitative measure of the way a board is run on the inside.[207] Hence a practitioner's interpretation of the results of this empirical literature might be that the studies have simply failed to measure the dimension of boards that matters most for corporate performance – their functioning.

7.4.5. International evidence

The international evidence on the role of boards in corporate governance and their impact on corporate performance is sketchy or the relevant studies are not easily accessible. A notable exception is the UK where a number of studies have broadly confirmed the findings for the USA [Franks, Mayer and Renneboog (2001)].

7.5. Executive compensation and careers [208]

7.5.1. Background and descriptive statistics

Executive compensation in the USA has risen continuously since 1970 [see Murphy (1999)] and in 2000 reached an all-time high, with the bulk of the increase stemming from option plans.[209] Compensation consultants estimate that for a comparable US CEO the basic compensation package alone is higher than the total package in Germany, Spain, Sweden and Switzerland, and not much lower than in France or Japan (Figure 2).[210] In contrast, the total compensation of other management is similar across OECD countries and higher in Italy than in the USA [Abowd and Kaplan (1999)]. The differential remains large when data are adjusted for company size.[211]

---

[207] Vafeas (1999) finds a positive relationship between the frequency of board meetings and corporate performance, but obviously this too is a very crude measure of the effectiveness of the working of the board. In a study that has been very influential in the management literature, Lorsch and MacIver (1989) use the survey method to provide direct evidence on the working of boards. Adams (2003) uses board remuneration as a proxy for board effort, but doesn't control for endogeneity.

[208] For recent surveys see Bebchuk, Fried and Walker (2002), Gugler (2001, p. 42), Perry and Zenner (2000), Loewenstein (2000), Abowd and Kaplan (1999) and Murphy (1999). Core, Guay and Larcker (2003) survey the specialized literature on equity-based compensation and incentives.

[209] Total compensation for the average US CEOs increased from $1 770 000 in 1993 to $3 747 000 in 1997 (in 1992 CPI-deflated dollars). The value of options in this package rose from $615 000 to $1 914 000 and bonuses from $332 000 to $623 000; [Perry and Zenner (2001, p. 461, Table 1)].

[210] The value of an executive compensation package is typically measured by the "after-tax value of salaries, short-term bonuses, deferred retirement bonuses, stockholdings, stock bonuses, stock options, dividend units, phantom shares, pension benefits, savings plan contributions, long term performance plans, and any other special items (such as a loan to the executive made at a below market rate)" [Antle and Smith (1985)]. As we shall see, the most important and controversial item are stock options, an unprecedented rise in their use throughout the 90s and the terms on which they are granted.

[211] Cheffins (2003) explores whether there will be global convergence to U.S. pay levels and practices: how can U.S. pay levels remain so much higher than anywhere else, and why has this gap only opened up in the last decade and not earlier.

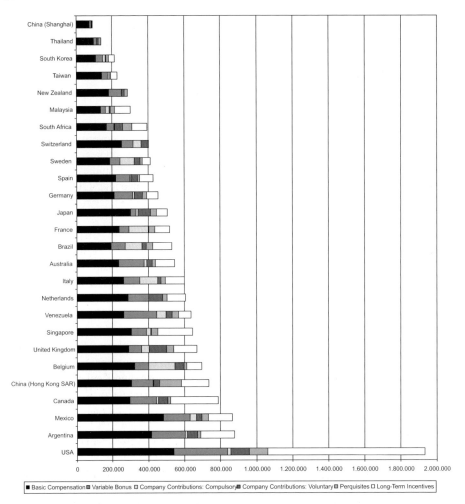

Fig. 2. Total remuneration of Chief Executive Officer. Data based on remuneration consultants' estimate for a typical CEO in a large industrial company. Source: Tower Perrins Worldwide Total Remuneration Survey 2000. See Murphy (1999, p. 2495) or http://www.towersperrin.com for more information.

Executive contracts are supposed to provide explicit and implicit incentives that align the interests of managers with those of shareholders, as discussed in Section 5. The bulk of the empirical literature has focused on sensitivity of pay[212] (explicit incentives)

---

[212] See Rosen (1992) for an early survey of this literature.

and the dismissal of executives (implicit incentive) to corporate performance.[213] High levels of pay were justified with the extraordinary gains in wealth shareholders reaped through most of the 1990s and incentive pay was characterized as one of the drivers behind the high market valuation of USA corporations [Holmstrom and Kaplan (2001)]. Recently, while stock prices plummeted and executive pay did not, attention has shifted to asymmetries in the pay–performance relationship and the potential for self-dealing by CEOs.

7.5.2. Pay–performance sensitivity

In the early 1990s the consensus view in the literature was that the sensitivity of pay to performance in the USA was too low [see Baker et al. (1988), Jensen and Murphy (1990)].[214] Executives did not receive enough cash after good corporate performance and did not incur sufficient losses, through dismissal, after poor performance. The same conclusions were reached for other countries, most notably Japan [see Kaplan (1994a)]. In the USA the sensitivity of executive pay to performance reached levels 2 to 10 times higher than in 1980 by 1994 [see Hall and Liebman (1998)]. The dollar change in executive wealth normalized by the dollar change in firm value appears small and falls by a factor of ten with firm size, but the change in the value of the CEO's equity stake is large and increases with firm size.[215] The probability of dismissal remained unchanged between 1970 and 1995 [Murphy (1999)].[216]

The sensitivity of equity-based compensation with respect to firm value is about 53 times higher than that of the salary and bonus components [Hall and Liebman (1998)]. However, even for median performance the annualized percentage increase in mean wealth for CEOs has been 11.5% for the period between 1982 and 1994 [Hall and Liebman (1998)] and the size of CEO losses relative to the average appreciation of their stock holdings has been modest.

In other countries too, the use of equity-based compensation and pay–performance sensitivity has risen, but nowhere close to the USA level. In the UK the percentage of companies with an option plan has risen from 10% in 1979 to over 90% in 1985

---

[213] The accounting literature also emphasizes the technical problem of estimating the monetary value of top executive compensation packages. See Antle and Smith (1985), based on early work by Burgess (1963) and Lewellen (1968).

[214] The point was also emphasized in an early survey by Jensen and Zimmerman (1985).

[215] Baker and Hall (1998) document the firms size effect and discuss the merits of each measure. During 1974–86 the median CEO gained or lost \$3.25 for \$1000 gained or lost by shareholders, adjusted for the risk of dismissal; but money equivalent of this threat was only \$0.30 [Jensen and Murphy (1990)]. In 1997 and 1998 the gain or loss was \$10–11 per \$1000 (unadjusted) [Perry and Zenner (2000), Hall and Liebman (2000)]. For an executive holding stock and options worth \$20 000 000, a 10% change in stock prices implies a \$2 000 000 change in wealth.

[216] Among S&P 500 firms average CEO turnover rates for low performers were 15% on and 11% from the 25th performance percentile upwards [Murphy (1999)].

[Main (1999)]. However, the level of shareholdings and pay–performance sensitivity are about six times lower than in the USA [Conyon and Murphy (2000)].

7.5.3. Are compensation packages well-designed?

Agency theory predicts that incentive pay should be tied to performance relative to comparable firms, not absolute performance. And indeed, early studies found that changes in CEO cash compensation were negatively related to industry and market performance, but positively related to firm performance [Gibbons and Murphy (1990)].[217] In contrast, equity-based compensation is hardly ever corrected for industry or market stock index movements, leading to a solid rejection of the relative performance evaluation (RPE) hypothesis in all recent surveys [Core et al. (2003, pp. 38–39), Bebchuk, Fried and Walker (2002), Abowd and Kaplan (1999), Murphy (1999)].[218]

Agency theory can be used to determine the optimal exercise price of options when they are granted. The optimal price is a function of numerous factors and not the same for different firms. In practice most options are granted at the money (i.e., with an exercise price equal to the company's stock price on the day), a clear contradiction of the predictions of theory [Bebchuk, Fried and Walker (2002, p. 818)].

Theory also predicts that incentive schemes and the adoption of such schemes should result in net increases in shareholder wealth. The latest evidence (based on "abnormal Q" regressions) rejects this prediction. An increase in CEO option holdings leads to a decrease in Tobin's Q, suggesting that CEOs hold too many options but not enough stock [Habib and Ljungqvist (2002)]. However, event study evidence generally supports the theory [Morgan and Poulsen (2001), DeFusco et al. (1990), Brickley, Bhagat and Lease (1985), Larcker (1983)].[219]

Agency theory further predicts that incentive pay and blockholder monitoring or takeover threats are substitutes. Firms subject to blockholder monitoring or with family representatives on the board are less likely to implement stock option plans [Mehran (1995), Kole (1997)] because more discipline substitutes for more sensitivity of pay. In contrast, without blockholder monitoring, CEOs are not paid as the theory predicts [Bertrand and Mullainathan (2001, 2000)]. Boards protected by state anti-takeover laws [Bertrand and Mullainathan (1998)] or anti-takeover amendments [Borokhovich, Brunarski and Parrino (1997)] (see Section 7.1) provide more incentive pay to

---

[217] See Murphy (1999, p. 2535)] for additional references.

[218] Several explanations of this puzzle have been put forward including accounting problems, tax considerations, the difficulty in obtaining performance data from rivals, worries about collusion between companies, the ability of managers to get back to absolute performance plans with appropriate financial instruments, but not a single one is very satisfactory.

[219] Note that DeFusco et al. (1990) found a negative reaction in bond prices, interpreting the adoption of stock option plans as means for transferring wealth from bondholders to stockholders. An influential early study is Masson (1971).

compensate for less discipline from hostile takeovers, while in the UK takeover threats are higher while incentive pay and the level of pay are lower than in the USA [Conyon and Murphy (2000)]. However, there are inconsistencies. Companies in industries with more disciplining takeovers should pay less, while in fact they pay more [Agrawal and Walkling (1994), Agrawal and Knoeber (1998)]. Although these results are suggestive, self-dealing is a plausible rival explanation – boards that are monitored less give more pay to their CEO cronies. [220]

7.5.4. Are managers paying themselves too much?

Few direct tests of the rival 'self-serving manager' explanation of USA pay practices are available, but some studies attempt to get at the issue indirectly. Thus, there is evidence that management manipulates the timing of stock option grants [Yermack (1997)] and times the flow of good and bad news prior to the option grant [Aboody and Kasznik (2000)]. This can be interpreted as evidence of self-dealing [Shleifer and Vishny (1997a)].

Another way of determining whether there has been self-dealing is to see whether CEO stock option plans (or bonus packages) have been approved by a shareholder vote. Even though in 2000 almost 99% of the plans proposed at major US corporations received shareholder approval, the average percentage of votes cast against stock-option plans has increased from 4% in 1988 to about 18% in 1995–1999 [IRRC (2000b)], 20.2% in 1999 and 23.3% in 2001 [IRRC (2002)]. In some cases dilution levels are 70% or more, especially in the technology sector, often associated with "evergreen" features [IRRC (2002)]. There is rising concern about exemptions for "broadly based plans", [221] potential dilution of voting rights, [222] broker voting, [223] option repricing, payments in restricted stock, loans for share purchases, "evergreen plans" [224] and discount options [Thomas and Martin (2000)]. In addition, activists are now worried that "at the same time that stock prices are falling, CEO pay continues

---

[220] Bebchuk, Fried and Walker (2002) express general skepticism about the substitution effect between incentive pay and disciplining through takeovers. They argue that boards can pay themselves and the CEO large amounts of money without reducing the value of the company enough to justify a takeover.

[221] Stock option plans that do not need shareholder approval if they benefit more than a certain proportion of non-officer employees.

[222] The IRRC (2001) estimates that the average potential dilution of the voting power of the currently outstanding shares from stock option plans was 13.1% for the S&P 500 and 14.6% for the S&P 1500 in 2000, higher than in previous years.

[223] Under NYSE rules brokers can vote shares without instructions from the beneficial owners. A recent study estimates that routine proposals that benefit from broker votes receive 14.2% more "yes" votes than other routine proposals of the same kind, making broker votes marginal for 5.2% of routine proposals [Bethel and Gillan (2002)].

[224] Evergreen plans reserve a small percentage of stock for award each year. Once approved the awards are made without shareholder approval. "Quasi-evergreen plans" have a limited lifetime, regular plans run indefinitely [Thomas and Martin (2000, p. 62)].

to rise" [AFL-CIO (2001)].[225] These results are not strong direct-evidence support for the self-serving manager hypothesis, but they can be re-interpreted as yet another failure of shareholder monitoring in the USA.

In parallel with the takeover literature, yet another approach for distinguishing between self-serving and efficient behavior brings in board composition and the power of the CEO vis-à-vis the board. Outside and independent directors on the board or on remuneration committees are thought to be (more) resistant to awarding self-serving compensation packages. In contrast, CEOs who are also the chairman of the board ("duality") are thought to lean more towards self-dealing. In the USA, most corporations have a compensation committee comprising outside directors.[226] As a direct result of the Cadbury Committee (1992) and Greenbury Committee (1995) reports, UK issuers have remuneration committees[227] and in 1994 already they were 91% staffed with outside directors. Similarly, during 1991–1994 the proportion of UK boards with "duality" fell from 52% to 36% [Conyon and Peck (1998)]. Both developments are also gaining ground in continental Europe.[228] So far, empirical studies have failed to detect that institutions and reforms have any impact on pay structure. In the USA committees staffed with directors close to management do not grant unusually generous compensation packages [Daily et al. (1998)]. In the UK in 1991–1994, the proportion of non-executive directors serving on boards and duality had no effect on compensation structure [Conyon and Peck (1998)].[229] CEOs monitored by a board with interlocking directors get more pay [Hallock (1997)].[230]

There is evidence that the extensive use of compensation experts and peer review increases pay in excess of what is warranted from a pure agency perspective. For example, CEOs with pay packages that lie below the median of their peers see their pay increase more quickly, *ceteris paribus* [Bizjak, Lemmon and Naveen (2000)].

7.5.5. Implicit incentives

Implicit incentives typically take the form of executive dismissal or post-retirement board services. Post-retirement appointment to a board can be a powerful implicit incentive or, once again, a sign of self-dealing. In the USA, CEO careers continue after retirement with 75% holding at least one directorship after two years. Almost

---

[225] The AFL-CIO has recently opened a Website campaigning against "runaway pay" in the USA, see (http://www.paywatch.org).
[226] If not, under U.S. tax law compensation is not tax deductible for executives mentioned in the proxy statement [Murphy (1999)].
[227] See Conyon and Mallin (1997).
[228] See http://www.cgcodes.org for reports on the implementation of the pertinent governance recommendations in continental Europe.
[229] We are not aware of a direct test that exploits the time series variation of the UK reforms.
[230] Fich and White (2001) investigate the determinants of interlocks.

half (49.5%) stay on their own board after retirement, in 18% of the cases as chairman [Brickley et al. (1999)].[231]

Most explicit and implicit incentives are written into CEO contracts that, under USA Federal Law, must be disclosed but had not been collected until recently [Minow (2000)]. Preliminary analysis reveals that contracts range from "short and to the point" [Minow (2000)] to guaranteed benefits and perks of epic proportions.[232] Implicit benefits include severance pay for dismissal without "cause"[233] or in case of changes in control (acquisition of 15, 20 or 51% of the voting shares).[234] We expect that more analytic studies based on this data will shed more light on these issues.

7.5.6. Conclusion

To conclude, it has become difficult to maintain the view, based on data from the bull market of the early 1990s, that US pay practices provide explicit and implicit incentives for aligning the interests of managers with those of shareholders. Instead, the rival view that US managers have the ability, the opportunity and the power to set their own pay at the expense of shareholders [Bebchuk, Fried and Walker (2002)], increasingly prevails. We know relatively less about pay practices in other countries, but attempts to implement USA practices are controversial, as the long-standing debate in the U.K.[235] and recent rows in France[236] show. The institutional investor community is drawing its own conclusions and has tabled global guidelines on executive pay,[237] while corporate America is under pressure to report earnings net of the cost of stock options.

---

[231] Many corporate governance codes oppose the appointment of CEOs to their own boards after retirement.

[232] See http://www.thecorporatelibrary.com/ceos/. One of the more lavish contracts included a $10 million signing bonus, $2 million stock options at $10 a share below market, a "guaranteed bonus" of at least half a million dollars a year, a Mercedes for the executive and his wife, a corporate jet for commuting and first class air for the family once a month, including the executive's mother [Minow (2000)].

[233] The definition of cause is often stringent, for example "felony, fraud, embezzlement, gross negligence, or moral turpitude" [Minow (2000)].

[234] The latter, once again, weakens the potential monitoring role of blockholders in the USA.

[235] Recently, coalitions of UK institutional investors have been successful at curbing pay packages, even in the case of perceived excess among their own kind: Andrew Bolger, *Prudential Bows to Revolt Over Executive Pay*, FT.com; May 08, 2002.

[236] Pierre Tran and David Teather, *Vivendi Shareholders Turn on Messier*, The Guardian; April 25, 2002.

[237] The proposed standard prescribes, *inter alia*, individual disclosure for individual executives, reporting of stock options as a cost to the company, shareholder voting on pay policy, appointment of an independent pay committee and limits on potential channels of self-dealing (e.g. loans to executives); ICGN (2002).

7.6. Multiple constituencies

In addition to shareholders there are four major other constituencies: creditors (and other non-equity investors), employees, suppliers and clients. In parallel to Section 5, we focus on the role and impact of the debtholder and employee constituencies in a comparative corporate governance perspective.

7.6.1. Debtholders

Many aspects of the role of debtholders in corporate governance are addressed in the empirical financial contracting literature.[238] These studies investigate the evolution impact and choice of general capital structures, or the effect of changes in leverage on stock prices, particularly in the context of corporate control transactions (see Section 7.1).

The main theoretical rationale for sharing control between managers, shareholder *and* debtholders is their different role in restructuring and, in particular during financial distress (see Section 5).

Is debt a commitment device for liquidation after poor performance? As usual, the role of debtholders differs appreciably between countries. For example, in the USA insolvency law is "softer" than in the UK,[239] and judges are more lenient [Franks and Sussman (1999)]. Furthermore, regulation in the USA is subject to political intervention and lobbying, which further weakens the usefulness of debt as a commitment device [Berglöf and Rosenthal (1999), Franks and Sussman (1999), Kroszner (1999)].[240] Basic statistics lend support to this view. In the USA the rate of deviation from absolute priority rules is 77–78%[241] but it is close to zero in the UK [Franks and Sussman (2000)].[242]

Recent work on venture capital financing lends more direct support to the importance of debtholder involvement by analysing the actual contracts signed between

---

[238] For a comprehensive earlier survey see Harris and Raviv (1992).

[239] Under Chapter 11 of the 1978 Bankruptcy Code the debtor is allowed to stay in control and try to raise new cash. In the UK floating charge holders take control through the appointment of an Administrative Receiver who acts in their interest and replaces the board [Franks and Sussman (2000), Davies et al. (1997)].

[240] Theory predicts that ex-ante commitment from dispersed debt is stronger than concentrated debt, yet systems that give creditors strong liquidation rights often do so through an agent, making it easier to renegotiate (e.g., the UK and Germany).

[241] See, for example, Franks and Torous (1989).

[242] Note that these basic statistics are methodologically problematic. The USA studies suffer from sample bias, looking primarily at large companies with publicly traded debt and conditional on the outcome of the bankruptcy procedure. Hence, the results could be distorted towards more or less actual commitment in the USA at large. The statistics of Franks and Sussman (2000) do not suffer from this problem because they were sponsored by a government-working group on the reform of insolvency law.

firms and the providers of finance.[243] Consistent with the theory they find that the financial constituencies[244] have control and liquidation rights that are contingent on performance and that control shifts between constituencies, again depending on performance [Kaplan and Strömberg (2003)].

7.6.2. Employees

The literature on employee involvement has focused on two questions: does employee involvement come at the expense of shareholders (reduce shareholder wealth), and if contracts are incomplete, is employee involvement efficient? There is little empirical evidence in support of the first question and, to our knowledge, no empirical evidence that would allow us to formulate an answer to the second question.

The incidence of employee involvement is often thought to be limited to Germany's mandatory codetermination and two-tier boards. In fact, employee involvement is also mandatory in Austria and the Netherlands[245] (two-tier boards), Denmark, Sweden, Luxembourg and France[246] (one-tier board). Companies operating in two or more member states of the European Union must have a "European Works Council".[247] Voluntary codetermination can be found in Finland and Switzerland [Wymeersch (1998)]. In contrast, employees in Japan are not formally represented on the board [Hoshi (1998)], although Japanese corporations are run, supposedly, in the employees' and not the shareholders' interest [Allen and Gale (2000)]. Compared to the wealth of opinions on employee involvement, the empirical literature is small, even for countries where such institutions are known to exist, such as Germany.

German codetermination provides for mandatory representation of employees on the supervisory board of corporations[248] with three levels of intensity: full parity for coal, iron and steel companies (since 1951),[249] quasi-parity for other companies with more

---

[243] Sahlman (1990), Black and Gilson (1998), Kaplan and Strömberg (2003).

[244] In theory a venture capitalist (universal bank) holding debt and equity represents two constituencies.

[245] In the Netherlands the board members of large *structuur* regime corporations have a duty to act "in the interest of the company" and shareholders do not appoint them. Formally the incumbent board members appoint new board members. In practice they are chosen jointly by capital and labor because the shareholders and the employees can challenge appointment in a specialised Court [Wymeersch (1998, p. 1146)].

[246] The French system provides for weak representation and has been called "a mockery" [Wymeersch (1998, p. 1149)].

[247] Council established under the European Works Council Directive (94/45/EC) to ensure that all company employees are "properly informed and consulted when decisions which affect them are taken in a Member State other than that in which they are employed". The Directive applies to companies and groups with at least 1000 employees in the European Economic Area (the EU15, Norway, Iceland and Liechtenstein) as a whole and at least 150 in each of two or more Member States.

[248] See Hopt et al. (1998) and Prigge (1998) for an overview; in what follows we only discuss corporations (AGs). The German-language literature is vast; see Streeck and Kluge (1999) or Frick et al. (1999) for recent examples.

[249] Shareholders and workers each appoint 50% of the board members. The chairman is nominated by the board and must be ratified by the general meeting and both sides of the board by majority vote.

than 2000 employees (since 1976)[250] and $\frac{1}{3}$ parity for those with 500–2000 employees (since 1994).[251] Media companies are exempt.

Does the degree of codetermination adversely affect shareholder wealth or company performance? If codetermination reduces shareholder wealth, shareholders will resent codetermination and they will try to bypass[252] or shift board rights to the general assembly. There is some evidence of the former but none for the latter. In 1976 most supervisory boards of corporations subject to the quasi-parity regime did not have to be consulted on important management decisions[253] [Gerum et al. (1988)], a clear violation of the recommendations in most corporate governance codes (see Section 6.2).[254]

If there are losses in shareholder wealth from codetermination, how large are they? Econometric studies of codetermination compare company or sector performance "before and after" the 1951, 1952, 1972 and 1976 reforms or their enforcement by the courts. These studies find no or small effects of codetermination [Svejnar (1981, 1982), Benelli et al. (1987), Baums and Frick (1999)] and/or their samples and methodology are controversial [Gurdon and Rai (1990), FitzRoy and Kraft (1993)].[255] A recent study relies on the cross-section variation of codetermination intensity, controlling for different types of equity control and company size. It finds codetermination reducing market-to-book-value and return on equity [Gorton and Schmid (2000a)]. Codetermination intensity and its incidence correlate with other factors that are known to matter for stock price and accounting measures of performance, in particular sector and company size, and it is doubtful that one can ever fully control for these factors.

8. Conclusion

As the length of this survey indicates, there has been an explosion of research on corporate governance in the past two decades. Having taken the reader through this lengthy overview it is only fair that we attempt to draw the main lessons from this massive research effort and also try to determine the main areas of agreement and disagreement.

[250] The chairman is chosen by the shareholder representatives and has a casting vote.
[251] Between 1952–1994 this regime applied to all corporations, and still does for corporations registered before 1994.
[252] For example, by delegating sensitive tasks to shareholder-dominated committees or allowing the shareholder appointed Chairman to add items to the agenda at will.
[253] The catalogue of decisions is long and includes mergers and acquisitions, patents and major contracts.
[254] In coal, iron and steel companies, where codetermination is most intense, more management decisions required formal approval from the supervisory board, an apparent contradiction to the general finding. However, one can argue that worker influence is so intense in these companies that the capital side of the supervisory board is too weak to apply a *de facto* opt-out of codetermination.
[255] Frick et al. (1999), Gerum and Wagner (1998).

If there is one point on which most researchers and policy commentators agree today it is that corporate governance is a pillar of wealth creation and a fundamental aspect of corporate finance. As the Asian and Russian financial crises of 1997–1998 or the recent collapse of the Enron corporation have dramatically highlighted, poor or corrupt corporate governance practices in banks and corporations can significantly worsen the depth of financial crises if not trigger them. It is now widely accepted that the textbook characterization of firms as profit maximizers subject to technological production constraints is a major oversimplification and that agency problems and corporate control issues are fundamental for corporate finance and the investment process. A major part of the story is left out by reducing securities to their cash-flow characteristics. Equity capital has valuable voting rights besides rights to residual cash flow and so does debt in the event of default. As we have highlighted, there are by now numerous empirical studies attempting to measure the value of these control rights by measuring block premia or voting rights premia in dual-class share structures. Another general point of agreement is that dispersed ownership results in a "power vacuum" and gives rise to a managerial agency problem. Unless corporate executives are given appropriate financial incentives or are adequately monitored they will not just take actions that maximize the net present value of the firm. They will also make decisions that benefit them at the expense of the firm.

Executive stock options have become an increasingly popular and controversial form of financial incentive for CEOs in the past decade. It is widely recognized, however, that these options are at best an inefficient financial incentive and at worst create new incentive or conflict-of-interest problems of their own. The options are inefficient if they are not based on some relative performance measure such as the excess stock performance relative to an industry or market index. They create new incentive problems by inducing CEOs to manipulate earnings or "cook the books" in order to support stock prices. Finally, they create major conflict-of-interest problems when the CEO borrows from the firm to "purchase" his or her stock options.

It is also widely recognized that boards of directors are weak and ineffective monitors of managers. As we have highlighted, the empirical research on boards and independent directors has produced disappointing results. The New York Stock Exchange is proposing to remedy this glaring deficiency by both increasing the number of independent directors that are required to sit on a board and by tightening the definition of "independent". Under the proposed new rules an independent director should have no "material" relationship with the company. This is likely to be seen as a step in the right direction by most commentators.

Board weakness calls for additional mechanisms for monitoring management. We have discussed extensively the role of hostile takeovers, large shareholders, shareholder activism in the form of proxy fights and shareholder suits, or the role of banks, large creditors and employee supervisory committees. It is fair to say that there is much less consensus on the effectiveness and relative benefits of each of these mechanisms.

It is generally accepted that hostile takeovers are rare and increasingly so. They are a rather blunt instrument of corporate control. Generally widely held companies are shielded from hostile takeovers through anti-takeover defenses (with the exception of the UK). It has been widely documented that the main beneficiaries of hostile takeovers are target company shareholders and the main losers acquiring company shareholders and target management. Also, the average combined value of the acquiring and target companies in hostile takeovers is not significantly different from zero. In other words, there is no robust evidence of net value creation in the average hostile takeover. Finally, existing evidence suggesting that threat of hostile takeovers has a disciplining effect on management is weak.

Another widely documented fact is that most companies around the world (except in the USA, and to a lesser extent the UK and Japan) have at least one blockholder with concentrated voting power. Also, deviations from "one-share–one-vote" are commonly observed but there are major variations across countries. It is generally accepted that large shareholders tend to use their control rights to both monitor management and to divert resources disproportionately to themselves. To what extent large shareholders benefit the firm on net, however, is disputed. One complication is that there are large variations across countries. In countries where "self-dealing" by large shareholders is tightly regulated the net contribution of large shareholders is likely to be positive according to some observers. In countries where it is not, large shareholders are often seen as the source of the corporate governance problem rather than the solution. Empirical research on these issues is held back by the lack of reliable and systematic panel data on control rights around the world. No doubt more evidence will emerge as more data becomes available over time.

It is generally agreed that direct shareholder intervention is difficult and only modestly effective. Proxy fights challenging incumbent management are immensely difficult to win. Shareholder suits are similarly challenged in the absence of strong evidence of malfeasance; and empirical evidence, available for the USA only, shows that while the lawyers involved undoubtedly benefit, the gain to the shareholders they represent are less clear; moreover the disciplinary effects of shareholder legal action on managerial wealth and position are minimal, and the impact on alternative forms of monitoring is ambiguous. Meanwhile, empirical studies find the impact of shareholder activism by large pension funds to be minimal.

Regarding the role of banks and large creditors, there is an emerging consensus that they have an important role to play in corporate governance, but only if they are themselves well managed. The East Asia crisis of the late 1990s has demonstrated that bad corporate governance, as exemplified by cronyism and connected lending, can be a source of major corporate governance failures throughout the economy. Meanwhile, where banks are sound and well-managed, as for instance Germany, there is evidence of their effectiveness in disciplining management.

Turning now to open issues, one of the most hotly debated topics is the relative merit of market-based and bank-based systems of corporate governance. There is no evidence that the cost of capital is lower in the USA or the UK. It is commonly argued that the Anglo-Saxon market-based setting provides a better environment for startups, new technologies and the redeployment of resources into new, more profitable lines of business, while bank-based systems are perhaps more suitable for effective management of existing technologies. No convincing evidence on these points is available.

Open questions also arise in the context of findings that better legal enforcement of minority shareholder rights is associated with greater reliance on stock market financing. How important is this finding for the availability of suitable financing? And which way does the causality run?

Very recently, problems associated with the growth in both levels of executive pay and CEO stock participation via option plans have come to the fore. It is not clear whether the intended effect on efficiency has outweighed the negative impact of self-serving behavior by unmonitored CEOs, whose ability to manipulate earnings creates a whole new set of incentive problems. Similarly the role of executive pay in encouraging excessive merger activity needs attention. Both theory and empirical research need to be brought into this general area.

Some neglected issues in corporate governance research have recently become focal points in the debate about the Enron collapse. The role of large auditing firms in corporate governance is under scrutiny, and better ways to manage the tradeoffs between toughness in auditing and generating consulting business are being discussed. Similarly, there are conflict of interest issues relating to Wall Street analysts whose firms are also involved in corporate financing. For both the accounting profession and the financial services industry, this raises underresearched issues such as the potential impact of excessive scope of activities concentrated on one firm, and the degree to which self-regulation is effective in limiting inappropriate behavior.

There is also surprisingly little theoretical and empirical research on the role of boards, given that the codes of practice and other reform proposals formulated by practitioners focus mainly on this area. There is a need for theoretical or empirical work that gives insight into appropriate ways to enhance board effectiveness.

Lastly, progress is needed in modelling and measuring how different monitoring mechanisms interact: and in garnering non-USA evidence on the roles of shareholder suits and regulatory change.

Regarding policy issues, steps that could be taken in the USA include a reduction in the costs and risks of large investor intervention, the strengthening of boards and their independence, a possibly greater degree of employee representation, a re-evaluation of the trend towards greater anti-takeover protection, and facilitation of shareholder activism in general.

In Europe, there is again a battle to be fought against excessive arsenals of anti-takeover devices. Other policy measures that might be of benefit include measures to proscribe self-dealing by large shareholders in some countries, and the strengthening of boards. In many respects the UK model of regulation seems to be the most appealing, though it has not resolved the problems of institutional investor passivity and fund governance; even so, EU policy proposals have generally tended in the UK direction.

To conclude, corporate governance is concerned with the resolution of collective action problems among dispersed investors and the resolution of conflicts of interest between various corporate claimholders. In this survey we have reviewed the theoretical and empirical research on the main mechanisms of corporate control, discussed the main legal and regulatory institutions in different countries, and examined the comparative corporate governance literature. A fundamental dilemma of corporate governance emerges from this overview: regulating large shareholder intervention appears necessary, especially in Continental Europe, Asia and emerging markets; but limiting the power of large investors can also result in greater managerial discretion and scope for abuse. This is of particular concern in the USA as the recent corporate governance crisis has highlighted.

References

Aboody, D., and R. Kasznik (2000), "CEO stock option awards and the timing of corporate voluntary disclosures", Journal of Accounting and Economics 29(1):73–100.

Abowd, J.M., and D.S. Kaplan (1999), "Executive compensation: six questions that need answering", Journal of Economic Perspectives 13(4):145–168.

Adams, R. (2001), "The dual role of boards as advisers and monitors", PhD dissertation (University of Chicago, IL).

Adams, R.B. (2003), "What do boards do? Evidence from board committee and director compensation data", Mimeo (Federal Reserve Bank of New York).

Admati, A.R., P. Pfleiderer and J. Zechner (1994), "Large shareholder activism, risk sharing, and financial market equilibrium", Journal of Political Economy 102:1097–1130.

Aghion, P., and P. Bolton (1987), "Contracts as a barrier to entry", American Economic Review 77:388–401.

Aghion, P., and P. Bolton (1992), "An incomplete contracts approach to financial contracting", Review of Economic Studies 59:473–494.

Aghion, P., and B. Hermalin (1990), "Legal restrictions on private contracts can enhance efficiency", Journal of Law, Economics and Organization 6:381–409.

Aghion, P., and J. Tirole (1997), "Formal and real authority in organizations", Journal of Political Economy 105:1–29.

Aghion, P., P. Bolton and S. Fries (1999), "Optimal design of bank bailouts: the case of transition economies", Journal of Institutional and Theoretical Economics 155:51–70.

Aghion, P., P. Bolton and J. Tirole (2000), Exit Options in Corporate Finance: Liquidity versus Incentives (Harvard University, Cambridge, MA).

Agrawal, A., and C.R. Knoeber (1998), "Managerial compensation and the threat of takeover", Journal of Financial Economics 47(2):219–239.

Agrawal, A., and R.A. Walkling (1994), "Executive careers and compensation surrounding takeover bids", Journal of Finance 49(3):985–1014.

Allen, F., and D. Gale (2000), Comparing Financial Systems (MIT Press, Cambridge, MA).

American Federation of Labor and Industrial Organizations (2001), Runaway CEO Pay: What's Happening and What You Can Do About It. http://www.aflcio.org/paywatch/.

Amihud, Y., and H. Mendelson (1986), "Asset pricing and the bid-ask spread", Journal of Financial Economics 17:223–249.

Amihud, Y., H. Mendelson and J. Uno (1999), "Number of shareholders and stock prices: evidence from Japan", Journal of Finance 54:1169–1184.

Andenas, M., K.J. Hopt and E. Wymeersch, eds (2003), Free Movement of Companies in EC Law (Oxford University Press, Oxford) forthcoming.

Anderson, R.C., and D.S. Lee (1997), "Ownership studies: the data source does matter", Journal of Financial and Quantitative Analysis 32.

Andrade, G., M. Mitchell and E. Stafford (2001), "New evidence and perspectives on mergers", Journal of Economic Perspectives 15:103–120.

Angelini, P., R. Di Salvo and G. Ferri (1998), "Availability and cost of credit for small businesses: customer relationships and credit cooperatives", Journal of Banking and Finance 22(6–8):925–954.

Antle, R., and A. Smith (1985), "Measuring executive compensation: methods and an application", Journal of Accounting Research 23(1):296–325.

Aoki, M. (1990), "Toward an economic model of the Japanese firm", Journal of Economic Literature 28:1–27.

Aoki, M., H. Patrick and P. Sheard (1994), "The Japanese main bank system: an introductory overview", in: M. Aoki and H. Patrick, eds., The Japanese Main Bank System: Its Relevance for Developing and Transforming Economies (Oxford University Press, Oxford).

Asquith, K.P., and E.H. Kim (1982), "The impact of merger bids on the participating firms' security holders", Journal of Finance 37:1209–1228.

Avilov, G., B. Black, D. Carreau, O. Kozyr, S. Nestor and S. Reynolds (1999), "General principles of company law for transition economies", Journal of Corporation Law 24:190–293.

Ayres, I., and P. Cramton (1994), "Relational investing and agency theory", Cardozo Law Review 15:1033–1066.

Ayres, I., and R. Gertner (1989), "Filling gaps in incomplete contracts: an economic theory of default rules", Yale Law Journal 99(1):87–130.

Bacon, J., and J. Brown (1975), Corporate Directorship Practices: Role, Selection, and Legal Status of the Board (American Society of Corporate Secretaries, New York).

Bagnoli, M., and B.L. Lipman (1988), "Successful takeovers without exclusion", Review of Financial Studies 1:89–110.

Bajaj, M., S.C. Mazumdar and A. Sarin (2000), "Securities class action settlements: an empirical analysis", Mimeo (Haas School of Business, University of California-Berkeley).

Baker, G.P., and B.J. Hall (1998), "CEO incentives and firm size", NBER Working Paper 6868 (Harvard Business School and NBER).

Baker, G.P., M.C. Jensen and K.J. Murphy (1988), "Compensation and incentives: practice vs. theory", Journal of Finance 43:593–616.

Barca, F., and M. Becht, eds (2001), The Control of Corporate Europe (Oxford University Press, Oxford).

Baron, D.P. (1983), "Tender offers and management resistance", Journal of Finance 38:331–343.

Bartlett, J. (1994), Venture Capital: Law, Business Strategies, and Investment Planning (Wiley, New York).

Baums, T. (1998), "Shareholder representation and proxy voting in the European Union: a comparative study", in: K.J. Hopt, H. Kanda, M.J. Roe, E. Wymeersch and S. Prigge, eds., Comparative Corporate Governance. The State of the Art and Emerging Research (Clarendon Press, Oxford) pp. 545–564.

Baums, T., and C. Fraune (1995), "Institutionelle Anleger und Publikumsgesellschaft: Eine Empirische Untersuchung", Die Aktiengesellschaft 3:97–112.

Baums, T., and B. Frick (1999), "The market value of the codetermined firm", in: M.M. Blair and M.J. Roe, eds., Employees and Corporate Governance (Brookings Institution Press, Washington DC) pp. 206–235.

Bebchuk, L.A. (1992), "Federalism and the corporation: the desirable limits on state competition in corporate law", Harvard Law Review 105:1435.

Bebchuk, L.A. (1999), A Rent-Protection Theory of Corporate Ownership and Control (NBER, Cambridge, MA).

Bebchuk, L.A. (2000), "Using options to divide value in corporate bankruptcy", European Economic Review 44:829–843.

Bebchuk, L.A., and A. Ferrell (1999), "Federalism and corporate law: the race to protect managers from takeovers", Columbia Law Review 99:1168–1199.

Bebchuk, L.A., and A. Ferrell (2001), "A new approach to takeover law and regulatory competition", Virginia Law Review 87:1168.

Bebchuk, L.A., and O. Hart (2001), "Takeover bids vs. Proxy fights in contests for corporate control", NBER Working Paper Series (NBER, Cambridge, MA).

Bebchuk, L.A., and M. Roe (1999), "A theory of path dependence in corporate ownership and governance", Stanford Law Review 52:127–170.

Bebchuk, L.A., R. Kraakman and G. Trianis (2000), "Stock pyramids, cross-ownership, and dual class equity", in: R.K. Morck, ed., Concentrated Corporate Ownership (NBER Conference Report Series, University of Chicago Press, Chicago).

Bebchuk, L.A., J.M. Fried and D.I. Walker (2002), "Managerial power and rent extraction in the design of executive compensation", The University of Chicago Law Review 69:751–846.

Bebchuk, L.A., J. Coates and G. Subramanian (2002), "The powerful antitakeover force of staggered boards: theory, evidence and policy", Stanford Law Review 54:887–951.

Bechmann, K., and J. Raaballe (2000), "A regulation of bids for dual class shares. Implication: two shares – one price", WP 2000-5 (Department of Finance, Copenhagen Business School).

Becht, M. (1999), "European corporate governance: trading off liquidity against control", European Economic Review 43:1071–1083.

Becht, M. (2001), "Beneficial ownership in the U.S.", in: F. Barca and M. Becht, eds., The Control of Corporate Europe (Oxford University Press, Oxford) pp. 285–299.

Becht, M., and E. Böhmer (2003), "Voting control in German corporations", International Review of Law and Economics 23:1–29.

Becht, M., and C. Mayer (2001), "Introduction", in: F. Barca and M. Becht, eds., The Control of Corporate Europe (Oxford University Press, Oxford) pp. 1–45.

Benelli, G., C. Loderer and T. Lys (1987), "Labor participation in corporate policy-making decisions: West Germany's experience with codetermination", Journal of Business 60:553–575.

Benston, G.J., and R.L. Hagerman (1974), "Determinants of bid-asked spreads in the over-the-counter market", Journal of Financial Economics 1:353–364.

Berger, P.G., and E. Ofek (1995), "Diversification's effect on firm value", Journal of Financial Economics 37:39–65.

Berglöf, E. (1990), "Corporate control and capital structure - essays on property rights and financial contracts", Dissertation for the Doctor's Degree in Business Administration (Stockholm School of Economics, Stockholm).

Berglöf, E. (1994), "A control theory of venture capital finance", Journal of Law, Economics, and Organization 10:247–267.

Berglöf, E., and H. Rosenthal (1999), "The political economy of American bankruptcy: the evidence from roll call voting, 1800–1978", Mimeo (Princeton University).

Berglöf, E., and E.-L. von Thadden (1994), "Short-term versus long-term interests: capital structure with multiple investors", Quarterly Journal of Economics 109:1055–1084.

Bergstrom, C., P. Hogfeldt and J. Molin (1997), "The optimality of the mandatory bid rule", Journal of Law, Economics, and Organization 13:433–451.

Berkovitch, E., and R. Israel (1996), "The design of internal control and capital structure", Review of Financial Studies 9:209–240.

Berle, A.A. (1931), "Corporate powers as powers in trust", Harvard Law Review 44:1049.

Berle, A.A. (1932), "For whom corporate managers are trustees: a note", Harvard Law Review 45:1365.

Berle, A.A. (1954), The 20th Century Capitalist Revolution (Harcourt Brace, New York).

Berle, A.A., and G. Means (1932), The Modern Corporation and Private Property (Macmillan, New York).

Berle, A.A., and G.C. Means (1930), "Corporations and the public investor", The American Economic Review 20:54–71.

Bernheim, B.D., and M. Whinston (1985), "Common marketing agency as a device for facilitating collusion", RAND Journal of Economics 16:269–281.

Bernheim, B.D., and M. Whinston (1986a), "Menu auctions, resource allocation, and economic influence", Quarterly Journal of Economics 101:1–31.

Bernheim, B.D., and M. Whinston (1986b), "Common agency", Econometrica 54(4):923–942.

Bertrand, M., and S. Mullainathan (1998), "Executive compensation and incentives: the impact of takeover legislation", NBER Working Paper W6830 (NBER).

Bertrand, M., and S. Mullainathan (2000), "Agents with and without principals", American Economic Review 90:203–208.

Bertrand, M., and S. Mullainathan (2001), "Are CEOs rewarded for luck? The ones without principals are", Quarterly Journal of Economics 116:901–932.

Best, R., and H. Zhang (1993), "Alternative information sources and the information content of bank loans", Journal of Finance 48(4):1507–1522.

Bethel, J.E., and S. Gillan (2002), "The impact of the institutional and regulatory environment on shareholder voting", Financial Management Journal 31(4):29–54.

Bhagat, S., and B.S. Black (1999), "The uncertain relationship between board composition and firm performance", Business Lawyer 54:921–963.

Bharadwaj, A., and A. Shivdasani (2003), "Valuation effects of bank financing in acquisitions", Journal of Financial Economics 67(1):113–148.

Bhide, A. (1993), "The hidden costs of stock market liquidity", Journal of Financial Economics 34:31–51.

Biais, B., and E. Perotti (2002), "Machiavellian privatization", American Economic Review 92:240–258.

Bianco, M., P. Casavola and A. Ferrando (1997), "Pyramidal groups and external finance: an empirical investigation", Working Paper (Servizio Studi Banca d'Italia, Rome, Italy).

Billett, M.T., M.J. Flannery and J.A. Garfinkel (1995), "The effect of lender identity on a borrowing firm's equity return", Journal of Finance 50(2):699–718.

Bizjak, J.M., M.L. Lemmon and L. Naveen (2000), Has the Use of Peer Groups Contributed to Higher Levels of Executive Compensation? http://papers.ssrn.com/sol3/papers.cfm?abstract_id=252544.

Black, B.S. (1990), "Shareholder passivity reexamined", Michigan Law Review 89:520.

Black, B.S. (1992), "Agents watching agents: the promise of institutional investor voice", UCLA Law Review 39:811–892.

Black, B.S. (1998), "Shareholder activism and corporate governance in the U.S.", in: P. Newman, ed., The New Palgrave Dictionary of Economics and the Law (Macmillan Reference Limited, London and Basingstoke).

Black, B.S. (2000a), "The core institutions that support strong securities markets", Business Lawyer 55:1565–1607.

Black, B.S. (2000b), "Strengthening Brazil's securities markets", Revista de Direito Mercantil, Economico e Financiero 120:41–55. Also available at: http://ssrn.com/abstract=247673.

Black, B.S., and J.C. Coffee Jr (1994), "Hail Britannia?: institutional investor behavior under limited regulation", Michigan Law Review 92:1997–2087.

Black, B.S., and R.J. Gilson (1998), "Venture capital and the structure of capital markets: banks versus stock markets", Journal of Financial Economics 47:243–277.

Black, B.S., R. Kraakman and J. Hay (1996), "Corporate law from scratch", in: R. Frydman, C.W. Gray and A. Rapaczynski, eds., Corporate Governance in Central Europe and Russia, Vol. 2: Insiders and the State (Central European University Press; distributed by Oxford University Press, New York, Budapest) pp. 245–302.

Black, B.S., R. Kraakman and A. Tarassova (2000), "Russian privatization and corporate governance: what went wrong?", Stanford Law Review 52:1731–1808.

Bloch, F., and U. Hege (2000), "Multiple shareholders and control contests", Mimeo (Tilburg University, Netherlands).

Böhmer, E. (2000), "Business groups, bank control, and large shareholders: an analysis of German takeovers", Journal of Financial Intermediation 9:117–148.

Bolton, P. (1995), "Privatization, and the separation of ownership and control: lessons from Chinese enterprise reform", Economics of Transition 3(1):1–12.

Bolton, P., and X. Freixas (2000), "Equity, bonds, and bank debt: capital structure and financial market equilibrium under asymmetric information", Journal of Political Economy 108:324–351.

Bolton, P., and D.S. Scharfstein (1996), "Optimal debt structure and the number of creditors", Journal of Political Economy 104:1–25.

Bolton, P., and E.-L. von Thadden (1998a), "Liquidity and control: a dynamic theory of corporate ownership structure", Journal of Institutional and Theoretical Economics 154:177–211.

Bolton, P., and E.-L. von Thadden (1998b), "Blocks, liquidity, and corporate control", Journal of Finance 53:1–25.

Bolton, P., and C. Xu (2001), "Ownership and managerial competition: employee, customer, or outside ownership", STICERD Discussion Paper No. TE/01/412 (London School of Economics).

Boot, A.W.A. (2000), Relationship banking: what do we know?", Journal of Financial Intermediation 9:7–25.

Borokhovich, K.A., K.R. Brunarski and R. Parrino (1997), "CEO contracting and antitakeover amendments", Journal of Finance 52:1495–1517.

Börsch-Supan, A., and J. Köke (2002), "An applied econometricians' view of empirical corporate governance studies", German Economic Review 3(3):295–326.

Borstadt, L.F., and T.J. Zwirlein (1992), "The efficient monitoring role of proxy contests: an empirical analysis of post-contest control changes and firm performance", Financial Management 21(3):22–34.

Bortolotti, B., M. Fantini and D. Siniscalco (2000), "Privatisation and institutions: a cross country analysis", CESifo Working Paper Series No. 375 (CESifo, Munich, Germany).

Bower, T. (1995), Maxwell: The Final Verdict (HarperCollins, London).

Bradley, M. (1980), "Interfirm tender offers and the market for corporate control", Journal of Business 53:345–376.

Bradley, M., A. Desai and E.H. Kim (1983), "The rationale behind interfirm tender offers: information or synergy", Journal of Financial Economics 11:183–206.

Bradley, M., A. Desai and E.H. Kim (1988), "Synergistic gains from corporate acquisitions and their division between the stockholders of the target and acquiring firms", Journal of Financial Economics 21:3–40.

Bratton, W.W., and J.A. McCahery (1999), "Comparative corporate governance and the theory of the firm: the case against global cross reference", Columbia Journal of Transnational Law 38:213–297.

Brickley, J.A., S. Bhagat and R.C. Lease (1985), "The impact of long-range managerial compensation plans on shareholder wealth", Journal of Accounting and Economics 7:115–129.

Brickley, J.A., J.S. Linck and J.L. Coles (1999), "What happens to CEOs after they retire? New evidence on career concerns, horizon problems, and CEO incentives", Journal of Financial Economics 52:341–377.

Bris, A., and C. Cabolis (2002), "Adopting better corporate governance: evidence from cross-border mergers", ICF Working Paper No. 02-32 (Yale University, New Haven).

Bulow, J., M. Huang and P. Klemperer (1999), "Toeholds and takeovers", Journal of Political Economy 107:427–454.

Burgess, L.R. (1963), Top Executive Pay Packages (Free Press, New York).

Burkart, M. (1995), "Initial shareholdings and overbidding in takeover contests", Journal of Finance 50(5):1491–1515.

Burkart, M. (1999), "The economics of takeover regulation", Discussion Paper (Stockholm School of Economics, Stockholm).

Burkart, M., and F. Panunzi (2000), "Agency conflicts, ownership concentration, and legal shareholder protection", Discussion Paper (Stockholm School of Economics, Stockholm).

Burkart, M., D. Gromb and F. Panunzi (1997), "Large shareholders, monitoring, and the value of the firm", Quarterly Journal of Economics 112:693–728.

Burkart, M., D. Gromb and F. Panunzi (1998), "Why higher takeover premia protect minority shareholders", Journal of Political Economy 106:172–204.

Byrd, J.W., and K.A. Hickman (1992), "Do outside directors monitor managers? Evidence from tender offer bids", Journal of Financial Economics 32:195–221.

Cable, J.R. (1985), "Capital market information and industrial performance: the role of West German banks", Economic Journal 95(377):118–132.

Cadbury Committee (1992), Report of the Committee on the Financial Aspects of Corporate Governance (Gee and Co., London).

Calomiris, C.W. (2000), U.S. Bank Deregulation in Historical Perspective (Cambridge University Press).

Calomiris, C.W., and C.M. Kahn (1991), "The role of demandable debt in structuring optimal banking arrangements", American Economic Review 81:497–513.

Cardon Report (1998), Report of the Belgian Commission on Corporate Governance (Brussels Stock Exchange). Now included as Part I of the Dual Code of the Brussels Stock Exchange and the Belgian Banking and Finance Commission, Corporate Governance for Belgian Listed Companies. www.cbf.be/pe/pec/en_ec01.htm.

Carleton, W.T., J.M. Nelson and M. Weisbach (1998), "The influence of institutions on corporate governance through private negotiations: evidence from TIAA-CREF", Journal of Finance 53:1335–1362.

Carlin, W., and C. Mayer (2003), "Finance, investment and growth", Journal of Financial Economics 69, forthcoming.

Carosso, V. (1970), "Washington and Wall Street: The New Deal and investment bankers, 1933–1940", Business History Review 44:425–445.

Carosso, V.P. (1973), "The Wall Street money trust from Pujo through Medina", Business History Review 47:421–437.

Carosso, V.P. (1985), "American private banks in international banking and industrial finance, 1870–1914", in: J. Atack, ed., Business and Economic History, 2nd Series, Vol. 14 (University of Illinois, Champaign).

Carver, T.N. (1925), The Present Economic Revolution in the U.S. (Little Brown and Company, Boston).

Cary, W.L. (1974), "Federalism and corporate law: reflections upon Delaware", The Yale Law Journal 83:663.

Chandler, A.D. (1976), "The development of modern management structure in the U.S. and the U.K.", in: L. Hannah, ed., Management Strategy and Business Development: An Historical and Comparative Study (Macmillan, London).

Chang, C. (1992), "Capital structure as an optimal contract between employees and investors", Journal of Finance 47:1141–1158.

Cheffins, B.R. (2002), "Putting Britain on the Roe Map: the emergence of the Berle–Means Corporation in the U.K.", in: J.A. McCahery, P. Moerland, T. Raaijmakers and L. Renneboog, eds., Corporate Governance Regimes: Convergence and Diversity (Oxford University Press, Oxford).

Cheffins, B.R. (2003), "Will executive pay globalize along American lines?" Corporate Governance: An international Review 11:12–24.

Chemla, G. (1998), "Hold-up, industrial relations and takeover threats", Discussion Paper (University of British Columbia, Canada).

Chernow, R. (1990), The House of Morgan (Simon and Schuster, London).

Chidambaran, N.K., and K. John (1998), "Relationship investing: large shareholder monitoring with managerial cooperation", Working Paper FIN-98-044 (Stern School of Business, New York University).

Cho, M.-H. (1998), "Ownership structure, investment, and the corporate value: an empirical analysis", Journal of Financial Economics 47:103–121.

Chung, K.H., and J.-K. Kim (1999), "Corporate ownership and the value of a vote in an emerging market", Journal of Corporate Finance: Contracting, Governance and Organization 5:35–54.

Claessens, S., S. Djankov and L.H.P. Lang (2000), "The separation of ownership and control in East Asian corporations", Journal of Financial Economics 58:81–112.

Claessens, S., S. Djankov, J. Fan and L. Lang (2002), "Expropriation of minority shareholders in East Asia", Journal of Finance 57:2741–2771.

Clark, R.C. (1986), Corporate Law (Little and Brown, Boston).

Coates IV, J.C. (1999), "The contestability of corporate control: a critique of the scientific evidence on takeover defenses", Discussion Paper No. 265 (Harvard John M. Olin Center for Law, Economics and Business, Cambridge, MA).

Coffee, J.C. (1991), "Liquidity versus control: the institutional investor as corporate monitor", Columbia Law Review 91:1277–1366.

Coffee, J.C. (1999), "The future as history: the prospects for global convergence in corporate governance and its implications", Northwestern University Law Review 93:641–708.

Coffee, J.C. (2002), "Convergence and its critics: what are the preconditions to the separation of ownership and control?", in: J.A. McCahery, P. Moerland, T. Raaijmakers and L. Renneboog, eds., Corporate Governance Regimes: Convergence and Diversity (Oxford University PresPress, Oxford, UK).

Cole, R.A. (1998), "The importance of relationships to the availability of credit", Journal of Banking and Finance 22(6–8):959–977.

Comment, R., and G.W. Schwert (1995), "Poison or placebo? Evidence on the deterrence and wealth effects of modern antitakeover measures", Journal of Financial Economics 39:3–43.

Committee on the Financial Aspects of Corporate Governance (Cadbury Committee) (1992), The Financial Aspects of Corporate Governance – The Cadbury Report (Committee on the Financial Aspects of Corporate Governance, and Gee and Co., London).

Confederation of Indian Industry (1998), Desirable Corporate Governance: A Code (CII, New Delhi). http://www.combinet.org/governance/finalver/listof.htm.

Conyon, M., and C. Mallin (1997), "A review of compliance with Cadbury", Journal of General Management 22:24–37.

Conyon, M.J., and K.J. Murphy (2000), "The prince and the pauper? CEO pay in the U.S. and U.K.", Economic Journal 110:640–671.

Conyon, M.J., and S.I. Peck (1998), "Recent developments in U.K. corporate governance", in: T. Buxton, P. Chapman and P. Temple, eds., Britain's Economic Performance (Routledge, London, New York).

Core, J.E., W. Guay and D.F. Larcker (2003), "Executive equity compensation and incentives: a survey", Federal Reserve Bank of New York Economic Policy Review 8(1):27–50.

Cornelli, F., and D.D. Li (1998), Risk Arbitrage in Takeovers (London Business School, UK).

Cosh, A.D., and A. Hughes (1989), "Ownership, management incentives and company performance: an empirical analysis for the UK, 1968–1980", Discussion Paper No. 11/89 (University of Cambridge, UK).

Cotter, J.F., A. Shivdasani and M. Zenner (1997), "Do independent directors enhance target shareholder wealth during tender offers?", Journal of Financial Economics 43:195–218.

Cubbin, J.S., and D. Leech (1983), "The effect of shareholding dispersion on the degree of control in British companies: theory and measurement", Economic Journal 93:351–369.

Cushing, H.A. (1915), Voting Trusts; A Chapter in Recent Corporate History (MacMillan, New York).

Da Rin, M., and T. Hellmann (2002), "Banks as a catalyst for industrialization", Journal of Financial Intermediation 11:366–397.

Dahlquist, M., L. Pinkowitz, R.M. Stulz and R. Williamson (2003), "Corporate governance, investor protection, and the home bias", Journal of Financial and Quantitative Analysis, forthcoming.

Daily, C., J.L. Johnson, A.E. Ellstrand and D.R. Dalton (1998), "Compensation committee composition as a determinant of CEO compensation", Academy of Management Journal 41:209–220.

Danielson, M.G., and J.M. Karpoff (1998), "On the uses of corporate governance provisions", Journal of Corporate Finance, Contracting, Governance and Organization 4:347–371.

David, R., and J.E.C. Brierley (1985), Major Legal Systems in the World Today: An Introduction to the Comparative Study of Law, 3rd Edition (Stevens, London).

Davies, P.L., D.D. Prentice and L.C.B. Gower (1997), Gower's Principles of Modern Company Law, 6th Edition (Sweet and Maxwell, London).

Davis, G.F., and M. Useem (2002), "Top management, company directors, and corporate control", in: A. Pettigrew, H. Thomas and R. Whittington, eds., Handbook of Strategy and Management (Sage Publications, London) pp. 233–259.

De Jong, A., D.V. DeJong, G. Mertens and C.E. Wasley (2001), "The role of self-regulation in corporate governance: evidence from the Netherlands", Working Paper No. FR 00-20 (Simon School of Business, University of Rochester, NY).

DeAngelo, H., and L. DeAngelo (1985), "Managerial ownership of voting rights: a study of public corporations with dual classes of common stock", Journal of Financial Economics 14:33–69.

DeAngelo, H., and L. DeAngelo (1989), "Proxy contests and the governance of publicly held corporations", Journal of Financial Economics 23(1):29–59.

Debreu, G. (1959), Theory of Value: An Axiomatic Analysis of Economic Equilibrium (Yale University Press, New Haven, London).

DeFusco, R.A., R.R. Johnson and T.S. Zorn (1990), "The effect of executive stock option plans on stockholders and bondholders", Journal of Finance 45:617–627.

DeGryse, H., and P. Van Cayseele (1998), "Informatie en de rol van financiele intermediatie", in: R. De Bondt and R. Veugelers, eds., Informatie en Kennis in de Economie (Leuvense Universitaire Pers, Belgium) pp. 463–477.

DeGryse, H., and P. Van Cayseele (2000), "Relationship lending within a bank-based system: evidence from European small business data", Journal of Financial Intermediation 9:90–109.

DeLong, J.B. (1991), "Did J.P. Morgan's men add value? An economist's perspective on financial capitalism", in: P. Temin, ed., Inside the Business Enterprise: Historical Perspectives on the Use of Information (University of Chicago Press for National Bureau of Economic Research, Chicago, London) pp. 205–236.

DeLong, J.B. (1998), "Robber barons", in: A. Aslund, ed., Perspectives on Russian Economic Development (Carnegie Endowment, Washington, DC).

Demsetz, H. (1968), "The cost of transacting", The Quarterly Journal of Economics 82:33–53.

Demsetz, H. (1986), "Corporate control, insider trading, and rates of return", American Economic Review 76:313–316.

Demsetz, H., and K. Lehn (1985), "The structure of corporate ownership: causes and consequences", Journal of Political Economy 93:1155–1177.

Demsetz, H., and B. Villalonga (2001), "Ownership structure and corporate performance", Journal of Corporate Finance 7:209–233.

Deutsche Schutzvereinigung für Wertpapierbesitz (2000), DSW Europe Study. A Study Comparing Minority Shareholders' Rights, Voting Rights and Proxy Voting in Europe (DSW and IRRC, Duesseldorf and Washington, DC).

Dewatripont, M. (1993), "The 'Leading Shareholder' strategy, takeover contests and stock price dynamics", European Economic Review 37:983–1004.

Dewatripont, M., and E. Maskin (1995), "Contractual contingencies and renegotiation", Rand Journal of Economics 26:704–719.

Dewatripont, M., and J. Tirole (1994), "A theory of debt and equity: diversity of securities and manager–shareholder congruence", Quarterly Journal of Economics 109:1027–1054.

Dey Committee (1994), Guidelines for Improved Corporate Governance (Toronto Stock Exchange Committee on Corporate Governance in Canada, Toronto, Canada).

Diamond, D.W. (1984), "Financial intermediation and delegated monitoring", Review of Economic Studies 51:393–414.

Diamond, D.W. (1989), "Reputation acquisition in debt markets", Journal of Political Economy 97:828–862.

Diamond, D.W. (1991), "Monitoring and reputation: the choice between bank loans and directly placed debt", Journal of Political Economy 99:689–721.

Diamond, D.W. (1993), "Bank loan maturity and priority when borrowers can refinance", in: C. Mayer and X. Vives, eds., Capital Markets and Financial Intermediation (Cambridge University Press, Cambridge, New York, Melbourne) pp. 46–68.

Diamond, D.W., and R.G. Rajan (2001), "Liquidity risk, liquidity creation and financial fragility: a theory of banking", Journal of Political Economy 109:287–327.

Dodd, M. (1932), "For whom are corporate managers trustees?", Harvard Law Review 45:1145.

Dodd, P., and J.-B. Warner (1983), "On corporate governance: a study of proxy contests", Journal of Financial Economics 11(1–4):401–438.

Dunlavy, C.A. (1998), "Corporate governance in late 19th century Europe and the U.S.: the case of shareholder voting rights", in: K.J. Hopt, H. Kanda, M.J. Roe, E. Wymeersch and S. Prigge, eds., Comparative Corporate Governance. The State of the Art and Emerging Research (Oxford University Press, Oxford) pp. 5–40.

Dyck, A., and L. Zingales (2003), "Private benefits of control: an international comparison", Journal of Finance, forthcoming.

Easterbrook, F.H. (1997), "International corporate differences: market or law?", Journal of Applied Corporate Finance 9:23–29.

Easterbrook, F.H., and D.R. Fischel (1981), "The proper role of target's management in responding to a tender offer", Harvard Law Review 94:1161–1204.

Easterbrook, F.H., and D.R. Fischel (1991), The Economic Structure of Corporate Law (Harvard University Press, Cambridge, MA).

Edwards, F.R., and R.G. Hubbard (2000), "The growth of institutional stock ownership: a promise unfulfilled", Journal of Applied Corporate Finance 13:92–104.

Edwards, J., and K. Fischer (1994), Banks, Finance and Investment in Germany (Cambridge University Press, Cambridge, MA).

Edwards, J., and S. Ogilvie (1996), "Universal banks and German industrialization: a reappraisal", Economic History Review 49:427–446.

Eells, R.S.F. (1960), The Meaning of Modern Business: An Introduction to the Philosophy of Large Corporate Enterprise (Columbia University Press, NY).

Eisenberg, M.A. (1976), The Structure of the Corporation (Little and Brown, Boston).

Elsas, R.K., and J.P. Krahnen (1998), "Is relationship lending special? Evidence from credit-file data in Germany", Journal of Banking and Finance 22:1283–1316.

European Association of Securities Dealers (2000), EASD Corporate Governance Principles and Recommendations (EASD, Brussels).

European Corporate Governance Network (1997), "The Separation of ownership and control: a survey of 7 European countries", Preliminary Report to the European Commission (European Corporate Governance Network, Brussels).

European Counsel (2000), European Counsel Mergers and Acquisitions Handbook (Practical Law Company Limited, London).

European Shareholders Group (2000), Euroshareholders Corporate Governance Guidelines 2000 (European Shareholders Group, Brussels).

Faccio, M., and H.P. Lang (2002), "The ultimate ownership of western European corporations", Journal of Financial Economics 65(3):365–395.

Faure-Grimaud, A., and D. Gromb (1999), "Private incentives and public trading", Working Paper (Sloan School, MIT, MA).

Fich, E.M., and L.J. White (2001), "Why do CEO's reciprocally sit on each other's board?", Research Paper No 01-002 (NYU Center for Law and Business, NY) http://papers.ssrn.com/sol3/papers.cfm?abstract_id=249975.

Fischel, D., and M. Bradley (1986), "The role of liability rules and the derivative suit in corporate law: a theoretical and empirical analysis", 71 Common Law Review 261.

Fishman, M.J. (1988), "A theory of preemptive takeover bidding", Rand Journal of Economics 19: 88–101.

FitzRoy, F.R., and K. Kraft (1993), "Economic effects of codetermination", Scandinavian Journal of Economics 95:365–375.

Florence, P.S. (1947), "The statistical analysis of joint stock company control", Journal of the Royal Statistical Society 110:1–26.

Florence, P.S. (1953), The Logic of British and American Industry; A Realistic Analysis of Economic Structure and Government (Routledge and K. Paul, London).

Florence, P.S. (1961), Ownership, Control and Success of Large Companies: An Analysis of English Industrial Structure and Policy, 1936–1951 (Sweet and Maxwell, London).

Fohlin, C. (1997), "Bank securities holdings and industrial finance before World War I: Britain and Germany compared", Business and Economic History 26:463–475.

Fohlin, C. (1999a), "Capital mobilisation and utilisation in latecomer economies: Germany and Italy compared", European Review of Economic History 3:139–174.

Fohlin, C. (1999b), "The rise of interlocking directorates in imperial Germany", Economic History Review 52:307–333.

Franks, J.R., and R.S. Harris (1989), "Shareholder wealth effects of corporate takeovers: the U.K. experience 1955–1985", Journal of Financial Economics 23(2):225–249.

Franks, J.R., and C. Mayer (1995), "Ownership and control", in: H. Siebert, ed., Trends In Business Organization: Do Participation and Cooperation Increase Competitiveness? (Mohr (Siebeck), Tübingen, Germany).

Franks, J.R., and C. Mayer (1996), "Hostile takeovers and the correction of managerial failure", Journal of Financial Economics 40:163–181.

Franks, J.R., and C. Mayer (2001), Ownership and control of German corporations", Review of Financial Studies 14(4):943–977.

Franks, J.R., and O. Sussman (1999), "Financial innovations and corporate insolvency", Mimeo (Said Business School, Oxford University, UK).

Franks, J.R., and O. Sussman (2000), "Resolving financial distress by way of a contract: an empirical study of small U.K. companies", Mimeo (London Business School, and Said Business School, Oxford).

Franks, J.R., and W.N. Torous (1989), "An empirical investigation of U.S. firms in reorganization", Journal of Finance 44:747–769.

Franks, J.R., C. Mayer and L. Renneboog (2001), "Who disciplines management in poorly performing companies?", Journal of Financial Intermediation 10:209–248.

Franks, J.R., C. Mayer and G. Rossi (2003), "The origination and evolution of ownership and control", Finance Working Paper No. 09/2003 (European Corporate Governance Institute).

Freeman, R.B., and E.P. Lazear (1995), "An economic analysis of works councils", in: J. Rogers and W. Streeck, eds., Works Councils: Consultation, Representation, and Cooperation in Industrial Relations. National Bureau of Economic Research Comparative Labor Markets Series (University of Chicago Press, Chicago, London).

Frick, B., N. Kluge and W. Streeck, eds (1999), Die Wirtschaftlichen Folgen der Mitbestimmung (Campus Verlag, Frankfurt/Main, New York).

Fukao, M. (1995), Financial Integration, Corporate Governance, and the Performance of Multinational Companies (Brookings Institution, Washington DC).

Galbraith, J.K. (1967), The New Industrial State (Hamilton, London).

Gerschenkron, A. (1962), Economic Backwardness in Historical Perspective: A Book of Essays (Harvard University Press, Cambridge, MA).

Gerum, E., and H. Wagner (1998), "Economics of labor co-determination in view of corporate governance", in: K.J. Hopt, H. Kanda, M.J. Roe, E. Wymeersch and S. Prigge, eds., Comparative Corporate Governance: The State of the Art and Emerging Research (Oxford University Press, UK; Clarendon Press, New York) pp. 341–360.

Gerum, E., H. Steinmann and W. Fees (1988), Der Mitbestimmte Aufsichtsrat: Eine Empirische Untersuchung (Poeschel, Stuttgart).

Gibbons, R., and K.J. Murphy (1990), "Relative performance evaluation for chief executive officers", Industrial and Labor Relations Review 43:30S–51S.

Gibbons, R., and K.J. Murphy (1992), "Optimal incentive contracts in the presence of career concerns: theory and evidence", Journal of Political Economy 100:468–505.

Gillan, S., and L. Starks (1998), "A survey of shareholder activism: motivation and empirical evidence", Contemporary Finance Digest 2:10–34.

Gilson, R. (1981), "A structural approach to corporations: the case against defensive tactics in tender offers", Stanford Law Review 33:819–891.

Gilson, R., and R. Kraakman (1991), "Reinventing the outside director: an agenda for institutional investors", Stanford Law Review 43:863–906.

Gilson, R.J. (2000), "Unocal fifteen years later (and what we can do about it)", Working Paper 177 (Columbia Law School); Research Paper 201 (Stanford Law School, CA).

Gilson, R.J. (2002), "Lipton and Rowe's apologia for Delaware: a short reply", Delaware Journal of Corporate Law 27:37–52.

Gilson, R.J., and A. Schwartz (2001), "Sales and elections as methods for transferring corporate control", Working Paper 206 (Stanford Law School, CA).

Goergen, M., and L. Renneboog (2001), "Strong managers and passive institutional investors in the U.K.", in: F. Barca and M. Becht, eds., The Control of Corporate Europe (Oxford University Press, Oxford) pp. 259–284.

Goergen, M., and L. Renneboog (2003), "Why are the levels of control (so) different in German and UK companies? Evidence from initial public offerings", Journal of Law, Economics and Organization 19(1):141–175.

Goldberg, V.P. (1976), "Regulation and administered contracts", Bell Journal of Economics and Management Science 7(426):439–441.

Gomes, A., and W. Novaes (2000), "Sharing of control as a corporate governance mechanism", Discussion Paper (Wharton School of Business, Philadelphia, PA).

Gompers, P., and J. Lerner (1999), The Venture Capital Cycle (MIT Press, Cambridge, MA).

Gompers, P.A., J. Ishii and A. Metrick (2001), "Corporate governance and equity prices", Working Paper 8449 (NBER, Cambridge, MA).

Gordon, R.A. (1945), Business Leadership in the Large Corporation (The Brookings Institution, Washington, DC).

Gorton, G., and F. Schmid (1999), "Corporate governance, ownership dispersion and efficiency: empirical evidence from Austrian cooperative banking", Journal of Corporate Finance, Contracting, Governance and Organization 5:119–140.

Gorton, G., and F.A. Schmid (2000a), "Class struggle inside the firm: a study of German codetermination", NBER Working Paper No. 7945 (NBER, Cambridge, MA).

Gorton, G., and F.A. Schmid (2000b), "Universal banking and the performance of German firms", Journal of Financial Economics 58:29–80.

Gorton, G., and A. Winton (1998), "Banking in transition economies: does efficiency require instability?", Journal of Money, Credit, and Banking 30(3):621–650.

Greenbury Committee (1995), Study Group on Directors' Remuneration, Final Report (Gee and Co, London).

Greenslade, R. (1992), Maxwell's Fall (Simon and Schuster, London).

Gregory, H.J. (2000), International Comparison of Corporate Governance: Guidelines and Codes of Best Practice in Developing and Emerging Markets (Weil, Gotshal and Manges LLP, New York).

Gregory, H.J. (2001a), International Comparison of Corporate Governance: Guidelines and Codes of Best Practice in Developed Markets (Weil, Gotshal and Manges LLP, New York).

Gregory, H.J. (2001b), International Comparison of Board 'Best Practices' – Investor Viewpoints (Weil, Gotshal and Manges LLP, New York).

Gregory, H.J. (2002), Comparative Study of Corporate Governance Codes Relevant to the European Union and its Member States, Report to the European Commission (Weil, Gotshal and Manges LLP, New York).

Gromb, D. (1993), "Is one share–one vote optimal?", Discussion Paper No. 177 (Financial Markets Group, London School of Economics, London, UK).

Grossman, S., and O. Hart (1980), "Takeover bids, the free-rider problem and the theory of the corporation", Bell Journal of Economics 11:42–64.

Grossman, S.J., and O.D. Hart (1983), "An analysis of the principal-agent problem", Econometrica 51:7–45.

Grossman, S.J., and O.D. Hart (1986), "The costs and benefits of ownership: a theory of vertical and lateral integration", Journal of Political Economy 94:691–719.

Grossman, S.J., and O.D. Hart (1988), "One share–one vote and the market for corporate control", Journal of Financial Economics 20:175–202.

Grundfest, J.A. (1990), "Subordination of American capital", Journal of Financial Economics 27:89–114.

Grundfest, J.A. (1993), "Just vote no: a minimalist strategy for dealing with barbarians inside the gates", Stanford Law Review 45:857–937.

Gugler, K., ed. (2001), Corporate Governance and Economic Performance (Oxford University Press, Oxford).

Guinnane, T.W. (2001), "Large and small: the development of Germany's banking system, 1800–1914", Center for Economic Studies Paper No. 565 (Center for Economic Studies, Munich, Germany).

Gurdon, M.A., and A. Rai (1990), "Codetermination and enterprise performance: empirical evidence from West Germany", Journal of Economics and Business 42:289–302.

Gutiérrez, M. (2000), "A contractual approach to the regulation of corporate directors' fiduciary duties", Working Paper 13 (CEMFI, Madrid).

Gutiérrez, M. (2003), "An economic analysis of corporate directors' fiduciary duties", Rand Journal of Economics, forthcoming.

Habib, M.A., and A.P. Ljungqvist (2002), "Firm value and managerial incentives", Mimeo (NYU and London Business School).

Hall, B.J., and J.B. Liebman (1998), "Are CEOs really paid like bureaucrats?", Quarterly Journal of Economics 113:653–691.

Hall, B.J., and J.B. Liebman (2000), "The taxation of executive compensation", Working Paper Series 7596 (National Bureau of Economic Research, Cambridge, MA).

Hallock, K.F. (1997), "Reciprocally interlocking boards of directors and executive compensation", Journal of Financial and Quantitative Analysis 32(3):331–344.

Hallock, K.F., and K.J. Murphy, eds (1999), The Economics of Executive Compensation (Elgar; distributed by American International Distribution Corporation Williston, Cheltenham, U.K. and Northampton, MA) 2 volumes.

Hampel Committee (1998), Committee on Corporate Governance, Final Report (Gee and Co, London).

Hannah, L. (1974), "Takeover bids in Britain before 1950: an exercise in business 'pre-history' ", Business History 16:65–77.

Hannah, L., ed. (1976), Management Strategy and Business Development: An Historical and Comparative Study (Macmillan, London).

Hansmann, H. (1996), The Ownership of Enterprise (The Belknap Press of Harvard University Press, Cambridge, MA).

Hansmann, H., and R. Kraakman (2001), "The end of history for corporate law", Georgetown Law Journal 89:439–468.

Harhoff, D., and T. Korting (1998), "Lending relationships in Germany – empirical evidence from survey data", Journal of Banking and Finance 22(10,11):1317–1353.

Harris, M., and A. Raviv (1988a), "Corporate control contests and capital structure", Journal of Financial Economics 20:55–86.

Harris, M., and A. Raviv (1988b), "Corporate governance: voting rights and majority rules", Journal of Financial Economics 20:203–235.

Harris, M., and A. Raviv (1992), "Financial contracting theory", in: J.J. Laffont, ed., Advances in Economic Theory: Sixth World Congress, Vol. 2, Econometric Society Monographs 21 (Cambridge University Press, Cambridge, New York, Melbourne) pp. 64–150.

Hart, O. (1988), "On SEC's one-share-one-vote decision", Wall Street Journal, July 14.

Hart, O. (1995), Firms, Contracts, and Financial Structure (Oxford University Press, London).

Hart, O., and J. Moore (1990), "Property rights and the nature of the firm", Journal of Political Economy 98:1119–1158.

Hart, O., and J. Moore (1995), "Debt and seniority: an analysis of the role of hard claims in constraining management", American Economic Review 85:567–585.

Hart, O., and J. Moore (1996), "The governance of exchanges: members' cooperatives versus outside ownership", Oxford Review of Economic Policy 12(4):53–69.

Hart, O., and J. Moore (1998), "Cooperatives vs. outside ownership", NBER Working Paper No.w6421 (NBER, Cambridge, MA).

Hart, O., A. Shleifer and R. Vishny (1997), "The proper scope of government: theory and an application to prisons", Quarterly Journal of Economics 112(4):1126–1161.

Hartzell, J.C., and L.T. Starks (2002), "Institutional investors and executive compensation", Mimeo (Department of Finance, University of Texas, Austin, TX).

Healy, P.M., and K.G. Palepu (2001), "Information asymmetry, corporate disclosure, and the capital markets: a review of the empirical disclosure literature", Journal of Accounting and Economics (31)1–3:405–440.

Heflin, F., and K.W. Shaw (2000), "Blockholder ownership and market liquidity", Journal of Financial and Quantitative Analysis 35:621–633.

Hellman, T. (1997), A Theory of Corporate Venture Capital (Stanford University Graduate School of Business, CA).

Hellwig, M. (2000b), "On the economics and politics of corporate finance and control", in: X. Vives, ed., Corporate Governance. Theoretical and Empirical Perspectives (Cambridge University Press, Cambridge) pp. 95–134.

Hellwig, M.F. (2000a), "Financial intermediation with risk aversion", Review of Economic Studies 67:719–742.

Hennessy, C.A., and A. Levy (2002), "A unified model of distorted investment: theory and evidence", Mimeo (Haas School of Business, University of California, Berkeley).

Hermalin, B.E., and M.S. Weisbach (1991), "The effects of board composition and direct incentives on firm performance", Financial Management 20:101–112.

Hermalin, B.E., and M.S. Weisbach (1998), "Endogenously chosen boards of directors and their monitoring of the CEO", American Economic Review 88:96–118.

Hermalin, B.E., and M.S. Weisbach (2003), "Boards of directors as an endogenously determined institution: a survey of the economic literature", Federal Reserve Bank of New York Economic Policy Review 9:7–26.

Herman, E.S. (1981), Corporate Control, Corporate Power (Cambridge University Press, New York).

Hessen, R. (1983), "The modern corporation and private property: a reappraisal", Journal of Law and Economics 26:273–289.

Higgins, R.C., and L.D. Schall (1975), "Corporate bankruptcy and conglomerate merger", Journal of Finance 30(1):93–113.

High Level Finance Committee on Corporate Governance (1999), The Malaysian Code on Corporate Governance (High Level Finance Committee Report on Corporate Governance, Kuala Lumpur) Chapter 5. http://www.combinet.org/governance/finalver/listof.htm.

Himmelberg, C.P., R.G. Hubbard and D. Palia (1999), "Understanding the determinants of managerial ownership and the link between ownership and performance", Journal of Financial Economics 53:353–384.

Hirschman, A.O. (1970), Exit, Voice, and Loyalty: Responses to Decline in Firms, Organizations, and States (Harvard University Press, Cambridge, MA).

Hirshleifer, D. (1995), "Mergers and acquisitions: strategic and informational issues", in: R.A. Jarrow, V. Maksimovic and W.T. Ziemba, eds., Handbooks of Operations Research and Management Science (Elsevier, Amsterdam) pp. 839–885.

Hirshleifer, D., and A.V. Thakor (1994), "Managerial performance, boards of directors and takeover bidding", Journal of Corporate Finance, Contracting, Governance and Organization 1:63–90.

Hirshleifer, D., and S. Titman (1990), "Share tendering strategies and the success of hostile takeover bids", Journal of Political Economy 98:295–324.

Hoffmann-Burchardi, U. (1999), "Corporate governance rules and the value of control – a study of German dual-class shares", Financial Markets Group Discussion Paper 315 (London School of Economics, London).

Hoffmann-Burchardi, U. (2000), "Unlocking Germany's corporate gates: the Vodafone–Mannesmann takeover and German corporate governance", Financial Markets Group Review (London School of Economics, London).

Holderness, C. (2003), "A survey of blockholders and corporate control", Federal Reserve Bank of New York Economic Policy Review 9:51–64.

Holderness, C.G., and D.P. Sheehan (1988), "The role of majority shareholders in publicly held corporations: an exploratory analysis", Journal of Financial Economics 20:317–346.

Holl, P. (1975), "Effect of control type on the performance of the firm in the U.K.", Journal of Industrial Economics 23:257–271.

Holmstrom, B. (1979), "Moral hazard and observability", Bell Journal of Economics 10:74–91.

Holmstrom, B. (1999), "Managerial incentive problems – a dynamic perspective", Review of Economic Studies 66(1):169–182.

Holmstrom, B., and S.N. Kaplan (2001), "Corporate governance and merger activity in the United States: making sense of the 1980s and 1990s", Journal of Economic Perspectives 15(2):121–144.

Holmstrom, B., and B. Nalebuff (1992), "To the raider goes the surplus: a re-examination of the free-rider problem", Journal of Economics and Management Strategy (1)1:37–62.

Holmstrom, B., and J. Ricart i Costa (1986), "Managerial incentives and capital management", Quarterly Journal of Economics 101:835–860.

Holmstrom, B., and J. Tirole (1993), "Market liquidity and performance monitoring", Journal of Political Economy 101:678–709.

Hopt, K., H. Kanda, M.J. Roe, E. Wymeersch and S. Prigge, eds (1998), Comparative Corporate Governance: The State of the Art and Emerging Research (Clarendon Press, Oxford, New York).

Hopt, K.J., and E. Wymeersch, eds (2003), Capital Markets and Company Law (Oxford University Press, Oxford).

Horiuchi, A., F. Packer and S. Fukuda (1988), "What role has the 'main bank' played in Japan?", Journal of the Japanese and International Economy 2(2):159–180.

Hoshi, T. (1998), "Japanese corporate governance as a system", in: K.J. Hopt, H. Kanda, M.J. Roe, E. Wymeersch and S. Prigge, eds., Comparative Corporate Governance. The State of the Art and Emerging Research (Clarendon Press, Oxford) pp. 847–875.

Hoshi, T., and A. Kashyap (2001), Corporate Financing and Governance in Japan (MIT Press, Cambridge, MA).

Hoshi, T., A. Kashyap and D. Scharfstein (1990), "The role of banks in reducing the costs of financial distress in Japan", Journal of Financial Economics 27:67–88.

Huddart, S. (1993), "The effect of a large shareholder on corporate value", Management Science 39(11):1407–1421.

Ikenberry, D., and J. Lakonishok (1993), "Corporate governance through the proxy contest: evidence and implications", Journal of Business 66(3):405–435.

International Corporate Governance Network (2002), "Executive remuneration – the caucus race?", Consultative Document (ICGN, London). www.icgn.org.

Investor Responsibility Research Center (IRRC) (2000a), Takeover Defences 2000 (IRRC, Washington DC).

Investor Responsibility Research Center (IRRC) (2000b), Management Proposals on Executive Compensation Plans. IRRC Governance Service Background Report A (IRRC, Washington DC).

Investor Responsibility Research Center (IRRC) (2001), Losing Value (IRRC, Washington DC).

Investor Responsibility Research Center (IRRC) (2002), Stock Plan Dilution 2002: Overhang from Stock Plans at S&P Super 1500 Companies (IRRC, Washington DC).

Jacquemin, A., and E. de Ghellinck (1980), "Familial control, size and performance in the largest French firms", European Economic Review 13(1):81–91.

James, C. (1987), "Some evidence on the uniqueness of bank loans", Journal of Financial Economics 19(2):217–235.

Jarrell, G.A., and A.B. Poulsen (1987), "Shark repellents and stock prices: the effects of antitakeover amendments since 1980", Journal of Financial Economics 19:127–168.

Jarrell, G.A., J.A. Brickley and J.M. Netter (1988), "The market for corporate control: the empirical evidence since 1980", Journal of Economic Perspectives 2:49–68.

Jeidels, O. (1905), Das Verhältnis der Deutschen Grossbanken zur Industrie: mit besonderer Berücksichtigung der Eisenindustrie (Duncker and Humblot, Leipzig).

Jenkinson, T.J., and A. Ljungqvist (2001), "The role of hostile stakes in German corporate governance", Journal of Corporate Finance 7(4):397–446.

Jensen, M.C. (1986), "Agency costs of free cash flow, corporate finance, and takeovers", American Economic Review 76:323–329.

Jensen, M.C. (1989), "The eclipse of the public corporation", Harvard Business Review 67:61–74.

Jensen, M.C. (2002), "Value maximization and the corporate objective function", in: J. Andriof, S. Waddock, S. Rahman and B. Husted, eds., Unfolding Stakeholder Thinking (Greenleaf Publishing, Sheffield, UK).

Jensen, M.C., and W.H. Meckling (1976), "Theory of the firm: managerial behavior, agency costs and ownership structure", Journal of Financial Economics 3:305–360.

Jensen, M.C., and K.J. Murphy (1990), "Performance pay and top-management incentives", Journal of Political Economy 98:225–264.

Jensen, M.C., and R.S. Ruback (1983), "The market for corporate control: the scientific evidence", Journal of Financial Economics 11:5–50.

Jensen, M.C., and J.L. Zimmerman (1985), "Management compensation and the managerial labor market", Journal of Accounting and Economics 7(1–3):3–9.

Jog, V., and A. Riding (1986), "Price effects of dual-class shares", Financial Analysis Journal 42:58–67.

John, K., and S. Kedia (2000), "Design of corporate governance: role of ownership structure, takeovers, bank debt and large shareholder monitoring", Working Paper FIN-00-048 (Stern School of Business, New York University).

John, K., and L. Senbet (1998), "Corporate governance and board effectiveness", Journal of Banking and Finance 22(4):371–403.

Johnson, S. (2000), "Corporate governance in the Asian financial crisis", Journal of Financial Economics 58:141–186.

Josephson, M. (1934), The Robber Barons; The Great American Capitalists, 1861–1901 (Harcourt Brace, New York).

Kahn, C., and A. Winton (1998), "Ownership structure, speculation, and shareholder intervention", Journal of Finance 53:99–129.

Kamar, E. (1998), "A regulatory competition theory of indeterminacy in corporate law", Columbia Law Review 98:1908–1959.

Kamerschen, D.R. (1968), "The influence of ownership and control on profit rates", The American Economic Review 58:432–447.

Kang, J.-K., and R.M. Stulz (2000), "Do banking shocks affect borrowing firm performance? An analysis of the Japanese experience", Journal of Business 73:1–23.

Kang, J.-K., A. Shivdasani and T. Yamada (2000), "The effect of bank relations on investment decisions: an investigation of Japanese takeover bids", Journal of Finance 55(5):2197–2218.

Kaplan, S.N. (1994a), "Top executive rewards and firm performance: a comparison of Japan and the U.S.", Journal of Political Economy 102(3):510–546.

Kaplan, S.N. (1994b), Federated's acquisition and bankruptcy: lessons and implications", Washington University Law Quarterly 72:1103–1126.

Kaplan, S.N., ed. (2000), Mergers and Productivity (The University of Chicago Press, Chicago).

Kaplan, S.N., and P. Strömberg (2003), "Financial contracting theory meets the real world: an empirical analysis of venture capital contracts", Review of Economic Studies 70(2):281–315.

Karpoff, J.M. (1998), The Impact of Shareholder Activism on Target Companies: A Survey of Empirical Findings (University of Washington School of Business).

Kim, E.H., and J.J. McConnell (1977), "Corporate mergers and the co-insurance of corporate debt", Journal of Finance 32:349–365.

King Committee (1994), The King Report on Corporate Governance (Institute of Directors of Southern Africa, Johannesburg).

Klein, B., R. Crawford and A.A. Alchian (1978), "Vertical integration, appropriable rents, and the competitive contracting process", Journal of Law and Economics 21(2):297–326.

Klein, W.A., and J.C. Coffee (2000), Business Organization and Finance. Legal and Economic Principles (Foundation Press, New York).

Knoeber, C.R. (1986), "Golden parachutes, shark repellents, and hostile tender offers", American Economic Review 76:155–167.

Kole, S.R. (1995), "Measuring managerial equity ownership: a comparison of sources of ownership data", Journal of Corporate Finance, Contracting, Governance and Organization 1:413–435.

Kole, S.R. (1997), "The complexity of compensation contracts", Journal of Financial Economics 43: 79–104.

Kovenock, D. (1984), A Note on Takeover Bids (Purdue University, IN).

Kraakman, R., P. Davies, H. Hansmann, G. Hertig, K.J. Hopt, H. Kanda and E.B. Rock (2003), The Anatomy of Corporate Law: A Comparative and Functional Approach (Oxford University Press) forthcoming.

Kraakman, R.H., H. Park and S. Shavell (1994), "When are shareholder suits in shareholders' interests?", Georgetown Law Review, pp. 1733–1775.

Krasa, S., and A.P. Villamil (1992), "Monitoring the monitor: an incentive structure for a financial intermediary", Journal of Economic Theory 57:197–221.

Kreps, D.M. (1990), "Corporate culture and economic theory", in: J.E. Alt and K.A. Shepsle, eds., Perspectives on Positive Political Economy (Cambridge University Press) pp. 90–143.

Kroszner, R. (1999), "Is the financial system politically independent? Perspectives on the political economy of banking and financial regulation", Working Paper (George J. Stigler Center for the Study of the Economy and the State Working Papers Series, University of Chicago).

Kroszner, R.S., and R.G. Rajan (1994), "Is the Glass–Steagall Act justified? A study of the U.S. experience with universal banking before 1933", American Economic Review 84:810–832.

Kroszner, R.S., and R.G. Rajan (1997), "Organization structure and credibility: evidence from commercial bank securities activities before the Glass–Steagall Act", Journal of Monetary Economics 39:475–516.

Kroszner, R.S., and P.E. Strahan (2001), "Obstacles to optimal policy: the interplay of politics and economics in shaping bank supervision and regulation reforms", in: F.S. Mishkin, ed., Prudential Supervision: What Works and What Doesn't. NBER Conference Report Series 5 (University of Chicago Press, Chicago, London).

Kunz, R.M., and J.J. Angel (1996), "Factors affecting the value of the stock voting right: evidence from the Swiss equity market", Financial Management 25:7–20.

Kyle, A.S., and J.-L. Vila (1991), "Noise trading and takeovers", Rand Journal of Economics 22:54–71.

La Porta, R., F. Lopez-de-Silanes, A. Shleifer and R.W. Vishny (1997), "Legal determinants of external finance", Journal of Finance 52:1131–1150.

La Porta, R., F. Lopez-de-Silanes and A. Shleifer (1998), "Law and finance", Journal of Political Economy 106:1113–1155.

La Porta, R., F. Lopez-de-Silanes and A. Shleifer (1999), "Corporate ownership around the world", Journal of Finance 54:471–517.

La Porta, R., F. Lopez-de-Silanes, A. Shleifer and R.W. Vishny (2000a), "Agency problems and dividend policies around the world", Journal of Finance 55:1–33.

La Porta, R., F. Lopez-de-Silanes, A. Shleifer and R.W. Vishny (2000b), "Investor protection and corporate governance", Journal of Financial Economics 58:3–27.

La Porta, R., F. Lopez-de-Silanes and A. Shleifer (2002), "Investor protection and corporate valuation", Journal of Finance 57:1147–1170.

Larcker, D.F. (1983), "The association between performance plan adoption and corporate capital investment", Journal of Accounting and Economics 5(1):3–30.

Larner, R.J. (1966), "Ownership and control in the 200 largest non-financial corporations, 1929–1963", The American Economic Review 16:781–782.

Larner, R.J. (1970), Management Control and the Large Corporation (Dunellen, New York).

Lease, R.C., J.J. McConnell and W.H. Mikkelson (1983), "The market value of control in publicly-traded corporations", Journal of Financial Economics 11:439–471.

Lease, R.C., J.J. McConnell and W.H. Mikkelson (1984), "The market value of differential voting rights in closely held corporations", Journal of Business 57:443–467.

Leech, D. (1987a), "Ownership concentration and the theory of the firm: a simple-game-theoretic approach", Journal of Industrial Economics 35:225–240.

Leech, D. (1987b), "Corporate ownership and control: a new look at the evidence of Berle and Means", Oxford Economic Papers N.S. 39:534–551.

Leech, D. (1987c), "Ownership concentration and control in large U.S. corporations in the 1930s: an analysis of the TNEC sample", Journal of Industrial Economics 35:333–342.

Leech, D. (2003), "Incentives to corporate governance activism", in: M. Waterson, ed., Competition, Monopoly and Corporate Governance, Essays in Honour of Keith Cowling (Edward Elgar) forthcoming.

Leech, D., and J. Leahy (1991), "Ownership structure, control type classifications and the performance of large British companies", Economic Journal 101:1418–1437.

Leland, H.E., and D.H. Pyle (1977), "Informational asymmetries, financial structure, and financial intermediation", Journal of Finance 32:371–387.

Levin, J. (1995), Structuring Venture Capital, Private Equity, and Entrepreneurial Transactions (Little-Brown, Boston) Chapter 9.

Levy, H. (1983), "Economic evaluation of voting power of common stock", Journal of Finance 38:79–93.

Lewellen, W.G. (1968), Executive Compensation in Large Industrial Corporations (Columbia University Press, NY).

Liefmann, R. (1909), Beteiligungs und Finanzierungsgesellschaften; eine Studie über den modernen Kapitalismus und das Effektenwesen (in Deutschland, den Vereinigten Staaten, England, Frankreich, Belgien und der Schweiz) (G. Fischer, Jena).

Liefmann, R. (1920), Kartelle und Trusts: und die Weiterbildung der volkswirtschaftlichen Organisation (E. Moritz, Stuttgart).

Lippmann, W. (1914), Drift and Mastery; an Attempt to Diagnose the Current Unrest (Holt & Co., New York).

Lipton, M., and P.K. Rowe (2001), "Pills, polls and professors: a reply to Professor Gilson", Working Paper CLB-01-006 (New York University).

Loderer, C., and U. Peyer (2002), "Board overlap, seat accumulation and share prices", European Financial Management 8:165–192.

Loewenstein, M.J. (2000), "The conundrum of executive compensation", Wake Forest Law Review 35(1):1–30.

Lorsch, J., and E. MacIver (1989), Pawns or Potentates (Harvard Business School Press, Boston, MA).

Lummer, S.L., and J.J. McConnell (1989), "Further evidence on the bank lending process and the capital-market response to bank loan agreements", Journal of Financial Economics 25(1):99–122.

Macey, J.R. (1992), "An economic analysis of the various rationales for make shareholders the exclusive beneficiaries of corporate fiduciary duties", Stetson Law Review 21:23–44.

Macey, J.R., and F.S. McChesney (1985), "A theoretical analysis of corporate greenmail", Yale Law Journal 95:13–61.

Maher, M., and T. Andersson (2000), "Corporate governance: effects on firm performance and economic growth", Discussion Paper (OECD, Paris).

Main, B.G. (1999), "The rise and fall of executive share options in Britain", in: J. Carpenter and D. Yermack, eds., Executive Compensation and Shareholder Value: Theory and Evidence (Kluwer Academic Press, Dordrecht) pp. 83–113.

Manne, H.G. (1964), "Some theoretical aspects of share voting", Columbia Law Review 64:1427–1445.

Manne, H.G. (1965), "Mergers and the market for corporate control", Journal of Political Economy 73:110–120.

Manning, B. (1958), "Book review: The American Stockholder, by J.A. Livingston", Yale Law Journal 67:1477–1496.

Marris, R. (1964), The Economic Theory of Managerial Capitalism (Free Press of Glencoe, IL).

Mason, E.S., ed. (1959), The Corporation in Modern Society (Harvard University Press, Cambridge, MA).

Masson, R.T. (1971), "Executive motivations, earnings, and consequent equity performance", Journal of Political Economy 79(6):1278–1292.

Maug, E. (1997), "Boards of directors and capital structure: alternative forms of corporate restructuring", Journal of Corporate Finance, Contracting, Governance and Organization 3:113–139.

Maug, E. (1998), "Large shareholders as monitors: is there a trade-off between liquidity and control?", Journal of Finance 53:65–98.

Mayer, C. (1988), "New issues in corporate finance", European Economic Review 32:1167–1183.

McCahery, J.A., P. Moerland, T. Raaijmakers and L. Renneboog, eds (2002), Corporate Governance Regimes: Convergence and Diversity (Oxford University Press, Oxford, UK).

McCauley, R.N., and S.A. Zimmer (1994), "Exchange rates and international differences in the cost of capital", in: Y. Amihud and R.M. Levich, eds., Exchange Rates and Corporate Performance (New York University, NY) pp. 119–148.

McConnell, J.J., and H. Servaes (1990), "Additional evidence on equity ownership and corporate value", Journal of Financial Economics 27:595–612.

Mead, E.S. (1903), Trust Finance; A Study of the Genesis, Organization, and Management of Industrial Combinations (Appleton, New York).

Mead, E.S. (1912), Corporation Finance, 2nd Edition (Appleton, New York, London).

Mead, E.S. (1928), Corporation Finance, 6th Edition (Appleton, New York, London).

Means, G.C. (1930), "The diffusion of stock ownership in the U.S.", Quarterly Journal of Economics 44:561–600.

Means, G.C. (1931a), "The growth in the relative importance of the large corporation in American economic life", The American Economic Review 21:10–42.

Means, G.C. (1931b), "The separation of ownership and control in American industry", Quarterly Journal of Economics 46:68–100.

Megginson, W.L. (1990), "Restricted voting stock, acquisition premiums, and the market value of corporate control", Financial Review 25:175–198.

Mehran, H. (1995), "Executive compensation structure, ownership, and firm performance", Journal of Financial Economics 38:163–184.

Mikkelson, W.H., and M.M. Partch (1997), "The decline of takeovers and disciplinary managerial turnover", Journal of Financial Economics 44:205–228.

Minow, N. (2000), CEO Contracts 1999. Introduction (http://www.thecorporatelibrary.com/).

Mirrlees, J.A. (1976), "The optimal structure of incentives and authority within an organization", Bell Journal of Economics 7:105–131.

Mirrlees, J.A. (1999), "The theory of moral hazard and unobservable behaviour: Part I", Review of Economic Studies 66:3–21.

Mitchell, J. (1990), "Perfect equilibrium and intergenerational conflict in a model of cooperative enterprise growth", Journal of Economic Theory 51:48–76.

Mitchell, J. (2000), "Bad debts and the cleaning of banks' balance sheets: an application to economies in transition", Revised version (http://www.ecare.ulb.ac.be/ecare/Janet/janet.htm).

Moeller, S.B., F.P. Schlingemann and R.M. Stulz (2003a), "Firm size and the gains from acquisitions", Journal of Financial Economics, forthcoming.

Moeller, S.B., F.P. Schlingemann and R.M. Stulz (2003b), "Wealth destruction on a massive scale: a study of acquiring-firm returns in the merger wave of the late 1990s", unpublished (Ohio State University).

Monks, R.A.G., and N. Minow (2001), Corporate Governance, 2nd Edition (Blackwell Publishing, Oxford, UK; Cambridge, MA).

Monsen, R.J., J.S. Chiu and D.E. Cooley (1968), "The effect of separation of ownership and control on the performance of the large firm", Quarterly Journal of Economics 82:435–451.

Morck, R., A. Shleifer and R.W. Vishny (1988), "Management ownership and market valuation: an empirical analysis", Journal of Financial Economics 20:293–315.

Morgan, A.G., and A.B. Poulsen (2001), "Linking pay to performance – compensation proposals in the S&P 500", Journal of Financial Economics 62(3):489–523.

Mukherji, S., Y.H. Kim and M.C. Walker (1997), "The effect of stock splits on the ownership structure of firms", Journal of Corporate Finance, Contracting, Governance and Organization 3:167–188.

Mulherin, H.-J., and A.-B. Poulsen (1998), "Proxy contests and corporate change: implications for shareholder wealth", Journal of Financial Economics 47(3):279–313.

Muller, H., and K. Warneryd (2001), "Inside versus outside ownership: a political theory of the firm", RAND Journal of Economics 32:527–541.

Murphy, K. (1999), "Executive compensation", in: O.C. Ashenfelter and D. Card, eds., Handbook of Labor Economics, Vol. 3 (Elsevier, Amsterdam) pp. 2485–2563.

Muus, C.K. (1998), "Non-voting shares in France: an empirical analysis of the voting premium", Working Paper Series Finance & Accounting (Johann Wolfgang Goethe Universität, Frankfurt am Main, Germany).

Myers, S.C. (1977), "Determinants of corporate borrowing", Journal of Financial Economics 5:147–175.

Myners, P. (2001), Institutional Investment in the U.K.: A Review (H.M. Treasury, London).

Narayanan, M.P. (1985), "Managerial incentives for short-term results", Journal of Finance 40(5):1469–1484.

Neher, D.V. (1999), "Staged financing: an agency perspective", Review of Economic Studies 66:255–274.

Nenova, T. (2000), "The value of corporate votes and control benefits: a cross-country analysis", Mimeo (Harvard University, Cambridge, MA).

Nicodano, G. (1998), "Corporate groups, dual-class shares and the value of voting rights", Journal of Banking and Finance 22:1117–1137.

Nicodano, G., and A. Sembenelli (2000), "Private benefits, block transaction premiums and ownership structure", Mimeo (Università degli Studi di Torino, Turin, Italy).

Noe, T.H., and M.J. Rebello (1996), "The design of corporate boards: composition, compensation, factions and turnover", Mimeo (Georgia State University, Atlanta, GA).

Odegaard, B.A. (2002), "Price differences between equity classes. Corporate control, foreign ownership or liquidity? Evidence from Norway", Mimeo (Norwegian School of Management, Oslo).

Olivencia Report (1998), Comisión Especial para el Estudio de un Código Etico de los Consejos de Administración de las Sociedades (El Gobierno de las Sociedades Cotizadas, Spain). www.ecgi.org.

Ongena, S., and D.C. Smith (1998), "Quality and duration of banking relationships", in: D. Birks, ed., Global Cash Management in Europe (MacMillan, London) pp. 225–235.

Ongena, S., and D.C. Smith (2000), "Bank relationships: a review", in: S.A. Zenios and P. Harker, eds., Performance of Financial Institutions (Cambridge University Press, Cambridge) pp. 221–258.

Organisation for Economic Co-operation and Development (1999), OECD Principles of Corporate Governance (OECD, Paris).

Pagano, M., and A. Röell (1998), "The choice of stock ownership structure: agency costs, monitoring, and the decision to go public", Quarterly Journal of Economics 113:187–225.

Pagano, M., and P.F. Volpin (1999), "The political economy of corporate governance", CSEF Working Paper 29 (University of Salerno, Salerno, Italy).

Pagano, M., and P.F. Volpin (2002), "Managers, workers, and corporate control", CSEF Working Paper 75 (University of Salerno, Salerno, Italy).

Pagano, M., A. Röell and J. Zechner (2002), "The geography of equity listing: why do companies list abroad?", Journal of Finance 57:2651–2694.

Perotti, E.C., and K.E. Spier (1993), "Capital structure as a bargaining tool: the role of leverage in contract renegotiation", American Economic Review 83:1131–1141.

Perry, T., and M. Zenner (2000), "CEO compensation in the 1990s: shareholder alignment or shareholder expropriation?", Wake Forest Law Review 35(1):123–152.

Perry, T., and M. Zenner (2001), Pay for performance? Government regulation and the structure of compensation contracts", Journal of Financial Economics 62(3):453–488.

Peters Report (1997), Corporate Governance in the Netherlands – Forty Recommendations (Secretariat Committee on Corporate Governance, Netherlands). www.ecgi.org.

Petersen, M.A. (1992), "Pension reversions and worker-stockholder wealth transfers", Quarterly Journal of Economics 107:1033–1056.

Petersen, M.A., and R.G. Rajan (1994), "The benefits of lending relationships: evidence from small business data", Journal of Finance 49:3–37.

Pettigrew, A., H. Thomas and R. Whittington, eds (2002), Handbook of Strategy and Management (Sage Publications, London).

Pfannschmidt, A. (1993), Personelle Verflechtungen über Aufsichtsräte: Mehrfachmandate in deutschen Unternehmen (Gabler, Wiesbaden).

Pistor, K. (2000), "Patterns of legal change: shareholder and creditor rights in transition economies", The European Business Organisation Law Review 1(1):59–108.

Pontiff, J., A. Shleifer and M.S. Weisbach (1990), "Reversions of excess pension assets after takeovers", Rand Journal of Economics 21:600–613.

Porter, M.E. (1992a), "Capital disadvantage: America's failing capital investment system", Harvard Business Review, pp. 65–82.

Porter, M.E. (1992b), "Capital choices: changing the way America invests in industry", Journal of Applied Corporate Finance 4.

Pound, J. (1988), "Proxy contests and the efficiency of shareholder oversight", Journal of Financial Economics 20(1/2):237–265.

Prigge, S. (1998), "A survey of German corporate governance", in: K.J. Hopt, H. Kanda, M.J. Roe, E. Wymeersch and S. Prigge, eds., Comparative Corporate Governance. The State of the Art and Emerging Research (Clarendon Press, Oxford) pp. 943–1044.

Prowse, S.D. (1990), "Institutional investment patterns and corporate financial behavior in the U.S. and Japan", Journal of Financial Economics 27:43–66.

Pujo Committee (1913), Report of the Committee Appointed Pursuant to House Resolutions 429 and 504 to Investigate the Concentration of Control of Money and Credit. United States Congress House Committee on Banking and Currency (Government Printing Office, Washington DC).

Radice, H.K. (1971), "Control type, profitability and growth in large firms: an empirical study", Economic Journal 81:547–562.

Raheja, C.G. (2002), "The interaction of insiders and outsiders in monitoring: a theory of corporate boards", Working Paper (Vanderbilt University, Nashville, TN).

Rajan, R.G., and L. Zingales (2000), "The governance of the new enterprise", in: X. Vives, ed., Corporate Governance. Theoretical and Empirical Perspectives (Cambridge University Press, Cambridge).

Rajan, R.G., and L. Zingales (2001), "The great reversals: the politics of financial development in the 20th century", Working Paper Series No. 8178 (National Bureau of Economic Research, Cambridge, MA) pp. 1–72.

Ramirez, C.D. (1995), "Did J.P. Morgan's men add liquidity? Corporate investment, cash flow, and financial structure at the turn of the twentieth century", Journal of Finance 50:661–678.

Ramirez, C.D., and J.B. DeLong (2001), "Understanding America's hesitant steps toward financial capitalism: politics, the depression, and the separation of commercial and investment banking", Public Choice 106:93–116.

Ripley, W.Z. (1927), Main Street and Wall Street (Little and Brown, Boston).

Roberts, J., and E. Van den Steen (2000), "Shareholder interests, human capital investments and corporate governance", Working Paper 1631 (Stanford University Graduate School of Business, Stanford, CA).

Robinson, C., J. Rumsey and A. White (1996), "Market efficiency in the valuation of corporate control: evidence from dual class equity", Revue Canadienne des Sciences de l'Administration/Canadian Journal of Administrative Sciences 13:251–263.

Roe, M.J. (1990), "Political and legal restraints on ownership and control of public companies", Journal of Financial Economics 27:7–41.

Roe, M.J. (1991), "A political theory of American corporate finance", Columbia Law Review 91:10–67.

Roe, M.J. (1994), Strong Managers, Weak Owners: The Political Roots of American Corporate Finance (Princeton University Press, Princeton, NJ).

Roe, M.J. (1996), "From antitrust to corporation governance? The corporation and the law: 1959–1994", in: C. Kaysen, ed., The American Corporation Today (Oxford University Press, New York) pp. 102–127.

Roe, M.J. (2002), "Corporate law's limits", Mimeo (Harvard Law School, Cambridge, MA).

Roll, R. (1986), "The hubris hypothesis of corporate takeovers", Journal of Business 59:197–216.

Romano, R. (1991), "The shareholder suit: litigation without foundation?", Journal of Law, Economics and Organization 7:55–87.

Romano, R. (1993), The Genius of American Corporate Law (AEI Press, Washington, DC).

Romano, R. (1996), "Corporate law and corporate governance", Industrial and Corporate Change 5(2):277–339.

Romano, R. (1998), "Empowering investors: a market approach to securities regulation", Yale Law Journal 107:2359–2430.

Romano, R. (2001), "Less is more: making institutional investor activism a valuable mechanism of corporate governance", Yale Journal on Regulation 18:174–251.

Rosen, S. (1992), "Contracts and the market for executives", in: L. Werin and H. Wijkander, eds., Contract Economics (Blackwell, Cambridge, MA, Oxford) pp. 181–211.

Rosenbaum, V. (2000), Corporate Takeover Defenses 2000 (Investor Responsibility Research Center, Washington, DC).

Rosenstein, S., and J.G. Wyatt (1990), "Outside directors, board independence, and shareholder wealth", Journal of Financial Economics 26:175–191.

Rossi, S., and P. Volpin (2003), "Cross-country determinants of mergers and acquisitions", IFA Working Paper 339 (London Business School, UK).

Rostow, E.V. (1959), "To whom and for what ends are corporate managements responsible?", in: E.S. Mason, ed., The Corporation in Modern Society (Harvard University Press, Cambridge, MA).

Rydqvist, K. (1992), "Dual-class shares: a review", Oxford Review of Economic Policy 8:45–57.

Rydqvist, K. (1996), "Takeover bids and the relative prices of shares that differ in their voting rights", Journal of Banking and Finance 20:1407–1425.

Sabel, C. (1996), "Ungoverned production: an American view of the novel universalism of Japanese production methods and their awkward fit with current forms of corporate governance". Worldspeak (electronic magazine).

Sahlman, W.A. (1990), "The structure and governance of venture-capital organizations", Journal of Financial Economics 27:473–521.

Sarin, A., K.A. Shastri and K. Shastri (1999), "Ownership structure and stock market liquidity", Mimeo (Santa Clara University, CA).

Scharfstein, D. (1988), "The disciplinary role of takeovers", Review of Economic Studies 55:185–199.

Schmidt, K. (1996), "The costs and benefits of privatization – an incomplete contracts approach", Journal of Law, Economics and Organization 12:1–24.

Schnitzer, M. (1995), " 'Breach of trust' in takeovers and the optimal corporate charter", Journal of Industrial Economics 43:229–259.

Schumpeter, J.A. (1934), The Theory of Economic Development: An Inquiry into Profits, Capital, Credit, Interest, and the Business Cycle (Harvard University Press: H. Milford, Cambridge, MA, London).

Schumpeter, J.A. (1939), Business Cycles: A Theoretical, Historical, and Statistical Analysis of the Capitalist Process (McGraw-Hill, New York, London).

Schwert, G.W. (2000), "Hostility in takeovers: in the eyes of the beholder?", Journal of Finance 55: 2599–2640.

Seligman, J. (1986), "Equal protection in shareholder voting rights : the one-share–one-vote controversy", George Washington Law Review 54:687.

Shapiro, C., and R.D. Willig (1990), "Economic rationales for the scope of privatization", in: E.N. Suleiman and J. Waterbury, eds., The Political Economy of Public Sector Reform and Privatization (Westview Press, London) pp. 55–87.

Shinn, J. (2001), "Private profit or public purpose? Shallow convergence on the shareholder model", Ph.D. Dissertation (Princeton University, NJ).

Shinn, J., and P. Gourevitch (2002), How Shareholder Reforms Can Pay Foreign Policy Dividends (Council on Foreign Relations, New York).

Shleifer, A., and L.H. Summers (1988), "Breach of trust in hostile takeovers", in: A.J. Auerbach, ed., Corporate Takeovers: Causes and Consequences (University of Chicago Press, National Bureau of Economic Research Project Report series, Chicago, London).

Shleifer, A., and R.W. Vishny (1986), "Large shareholders and corporate control", Journal of Political Economy 94:461–488.

Shleifer, A., and R.W. Vishny (1988), "Value maximization and the acquisition process", Journal of Economic Perspectives 2:7–20.

Shleifer, A., and R.W. Vishny (1989), "Equilibrium short horizons of investors and firms", American Economic Review 80(2):148–153.

Shleifer, A., and R.W. Vishny (1997a), "A survey of corporate governance", Journal of Finance 52: 737–783.

Shleifer, A., and R.W. Vishny (1997b), "The takeover wave of the 1980s", in: D.H. Chew, ed., Studies in International Corporate Finance and Governance Systems (Oxford University Press, New York) pp. 98–105.

Shockley, R., and A.J. Thakor (1997), "Bank loan commitments: data, theory, and tests", Journal of Money, Credit and Banking 29(4):517–534.

Short, H. (1994), "Ownership, control, financial structure and the performance of firms", Journal of Economic Surveys 8:203–249.

Short, H., and K. Keasey (1999), "Managerial ownership and the performance of firms: evidence from the U.K.", Journal of Corporate Finance, Contracting, Governance and Organization 5:79–101.

Smith, B.F., and B. Amoako-Adu (1995), "Relative prices of dual class shares", Journal of Financial and Quantitative Analysis 30:223–239.

Spier, K.E. (1992), "Incomplete contracts and signalling", Rand Journal of Economics 23:432–443.

Stapledon, G. (1996), Institutional Shareholders and Corporate Governance (Clarendon Press, Oxford).

Steer, P.S., and J.R. Cable (1978), "Internal organization and profit: an empirical analysis of large U.K. companies", Journal of Industrial Economics 27:13–30.

Stein, J.C. (1988), "Takeover threats and managerial myopia", Journal of Political Economy 96:61–80.

Stein, J.C. (1989), "Efficient capital markets, inefficient firms: a model of myopic corporate behavior", Quarterly Journal of Economics 104:655–669.

Stock Exchange of Singapore (1998), Listing Manual (as amended) and Best Practices Guide (Stock Exchange of Singapore, Singapore). http://www.combinet.org/governance/finalver/listof.htm.

Stock Exchange of Thailand (SET) (1998), The SET Code of Best Practice for Directors of Listed Companies (SET, Bangkok). http://www.combinet.org/governance/finalver/listof.htm.

Stoll, H.R., and R.E. Whaley (1983), "Transaction costs and the small firm effect", Journal of Financial Economics 12:57–79.

Streeck, W., and N. Kluge, eds (1999), Mitbestimmung in Deutschland. Tradition und Effizienz (Campus Verlag, Frankfurt/Main, New York).

Stulz, R.M. (1988), "Managerial control of voting rights: financing policies and the market for corporate control", Journal of Financial Economics 20:25–54.

Stulz, R.M., and R. Williamson (2003), "Culture, openness and finance", Journal of Financial Economics, forthcoming.

Svejnar, J. (1981), "Relative wage effects of unions, dictatorship and codetermination: econometric evidence from Germany", Review of Economics and Statistics 63:188–197.

Svejnar, J. (1982), "Codetermination and productivity: evidence from the Federal Republic of Germany", in: D. Jones and J. Svejnar, eds., Participatory and Self-Managed Firms (Heath, Lexington, MA).

Tabarrok, A. (1998), "The separation of commercial and investment banking: the Morgans vs. the Rockefellers", Quarterly Journal of Austrian Economics 1:1–18.

Tallman, E.W. (1991), "The House of Morgan: an American banking dynasty and the rise of modern finance: review article", Federal Reserve Bank of Atlanta Economic Review 76:28–32.

Temporary National Economic Committee (TNEC) (1940), The Distribution of Ownership in the 200 Largest Nonfinancial Corporations (U.S. Government Printing Office, Washington, DC).

Thomas, R.S., and K.J. Martin (2000), "The determinants of shareholder voting on stock option plans", Wake Forest Law Review 35(1):31–73.

Tilly, R.H. (1989), "Banking institutions in historical and comparative perspective: Germany, Great Britain and the U.S. in the 19th and early 20th century", Journal of Institutional and Theoretical Economics 145:189–209.

Tinic, S.M. (1972), "The economics of liquidity services", Quarterly Journal of Economics 86:79–93.

Tirole, J. (1986), "Hierarchies and bureaucracies", Journal of Law, Economics and Organization 2: 181–214.

Tirole, J. (2001), "Corporate governance", Econometrica 69:1–35.

Twain, M., and C.D. Warner (1873), The Gilded Age. A Tale of Today (American Pub. Co.; F.G. Gilman, Hartford, Chicago, IL).

Vafeas, N. (1999), "Board meeting frequency and firm performance", Journal of Financial Economics 53(1):113–142.

Van-Nuys, K. (1993), "Corporate governance through the proxy process: evidence from the 1989 Honeywell proxy solicitation", Journal of Financial Economics 34(1):101–132.

Veblen, T. (1923), Absentee Ownership and Business Enterprise in Recent Times: The Case of America (B.W. Huebsch Inc., New York).

Viénot Report (1995), The Boards of Directors of Listed Companies in France – Viénot I (Conseil National du Patronat Français ('CNPF') & Association Française des Entreprises Privéss ('AFEP'), France). www.ecgi.org.

Viénot Report (1999), Report of the Committee on Corporate Governance – Viénot II (Association Française des Entreprises Privéss ('AFEP') & Mouvement des Entreprises de France ('MEDEF'), France). www.ecgi.org.

Warga, A., and I. Welch (1993), "Bondholder losses in leveraged buyouts", Review of Financial Studies 6:959–982.

Warshow, H.T. (1924), "The distribution of corporate ownership in the U.S.", Quarterly Journal of Economics 39:15–38.

Warther, V.A. (1998), "Board effectiveness and board dissent: a model of the board's relationship to management and shareholders", Journal of Corporate Finance, Contracting, Governance and Organization 4:53–70.

Weiner, J.L. (1964), "The Berle–Means dialogue on the concept of the corporation", Columbia Law Review 64:1459–1467.

Weisbach, M.S. (1988), "Outside directors and CEO turnover", Journal of Financial Economics 20: 431–460.

Weston, J.F., J.A. Siu and B.A. Johnson (2001), Takeovers, Restructuring & Corporate Governance (Prentice Hall, Upper Saddle River, NJ).

Williamson, O. (1984), "Corporate governance", Yale Law Journal 93:1197–1230.

Williamson, O.E. (1971), "The vertical integration of production: market failure considerations", American Economic Review 61:112.

Williamson, O.E. (1975), Markets and Hierarchies: Analysis and Antitrust Implications (The Free Press, New York).

Williamson, O.E. (1979), "Transaction cost economics: the governance of contractual relations", Journal of Law and Economics 22:233–261.

Williamson, O.E. (1985a), The Economic Institutions of Capitalism (Free Press, New York).

Williamson, O.E. (1985b), "Employee ownership and internal governance: a perspective", Journal of Economic Behavior and Organization 6:243–245.

Williamson, O.E. (1988), "Breach of trust in hostile takeovers: comment", in: A.J. Auerbach, ed., Corporate Takeovers: Causes and Consequences (Chicago University Press, Chicago) pp. 61–67.

Wolfenzon, D. (1999), "A theory of pyramidal ownership", Mimeo (Stern School of Business, New York University).

Womack, J.P., D.T. Jones and D. Roos (1991), The Machine that Changed the World: How Japan's Secret Weapon in the Global Auto Wars Will Revolutionize Western Industry (HarperPerennial, NY).

Wormser, I.M. (1931), Frankenstein, Incorporated (McGraw-Hill, New York, London).

Wymeersch, E. (1998), "A status report on corporate governance rules and practices in some continental European states", in: K.J. Hopt, H. Kanda, M.J. Roe, E. Wymeersch and S. Prigge, eds., Comparative Corporate Governance. The State of the Art and Emerging Research (Clarendon Press, Oxford) pp. 1046–1199.

Wymeersch, E. (2003), "Do we need a law on groups of companies?", in: K.J. Hopt and E. Wymeersch, eds., Capital Markets and Company Law (Oxford University Press).

Yermack, D. (1997), "Good timing: CEO stock option awards and company news announcements", Journal of Finance 52:449–476.

Yilmaz, B. (2000), "Strategic voting and proxy contests", Rodney L. White Center for Financial Research Working Paper No. 05-00 (Wharton School, University of Pennsylvania, Philadelphia, PA).

Zender, J.F. (1991), "Optimal financial instruments", Journal of Finance 46:1645–1663.

Zingales, L. (1994), "The value of the voting right: a study of the Milan Stock Exchange experience", Review of Financial Studies 7:125–148.

Zingales, L. (1995), "What determines the value of corporate votes?", Quarterly Journal of Economics 110:1047–1073.

Zingales, L. (1998), "Corporate governance", in: P. Newman, ed., The New Palgrave Dictionary of Economics and the Law (MacMillan, New York).

Zwiebel, J. (1995), "Block investment and partial benefits of corporate control", Review of Economic Studies 62:161–185.

Chapter 2

AGENCY, INFORMATION AND CORPORATE INVESTMENT

JEREMY C. STEIN*

Harvard University and NBER

Contents

* I am grateful to the NSF for financial support, and to Geoff Tate and Ann Richards for research assistance. Thanks also to Judy Chevalier, Milt Harris, Oliver Hart, Bengt Holmström, Steve Kaplan, Owen Lamont, Raghu Rajan, David Scharfstein, Andrei Shleifer and René Stulz for their input.

Handbook of the Economics of Finance, Edited by G.M. Constantinides, M. Harris and R. Stulz

Abstract

This essay surveys the body of research that asks how the efficiency of corporate investment is influenced by problems of asymmetric information and agency. I organize the material around two basic questions. First, does the external capital market channel the right amount of money to each firm? That is, does the market get *across-firm* allocations right, so that the marginal return to investment in firm i is the same as the marginal return to investment in firm j? Second, do internal capital markets channel the right amount of money to individual projects within firms? That is, does the internal capital budgeting process get *within-firm* allocations right, so that the marginal return to investment in firm i's division A is the same as the marginal return to investment in firm i's division B? In addition to discussing the theoretical and empirical work that bears most directly on these questions, the essay also briefly sketches some of the implications of this work for broader issues in both macroeconomics and the theory of the firm.

Keywords

external capital markets, internal capital markets, underinvestment, overinvestment, moral hazard, agency problems, asymmetric information, adverse selection

JEL classification: G31, G32

1. Introduction

A fundamental question in corporate finance is this: to what extent does capital get allocated to the right investment projects? In a perfect world, with frictionless capital markets of the sort envisioned in Modigliani and Miller (1958), funds flow in such a way that the marginal product of capital is equated across every project in the economy. Of course, in the real world, there are a variety of distortionary forces that prevent things from working this well. Taxes and transactions costs are examples of such frictions. But perhaps the most pervasive and important factors influencing the efficiency of corporate investment are those that arise from informational asymmetries and agency problems.

This essay surveys research – both theoretical and empirical – that speaks to the influence of asymmetric information and agency on investment behavior. I organize the material by noting that the fundamental question posed above can be divided into two sub-questions. First, does the external capital market channel the right amount of money to each firm? In other words, does the market get *across-firm* allocations right, so that the marginal return to investment in firm i is the same as the marginal return to investment in firm j?

Second, do internal capital markets channel the right amount of money to individual projects within firms? In other words, does the internal capital budgeting process get *within-firm* allocations right, so that the marginal return to investment in, say, firm i's division A is the same as the marginal return to investment in firm i's division B?

Although these two questions are logically distinct – in the sense that the workings of the external capital market appear in many ways to be quite different from those of the internal capital market – an overarching goal of this essay is to emphasize the common elements of the capital-allocation problem across and within firms. For example, just as investors in the external capital market have to be wary of dealing with a CEO who is better informed about firm prospects than they, and whose incentives diverge from theirs, so must a CEO overseeing the internal capital budgeting process be wary of dealing with subordinates who are better informed about divisional prospects than she, and whose incentives diverge from hers. While the external capital market may ultimately resolve this problem through different means than the internal capital market – with different consequences for investment behavior – it is nevertheless important to appreciate that the underlying problem may well be the same one in both cases.

Both of the sub-questions have been the subject of extensive theoretical and empirical work. Still, it is fair to say that research on the first sub-question – that having to do with the efficiency of across-firm capital allocation – is currently at a more mature stage. On the notion that life is more exciting near the frontier, I will thus devote a somewhat disproportionate share of my attention to surveying work on the second sub-question, that of within-firm capital allocation. On the first, and especially when it comes to empirical work, I will defer more to existing survey papers [e.g., Hubbard (1998)].

1.1. Scope of the essay: what's covered and what's left out

As much as possible, I am going to focus on research that speaks directly to the impact of information and agency problems on *investment behavior.* To oversimplify, but not by much, most of the empirical papers that I will touch on have some measure of investment as the left-hand-side variable. Of course, the concepts of asymmetric information and agency are central to virtually every major topic in corporate finance, including corporate governance, capital structure, the design of incentive contracts, financial intermediation, etc. Indeed, one can think of governance, capital structure, incentive contracts and intermediation as a variety of curative mechanisms that arise endogenously to mitigate the effects of information and agency problems on investment outcomes. Thus, at some level, it is difficult to satisfactorily address the subject of investment without taking on these other topics as well.

Nevertheless, although this will no doubt lead to some awkwardness and many omissions, I will for the most part leave these curative mechanisms lurking in the background.[1] This can be thought of as a partial equilibrium approach, where it is implicitly assumed that certain types of information and agency distortions are not fully resolved by the curative mechanisms, and thus – for reasons that are exogenous to the model – remain relevant in equilibrium. This partial equilibrium approach is the only way I can think of to keep the scope of this essay manageable.

Moreover, in much of what follows, I will give primary emphasis to those types of investment distortions that are the most pervasive and stubborn, in the sense that they are likely to exist even when agency and information problems are relatively "mild" – that is, even when the legal, auditing, and contracting environment is highly evolved. (Think of the USA environment, for example). I will have less to say about more extreme distortions that arise in economies and situations where investors are poorly protected, and where managers are left with significant scope for looting their firms.[2]

Finally, although I will discuss the general consequences of high leverage for investment, I will not address the details of how financially distressed companies restructure their assets, either inside or outside of formal bankruptcy. So perhaps the best way to interpret much of what I am doing is to think of a financially healthy firm operating in an environment where governance and other curative mechanisms are about as good as they can be, and to ask: what can still go wrong?

---

[1] Fortunately, there are already several surveys on these topics. In addition to the essays in this volume, see, e.g., Shleifer and Vishny (1997) on governance, and Harris and Raviv (1991) on capital structure.

[2] See Johnson, LaPorta, Lopez-de-Silanes and Shleifer (2000) for several examples of such looting behavior. Of course, even in economies such as the USA where it is not often observed in equilibrium, the out-of-equilibrium threat of such very bad behavior may do a lot to explain various features of governance, law, disclosure policies, etc.

1.2. Organization

The remainder of this essay is divided into two main parts. Part A deals with investment at the firm level, and contains three sections. I begin in Section 2 by reviewing the various major classes of theories that are relevant for understanding investment at the firm level. In Section 3, I discuss the empirical evidence that speaks to these theories. In Section 4, I touch briefly on the macroeconomic implications of this research.

Part B of the essay deals with investment inside firms. Section 5 covers the theoretical work, and Section 6 the associated empirical work.

Finally, in Section 7, I conclude by offering some tentative thoughts on how the central ideas in the essay can be used to think about the boundaries of the firm.

Part A. Investment at the firm level

2. Theoretical building blocks: investment at the firm level

There are many, many theoretical models that have implications for investment at the firm level, and there a variety of ways that one could go about grouping them. For the purposes of the discussion that follows, I will take an empirically-oriented approach to organizing the theories. That is, I will cluster together those models that have similar empirical implications, even if the underlying theoretical mechanisms are quite distinct. The converse and potentially awkward feature of this approach is that sometimes models that are quite close in terms of their underlying logic will get placed into different categories. To take a concrete example, the models of Myers (1977) and Hart and Moore (1995) are both built on the same foundation–the idea that a large debt burden can prevent a company from raising the funds to undertake new investment. But in the former paper, managers are benevolent towards outside shareholders, and there is always underinvestment in equilibrium; in contrast, in the latter, managers are self-interested and there can be either underinvestment or overinvestment, depending on the state of the world. Thus, although the formal structure of these models is quite similar, I will put them into different groupings.

2.1. Models of costly external finance

The first broad class of models to be considered are those that unambiguously predict underinvestment relative to a first-best benchmark. In these models, managers can for the most part be thought of as acting in the interests of current shareholders, at least in equilibrium.[3] Thus when managers have access to unlimited discretionary resources,

---

[3] Though in some cases [e.g., Townsend (1979), Gale and Hellwig (1985), Bolton and Scharfstein (1990), Hart and Moore (1998)], managers act on behalf of shareholders only because they are in equilibrium the *only* shareholders. In these entrepreneurial-firm models, agency problems are so severe as to rule out the use of outside equity finance.

investment converges to the efficient level. However, when managers are resource-constrained in some way or another, there will be too little investment, because there are frictions associated with raising finance externally.

2.1.1. Costs of equity finance

An important insight, due to Myers and Majluf (1984), Myers (1984) and Greenwald, Stiglitz and Weiss (1984), is that raising equity externally will generally be problematic due to an adverse-selection problem of the sort first identified by Akerlof (1970).[4] To the extent that managers favor their current stockholders at the expense of potential future investors, they will wish to sell new shares at times when their private information suggests that these new shares are most overvalued. As a result, equity issues are rationally interpreted by the market as bad news [see Asquith and Mullins (1986), Masulis and Korwar (1986), Mikkelson and Partch (1986) for empirical evidence], which in turn can make managers of good firms (those with favorable realizations of their private information) reluctant to sell equity in the first place. The bottom line is that even firms that are badly in need of new equity – say because they have good investment opportunities but scarce internal resources – may be unable or unwilling to raise it.

2.1.2. Costs of debt finance

Of course, an inability to access new equity would not compromise investment if firms could frictionlessly raise unlimited amounts of debt financing. However, a variety of theories suggest that this is unlikely to be the case.

2.1.2.1. Adverse selection, moral hazard and credit rationing in the debt market. The same basic adverse selection argument that is used by Myers and Majluf (1984) for the equity market can be applied to the debt market, to the extent that the debt involved has some default risk: at any given interest rate, managers will be more likely to borrow if their private information suggests that they are relatively prone to default. Or, as a variation on the theme, there can be moral hazard, whereby those managers who borrow have an increased incentive to take the sort of risks that lead to default. As has been shown by Jaffee and Russell (1976), Stiglitz and Weiss (1981, 1983), and others, these sorts of considerations can lead to credit rationing, whereby firms are simply unable to obtain all the debt financing they would like at the prevailing market interest rate.[5]

---

[4] The Myers–Majluf model has been extended and refined by many authors [e.g., Krasker (1986)]. See Harris and Raviv (1991) for a discussion and references. Dybvig and Zender (1991) have questioned the microfoundations of the assumption that managers act on behalf of existing shareholders, while Persons (1994) has offered a rationalization of this assumption.

[5] In spite of the similarities, Myers (1984) and Myers and Majluf (1984) argue that adverse selection problems are generally likely to be more severe in the equity market, because equity values are more sensitive than debt values to managers' private information.

2.1.2.2. Debt overhang. Myers (1977) is another paper that speaks to the limitations of debt finance. Here the problem is not so much in accessing the debt market ex ante, but rather in what happens after the money is borrowed. In particular, a large debt burden on a firm's balance sheet discourages further new investment, particularly if this new investment is financed by issuing claims that are junior to the existing debt. This is because if the existing debt is trading at less than face value, it acts as a tax on the proceeds of the new investment: part of any increase in value generated by the new investment goes to make the existing lenders whole, and is therefore is unavailable to repay those claimants who put up the new money. [6]

Debt overhang models can be thought of as having two distinct sorts of empirical implications: ex post (once the debt burden is in place) they suggest that highly-leveraged firms, such as those that have recently undergone leveraged buyouts, will be particularly prone to underinvestment. Ex ante, they offer a reason why even more modestly-levered firms, particularly those with attractive future investment opportunities, may be reluctant to raise much debt in the first place, even if this means foregoing some current investment projects. [7]

2.1.2.3. Optimal contracting models of debt: underinvestment in entrepreneurial firms.
The above-discussed models of debt and equity finance take the existence of these types of financial claims as given, and then go on to derive implications for investment, capital structure, etc. Another branch of the literature seeks to endogenize the financial contract, typically by positing some specific agency problem (e.g., managers' penchant for diverting the firm's cashflow to themselves) and asking what sort of claim represents an optimal response to this agency problem.

In much of this work, the optimal contract that emerges resembles a standard debt contract, and there is no outside equity financing. [8] Thus, the firms in question should be interpreted as "entrepreneurial", in the sense that their only stockholders are their

---

[6] The basic debt overhang concept has proved to be enormously useful in addressing a wide range of questions having to do with: i) debt structure (seniority, security, etc.); as well as ii) the more specific details of how financial distress plays itself out and is resolved. For a few examples from a very large literature, see Stulz and Johnson (1985), Berkovitch and Kim (1990), Bergman and Callen (1991), Hart and Moore (1995) and Gertner and Scharfstein (1991). Again, see Harris and Raviv (1991) for more complete references.

[7] Fama and Miller (1972) and Jensen and Meckling (1976) offer another reason why firms might be unwilling to take on too much debt ex ante: the so-called "asset substitution" effect, whereby an excessive debt burden can create incentives for managers, acting on behalf of shareholders, to take on risky negative-NPV projects at the expense of lenders.

[8] Debt tends to be an attractive contract when verification of cashflows is costly or impossible, so that managers have broad scope for diverting these cashflows to themselves. However, Fluck (1998) and Myers (2000) show how outside equity financing can also be sustained in such a setting, provided there is an infinite horizon [see also Gomes (2000) for a related argument]. In other cases, when cashflows can be more readily verified, optimal financing schemes can involve a richer mix of claims. See, e.g., Dewatripont and Tirole (1994).

managers. Early examples include Townsend (1979) and Gale and Hellwig (1985), who assume that outside investors can only verify a firm's cashflows by paying some fixed auditing cost. As long as the manager turns over the stipulated debt payments, there is no audit, and the manager gets to keep the rest of the firm's cashflow. However, if the manager fails to make the debt payment, the lender audits, and keeps everything he finds; this can be interpreted as costly bankruptcy. The implications for investment follow from the auditing/bankruptcy cost. In particular, the less wealth the manager is able to put up, and hence the more he must borrow, the greater is the likelihood of the auditing cost being incurred. Thus, less managerial wealth translates into greater deadweight costs of external finance, and less investment.

More recently, following the work of Grossman and Hart (1986), Hart and Moore (1990), and Hart (1995) on incomplete contracting, the emphasis has shifted to thinking of financial contracts in terms of the allocation of control rights that they embody; Aghion and Bolton (1992) were among the first to take this point of view. In this context, debt is often seen as an incentive scheme that rewards management with continued control if it makes the required debt payments, and punishes it with loss of control otherwise. In a multi-period framework, this type of incentive scheme enables outside lenders to extract payments from managers even in the extreme case where cashflows are completely unverifiable. Well-known papers in this vein include Bolton and Scharfstein (1990) and Hart and Moore (1994, 1998).

Like the costly-state-verification models, these models also have the feature that there is underinvestment ex ante, with this problem being a decreasing function of managers' wealth. Moreover, given the multi-period nature of the models, one can also interpret some of them as implying a form of ex-post underinvestment as well, with assets sometimes being prematurely seized and liquidated by lenders when managers are unable to meet their debt payments.[9]

2.1.3. Synthesis: a reduced-form model of costly external finance

In spite of the wide variety of modeling approaches, all the theories surveyed thus far have broadly similar empirical implications for investment. Indeed, the essence of what these theories have to say about investment can be captured in a very simple reduced-form model. Although the model may appear ad hoc, Froot, Scharfstein and Stein (1993) demonstrate that it can be mapped precisely into a variant of the Townsend (1979) and Gale–Hellwig (1985) costly-state-verification models. Also, Stein (1998) shows that an appropriately parameterized version of the Myers–Majluf (1984) adverse-selection model leads to essentially the same reduced form.

The setup is as follows. The firm invests I at time 1, which yields a gross return of $f(I)$ at time 2, where $f()$ is an increasing, concave function. Of the investment I, an amount w is financed out of internal resources (managers' wealth, or the firm's retained

---

[9] See also Diamond (1991) for a model with excessive ex post liquidation by lenders.

earnings) and an amount e is raised externally, via new issues of debt, equity or some other claim. Thus, the budget constraint is $I = e + w$. In a first-best world, managers would seek to maximize:

$$\max f(I)/(1+r) - I, \tag{1}$$

where r is the risk-adjusted discount rate. This involves setting the marginal product of capital, f_1, equal to $(1+r)$.

One can loosely capture some of the financing frictions discussed above by assuming that there are deadweight costs associated with funds raised externally, and that these costs are given by $\theta C(e)$, where $C()$ is an increasing convex function, and θ is a measure of the degree of the financing friction. Thus, the firm's problem becomes:

$$\max f(I)/(1+r) - I - \theta C(e). \tag{2}$$

Kaplan and Zingales (1997) show that the solution in this case has the following properties. First, I is always less than or equal to the first best. Also, $dI/dw \geqslant 0$ and $dI/d\theta \leqslant 0$: I is (weakly) increasing in the firm's internal resources w, and (weakly) decreasing in the degree of the financing friction θ. These features are exactly what one would expect. However, there is more subtlety in the behavior of some the higher-order derivatives of I. In particular, d^2I/dw^2 cannot be unambiguously signed. Thus while the local sensitivity of investment to internal cash, dI/dw, eventually converges to zero for w high enough, this convergence need not be monotonic. Similarly, one cannot in general sign $d^2I/dwd\theta$. As Kaplan and Zingales (1997) emphasize, the important message for empirical work is that one has to be careful in using measures of dI/dw as proxies for θ. That is, in comparing two firms, it is not necessarily true that the one with the higher empirically-measured sensitivity of investment to internal cash should be thought of as the one facing the more severe financing frictions. I will return to this caveat below.

2.2. The agency conflict between managers and outside stockholders

In the models discussed so far, there is in equilibrium no meaningful conflict between managers and stockholders. This is either because managers are simply assumed to act in the interests of stockholders [as in Myers and Majluf (1984) and Myers (1977)] or, at the other extreme, because the threat of managerial expropriation of outside stockholders is so great that equity financing is not viable in equilibrium, and the firm remains owner-managed. But a central theme in much of the corporate-finance literature – with a lineage going back to Berle and Means (1932), and including the influential work of Jensen and Meckling (1976) – is that the managers of publicly-traded firms pursue their own private objectives, which need not coincide with those of outside stockholders.

There are many possible manifestations of the manager–stockholder agency conflict. For example, managers may simply not exert as much effort as they would in a first-best world [Holmström (1979)]. Given the focus of this essay, however, I restrict attention to those variants of the agency problem that have the most direct implications for investment.

2.2.1. Empire-building

2.2.1.1. Empire-building and overinvestment. One way in which managers' interests may diverge from those of stockholders is that managers may have an excessive taste for running large firms, as opposed to simply profitable ones. This "empire-building" tendency is emphasized by Baumol (1959), Marris (1964), Williamson (1964), Donaldson (1984) and Jensen (1986, 1993), among many others.

Jensen (1986, 1993) argues that empire-building preferences will cause managers to spend essentially all available funds on investment projects. This leads to the prediction that investment will be increasing in internal resources. It also implies that investment will decrease with leverage, because high current debt payments force cash out of the firm, thereby reducing managers' discretionary budgets. Note that these are the same basic predictions that emerge from the costly-external-finance genre of models described in Section 2.1 above, though of course the welfare implications are very different.

Jensen's ideas have been further developed and refined in formal models by Stulz (1990), Harris and Raviv (1990), Hart and Moore (1995) and Zwiebel (1996). [10] These models typically incorporate empire-building preferences by using the modeling device of managerial private benefits of control [Grossman and Hart (1988)], and assuming that these private benefits are proportional to either the amount the firm invests [Hart and Moore (1995)], or the gross output from investment [Stulz (1990)]. [11] One insight that comes from these models is that no matter how strong the underlying agency problem, it would be wrong to conclude that empire-building tendencies necessarily lead to an empirical prediction of *overinvestment on average.* Rather, the usual outcome in the models is an endogenously determined level of debt that attempts to balance ex post over- and underinvestment distortions. Thus, the models predict ex post overinvestment in some states of the world (when the level of free cashflow relative to investment opportunities is higher than expected), and ex post underinvestment in others.

As a very loose heuristic way of comparing the empirical content of empire-building models to those of costly external finance, one can modify Equation (2) above in the spirit of Stulz (1990) and Hart and Moore (1995) by adding a term equal to $\gamma f(I)$ to the objective function. This captures the idea that managers derive private benefits

---

[10] With respect to the general idea that debt can serve as a disciplinary device, an important precursor to these papers is Grossman and Hart (1982).

[11] The latter formulation – private benefits proportional to output – implies that managers overinvest, but that conditional on the level of investment, they rank projects in the right order, from high to low NPV. This seems to capture the behavior described by Donaldson (1984).

from gross investment output, as in Stulz (1990), with γ measuring the intensity of the agency conflict. Thus, Equation (2) becomes:

$$\max(1 + \gamma)f(I)/(1 + r) - I - \theta C(e). \tag{3}$$

As internal resources w go to infinity, the marginal product of capital now asymptotes at $(1+r)/(1+\gamma)$, rather than at $(1+r)$ – i.e., there is overinvestment. However, more generally, there can be either over- or underinvestment, depending on the realization of w relative to other parameter values.[12] And importantly, most of the other comparative statics of the model – having to do with dI/dw, $dI/d\theta$, d^2I/dw^2 and $d^2I/dwd\theta$ – are the same as before. Again, this underscores the challenges associated with empirically distinguishing the two classes of theories.[13]

2.2.1.2. Empire-preservation, entrenchment and diversification. If managers do in fact derive private benefits from being in charge of large corporate empires, this is likely to show up not just as an overall tendency toward overinvestment. Rather, some specific types of investments will seem especially attractive to managers. For example, Amihud and Lev (1981) argue that there will be a managerial preference for diversification, as this reduces the risk of the empire going out of business. And Shleifer and Vishny (1989) suggest that managers will be particularly keen to invest in projects that require their specific human capital, thereby strengthening their chances of keeping their jobs.

2.2.2. Reputational and career concerns

Another source of conflict between managers and shareholders is that managers may be concerned with how their actions affect their reputations, and ultimately their perceived value in the labor market.[14] This idea, elegantly modeled by Holmström (1999a), has a variety of specific applications to investment.[15]

2.2.2.1. Short-termism. Narayanan (1985) observes that managers concerned with their labor-market reputations may have incentives to take actions that boost measures of short-term performance at the expense of long-run shareholder value. Stein (1989) makes a similar point about managers concerned not with their own reputations per se,

---

[12] The models discussed above suggest that w will be in part endogenously determined by the firm's choice of capital structure policy.

[13] Hadlock (1998) argues that empire-building models have the property that dI/dw is decreasing in managerial incentives, while a costly-external-finance model of the Myers–Majluf (1984) type has the opposite property, and uses this insight to construct a differentiating test.

[14] Fama (1980) is one of the first to discuss how career concerns might affect agents' incentives. He stresses how career concerns can in some cases lead to better-behaved agents.

[15] See Dewatripont, Jewitt and Tirole (1999) for a recent extension of Holmström's model to more complex information structures.

but rather with their firms' stock prices over a near-term horizon.[16] In both cases, the key to the argument is that managers can do things that are unobservable to outside shareholders. For example, managers may be able to boost reported earnings by underinvesting in hard-to-measure assets, such as maintenance, customer loyalty, employee training, etc. From the perspective of outside investors, such myopic behavior cannot be disentangled from other, more positive shocks (e.g., increases in customer demand) that also lead to higher reported profits. Consequently underinvestment is rewarded with an increase in either the stock price, or in managers' personal reputations.

The model of Bebchuk and Stole (1993) also shares the general idea that a concern with near-term stock prices or reputation can lead to investment distortions. However, they point out that the nature of the investment distortion can be quite sensitive to the information structure. In particular, a desire to impress the stock market or the labor market in the short run can in some circumstances lead to overinvestment, rather than underinvestment. This will happen if, for example, the act of investment itself is observable and the asymmetry of information instead has to do with managers' ability to generate good investment opportunities. Now, managers seeking to boost their reputations will want to invest more, rather than less.

The most basic empirical implications of short-termism models flow from the comparative-static proposition that investment distortions will be greatest when the concern with impressing the market is most pronounced. Thus, Stein (1988, 1989) suggests that underinvestment will be particularly acute when firms are either subject to takeover pressure, or are preparing to issue new equity; in either case, the fact that shares will actually be sold at the current market price makes maximizing this price more of a pressing concern to managers. In a similar vein, Gompers (1996) and Baker (2000) argue that young venture capital firms – who do not yet have well-established track records, and who must boost their reputations if they are to attract more capital – are more likely than older venture firms to take distortionary actions to enhance their near-term performance.

2.2.2.2. Herding. Another manifestation of managers' career concerns is that they may exhibit an excessive tendency to "herd" in their investment decisions, with any given manager ignoring his own private information about payoffs, and blindly copying the decisions of previous movers. Scharfstein and Stein (1990) show how the herding incentive can arise in a reputation-based model. They assume that "smart" agents receive signals about future payoffs that are informative, but that contain a common

---

[16] In Stein (1989), managers maximize a weighted average of near-term stock prices and long-run value. Thus, although the modeling apparatus is taken from Holmström (1999a), the conflict of interest is not the classic agency conflict between managers and their principals, but rather one between short-term and long-term stockholders. Other models of underinvestment with a similar structure include Miller and Rock (1985) and Stein (1988). Bizjak, Brickley and Coles (1993) explore some of the implications of this framework for the design of optimal managment compensation schemes.

error component. In contrast, "dumb" agents receive signals that are uncorrelated noise. This information structure has the property that, holding fixed the absolute payoff to an agent's investment choice, the labor market should rationally infer that he is more likely to be smart if his choice was the same as that of other agents. This form of endogenous relative performance evaluation generates an incentive for all agents to mimic each other, regardless of their actual signals. [17]

As with short-termism models, one way to generate empirical predictions from reputational herding models is to think about cross-sectional variation in managers' incentives to boost their reputations. For example, one might posit that younger managers with less of a track record have more to gain from trying to manipulate the labor market's assessment of their ability. [18] If so, it follows that there should be more herd-like behavior among young managers than among older managers.

2.2.2.3. Other distortions induced by career concerns. As the above discussion suggests, models of career concerns can deliver a wide range of outcomes, depending on the specific assumptions that are made about information structure, etc. Holmström and Ricart i Costa (1986) demonstrate that career concerns may induce a general reluctance on the part of managers to undertake new investment projects. This is because the performance of a new project will reveal information about managerial ability; in contrast, if no project is undertaken, no information is revealed. If managers are risk-averse, they will prefer to avoid the variation in wages that accompanies any labor-market updating about their ability. Hirshleifer and Thakor (1992) build a related model of excessive conservatism in which reputational considerations lead managers to favor safe projects over riskier ones.

Career concerns can also come into play when the decision at hand is not whether to initiate a new project, but rather, whether to kill an existing one. Boot (1992) and Baker (2000) both argue that managers may be reluctant to either liquidate or divest poorly-performing lines of business, for fear that such actions will be interpreted as an admission of failure on their part.

2.2.3. The quiet life

Although empire-building and career-concerns theories have probably received the most attention, there are other variations on the classic manager–shareholder agency conflict that also have implications for investment. A recent paper by Bertrand and Mullainathan (2003) considers an especially simple variant: managers prefer the "quiet

---

[17] Zwiebel (1995) builds a related model of reputational herding. Given his setup, herding requires managerial risk aversion, unlike in Scharfstein and Stein (1990). See also Trueman (1994) on herding among security analysts. By contrast, Banerjee (1992) and Bikhchandani, Hirshleifer and Welch (1992) generate herding without appealing to agency considerations.

[18] For a more detailed analysis of how herding incentives can vary over the course of an agent's career, see Prendergast and Stole (1996) and Avery and Chevalier (1999).

life", and thus are prone to excessive inertia when it comes to making tough decisions. On the one hand, this can lead to something that looks much like empire-building overinvestment, if the decision at hand is whether to shut down an existing, poorly-performing plant. On the other hand, it can also lead to underinvestment if the decision concerns whether to enter a new line of business. [19]

2.2.4. Overconfidence

A final – and potentially very promising – agency theory of investment builds on the premise that managers are likely to be overly optimistic about the prospects of those assets that are under their control. That such overconfidence exists at the individual level has been repeatedly established in the psychology literature. [20] Moreover, unlike in the asset-pricing arena, one cannot easily appeal to arbitrage considerations to argue that the effects of individual-level overconfidence will not show up in aggregate corporate investment.

Roll (1986) is one of the first papers to explicitly introduce overconfidence into a corporate-finance context. [21] Roll argues that managerial "hubris" can explain a particular form of overinvestment, namely overpayment by acquiring firms in takeovers, but his general logic would seem to carry over to other forms of investment as well. Malmendier and Tate (2002a) provide evidence consistent with Roll's theory.

More recently, Heaton (2002) demonstrates that an overconfidence model can deliver not only a broad tendency towards overinvestment, but also many of the liquidity-constraints-type patterns associated with the costly-external finance models reviewed in Section 2.1. Heaton's insight is that when managers make overly optimistic assessments of their firms' prospects, they will be reluctant to issue new equity, as the stock price will often seem unfairly low to them. This leads to very much the same conclusions as in Myers–Majluf (1984) – there will be little external equity financing, and investment will increase with internal resources. [22] Thus, an assumption of overconfidence can be an alternative and relatively parsimonious way to generate a reduced form that looks very much like the unified empire-building/costly-external-finance model summarized in Equation (3). This idea is explored empirically by Malmendier and Tate (2002b).

One reason for taking overconfidence seriously in a corporate-finance setting is that, compared to other agency problems, it is likely to be relatively impervious to some of the obvious remedies. This is because overconfident managers will think that they

---

[19] Aggarwal and Samwick (1999) build a model in which underinvestment is a result of managerial laziness.

[20] See, e.g., Weinstein (1980).

[21] See also Cooper, Woo and Dunkelberg (1988) and Bernardo and Welch (2001) on the subject of entrepreneurial overconfidence.

[22] In contrast, one weakness of pure empire-building models is that they have a hard time explaining why managers – disregarding shareholders' preferences – don't simply issue large amounts of external equity so that they can grow their empires faster.

are acting benevolently on behalf of shareholders, even though from the perspective of objective outsiders their decisions may destroy value. As a result, the distortions associated with overconfidence cannot be easily resolved by, e.g., giving managers higher-powered incentive contracts.

2.3. Investment decisions when stock prices deviate from fundamentals

All of the theories discussed to this point share the common premise that financial markets are informationally efficient – i.e., that the prices of debt and equity accurately reflect fundamental values – even if individual managers are prone to making mistakes, as in Roll (1986) and Heaton (2002). However, a growing body of work in behavioral finance [surveyed in Shleifer (2000)] suggests that one might wish to view this market-efficiency premise with some skepticism. If so, the relevant question for our purposes is how the presence of non-fundamental noise in asset prices might influence the behavior of corporate investment, and thereby alter some of the conclusions offered above. Although this topic is beginning to generate some interest among finance researchers, the existing literature on it is quite small. So I will just briefly mention a few of the most prominent themes.

First, a market-inefficiency perspective can potentially shed light on the empirical relationship between stock prices and investment, which has been studied in a number of papers, including Fischer and Merton (1984), Barro (1990), Morck, Shleifer and Vishny (1990a) and Blanchard, Rhee and Summers (1993). According to traditional efficient-market theories, one should expect to see a strong association between Tobin's (1969) q and firm investment, since q is a summary statistic for the market's information about investment opportunities. Although there is certainly a significant positive relationship in the data, this relationship (after controlling for fundamentals like firm profitability) has been characterized by some as relatively limited in economic terms – e.g., Morck, Shleifer and Vishny argue that the stock market is something of a sideshow in terms of its influence on investment. Such a sideshow outcome can be easily rationalized in the context of an inefficient market, to the extent that managers are relatively rational and far-sighted, and therefore do not let investment respond to noise in stock prices.

Second, and perhaps more interestingly, market inefficiencies can interact with some of the other financing frictions discussed above to produce a variety of cross-sectional and time-series patterns in investment. For example, Stein (1996) hypothesizes that firms that are heavily dependent on external equity (i.e., those that are growing fast relative to their retained earnings, and that have little debt capacity) will have investment that is more sensitive to non-fundamental variations in stock prices than firms that have plenty of cash on hand. Intuitively, when stock prices are below fundamental values, rational managers of equity-dependent firms are very reluctant to invest, because for them investment requires the issuance of stock at a too-low price. This is effectively the same mechanism as in the Myers–Majluf (1984) model, but now it works with a vengeance. In contrast, when stock prices are above fundamental values, the problems identified by Myers and Majluf go away, and equity-dependent firms find it more attractive to issue new shares and invest.[23] In this story, the stock market may well be a sideshow for some firms – those with ample cash or debt capacity – but it is a much more important determinant of investment for the subset of equity-dependent firms. Baker, Stein and Wurgler (2003) provide evidence supportive of this prediction.

Finally, Shleifer and Vishny (2003) argue that stock-market inefficiencies may explain a variety of facts about mergers and acquisitions, such as the tendency for aggregate M&A activity to be clustered in periods when market prices are high relative to observable fundamentals. Their idea is that at such times, the manager of an overvalued firm would like to issue large amounts of equity, but needs an excuse for doing so – simply issuing stock and parking the proceeds in T-bills won't work. Given the adjustment costs associated with physical investment, a stock-for-stock acquisition of another less-overvalued firm may be the best way to go.

3. Evidence on investment at the firm level

3.1. Financial slack and investment

3.1.1. What we know: firms with more cash and less debt invest more

According to the Modigliani–Miller (1958) paradigm, a firm's investment should depend only on the profitability of its investment opportunities as measured, e.g., by its value of Tobin's (1969) q. Nothing else should matter: not the firm's mix of debt and equity financing, nor its reserves of cash and securities, nor financial market "conditions", however defined. Perhaps the one clearest empirical finding emerging from research on investment over the last 15 or so years is that this theoretical proposition is false. In fact, controlling for investment opportunities, firms with more cash on hand invest more, as do firms with lower debt burdens.

The literature that establishes these results is by now very large, and includes important contributions by Meyer and Kuh (1957), Fazzari, Hubbard and Petersen (1988), Hoshi, Kashyap and Scharfstein (1991), Whited (1992), Schaller (1993), Bond and Meghir (1994), Calomiris and Hubbard (1995), Chirinko (1995), Gilchrist and Himmelberg (1995), Hubbard, Kashyap and Whited (1995) and Lang, Ofek and Stulz (1996). This work is surveyed in detail by Hubbard (1998), so I will confine myself to a few brief observations.

First, it is important to recognize that the evidence speaks to the effect of financial slack on a wide range of investments, not just expenditures on plant and equipment. These include investments in inventories [Carpenter, Fazzari and Petersen (1994),

---

[23] Many studies have documented that there is a strong positive link between stock prices and the propensity of firms to issue equity. See Baker and Wurgler (2002) for a recent treatment and further references.

Kashyap, Lamont and Stein (1994)], in R&D [Hall (1992), Himmelberg and Petersen (1994)], in pricing for market share [Chevalier (1995a,b), Chevalier and Scharfstein (1995, 1996), Phillips (1995)], and in labor hoarding during recessions [Sharpe (1994)].

Second, taken as a whole, the literature has convincingly dealt with a fundamental endogeneity problem, namely that a firm's cash position or its debt level may contain information about its investment opportunities. For example, firms will tend to accumulate cash when they are abnormally profitable, and high profitability may be an indicator that marginal q (which is hard to measure accurately) is high as well.[24] Or firms may take on debt precisely at those times when they plan to cut investment, so that it can be tricky to infer causality from, e.g., the finding that dramatic increases in leverage are associated with sharply reduced investment [Kaplan (1989)].

Different papers have addressed this endogeneity problem in different ways, and there has been some debate as to the merits of various approaches to identification. But at this point, even a skeptic would have to concede that the case has been made. Perhaps the cleanest evidence comes from a series of "natural experiments" which isolate shocks to firms' financial positions that appear obviously unrelated to (at least a subset of) their investment opportunities. For example, Blanchard, Lopez-de-Silanes and Shleifer (1994) show that firms' acquisition activity responds to large cash windfalls coming from legal settlements unrelated to their ongoing lines of business. Peek and Rosengren (1997) document that declines in the Japanese stock market lead to reductions in the USA-lending-market share of USA branches of Japanese banks, with these reductions being larger for banks with weaker balance sheets. Similarly, Froot and O'Connell (1997) find that reinsurance companies cut back on their supply of earthquake insurance after large hurricanes impair their capital positions.[25]

A related natural-experiment approach to identification, pioneered by Lamont (1997), involves looking at how investment in one division of a firm responds to shocks originating in another, ostensibly unrelated division. As has been found by Lamont (1997), Lang, Ofek and Stulz (1996), Houston, James and Marcus (1997), Shin and Stulz (1998) among others, increases in cashflow or decreases in leverage attributable to one of a firm's divisions translate into significant increases in the investment of other divisions. As these papers ultimately speak more to the topic of the second part of this essay–within-firm investment allocation – I defer a more complete discussion of them until later. For the time being, suffice it to say that they represent one more nail in the coffin of the Modigliani–Miller null hypothesis that a firm's investment is unrelated to its liquidity position or its leverage ratio.

---

[24] See Erickson and Whited (2000) for a recent analysis of the biases arising from measurement errors in q.

[25] Other work that can arguably be thought of in this natural-experiment spirit includes Froot and Stein (1991) and Calomiris and Hubbard (1995).

3.1.2. What we don't know: why firms with more cash and less debt invest more

While it is becoming very hard to argue with the proposition that financial slack matters for investment, it is much less clear what the precise mechanism is that drives this relationship. Most of the empirical findings discussed above can be loosely understood in the context of Equation (3), which nests both the empire-building and costly-external-finance models, and which contains the latter as a special case (where $\gamma = 0$). Consequently, these findings do not for the most part allow one to sharply discriminate between the two.[26]

Indeed, given that the models can be so naturally nested, it is not even clear that it is a sensible goal to try to universally reject one in favor of the other. The only way to do so would be to establish that $\gamma = 0$ always, i.e., that managers never seek to empire-build. As is discussed in more detail below, there is a variety of other evidence that appears to directly contradict this hypothesis. And if it is the case that $\gamma > 0$, then the unified empire-building/costly-external-finance model in Equation (3) admits either over- or underinvestment, and a more interesting question to ask is simply this: as an empirical matter, which distortion is more prevalent?

On this point, some helpful evidence is provided by McConnell and Muscarella (1985). They look at how the stock market responded to firms' announcements of new capital expenditures during the period 1975–81. In most cases, the market reaction was positive.[27] However, in the oil industry – in which, according to Jensen (1986), there was systematic overinvestment during the sample period – the market reaction to new investment was negative. A simple and appealing interpretation of these findings is that the unified model with both empire-building and financing constraints is the right one, and that in many, but not all cases, the parameters line up in such a way that the typical firm is in the underinvestment region, where the net present value (NPV) of the marginal investment is positive.[28]

Unfortunately, the full story for why investment is related to financial slack is likely to be somewhat more complicated. Kaplan and Zingales (2000) point to the case of Microsoft, which over the period 1986–1997, had a very high sensitivity of investment to cashflow. On the one hand, given Microsoft's extraordinarily strong financial position – no debt and almost $9 billion in cash on hand in 1997 – this underscores Kaplan and Zingales' (1997) warning that one cannot assume that high values of dI/dw are necessarily indicative of tightly binding financing constraints.[29]

---

[26] It should be noted that on this point, my reading of the literature differs from that of Hubbard (1998). Hubbard interprets the evidence almost entirely in terms of models of costly external finance, and concludes that: "the free cash flow (empire-building) story does not appear to explain the link between net worth and investment ..." (p. 214).

[27] As discussed below, the stock market often seems more skeptical about another form of corporate investment – mergers and acquisitions.

[28] Alternatively, one could say the same thing about Heaton's (2002) overconfidence model, since, as argued above, it delivers a reduced form similar to that in Equation (3).

[29] See also Cleary (1999) and Almeida and Campello (2001) for more on this point.

But the puzzle goes deeper than this. In light of the high level of inside ownership (by Bill Gates and other top managers) it is also hard to believe that the high investment–cashflow correlation is telling us that Microsoft is a worst-case example of the traditional agency/empire-building effect. One is thus tempted to conclude that even if the unified model in Equation (3) describes a good part of what is going on, there must be something else at work in the data as well.

3.2. Direct evidence of agency-related overinvestment

While much of the evidence discussed above – on the correlation between investment and measures of financial slack – does not speak to the question of whether empire-building tendencies exert an important influence on investment, there are a variety of other studies that do. I now briefly review some of this work.

3.2.1. Acquisitions as a form of empire-building

There are a number of studies that suggest that acquiring firms often overpay when buying other companies. For example, in many deals, the acquiror's stock price falls upon announcement of the transaction [see Roll (1986) for references to this work]. Moreover, it appears that the tendency towards this particular form of overinvestment is linked to agency conflicts. Lewellen, Loderer and Rosenfeld (1985) document that negative announcement effects are most pronounced for those acquirors where management has a small equity stake. Similarly, Lang, Stulz and Walkling (1991) find that negative announcement effects are stronger when the acquiror has a low value of q and relatively high cashflows – precisely the configuration of excess cashflow relative to investment opportunities that, according to Jensen (1986), exacerbates empire-building overinvestment. And Morck, Shleifer and Vishny (1990b) find more negative announcement effects when acquirors are engaging in unrelated diversification. As noted above, unrelated diversification represents a type of merger for which there is a natural presumption of an agency motivation, with managers seeking to build not only larger, but more stable empires. [30]

Blanchard, Lopez-de-Silanes and Shleifer (1994) look at how a small sample of firms respond to large cash windfalls coming from legal settlements. The firms in their sample have for the most part very poor investment opportunities as measured by low values of q. Yet rather than turning over the windfalls to their shareholders, they typically spend the cash on acquisitions, in many cases on deals that represent unrelated diversification. This is a clear-cut violation of the Modigliani–Miller theorem – exogenous cash shocks have a big impact on investment – and it also seems very consistent with an empire-building view of the world. But just to restate a point stressed above: while this sort of evidence goes a long way toward rejecting the hypothesis that

---

[30] See Section 6 below for more about empirical work on unrelated diversification.

$\gamma = 0$, it does not imply that, across the entire universe of firms, the dominant problem is one of overinvestment. It is quite possible that, were firms with high values of q and scarce internal resources to receive similar windfalls, they would spend them on value-creating investment in their own line of business, as suggested by models of costly external finance.[31]

3.2.2. Is agency-related overinvestment always empire-building?

Although it has become commonplace in the literature to associate overinvestment with the specific mechanism of empire-building, there are, as noted above, other agency effects that can also give rise to overinvestment under some circumstances. Bertrand and Mullainathan (2003) argue that a managerial preference for the "quiet life" – effectively, a resistance to change – can lead to excessive continuation of existing negative-NPV projects. Consistent with this hypothesis, and in contrast to a naive empire-building story, they find that when discipline on managers (in the form of takeover pressure) decreases, firms are less likely to shut down old plants, but also less likely to build new ones. In a somewhat similar vein, Baker (2000) builds a model in which reputational concerns deter managers from discontinuing negative-NPV projects, as this would be an admission of failure. He then finds evidence which suggests that the youngest venture-capital firms – who are presumably the most concerned about reputation-building – are also the most reluctant to liquidate bad investments.

3.3. Evidence on reputational models of investment

3.3.1. Short-termism

Short-termism models such as that of Stein (1989) can be difficult to test directly. This is because their central prediction is that there will be underinvestment in *those types of activities that are not directly observable by the market.* For example, a firm may skimp on maintenance, advertising, worker training, etc., because the resulting cost savings are interpreted by investors not as reduced investment per se, but rather as increases in firm profitability. But to the extent that an econometrician's information set is no better than that of investors, this makes it difficult to actually document the underinvestment behavior explicitly.

Nevertheless, there is a good deal of circumstantial evidence consistent with the main comparative-static prediction of the theory, namely that underinvestment will be most pronounced in circumstances when managers are most concerned with hyping

---

[31] Indeed, Holtz-Eakin, Joulfaian and Rosen (1994) find evidence to just this effect: small businesses whose owners receive windfalls in the form of inheritances are more likely to survive, and to grow rapidly, than their peers.

their stock prices or labor-market reputations. Perhaps the best example comes from studies that examine the operating performance of firms around the time of equity offerings. A number of papers, including Hansen and Crutchley (1990), DeGeorge and Zeckhauser (1993) and Loughran and Ritter (1997) find that firms typically have abnormally strong operating performance relative to their peers in the year or two preceding an equity issue (either a seasoned issue or an IPO), and abnormally weak performance in the years after the issue. Although this is not definitive proof, it is exactly the pattern that one would expect to see if the desire to elevate the stock price at the time of the issue were leading managers to sacrifice long-run value for higher current profits. [32]

Also noteworthy is the work of Gompers (1996). He observes that for venture-capital firms, having the startup companies in their portfolio go public is often one of the most visible and credible signs of strong performance. He then documents that younger venture firms take their startups public at an earlier stage of their life-cycle than do older, more established venture firms. If there is an optimal time for startups to go public, and going too soon is therefore costly, this would represent another form of distortionary short-run performance boosting.

3.3.2. Herding

A number of recent papers provide evidence supportive of reputational herding models. For the most part, this evidence comes not from garden-variety corporate investment decisions, but rather from either: i) the investment choices of institutional investors; or ii) the recommendations of security analysts. In some of the work [Lakonishok, Shleifer and Vishny (1992), Grinblatt, Titman and Wermers (1995), Falkenstein (1996), Nofsinger and Sias (1999), Wermers (1999), Welch (2000)], the aim is simply to determine whether certain groups of agents look like they are herding – e.g., whether all money managers try to buy the same stocks at the same time – without relating this herding behavior to career concerns. However, there are also several papers that tie actions directly to measures of agents' reputations, thereby providing sharper tests of the reputational herding mechanism. Notable work in this latter category includes Stickel (1990), Ehrbeck and Waldmann (1996), Graham (1999), Chevalier and Ellison (1999), Hong, Kubik and Solomon (2000) and Lamont (2002).

The Chevalier–Ellison (1999) and Hong–Kubik–Solomon (2000) papers are especially interesting from a career-concerns perspective in that they both: i) identify the implicit labor-market incentives that agents face; and ii) show how these implicit incentives color behavior. For example, in their study of mutual fund managers, Chevalier and Ellison find that young managers (with presumably less well-established reputations) are more likely to be fired if their portfolio choices differ from those of their peers, *even after controlling for the absolute performance of these portfolios.* The

---

[32] See also Teoh, Welch and Wong (1998a,b) for closely related evidence.

result that, controlling for absolute performance, an agent is punished for a decision that differs from the herd, is precisely what is predicted by the model of Scharfstein and Stein (1990). Chevalier and Ellison then go on to show that consistent with the incentives they face, younger money managers are indeed less likely to take positions that differ from benchmark weightings. In a similar vein, Hong, Kubik and Solomon demonstrate that inexperienced security analysts are more likely to be fired for earnings forecasts that deviate from the consensus, controlling for forecast accuracy. And, in the face of these incentives, inexperienced analysts tend to issue earnings forecasts that are in fact closer to the consensus.

4. Macroeconomic implications

Thus far, I have been taking a very microeconomic perspective on corporate investment, focusing on the extent to which information or agency problems can lead a single firm's investment to deviate from its first-best value. But the work surveyed thus far has important and far-reaching macroeconomic implications as well. Unfortunately, giving a complete and satisfactory treatment of these macro implications – which are fleshed out in a what has become a very large literature in its own right – would take me well outside the scope of this essay. So what follows is intended to be only an extremely cursory and selective review.

4.1. The financial accelerator

Over the years, many macroeconomists, including Fisher (1933), Bernanke (1983) and Eckstein and Sinai (1986), have argued that financial-market imperfections can play an important role in propagating and amplifying business-cycle fluctuations. More recently, researchers have begun explicitly embedding financing frictions of the sort discussed in Section 2 into formal macro models. One of the first and most significant papers in this genre is Bernanke and Gertler (1989). Using an adaptation of Townsend's (1979) costly-state-verification model, they show how economy-wide movements in firms' internal resources can be a source of output dynamics. In particular, an initial positive shock to the economy improves firms' profits and retained earnings; this in turn leads to increased investment and output, which amplifies the upturn, and so forth. A converse effect plays out during recessions.

Kiyotaki and Moore (1997) add a substantial kick to the Bernanke–Gertler story by noting that movements in asset values – as opposed to just cashflows – can also exert a strong influence on firms' ability to fund their investments. In the language of the heuristic model sketched above, Kiyotaki and Moore would say that a firm's internal resources w can be a function of asset prices, if, for example, the firm owns substantial amounts of land. In such a scenario, an initial positive shock is further amplified by an increase in land prices, which then feeds back into more investment and output, further increases in land prices, and so on. There is also now an added intertemporal ingredient, as land prices respond not only to current movements in output, but also to expectations of future movements.

The large body of work in this "financial-accelerator" genre is surveyed by, among others, Bernanke, Gertler and Gilchrist (1996, 1999). One point worth noting is that in most cases, the financing imperfections considered in the macro literature are ones that fit in the costly-external finance genre – i.e., that have reduced forms similar to that given in Equation (2) – while empire-building tendencies have been given less attention. Nevertheless, it is unlikely that adding empire building into the macro models would dramatically change their most basic *positive* implications. After all, whether or not one allows for $\gamma > 0$, the link between investment and financial slack – which is the mechanism at the heart of the macro models – is much the same.

What would probably change with the addition of empire-building preferences, however, are the *welfare* implications of the macro models. For example, one might imagine that there could be a silver-lining aspect to recessions, to the extent that they lead certain firms to curtail wasteful overinvestment. [33]

4.2. When banks face financing frictions

The same external-financing frictions which make life difficult for non-financial firms are also likely to affect banks. This observation underlies recent research in two related areas: on the effects of "capital crunches" in banking; and on the so-called "bank lending channel" of monetary-policy transmission.

4.2.1. Capital crunches in banking

Suppose that banks in a particular region are heavily exposed to local real estate, and that land prices crash, leading to large loan losses and depleted equity capital for the banks. What happens to their subsequent ability to make new loans? Clearly, it depends on the extent to which they are able to promptly rebuild their capital bases with new equity issues. If, for example, banks face the sort of adverse-selection problems in the equity market described by Myers and Majluf (1984), it may take a while to repair their balance sheets, and in the meantime, their lending may be sharply reduced, with attendant effects on their borrowers' investment, the regional economy, etc. This would be a classic example of a bank capital crunch.

This mechanism is at the heart of Bernanke's (1983) account of the Great Depression. More recently, research interest in bank capital crunches surged in the early 1990s, in the wake of widespread capital-adequacy problems in the USA banking industry, and has continued to draw motivation from episodes like the Asian financial crises of the late 1990s. Among the many empirical papers on the topic are Bernanke

---

[33] Loosely speaking, such a silver lining can arise if, in a recession, firms' cashflows decline *relative* to the rate at which their positive-NPV investment opportunities dry up.

and Lown (1991) and Peek and Rosengren (1995, 1997). Holmström and Tirole (1997) build a formal theoretical model of a capital crunch.

4.2.2. The bank lending channel of monetary policy transmission

As developed by Bernanke and Blinder (1988) and Stein (1998), the idea behind the bank lending channel is that central bank open-market operations have independent consequences for the supply of loans by banks – and hence for the investment of bank-dependent firms – above and beyond any impact due to standard "money channel" increases in bond-market rates of interest. The logic goes as follows. When the central bank drains reserves from the banking system, this obviously compromises banks' ability to raise money with *reservable* sources of financing, such as insured deposits. In a Modigliani–Miller world, this shock to the liability side of banks' balance sheets would have no independent effect on lending, since a bank losing a dollar of insured deposits could simply offset this by raising a dollar of nonreservable uninsured debt finance, e.g., by issuing commercial paper, or medium-term notes.

However, if banks are subject to adverse-selection problems, they will have difficulty replacing insured deposits with these other forms of uninsured debt finance, since the latter expose investors to default risk. As a result, contractionary open-market operations which shrink banks' deposit bases ultimately translate into declines in bank lending, and in turn into reductions in the investment of those non-financial firms that depend on banks.

A wide variety of evidence consistent with these ideas is documented by, among others, Bernanke and Blinder (1992), Kashyap, Stein and Wilcox (1993), Kashyap and Stein (1995, 2000), Ludvigson (1998), Morgan (1998) and Kishan and Opiela (2000). More complete surveys include Kashyap and Stein (1994), Bernanke and Gertler (1995), Cecchetti (1995) and Hubbard (1995).

4.3. Cross-country differences in financial development, investment and growth

Implicit in many of the theories discussed in Section 2 above is the idea that the efficiency of corporate investment is ultimately a function of institutional factors such as: the quality of auditing and disclosure; and the degree to which the legal and regulatory system enforces contracts and otherwise protects outside investors from abuse by managers. For example, in the context of an adverse-selection model, one would predict that better accounting standards and more timely disclosure would reduce the information asymmetry between managers and outsiders, and thus free up the flow of external finance to positive-NPV projects.

Alternatively, note that models such as Bolton and Scharfstein (1990) and Hart and Moore (1998) – in which managers can simply steal all of a firm's operating cashflows because these cashflows cannot be verified in a court of law – correspond to an extremely weak auditing/contract-enforcement technology. Thus, taken literally, these models might be most appropriate for thinking about firms in economies where the legal system offers investors very little in the way of protection from managerial misbehavior. Again, the obvious prediction that follows from this observation is that raising external finance for good projects ought to be easier when investors are better protected.

A natural way to test such propositions empirically is with cross-country comparisons. LaPorta et al. (1997, 1998) show that there is indeed substantial variation across countries in measures of legal protection and accounting standards. They also establish the key link between these institutional factors and "financial development", demonstrating that countries which score better on their legal and accounting criteria also have more extensively developed debt and equity markets.

Having established this link, the next important empirical question becomes: what are the consequences of such financial development for investment? The answer, which is beginning to emerge convincingly in a series of recent papers, is that financial development seems to be quite important for real activity.[34] In particular, King and Levine (1993) and Levine and Zervos (1998) find that the predetermined component of a country's financial development is a strong predictor of its future growth, capital accumulation and productivity improvements.

More detail on the mechanisms by which financial development exerts these beneficial effects is provided by Rajan and Zingales (1998), Demirguc-Kunt and Maksimovic (1998) and Wurgler (2000). The first two papers show that countries with more developed financial systems do a better job of channeling funds to, and promoting the growth of, externally-dependent industries and firms – i.e., those with strong investment opportunities but scarce internal resources. In a similar vein, Wurgler (2000) finds that in countries with more developed financial markets, investment is more sensitive to measures of the quality of investment opportunities, such as value-added. Thus overall, financial development seems to help growth in just the way that the theory would lead one to expect: by relaxing external financing constraints, and thereby allowing capital to flow to the best investment projects.

Part B. Investment inside firms

5. Theoretical work on internal capital allocation

I now turn to the topic of within-firm capital allocation, beginning with the theoretical work in this area. To organize the discussion, I first give an overview of the primitive differences between internal and external capital markets, focusing heavily on the control rights held by the provider of finance in either case. I then go on to examine

---

[34] See Levine (1997) for a more complete survey. Earlier work hypothesizing a causal relationship between financial development and growth includes Schumpeter (1911), Goldsmith (1969), McKinnon (1973) and Shaw (1973).

in more detail the specific implications of these differences for the efficiency of within-firm investment outcomes. Finally, I very briefly touch on a related literature, that which seeks to explain observed capital budgeting practices by appealing to information and agency problems inside firms.

5.1. Fundamental differences between internal and external capital markets

Consider a particular line of business, denoted by $B1$, which has both assets in place, as well as future investment opportunities. $B1$ is run by manager $M1$, who, in the spirit of much of the work surveyed in Section 2, may both have empire-building tendencies (i.e., may derive private benefits from the assets under his control), as well as private information about the value of either the assets in place or the future investment opportunities. $B1$ can be financed as a stand-alone entity in the external capital market – in which case it goes to, e.g., a bank, a venture capitalist, or the public debt or equity market – or it can be financed in an internal capital market. In the internal market, $M1$ always approaches the CEO of the parent firm for funding.

5.1.1. Simplest case: a benevolent CEO overseeing just one division

Let us begin with the simplest possible case, in which the CEO acts benevolently on behalf of her ultimate shareholders (so that the only agency problem is that between $M1$ and the CEO) and in which $B1$ is the only division reporting to the CEO. How do the workings of the internal capital market differ in this case from those of the external capital market?

A first observation is that when $M1$ deals with the CEO, he is dealing with a single centralized provider of finance, as opposed to a (possibly) large group of investors, such as in the public debt or equity market. Standard free-riding arguments therefore suggest that the CEO might be expected to devote more effort to monitoring, i.e., to uncovering information about either $B1$'s current performance or future prospects. This would be a benefit of internal capital allocation. On the other hand, as has been pointed out by Dewatripont and Maskin (1995), Bolton and Scharfstein (1996) and others, there is also a potential downside to centralized finance and the accompanying lack of free-riding. In particular, the CEO's inability to precommit not to renegotiate with $M1$ can lead to a "soft budget constraint" whereby projects are not liquidated even following poor managerial performance; this in turn weakens ex ante incentives for $M1$.

While the centralized-finance aspect of an internal capital market is important, it is at best only a part of the story. After all, if one focuses only on the degree of centralization, there is no distinction between $M1$ approaching the CEO of his firm and, say, a single bank lender, or a single venture capitalist. Motivated by this observation, Gertner, Scharfstein and Stein (1994) argue that what distinguishes the CEO from these other centralized providers of finance is that the CEO has total and unconditional control rights in the sense of GHM [short for Grossman and Hart (1986), Hart and

Moore (1990) and Hart (1995)]. That is, the CEO can unilaterally decide what to do with $B1$'s physical assets, while the same is not true of a banker if the firm is not currently in default.

Gertner, Scharfstein and Stein (1994) argue that these strong control rights have two consequences. First, the CEO will have greater monitoring incentives than even other centralized providers of finance; that is, control and monitoring are complements. This is because when the monitor (i.e., the CEO) also has control rights, she can ensure that any value-enhancing ideas that occur to her in the course of monitoring are implemented, something which a financier without control rights cannot do. For example, suppose that the CEO decides that some of $B1$'s assets should be reconfigured, or put to different uses. With full control rights over these assets, she can implement such a restructuring directly. In contrast, a bank lender making the same judgement cannot (outside of default) do anything with $B1$'s assets; the bank is limited to just making suggestions that $M1$ may or may not want to take up. As a result, the bank has less incentive to invest in learning about the business in the first place. This formalizes an old line of argument, due to Alchian (1969) and Williamson (1975), that the internal capital market brings a higher quality of information to bear on decisions than the external market.

Second, however, a direct application of the GHM logic suggests that there will also be an offsetting cost of the CEO's strong control rights. The presence of the CEO on top of him in the chain of command is likely to blunt $M1$'s entrepreneurial incentives, i.e., to discourage him from taking a variety of costly but non-contractible actions that raise the overall value of the business. This point is also made by Aghion and Tirole (1997). [35]

5.1.2. More interesting case: a benevolent CEO overseeing multiple divisions

The case in which the CEO oversees only one division is a helpful starting point in thinking about the fundamental differences in control rights between the internal and external markets. But this case obviously does not leave much room for thinking about within-firm capital reallocations per se. So the next step is to consider a situation in which the CEO oversees multiple lines of business, each with their own managers.

Stein (1997) argues that, in this case, the key distinction between the CEO and a banker is that the CEO has greater scope to redistribute resources across the lines of business. To be concrete, suppose that there are now two businesses, $B1$ and $B2$, each of which has adequate collateral/pledgeable income to raise one unit of financing on its own. A CEO who controls both businesses can, if she wants, raise two units of

---

[35] Aghion and Tirole (1997) further explain why a manager reporting to a CEO is more likely to be discouraged than one reporting directly to outside shareholders. Although diffuse shareholders also have complete control rights in a formal (i.e., legal) sense, their de facto control is likely to be much weaker than a CEO's, since they are less well-informed. See also Burkart, Gromb and Panunzi (1997) for a similar argument.

financing against the combined collateral, and give both units to $B1$. In other words, the CEO can engage in a strong form of winner-picking.[36] Note that if the two businesses were separate entities borrowing from a bank, the bank could not impose the same outcome – if it tried to hold $B2$ to a zero allocation, $M2$ would be free to go to another bank and seek a better offer. In contrast, the CEO's control rights enable it to keep $M2$ from seeking competing financing offers. After all, the CEO "owns" the assets of $B2$ and can thus forbid $M2$ to use these assets as collateral in a transaction that the CEO does not approve of. This idea builds on Hart and Moore's (1990, p. 1121) observation that "... the sole right possessed by an owner of an asset is his ability to exclude others from the use of that asset".

Whether the CEO ultimately uses her reallocative authority to good or bad ends is of course the central question to be addressed here. There are arguments on either side, and I take these up momentarily. But first, note that the very existence of this authority can also have further incentive effects – either positive or negative – above and beyond any direct consequences for ex post investment efficiency. On the negative side, as emphasized by Milgrom (1988), Milgrom and Roberts (1988) and Meyer, Milgrom and Roberts (1992), division managers may engage in wasteful influence activities in an effort to convince the CEO to give them a larger share of the capital budget. Alternatively, Brusco and Panunzi (2000) argue that the potential threat of reallocation away from, say, $M2$ can weaken his incentives. For if he is not sure he will get to reinvest all of the profits generated by his line of business – because they might get steered to $B1$ instead – he will not want to work as hard to create such profits in the first place.[37]

In contrast, Stein (2002) argues that the CEO's reallocative authority may also have positive ex ante effects. To the extent that their desire to convince the CEO to grant them a larger share of the firm's capital budget leads division managers to act as honest advocates, and to produce additional legitimate "hard" (i.e., verifiable) information about project prospects, overall efficiency can in some circumstances be enhanced.[38]

5.1.3. The CEO is herself an agent

A final and very important aspect of internal capital allocation is that the party making the allocation decisions (the CEO) is herself an agent of outside shareholders, so

---

[36] A distinct point, due to Gertner, Scharfstein and Stein (1994), is that a CEO overseeing two related lines of business can, when $B1$ is in trouble, combine its assets with those of $B2$, and put $M2$ in charge of everything – a form of internal restructuring that cannot be as simply accomplished by a bank lending to two separate firms.

[37] See also Rotemberg and Saloner (1994) and Inderst and Laux (2000) for somewhat related analyses.

[38] But this advocacy mechanism is a delicate one: the private returns to division managers from producing hard information – and thereby possibly increasing their capital budgets – are potentially much greater than the social returns, so there is the danger that they waste too much time on this activity.

that one cannot simply assume that she will act benevolently on their behalf. Thus, a complete model of the within-firm allocation process should incorporate at least two layers of agency – one between the CEO and shareholders, and one between the division managers and the CEO.

This two-tiered agency feature is not unique to models of internal capital allocation; consider for example Diamond's (1984) well-known model of a bank, which explicitly recognizes the agency problem between the bank and its ultimate investors.[39] But, as will become clear below, the ultimate effect of the top-level agency problem between the principals and the "supervisor" (i.e., either the bank, or the CEO) can depend crucially on the structure of control rights in the lower-level agency relationship. For example, in Diamond's model – in which the bank does not have the authority to take all the money away from some of its clients in order to give it to others – diversification across multiple projects emerges as a device which is helpful in mitigating the top-level agency problem. In contrast, in an internal capital market, where the CEO has much broader reallocative authority, diversification can in some cases actually exacerbate top-level agency problems [Scharfstein and Stein (2000)].

5.2. Implications for the efficiency of capital allocation

The literature has identified several mechanisms by which the allocation of investment funds in an internal capital market can lead to either increases or reductions in efficiency, as compared to an external-capital-markets benchmark. I consider the bright and dark sides of internal capital markets in turn.

5.2.1. The bright side of internal capital markets

Absent any direct operating synergies, there are two basic financing-related ways that value can be created by bringing together multiple business under the roof of a single parent company. First, integration of this sort may allow *more* total external financing to be raised than could be raised by the individual businesses operating as stand-alones; this "more-money" effect is beneficial if there is an underinvestment problem on average. Second, an internal capital market may do a better job of allocating *a given amount* of funding across projects, which one might call a "smarter-money" effect.

With respect to the more-money effect, Lewellen (1971) argues that coinsurance across imperfectly correlated divisions increases the debt capacity of integrated firms.[40] However, Berger and Ofek (1995) and Comment and Jarrell (1995) cast doubt on the importance of this story by documenting that, empirically, integrated firms

---

[39] There are also other multi-tier agency models – Tirole (1986) is an early example – which do not focus on capital allocation issues.

[40] Inderst and Muller (2003) provide a modern treatment of this and related issues, showing how the existence of an internal capital market shapes the nature of the optimal financial contract between a firm and its outside investors.

borrow only a trivial amount more than their stand-alone counterparts. Alternatively, Hadlock, Ryngaert and Thomas (2001) build a model in which diversification – by pooling risks and therefore reducing the variance of managers' inside information – helps to alleviate adverse-selection problems of the Myers–Majluf (1984) type in the external equity market.[41] In support of this hypothesis, they find that equity issues by diversified firms have a smaller price impact than equity issues by comparable stand-alone firms. Again, though, there is little direct evidence as to whether this ultimately translates into more external finance being raised by diversified firms.

The smarter-money effect has a long tradition and has been discussed by a number of authors, including Alchian (1969), Weston (1970), Williamson (1975) and Donaldson (1984). It is based on two related premises: first, that the CEO in an internal capital market will become relatively well-informed about the prospects of the firm's divisions; and second, that the CEO will use her high-quality information as the basis for making value-enhancing reallocations across divisions – i.e., will engage in active winner-picking. As discussed above, more recent theoretical treatments [e.g., Gertner, Scharfstein and Stein (1994), Li and Li (1996), Stein (1997) and Matsusaka and Nanda (2002)] explicitly link the performance of one or both of these functions – monitoring and winner-picking – to the strong control rights held by the CEO in an internal capital market.

Stein (1997) goes on to suggest that the CEO will be more likely to do a good job of winner-picking when the firm operates in related lines of business. The logic is one of relative performance evaluation: if the task is to most efficiently distribute a fixed amount of capital, it is not important to know the *absolute* merits of the competing investment projects, all that matters is their *relative* merits. And assessing relative value may be easier when comparing projects in related lines of business.

The smarter-money effect arises naturally in a setting where the CEO acts in the interests of outside shareholders. But it can also come through even when the CEO is self-interested. This point is emphasized by Stein (1997), who notes that CEO's with certain kinds of empire-building preferences (such as private benefits that are proportional to gross output) may actually have very good intrinsic incentives for doing intra-firm resource allocation – though they may want to do more total investment than their principals would like, their desire to have large and profitable empires can lead them to rank projects in the right order from the principals' perspective. Although one can think of counterexamples [e.g., a CEO who only wants to invest in projects which make use of her specific human capital, as in Shleifer and Vishny (1989)], the general conclusion to be taken away is that CEO self-interest, *taken alone,* is not necessarily inimical to efficient capital allocation.

---

[41] As a counterpoint to this idea, practitioners often argue that diversified firms have a harder time raising equity, because their complexity makes them difficult for investors to value accurately. See Nanda and Narayanan (1999).

5.2.2. The dark side of internal capital markets

Parallel to the discussion of its potential benefits, there are two broad ways in which an internal capital market can reduce value. First, if one believes that there is a general tendency towards overinvestment, then the more-money effect – the potential for integrated firms to have larger capital budgets than their stand-alone peers – is seen as a bad thing. Second, holding fixed the overall level of investment, there is the concern that the internal capital market does a worse job of allocating funds to individual divisions or projects.

Recent theoretical research has focused almost exclusively on the latter possibility, which makes sense, given the paucity of direct evidence to support the more-money hypothesis. This work, which includes Rajan, Servaes and Zingales (2000), Scharfstein and Stein (2000) and Wulf (1999), goes a level further down into the organization and stresses the agency conflict between division managers (i.e., $M1$ and $M2$ in our earlier notation) and the CEO as being a central part of the problem. Following the papers on influence activities by Milgrom (1988), Milgrom and Roberts (1988) and Meyer, Milgrom and Roberts (1992), division managers in these models are portrayed as rent-seeking agents who try to actively sway the CEO to give them more in the way of compensation, power, or resources.[42]

Although introducing rent-seeking at the division-manager level is a helpful step in building a model of inefficient within-firm capital allocations, it is by itself not sufficient. For example, in the model of Meyer, Milgrom and Roberts (1992), division managers try to influence the CEO to give them more capital by overstating their divisions' prospects, but the CEO rationally sees through the hype. The only inefficiency in the model is the fact that division managers waste their time and effort in the futile attempt to influence the CEO. Alternatively, think of models where division managers expend effort to increase their bargaining positions vis-a-vis the CEO, perhaps by building up their outside options, or by making it harder for a successor to take over their jobs [Shleifer and Vishny (1989), Edlin and Stiglitz (1995)]. Such models make it clear how rent-seeking division managers might be able to extract larger compensation packages from the CEO, but they do not say much about why the extra compensation comes in the form of increased capital allocations, as opposed to just cash.

Rajan, Servaes and Zingales (2000) address this why-distort-the-capital-budget question in a model in which the CEO acts on behalf of shareholders – i.e., where the only agency conflict is the lower-level one between the CEO and division managers. They argue that when divisions have different investment opportunities, the CEO will want to tilt the capital budget away from the efficient point, and towards a "socialist" outcome in which the weaker division gets relatively more than it would under the first-best. This is because in their setup, the technology is such that a more equal capital

---

[42] See also Bagwell and Zechner (1993) for an application of influence-cost ideas.

budget increases division managers' incentives to engage in cooperative, joint-surplus-maximizing behavior, as opposed to self-interested, rent-seeking forms of behavior.

Thus, loosely speaking, Rajan, Servaes and Zingales (2000) view the capital budget as a tool that the CEO, acting as a principal, uses in part to design a more effective incentive scheme to control division-manager rent-seeking. A similar observation can be made about Wulf (1999). Although her model works somewhat differently, it shares the feature that the CEO is a principal who uses capital allocation rules as part of an incentive scheme to make rent-seeking division managers behave better. [43]

In contrast, the key assumption in Scharfstein and Stein (2000) is that there are two levels of agency, with the CEO acting in her own private interests, rather than those of shareholders. In their framework, managers of weak divisions spend more effort building up their outside options, which in turn forces the CEO to compensate them more highly in order to retain them. If the CEO were herself the principal, she would pay this added compensation in the form of cash, and capital would still be allocated efficiently. But as an agent, she may view it as less personally costly to tilt the capital budget in the direction of the weaker division; this allows her to save the firm's cash to use for other, more privately attractive purposes. [44]

This model shares with Rajan, Servaes and Zingales (2000) the general implication of socialism in internal capital allocation, with weaker divisions being cross-subsidized by stronger ones. Moreover, both models also imply that problems will be most acute when the divisions in question have widely divergent investment opportunities (as measured, e.g., by industry q). The most obvious empirical distinction between the two is that Scharfstein and Stein (2000) predict that socialism will be most pronounced when the CEO has poorly aligned incentives, while Rajan, Servaes and Zingales (2000), who cast the CEO as a principal, make no such prediction.

5.2.3. Pulling it together: when are internal capital markets most likely to add value?

Rather than viewing the bright-side and dark-side models as competing directly with one another, a more fruitful way to synthesize the theoretical work in this area is to ask a cross-sectional question. Specifically: under what conditions is an internal capital market most (or least) likely to add value relative to an external capital markets benchmark?

First, an internal capital market should, all else equal, be more valuable in situations where the external capital market is underdeveloped, either because of weaknesses in the legal and contracting environment, inadequate accounting and disclosure practices,

---

[43] In this regard, these papers bear some similarity to Rotemberg (1993).

[44] This conclusion requires the assumption that the CEO has less ability to divert private benefits from the firm's capital budget than from spare cash. Alternatively, the CEO may prefer to compensate division managers with capital instead of higher salaries because, as in Stein (1989), this is a way of pumping up reported earnings and hence boosting either her bonus or the short-run value of her stock options.

etc. To see the logic most clearly, consider an extreme case where outside investors are so poorly protected that they are unwilling to put up any financing, and hence firms can only invest out of their retained earnings. In this case, an internal capital market represents the only way to move money from those lines of business that have surpluses relative to their investment needs to those in the opposite situation.[45]

Second, the dark-side theories reviewed above suggest that the internal capital market is most likely to run into problems when the firm's divisions have sharply divergent investment prospects. Third, these problems may be exacerbated when divisional managers both: i) have a strong incentive to maximize their own division's capital allocation as opposed to profits; and ii) are powerful relative to the CEO – i.e., have valuable specific human capital (either expertise or internal political clout), and so can threaten to disrupt the firm's activities.

As an example of the latter point, consider this bit of folklore about General Electric, which is widely viewed to be one of the most successful diversified conglomerates. GE apparently follows a policy of rotating its senior managers across different divisions on a regular basis. According to the logic above, there are two distinct potential benefits of such a policy. First, managers' incentives to lobby for a lot of capital in any given division will be reduced if they think that they will be leaving the division soon anyway. Second, a job-rotation policy may prevent managers from accumulating a great deal of specific expertise and political capital in a given division, thereby reducing their bargaining power relative to that of the CEO.

This discussion suggests a fundamental tradeoff in organizational design and capital allocation: that between expertise and parochialism. One way to see this tradeoff is to think of a CEO who has to allocate a fixed capital budget across four competing projects. The CEO's first option is to do the whole job herself – i.e., to assess each project and then make a decision. Alternatively, she might hire two division managers, each of whom would be given the responsibility of evaluating two of the four projects in more detail. In this hierarchical case, the CEO would make a division-level allocation to each of the two managers, and these managers would then choose how much to give to the individual projects within their divisions. The latter option has the obvious advantage of more total information production. But it also has the potential disadvantage that each division manager may be preoccupied with landing his division a larger share of the overall capital budget, with the adverse consequences discussed above. In contrast, in the case where the CEO makes all the decisions, there may be less total information brought to bear, but there is also less parochialism, because the CEO has a broader span of control and thus does not have a vested interest as to which division gets more capital.

---

[45] Hubbard and Palia (1999) use this reasoning to argue that the conglomerate mergers of the 1960s and 1970s in the USA made sense at the time that they were done, even though later it became optimal to undo them – there was a change in the environment, in that external capital markets became more developed over time.

5.3. How information and agency problems shape firms' capital budgeting practices

While I have been emphasizing how information and agency problems shape *investment outcomes* inside firms, there is a closely related literature that seeks to rationalize observed *capital budgeting practices* based on the same primitive frictions. A broad set of anecdotal and field-based evidence suggests that firms often do not follow the textbook prescription of allocating capital to projects based on a simple net-present-value (NPV) criterion; instead, they often rely at least in part on other methods, such as rationing capital to individual division managers, imposing payback requirements, and so forth.

These alternative capital budgeting practices can in many cases be understood by reference to the canonical model laid out above – one in which lower-level managers (e.g., division managers) have better information about project prospects than their superiors, but also have empire-building preferences, and hence cannot be relied on to truthfully report their private information. In such a setting, capital budgeting procedures can be thought of as part of a mechanism to elicit truthful revelation of this private information.[46] Among the papers to take this point of view are Harris, Kriebel and Raviv (1982), Antle and Eppen (1985), Harris and Raviv (1996, 1998) and Bernardo, Cai and Luo (2001).

For example, internal capital rationing can emerge in the sense that even when the firm as a whole has plenty of cash, the allocation to a given division will increase relatively little as its reported prospects improve; this type of underinvestment in strong divisions is needed to preserve incentive compatibility. And as argued by Bernardo, Cai and Luo, if it is harder to get managers to be honest about the prospects of longer-horizon projects (because their forecasts cannot be contradicted by data in the short run), then firms may want to adopt payback-like criteria that effectively punish distant cashflows more heavily than does the NPV method.[47]

6. Empirical work on internal capital allocation

6.1. The value consequences of diversification

There is a large empirical literature which, broadly speaking, asks the following question: what are the consequences of diversification for shareholder value? While this literature does not get directly at the efficiency of the internal capital market – diversification may impact value for a variety of other reasons unrelated to investment

---

[46] Often the optimal design also includes other features, such as auditing by headquarters [Harris and Raviv (1996, 1998)], or incentive compensation [Bernardo, Cai and Luo (2001)].

[47] See also Thakor (1990) and Berkovitch and Israel (1998) for alternative rationalizations of the payback criterion.

efficiency, such as operating or organizational synergies, etc. – it is nonetheless informative. And for the most part, the picture painted is one that is unfavorable to diversification, especially if one focuses on unrelated diversification and data after around, say, 1980. For example, the stock market seems to encourage and reward focus-increasing transactions, but to punish the stocks of acquirors in diversifying mergers.[48]

One particular measure of the value effect of diversification that has received a great deal of attention in recent work is the so-called "diversification discount". As developed by Lang and Stulz (1994) and Berger and Ofek (1995), the diversification discount compares the stock price of a diversified firm to the imputed stand-alone values of its individual segments, where these imputed values are based on multiples (such as price-to-book, or price-to-sales) of comparable pure-play firms in the same industries as the diversified firm's segments. Using data from the USA, these authors find substantial mean discounts, on the order of 15%, which they interpret as evidence of value destruction by diversified firms. This work has been extended to a variety of other sample periods and countries by Servaes (1996), Lins and Servaes (1999, 2002), Fauver, Houston and Naranjo (1998) and Claessens et al. (1999) among others, and the results suggest that the diversification discount is a pervasive phenomenon.[49]

However, a number of other papers have taken issue with the idea that the diversification discount reflects value destruction. Villalonga (1999), Burch, Nanda and Narayanan (2000), Campa and Kedia (2002), Graham, Lemmon and Wolf (2002) and Hyland and Diltz (2002) all argue in one way or another that the discount is tainted by endogeneity bias, because relatively weak firms are the ones that choose to diversify in the first place.[50] Lamont and Polk (2001) show that the discount also is partly driven by the fact that stocks of diversified firms have higher expected returns than their pure-play counterparts; this could be because the cashflows of diversified firms are inefficiently undervalued by the market. A balanced reading of these papers suggests that taking these caveats into account significantly reduces – though may not eliminate – that part of the discount which one can think of as reflecting a causal link from diversification to fundamental value. Such skepticism about the causal significance of the diversification

---

[48] See, e.g., Wernerfelt and Montgomery (1988), Bhagat, Shleifer and Vishny (1990), Morck, Shleifer and Vishny (1990b), Kaplan and Weisbach (1992), Liebeskind and Opler (1993), John and Ofek (1995), Comment and Jarrell (1995), Berger and Ofek (1996, 1999) and Denis, Denis and Sarin (1997). In contrast, Matsusaka (1993) finds positive event returns for diversifying acquirors in the 1960s.

[49] Some of these papers have also tried to test a hypothesis discussed above – that internal capital markets will be relatively more valuable when external capital markets are poorly developed – by regressing the diversification discount against various country-level measures of financial development. Taken together, the results from this effort thus far seem inconclusive.

[50] Fluck and Lynch (1999) offer a theoretical explanation for why weak firms might find it optimal to merge. It should be noted, however, that there is another less well-explored bias which cuts in the opposite direction. Even if it occurs more among weak firms, diversification will still only be chosen by those for whom it is most valuable. This implies that the observed discount could actually be *less* than would occur if random firms were forced to merge.

discount is also reinforced by the fact that although the stocks of acquirors tend to drop upon announcement of a diversifying transaction, studies looking at the *combined return* to acquirors and targets in such deals generally find it to be either close to zero or slightly positive [Chevalier (2000)].

While this methodological debate over the correct mean value of the diversification discount is interesting, it should be noted that, from the perspective of testing the theories discussed in Section 5 above, the mean value of the discount is not necessarily the most informative item. After all, taken as a whole, the theoretical work does not lead to a clear-cut prediction that diversification (and the associated creation of an internal capital market) is on average good or bad. Rather, the theory has more bite in the cross-section, pointing to the specific circumstances under which internal capital markets are most likely to destroy value. Thus, the diversification discount may indeed be a useful measure, but perhaps one should pay less attention to its mean value, and more to its cross-sectional variation.[51] As an example in this vein, Rajan, Servaes and Zingales (2000) and Lamont and Polk (2002) both find that the discount increases with measures of the diversity of a firm's investment opportunities. These results provide indirect support for one of the dark-side theories' main cross-sectional implications, namely that greater divergence in investment opportunities leads to less efficient internal capital allocation.

6.2. Evidence on investment at the divisional and plant level

6.2.1. Is there an active internal capital market?

I turn next to evidence which speaks directly to investment outcomes. The first question to ask is this: is it in fact true that – as both bright-side and dark-side theories presuppose – that the internal capital market actively reallocates funds across a firm's divisions? Operationally, this question can be rephrased as: holding fixed $B1$'s investment prospects and cashflow, is it the case that $B1$'s investment is influenced by $B2$'s cashflow?

The first paper to provide an answer to this question is Lamont (1997). He finds that when oil prices decline, integrated oil companies cut investment across the board in all of their divisions. These divisions include not only lines of business that appear totally unrelated to oil (such as Mobil's Montgomery Ward department-store business), but also petrochemical divisions. What is particularly interesting here is that the petrochemical industry is one which takes oil as an input, and hence whose investment prospects should *benefit* when oil prices fall. And indeed, the operating cashflows of oil companies' non-oil segments generally rise at such times. The fact that they

---

[51] Berger and Ofek (1996) find that firms with higher diversification discounts are more likely to be taken over and busted up. This suggests that even if there is an endogeneity bias in the mean value of the discount, there is useful information in its cross-section.

nonetheless see their investment reduced seems to be very clean evidence that the cashflow of one of a firms' divisions affects the investment of its other divisions.

Further work, including Houston, James and Marcus (1997) and Shin and Stulz (1998) has found that Lamont's (1997) results generalize to other industries. Chevalier (2000) raises a methodological caveat about some of this work, particularly insofar as the relatedness or unrelatedness of divisions is established using measures like standard industrial classification (SIC) codes. Chevalier's point is that if a single firm owns two divisions in apparently unrelated SIC codes, they may still be related because of a common factor at the firm level. The example she uses is of a firm based in Texas that owns both local restaurants and oilfields, which, though they belong to different SIC codes, are both influenced by the same regional economic conditions. In this case, it would be unsurprising if the restaurant division's investment is related to the oil division's cashflow, as the latter may contain information about the common component of investment opportunities.

Nevertheless, while this critique contains an important message about experiment design – that one should be careful not to measure relatedness too mechanically – it does not appear that it undermines the basic qualitative message of Lamont's (1997) original work. [52] The bottom line is that it seems very hard to argue with the simple statement that the internal capital market actively reallocates funds across divisions.

6.2.2. Is it efficient?

Of course, the harder question is whether these internal reallocations are value-increasing or value-reducing. That is, compared to the external capital market, does the internal market move money at the margin from less to more deserving divisions, or is it the other way around? Before turning to the evidence, note that this question can be framed a couple of different ways. First, one might ask an "on average" version of the question: across a large sample, does it look like the internal capital market of the typical firm is doing a good job? This version of the question is certainly interesting, but as with the mean value of the diversification discount, it is not one for which a synthesis of the theoretical work yields strong priors one way or another. Alternatively, one can ask various cross-sectional versions of the question. For example, under what circumstances does it look like the internal capital market makes the worst allocations? And are the investment outcomes in these bad scenarios sufficiently value-destroying that they can plausibly be the leading explanation for large diversification discounts, bustups, etc.?

6.2.2.1. On-average statements. Most papers that pose the on-average version of the question [Shin and Stulz (1998), Scharfstein (1998), Rajan, Servaes and Zingales

---

[52] Lamont in fact takes pains to hand-clean the data in such a way as to eliminate observations which appear to fit the Chevalier restaurants/oilfields characterization.

(2000), Billett and Mauer (2003)] come to the conclusion that the internal capital market in the typical diversified firm engages in "socialist" cross-subsidization, allocating too much to low-q divisions and too little to high-q divisions.[53] For example, Rajan, Servaes and Zingales (2000) find that the industry-adjusted investment of low-q divisions within conglomerates is higher than the industry-adjusted investment of high-q divisions. Similarly, Scharfstein (1998) shows that the sensitivity of investment to industry q is much lower for divisions of a conglomerate than it is for stand-alone firms.

However, as in the case of the diversification discount, this on-average conclusion of socialism has been challenged on methodological grounds. The concerns have to do with the endogeneity of the diversification decision, and the resulting possibility that conglomerate divisions are systematically different from their stand-alone counterparts in the same industry. To take one concrete example of the sorts of issues that come up, Whited (2001) and Chevalier (2000) argue that industry q's may be better measures of the investment opportunities of stand-alone firms than those of conglomerate divisions. If this is so, it could explain Scharfstein's (1998) findings.

Chevalier (2000) investigates the importance of these effects by looking at the investment behavior of conglomerate divisions in the years before they merged. In this pre-merger phase – when the divisions were still stand-alone firms and by definition there could have been no reallocation – she finds some of the same patterns as Rajan, Servaes and Zingales (2000) and Scharfstein (1998), albeit in a weaker form. This suggests that correcting for various econometric biases weakens, though does not necessarily overturn, the evidence of on-average socialism in these papers.

Thus overall, someone with relatively neutral priors might say that the weight of the current evidence favors the view that there is on average some degree of socialist cross-subsidization in diversified firms, at least at the divisional level.[54] At the same time, a skeptic could reasonably remain skeptical at this point. But again, it is important to recognize that if one is interested in testing the distinctive predictions of the dark-side theories, then trying to definitively nail down the average degree of socialism may not be the best way to go. Instead, it can be more helpful to look at the cross-section.

6.2.2.2. The cross-section.
6.2.2.2.1. Diversity of investment opportunities. In addition to simply computing an average measure of cross-subsidization, Rajan, Servaes and Zingales (2000) also

---

[53] A more positive view of the internal capital market emerges in Maksimovic and Phillips (2002). Using plant-level data from manufacturing firms, they find that when a division that has high productivity relative to its industry experiences a positive demand shock, this reduces the growth of the other divisions in the same firm. Thus, the internal capital market seems to take money away from other divisions to feed the strong ones when they most need it.

[54] It is of course quite possible that the internal capital market does a poor job of allocating funds at the divisional level, but at the same time, is quite efficient with respect to within-division allocations – e.g., across manufacturing plants in the same line of business.

investigate how this measure is correlated with other variables. Two key findings stand out. First, socialist cross-subsidization (roughly defined as the industry-adjusted investment of low-q divisions minus the industry-adjusted investment of high-q divisions) is more pronounced when there is a greater diversity of investment opportunities within the firm, i.e., when there is a greater spread in the industry q's of the divisions. This pattern is, as noted above, precisely what is predicted by the theoretical models. It is also particularly noteworthy in light of the methodological critiques of Whited (2001) and Chevalier (2000). For even if one takes these critiques seriously and worries that there is a bias in the average estimate of cross-subsidization, there is no clear reason to expect a positive bias in the correlation between the cross-subsidization measure and the diversity measure.

The second important fact is that the cross-subsidization measure is significantly correlated with the diversification discount. That is, firms whose investment behavior looks more socialistic suffer greater discounts. Again, even if one is skeptical about putting too much inferential weight on the average values of either the diversification discount or the cross-subsidization measure, this suggests that there is valuable information in their cross-sectional variation. And at a minimum, it appears that one can say that in those cases where socialist tendencies are the strongest, this has a negative effect on firm value.

6.2.2.2.2. CEO incentives. Using his somewhat different measure of cross-subsidization, Scharfstein (1998) finds that socialism is more pronounced in those diversified firms in which top management has a small equity stake. Palia (1999) comes to a similar conclusion, and also shows that there is more socialism when firms have large (and, he presumes, less effective) boards of directors. These governance-related patterns are consistent with the two-tier agency model of Scharfstein and Stein (2000), though not with the CEO-as-principal models of Rajan, Servaes and Zingales (2000) or Wulf (1999). And once again, these kinds of cross-sectional tests help to address the econometric issues raised by Whited (2001) and Chevalier (2000): even if one believes that Scharfstein's measure of socialism is biased upwards, it is hard to see why it would be spuriously correlated with top-management ownership.

6.2.2.2.3. Division-manager incentives. In a similar vein, Palia (1999) also finds that there is more socialist cross-subsidization when division managers' compensation is less closely linked to overall firm performance, either through stock ownership or options. To the extent that one is willing to take division-manager compensation as exogenous, this fits with a central prediction of all the dark-side theories, since all of them are predicated in part on an agency problem at the division-manager level.

Of course, it is more natural to think of division-manager compensation as endogenous. Though this suggests that one needs to interpret results like Palia's very cautiously, it may actually make them all the more striking, since the most obvious endogeneity story is one that would lead to a bias that works in the opposite direction to these results. In particular, the theory suggests that a principal would want to offer more high-powered incentive compensation (based on overall firm performance) to those division managers who have the greatest ability to rent-seek, or to otherwise engage in distortionary influence activities designed to increase their share of the capital budget. And indeed, Wulf (2002) presents a variety of empirical evidence consistent with the hypothesis that division managers' compensation contracts are designed to reduce rent-seeking incentives.

6.2.2.2.4. Spinoff firms. Another way to address the methodological critiques of Whited (2001) and Chevalier (2000) is to look at the investment behavior of a division before and after it is spun out of a conglomerate firm. Recall that the heart of the critique is that conglomerate divisions are somehow endogenously different than stand-alone firms, and that as a result, one cannot use the investment behavior of the latter as a benchmark for the former. But by focusing on spinoffs, one isolates a pure change in the degree of integration, while holding fixed the division in question. This approach is taken by Gertner, Powers and Scharfstein (2002). They find that once a division is spun off from its parent, its investment becomes markedly more sensitive to industry q. Most of the effect is driven by the behavior of divisions in low-q industries, which sharply cut investment after a spinoff. Moreover, the change in investment behavior is most pronounced for those spinoffs to which the stock market reacts favorably. Overall, this would seem to be quite convincing evidence that there is inefficient overinvestment in the weak divisions prior to spinoff.[55]

However, an important caveat with this research design is that those divisions that are spun off from their parents are far from a random sample; spinoffs are likely to occur precisely in those situations where it becomes clear that integration is destroying value. Thus, the results of Gertner, Powers and Scharfstein (2002) do not really speak to the question of whether there is socialism on average. Rather they make a somewhat different point: in those particular cases where integration appears to be a bad idea, the problems are at least in part attributable to socialist-type inefficiencies in the internal capital market.[56]

6.2.2.2.5. Relatedness. In an interesting counterpoint to much of the recent work in this area – which has tended to look at instances of unrelated diversification (i.e., conglomerates) and has come to largely negative conclusions about the efficiency of the internal capital market – Khanna and Tice (2001) focus on firms that operate in multiple divisions within the same broad industry, retailing. An example of an integrated firm in this context would be Dayton Hudson, which operates both a discount department store chain (Target) and a more exclusive chain (Hudson). Khanna and Tice find that such integrated retailers react quite efficiently when they experience a negative shock to their discount business, in the form of Wal-Mart entering their markets. In particular, they document that the subsequent investment decisions of the integrated firms are *more responsive* to division profitability than those of the

---

[55] For related analyses of spinoffs, see also McNeil and Moore (2000) and Burch and Nanda (2003).

[56] On a somewhat related note, Peyer and Shivdasani (2001) find that one of the costs of high leverage is that it also can lead to distortions in the internal capital market – after leveraged recapitalizations, firms allocate more resources to low-growth, high-cashflow segments.

specialized firms that operate only discount businesses. These results thus have the opposite flavor of the empirical "socialism" findings of Scharfstein (1998) and Rajan, Servaes and Zingales (2000). Khanna and Tice interpret them as being consistent with a comparative static of Stein's (1997) model, namely that the positive, winner-picking function of the internal capital market will work best if the firm in question operates in related lines of business.

6.2.3. Where things stand

Empirical work on investment inside firms is at a very early stage, and many of the most interesting and important questions remain incompletely resolved. Nevertheless, a few conclusions can be ventured with some confidence. First, it is clear that the internal capital market can generate economically significant reallocations of resources across a firm's operating segments – i.e., divisions that are part of a larger firm can have markedly different investment patterns than they would as stand-alones. Second, in those cases where there is a large value loss associated with integration, this value loss is often due in part to inefficiencies in the internal capital allocation process. Third, when such inefficiencies do occur, they tend to be socialist in nature, with weak divisions receiving too much capital, and strong divisions too little. (There is little evidence to date of the reverse kind of inefficiency, excessive Darwinism, whereby strong divisions get too much capital, and weak ones too little). Finally, and most tentatively, socialism appears to be more of a problem when a firm's divisions are in unrelated lines of business, and have widely divergent investment prospects.

Looking to the future, it would seem that one particularly promising line of research is that which pushes beyond the divisional level, and looks at investment patterns *within* operating segments, e.g., at the plant level. Such work is just getting started, in papers by Maksimovic and Phillips (2002) and Schoar (2002). Among the many kinds of questions that one might hope to answer with it are the following: are there cases in which capital is allocated relatively inefficiently across divisions, but relatively efficiently within divisions? If so, what aspects of organizational structure appear to be driving the outcome? For example, in a heuristic extension of the dark-side models discussed above, one might conjecture that this sort of pattern would result if division-level managers are very powerful in the capital budgeting process, while lower-level managers (e.g., plant managers) have less influence.

7. Conclusions: implications for the boundaries of the firm

The process of allocating capital to investment projects is made difficult by the existence of information asymmetries and agency conflicts. Put most simply, the fundamental problem is that the manager closest to a project is likely to know more about its prospects, but at the same time may have incentives to misrepresent this information – e.g., to say that the outlook is better than it really is. This fundamental problem arises both when capital is allocated across firms via external debt and equity markets, and when capital is allocated within firms via the internal capital market. Internal and external markets differ in how they address the problem, but it is important to recognize that they are both trying to accomplish the same objective.

This observation suggests a particular perspective on Coase's (1937) enduring question about what determines the boundaries of the firm: loosely speaking, a collection of assets should optimally reside under the roof of a single firm to the extent that the firm's internal capital market can do a more efficient job of allocating capital to these assets than would the external capital market, if the assets were located in distinct firms.

Such a capital-allocation-centric point of view on the boundaries question appears in recent papers by Bolton and Scharfstein (1998) and Holmström and Kaplan (2001).[57] Bolton and Scharfstein write (p. 111):

> ... integration fundamentally changes the resource allocation process by increasing centralized decision making under corporate headquarters ... integration can lead to inefficient outcomes from decision-making processes (in this case the allocation of capital) in contrast to the efficient outcomes from bargaining that always occur in the Grossman–Hart–Moore paradigm. In our view, corporate headquarters, agency problems, and the resource allocation process must play a key role in any realistic theory of the firm."

In a similar spirit, Holmström and Kaplan give this example of the limits of integration:

> It would make little sense for shareholders to become directly involved in General Motors' choice of car models ... But if resources are to shift from car manufacturing to computer manufacturing, there is little reason to believe that having General Motors start making computers, an area in which the company currently has little expertise, would make economic sense. Instead, the market may have a role to play in funneling capital toward the new companies.

While there may yet be no single fully-articulated model of firm boundaries which captures all the important nuances of this capital-allocation-based perspective, several bits and pieces of the theory are clearly present in the work surveyed above. For example, one reason why it may make sense for GM's CEO to be the one to allocate resources across different lines of cars and trucks – even though some of these lines could in principle be housed in stand-alone firms – flows from the complementarity of authority and monitoring incentives. This is the idea that a CEO's authority will make

---

[57] Bolton and Scharfstein (1998) provide a nice discussion of how this approach differs from the GHM property-rights paradigm [Grossman and Hart (1986), Hart and Moore (1990), Hart (1995)]. The common element is the heavy reliance on GHM notions of authority and control in an incomplete-contracting environment. One important distinction is that in GHM, everything is driven by the impact of asset ownership on agents' ex ante incentives. This tends to imply that assets should be owned on a very individual basis, making the GHM model hard to reconcile with large firms where virtually none of the employees other than the CEO have clear-cut control rights [see also Holmström and Roberts (1998) and Holmström (1999b)]. Also, the capital-allocation perspective emphasizes ex post inefficiencies – namely, misallocations of capital – in addition to the sort of ex ante incentive effects seen in GHM.

her more willing to invest in learning about any given business that she oversees than would be say, a bank lender, or an atomistic shareholder. A natural corollary to this idea is that if the CEO is to be given authority over multiple lines of business, these should be lines of business that can potentially be well-monitored and well-understood by a single properly-motivated individual.

Moreover, if the CEO's authority-based incentives help lead her to become an expert with respect to multiple lines of business that report to her, this can in turn have beneficial incentive effects on the agents further down in the hierarchy. Stein (2002) argues that the desire of these lower-ranking agents (e.g., division managers) to attract a larger share of the overall capital budget need not always have adverse consequences. In particular, the more expert is the CEO – in terms of being able to assess the value implications of data presented to her by her subordinates – the more likely it is that the subordinates' attempts at advocacy will take the form of useful information creation as opposed to wasteful and uninformative lobbying.

In contrast, if the CEO is not able to develop significant expertise across lines of business (as might be the case in the Holmström–Kaplan example of an integrated car/computer company), the potential bright side of giving authority to the CEO is obviously not exploited. And indeed, when an ill-informed CEO allocates capital, the outcome can be *strictly worse* than one in which capital is allocated by an equally ill-informed capital market. Now the fact that the CEO has the authority to move resources around inside the firm, but no expertise, suggests that the sorts of rent-seeking problems identified by Meyer, Milgrom and Roberts (1992), Rajan, Servaes and Zingales (2000) and Scharfstein and Stein (2000) are most likely to come to the fore. In this context, the capital market has the advantage that even if it is no better informed, its impersonal and hence objective nature – there is no single identifiable person vested with so much authority over resources – makes it much less subject to such rent-seeking distortions.

In sum, according to this informal theory, the boundaries of the firm are determined by the following tradeoff between managers vs. markets as allocators of capital. On the one hand, by giving a CEO control over a set of assets, and the authority to redistribute capital across these assets, one sets her up with high-powered incentives to become a delegated expert. On the other hand, the very fact that she has the authority to move capital around makes her vulnerable to rent-seeking on the part of her subordinates; all the more so because she is herself only an agent of investors and hence will not necessarily respond to the rent-seeking pressure as a principal might want her to.

This managers vs. markets tradeoff can be thought of as loosely analogous to the question of what types of political issues should be put to a direct vote of the general electorate, as opposed to being decided by previously-elected representatives (e.g., in Congress). Since elected officials are vested with legislative powers, they have more incentive to become informed about the details of the issues before them – their power will allow them to put their information to good use. It is hard to imagine, for example, that the average citizen would devote as much time as a Congressman to learning the arcane details of a banking deregulation bill. However, precisely because they as agents are vested with legislative powers, elected officials are more subject to lobbying and the potential for corruption than ordinary citizens. The general electorate, like the capital market, may be less well-informed than the delegated experts, but it is also less vulnerable to rent-seeking. As with the boundaries of the firm, the goal is to strike a proper balance.

References

Aggarwal, R.K., and A.A. Samwick (1999), "Empire-builders and shirkers: investment, firm performance, and managerial incentives", Working Paper 7335 (National Bureau of Economic Research, Cambridge, MA).

Aghion, P., and P. Bolton (1992), "An incomplete contracts approach to financial contracting", Review of Economic Studies 59:473–494.

Aghion, P., and J. Tirole (1997), "Formal and real authority in organizations", Journal of Political Economy 105:1–29.

Akerlof, G. (1970), "The market for 'lemons': quality and the market mechanism", Quarterly Journal of Economics 84:488–500.

Alchian, A.A. (1969), "Corporate management and property rights", in: H. Manne, ed., Economic Policy and the Regulation of Corporate Securities (American Enterprise Institute, Washington, DC) pp. 337–360.

Almeida, H., and M. Campello (2001), "Financial constraints and investment-cash flow sensitivities: new theoretical foundations", Working Paper (New York University, NY).

Amihud, Y., and B. Lev (1981), "Risk reduction as a managerial motive for conglomerate mergers", Bell Journal of Economics 12:605–617.

Antle, R., and G. Eppen (1985), "Capital rationing and organizational slack in capital budgeting", Management Science 31:163–174.

Asquith, P., and D. Mullins (1986), "Equity issues and offering dilution", Journal of Financial Economics 15:61–89.

Avery, C.N., and J.A. Chevalier (1999), "Herding over the career", Economics Letters 63:327–333.

Bagwell, L.S., and J. Zechner (1993), "Influence costs and capital structure", Journal of Finance 48: 975–1008.

Baker, M. (2000), "Career concerns and staged investment: evidence from the venture capital industry", Working Paper (Harvard University, MA).

Baker, M., and J. Wurgler (2002), "Market timing and capital structure", Journal of Finance 57:1–32.

Baker, M., J.C. Stein and J. Wurgler (2003), "When does the market matter? Stock prices and the investment of equity-dependent firms", Quarterly Journal of Economics, forthcoming.

Banerjee, A.V. (1992), "A simple model of herd behavior", Quarterly Journal of Economics 107: 797–818.

Barro, R.J. (1990), "The stock market and investment", Review of Financial Studies 3:115–131.

Baumol, W. (1959), Business Behavior, Value, and Growth (Macmillan, New York).

Bebchuk, L.A., and L.A. Stole (1993), "Do short-term objectives lead to under- or overinvestment in long-term projects", Journal of Finance 48:719–729.

Berger, P., and E. Ofek (1995), "Diversification's effect on firm value", Journal of Financial Economics 37:39–65.

Berger, P., and E. Ofek (1996), "Bust-up takeovers of value-destroying diversified firms", Journal of Finance 51:1175–1200.

Berger, P., and E. Ofek (1999), "Causes and effects of corporate refocusing programs", Review of Financial Studies 12:311–345.

Bergman, Y.A., and J.L. Callen (1991), "Opportunistic underinvestment in debt renegotiation and capital structure", Journal of Financial Economics 29:137–171.

Berkovitch, E., and R. Israel (1998), "Why the NPV criterion does not maximize NPV", Working Paper (Tel Aviv University, Israel).

Berkovitch, E., and E.H. Kim (1990), "Financial contracting and leverage induced over- and under-investment incentives", Journal of Finance 45:765–794.

Berle, A., and G. Means (1932), The Modern Corporation and Private Property (Macmillan, New York).

Bernanke, B. (1983), "Nonmonetary effects of the financial crisis in propagation of the great depression", American Economic Review 73:257–276.

Bernanke, B., and A. Blinder (1988), "Credit, money, and aggregate demand", American Economic Review 78:435–439.

Bernanke, B., and A. Blinder (1992), "The Federal Funds rate and the channels of monetary transmission", American Economic Review 82:901–921.

Bernanke, B., and M. Gertler (1989), "Agency costs, net worth, and business fluctuations", American Economic Review 79:14–31.

Bernanke, B., and M. Gertler (1995), "Inside the black box: the credit channel of monetary policy transmission", Journal of Economic Perspectives 9:27–48.

Bernanke, B., and C. Lown (1991), "The credit crunch", Brookings Papers on Economic Activity, pp. 204–239.

Bernanke, B., M. Gertler and S. Gilchrist (1996), "The financial accelerator and the flight to quality", Review of Economic Studies 78:1–15.

Bernanke, B., M. Gertler and S. Gilchrist (1999), "The financial accelerator in a quantitative business cycle framework", in: J.B. Taylor and M. Woodford, eds., Handbook of Macroeconomics, Vol. 1C (Elsevier, Amsterdam) pp. 1341–1393.

Bernardo, A.E., and I. Welch (2001), "On the evolution of overconfidence and entrepreneurs", Journal of Economics and Management Strategy 10:301–330.

Bernardo, A.E., H. Cai and J. Luo (2001), "Capital budgeting and compensation with asymmetric information and moral hazard", Journal of Financial Economics 61:311–344.

Bertrand, M., and S. Mullainathan (2003), "Enjoying the quiet life? Corporate governance and managerial preferences", Journal of Political Economy, forthcoming.

Bhagat, S., A. Shleifer and R.W. Vishny (1990), "Hostile takeovers in the 1980s: the return to corporate specialization", Brookings Papers on Economic Activity: Microeconomics, pp. 1–72.

Bikhchandani, S., D. Hirshleifer and I. Welch (1992), "A theory of fads, fashion, custom and cultural change as informational cascades", Journal of Political Economy 100:992–1026.

Billett, M., and D. Mauer (2003), "Cross subsidies, external financing constraints, and the contribution of the internal capital market to firm value", Review of Financial Studies, forthcoming.

Bizjak, J., J. Brickley and J. Coles (1993), "Stock-based incentive compensation, asymmetric information and investment behavior", Journal of Accounting and Economics 16:349–372.

Blanchard, O.J., C. Rhee and L.H. Summers (1993), "The stock market, profit and investment", Quarterly Journal of Economics 108:115–136.

Blanchard, O.J., F. Lopez-de-Silanes and A. Shleifer (1994), "What do firms do with cash windfalls?", Journal of Financial Economics 36:337–360.

Bolton, P., and D.S. Scharfstein (1990), "A theory of predation based on agency problems in financial contracting", American Economic Review 80:93–106.

Bolton, P., and D.S. Scharfstein (1996), "Optimal debt structure and the number of creditors", Journal of Political Economy 104:1–25.

Bolton, P., and D.S. Scharfstein (1998), "Corporate finance, the theory of the firm, and organizations", Journal of Economic Perspectives 12:95–114.

Bond, S., and C. Meghir (1994), "Dynamic investment models and the firm's financial policy", Review of Economic Studies 61:197–222.

Boot, A.W. (1992), "Why hang on to losers? Divestitures and takeovers", Journal of Finance 47: 1401–1423.

Brusco, S., and F. Panunzi (2000), "Reallocation of corporate resources and managerial incentives in internal capital markets", Discussion Paper 2532 (CEPR, London).

Burch, T., and V. Nanda (2003), "Divisional diversity and the conglomerate discount: the evidence from spin-offs", Journal of Financial Economics, forthcoming.

Burch, T., V. Nanda and M.P. Narayanan (2000), "Industry structure and the conglomerate discount: theory and evidence", Working Paper (University of Michigan Business School).

Burkart, M., D. Gromb and F. Panunzi (1997), "Large shareholders, monitoring, and the value of the firm", Quarterly Journal of Economics 112:693–728.

Calomiris, C.W., and R.G. Hubbard (1995), "Internal finance and investment: evidence from the undistributed profits tax of 1936–37", Journal of Business 68:443–482.

Campa, J., and S. Kedia (2002), "Explaining the diversification discount", Journal of Finance 57: 1731–1762.

Carpenter, R.E., S.M. Fazzari and B.C. Petersen (1994), "Inventory investment, internal-finance fluctuations, and the business cycle", Brookings Papers on Economic Activity, pp. 75–122.

Cecchetti, S.G. (1995), "Distinguishing theories of the monetary transmission mechanism", Federal Reserve Bank of St. Louis Review 77:83–97.

Chevalier, J.A. (1995a), "Do LBO supermarkets charge more?: An empirical analysis of the effects of LBOs on supermarket pricing", Journal of Finance 50:1095–1112.

Chevalier, J.A. (1995b), "Capital structure and product-market competition: empirical evidence from the supermarket industry", American Economic Review 85:415–35.

Chevalier, J.A. (2000), "What do we know about cross-subsidization? Evidence from the investment policies of merging firms", Working Paper (University of Chicago GSB).

Chevalier, J.A., and G. Ellison (1999), "Career concerns of mutual fund managers", Quarterly Journal of Economics 114:389–432.

Chevalier, J.A., and D.S. Scharfstein (1995), "Liquidity constraints and the cyclical behavior of markups", American Economic Review 85:390–396.

Chevalier, J.A., and D.S. Scharfstein (1996), "Capital-market imperfections and countercyclical markups: theory and evidence", American Economic Review 86:703–725.

Chirinko, R.S. (1995), "Why does liquidity matter in investment equations?", Journal of Money, Credit, and Banking 27:527–548.

Claessens, S., S. Djankov, J.P.H. Fan and L.H.P. Lang (1999), "The benefits and costs of internal markets: evidence from Asia's financial crisis", Working Paper (World Bank, Washington, DC).

Cleary, S. (1999), "The relationship between firm investment and financial status", Journal of Finance 54:673–692.

Coase, R. (1937), "The nature of the firm", Economica 4:386–405.

Comment, R., and G.A. Jarrell (1995), "Corporate focus and stock returns", Journal of Financial Economics 37:67–87.

Cooper, A.C., C.A. Woo and W. Dunkelberg (1988), "Entrepreneurs' perceived chances for success", Journal of Business Venturing 3:97–108.

DeGeorge, F., and R. Zeckhauser (1993), "The reverse LBO decision and firm performance: theory and evidence", Journal of Finance 48:1323–1348.

Demirguc-Kunt, A., and V. Maksimovic (1998), "Law, finance, and firm growth", Journal of Finance 53:2107–2137.

Denis, D.J., D.K. Denis and A. Sarin (1997), "Agency problems, equity ownership, and corporate diversification", Journal of Finance 52:135–160.

Dewatripont, M., and E. Maskin (1995), "Credit and efficiency in centralized and decentralized economies", Review of Economic Studies 62:541–555.

Dewatripont, M., and J. Tirole (1994), "A theory of debt and equity: diversity of securities and manager–shareholder congruence", Quarterly Journal of Economics 109:1027–54.

Dewatripont, M., I. Jewitt and J. Tirole (1999), "The economics of career concerns, Part I: Comparing information structures", Review of Economic Studies 66:183–198.

Diamond, D. (1984), "Financial intermediation and delegated monitoring", Review of Economic Studies 51:393–414.

Diamond, D. (1991), "Debt maturity structure and liquidity risk", Quarterly Journal of Economics 106:709–737.

Donaldson, G. (1984), Managing Corporate Wealth (Praeger, New York).

Dybvig, P., and J. Zender (1991), "Capital structure and dividend irrelevance with asymmetric information", Review of Financial Studies 4:201–219.

Eckstein, O., and A. Sinai (1986), "The mechanisms of the business cycle in the postwar era", in: R.J. Gordon, ed., The American Business Cycle: Continuity and Change (University of Chicago Press, Chicago) pp. 39–105.

Edlin, A.S., and J.E. Stiglitz (1995), "Discouraging rivals: managerial rent seeking and economic inefficiencies", American Economic Review 85:1301–1312.

Ehrbeck, T., and R. Waldmann (1996), "Why are professional forecasters biased? Agency versus behavioral explanations", Quarterly Journal of Economics 111:21–40.

Erickson, T., and T. Whited (2000), "Measurement error and the relationship between investment and q", Journal of Political Economy 108:1027–1057.

Falkenstein, E.G. (1996), "Preferences for stock characteristics as revealed by mutual fund portfolio holdings", Journal of Finance 51:111–135.

Fama, E.F. (1980), "Agency problems and the theory of the firm", Journal of Political Economy 88: 288–307.

Fama, E.F., and M.H. Miller (1972), The Theory of Finance (Holt, Rinehart and Winston, New York).

Fauver, L., J. Houston and A. Naranjo (1998), "Capital market development, legal systems and the value of corporate diversification: a cross-country analysis", Working Paper (University of Florida).

Fazzari, S.M., R.G. Hubbard and B.C. Petersen (1988), "Financing Constraints and corporate investment", Brookings Papers on Economic Activity, pp. 141–195.

Fischer, S., and R. Merton (1984), "Macroeconomics and finance: the role of the stock market", Carnegie Rochester Conference Series on Public Policy 21:57–108.

Fisher, I. (1933), "The debt-deflation theory of great depressions", Econometrica 1:337–357.

Fluck, Z. (1998), "Optimal financial contracting: debt versus outside equity", Review of Financial Studies 11:383–418.

Fluck, Z., and A.W. Lynch (1999), "Why do firms merge and then divest? A theory of financial synergy", Journal of Business 72:319–346.

Froot, K., and P. O'Connell (1997), "On the pricing of intermediated risks: theory and application to catastrophe reinsurance", NBER Working Paper 6011 (NBER, Cambridge, MA).

Froot, K., and J.C. Stein (1991), "Exchange rates and foreign direct investment: an imperfect capital markets approach", Quarterly Journal of Economics 106:1191–1217.

Froot, K., D. Scharfstein and J.C. Stein (1993), "Risk management: coordinating corporate investment and financing policies", Journal of Finance 48:1629–1658.

Gale, D., and M. Hellwig (1985), "Incentive-compatible debt contracts: the one-period problem", Review of Economic Studies 52:647–663.

Gertner, R., and D. Scharfstein (1991), "A theory of workouts and the effects of reorganization law", Journal of Finance 46:1189–1222.

Gertner, R., E. Powers and D. Scharfstein (2002), "Learning about internal capital markets from corporate spinoffs", Journal of Finance 57:2479–2506.

Gertner, R.H., D.S. Scharfstein and J.C. Stein (1994), "Internal versus external capital markets", Quarterly Journal of Economics 109:1211–1230.

Gilchrist, S., and C.P. Himmelberg (1995), "Evidence on the role of cash flow for investment", Journal of Monetary Economics 36:531–572.

Goldsmith, R.W. (1969), Financial Structure and Development (Yale University Press, New Haven, CT).

Gomes, A. (2000), "Going public without governance: managerial reputation effects", Journal of Finance 50:615–646.

Gompers, P.A. (1996), "Grandstanding in the venture capital industry", Journal of Financial Economics 42:133–156.

Graham, J.R. (1999), "Herding among investment newsletters: theory and evidence", Journal of Finance 54:237–268.

Graham, J.R., M.L. Lemmon and J. Wolf (2002), "Does corporate diversification destroy value", Journal of Finance 57:695–720.

Greenwald, B., J.E. Stiglitz and A. Weiss (1984), "Informational imperfections in the capital market and macroeconomic fluctuations", American Economic Review 74:194–199.

Grinblatt, M., S. Titman and R. Wermers (1995), "Momentum investment strategies, portfolio performance, and herding: a study of mutual fund behavior", American Economic Review 85:1088–1105.

Grossman, S., and O. Hart (1982), "Corporate financial structure and managerial incentives", in: J.J. McCall, ed., The Economics of Information and Uncertainty (University of Chicago Press, Chicago, IL) pp. 107–140.

Grossman, S., and O. Hart (1988), "One share–one vote and the market for corporate control", Journal of Financial Economics 20:175–202.

Grossman, S.J., and O.D. Hart (1986), "The costs and benefits of ownership: a theory of vertical and lateral integration", Journal of Political Economy 94:691–719.

Hadlock, C., M. Ryngaert and S. Thomas (2001), "Corporate structure and equity offerings: are there benefits to diversification?", Journal of Business 74:613–635.

Hadlock, C.J. (1998), "Ownership, liquidity, and investment", RAND Journal of Economics 29:487–508.

Hall, B.H. (1992), "Investment and research and development at the firm level: does the source of funding matter?", NBER Working Paper 4096 (NBER, Cambridge, MA).

Hansen, R., and C. Crutchley (1990), "Corporate earnings and financings: an empirical analysis", Journal of Business 63:347–371.

Harris, M., and A. Raviv (1990), "Capital structure and the informational role of debt", Journal of Finance 45:321–350.

Harris, M., and A. Raviv (1991), "The theory of capital structure", Journal of Finance 46:297–355.

Harris, M., and A. Raviv (1996), "The capital budgeting process: incentives and information", Journal of Finance 51:1139–1174.

Harris, M., and A. Raviv (1998), "Capital budgeting and delegation", Journal of Financial Economics 50:259–289.

Harris, M., C.H. Kriebel and A. Raviv (1982), "Asymmetric information, incentives and intrafirm resource allocation", Management Science 28:604–620.

Hart, O. (1995), Firms, Contracts, and Financial Structure (Oxford University Press, London).

Hart, O., and J. Moore (1990), "Property rights and the nature of the firm", Journal of Political Economy 98:1119–1158.

Hart, O., and J. Moore (1994), "A theory of debt based on the inalienability of human capital", Quarterly Journal of Economics 109:841–879.

Hart, O., and J. Moore (1995), "Debt and seniority: an analysis of the role of hard claims in constraining management", American Economic Review 85:567–585.

Hart, O., and J. Moore (1998), "Default and renegotiation: a dynamic model of debt", Quarterly Journal of Economics 113:1–41.

Heaton, J.B. (2002), "Managerial optimism and corporate finance", Financial Management 31:33–45.

Himmelberg, C.P., and B. Petersen (1994), "R&D and internal finance: a panel study of small firms in high-tech industries", Review of Economics and Statistics 76:38–51.

Hirshleifer, D., and A.V. Thakor (1992), "Managerial conservatism, project choice, and debt", Review of Financial Studies 5:437–470.

Holmström, B. (1979), "Moral hazard and observability", Bell Journal of Economics 10:74–91.

Holmström, B. (1999a), "Managerial incentive problems: a dynamic perspective", Review of Economic Studies 66:169–182.

Holmström, B. (1999b), "The firm as a subeconomy", Journal of Law, Economics and Organization 15:74–102.

Holmström, B., and S.N. Kaplan (2001), "Corporate governance and merger activity in the U.S.: making sense of the 1980s and 1990s", Journal of Economic Perspectives 15:121–144.

Holmström, B., and J. Ricart i Costa (1986), "Managerial incentives and capital management", Quarterly Journal of Economics 101:835–860.

Holmström, B., and J. Roberts (1998), "The boundaries of the firm revisited", Journal of Economic Perspectives 12:73–94.

Holmström, B., and J. Tirole (1997), "Financial intermediation, loanable funds, and the real sector", Quarterly Journal of Economics 112:663–691.

Holtz-Eakin, D., D. Joulfaian and H.S. Rosen (1994), "Sticking it out: entrepreneurial survival and liquidity constraints", Journal of Political Economy 102:53–75.

Hong, H., J.D. Kubik and A. Solomon (2000), "Security analysts' career concerns and herding of earnings forecasts", RAND Journal of Economics 31:121–144.

Hoshi, T., A. Kashyap and D. Scharfstein (1991), "Corporate structure, liquidity, and investment: evidence from Japanese industrial groups", Quarterly Journal of Economics 106:33–60.

Houston, J., C. James and D. Marcus (1997), "Capital market frictions and the role of internal capital markets in banking", Journal of Financial Economics 46:135–164.

Hubbard, R.G. (1995), "Is there a 'credit channel' for monetary policy?", Federal Reserve Bank of St. Louis Review 77:63–77.

Hubbard, R.G. (1998), "Capital-market imperfections and investment", Journal of Economic Literature 36:193–225.

Hubbard, R.G., and D. Palia (1999), "A re-examination of the conglomerate merger wave in the 1960s: an internal capital markets view", Journal of Finance 54:1131–1152.

Hubbard, R.G., A.K. Kashyap and T.M. Whited (1995), "Internal finance and firm investment", Journal of Money, Credit, and Banking 27:683–701.

Hyland, D.C., and J.D. Diltz (2002), "Why firms diversify: an empirical examination", Financial Management 31:51–81.

Inderst, R., and C. Laux (2000), "Incentives in internal capital markets: capital constraints, competition, and investment opportunities", Working Paper (University College London).

Inderst, R., and H.M. Muller (2003), "Corporate borrowing and financing constraints", Journal of Finance, forthcoming.

Jaffee, D.M., and T. Russell (1976), "Imperfect information, uncertainty, and credit rationing", Quarterly Journal of Economics 90:651–666.

Jensen, M.C. (1986), "Agency costs of free cash flow, corporate finance, and takeovers", American Economic Review 76:323–329.

Jensen, M.C. (1993), "The modern industrial revolution, exit, and the failure of internal control systems", Journal of Finance 48:831–880.

Jensen, M.C., and W.H. Meckling (1976), "Theory of the firm: managerial behavior, agency costs and ownership structure", Journal of Financial Economics 3:305–360.

John, K., and E. Ofek (1995), "Asset sales and increase in focus", Journal of Financial Economics 37:105–126.

Johnson, S., R. LaPorta, F. Lopez-de-Silanes and A. Shleifer (2000), "Tunnelling", American Economic Review Papers and Proceedings 90:22–27.

Kaplan, S. (1989), "The effects of management buyouts on operating performance and value", Journal of Financial Economics 24:217–254.

Kaplan, S., and M. Weisbach (1992), "The success of acquisitions: evidence from divestitures", Journal of Finance 47:107–138.

Kaplan, S.N., and L. Zingales (1997), "Do investment-cash flow sensitivities provide useful measures of financing constraints?", Quarterly Journal of Economics 112:159–216.

Kaplan, S.N., and L. Zingales (2000), "Investment-cash flow sensitivities are not valid measures of financing constraints", Quarterly Journal of Economics 115:707–712.

Kashyap, A., and J.C. Stein (1994), "Monetary policy and bank lending", in: N.G. Mankiw, ed., Monetary Policy (University of Chicago Press, Chicago) pp. 221–256.

Kashyap, A., and J.C. Stein (1995), "The impact of monetary policy on bank balance sheets", Carnegie-Rochester Conference Series on Public Policy 42:151–195.

Kashyap, A., and J.C. Stein (2000), "What do a million observations on banks say about the transmission of monetary policy?", American Economic Review 90:407–428.

Kashyap, A., J.C. Stein and D. Wilcox (1993), "Monetary policy and credit conditions: evidence from the composition of external finance", American Economic Review 83:78–98.

Kashyap, A.K., O.A. Lamont and J.C. Stein (1994), "Credit conditions and the cyclical behavior of inventories", Quarterly Journal of Economics 109:565–592.

Khanna, N., and S. Tice (2001), "The bright side of internal capital markets", Journal of Finance 56:1489–1528.

King, R.G., and R. Levine (1993), "Finance and growth: schumpeter might be right", Quarterly Journal of Economics 108:717–737.

Kishan, R., and T. Opiela (2000), "Bank size, bank capital, and the bank lending channel", Journal of Money, Credit and Banking 32:121–141.

Kiyotaki, N., and J. Moore (1997), "Credit cycles", Journal of Political Economy 105:211–248.

Krasker, W.S. (1986), "Stock price movements in response to stock issues under asymmetric information", Journal of Finance 41:93–105.

Lakonishok, J., A. Shleifer and R. Vishny (1992), "The impact of institutional trading on stock prices", Journal of Financial Economics 32:23–43.

Lamont, O. (1997), "Cash flow and investment: evidence from internal capital markets", Journal of Finance 52:83–109.

Lamont, O. (2002), "Macroeconomic forecasts and microeconomic forecasters", Journal of Economic Behavior and Organization 48:265–280.

Lamont, O., and C. Polk (2001), "The diversification discount: cash flows vs. returns", Journal of Finance 56:1693–1721.

Lamont, O., and C. Polk (2002), "Does diversification destroy value? Evidence from industry shocks", Journal of Financial Economics 63:51–77.

Lang, L.H.P., and R. Stulz (1994), "Tobin's q, corporate diversification, and firm performance", Journal of Political Economy 102:1248–1280.

Lang, L.H.P., R.M. Stulz and R.A. Walkling (1991), "A test of the free cash flow hypothesis: the case of bidder returns", Journal of Financial Economics 29:315–335.

Lang, L.H.P., E. Ofek and R. Stulz (1996), "Leverage, investment, and firm growth", Journal of Financial Economics 40:3–30.

LaPorta, R., F. Lopez-de-Silanes, A. Shleifer and R. Vishny (1997), "Legal determinants of external finance", Journal of Finance 52(3):1131–1150.

LaPorta, R., F. Lopez-de-Silanes, A. Shleifer and R. Vishny (1998), "Law and finance", Journal of Political Economy 106:1113–1155.

Levine, R. (1997), "Financial development and economic growth: views and agenda", Journal of Economic Literature 35:688–726.

Levine, R., and S. Zervos (1998), "Stock markets, banks, and economic growth", American Economic Review 88:537–558.

Lewellen, W.G. (1971), "A pure financial rationale for the conglomerate merger", Journal of Finance 26:521–537.

Lewellen, W.G., C. Loderer and A. Rosenfeld (1985), "Merger decisions and executive stock ownership in acquiring firms", Journal of Accounting and Economics 7:209–231.

Li, D.D., and S. Li (1996), "A theory of corporate scope and financial structure", Journal of Finance 51:691–709.

Liebeskind, J., and T. Opler (1993), "The causes of corporate refocusing", Working Paper (Ohio State University).

Lins, K., and H. Servaes (1999), "International evidence on the value of corporate diversification", Journal of Finance 54:2215–2239.

Lins, K., and H. Servaes (2002), "Is corporate diversification beneficial in emerging markets?", Financial Management 31:5–31.

Loughran, T., and J. Ritter (1997), "The operating performance of firms conducting seasoned equity offerings", Journal of Finance 52:1823–1850.

Ludvigson, S. (1998), "The channel of monetary transmission to demand: evidence from the market for automobile credit", Journal of Money, Credit and Banking 30:365–383.

Maksimovic, V., and G.M. Phillips (2002), "Do conglomerate firms allocate resources inefficiently across industries? Theory and evidence", Journal of Finance 57:721–767.

Malmendier, U., and G. Tate (2002a), "Who makes acquisitions? CEO overconfidence and the market's reaction", Working Paper (Harvard University, Cambridge, MA).

Malmendier, U., and G. Tate (2002b), "CEO overconfidence and corporate investment", Working Paper (Harvard University, Cambridge, MA).

Marris, R. (1964), The Economic Theory of Managerial Capitalism (Free Press, Glencoe, IL).

Masulis, R., and A.N. Korwar (1986), "Seasoned equity offerings: an empirical investigation", Journal of Financial Economics 15:91–119.

Matsusaka, J. (1993), "Takeover motives during the conglomerate merger wave", RAND Journal of Economics 24:357–379.

Matsusaka, J., and V. Nanda (2002), "Internal capital markets and corporate refocusing", Journal of Financial Intermediation 11:176–216.

McConnell, J.J., and C.J. Muscarella (1985), "Corporate capital expenditure decisions and the market value of the firm", Journal of Financial Economics 14:399–422.

McKinnon, R.I. (1973), Money and Capital in Economic Development (Brookings Institute, Washington, DC).

McNeil, C.R., and W. Moore (2000), "Spinoff wealth effects and the dismantling of internal capital markets", Working Paper (University of Miami).

Meyer, J.R., and E. Kuh (1957), The Investment Decision (Harvard University Press, Cambridge, MA).

Meyer, M., P. Milgrom and J. Roberts (1992), "Organizational prospects, influence costs, and ownership changes", Journal of Economics and Management Strategy 1:9–35.

Mikkelson, W.H., and M.M. Partch (1986), "Valuation effects of security offerings and the issuance process", Journal of Financial Economics 15:31–60.

Milgrom, P. (1988), "Employment contracts, influence activities, and efficient organization design", Journal of Political Economy 96:42–60.

Milgrom, P., and J. Roberts (1988), "An economic approach to influence activities in organizations", American Journal of Sociology 94:154–179.

Miller, M.H., and K. Rock (1985), "Dividend policy under information asymmetry", Journal of Finance 40:1031–1051.

Modigliani, F., and M. Miller (1958), "The cost of capital, corporation finance, and the theory of investment", American Economic Review 48:261–297.

Morck, R., A. Shleifer and R. Vishny (1990a), "The stock market and investment: is the market a sideshow?", Brookings Papers on Economic Activity, pp. 157–215.

Morck, R., A. Shleifer and R. Vishny (1990b), "Do managerial objectives drive bad acquisitions?", Journal of Finance 45:31–48.

Morgan, D. (1998), "The credit effects of monetary policy: evidence using loan commitments", Journal of Money, Credit and Banking 30:102–118.

Myers, S.C. (1977), "Determinants of corporate borrowing", Journal of Financial Economics 5:147–175.

Myers, S.C. (1984), "The capital structure puzzle", Journal of Finance 39:575–592.

Myers, S.C. (2000), "Outside equity", Journal of Finance 55:1005–1037.

Myers, S.C., and N.C. Majluf (1984), "Corporate financing and investment decisions when firms have information that investors do not have", Journal of Financial Economics 13:187–222.

Nanda, V., and M.P. Narayanan (1999), "Disentangling value: financing needs, firm scope, and divestitures", Journal of Financial Intermediation 8:174–204.

Narayanan, M.P. (1985), "Managerial incentives for short-term results", Journal of Finance 40:1469–1484.

Nofsinger, J., and R. Sias (1999), "Herding and feedback trading by institutional and individual investors", Journal of Finance 54:2263–2295.

Palia, D. (1999), "Corporate governance and the diversification discount", Working Paper (UCLA, CA).

Peek, J., and E. Rosengren (1995), "The capital crunch: neither a borrower nor a lender be", Journal of Money, Credit and Banking 27:625–638.

Peek, J., and E. Rosengren (1997), "The international transmission of financial shocks: the case of Japan", American Economic Review 87:495–505.

Persons, J. (1994), "Renegotiation and the impossibility of optimal investment", Review of Financial Studies 7:419–449.

Peyer, U., and A. Shivdasani (2001), "Leverage and internal capital markets: evidence from leveraged recapitalizations", Journal of Financial Economics 59:477–515.

Phillips, G.M. (1995), "Increased debt and industry product markets: an empirical analysis", Journal of Financial Economics 37:189–238.

Prendergast, C., and L. Stole (1996), "Impetuous youngsters and jaded old-timers: acquiring a reputation for learning", Journal of Political Economy 104:1105–1134.

Rajan, R., H. Servaes and L. Zingales (2000), "The cost of diversity: the diversification discount and inefficient investment", Journal of Finance 55:35–80.

Rajan, R.G., and L. Zingales (1998), "Financial dependence and growth", American Economic Review 88:559–586.

Roll, R. (1986), "The hubris hypothesis of corporate takeovers", Journal of Business 59:197–216.

Rotemberg, J. (1993), "Power in profit-maximizing organizations", Journal of Economics and Management Strategy 2:165–198.

Rotemberg, J., and G. Saloner (1994), "Benefits of narrow business strategies", American Economic Review 84:1330–1349.

Schaller, H. (1993), "Asymmetric information, liquidity constraints and Canadian investment", Canadian Journal of Economics 26:552–574.

Scharfstein, D.S. (1998), "The dark side of internal capital markets II: evidence from diversified conglomerates", NBER Working Paper 6352 (NBER, Cambridge, MA).

Scharfstein, D.S., and J.C. Stein (1990), "Herd behavior and investment", American Economic Review 80:465–479.

Scharfstein, D.S., and J.C. Stein (2000), "The dark side of internal capital markets: divisional rent-seeking and inefficient investment", Journal of Finance 55:2537–2564.

Schoar, A.S. (2002), "Effects of corporate diversification on productivity", Journal of Finance 57: 2379–2403.

Schumpeter, J.A. (1911), The Theory of Economic Development (Harvard University Press, Cambridge, MA).

Servaes, H. (1996), "The value of diversification during the conglomerate merger wave", Journal of Finance 51:1201–1225.

Sharpe, S.A. (1994), "Financial market imperfections, firm leverage, and the cyclicality of employment" American Economic Review 84:1060–1074.

Shaw, E.S. (1973), Financial Deepening in Economic Development (Brookings Institute, Washington, DC).

Shin, H., and R. Stulz (1998), "Are internal capital markets efficient?", Quarterly Journal of Economics 113:531–552.

Shleifer, A. (2000), Inefficient Markets: An Introduction to Behavioral Finance (Oxford University Press, Oxford).

Shleifer, A., and R.W. Vishny (1989), "Management entrenchment: the case of manager-specific investments", Journal of Financial Economics 25:123–139.

Shleifer, A., and R.W. Vishny (1997), "A survey of corporate governance", Journal of Finance 52: 737–783.

Shleifer, A., and R.W. Vishny (2003), "Stock market driven acquisitions", Journal of Financial Economics, forthcoming.

Stein, J.C. (1988), "Takeover threats and managerial myopia", Journal of Political Economy 96:61–80.

Stein, J.C. (1989), "Efficient capital markets, inefficient firms: a model of myopic corporate behavior", Quarterly Journal of Economics 104:655–669.

Stein, J.C. (1996), "Rational capital budgeting in an irrational world", Journal of Business 69:429–455.

Stein, J.C. (1997), "Internal capital markets and the competition for corporate resources", Journal of Finance 52:111–133.

Stein, J.C. (1998), "An adverse-selection model of bank asset and liability management with implications for the transmission of monetary policy", RAND Journal of Economics 29:466–486.

Stein, J.C. (2002), "Information production and capital allocation: decentralized vs. hierarchical firms", Journal of Finance 57:1891–1921.

Stickel, S. (1990), "Predicting individual analyst earnings forecasts", Journal of Accounting Research 28:409–417.

Stiglitz, J.E., and A. Weiss (1981), "Credit rationing and markets with imperfect information", American Economic Review 71:393–411.

Stiglitz, J.E., and A. Weiss (1983), "Incentive effects of terminations: applications to the credit and labor markets", American Economic Review 73:912–927.

Stulz, R.M. (1990), "Managerial discretion and optimal financing policies", Journal of Financial Economics 26:3–27.

Stulz, R.M., and H. Johnson (1985), "An analysis of secured debt", Journal of Financial Economics 14:501–521.

Teoh, S., I. Welch and T.J. Wong (1998a), "Earnings management and the underperformance of seasoned equity offerings", Journal of Financial Economics 50:63–99.

Teoh, S., I. Welch and T.J. Wong (1998b), "Earnings management and the long-run underperformance of initial public offerings", Journal of Finance 53:1935–1974.

Thakor, A.V. (1990), "Investment 'myopia' and the internal organization of capital allocation decisions", Journal of Law, Economics and Organization 6:129–154.

Tirole, J. (1986), "Hierarchies and bureaucracies: on the role of collusion in organizations", Journal of Law, Economics and Organization 2:181–214.

Tobin, J. (1969), "A general equilibrium approach to monetary theory", Journal of Money, Credit and Banking 1:15–29.

Townsend, R.M. (1979), "Optimal contracts and competitive markets with costly state verification", Journal of Economic Theory 21:265–293.

Trueman, B. (1994), "Analyst forecasts and herding behavior", Review of Financial Studies 7:97–124.

Villalonga, B. (1999), "Does diversification cause the 'diversification discount'", Working Paper (UCLA Anderson Graduate School of Management, CA).

Weinstein, N. (1980), "Unrealistic optimism about future life events", Journal of Personality and Social Psychology 39:806–820.

Welch, I. (2000), "Herding among security analysis", Journal of Financial Economics 58:369–396.

Wermers, R. (1999), "Mutual fund herding and the impact on stock prices", Journal of Finance 54: 581–622.

Wernerfelt, B., and C.A. Montgomery (1988), "Tobin's q and the importance of focus in firm performance", American Economic Review 78:246–254.

Weston, J.F. (1970), "Diversification and merger trends", Business Economics 5:50–57.

Whited, T. (1992), "Debt, liquidity constraints, and corporate investment: evidence from panel data", Journal of Finance 47:1425–1460.

Whited, T. (2001), "Is it inefficient investment that causes the diversification discount?", Journal of Finance 56:1667–1691.

Williamson, O.E. (1964), The Economics of Discretionary Behavior: Managerial Objectives in a Theory of the Firm (Prentice Hall, Englewood Cliffs, NJ).

Williamson, O.E. (1975), Markets and Hierarchies: Analysis and Antitrust Implications (Collier Macmillan Publishers, Inc., NY).

Wulf, J. (1999), "Influence and inefficiency in the internal capital market: theory and evidence", Working Paper (University of Pennsylvania).

Wulf, J. (2002), "Internal capital markets and firm-level compensation incentives for division managers", Journal of Labor Economics 20:5219–5262.

Wurgler, J. (2000), "Financial markets and the allocation of capital", Journal of Financial Economics 58:187–214.

Zwiebel, J. (1995), "Corporate conservatism and relative compensation", Journal of Political Economy 103:1–25.

Zwiebel, J. (1996), "Dynamic capital structure under management entrenchment", American Economic Review 86:1197–1215.

Chapter 3

CORPORATE INVESTMENT POLICY

MICHAEL J. BRENNAN*

University of California, Los Angeles; London Business School

Contents

* Goldyne and Irwin Hearsh Professor of Banking and Finance, University of California, Los Angeles, and Professor of Finance, London Business School. I am grateful to John Cochrane, George Constantinides, Avinash Dixit, Milt Harris, Pedro SantaClara and Eduardo Schwartz for comments and suggestions.

Handbook of the Economics of Finance, Edited by G.M. Constantinides, M. Harris and R. Stulz

Abstract

This chapter is concerned with the classical applied problem of capital allocation by a corporation whose securities are traded in competitive and frictionless markets. Under reasonable assumptions that are discussed, this amounts to choosing projects whose market value exceeds their cost, so that the problem becomes one of valuing uncertain future cash flows. Valuation by discounting at a risk-adjusted discount rate is shown to be admissible under certain assumptions, and the practical problems of estimating risk premia are discussed. More general valuation approaches are introduced under the rubric of certainty equivalent pricing, which is based on the martingale pricing theory of Harrison and Pliska (1981), which allows, for example, for stochastic interest rates and risk premia. This leads naturally to a discussion of real options and of the role of competition and strategic considerations in investment policy.

Keywords

cost of capital, net present value, certainty equivalent valuation, cost of equity, equity premium, risk premium, martingale

JEL classification: G31, G32

1. Introduction

The allocation of capital to its highest value use is one of the most important roles of capital markets, and the investment policy of corporations is a major element of the allocation process. In this survey we are primarily concerned with the normative approach to corporate investment policy – what investment policy *should* firms follow, given their legal and ownership structures, and given that security prices are set in markets populated by rational investors. Therefore, for the most part we shall neglect considerations of agency, and assume that managers are concerned with maximizing the interests of stockholders. [1] We shall also generally ignore the problems that are raised by asymmetries of information between insiders and outsiders in the firm. In other words, after considering the issues that underlie the appropriate choice of objective function for a corporation in Section 2, we shall then adopt assumptions that make the selection of projects with the highest net-present-value (NPV) optimal for investors, and concern ourselves mainly with the practical problems that arise in assessing project value. [2]

Significant advances have been made in developing theories of asset pricing over the past 35 years. Nonetheless, there is still dispute about the correct theoretical asset pricing model, and there is considerable uncertainty about the parameters of the individual models. Attacks have been mounted in recent years on the whole rational markets paradigm which asserts that security prices are set by rational investors using the best information that is available. [3] However, the implications of irrational markets for corporate investment policy have yet to be developed, [4] and it remains to be seen whether behavioral theories offer a more fruitful approach to the analysis of markets than does the rational markets paradigm. Therefore, this survey is firmly within the rational markets paradigm. We shall not attempt to survey the considerable literature on theoretical and empirical asset pricing, but will explore the implications of the different asset pricing models for corporate discount rates, and appraise the empirical evidence that bears on the practical application of asset pricing models in investment appraisal.

Until recently, most applied work concerned with investment appraisal has relied on *ad hoc* adjustments to *single-period* asset pricing models in order to apply them to the multi-period context in which real investment appraisal must take place. As a result, there have been disagreements, not only over empirical issues such as how large is the equity risk premium, but also over such basic theoretical issues as whether the equity risk premium should be measured relative to the returns on long term bonds or relative to the returns on short term securities such as Treasury Bills, and whether risk premia

---

[1] We shall generally ignore conflicts of interest that may arise between shareholders and other security holders in the firm.

[2] See Chapter 2 in this volume by Jeremy Stein for a discussion of the role of agency and information.

[3] For example, DeBondt and Thaler (1995).

[4] For an early effort in this direction see Stein (1996).

should be estimated as arithmetic means or as geometric means of the time series of realized excess returns. In Section 3 we shall consider the conditions under which traditional discounted cash-flow analysis is warranted, and show how the discount rate should be related to the characteristics of the cash flow that is being discounted under different asset pricing theories.

Section 4 is concerned with the practical problems of estimating the discount rates to be used in discounted cash flow analysis; both asset-pricing model-based, and direct, or discounted cash flow (DCF), estimates of the cost of equity capital are considered; asset-pricing model-based estimates rely on estimates of the risk premia associated with different risk factors, the most important of which is the equity-risk premium, or reward for market risk; they also rely on estimates of factor loadings. DCF estimates of the cost of equity capital on the other hand do not depend on a particular asset pricing model or estimates of risk, but rely instead on direct forecasts of the cash flows of the individual firm. An intermediate approach is to estimate the market risk premium using a DCF approach for all the firms in the "market portfolio" and then to arrive at a cost of equity capital for an individual firm by adjusting for its relative risk. The DCF and asset-pricing model estimates are based on quite different paradigms and it is not surprising that the resultant estimates should differ considerably. It is more surprising to find that there are considerable differences in the cost of equity capital estimates obtained from the Capital Asset Pricing Model and the Arbitrage Pricing Theory. The continuing existence of the different approaches reflects both the unsatisfactory state of asset-pricing theory and the difficulties of applying it in practice.

The cost of equity capital is only one component of a firm's cost of capital and it is important to relate the cost of equity capital to the firm's overall cost of capital for two reasons. First, it is the overall cost of capital, not the cost of equity capital, that is relevant for discounting cash flows with similar risk characteristics to the firm's existing assets; secondly, it is often important to be able to assess the cost of capital for several different firms in a single industry in order to obtain an estimate for the cost of capital of a single division of a multi-divisional firm. To the extent that the sample firms have different capital structures, their costs of equity capital will differ, and it is necessary to be able to adjust for this capital-structure effect to determine the cost of capital that is appropriate for a particular line of business. Therefore, the effects of corporate and personal taxes on the relation between cost of equity and cost of capital are analyzed.

In recent years an alternative to the standard discounted cash-flow approach to project evaluation has begun to gain popularity. This is the theory of martingale, or certainty equivalent, pricing that has evolved from the option-pricing paradigm, and which provides a more general framework for asset valuation. This theory has begun to find practical application under the rubric of "real options" because it is particularly well suited for analyzing projects whose future cash flows can be affected by subsequent decisions of the firm that will be made as more information becomes available. It is these future decision contingencies that constitute the "real options". However, even when there are no real options in a project, the certainty equivalent approach provides a conceptually more satisfactory framework for dealing with risk than does traditional discounted cash flow. Section 5 discusses the principles that underlie certainty equivalent or martingale pricing, and presents some examples of this approach. It also considers the application of martingale pricing to situations in which risk premia are subject to stochastic variation.

Throughout the survey we assume that the firm is publicly traded in competitive security markets and has access to a perfectly elastic supply of capital for its investment projects. These assumptions allow us to ignore the mainly intractable problems of project selection that arise when a firm faces a limited supply of capital.

As a prelude to the discussion of the valuation of real assets that occupies most of this survey, we start in Section 2 with a discussion of the objective of the firm and the conditions under which value maximization is an appropriate objective.

2. The objective of the firm and the net-present-value rule

In the standard neoclassical theory of the firm under certainty there is no distinction between debt and equity, so that the objective of the firm in a competitive capital market is simple and unequivocal: by choosing policies that maximize its value, the firm maximizes the budget sets of its investors and hence their welfare; as a result, owners of the firm are unanimous in supporting the investment policy that maximizes the value of the firm. [5] This theory extends naturally to allow for uncertainty about asset payoffs if potential conflicts of interest between bondholders and stockholders can be ignored, and if the capital market is both competitive and permits a Pareto-optimal allocation. [6] Under these conditions also, there exists unanimous support among shareholders for value-maximizing policies.

When the capital market is incomplete and does not permit an unconstrained Pareto-optimal allocation, the objective of the firm is less clear; shareholders may disagree about the best policy and will in general not support the policy that maximizes the value of the firm, or even of the firm's equity. As an example, consider a firm that is contemplating an investment in an exploratory oil well. If we assume that there are no nearby drillers, the success of this venture will be largely independent of the returns on the securities of any other firm in the capital market. We say that the firm is "creating a

---

[5] See Fisher (1930, p. 141), or Hirshleifer (1970, p. 14). Rubinstein (1978) emphasizes the stringent conditions that must be satisfied if value maximization is to maximize the budget sets of all investors even under certainty; for small shareholders, the effect on their budget sets of even a small change in the interest rate may outweigh the direct effect of a change in the value of their investment in a firm.

[6] See Nielsen (1976). A Pareto-optimal allocation will be achieved in a competitive market if the market is complete or if there exists a riskless security and the conditions for two-fund separation are met. Under two-fund separation all investors hold linear combinations of the riskless security and the same portfolio of risky assets; sufficient conditions for two-fund separation are that all investors have HARA (hyperbolic absolute risk aversion) utility with identical cautiousness and have identical beliefs: the capital asset pricing model is a special case of two-fund separation. See also Ross (1978).

new security" by investing in the oil well, because the payoff from this project cannot be spanned or replicated by investing in any portfolio of existing securities. Under such conditions, an individual investor who is particularly optimistic about the prospects for the oil well may support the project even though announcement that the project is going to be undertaken will *reduce the current wealth of all shareholders* because the market does not rate the prospects of finding oil highly, and places a corresponding low value on the prospective cash flows from the well; the optimistic investor values the new security highly because it allows him to do something he wants to do that is otherwise impossible: to gamble on the prospect of oil in this location. It is clear that the unanimity of investors that is a property of complete markets for risk, does not exist in this case: the optimistic shareholder may support the project while pessimists oppose it.[7] Unanimity in favor of value-maximizing decisions will be re-established, even in an incomplete market, if the payoffs of the project are spanned by the existing securities so that no new security is created, and the market is competitive. However, spanning seems an unlikely property for investment projects in general, and therefore it is important to consider the conditions under which unanimity among shareholders will hold in incomplete markets without either Pareto-optimality or spanning.

The strongest result is obtained by Makowski (1983) who shows that shareholders will unanimously agree on a policy of value maximization, even in incomplete markets without spanning, provided that no short sales are allowed and that the demand curve for the firm's shares is perfectly elastic. The perfect elasticity of the demand curve means that no purchaser of the firm's shares enjoys a consumer surplus, so that the availability or unavailability of the firm's shares is a matter of indifference to any potential buyer (and there are no short sellers); on the other hand, any initial shareholder is made better or worse off by the investment decision according to whether or not it increases his wealth. In terms of our oil well example, the Makowski conditions imply that if one shareholder is optimistic about the prospects for oil, there are enough other equally optimistic individuals that the capital market will value the opportunity at the optimist's valuation, leaving him no consumer surplus; under these conditions, his welfare (like that of other shareholder's who will sell their shares) is affected only by his wealth, so that all shareholders unanimously support a policy of value maximization.

If the capital market is not competitive even if it is complete, there will in general be no unanimity among shareholders about the optimal investment decision.[8] Further complications arise if there is asymmetric information about project returns.

---

[7] The introduction of a new security into an incomplete market also has the potential to change the prices of all other securities which will have additional effects on the wealth of shareholders who also hold shares in other firms.

[8] *Local* unanimity (agreement on the direction of change of a decision variable) may exist among the investors in a firm in an imperfect capital market if market equilibrium has been achieved and either the marginal investment is spanned or portfolio separation obtains; however, this will not be unanimity in favor of value-maximizing decisions [Ekern and Wilson (1974), Leland (1974)], and Nielsen (1976)

In an important, but relatively neglected paper, Leland (1974) considers the issue of unanimity when markets are competitive but incomplete and corporate managers have more information about project-specific risks than do shareholders. He shows that if the manager is allowed to trade to his optimal firm shareholding, then for "small" decisions the shareholders will unanimously support decisions that maximize the expected utility of the manager.[9] Other authors[10] have assumed without proof that, when managers have inside information, an appropriate objective function for the corporation is the maximization of a weighted average of the market and intrinsic values of the firm's shares, where the latter is determined using the manager's information.

Despite evidence that even developed capital markets are less than perfectly competitive,[11] and that managers do have inside information about firm returns, market value maximization seems a reasonable practical objective for the firm, and that is the one on which most of the theory of corporate investment policy is based. It is the one that we shall take for granted in the rest of this survey. We shall assume that the market has access to the same information about future cash flows as does the manager, so that in assessing market values the manager is warranted in using his expectations about future cash flows.

The firm objective of value maximization gives rise to what has come to be known as the Net Present Value Rule:

Net Present Value Rule. *An investment project should be adopted if and only if its net present value is positive; if two projects are mutually exclusive, then the one having the higher net present value should be adopted.*

Consistent implementation of the Net Present Value rule will ensure that the value of the shareholders' interest is maximized, provided that two conditions are met:
(i) adoption of the new project must have no effect on the value of the firm's outstanding debt or other securities except the common equity;
(ii) the new equity (or other securities) that are sold to finance the project must be sold on fair terms, so that the price at which they are sold is equal to the price at which they trade.

To see the importance of (i), suppose that the new project improves the security of the outstanding debt so that its expected payoff and current value rise. In this case, part of the benefits of the project accrue to the holders of the firm's debt, reducing the benefits that are left for the stockholders; in extreme cases this potential "wealth transfer" to debtholders can be so great that the net gain to the shareholders is negative,

---

shows that *local* unanimity does not imply *global* unanimity (agreement on the magnitude of the change), so that in general there is no unanimously supported objective function in imperfect capital markets.

[9] This is a *local* unanimity result. See footnote 7.

[10] See, for example, Miller and Rock (1985).

[11] Bagwell (1992) and Shleifer (1986) provide evidence that the demand curve for a firm's shares is downward sloping.

even though the NPV is positive; then shareholders will be unwilling to finance a project even though it has a positive NPV. [12]

To see the importance of (ii), suppose that the market value of the equity does not rise when the project is announced despite the fact that NPV > 0, perhaps because the market does not have access to the same information as the manager and does not recognize the value of the project cash flows. In this case, the original shareholders will gain only a fraction of the NPV of the project if it is financed by issuing (underpriced) equity. In more extreme cases, in which the original equity is selling below the value of the existing assets, the gain to the old shareholders from the project may even be negative if it is financed by issuing equity. [13]

In what follows we shall ignore completely issues raised by wealth transfers to other security holders and problems caused by asymmetric information. Then the simple NPV Rule described above leads to the maximization of the wealth of old shareholders.

Under certain circumstances, [14] the NPV will be positive whenever the Internal Rate of Return (IRR) on the project exceeds the appropriate discount rate for valuing the cash flows from the project, or the project's "cost of capital". However, it is well known that if two projects are mutually exclusive, the project with the higher Internal Rate of Return is not necessarily the one with the higher Net Present Value, so the IRR is at best an uncertain guide to action. One important way in which mutually exclusive projects can arise is through the 'timing option' – the consideration that a project may be undertaken today or at some time in the future, but not on both occasions. Thus, to take account of this timing option we should modify the NPV Rule to add the condition that a project should not be undertaken today even if its NPV is positive, if the NPV is higher under the policy of postponing the project. [15]

The foregoing discussion implies that the fundamental problem of the capital allocation process is the valuation of the different capital projects that are available for consideration. Occasionally, a cash-flow claim can be valued by arbitrage as a function only of the observables, time, the interest rate, and the value of another asset. [16] Most often however, valuation must be based on a model of equilibrium. We shall consider the two major approaches to valuation in turn, and show how these are related to standard models of capital market equilibrium. The traditional, and by far the most commonly employed approach in practice, is valuation by discounting, using a

---

[12] This situation is analyzed by Myers (1977). The same considerations apply if the project is financed with debt so long as the new debt is sold at fair market value.

[13] See Myers and Majluf (1984).

[14] Basically, whenever the discounted present value of the project is a monotone decreasing function of the discount rate.

[15] For further discussion of the timing option see Section 5.

[16] Ross (1978) presents necessary and sufficient conditions; these are that the cash flow be a linear function of the value of the asset whose price is known, and that the cash flow yield of that asset be deterministic.

discount rate that is adjusted for the risk of the cash flows. The more recent approach, which has its roots in the Black–Scholes–Merton stock option pricing paradigm, is a certainty-equivalent approach in which expected cash flows are first adjusted for risk using the martingale approach and are then discounted at a risk-free interest rate; for historical reasons, this has come to be called the "real options" approach. This is something of a misnomer since the principles apply whether or not there are options involved, and we shall use the more neutral term, "certainty equivalent" approach. We consider first the conditions under which valuation by discounting is warranted.

3. Valuation by discounting

As we have seen, investment decision making is essentially concerned with the valuation of investment projects. If, as is most likely, the returns on an investment project are not spanned by the returns on existing securities, the analyst must *estimate* the (present) value of the project cash flows. Since an unspanned project is by definition unique, some asset pricing theory is required to predict the price at which claims to the returns from the project would trade. In practice, estimates of value are most commonly arrived at by discounting the expected cash flows from the project at a "risk-adjusted discount rate" or "cost of capital".[17] In this section we consider the conditions under which a stream of cash flows can be valued by applying a discount rate derived from one of the classic asset pricing models.

The simplest approach to valuing a stream of future cash flows is to apply a single discount rate, ρ^*, which is appropriate for the risk of the cash flows, to the expected future cash flows, so that V_t, the value of the stream at time t, can be written as

$$V_t = \sum_{s=t+1}^{T} \frac{y_{t,s}}{(1+\rho^*)^{(s-t)}},\tag{1}$$

where $y_{t,s} \equiv E_t[C_s]$ is the expected value at time t of the cash flow that will be received at time s. This expression does not take account of the term structure of riskless interest rates. Therefore, a natural generalization of expression (1) is to assume that the discount rate for a particular cash flow is equal to the spot riskless rate for that

---

[17] This approach to valuation is basically a heuristic extension of established methods for valuing bonds. It has a long history, and is to be found in such investment classics as J.B. Williams (1938) who proposed a risk premium of 13/4% for General Motors "in view of this risk (of "going to seed")" (p. 406). The alternative to the discounted cash flow approach is the "real options" or certainty equivalent approach which is discussed in Section 5.

maturity plus a constant risk premium. In this case the value of the cash-flow stream may be written as

$$V_t = \sum_{s=t+1}^{T} \frac{y_{t,s}}{(1 + R_{t,s} + \lambda)^{(s-t)}}, \tag{2}$$

where λ is the risk premium and $R_{t,s}$ is the spot interest rate at time t for a loan of $(s-t)$ periods.

The first issue is the conditions under which asset values can be consistently expressed as expected cash flows discounted at a risk adjusted discount rate as in the formulation (2). It is convenient to work with the continuous compounding equivalents of Equations (1) and (2). Then the issue is the conditions under which $V_{t,s}$, the value at time t of a single cash flow expected to be received at time s, can be expressed as

$$V_{t,s} = y_{t,s} \exp[-(r_{t,s} + \lambda)(s-t)] \equiv y_{t,s} B(t,s) \exp[-\lambda(s-t)] \approx \frac{y_{t,s}}{(1 + R_{t,s} + \lambda)^{(s-t)}}, \tag{3}$$

where $r_{t,s}$ is the continuously compounded spot rate and $B(t,s)$ is the value at time t of a pure discount bond that pays \$1 at time s. We shall drop the time subscripts from the current expectation variable, $y_{t,s}$, and the bond price, $B(t,s)$. Then consider a continuous-time economy in which y, the expectation of the cash flow at time τ which is to be valued, the pricing kernel, M,[18] the price B of the bond maturing at time s, and a generic state variable, X, follow the following correlated stochastic processes:

$$\frac{dy}{y} = \sigma_y(X) \, dz_y, \tag{4a}$$

$$\frac{dM}{M} = -r(X) \, dt + \sigma_M(X) \, dz_M, \tag{4b}$$

$$\frac{dB}{B} = \mu_B(X) \, dt + \sigma_B(X) \, dz_B, \tag{4c}$$

$$dX = \mu_x(X) \, dt + \sigma_x \, dz_X, \tag{4d}$$

where dz_y, dz_M, etc., are increments to Gauss–Wiener processes.

---

[18] Also known as the stochastic discount factor, the pricing kernel can be thought of as corresponding to the marginal utility of a representative investor.

Note that we have imposed a martingale or zero drift property on y, since it is an expectation. Since the pricing kernel, M, prices both the cash flow claim and the bond, we have that:

$$E[d(MV)] = 0, \tag{5}$$
$$E[d(MB)] = 0. \tag{6}$$

Substituting $yB\exp[-\lambda(s-t)]$ for V in Equation (5) and using Ito's Lemma implies that

$$\lambda - r + \mu_B + \sigma_{By} + \sigma_{My} + \sigma_{BM} = 0. \tag{7}$$

But, using Ito's Lemma in Equation (6) implies that

$$\mu_B - r + \sigma_{BM} = 0. \tag{8}$$

Finally, combining Equations (7) and (8), we have

$$\lambda = -\sigma_{By} - \sigma_{My}. \tag{9}$$

This leads to the following

Theorem. *The value at time t of a claim to an expected cash flow at time s, $V_{t,s}$, may be expressed as the expected value of the cash flow, $y_{t,s}$, discounted at the $(s-t)$-period spot riskless rate, $r_{t,s}$, plus a risk premium λ that is constant and independent of the maturity of the claim, $V_{t,s} = y_{t,s}\exp[-(r_{t,s} + \lambda)(s-t)]$, if and only if the sum of the covariances of the cash flow expectation, y, with the $(s-t)$-period bond price, B, and with the pricing kernel, M, $(\sigma_{By} + \sigma_{My})$, is constant.*

The theorem thus provides necessary and sufficient conditions for valuation using the risk-adjusted discount rate approach with a constant risk adjustment.

Consider first the case in which interest rates are non-stochastic, so that $\sigma_{By} = 0$. Then the conditions of the theorem are satisfied if and only if σ_{My} is constant. We shall assume until Section 5.2.3 that the pricing kernel has constant volatility. [19] Then σ_{My} will be constant if the 'beta' in a regression of changes in the expectation of the cash flow on the innovations in the pricing kernel is constant; roughly speaking, the flow of priced information must be constant over time. [20] We shall say that a cash flow

---

[19] This assumption is roughly equivalent to the assumption that risk premia are constant over time.

[20] Fama (1977) gives a similar condition for the CAPM to yield the cost of capital for a cash flow stream. Brennan (1977) and Myers and Turnbull (1977) provide related examples in which the CAPM may be used to obtain the discount rate. Myers and Robichek (1966) recognized the relation between information flows and discount rates. Ross (1989) points out that the value of a cash flow claim is independent of the *timing* of the resolution of its uncertainty.

satisfies the *Constant Relative Risk Condition* (CRRC) if and only if σ_{My} is constant. If the correlation between the innovations in the expected cash flow and in the pricing kernel is constant, the CRRC will be satisfied if and only if σ_y is constant so that the cash flow expectation follows a geometric Brownian motion. This is inconsistent, for example, with a cash flow that consists of a risky and a riskless component – in this setting, only "pure" risky cash flows can be discounted with a constant risk premium. Note that a T-period distant cash flow for which σ_y is constant will have a lognormal conditional distribution with parameters $(\ln y - (T/2)\,\sigma_y^2,\ T\sigma_y^2)$. This implies that the distribution of the cash flow will be positively skewed. [21]

When interest rates are stochastic, the theorem requires that $(\sigma_{By} + \sigma_{My})$ be constant. However, σ_{By}, the covariance of the bond price with the expected future cash flow, will not in general be constant unless either σ_{My} or σ_{BM} are equal to zero. The former corresponds to the case in which the expected cash flow is uncorrelated with the pricing kernel and the latter corresponds to the situation in which the pure expectations theory of interest rates holds. [22]

Reverting to the case in which interest rates are non-stochastic, the theorem places an upper bound on the risk premium; when the innovation of the cash flow expectation is perfectly correlated with the pricing kernel, the risk premium is equal to $\sigma_y \sigma_M$. Thus, knowing the volatility of the cash flow, the risk premium can be bounded for a given model of the pricing kernel. This property has not been widely exploited. [23]

In order to proceed further, it is necessary to specify the pricing kernel. The two most popular models of the pricing kernel are the Capital Asset Pricing Model of Lintner (1965) and Sharpe (1964), [24] and the Multi-Factor Asset Pricing Models which are based on either the Intertemporal Capital Asset Pricing Model of Merton (1973) or the Arbitrage Pricing Theory developed by Ross (1976). [25]

3.1. Multi-factor asset pricing models

Suppose that the pricing kernel is such that $\frac{dM}{M} = -r\,dt - \sum_{k=1}^{K} \gamma_k\,df_k$, where r is the instantaneously riskless interest rate and $E[df_k] = df_k\,df_l = 0$ for $k \neq l$ and $df_k\,df_k = 1$.

---

[21] See Fama (1996) for a similar point. Of course a cash flow could be the algebraic sum of several component cash flows, each of which satisfy the CRRC condition. If all the components have the same risk premium it will be appropriate to discount the aggregate cash flow at the same rate and there is no need for the aggregate cash flow to be positively skewed; however, in this case the correlation between the aggregate cash flow expectation and the pricing kernel will be stochastic.

[22] This is because the volatility of the bond return, σ_B, is decreasing in the maturity of the bond for typical bond pricing models such as Vasicek (1977) or Cox, Ingersoll and Ross (1985)

[23] But see Cochrane and Saa-Requejo (2000).

[24] "The only asset pricing model that has been applied widely in practice is the capital asset pricing model" [Cornell et al. (1997, p. 12)].

[25] It is common to treat the Merton and Ross models as empirically indistinguishable, neglecting the restriction of the Merton framework that the factors are innovations in state variables *that predict future investment opportunities*. The factors in Ross's model may have no relation to future investment opportunities.

Then Equation (5) implies that, if the interest rate is non-stochastic and the innovations in the expected cash flow for project i satisfy the factor model [Leland (1977)]:

$$\frac{\mathrm{d}y^i_{t,\tau}}{y^i_{t,\tau}} = \sum_{k=1}^{K} \beta_{ik}\, \mathrm{d}f_k + \sigma_i(t,\tau)\, \mathrm{d}z^i_{t,\tau},$$ (10)

where $\mathrm{d}z^i_{t,\tau}\, \mathrm{d}f_k = 0$, then the risk premium, λ_i, is given by the linear pricing relation

$$\lambda_i = \sum_{k=1}^{K} \gamma_k \beta_{ik}.$$ (11)

3.2. The capital asset pricing model

Now suppose that the pricing kernel may be written as $\mathrm{d}M/M = -r\,\mathrm{d}t - S_m\,\mathrm{d}z_m$, where the return on the market portfolio is given by $\mathrm{d}V_m/V_m = \mu_m\,\mathrm{d}t + \sigma_m\,\mathrm{d}z_m$, and $S_m \equiv (\mu_m - r)/\sigma_m$ is the Sharpe ratio for the market portfolio.

Then, if the innovations in the cash flow expectations for project i satisfy the market model:

$$\frac{\mathrm{d}y^i_{t,\tau}}{y^i_{t,\tau}} = \beta_i \left[\frac{\mathrm{d}V_m}{V_m} - \mu_m\,\mathrm{d}t \right] + \eta_i\,\mathrm{d}z_i,$$ (12)

where $\mathrm{d}z_i\, \mathrm{d}V_m = 0$, condition (5) implies that the risk premium for the project satisfies the CAPM relation:

$$\lambda_i = \beta_i(\mu_m - r).$$ (13)

Note that if the CAPM is used to estimate a discount rate, the rate should be equal to the corresponding spot interest rate plus a risk premium equal to beta times the market risk premium, $(\mu_m - r)$, where the market risk premium is measured relative to the instantaneously riskless interest rate.[26]

Simple manipulations show that the *maximum* risk premium for a cash flow is $S_m \sigma_y$ where σ_y is the cash flow volatility. Using a Sharpe ratio of 0.3,[27] a 4 year distant cash flow with a 4-year volatility of 40% which satisfied the CRRC would have a one-year

---

[26] This corresponds roughly to one of the procedures employed by practitioners who use the term structure of forward rates to forecast future short rates, and then add to these a market risk premium. See Cornell et al. (1997). It is inconsistent with estimating the risk premium as the difference in expected returns between the market portfolio and a *long-term* bond, even when the long term bond yield is used as the riskless rate [see Kaplan and Ruback (1995) for an example of this procedure].

[27] MacKinlay (1995) reports an estimate of the Sharpe ratio for the CRSP value weighted index of around 0.3 for the period 1963–1991.

volatility of 20%, and this would imply a *maximum* risk premium of $0.3 \times 20\% = 6\%$. Similarly, a 16 year cash flow with a 16 year volatility of 80% would also have a maximum risk premium of 6%. This seems low compared with anecdotal evidence of corporate discount rates.[28]

Consider a situation in which the term structure of riskless interest rates is constant and a firm's shares promise a series of aggregate dividends, D_1, D_2, etc., whose expected values at time t are denoted by $y_{t,sT}, s = t + 1, \ldots$ If each dividend satisfies the *Constant Relative Risk Condition* with the same value of σ_{My}, the value of the equity at time t, E_t, will be given by the standard DCF formula:

$$E_t = \sum_{s=t+1}^{\infty} \frac{y_{t,s}}{(1 + r + \lambda)^s},$$
(14)

and $k \equiv r + \lambda$ is the firm's *cost of equity capital*. Even though there is no theoretical relation between a firm's cost of equity and the discount rate that is appropriate for discounting the expected cash flows from a new investment project, estimates of a firm's costs of equity capital are an important element in most estimates of project value. Therefore we will consider how a firm's cost of equity capital can be estimated.

4. Practical approaches to estimating discount rates

Estimation of the risk-adjusted discount rate or cost of capital for an investment project typically involves three steps:
(1) Estimation of the cost of *equity* capital for a firm or a group of firms;
(2) Estimation of the overall cost of capital for the firm or firms – this requires adjustments to the cost of equity capital to take account of other sources of finance as well as the effect of taxes and non-traded securities.
(3) Estimation of the cost of capital for a project or for a division of a firm from what is known about the costs of capital for the firm itself and possibly for other firms in similar industries.

In Section 4.1 we shall consider the problem of estimating the cost of equity capital for a *firm,* assuming that the firm's cash flows satisfy the CRRC.

4.1. Estimating equity discount rates in practice

There are essentially two different approaches to estimating costs of equity capital, the discount rates that investors implicitly use to value equity securities. The older method,

---

[28] Summers (1987) reports a median corporate hurdle rate for investment projects of 15%. An alternative explanation for high corporate hurdle rates is that they represent a heuristic for allowing for the timing option in investment projects. See footnote 78.

which is currently experiencing a revival, is to forecast the cash flows that investors could reasonably expect to receive from a share of common stock, and to find the discount rate that equates the value of the stream of expected cash flows to the stock price – this is sometimes referred to as the discounted cash flow or DCF method. With the development of the CAPM and multi-factor asset pricing models, attention shifted from these techniques to (asset pricing) model-based estimates of the cost of equity capital. Graham and Harvey (2001), who survey 392 Chief Financial Officers of large corporations, report that "the CAPM is by far the most popular method of estimating the cost of equity capital: 73.5% of respondents always or almost always use the CAPM". However, asset-pricing model-based estimates of the cost of equity require estimates of factor (market) risk premia as well as factor loadings, and an intermediate approach is to estimate these premia using DCF methods. We shall first discuss asset-pricing model-based estimates and then the more traditional DCF approach.

4.1.1. Using asset-pricing models

Most published studies of the use of asset-pricing models to estimate costs of equity capital have been restricted to regulated USA utility companies for which the estimated cost of equity capital is a major determinant of allowed profit rates and prices.[29] However, Fama and French (1997) use both the CAPM and the Fama–French (1995, 1997) three factor model[30] to estimate the costs of equity capital for industry portfolios. They are somewhat discouraged by the results they obtain:

> The first problem is imprecise estimates of risk loadings. Estimates of CAPM and three-factor risk loadings would be precise if the loadings were constant. We find, however, that there is strong variation through time in the CAPM and three-factor risk loadings of industries … estimates from full sample (1963–1994) regressions are no more accurate than the imprecise estimates from regressions that use only the latest three years of data. And industries give an understated picture of the problems that will arise in estimating risk loadings for individual firms and investment projects.
>
>   The second problem is imprecise estimates of factor risk premiums. For example, the price of risk in the CAPM is the expected return on the market minus the risk-free rate, $E(R_M) - R_f$. The

---

[29] See Bower, Bower and Logue (1984), Goldenberg and Robin (1991) and Elton, Gruber and Mei (1994). See Brennan and Schwartz (1982) for a critique of the cost of capital approach to utility rate regulation.

[30] The Fama–French factors are the return on the equity market portfolio, and the returns on two zero net investment portfolios: the first, HML, is a portfolio that is long high book-to-market stocks and short low book-to-market stocks; the second, SMB, is long in small stocks and short in large stocks. As yet there is no theoretical justification for these factors although [Davis, Fama and French (2000, p. 390)] claim that "the model largely captures the average returns on USA portfolios formed on size, BE/ME and other variables known to cause problems for the CAPM". Daniel and Titman (D–T) (1997) have questioned whether the FF portfolios represent priced risk factors; Davis, Fama and French (2000) present evidence in favor of their risk interpretation and against the D–T characteristics (size, book-to-market) model of expected returns.

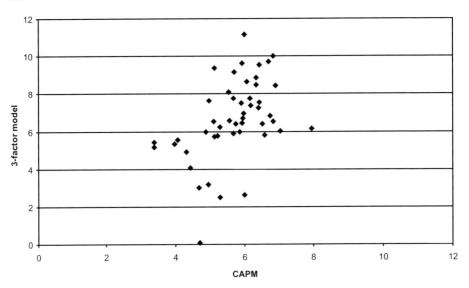

Fig. 1. Industry costs of equity capital (%). Risk premia for the CAPM and 3-factor model are based on the average monthly excess return on the market portfolio and the average monthly returns on the Fama–French SMB and HML portfolios for the period July 1963 to December 1994. Data from Fama and French (1997, Table 7).

annualized average excess return on the CRSP value-weight market portfolio ... for our 1963–1994 sample period is 5.16%; its standard error is 2.71%. Thus, if we use the historical market risk premium to estimate the expected premium, the traditional plus and minus two standard error interval ranges from less than zero to more than 10.0%.

Our message is that uncertainty of this magnitude about risk premiums, coupled with the uncertainty about risk loadings, implies woefully imprecise estimates of the cost of equity capital.

Fama and French (1997, p. 154)

We should not be surprised that the industry risk loadings vary over time: even if the assets underlying the firms have the CRRC property that would give them constant risk loadings, time variation in corporate leverage would be enough to create time variation in equity risk loadings. Figure 1 plots the estimated costs of equity from the CAPM and three-factor models from the Fama–French paper. The correlation between the two sets of estimates is only 0.45 and an even lower correlation would be found between estimates from the two models for individual firms.

Pastor and Stambaugh (1999) employ a Bayesian approach to consider, not only uncertainty about the parameters of the asset-pricing model, but also uncertainty about the degree to which a given pricing model misprices the risk of a given stock, and uncertainty about which pricing model to use.[31] They find that model mispricing

---

[31] In addition to the CAPM they consider the Fama–French three-factor model and a version of the APT based on statistical factors.

uncertainty is typically less important than uncertainty about the parameters (risk loadings and risk premia) of the model. Like Fama and French (1997)[32] they conclude that uncertainty about risk premia is much more important than uncertainty about risk loadings even when the unit of analysis is the individual firm rather than an industry portfolio. Ignoring model error, and using data for the period 1963–1995, they find that the average posterior standard deviation of the equity premium for individual stocks · is around 2.9% for the CAPM, and 3.9% for the Arbitrage Pricing Theory (APT) models; however, the average premium estimated from the APT models is 8.2–9.0% as compared with only 5.57% for the CAPM. This difference reflects the fact that the APT models allow for size and book-to-market effects that are not captured by the CAPM.[33] When they assign equal probability to the CAPM and one of the APT models they find that this additional model uncertainty adds on average about 0.71% to the standard deviation of the posterior distribution of the premium of the average stock.

Given the importance of the equity premium for cost of capital estimates that use the CAPM, it is not surprising to find that considerable effort has been devoted to pinning down this elusive expectational variable. In contrast, relatively little effort has been expended in estimating the premia associated with the factors of multi-factor models – one reason for this is that there is no canonical set of risk factors, and until recently the available time series for the Fama–French factors, which are currently the most widely used, dated only from 1963.[34]

4.1.1.1. The equity risk premium. Two main approaches have been taken to the estimation of the equity risk premium: an historical approach that typically assumes that the premium is constant over time; and a forward-looking approach that allows for time variation in the premium and relies on forecasts of future dividends from the stocks that make up the market portfolio. However, neither approach allows for stochastic variation in the premium although there is now extensive evidence of predictability of excess returns on stocks.[35] The two approaches yield quite different results.

Typical *historical based estimates* of the equity premium for the USA since 1926 fall around 8%, if the arithmetic mean is used and around 6% if the geometric mean is used. The arithmetic mean is an unbiased estimate of the one period premium and many authors recommend that it be used in estimating discount rates. As Cooper (1996) points out, this procedure rests on three assumptions: that the arithmetic expected return (risk premium) is constant; that returns are serially independent; and that

---

[32] See also Ferson and Locke (1998).

[33] The averages are *equally weighted averages,* and are therefore affected by the higher average returns on small firms.

[34] Ibbotson Associates (1997) reports estimates of the premia for the Fama–French factors: 3.70% for SMB and 5.04% for HML. Davis, Fama and French (2000) extend the series back to 1929.

[35] See for example, Fama and French (1989) and Kothari and Shanken (1997). Section 5.2.3 discusses valuation under stochastic variation in interest rates and risk premia.

the expected return is known. However, in valuing a future cash flow the discount factor is raised to a power that depends on the number of periods, and an unbiased estimate of the risk premium cannot be used directly to obtain an unbiased estimate of the T-period discount factor on account of Jensen's inequality. Cooper proposes the following unbiased estimator of the T-period *discount factor* when returns are serially independent and the expected return is constant. Let G and A denote the geometric and arithmetic mean (gross) returns estimated from a T-period sample. Then the unbiased estimate of the N-period discount factor, D^N, is a weighted average of these two estimates:

$$D^N = bA^{-N} + (1 - b)G^{-N}, \tag{15}$$

where $b = (N + T)/(T - 1)$. For large sample sizes, T, this converges to the arithmetic mean. However, this formula does not take account of serial correlation or other types of predictability in returns for which there is now quite extensive evidence.[36] Brennan (1997) suggests Monte-Carlo simulation of a vector autoregression of the predictive variables, interest rates, and market returns to obtain estimates of long horizon discount factors. However, his procedure ignores the fact that the parameters of the VAR are estimated rather than known. Indro and Lee (1997) present an analysis of the effects of (negative) autocorrelation in returns, and suggest that the horizon weighted average of arithmetic and geometric mean estimators proposed by Blume (1974) has the least bias for expected wealth relatives.

Brown et al. (1995) cast doubt on any use of historical estimates of the risk premium which, they argue, contain a survival bias; for example, the 8% historical equity premium for the surviving USA market is consistent with a true ex-ante equity premium of 4% and a survival probability of 80%. Fama and French (2002) also argue that historical estimates of the equity risk premium have a positive bias. They compare realized average real returns with "Gordon" estimates[37] which are obtained by averaging across years the sum of the dividend yield at the beginning of the year and the dividend growth rate for the year. The Gordon approach and realized average returns yield similar estimates of the premium of around 4% for the period 1872–1949; however, the two methods yield divergent estimates for the period 1950–1999. The Gordon estimate of 3.40% is less than half the estimate of 8.28% that is obtained from realized real returns because the average growth rate in stock prices has exceeded the average growth in dividends causing the dividend yield to fall substantially. The authors argue that this decline in the dividend yield is due to the fact that the equity premium has fallen as stock volatility has fallen, giving rise to a once for all capital gain. Their estimates of the forward looking premium in 1999 are in the range of 0.69% to 2.31%; these estimates are based on the current dividend yield and historical

---

[36] See, for example, Campbell and Cochrane (1999).
[37] See Gordon (1962).

estimates of the real dividend growth rate. However, despite the problems associated with historical estimates of the equity premium, they continue to be widely used, in part because they are so easily available. [38]

Discounted Cash Flow estimates of the equity risk premium rely on forecasts of corporate earnings and dividends which are then converted into internal rates of return on investment and compared with bond yields. Thus Kaplan and Ruback (1995) find that the market risk premium implied by CAPM-based discount rates that are consistent with the prices paid, and the cash flow forecasts made, in highly levered transactions in the 1980s was 7.75%. Cornell et al. (1997), using a three-stage dividend discount model based on forecasts of future dividends, [39] estimated the expected nominal return on the S&P500 in December 1996 at 10.92%; this corresponds to a premium of 4.19% over long-term Treasury Bonds and 5.56% over the 'expected' long-run Treasury Bill rate.

4.1.2. DCF estimates of the cost of equity capital

There is a long history of using the dividend discount model to estimate the cost of equity capital for the individual firm. [40] The general form of the model may be written:

$$P_t = \sum_{s=1}^{\infty} \frac{E_t[d_{t+s}]}{(1+k)^s}, \tag{16}$$

where P_t is the share price at time t, d_t is the dividend per share payable at time t, and k is the cost of equity capital. Note that in applying such a formula to estimate a single number as the cost of equity capital, the analyst is implicitly assuming not only that the spot yield curve is flat but that each period's dividends satisfy the *Constant Relative Risk Condition*. This seems quite unlikely in view of the tendency of firms to adjust their dividends slowly. However, the importance of these implicit assumptions has not been quantified.

In order to use Equation (16) to estimate the cost of equity capital it is necessary to have some model for forming dividend expectations. Two main approaches have been followed. The first is to project either a constant or time-varying dividend growth rate, perhaps constructed from analysts' earnings forecast growth rates. The second approach is to use analyst estimates of future earnings to make forecasts of future

---

[38] The views of academic financial economists seem to be strongly related to the historical data: Welch (2000) reports that a sample of 226 academic financial economists forecasts an arithmetic equity premium of 7% per year over 10 and 30 year horizons.

[39] Dividend growth rates for the first five years were based on analyst forecasts; from year 20 on the growth was assumed to be 5.61% based on long run forecasts in the national economy; for years 6–19 growth rates were linearly interpolated. See also Cornell (1999b).

[40] Cragg and Malkiel (1982).

accounting rates of return, and from these, together with a dividend payout assumption, to make forecasts of earnings and dividends. We discuss them in turn.

Harris and Marston (1992) estimate costs of equity capital for individual firms each month for the period 1982–1991, by adding to the dividend yield, analysts' estimates of the 5-year earnings growth rate. The estimated average risk premium over long-term Treasury bonds is 6.47% but shows considerable time series variability that is related to the level of interest rates and to the corporate bond yield spread over Treasuries. They also regress estimated costs of equity capital on betas for 20 portfolios of S&P500 firms formed on the basis of prior beta estimates for each of the 72 months from 1982 to 1987. The average R^2 from the cross-sectional regression is 0.50; the average intercept is 14.06% and the average coefficient of beta is 2.78%. Thus, it appears that the DCF estimates of the cost of equity are related to betas, and therefore to CAPM estimates, but that the DCF estimates are much less sensitive to beta than standard applications of the CAPM would imply.

Gordon and Gordon (1997) use a finite-horizon growth model: given that the current dividend, d_0, and next year earnings per share, e_1, will grow at the rate g for N years, after which the firm will earn exactly its cost of equity, k, they show that the current share price is given by:

$$P_0 = \sum_{\tau=1}^{N} \frac{d_0(1+g)^\tau}{(1+k)^\tau} + \frac{e_1(1+g)^N}{k(1+k)^N}. \tag{17}$$

Using analyst estimates of growth rates, they find in quarterly cross-section regressions for individual securities of the estimated cost of equity on estimated betas and dividend yields for the period 1985–1991 a coefficient of about 2% on beta and a positive coefficient on the dividend yield.[41]

Instead of projecting dividends directly, Gebhardt et al. (2001) (GLS) use analysts' forecasts to project accounting rates of return, and from these arrive at estimates of the cost of equity capital. As long as a firm's earnings and book value are forecast in a manner that is consistent with "clean surplus" accounting, the price of a share can be related to the book value per share, B_t, the accounting return on equity, ROE_t, and the cost of equity capital:[42]

$$P_0 = B_0 + \sum_{t=1}^{\infty} \frac{E_0[(\text{ROE}_t - k)B_{t-1}]}{(1+k)^t}, \tag{18}$$

where ROE_t is equal to the net income for period t divided by the book value at the end of period $t-1$. The authors use analyst earnings estimates and historical

---

[41] Unfortunately, these authors make no attempt to adjust for the errors-in-variables problem caused by the fact that security betas are estimated and that the current dividend enters on both sides of the regression.

[42] Clean surplus accounting requires that the change in book value for the period be equal to net income minus dividends. The resulting valuation model is essentially the same as the Miller and Modigliani (1961) "investment opportunities" approach to valuation.

dividend payout ratios to forecast ROE and book values for the next three years, and then assume that the ROE reverts to the industry mean over the next T years,[43] after which the firm is assumed to earn no further economic profits so that its period-T value can be determined as the value of a perpetuity. The authors estimate the costs of equity for a sample of over 1000 firms in June of each year from 1979 to 1995, and convert these to risk premia by subtracting the yield on a 30-year US Treasury security. The average implied risk premium over their sample period is around 2–3%; even adding 1.5% to adjust for the risk premium on the long term Treasury security,[44] this is far lower than typical historically based estimates of the market risk premium.[45] Conveniently, they calculate the average risk premia over their sample period for the Fama–French (1997) (FF) industries; although FF calculate the risk premium relative to a Treasury Bill rate while GLS use a 30-year rate, and although the sample periods are different, we should expect a close relation between the two sets of estimates if risk is reasonably constant and the two approaches yield reasonably good estimates. Unfortunately, Figure 2 shows that there is very little relation between the DCF cost of capital estimates and the CAPM estimates – indeed the simple correlations between the DCF estimates and either the CAPM or the three-factor model estimates is around *minus* 6%; this is consistent with the GLS finding of a negative relation between their cost of equity estimate and betas.

GLS estimate the following equation relating a firm's estimated cost of equity, k, to firm characteristics:

$$k = -0.15 + 0.39\beta + 0.11\ln(\text{Size}) - 0.77\ln(\text{Disp}) + 19.71\text{Ltg} + 5.88\ln(B/M), \quad R^2 = 0.57,$$
$$\quad (0.28) \quad (2.16) \quad (2.01) \qquad\qquad (7.78) \qquad\qquad (7.24) \qquad (23.53)$$

where t-ratios are in parentheses, β is the firm's estimated beta coefficient, Size is the market value of the firm, Disp is the dispersion of analysts' earnings forecasts, Ltg is the analyst consensus long-term growth estimate, and B/M is the market-to-book ratio. In this regression, the implied "market risk premium" is only 39 basis points, and it is clear that most significant variables are the firm's long-term growth prospects and book-to-market ratio.[46]

4.1.3. Summary

At this point there appears to be no clear consensus on whether asset-pricing model-based, or DCF based, estimates of the cost of equity capital are likely to be more

---

[43] Their results are largely insensitive to the choice of T.

[44] Cornell et al. (1997) report that the risk premium on the 20 year Treasury relative to the Treasury Bill was 1.37% for the period 1926–1996.

[45] See also Claus and Thomas (2000). The low level of the equity premium that is derived using analyst estimates is unlikely to be due to systematic analyst pessimism since there is strong evidence that analysts tend to be optimistic [Esterwood and Nutt (1999)].

[46] The coefficient on *Disp* is consistent with the theoretical models of E.M. Miller (1977) and Jarrow (1980) which allow for disagreement among investors and assume no short selling.

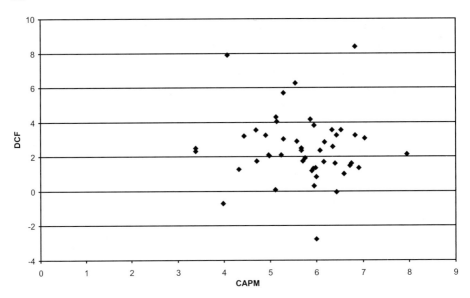

Fig. 2. Comparison of Gebhardt, Lee and Swaminathan (GLS) (2001) DCF estimates of equity risk premia for 48 industries with the Fama–French (FF) (1997) CAPM-based estimates. The GLS estimates are based on analyst forecasts of earnings growth and are annual averages for the period 1979–1995; risk premia are measured relative to the yield on 30-year US Treasury bonds. The FF estimates are the same as those used in Figure 1.

precise. The relative merits of the two approaches are likely to depend on how easy it is to make reasonable earnings and dividend forecasts for individual firms, and this will differ from firm to firm. A caveat for both approaches is that the cost of equity capital may depend on more than the risk of the firm. For example, Amihud and Mendelson (1986) and Brennan and Subrahmanyam (1996) have shown that the liquidity of the market for a firm's shares can have a very large effect on a firm's cost of equity capital; this is not taken into account in extant approaches to assessing discount rates for investment projects.

Historically-based estimates of the equity risk premium are typically unconditional and assume that it is constant over time.[47] Even DCF estimates that condition on the current levels of stock prices and analyst forecasts implicitly assume that the premium is an intertemporal constant *in the future,* and do not allow for any term structure of premia. Section 5.2.3 explores the implications of a stochastic equity risk premium.

4.2. From firm cost of equity to firm cost of capital

To this point we have assumed that the investment project whose cash flows are being valued is financed entirely by equity. While the classic paper of Modigliani and

---

[47] Brennan (1997) and Campbell and Shiller (1988) are exceptions.

Miller (1958) showed that the cost of capital is unaffected by leverage, this principle applies only in the absence of distortionary taxes, and even then it is useful to have an expression relating the overall cost of capital to the cost of equity capital.

Ross (1985, 1987) shows that the absence of arbitrage in a world in which income is taxed at the rate t_p implies the existence of an *after-tax* pricing kernel, M^*, which prices *after-tax* cash flows and whose dynamics may be written as

$$\frac{\mathrm{d}M^*}{M^*} = -r^e(X)\,\mathrm{d}t + \sigma_{M^*}\,\mathrm{d}z_{M^*}, \tag{19}$$

where $r^e(X) \equiv r(X)(1 - t_p)$, and t_p is to be interpreted as the implied marginal (personal) tax on income, and r^e is the return on "riskless equity".[48] Introducing a corporate income tax at the rate t_c, allowing for the tax deductibility of corporate interest payments, and assuming that equity returns are non-taxable, the value, V, of a firm which is financed by a fraction w_D of *riskless* (short-term) debt will satisfy the equilibrium pricing condition:

$$E[d(M^*V)] + M^*Dr\left(t_c - t_p\right)\,\mathrm{d}t = 0, \tag{20}$$

where $D = w_D V$. Dividing through by M^*V, we have:

$$E\left[\frac{\mathrm{d}M^*}{M^*} + \frac{\mathrm{d}V}{V} + \frac{\mathrm{d}M^*}{M^*}\frac{\mathrm{d}V}{V}\right] + r^e w_D \left(\frac{t_c - t_p}{1 - t_p}\right) = 0, \tag{21}$$

which implies that the overall cost of capital or proportionate drift in firm value, $\mu_V(w_D)$, is given by:

$$\mu_V(w_D) = r^e - \sigma_{M^*V} - r^e w_D \left(\frac{t_c - t_p}{1 - t_p}\right). \tag{22}$$

Suppose that the firm is a claim to a single (after tax) cash flow at time T whose expected value, y, follows the diffusion (4a) and satisfies the CRRC, and that the riskless interest rate is constant. Then it may be verified that if the firm maintains a constant debt ratio, w_D, the value of the firm at time t is $V_t(y) = y \exp(-\mu_V(T - t))$, so that, under these assumptions, the value of the firm is obtained by discounting the expected future cash flow, y, at a cost of capital which depends on the debt ratio.[49] Moreover, $\mu_V(w_D)$, the discount rate for the expected after tax cash flow, is the

---

[48] Alternatively, the instantaneously riskless municipal bond rate.
[49] We are implicitly assuming that the firm receives a tax rebate on its corporate interest payments.

traditional "weighted average cost of capital". Thus define the cost of equity, $\mu_E(w_D)$, by

$$\mu_E(w_D) = r^e - \sigma_{M^*E} \equiv r^e - (1-w_D)^{-1}\sigma_{M^*V}. \tag{23}$$

Then simple algebra establishes that[50]

$$\mu_V(w_D) = w_e\mu_E(w_D) + w_D r(1-t_c). \tag{24}$$

Moreover the cost of capital of a levered firm is related to the cost of capital of an unlevered firm by[51]

$$\mu_V(w_D) = \mu_V(0) - w_D r^e \left(\frac{t_c - t_p}{1 - t_p}\right), \tag{25}$$

and the cost of equity is related to the cost of capital of an unlevered firm by:

$$\mu_E(w_D) = \mu_V(0) + (\mu_V(0) - r^e)\left(\frac{w_D}{1 - w_D}\right). \tag{26}$$

If the after tax pricing kernel is perfectly (negatively) correlated with the return on the market portfolio, and can be written as $dM^*/M^* = -r^e dt - S^e_m\, dz_m$, where $S^e_m \equiv (\mu_m - r^e)/\sigma_m$ is the (after tax) Sharpe ratio of the market portfolio, then an after tax version of the Capital Asset Pricing Model holds,[52] which implies that, for any (untaxed) equity security i, the expected return is given by:

$$\mu_i = r^e + \beta_i(\mu_m - r^e). \tag{27}$$

The M.H. Miller (1977) equilibrium corresponds to the case in which $t_c = t_p$. Moreover, regardless of the implied personal tax rate, Equation (22) implies that the cost of capital for a riskless cash flow that is entirely debt financed ($w_D = 1$) is $r(1-t_c)$.[53]

---

[50] Fama and French (1999) estimate that the arithmetic (geometric) average annual returns on the aggregate value of the securities issued by non-financial USA corporations was 12.12% (11.51%) in nominal terms and 7.81% (7.09%) in real terms for period 1950–1996. To make these numbers comparable to estimates of the weighted average cost of capital they should be reduced by $w_D r t_c$ to account for the tax deductibility of interest payments.

[51] Miles and Ezzell (1980) first derived a similar formula ignoring personal taxes. There have been extensive and mostly inconclusive empirical tests of the effect of debt on the cost of capital. One paper concludes on the pessimistic note that "imperfect controls for profitability probably drive the negative relations between debt and value and prevent the regressions from saying anything about the tax benefits of debt" [Fama and French (1998, p. 839)]. More recently Kemsley and Nissim (2002) estimate the average net tax shield associated with corporate debt to be in the range of 38–42%.

[52] See Brennan (1970).

[53] Ruback (1986) establishes this by a direct arbitrage argument.

The foregoing analysis is predicated on the assumption that the firm maintains a constant debt ratio. Other valuation and cost of capital formulae have been derived assuming that the firm has a fixed known schedule of debt outstanding.[54] For example, if the level of debt outstanding at time s is D_s, the net tax savings rate at time s is $D_s(t_c - t_p)$ and the present value of the tax shield associated with the debt is $(t_c - t_p) \int_0^\infty D_s \exp(-r^e s) \, ds$. Myers (1974) has proposed that investment projects be evaluated by calculating the net present value assuming all equity financing so that discounting is done at the rate $\mu_V(0)$, and then adding to this the present value of the tax shield associated with a known schedule of debt financing; the resulting sum is known as the *Adjusted Present Value*. Ruback (2000) shows that discounting the after tax free cash flow from a project at the weighted average cost of capital, $\mu_V(w_D)$, is equivalent to discounting the *capital cash flows* from the project at the cost of capital of an unlevered firm, $\mu_V(0)$, where capital cash flows are defined to include the interest tax shields on debt.

4.3. Performance of CAPM-based valuations

The only published empirical evidence on the usefulness of CAPM-based discount rates in asset valuation is provided in a study of the valuation of 51 management buyouts and highly leveraged transactions by Kaplan and Ruback (1995). They compare the prices paid in these transactions with valuations that are obtained using CAPM-derived discount rates to discount managerial cash-flow projections augmented by their own terminal growth-rate assumption of 4%. The cash flows that are discounted are the aggregate after tax cash flows received by capital suppliers (debt as well as equity), and the beta that is used is not the equity beta but the aggregate firm or asset beta which is a weighted average of equity, debt and preferred betas.[55] The discount rate for all cash flows is taken as the long term Treasury bond yield *plus* a risk premium which is equal to the estimated beta times about 7.4%, which is the arithmetic average of the excess return of the S&P500 over the long term Treasury bond return for the period from 1926 to the date of each transaction (1980–89). With these assumptions, the median valuation error (estimated value minus transaction price) is about 6% with a standard deviation of around 28%. The authors compare their CAPM-based value estimates with those obtained by the crude method of using multiples for

---

[54] Taggart (1991) offers a clear presentation of the effects of different assumptions about debt policy on valuation and the cost of capital. The original Modigliani and Miller (1963) paper on the effect of taxes assumed that the firm's debt level was constant over time.

[55] The weights are based on the market value of equity and the book values of the other securities. The cash flows include tax shields generated by debt financing which are implicitly assumed to have the same risk as the firms' other cash flows. Following Cornell and Green (1991) the debt and preferred betas are taken as 0.25. They also use two other estimates of beta – slightly better results are obtained when an average market asset beta is used in place of firm specific betas.

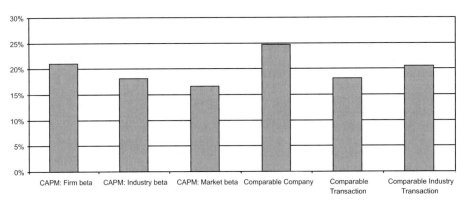

Fig. 3. Mean absolute valuation errors from CAPM and comparable approaches. CAPM discount rates are equal to the long-term Treasury yield plus a market risk premium that is equal to the arithmetic average premium of the S&P500 return over the long-term Treasury return from 1926 to the date of the transaction. Data from Kaplan and Ruback (1995, Table II), based on 51 highly leveraged buyout transactions between 1983 and 1989.

comparable companies. Figure 3, which reports the mean absolute valuation errors from the different valuation approaches, suggests that CAPM-based estimates perform at least as well as do the comparable based estimates. However, the results are sensitive to the 4% terminal growth-rate assumption. The authors also invert their procedure to determine the "implied" equity premium for each transaction that would make their CAPM-based value estimate equal to the transaction price. The median and mean implied equity premiums of 7.78% and 7.97% are close to the median premium of 7.42% that they estimated from historical data. They conclude that "there is no evidence that the use of lower risk premia, however obtained, would improve the accuracy of discounted cash flow techniques".

4.4. From firm cost of capital to project cost of capital

To value a new investment project by discounted cash flow, its expected cash flows should be discounted at a rate that reflects the risk of those cash flows, rather than at the firm's cost of capital which reflects the risk of the firm's pre-existing expected cash flows.

Even a firm that operates in a single industry may have reason to believe that the cost of capital for any single investment project is different from the firm's cost of capital. Cornell (1999a) analyzes Amgen, a biotech firm with high anticipated growth and a substantial R&D budget: he finds that, although innovations in the firm's cash flow have little relation to stock market returns, the company's beta is in excess of unity. Cornell attributes this to a discount rate effect – he argues, following Campbell and Mei (1993), that a significant component of a firm's beta is due to common innovations in discount rates rather than to common innovations in expectations about future cash flows, and that this effect is more pronounced the more distant are the cash flows.[56] If this is accepted, then the cost of capital of a firm whose individual investment projects are of short duration but which is expected to grow over time will exceed the discount rate applicable to any of the individual investment projects that it undertakes.[57]

Myers and Howe (1997) argue on the other hand that the reason that pharmaceutical firms like Amgen have high betas, despite the fact that the payoffs on their R&D investments have low betas, is that these firms have relatively fixed budgets for R&D. To illustrate, consider a firm with a single R&D project and denote the net present value of the expected R&D payoff by X; suppose that the investment in R&D required to achieve the payoff will be made over several years and is a fixed, known amount, with present value K. Then straightforward arguments imply that the beta of the firm, β_V, is related to the beta of the project payoff, β_X, by

$$\beta_V = \frac{X}{X-K}\beta_X. \tag{28}$$

In this case, the investment requirement, K, is essentially equivalent to leverage or a debt that does not appear on the balance sheet. If the Net Present Value of the project, $X - K$, is small relative to the required R&D investment it is clear that the firm's beta can be much larger than the beta of the payoff, X. Therefore a firm that attempts to value the project payoff using a discount rate based on the firm's beta will typically undervalue the project.

Some support for the Myers and Howe position is offered by Figure 4 which plots the estimated betas of deciles of firms in the machinery industry ranked by the ratio of R&D to sales; there is a strong relation between R&D intensity and betas as Myers and Howe would predict, and similar results hold for other industries. However, it is also possible that the higher betas of R&D intensive firms are due to their higher growth rates and thus their greater sensitivity to discount rate shocks as Cornell would predict. A third alternative is that the high betas of these firms are due to the fact that investment growth options are a major component of the value of the firms and that options have greater risk than the underlying assets. The fundamental determinants of firm systematic risk are still largely unknown.

Even if it is accepted that the risk characteristics of a relatively homogeneous firm provide an adequate guide for the discount rate that is appropriate for a typical project

---

[56] In support of this he notes that long term Treasury bonds, for which there are no (nominal) cash flow innovations, have betas of around 0.5 in recent years. A weakness of Cornell's analysis is that he measures the degree of association between innovations in Amgen's cash flows and the market return by the correlation coefficient rather than the beta; it is quite possible to have a high beta and a low correlation. Common innovations in discount rates are implied by the model developed in Section 5.2.3.

[57] As an example that goes the other way, consider a firm which has a franchise to sell ice-cream outside the New York Stock Exchange. If we assume that sales depend on the market movement for the day, the beta of the overnight investment in ice-cream will be high, while the beta of the franchise, and therefore of the firm, will be relatively low, since on any day there is only a small amount of news about the firm's value.

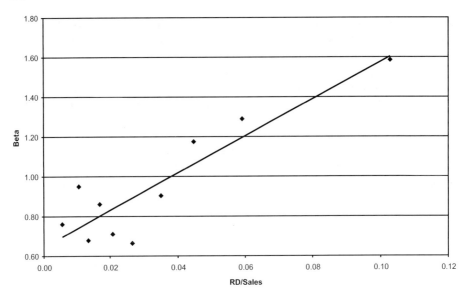

Fig. 4. 5-year equity betas for firms in the machinery industry against Research and Development intensity as measured by the ratio of R&D to sales in 1997. The 92 firms are grouped into deciles based on their R&D intensity. Data from Compustat.

in the firm, problems arise for multi-divisional firms where there can be no presumption that the risk or cost of capital of the firm is a good proxy for the risk or appropriate discount for typical projects in particular divisions of the firm. A common procedure is to estimate the cost of capital for several firms that are "pure plays" in an industry that corresponds to the division of the firm in question, and then to infer the cost of capital for the division by making adjustments for differences in leverage using Equation (25) above.[58]

5. The certainty equivalent approach to valuation

As suggested in footnote 18 above, the discounted cash-flow approach to project valuation originated as a heuristic extension of standard approaches to valuing bonds and, as we have seen in Section 3, the approach can be justified if interest rates are non-stochastic and cash flows satisfy a *Constant Relative Risk Condition* (CRRC). There are many situations in which the *CRRC* is likely to be violated. If the cash flow from a project is the sum of two cash flows, each of which satisfies the *CRRC*, the aggregate cash flow will not satisfy the condition. If the cash flow is a non-linear function of a variable which itself satisfies the *CRRC*, then the cash flow itself will not satisfy the

---

[58] See Fuller and Kerr (1981) and Harris et al. (1989).

CRRC – for example, if the after-tax cash flow is a non-linear function of the pre-tax cash flow because of restrictions in deducting losses, then the after-tax cash flow will not satisfy the *CRRC,* even if the pre-tax cash flow does. Strictly speaking, of course, the use of a single risk-adjusted discount rate also requires that the interest rate be non-stochastic and this condition will never be met in practice. Moreover, there will be many situations in which the underlying state variable(s) that determine cash flows do not satisfy the *CRRC.* In all of these cases the simple discounted cash flow approach to valuation is not warranted.

Finally, additional problems arise if a decision maker can make subsequent decisions that will affect the cash flow by, for example, deciding to abandon a project earlier than anticipated if it is unsuccessful, or to expand an already successful project. Such "real options" change, not only the expected cash flows from the project, but also the risk of those cash flows, and hence the discount rate that is applicable in valuing them.

Early attempts to refine discounted cash flow analysis focused on non-linearities between the stochastic state variables that drive project cash flows and the cash flows themselves, and on the effects of future state-contingent decisions. Non-linearities in the relation between the state variables that determine cash flows and the cash flows themselves make it difficult to calculate expected cash flows by analytical methods; this problem was dealt with by scenario analysis or its continuous state space equivalent, Monte-Carlo simulation.[59] Decision trees were applied to the analysis of problems in which a project's cash flows are affected by subsequent decisions to be taken in the light of new information.[60] However, neither of these approaches offered a sound basis for determining how cash flow non-linearities or future decision contingencies affect project risk and therefore the discount rate.

This discount rate problem was solved by Cox and Ross (1976) who, building on the financial option pricing work of Black and Scholes (1973) and Merton (1973), developed the technique of "certainty equivalent" or "martingale" pricing,[61] which implies that a cash flow may be valued by first calculating its "certainty equivalent", and then discounting this certainty equivalent back at the riskless interest rate.[62] The certainty-equivalent cash flow is calculated by reducing the drift or expected rate of change in the stochastic cash flow drivers, or state, variables by risk premia that depend on the risks of those variables. As we shall see, making this risk adjustment to the cash flow drivers is one of the major challenges in the application of martingale pricing, just as it is in determining discount rates in DCF analysis.

---

[59] Hertz (1964).

[60] Magee (1964).

[61] Developed further by Harrison and Pliska (1981).

[62] This simple description applies only if innovations in the interest rate are orthogonal to the cash flow.

5.1. The basic theory of martingale pricing

To illustrate the martingale approach to asset valuation, consider a claim to a cash-flow stream which is a function of a single stochastic state variable X, and time s: $C(X, s)$, $(s = 0, T)$ and assume that X follows a diffusion process:

$$\frac{\mathrm{d}X}{X} = \mu_X(X)\,\mathrm{d}t + \sigma_X(X)\,\mathrm{d}z_X. \tag{29}$$

Let $V(X, t)$ denote the value of the claim at time t. Then, using Ito's Lemma, Constantinides (1978) shows that if the continuously compounded riskless rate is a constant, r, then the value of the claim satisfies:

$$\frac{1}{V}\left\{\tfrac{1}{2}V_{XX}X^2\sigma_X^2 + \mu_X XV_X + V_t + C(X, t)\right\} = r + \frac{V_X}{V}X\lambda_X(X, t), \tag{30}$$

where $\lambda(X, t)$ is the risk premium associated with the state variable, X, and we have implicitly assumed that the risk premium depends only on time and the value of the state variable itself.[63] The left side of Equation (30) is the expected rate of return on the claim and the right side is its *equilibrium* expected return, given the risk premium on the underlying state variable X. Simplifying, Equation (30) may be written in a form that is reminiscent of the Black and Scholes (1973) partial differential equation:

$$\tfrac{1}{2}V_{XX}X^2\sigma_X^2 + (\mu_X - \lambda_X)XV_X + C(X, t) + V_t - rV = 0. \tag{31}$$

Thus the value of the cash-flow claim is the solution to the partial differential Equation (31) subject to the terminal boundary condition $V(X, T) = 0$. As Cox, Ingersoll and Ross (1985) point out,[64] the solution to Equation (31) can be written as a discounted expectation:

$$V(X, t) = E^*\left\{\int_t^T \exp(-r\tau)\,C(X, \tau)\,\mathrm{d}\tau\right\}, \tag{32}$$

where $E^*[\,]$ denotes that expectations are taken with respect to the "risk-adjusted" process:

$$\frac{\mathrm{d}X}{X} = (\mu_X(X) - \lambda_X(X))\,\mathrm{d}t + \sigma_X\,\mathrm{d}z_X. \tag{33}$$

Equations (32) and (33) represent the basic result of martingale pricing theory. They imply that, when the interest rate is deterministic,[65] a cash flow can be valued by first

---

[63] Equations (5) and (6) imply that the risk premium is determined by the covariance between the innovations in X and in the pricing kernel: $\lambda(X, t) = \mathrm{cov}(\mathrm{d}X/X, \mathrm{d}M/M)$.

[64] This is known as the Feynman–Kac formula. Black (1988) provides an early application of this rule to corporate capital budgeting.

[65] The expression is $V(X, t) = E^*[\int_t^T \exp\left(\int_t^\tau -r(s)\,\mathrm{d}s\right) C(X, \tau)\,\mathrm{d}\tau]$ when the interest rate is stochastic, and where the expectation must be taken with respect to the risk-adjusted stochastic process for all state variables, including the interest rate, $r(s)$.

calculating the "certainty-equivalent" cash flow, and then discounting this certainty equivalent at the *risk-free* interest rate. The certainty-equivalent cash flow itself is equal to the "expected" cash flow, where the expectation is calculated by first adjusting down the drift of all state variables by an amount that reflects their risk premium as shown in Equation (33).

The certainty-equivalent valuation approach (32–33) overcomes two major limitations of the more traditional discounted cash-flow approach represented by Equations (1) or (2). First, the certainty equivalent approach does not require that the risk premium, $\lambda_X(X)$, be constant or even deterministic, whereas the discounted cash-flow approach requires that the risk premium be constant, if the cash flows are to satisfy the *Constant Relative Risk Condition*. Even when the underlying state variable(s) satisfy the *Constant Relative Risk Condition* there is no reason to expect the cash flow, $C(X, t)$, to satisfy the condition. For example, if $C(X, t) = \max(X - K, 0)$, the cash flow will be relatively riskless if $X \ll K$, while its risk will approach that of X itself if $X \gg K$;[66] a similar problem will arise if the cash flow is equal to the product of two state variables (e.g., price and quantity) each of which satisfies the *Constant Relative Risk Condition*: in such cases there is no obvious way to value the cash flow by applying a fixed discount rate to its expected value. Secondly, the simple discounted cash-flow approach takes the distribution of the cash flows as given, whereas the cash flows are, at least in part, controllable, and the effects of contingent future decision possibilities on the risk of the cash flows must be taken into account when the project is initially analyzed: the certainty-equivalent approach does this in a simple and direct way.

5.2. Estimating risk-adjusted drifts

The certainty-equivalent approach requires estimates of the risk-adjusted drifts of the state variables, $\mu_X - \lambda_X$. If the underlying state variable, X, corresponds to the price of a traded asset, then it is usually relatively simple to determine the risk-adjusted drift, since this does not require estimation of the elusive risk premium, λ_X. Examples of state variables that correspond to the prices of traded assets include the prices of commodities which are held in storage, currency exchange rates, and the value of a completed project. We consider how risk-adjusted drifts may be estimated, first the case in which the state variable is the price of a traded asset, and then when it is not.

5.2.1. The state variable is the price of a traded asset

If the state variable, X, can be thought of as the price of a traded asset, the problem of determining the risk premium can be avoided, just as it is in the financial options

---

[66] Such non-linearities in the relation between the cash flow and the underlying state variable can easily arise from non-linearities in the corporate tax code or from managerial decisions that, for example, curtail output in low price states.

pricing literature. As a simple example, suppose that X is the value of a completed plant which produces a perpetual cash flow at the rate δX, where X follows the diffusion:

$$\frac{\mathrm{d}X}{X} = \mu_X \, \mathrm{d}t + \sigma \, \mathrm{d}z. \tag{34}$$

Then, if the interest rate, r, is constant, the expected rate of return on the plant, including both the cash flow and capital appreciation, is $\mu_X + \delta$, so that the risk premium is $\mu_X + \delta - r$; the risk-adjusted drift in X is $\mu_X - \lambda_X = \mu_X - (\mu_X + \delta - r) = r - \delta$, which depends only on observables and does not involve the risk premium itself.

Let $V(X)$ denote the value of the right or (real) option to construct the plant at a cost K at any future date. Then substituting for $\mu_X - \lambda_X$ in Equation (31), and noting that the value of the option does not depend on time and produces no cash flow, so that $\partial V/\partial t = C(X,t) = 0$, the value of the option satisfies the ordinary differential equation:

$$\tfrac{1}{2} V_{XX} X^2 \sigma_X^2 + (r - \delta) X V_X - rV = 0. \tag{35}$$

The solution to this equation depends on the boundary conditions, which are determined by the optimal policy for exercising the option to construct the plant; these are discussed in Section 5.3.

Brennan and Schwartz (1985) and Paddock, Siegel and Smith (1988) consider the case in which the underlying state variable is the price of a commodity; commodities that are held in inventory can be treated as assets which yield a flow of "convenience services", and the convenience yield,[67] which is analogous to the dividend yield on a stock, can be inferred from the relation between the spot and forward prices if forward markets exist for the commodity. Denoting the convenience yield by c, the risk-adjusted (proportional) drift, $\mu_X(X) - \lambda(X)$ in Equations (31) and (33), for a commodity price, S, is $(r - c)$.[68]

5.2.2. The state variable is not the price of a traded asset

When the stochastic state variables that drive cash flows do not correspond to the prices of traded assets, an equilibrium model must be used to assess the risk premium, or equivalently the risk-adjusted drift. Sick (1986, 1989a,b) has proposed using a factor-pricing model to evaluate certainty-equivalent cash flows. To illustrate, suppose that the interest rate is constant, that the single-period capital asset pricing model holds, and that the growth rate of some real state variable, X, such as automobile production,

---

[67] For the early development of this concept see Brennan (1958).
[68] For models in which the convenience yield is stochastic see Brennan (1991), Gibson and Schwartz (1990) and Schwartz (1997).

Table 1

Simulated cash-flow statement under the risk-neutral measure when the risk-free interest rate is 5% [a]

Component	Time						
	0	1	2	3	4	5	6
(1) $\bar{R}_{Mt} \sim N(0.05, \sigma_M)$ [b]		−0.01	0.03	0.05	−0.10	0.04	0.01
(2) $\varepsilon_t \sim N(0, \sigma_\varepsilon)$ [c]		0.01	−0.03	0.03	−0.04	0.02	0.02
(3) Base sales [d]	100						
(4) Sales growth [e]: $g_t = b_0 + b_1 R_{mt} + b_2 R_{mt-1} + b_2 R_{mt-1} + b_3 R_{mt-2} + \varepsilon_t$		0.04	0.03	0.02	0.04	−0.01	0.03
(5) $\text{Sales}_t = \text{Sales}_{t-1} * (1 + g_t)$ [f]		104	107.1	109.2	113.6	112.5	115.8
(6) Cost of Sales$_t$ = 0.90 * Sales$_t$ + 10		103.6	106.4	108.3	112.2	111.3	114.2
(7) Net cash flow$_t$ [g]		0.4	0.7	0.9	1.4	1.3	1.6
(8) Present value at 5% [h]	5.1						

[a] The table shows the cash flow and present value calculation for a single simulation under the martingale or risk-adjusted process when sales growth depends on current and lagged market returns (Equation 36).
[b] The market return is generated from a distribution with mean equal to the risk free rate of 5%.
[c] The error in Equation (36) has mean zero.
[d] The initial level of sales.
[e] Sales growth calculated from Equation (36).
[f] Sales.
[g] The series of net cash flows for a single simulation under the risk-adjusted process.
[h] The present value of the cash flows, discounted at the risk-free rate.

is related to current and lagged returns on the market portfolio, R_{Mt}, by the regression equation:

$$\tilde{g}_{Xt} = b_{X0} + b_{X1}\tilde{R}_{M,t} + b_{X2}\tilde{R}_{M,t-1} + b_{X3}\tilde{R}_{M,t-2} + \tilde{\varepsilon}_{Xt}. \tag{36}$$

Then, if a cash flow which is receivable at time T is $C(X_T)$, and the growth rate of X is given by Equation (36), the certainty equivalent at time τ of the cash flow, $CE_\tau(X_T)$ is given by $E_\tau^*[C(\tilde{X}_\tau \tilde{g}_{\tau+1} \tilde{g}_{\tau+2} \cdots \tilde{g}_{\tau+T-1})]$, where $E_\tau^*[]$ denotes that expectations are taken with respect to the risk-neutral process for R_M under which it has a mean equal to the risk-free rate, r. The expectation is easily evaluated by Monte-Carlo simulation. [69] Table 1 provides a simple example in which X is the level of sales whose growth rate is determined by Equation (36). The sales growth rates are calculated by drawing values of the market return from a (normal) distribution with a mean equal to the risk-free rate (the risk-adjusted expected return for the market). The resulting cash flows are realizations under the risk-adjusted distribution, and are therefore discounted

[69] Sick (1989b) provides analytic formulae when $C(X)$ is linear.

to the present at the riskless interest rate of 5%. The method is easily extended to accommodate non-linearities in the relation between the state variables and the cash flows, multiple state variables, stochastic interest rates, etc.

However, there has been little work relating real variables to market or factor returns. Figure 5 reports the results of some regressions of industrial output growth for different industries on current and lagged quarterly market returns. Figure 5a shows four quarter lag coefficients; Figure 5b shows the sum of the coefficients, and Figure 5c compares the summed coefficients for two different sample periods. Output growth in these industries is clearly related to lagged stock-market returns and is therefore a source of priced risk for these industries. There is much more work to be done in relating cash flow risks to the fundamental sources of priced risk in the economy.

5.2.3. Stochastic risk premia and interest rates

The *Constant Relative Risk Condition* introduced in Section 3 requires that σ_{My}, the covariance between innovations in the expectation of the cash flow and innovations in the pricing kernel, be constant. This condition will fail generically if σ_M, the volatility of the pricing kernel, is stochastic, since this will make all risk premia stochastic. Thus, the martingale property (5) implies that the expected return on any asset or portfolio is given by:

$$E\left[\frac{dV}{V}\right] \equiv \mu_V\, dt = r(X)\, dt - \sigma_M(X)\rho_{VM}\sigma_V\, dt, \tag{37}$$

and $\sigma_M(X)\rho_{VM}\sigma_V$ is the (negative of the) risk premium. Therefore variation in $\sigma_M(X)$ corresponds to common variation in risk premia across all assets. Moreover, since the correlation between the asset return and pricing kernel, ρ_{VM}, is bounded by unity, Equation (37) implies that $\sigma_M(X)$ is the maximum value of the Sharpe ratio, $\frac{\mu_V - r}{\sigma_V}$, across all assets: it is the slope of the capital-market line or "market" Sharpe ratio.

There is now substantial evidence of time variation in risk premia,[70] but so far little analysis of its implications for asset valuation. Brennan, Wang and Xia (BWX) (2002)[71] develop a simple valuation model in which both the Sharpe ratio and the interest rate are stochastic and follow correlated Ornstein–Uhlenbeck processes. Writing $\eta \equiv \sigma_M(X)$ for the Sharpe ratio, the stochastic process for the pricing kernel (4b,d) becomes:

$$\frac{dM}{M} = -r\, dt - \eta\, dz_M, \tag{38a}$$

$$d\eta = \kappa_\eta(\bar{\eta} - \eta)\, dt + \sigma_\eta\, dz_\eta, \tag{38b}$$

$$dr = \kappa_r(\bar{r} - r)\, dt + \sigma_r\, dz_r. \tag{38c}$$

---

[70] For example, Fama and Schwert (1977), Campbell and Shiller (1988), Fama and French (1989), Whitelaw (1997) and Perez-Quiros and Timmerman (2000).
[71] See also Bekaert and Grenadier (1999).

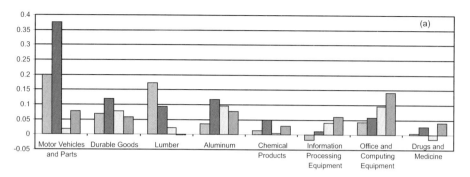

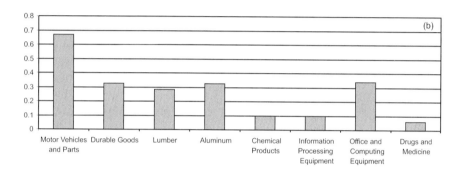

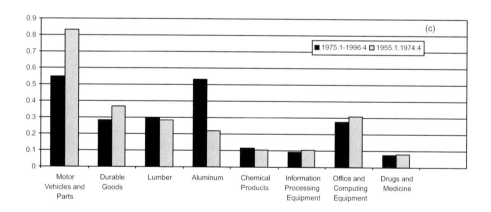

Fig. 5. Results from regressing quarterly industry output growth on current and 3 quarters of lagged stock market returns as in Equation (36) for different industries for the period 1955.1 to 1996.4: (a) coefficients on the current and lagged market returns; (b) sum of the coefficients on the current and lagged market returns; (c) summed coefficients for two different sample periods.

Let $V(Y, r, \eta, \tau)$ denote the value at time t of a claim to a single (real) cash flow, x, which is due at time $t + \tau$, where $Y \equiv E_t[x]$ is the time t expectation of the cash flow, which follows a driftless geometric Brownian motion with constant volatility:

$$\frac{dY}{Y} = \gamma \, dz_Y. \tag{39}$$

They show, using the martingale property that $M_t V(Y, r, \eta, \tau) = E_t[M_{t+\tau} x]$, that the value of the claim may be written as:

$$V(Y, r, \eta, \tau) \equiv Y \exp\left[A(\tau) - B(\tau) r - D(\tau) \eta\right], \tag{40}$$

where the maturity-dependent coefficients, A, B, and D, are functions of the parameters of the joint stochastic process of the pricing kernel and the cash-flow expectation. Equation (40) implies that assets may be valued by discounting expected cash flows of maturity τ at the continuously compounded rate $[-A(\tau) + B(\tau) r + D(\tau) \eta]/\tau$. Note that the discount rate depends, not only upon the risk characteristics of the cash flows and the current interest rate, r, but also upon the current risk-reward ratio as measured by the Sharpe ratio, η, and the maturity of the cash flow, τ. The same valuation framework may be applied to the valuation of nominal bonds if a stochastic process for the price level is specified. If the price level follows a geometric Brownian motion whose drift, π, the expected rate of inflation, follows an Ornstein–Uhlenbeck process, the price of a nominal bond with maturity τ, $P(r, \eta, \tau)$ is given by $\exp[\hat{A}(\tau) - \hat{B}(\tau) r - C(\tau) \pi - \hat{D}(\tau) \eta]$, where the coefficients are now functions of the joint stochastic process for the pricing kernel and the inflation process. BWX apply a Kalman filter to a time series of Treasury bond yields to obtain a time series of estimates of the state variable η (as well as r and π): these are shown in Figure 6. The

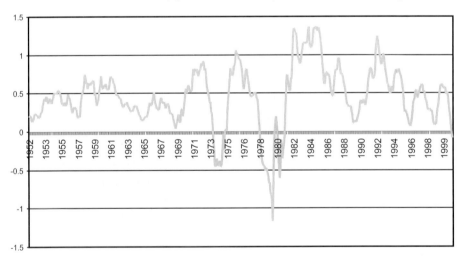

Fig. 6. Evidence of time variation in the Sharpe ratio, based on Brennan, Wang and Xia (2002). The series is obtained by applying a Kalman filter to panel data on constant maturity Treasury bond yields to estimate the real interest rate, the expected rate of inflation and the Sharpe ratio.

time series shows considerable variation which is consistent with similar findings by Whitelaw (1997) and by Perez-Quiros and Timmerman (2000). The implications for corporate investment policy of time variation in risk premia are yet to be explored, although there is some evidence that firms are influenced in their investment decisions by the state of the capital market. [72]

5.3. Some real options [73]

The prototypical real option is the timing option or the option to postpone an investment project until more information becomes available; [74] closely related is the option to postpone extraction of a mineral resource, or to abandon a project that is in operation. All three decisions have the characteristic that for practical purposes, they are *irreversible*. Therefore, when there is discretion over the timing of investment, or extraction, or abandonment, these decisions are formally examples of the mutually exclusive projects that were discussed in Section 2 above. Other examples include the option to convert a partially built nuclear-power station to fossil fuel, to lay up a tanker, to develop a real-estate site or an oil field, to enter a new product market, to file for a patent, or to develop a new product.

It is useful to distinguish between situations in which the cash flows of a project depend only on the actions of a decision-maker and uncontrollable moves by "nature", and situations in which the cash flows depend also on the decisions of other actors, such as the firm's competitors, which may be influenced by the firm's own decisions: in the latter case there is a strategic element to the firm's decisions. We shall consider these in turn.

5.3.1. Games against nature

As a simple example of a game against nature, consider the problem of the timing of an investment project introduced in Section 5.2.1. The general solution to Equation (35) is of the form

$$V(X) = A_1 X^{b_1} + A_2 X^{b_2}, \tag{41}$$

where A_1 and A_2 are constants to be determined, and

$$b_1 = \tfrac{1}{2} - (r - \delta)^2 + \sqrt{D} > 1, \quad b_2 = b_1 - 2\sqrt{D} < 0, \quad D = \left[\frac{r - \delta}{\sigma^2}\right]^2 + 2\frac{r}{\sigma^2}.$$

Since $X = 0$ is an absorbing boundary $V(0) = 0$, which implies that $A_2 = 0$. Let the investment decision rule be to invest when $X = X^*$; then $V(X^*)$ satisfies the "value-matching condition" $V(X^*) = A_1 X^{*b_1} - K$. The *optimal* value of X^*, the one that

[72] Lamont (2000).
[73] Dixit and Pindyck (1994) provide a comprehensive survey of the theory of real options. Schwartz and Trigeorgis (2001) collect the major articles.
[74] See Brennan and Schwartz (1985) and McDonald and Siegel (1986)

maximizes $V(X)$, is obtained by imposing the "high contact" condition,[75] $V'(X^*) = 1$. Imposing both conditions implies that the optimal rule is to invest when X attains the critical value, X^*, where

$$X^* = \frac{b_1}{b_1 - 1}K, \tag{42}$$

and that $A_1 = (X^* - K)/X^{*b_1}$.

Condition (42) implies that it is optimal to wait until the net present value of the investment opportunity, $(X - K)$, is strictly positive before investing. This contrasts with the simple prescription of the Marshallian Net Present Value Rule in Section 2 that a project should be undertaken if its net present value is positive.[76] This result, that when investment is irreversible, it is optimal to postpone investment relative to the Marshallian NPV rule, is the most general result from the "real options" literature.[77] Ingersoll and Ross (1992) show that a timing option may exist even for a riskless project if the interest rate is stochastic,[78] and Berk (1999) shows that the optimal decision in this case can be achieved by using the simple NPV Rule with a hurdle rate equal to the par coupon on an immediately callable bond. Boyarchenko (2000) shows that the optimal timing decision for an irreversible investment can be written as the Marshallian rule of invest as soon as the NPV is positive, if the NPV is calculated using the infimum process for the output price starting at the current price.[79]

The simple timing option model has been extended to account for the time to build the plant, allowing also for the possibility that building may be suspended and restarted; the "option" or stochastic control here is the rate of investment. In this case the value of the right to continue investing to complete the plant is a function of both the value of the completed plant, X, and the *remaining* investment that is required to complete the plant, K. Assuming constant returns to scale in the rate of investment, I, so that $dK = -I\,dt$, the optimal policy is 'bang-bang': invest either at the maximum rate, I^*, or set $I = 0$. The optimal investment policy and the value of the partially completed plant, are then determined by the solution of a pair of linked partial differential equations. Let $V(X,K)$ denote the value of the partially completed plant *when investment is occurring* at the rate I^*, let $v(X,K)$ be the corresponding value when no investment is being made, and let $X^*(K)$ be the value of X above which it is

---

[75] See Merton (1973) and Dumas (1991)
[76] Though not with the more sophisticated version of the rule that recognizes that investing now and investing later are mutually exclusive projects.
[77] McDonald (2000) suggests that the use by corporations of investment hurdle rates that exceed their cost of capital may represent a heuristic for dealing with the timing option.
[78] The authors demonstrate that the timing option may cause a reduction in interest rates to lead to a *fall* in investment.
[79] The infimum process for the price starting at P_0 is defined by $N_t = \inf_{0 \le s < t} P_t$.

optimal to invest when the remaining investment required is K. Then V and v satisfy the following linked partial differential equations: [80]

$$\frac{1}{2}\sigma^2 X^2 V_{XX} + (r - \delta) V_X - I^* V_K - I^* - rV = 0, \quad X \geqslant X^*(K),$$
$$\frac{1}{2}\sigma^2 X^2 v_{XX} + (r - \delta) v_X - rv = 0, \qquad\qquad X \leqslant X^*(K),$$

$$(43)$$

subject to the following boundary conditions:

$$V(X, 0) = X,$$
$$v(0, K) = 0,$$
$$V(X, K) \to X \exp\left(-\frac{\delta K}{I^*}\right) + \frac{I^*}{r}\left[\exp\left(\frac{rK}{I^*}\right) - 1\right], \quad \text{as } X \to \infty,$$
$$V(X^*, K) = v(X^*, K),$$
$$V_X(X^*, K) = v_X(X^*, K),$$
$$V_K(X^*, K) = v_K(X^*, K) = -1.$$

If there is no possibility of suspension, the investment threshold is identical to the instantaneous investment case (42); the possibility of suspending building reduces the investment threshold. [81] This reflects the general principle that the more reversible is a project, the lower will be the investment threshold; for example, if the underlying stochastic variable is output price, then the output price at which it will be optimal to invest in the project will be lower if production can be varied as a function of the output price or if the project can be abandoned. [82]

5.3.2. Multi-person games

The classic real options result that it is optimal to postpone an investment project relative to the Marshallian NPV Rule depends critically on the assumption that the firm is a monopolist with respect to the investment project, and that output prices are parametric. If the firm has a small number of competitors then the output price becomes endogenous, and must be solved for simultaneously with the optimal investment decision for all firms; in this setting, the firm must weigh the benefits of waiting against the risk of pre-emption. We will consider examples of the purely competitive and oligopolistic cases in turn. [83] Note that, once allowance is made for competitors, it

---

[80] This problem is closely related to the Brennan and Schwartz (1985) valuation of a mine which may either be operating or closed, and to Schwartz and Moon (2000) who determine the optimal policy for investing in drug development.

[81] See Milne and Whalley (2000).

[82] Abel et al. (1996) analyze the role of reversibility, and point out that "expandability" options will raise the investment threshold. Interactions created by the existence of multiple options are in general difficult to analyze and there are no general results. See Trigeorgis (1993) and Kulatilaka (1995).

[83] This section relies heavily on Dixit and Pindyck (1994).

is no longer possible to take either the present value of the investment opportunity or the output price as exogenous variables; they must be derived as part of an equilibrium which considers the equilibrium optimal strategies of all firms.

5.3.2.1. The purely competitive case. Consider an industry with a large number of competitive firms, each of which has rational expectations about the strategies of the other firms; the cost of entering the industry is K, and having paid K, each firm can produce a single unit of output at zero cost. Suppose that the output price is given by

$$P = XD(Q), \tag{44}$$

where X is a state variable that affects the industry inverse demand and follows the diffusion process (34), and Q is the number of active firms. When Q is constant (no entry is taking place), the output price follows a diffusion with (constant) relative drift $\mu_P = \mu_X$ and diffusion coefficient $\sigma_P = \sigma_X$, and the cash flow, $C(X,t)$, is equal to $XD(Q)$, so that from Equations (31) and (44) the value of an operating firm, $V(P) \equiv V(P(X)) \equiv G(X)$ satisfies

$$\tfrac{1}{2} V_{PP} P^2 \sigma_P^2 + (\mu_P - \lambda_P - r) P V_P + P - rV = 0. \tag{45}$$

If entry takes place at an output price $\overline{P}$, $\overline{P}$ will be a reflecting barrier for the output price; this requires that, to avoid arbitrage profits, $V_P(\overline{P}) = 0$. Given $\overline{P}$, and imposing the lower boundary condition $V(0) = 0$, the ordinary differential Equation (45) can be solved for $V(P)$:

$$V(P) = \frac{1}{r + \lambda_P - \mu_P} \left(P - \frac{1}{b_1} P^{b_1} \overline{P}^{1-b_1} \right), \tag{46}$$

where b_1 is the positive root of the fundamental quadratic equation $\tfrac{1}{2}\sigma_P^2 b(b-1) + (\mu - \lambda) b - r = 0$. To find the equilibrium entry price, $\overline{P}$, let $v(P)$ denote the value of the right to undertake the investment necessary to enter the industry. Then, noting that $v(P)$ has to satisfy the same differential Equation (31) with $C(X,t) = 0$, $v(P)$ is of the form AP^{b_1} where A is an undetermined constant. A, and the equilibrium value of $\overline{P}$, are determined by the value matching and smooth pasting conditions, $v(\overline{P}) = V(\overline{P}) - K$ and $v'(\overline{P}) = V'(\overline{P})$. The solution for the entry price is:

$$\overline{P} = \frac{b_1}{(b_1 - 1)(r + \lambda_P - \mu_P)} K. \tag{47}$$

Leahy (1993)[84] points out the surprising result that the entry price in this case is identical to the optimal entry price of a monopolist who takes the price process as exogenous and ignores the effects of future entry on the price process.

---

[84] See also Dixit and Pindyck (1994, Chapters 7 and 8).

Other real options models that analyze a competitive industry equilibrium include Grenadier (1995, 2000) who models real estate markets with and without time-to-build, and Tvedt (2000) who analyzes the effects of the layup option on the stochastic process for shipping freight rates when different vessels have different operating costs.

5.3.2.2. The oligopolistic case. When the number of competitors is small, each firm can influence the decisions of the others by its decisions, and these strategic interactions affect the optimal policies. As a simple example, consider an industry whose inverse demand curve is given by Equation (44) where the state variable X follows the diffusion (29), and suppose that there are only two firms that can enter the industry at unit scale with entry costs, $K_1 < K_2$ and zero marginal costs. The equilibrium is constructed as follows. First, find the value functions for the two firms when *both* firms are producing, by solving the differential Equation (31) with $C(X,t) = XD(2)$ and $V_t = 0$. Next find $\overline{X}_2$, the threshold value at which the *second* firm (the "follower") will enter, given that the first firm (the "leader") has already entered. Given the optimality of myopic behavior in the competitive case, the threshold price is of the form (47), and the value of the follower before it enters is of the form $v_2(X) = A_2 X^{b_1}$, where A_2 is a constant that is determined by the value-matching condition and b_1 is the positive root of the fundamental quadratic. The value of the leader, after it has entered, but before the follower has entered, is found by solving the standard differential Equation (31) with $C(X) = XD(1)$, and with a boundary condition corresponding to the value of the firm when both firms are producing at $\overline{X}_2$. Finally, the value of the leader prior to entry and the equilibrium entry strategy are found by noting that the value of the follower before entry is also of the form $v_1(X) = A_1 X^{b_1}$, where the constant A_1 and the threshold value for leader entry, $\overline{X}_1$, are determined by the value-matching and smooth-pasting conditions.

There are two types of equilibria in this model depending on parameter values: simultaneous entry equilibria, in which both firms invest at the same threshhold value of X, and sequential entry equilibria in which the leader enters first. We have described only the latter. Determination of the appropriate equilibrium requires checking the relevant incentive-compatibility conditions for the two firms, which would take us beyond the scope of this survey. The model can be further enriched by considering in more detail the nature of product market competition, and by allowing the firms to choose the optimal scale of investment.

Models of oligopolistic competition and the strategic exercise of investment options within a real options context include Smit and Ankum (1993), Kulatilaka and Perotti (1998), Trigeorgis (1996), Grenadier (1996) and Lambrecht (2000). This growing literature offers the prospect of an integration of the theory of the corporate investment decision with a theory of corporate strategy.

6. Summary

Under reasonable assumptions, the investment policy of the firm that will be supported by the shareholders who have control rights is a policy that maximizes the value of the firm's shares. This separation result[85] reduces the problem of corporate investment policy in perfect capital markets to the problem of valuing the cash flow streams that will result from different policies. Unfortunately, research in asset pricing[86] has been slow to yield results that are useful for valuing real assets. First, there is as yet no canonical model of asset pricing: the capital asset pricing model and its consumption based variant, despite their theoretical elegance, perform poorly in practice, and the empirically most successful asset pricing model[87] lacks a strong conceptual underpinning. Secondly, asset pricing theory has concentrated on the determination of the equilibrium expected rates of return on securities rather than on the determination of equilibrium prices. As a result, most applied work on investment appraisal has relied on the risk-adjusted discount rate approach, with the discount rate justified by *ad hoc* appeals to single period asset pricing models, particularly the capital asset pricing model. In Section 3 we showed that the typical risk-adjusted discount rate approach to valuation that uses a constant risk adjustment can be justified only under special assumptions.

Even accepting the risk-adjusted discount rate approach to valuation, the analyst is faced with the problem first, of determining the appropriate model for the risk premium, and secondly, of determining the appropriate model parameters. The practical problems of estimating discount rates were discussed in Section 4. The results of Pastor and Stambaugh (1999) suggest that parameter (risk premium) uncertainty is a likely to be a bigger problem than model uncertainty. A new challenge to the risk-adjusted discount rate approach is posed by recent evidence that risk premia are stochastic, and research is only just beginning on the consequences of this for asset valuation.

Perhaps the most significant development in asset valuation has been the importation of techniques from financial option pricing and industrial organization. Application of option or certainty-equivalent pricing techniques is straightforward when the principal stochastic cash flow drivers can be identified with the prices of traded securities for then the powerful principle of arbitrage pricing can be invoked. When this is not the case, the analyst is still faced with the problem of determining the risk premia that are associated with the cash flow drivers. However, there is no doubt that this is a more consistent approach to valuation than the simple use of risk-adjusted discount rates, since the net cash flows that are typically discounted in this approach are stochastic mixtures of cash flows with different risks, such as sales revenues, costs, and tax

---

[85] Hirshleifer (1965).
[86] For an excellent survey see Campbell, Lo and MacKinlay (1997).
[87] The Fama–French 3-factor model. See Fama and French (1995).

payments. The certainty-equivalent approach, by applying the risk premia directly to the underlying sources of risk, ensures that the risks of cash flows that are non-linear functions of the underlying drivers (such as taxes) are properly taken into account in valuation. Moreover, the closely related option pricing approaches to valuation focus attention directly on the future decision alternatives that are associated with asset ownership and that are often a major source of value. These approaches are increasingly finding their way into practice.[88] The most recent development is the incorporation of strategic considerations within the martingale pricing framework of asset valuation. While parameterization of these models poses fundamental challenges, they hold out the promise of placing traditional capital budgeting within the overall framework of corporate strategy.

References

Abel, A.B., A.K. Dixit, J.C. Eberly and R.S. Pindyck (1996), "Options, the value of capital, and investment", Quarterly Journal of Economics 111:753–777.

Amihud, Y., and H. Mendelson (1986), "Asset pricing and the bid-ask spread", Journal of Financial Economics 17:223–249.

Bagwell, L.S. (1992), "Dutch auction repurchases: an analysis of shareholder heterogeneity", Journal of Finance 47:71–106.

Bekaert, G., and S.R. Grenadier (1999), "Stock and bond pricing in an affine economy", Unpublished Manuscript (Stanford University, CA).

Berk, J.B. (1999), "A simple approach for deciding when to invest", American Economic Review 89:1319–1326.

Black, F. (1988), "A simple discounting rule", Financial Management 17:7–11.

Black, F., and M. Scholes (1973), "The pricing of options and corporate liabilities", Journal of Political Economy 81:637–659.

Blume, M. (1974), "Unbiased estimates of long-run expected rates of return", Journal of American Statistical Association 69:634–638.

Bower, D.H., R.S. Bower and D.E. Logue (1984), "Arbitrage pricing theory and utility stock returns", Journal of Finance 39:1041–1055.

Boyarchenko, S. (2000), "Capital accumulation under non-Gaussian processes and the Marshallian law", Unpublished Manuscript (University of Pennsylvania).

Brennan, M.J. (1958), "The supply of storage", American Economic Review 48:50–72.

Brennan, M.J. (1970), "Taxes, market valuation and corporate financial policy", National Tax Journal 23:417–427.

Brennan, M.J. (1977), "An approach to the valuation of uncertain income streams", Journal of Finance 28:661–674.

Brennan, M.J. (1991), "The price of convenience and the valuation of commodity contingent claims", in: D. Lund and B. Oksendal, eds., Stochastic Models and Option Values (Elsevier, Amsterdam) pp. 33–72.

Brennan, M.J. (1997), "The term structure of discount rates", Financial Management 26:81–90.

Brennan, M.J., and E.S. Schwartz (1982), "Consistent regulatory policy under uncertainty", Bell Journal of Economics and Management Science 13:507–521.

---

[88] See Triantis and Borison (2001).

Brennan, M.J., and E.S. Schwartz (1985), "Evaluating natural resource investments", Journal of Business 58:135–157.

Brennan, M.J., and A. Subrahmanyam (1996), "Market microstructure and asset pricing: on the compensation for illiquidity in stock returns", Journal of Financial Economics 41:441–464.

Brennan, M.J., A.W. Wang and Y. Xia (2002), "A simple model of intertemporal asset pricing", Unpublished Manuscript (Anderson School, University of California, Los Angeles).

Brown, S.J., W.N. Goetzmann and S.A. Ross (1995), "Survival", Journal of Finance 50:853–874.

Campbell, J.Y., and J.H. Cochrane (1999), "By force of habit: a consumption-based explanation of aggregate stock market behavior", Journal of Political Economy 107:205–251.

Campbell, J.Y., and J. Mei (1993), "Where do betas come from? Asset price dynamics and the sources of systematic risk", Review of Financial Studies 6:567–592.

Campbell, J.Y., and R. Shiller (1988), "The dividend price ratio and expectations of future dividends and discount factors", Review of Financial Studies 1:195–228.

Campbell, J.Y., A.W. Lo and A.C. MacKinlay (1997), The Econometrics of Financial Markets (Princeton University Press, Princeton, NJ).

Claus, J., and J. Thomas (2000), "Equity premia as low as 3%? Empirical evidence from analysts' earnings forecasts for domestic and international stock markets", Unpublished Manuscript (Columbia University).

Cochrane, J.H., and J. Saa-Requejo (2000), "Beyond arbitrage: good-deal asset price bounds in incomplete markets", Journal of Political Economy 108:79–119.

Constantinides, G.M. (1978), "Market risk adjustment in project valuation", Journal of Finance 33: 606–616.

Cooper, I. (1996), "Arithmetic versus geometric mean estimators: setting discount rates for capital budgeting", European Financial Management 2:157–167.

Cornell, B. (1999a), "Risk, duration, and capital budgeting: new evidence on some old questions", Journal of Business 72:183–200.

Cornell, B. (1999b), The Equity Risk Premium (Wiley, New York).

Cornell, B., and K. Green (1991), "The investment performance of low grade bond funds", Journal of Finance 46:29–48.

Cornell, B., J.I. Hirshleifer and E.P. James (1997), "Estimating the cost of equity capital", Contemporary Finance Digest 1:5–13.

Cox, J.C., and S.A. Ross (1976), "The valuation of options for alternative stochastic processes", Journal of Financial Economics 3:173–183.

Cox, J.C., J.E. Ingersoll and S.A. Ross (1985), "An intertemporal general equilibrium model of asset prices", Econometrica 53:363–384.

Cragg, J.G., and B.G. Malkiel (1982), Expectations and the Structure of Share Prices (University of Chicago Press, Chicago).

Daniel, K., and S. Titman (1997), "Evidence on the characteristics of cross-sectional variation in expected returns", Journal of Finance 52:1–33.

Davis, J.J., E.F. Fama and K.R. French (2000), "Characteristics, covariances,and average returns: 1929–1997", Journal of Finance 55:389–406.

DeBondt, W., and R. Thaler (1995), "Financial decision making in firms and markets: a behavioral perspective", in: R. Jarrow et al., eds., Handbooks in Operations Research and Management Science, Vol. 9 (Elsevier, Amsterdam) pp. 385–410.

Dixit, A.K., and R.S. Pindyck (1994), Investment under Uncertainty (Princeton University Press, Princeton, NJ).

Dumas, B. (1991), "Super contact and related optimality conditions", Journal of Economic Dynamics and Control 15:675–695.

Ekern, S., and R. Wilson (1974), "On the theory of the firm in an economy with incomplete capital markets", Bell Journal of Economics and Management Science 5:171–180.

Elton, E., M. Gruber and J. Mei (1994), "Cost of capital using arbitrage pricing theory: a case of nine New York utilities", Financial Markets, Institutions and Instruments 2.

Esterwood, J.C., and S.R. Nutt (1999), "Inefficiency in analysts' earnings forecasts: systematic misreaction or systematic optimism", Journal of Finance 54:1777–1798.

Fama, E.F. (1977), "Risk adjusted discount rates and capital budgeting under uncertainty", Journal of Financial Economics 5:3–24.

Fama, E.F. (1996), "Discounting under uncertainty", Journal of Business 69:415–429.

Fama, E.F., and K.R. French (1989), "Business conditions and expected returns on stocks and bonds", Journal of Financial Economics 25:23–49.

Fama, E.F., and K.R. French (1995), "Size and book-to-market factors in earnings and returns", Journal of Finance 50:131–155.

Fama, E.F., and K.R. French (1997), "Industry costs of equity", Journal of Financial Economics 43: 153–194.

Fama, E.F., and K.R. French (1998), "Taxes, financing decisions, and firm value", Journal of Finance 53:819–843.

Fama, E.F., and K.R. French (1999), "The corporate cost of capital and the return on corporate investment", Journal of Finance 5:1939–1967.

Fama, E.F., and K.R. French (2002), "The equity premium", Journal of Finance 57:637–659.

Fama, E.F., and G.W. Schwert (1977), "Asset returns and inflation", Journal of Financial Economics 5:115–146.

Ferson, W.E., and D.H. Locke (1998), "Estimating the cost of capital through time: an analysis of the sources of error", Management Science 44:485–500.

Fisher, I. (1930), The Theory of Interest as Determined by Impatience to Spend Income and Opportunity to Invest It (MacMillan, New York).

Fuller, R., and H. Kerr (1981), "Estimating the divisional cost of capital: an analysis of pure play techniques", Journal of Finance 36:997–1009.

Gebhardt, W.R., C.M.C. Lee and B. Swaminathan (2001), "Toward an implied cost of capital", Journal of Accounting Research 39:135–176.

Gibson, R., and E.S. Schwartz (1990), "Stochastic convenience yield and the pricing of oil contingent claims", Journal of Finance 45:959–976.

Goldenberg, D.H., and A.J. Robin (1991), "The arbitrage pricing theory and cost-of-capital estimation: the case of electric utilities", Journal of Financial Research 14:181–197.

Gordon, J.R., and M.J. Gordon (1997), "The finite horizon expected return model", Financial Analysts' Journal 53:52–61.

Gordon, M.J. (1962), The Investment, Financing and Valuation of the Corporation (Irwin, Homewood, IL).

Graham, J.R., and C.R. Harvey (2001), "The theory and practice of corporate finance: evidence from the field", Journal of Financial Economics 60:187–243.

Grenadier, S.R. (1995), "Valuing lease contracts: a real options approach", Journal of Financial Economics 38:297–331.

Grenadier, S.R. (1996), "The strategic exercise of options: development cascades and overbuilding in real estate markets", Journal of Finance 51:1653–1679.

Grenadier, S.R. (2000), "Equilibrium with time to build", in: M.J. Brennan and L. Trigeorgis, eds., Project Flexibility, Agency and Competition (Oxford University Press, Oxford) pp. 275–296.

Harris, R.S., and F.C. Marston (1992), "Estimating shareholder risk premia using analysts' growth forecasts", Financial Management 21:63–70.

Harris, R.S., T.J. O'Brien and D. Wakeman (1989), "Divisional cost of capital estimation for multi-industry firms", Financial Management 18:74–84.

Harrison, J.M., and S. Pliska (1981), "Martingales and arbitrage in the theory of continuous trading", Stochastic Processes and their Applications 11:215–260.

Hertz, D.B. (1964), "Risk analysis in capital investment", Harvard Business Review 42:95–106.

Hirshleifer, J. (1965), "Investment decision under uncertainty: choice-theoretic approaches", The Quarterly Journal of Economics 79:509–536.

Hirshleifer, J. (1970), Investment, Interest and Capital (Prentice-Hall, Englewood Cliffs).

Ibbotson Associates (1997), 1997 Yearbook (Ibbotson Associates, Chicago).

Indro, D.C., and W.Y. Lee (1997), "Biases in arithmetic and geometric averages as estimates of long-run expected returns and risk premia", Financial Management 26:81–90.

Ingersoll, J.E., and S.A. Ross (1992), "Waiting to invest", Journal of Business 65:1–30.

Jarrow, R.A. (1980), "Heterogeneous expectations, restrictions on short sales, and equilibrium asset prices", Journal of Finance 35:53–85.

Kaplan, S., and R. Ruback (1995), "The valuation of cash flow forecasts: an empirical analysis", Journal of Finance 50:1059–1094.

Kemsley, D., and D. Nissim (2002), "Valuation of the debt tax shield", Journal of Finance 57:2045–2073.

Kothari, S.P., and J. Shanken (1997), "Book-to-market, dividend yield, and expected market returns: a time series analysis", Journal of Financial Economics 44:169–203.

Kulatilaka, N. (1995), "Operating flexibilities in capital budgeting: substitutability and complementarity in real options", in: L. Trigeorgis ed., Real Options in Capital Investment (Praeger, New York) pp. 121–132.

Kulatilaka, N., and E.C. Perotti (1998), "Strategic growth options", Management Science 44:1021–1031.

Lambrecht, B. (2000), "Strategic sequential investments and sleeping patents", in: M.J. Brennan and L. Trigeorgis, eds., Project Flexibility, Agency and Competition (Oxford University Press, Oxford) pp. 297–323.

Lamont, O.A. (2000), "Investment plans and stock returns", Journal of Finance 55:2719–2745.

Leahy, J.V. (1993), "Investment in competitive equilibrium: the optimality of myopic behavior", Quarterly Journal of Economics 108:1105–1134.

Leland, H.E. (1974), "Production theory and the stock market", Bell Journal of Economics and Management Science 5:125–144.

Leland, H.E. (1977), "Information, managerial choice and stockholder unanimity", Review of Economic Studies 45:527–534.

Lintner, J. (1965), "The valuation of risky assets and the selection of risky investments in stock portfolios and capital budgets", Review of Economics and Statistics 47:13–37.

MacKinlay, A.C. (1995), "Multifactor models do not explain deviations from the CAPM", Journal of Financial Economics 38:3–28.

Magee, J. (1964), "How to use decision trees in capital investment", Harvard Business Review 42:79–96.

Makowski, L. (1983), "Competition and unanimity revisited", American Economic Review 73:329–339.

McDonald, R. (2000), "Real options and rules of thumb in capital budgeting", in: M.J. Brennan and L. Trigeorgis, eds., Project Flexibility, Agency and Competition (Oxford University Press, Oxford) pp. 13–33.

McDonald, R., and D.R. Siegel (1986), "The value of waiting to invest", Quarterly Journal of Economics 101:707–728.

Merton, R.C. (1973), "The theory of rational option pricing", Bell Journal of Economics and Management Science 4:141–183.

Miles, J.A., and J.R. Ezzell (1980), "The weighted average cost of capital, perfect capital markets and project life: a clarification", Journal of Financial and Quantitative Analysis 15:719–730.

Miller, E.M. (1977), "Risk, uncertainty, and divergence of opinion", Journal of Finance 32:1151–1168.

Miller, M.H. (1977), "Debt and taxes", Journal of Finance 32:261–275.

Miller, M.H., and F. Modigliani (1961), "Dividend policy, growth, and the valuation of shares", Journal of Business 34:411–433.

Miller, M.H., and K. Rock (1985), "Dividend policy under asymmetric information", Journal of Finance 40:1031–1051.

Milne, A., and A.E. Whalley (2000), "Time to build, option value and investment decisions", Journal of Financial Economics 56:325–332.

Modigliani, F., and M.H. Miller (1958), "The cost of capital, corporation finance and the theory of investment", American Economic Review 48:261–297.

Modigliani, F., and M.H. Miller (1963), "Corporate income taxes and the cost of capital: a correction", American Economic Review 53:433–443.

Myers, S.C. (1974), "Interactions of corporate investment and financing decisions – implications for capital budgeting", Journal of Finance 29:1–25.

Myers, S.C. (1977), "Determinants of corporate borrowing", Journal of Financial Economics 5:147–175.

Myers, S.C., and C.D. Howe (1997), "A life-cycle financial model of pharmaceutical R&D", Unpublished Paper (MIT, MA).

Myers, S.C., and N.S. Majluf (1984), "Corporate financing and investment decisions when firms have information that investors do not have", Journal of Financial Economics 13:187–221.

Myers, S.C., and A.A. Robichek (1966), "Conceptual problems in the use of risk-adjusted discount rates", Journal of Finance 21:727–730.

Myers, S.C., and S.M. Turnbull (1977), "Capital budgeting and the capital asset pricing model – good news and bad news", Journal of Finance 32:321–333.

Nielsen, N.C. (1976), "The investment decision of the firm under uncertainty and the allocative efficiency of capital markets", Journal of Finance 31:587–602.

Paddock, J.L., D.R. Siegel and J.L. Smith (1988), "Option valuation of claims on real assets", Quarterly Journal of Economics 103:479–508.

Pastor, L., and R.F. Stambaugh (1999), "Costs of equity capital and model mispricing", Journal of Finance 54:67–121.

Perez-Quiros, G., and A. Timmerman (2000), "Firm size and cyclical variation in returns", Journal of Finance 55:1229–1262.

Ross, S.A. (1976), "The arbitrage theory of capital asset pricing", Journal of Economic Theory 13: 341–360.

Ross, S.A. (1978), "Mutual fund separation and financial theory – the separating distributions", Journal of Economic Theory 17:254–286.

Ross, S.A. (1985), "Debt, taxes and uncertainty", Journal of Finance 60:637–656.

Ross, S.A. (1987), "Arbitrage and martingales with taxation", Journal of Political Economy 95:371–393.

Ross, S.A. (1989), "Information and volatility: the no-arbitrage martingale approach to timing and resolution irrelevancy", Journal of Finance 44:1–17.

Ruback, R. (1986), "Calculating the value of risk-free cash flows", Journal of Financial and Quantitative Analysis 21:323–339.

Ruback, R. (2000), "Capital cash flows: a simple approach to valuing risky cash flows", Unpublished Manuscript (Harvard University).

Rubinstein, M. (1978), "Competition and approximation", Bell Journal of Economics 9:280–286.

Schwartz, E.S. (1997), "The behavior of commodity prices: implications for valuation and hedging", Journal of Finance 52:923–973.

Schwartz, E.S., and M. Moon (2000), "Evaluating research and development investments", in: M.J. Brennan and L. Trigeorgis, eds., Project Flexibility, Agency and Competition (Oxford University Press, Oxford) pp. 85–106.

Schwartz, E.S., and L. Trigeorgis (2001), Real Options and Investment under Uncertainty (MIT Press, Cambridge, MA).

Sharpe, W.F. (1964), "Capital asset prices: a theory of market equilibrium under conditions of risk", Journal of Finance 19:425–442.

Shleifer, A. (1986), Do demand curves for stocks slope down?", Journal of Finance 41:579–590.

Sick, G. (1989a), "Capital budgeting with real options", Monograph Series in Finance and Economics (Salomon Bros. Centre, New York University).

Sick, G.A. (1986), "A certainty equivalent approach to capital budgeting", Financial Management 15:23–32.

Sick, G.A. (1989b), "Multiperiod risky project valuation: a mean-covariance certainty equivalent approach", Advances in Financial Planning and Forecasting 3:1–36.

Smit, H.T.J., and L.A. Ankum (1993), "A real options and game theoretic approach to corporate investment strategy under competition", Financial Management 22:241–250.

Stein, J.C. (1996), "Rational capital budgeting in an irrational world", Journal of Business 69:429–456.

Stein, J.C. (2003), "Agency, information, and capital investment", in: G.M. Constantinides, M. Harris and R.M. Stulz, eds., Handbook of the Economics of Finance, Vol. 1A (Elsevier, Amsterdam) Chapter 2, this volume.

Summers, L.H. (1987), "Investment incentives and the discounting of depreciation allowances", in: M. Feldstein, ed., The Effects of Taxation on Capital Accumulation (Chicago University Press, Chicago).

Taggart, R.A. (1991), "Consistent valuation and cost of capital expressions with corporate and personal taxes", Financial Management 20:8–20.

Triantis, A., and A. Borison (2001), "Real options: state of the practice", Journal of Applied Corporate Finance 14:8–24.

Trigeorgis, L. (1993), "The nature of real option interactions and the valuation of investments with multiple real options", Journal of Financial and Quantitative Analysis 28:1–20.

Trigeorgis, L. (1996), Real Options (MIT Press, Cambridge, MA).

Tvedt, J. (2000), "The ship Lay-up Option and Equilibrium Freight Rates", in: M.J. Brennan and L. Trigeorgis, eds., Project Flexibility, Agency and Competition (Oxford University Press, Oxford) pp. 340–348.

Vasicek, O. (1977), "An equilibrium characterization of the term structure", Journal of Financial Economics 5:177–188.

Welch, I. (2000), "Views of financial economists on the equity premium and other issues", Journal of Business 73:501–537.

Whitelaw, R.F. (1997), "Time variation in Sharpe ratios and market timing", Unpublished Paper (New York University).

Williams, J.B. (1938), Theory of Investment Value (Harvard University Press, Cambridge, MA).

Chapter 4

FINANCING OF CORPORATIONS

STEWART C. MYERS[*]

Sloan School of Management, MIT

Contents

[*] Some passages in this paper appeared in Myers (2001). I thank the *Journal of Economic Perspectives* for permission to repeat these passages. I also thank René Stulz for helpful comments and Neeti Nundi for excellent research assistance.

Handbook of the Economics of Finance, Edited by G.M. Constantinides, M. Harris and R. Stulz

Abstract

This review evaluates the four major theories of corporate financing: (1) the
Modigliani–Miller theory of capital-structure irrelevance, in which firm values and
real investment decisions are unaffected by financing; (2) the trade-off theory, in which
firms balance the tax advantages of borrowing against the costs of financial distress;
(3) agency theories, in which financing responds to managers' personal incentives; and
(4) the pecking-order theory, in which financing adapts to mitigate problems created
by differences in information.

   These theories are conditional, not general. It is easy to find examples of each theory
at work, but otherwise difficult to distinguish the theories empirically. Large, safe
firms with mostly tangible assets tend to borrow more. Firms with high profitability
and valuable growth opportunities tend to borrow less. Each of these tendencies is
consistent with two or more of the major theories of financing. It may be possible to
devise sharper tests by exporting the theories to developing economies, where agency
and information problems are more severe.

   Further progress in understanding corporate financing decisions will require a deeper
understanding of agency issues when value-maximizing operating and investment
decisions cannot be observed or verified. But managers are not just temporary agents
motivated by immediate pecuniary compensation or perquisites. Managers specialize
their human capital to the firm. Some recent research suggests how financing can
support the co-investment of human and financial capital.

Keywords

corporate financing, capital structure, trade-off theory, pecking-order theory, agency
costs, financing

JEL classification: G32

1. Introduction

This review covers corporate financing and capital structure, that is, the mix of securities and financing sources used to finance real investment by corporations.

The leading theories of capital structure attempt to explain the proportions of debt and equity observed on the right-hand side of corporations' balance sheets. Most research assumes that the corporations are public, non-financial firms raising capital primarily from outside investors, not from the firm's entrepreneurs, managers or employees. The firms are assumed to have access to "Anglo–Saxon" capital markets and institutions, characterized by a broad, efficient public market for shares and corporate debt, and by reasonably good protection of the rights of outside investors. Most tests of capital structure theories have examined debt ratios of established, public, USA corporations.

These theories and tests are really focusing on financing *strategy*, the determination of overall debt ratios for a particular type of firm in a particular institutional setting. This review will attempt to look beyond that setting where pertinent research is available. The review will also consider financing *tactics*, for example the design of specific security issues.

The diversity of financing tactics is remarkable. Innovation in security design continues apace. The composition of financing varies cross-sectionally, even within apparently homogeneous industries, and also over time, even when markets, institutions, regulation and taxation are apparently constant. Are these variations and fluctuations just tactical noise overlaying fixed, general principles of optimal financing strategy, or do the tactics dominate strategy?

If financing tactics are more than just noise, then tactics should provide circumstantial evidence for more general theories. Perhaps those theories are plausible not because they do a satisfactory job explaining differences in overall debt ratios, but because one can see the costs and benefits that drive the theories at work in financing tactics.

1.1. Theories of optimal financing

There is no universal theory of capital structure, and no reason to expect one. There are useful *conditional* theories, however. The theories differ in their relative emphasis on the factors that could affect the choice between debt and equity. These factors include agency costs, taxes, differences in information, and the effects of market imperfections or institutional or regulatory constraints. Each factor could be dominant for some firms or in some circumstances, yet unimportant elsewhere.

The leading theories of capital structure are as follows:

Capital-Structure Irrelevance. This theory holds that firm value and real investment decisions are, with few important exceptions, independent of financing. The choice between debt and equity is not totally unimportant – you can surely screw it up – but its effects on real decisions are second- or third-order. Differences among financing strategies are mostly tactical noise.

Trade-off theory. Firms choose target debt ratios by trading off the tax benefits of debt against the costs of bankruptcy and financial distress. Actual debt ratios move towards the targets.

Agency theory. Financing decisions have first-order real effects because they change managers' incentives and their investment and operating decisions. Agency costs drive financing – or at least they explain the effects of financing decisions.

Pecking-order theory. Financing adapts to mitigate problems created by differences in information between insiders (managers) and outside investors. The firm turns first to the financing sources where differences in information matter least.

Obviously these theories overlap. For example, most versions of the trade-off theory interpret the costs of financial distress as including agency costs encountered at high debt ratios. At the end of the day some blend of all of the theories may be needed to explain capital structure. Nevertheless, it is helpful to address the theories, and the evidence for and against them, one by one. The next three sections of this paper cover the value-irrelevance, trade-off and pecking-order theories, which are well-specified and well-understood, at least theoretically. Section 5 turns to agency theories of financing. These theories are not as tightly specified, but do address broader and deeper issues. Section 6 notes some new ideas and approaches. I conclude that significant progress in understanding financial structure will come only by modeling agency effects of financing at a more fundamental level.

The literature on capital structure is enormous. I have emphasized more recent work, but have not been able to cite, much less discuss, all relevant research. Harris and Raviv (1991) contains a comprehensive survey of research through 1990.

2. The Modigliani–Miller value-irrelevance propositions

The modern theory of optimal capital structure starts with Modigliani and Miller's (MM's) proof (1958) that financing doesn't matter in perfect capital markets. [1] Consider the market-value balance sheet on the next page. The market values of the firm's debt and equity, D and E, add up to total firm value V. MM's Proposition 1 says that V is a constant, regardless of the proportions of D and E, provided that the assets and

---

[1] "Perfect" requires that capital markets are not only competitive and frictionless, but also complete, so that the risk characteristics of every security issued by the firm can be matched in capital markets by purchase of another existing security or portfolio, or by a dynamic trading strategy. Titman (2002) points out that MM's argument can survive even in incomplete markets if the firm's securities can be repackaged costlessly by financial institutions or investors. A firm that attempts to exploit an area of incompleteness should get nowhere, because of competition from repackagers. But this amounts to saying that markets will quickly become complete with respect to any state of nature that is of interest to investors and that the firm's securities could pay off in.

growth opportunities on the left-hand side of the balance sheet are held constant.[2] Financial leverage or "gearing", that is, the proportion of debt financing, is irrelevant. This leverage-irrelevance result generalizes to any mix of securities issued by the firm. For example, it doesn't matter whether debt is short- or long-term, callable or call-protected, straight or convertible, in dollars or euros, or some mixture of all of these or other types.

Assets-in-place and growth opportunities	Debt (D)
	Equity (E)
	Firm value (V)

Proposition 1 also says that each firm's cost of capital is a constant, regardless of the debt ratio D/V. Let r_D and r_E be the "cost of debt" and the "cost of equity," that is, the expected rates of return demanded by investors in the firm's debt and equity securities. Then the overall (weighted-average) cost of capital is:

$$\text{Weighted Average Cost of Capital} = r_A = r_D \, D/V + r_E \, E/V. \tag{1}$$

The weighted-average cost of capital r_A is the expected return on a market-value-weighted portfolio of all the firm's outstanding securities. It is also the discount or "hurdle rate" for capital investment by the firm.[3]

Solving Equation (1) for the cost of equity gives MM's Proposition 2:

$$r_E = r_A + (r_A - r_D) \, D/E. \tag{2}$$

Proposition 2 shows why there is "No magic in financial leverage". Any attempt to substitute "cheap" debt for "expensive" equity fails to reduce the overall cost of capital, because it makes the remaining equity still more expensive – just enough more expensive to keep the overall cost of capital constant.

MM's propositions are no longer controversial as a matter of theory. The economic intuition is simple, equivalent to asserting that in a perfect-market supermarket "The

---

[2] Fama (1978) summarizes the conditions necessary for Proposition 1.

[3] Here I am ignoring taxes. Corporations actually use the after-tax weighted average cost of capital (WACC) as a discount or hurdle rate for capital investment:

$$\text{WACC} = r_D(1 - T_C) \, D/V + r_E \, E/V.$$

This incorporates the after-tax cost of debt, calculated at the marginal corporate rate T_C. WACC is the correct discount rate for after-tax cash flows from capital investments that do not change the firm's business risk or market-value debt ratio. See Brealey and Myers (2003, Chapter 19), Miles and Ezzell (1980) and Taggart (1991).

value of a pizza does not depend on how it is sliced". But are capital markets really sufficiently perfect? After all, the values of pizzas *do depend* on how they are sliced. Consumers are willing to pay more for the several slices than for the equivalent whole. Perhaps the value of the firm does depend on how its assets, cash flows and growth opportunities are sliced up and offered to investors. There are surely investors who would be willing to pay extra for particular types or mixes of corporate securities. For example, investors cannot easily borrow with limited liability, but corporations provide limited liability and can borrow on their stockholders' behalf.

We see constant innovation in the design of securities and new financing schemes.[4] Innovation proves that financing can matter. If new securities or financing tactics never added value, then there would be no incentive to innovate.

The practical relevance and credibility of MM's propositions cannot rest on a lack of demand for financial leverage or for specialized securities. The propositions' support must in the end come from the supply side. The key fact supporting MM is that the cost of supply is very small relative to the market value of the firm. Suppose there is a clientele of investors who would be willing to pay extra for the firm's debt and equity securities at a particular, "optimal" debt ratio. In equilibrium they do not have to pay extra, because public corporations' costs of manufacturing debt and equity securities, rather than equity only, are a small fraction of the securities' market values. Thus the supply of debt adjusts until the value added for the marginal investor is essentially zero. (If for some reason firms do not supply the equilibrium amount of debt, financial institutions will do so. They can buy a firm's securities, repackage them in the correct debt-equity proportions, and sell the repackaged securities to investors.)

MM's propositions are exceptionally difficult to test directly, but financial innovation provides strong circumstantial evidence. The costs of designing and creating new securities and financing schemes are low, and the costs of imitation are trivial. (Fortunately, securities and financing tactics cannot be patented.)[5] Thus temporary departures from Proposition 1 create the opportunity for financial innovation, but successful innovations quickly become "commodities", that is, standard, low-margin financial products. The rapid response of supply to a successful, innovative financial product should restore the MM equilibrium.[6] Firms may find it convenient to use these new products, but only the first users will increase value, or lower the cost of capital, by doing so.[7]

---

[4] See Persons and Warther (1997), Carow, Erwin and McConnell (1999), Finnerty and Emery (2002) and Tufano (1995).

[5] But the number of patents pertaining to other financial applications has been growing rapidly. See Lerner (2002).

[6] There are many clear examples showing the rapid response of supply following financial innovation. These examples cannot prove that *all* deviations from Proposition 1 trigger successful innovation, or that all supply responses completely restore MM's equilibrium. Deviations from Proposition 1 could persist because of transaction costs or segmented markets. See Titman (2002).

[7] Tufano (1989) found that issuers did not appear to capture the rewards of innovation, because the first issues of a new security were not sold on better terms than later issues. Investment banks still had

For regulators and policymakers, MM's leverage-irrelevance proposition is the ideal end result. If that result could be achieved in practice, then investors' diverse demands for specialized securities would be satisfied at negligible cost. All firms would have equal access to capital, and the cost of capital would not depend on financing, but only on business risk. Capital would flow directly to its most efficient use. Therefore public policy should accommodate financial innovation because it makes financing decisions unimportant.

But for corporate finance, the MM propositions are benchmarks, not end results. The propositions say that financing does not affect value *except for* specifically identified costs or imperfections. As Merton Miller (1989, p. 7), noted, "... showing what *doesn't* matter can also show, by implication, what *does*". Perhaps he should have said "what *may* matter". Identifying a fact or factor that affects some financing choices does not prove that MM's leverage-irrelevance theory is systematically wrong. Compared to real investment and operating decisions, most financing decisions have only second-order effects on value. Idiosyncratic financing decisions [8] may not be very harmful, and managers may not have the attention and discernment necessary to see the effects of financing on volatile stock-market values. Black (1986) describes how models based on fine-tuned optimizing can be confounded by "noise".

3. The trade-off theory

The trade-off theory changes MM's Proposition 1 to:

$$V = D + E = \overline{V} + PV \text{ (interest tax shields)} - PV \text{ (costs of financial distress)},$$

where $\overline{V}$ is firm value with all-equity financing, PV (interest tax shields) is the present value of future taxes saved because of interest tax deductions, and PV (costs of financial distress) is the present value of future costs attributable to the threat or occurrence of default. The firm chooses the level of debt that maximizes V.[9] The optimum requires that the firm borrow up to the point where PV (interest tax shields) and PV (costs of financial distress) are equal at the margin.

---

incentives to create new securities, however, because innovating banks gained larger shares of subsequent issues and trading.

[8] Bertrand and Schoar (2002) show that the background and training of top managers can predict their financing choices. This result is hard to square with the theories described below. The result fits the MM leverage-irrelevance hypothesis, where idiosyncratic financing has no effect on value.

[9] Optimal capital structure is sometimes defined as the debt ratio that minimizes the after-tax weighted average cost of capital (WACC). WACC is drawn as a shallow, U-shaped function of the debt ratio. The upward slope of WACC at high debt ratios is attributed to the costs of financial distress. This is not strictly correct. Maximizing V and minimizing WACC are not the same thing. WACC is a (tax-adjusted) expected rate of return. Financial distress reduces future cash flows and asset values, but does not necessarily increase the expected rates of return demanded by investors, which depend only on risk.

The trade-off theory has common-sense appeal. Interest tax shields appear to have significant value, at least under the USA corporate tax system, and there are ample examples of costs triggered by "excessive" debt. The trade-off theory therefore explains moderate, cautious borrowing. We can also identify the types of firms that should face especially high costs of distress, for example, firms facing above-average business risk [10] and firms with unusually valuable growth opportunities and intangible assets. The trade-off theory predicts that firms or industries with these characteristics should be especially cautious and operate at low target debt ratios.

Before considering the evidence for and against the trade-off theory, I will take a closer look at taxes and costs of financial distress.

3.1. Taxes

The USA double-taxes corporate income. The corporate income tax is followed by another tax on interest paid out to investors and on the dividends or capital gains realized by stockholders. Interest is tax-deductible, so it escapes the top (corporate) layer of taxation.

The value of corporate interest tax deductions may be offset at the bottom (investor) layer of taxation, because most equity income comes as capital gains, which are taxed only when realized, and at a lower rate than the tax rate on dividend or interest income. The tax advantage of debt vs. equity, considering both layers of tax, is:

$$\text{Tax advantage of debt} = (1 - T_P) - (1 - T_C)(1 - T_{PE}), \tag{3}$$

where T_C is the marginal corporate tax rate; T_P is the tax rate paid by investors on interest income; and T_{PE} is the effective tax rate on returns to shareholders.

Modigliani and Miller (1958, 1963) recognized the potential value of interest tax shields, but ignored taxes paid by investors (effectively assuming $T_P = T_{PE}$). In this case only the corporate interest tax shields matter. MM also assumed fixed debt and safe interest tax shields, which they discounted at the borrowing rate r_D. For perpetual debt, the resulting PV(interest tax shields) $= r_D T_C D/r_D = T_C D$.[11] With $T_C = .35$, for example, $1 million of additional debt would generate interest tax shields worth $350 000.

Tax savings of this magnitude would make interest tax shields the dominant force in capital structure decisions. MM's rule-of-thumb calculation is now understood as a

---

[10] Captial structure theory takes business risk as given. In fact risk can be managed. For example, oil and mining companies can lock in selling prices with forward commodity trades. The trade-off theory predicts that firms will reduce risk in order to increase debt capacity. I suspect that few firms manage business risk for that purpose. But I have not attempted to cover the theory or practice of risk management in this paper.

[11] The net tax savings, after taxes paid by shareholders, are $T_C(1 - T_{PE})$. Shareholders would discount this saving at an after-personal-tax rate $r_D(1 - T_{PE})$, so the value of the tax shields for a dollar of perpetual debt is $T_C r_D(1 - T_{PE})/r_D(1 - T_{PE}) = T_C$.

remote upper bound, however. First, any contribution to the current market value of the firm should come only from interest tax shields attaching to assets in place, which will not last forever. [12] Second, interest tax shields are proportional to the total future amount of debt outstanding, which depends on future debt capacity, which depends in turn on the future market value of the firm. Therefore interest tax shields are not safe. For example, if the firm maintains a fixed market-value debt ratio, future interest tax shields will be proportional to firm value and just as risky. [13] Third, the firm may not stay profitable. If it ends up with tax-loss carry-forwards, interest tax shields will be deferred or perhaps lost entirely. Thus the average future tax rate is less than the statutory rate. Fourth, the value of interest tax shields should be partially offset by the tax advantages of equity to individual investors, namely the ability to defer realization of capital gains and then to pay taxes at the relatively low capital gains rate.

Miller (1977) argues that the tax advantages of equity could completely offset the tax-deductibility of interest at the corporate level. Suppose $T_{\rm PE}$ is very low, say zero. Then firms would substitute debt for equity as long as the personal tax rate of the *marginal* investor in debt is less than the corporate tax rate ($T_{\rm P} < T_{\rm C}$). As the supply of debt from all corporations expands, investors in higher tax brackets have to be enticed to hold corporate debt, and interest rates rise. The supply of debt increases until there is no further net tax advantage. At that point, $T_{\rm P} = T_{\rm C}$ for the marginal investor in debt, the effects of personal and corporate taxes cancel out, and MM's Proposition 1 holds despite the tax-deductibility of interest.

This "Miller equilibrium" shows how the tax advantages of corporate debt could be eroded by supply responses and shifts in investors' portfolios. But it is not a complete theory of taxes and portfolio choice, [14] and actual tax rates do not appear to support this

---

[12] If interest tax shields are a subsidy to investment, then competition will drive up the cost of new assets and drive down their pre-tax returns. The firm will have to *pay for* the value of interest tax shields on future investments for replacement or growth. Therefore the value of interest tax shields on debt supported by these future investments will make no net contribution to firm value today.

What if a firm has market power, and does not have to pay for the full value of interest tax shields on debt supported by future investments? In that case, be careful not to double-count. The NPV of future growth opportunities is on the left-hand side of the firm's market-value balance sheet. NPVs calculated by standard methods, say by discounting at the after-tax WACC given in footnote 3 above, already include the value of interest tax shields supported by new investment.

[13] The assumption of a constant market-value debt ratio is not realistic. The assumption is nevertheless implicit in practice: the widely used formula for WACC (see footnote 3 above) assumes that the firm's debt is rebalanced period-by-period to keep the market-value debt ratio constant. See Miles and Ezzell (1980).

[14] Miller assumed that investors' choices between debt and equity are based only on a comparison of after-tax interest rates to after-tax equity returns. The equity returns were implicitly assumed safe. The risk and risk premiums of equity investment were not modeled. Modigliani (1982) presents a more general model of debt, taxes and portfolio choice.

If equity risk is measured by beta (β), the Miller equilibrium would require an after-tax capital asset pricing model (CAPM) of the form $r = (1 - T_{\rm C})r_{\rm f} + \beta[r_{\rm m} - (1 - T_{\rm C})r_{\rm f}]$, where r is expected return, $r_{\rm m}$ is the expected market return and $r_{\rm f}$ is the risk-free interest rate. The intercept of the security market

equilibrium. Graham (2000) examines the interest-rate spread between corporate bonds and tax-exempt municipal bonds to estimate the tax rate paid by marginal investors in corporate debt. The rate is about 30%, well below the top bracket of about 40%. He also estimates the effective tax rate on equity income at about 12%. [15] At these rates interest tax shields still have significant value:

$$\text{Tax advantage of debt} = (1 - 0.30) - [(1 - 0.35)(1 - 0.12)] = 0.13.$$

Graham's estimates are not definitive. We are not sure who the relevant marginal investors are, much less their effective tax rates. Yet there is a near-consensus, among both practitioners and economists, that there is a significant tax incentive for corporate borrowing. Therefore we should observe corporations borrowing to exploit interest tax shields. We should not observe corporations leaving interest tax shields "on the table" when the risk of financial distress is remote. Yet many of the most successful firms operate at very low, even negative debt ratios. ("Negative" means that investments in debt securities, typically money-market instruments, exceed total debt outstanding.)

Graham (2000) also examined a sample of firms listed on Compustat and paying taxes at the full statutory rate. He estimated that these companies could have added 7.5% on average to firm value by "levering up" to still-conservative debt ratios. [16] This is not small change. A 7.5% deviation from MM's leverage-irrelevance proposition should prompt a vigorous supply response – conservatively financed firms should issue massive amounts of debt and retire massive amounts of equity. But many mature, profitable corporations seem uninterested in the tax advantages of debt.

Yet we can quickly dismiss the idea that managers and investors don't pay at least tactical attention to taxes. Many securities are creatures of the tax code, for example floating-rate preferred shares, which are designed for purchase by other corporations with excess cash available for short-term investment. (The advantage is that only 30% of inter-corporate dividends are taxed.) [17]

---

line would be much smaller than in the standard, pre-tax CAPM, and the slope much higher. But tests of the standard CAPM seem to show higher-than-predicted intercepts and lower-than-predicted slopes. See Black (1993).

[15] Graham's estimate of the marginal rate on interest and dividends is an average from 1980 to 1994. The estimate for the effective rate on equity income varied over this sample period. I have quoted the rate for 1993 and 1994.

[16] Graham (2000, pp. 1916, 1934). The 7.5% estimate is probably overstated. I understand that Graham projected several years of future growth in interest tax shields, which is inappropriate in competitive industries. See footnote 12 above. He also discounts at a corporate borrowing rate, which assumes that the level of future debt is fixed rather than rebalanced as firm value changes.

[17] The financial innovators who first created floating-rate preferred shares thus created a partially tax-exempt security that acted like a safe, short-term, money-market instrument. Since then corporations and investment bankers have also figured out how to issue *tax-deductible* preferred shares. The corporation issues a bond to a special purpose trust, which in turn issues preferred stock to investors. The trust is designed to be a tax-free conduit. The issuing corporation deducts interest, and corporate investors can

Financial leases are also largely tax-driven. When the lessor's tax rate is higher than the lessee's, there is a net gain because the lessor's interest and depreciation tax shields are front-loaded, i.e., mostly realized earlier, than the taxes paid on the lease payments. [18] The tax advantage is due to the time value of money, and therefore increases in periods of high inflation and high nominal interest rates.

There are many further examples of tax-driven financing tactics. But finding clear evidence that taxes have a systematic effect on financing *strategy*, as reflected in actual or target debt ratios, is much more difficult. In 1984, after a review of the then-available empirical work, I concluded that there was "no study clearly demonstrating that a firm's tax status has a predictable, material effect on its debt policy. I think that the wait for such a study will be protracted" [Myers (1984, p. 588)].

A few such studies have since appeared, although some relate in part to financing tactics, and none gives conclusive support for the trade-off theory. MacKie-Mason (1990) tested whether companies with low marginal tax rates, for example companies with tax loss carry-forwards, were more likely to issue equity, compared to more profitable companies facing the full statutory tax rate. This was clearly true in his sample. [19]

MacKie-Mason's result is consistent with the trade-off theory, because it shows that tax-paying firms favor debt. But it is also consistent with a Miller (1977) equilibrium in which the value of corporate interest tax shields is entirely offset by the low effective tax rate on capital gains. In this case, a firm facing a low-enough tax rate would also use equity, because investors pay less taxes on equity income than on interest income. Thus we cannot conclude from MacKie-Mason's results that interest tax shields make a significant contribution to the market value of the firm or that debt ratios are determined by the trade-off theory.

Graham (1996) also finds evidence that changes in long-term debt are positively and significantly related to the firm's effective marginal tax rate. Again this shows that taxes affect financing decisions, at least at the tactical level. It does not show that the present value of interest tax shields is materially positive. An early paper by Miller and Modigliani (1966) did find that interest tax shields contributed significantly to market value in a sample of electric utilities. But Fama and French (1998), who examined a much larger sample from 1965 to 1992, found no significant link between taxes, financing and market value.

---

receive income taxed as inter-corporate dividends. The first tax-deductible preferred was designed and successfully issued in 1993. By the end of 1997, there were 285 more issues raising $27 billion – another example of rapid supply response to a successful financial innovation. See Khanna and McConnell (1998) and Irvine and Rosenfeld (2000).

[18] See Myers, Dill and Bautista (1976) and Schallheim (1994).

[19] This result has been confirmed in later studies, for example Jung, Kim and Stulz (1996).

3.2. Direct costs of financial distress

Costs of financial distress are incurred when the threat or occurrence of default reduces the market value of the firm's assets, operations or growth opportunities.

Direct costs of financial distress are incurred in bankruptcy and reorganization. These include legal and administrative costs and the costs of shutting down operations and disposing of assets [20] (but only costs that would not be incurred absent financial distress). Direct costs may also include continued operating losses while creditors and stockholders wrangle or legal processes unfold. (Some railroad bankruptcies took decades to resolve.) Weiss and Wruck (1998) describe how most of Eastern Airlines' remaining value dissipated during two years under the "protection" of the bankruptcy court.

But a few examples of meltdowns in bankruptcy do not prove that *direct* bankruptcy costs are generally large enough to make the trade-off theory work. Andrade and Kaplan (1998), who studied a sample of highly leveraged companies that fell into financial distress, found that most of the costs of financial distress occurred before bankruptcy was declared. In general, the bankruptcy process appeared to be reasonably efficient, [21] at least for large firms. There are economies of scale in bankruptcy.

3.3. Indirect costs of financial distress – conflicts between creditors and stockholders

Indirect costs of financial distress are mostly due to agency costs generated by conflicts of interest between debt and equity investors. If there is a chance of default, then shareholders can gain at the expense of debt investors. Equity is a residual claim, so shareholders gain when the value of existing debt falls, even when the value of the firm is constant.

Black and Scholes (1973) were first to show that common stock is equivalent to a call option on the firm's assets, with an exercise price equal to the face value of outstanding debt. The market value of debt equals its value if default-risk free minus a default put: $D = D(\text{risk-free}) - P$. The put value P depends on firm value V, the standard deviation of asset returns σ, the debt's time to maturity t and its face value (exercise price) F. Thus $P = P(V, \sigma, t, F)$, [22] and

$$E = V - D = V - D(\text{risk} - \text{free}) + P(V, \sigma, t, F). \tag{4}$$

---

[20] For example, the costs of a "fire sale" where assets are sold for less than their value to a going concern. See Pulvino (1998).

[21] For example, Weiss (1990) found bankruptcy costs averaging about 20% of equity value pre-bankruptcy. The expected costs for a healthy firm should be far less. An important earlier paper by Warner (1977) likewise finds that direct bankruptcy costs are relatively small. See also Franks and Torous (1994), Gilson (1997) and Maksimovic and Phillips (1998).

[22] For simplicity I assume that the firm has but one debt issue outstanding. Valuing the default put is more difficult when there are many issues with different maturities, terms and covenants, but the nature of the conflicts of interest between lenders and stockholders is unchanged.

Suppose that managers act in stockholders' interests, and that the risk of default is significant. There are several ways for managers to transfer value from the firm's creditors to its stockholders. First, managers could invest in riskier assets or shift to riskier operating strategies. This works because $dP/d\sigma > 0$. Higher risk increases the "upside" for stockholders. The downside is absorbed by the firm's creditors. Jensen and Meckling (1976) first stressed *risk shifting* as an agency problem.

Second, the managers may be able to borrow still more and pay out cash to stockholders. In this case the overall value of the firm is constant, but the market value of the existing debt declines because $dP/dF > 0$. (New debt does not suffer because it is issued at market value.) The cash received by stockholders more than offsets the decline in the value of their shares.

Third, the managers can cut back equity-financed capital investment. Optimal investment I is normally determined at $dV/dI = 1$. But investment at this margin makes debtholders better off, because $dP/dV < 0$. Part of the value generated by new investment goes to existing creditors, who are better protected once the investment is made. The gain in the market value of debt acts like a tax, which discourages investment and tempts managers to shrink the firm and pay out cash to stockholders. Myers (1977) was the first to stress this *underinvestment* or "debt overhang" problem.

Fourth, the managers can "play for time," for example by concealing problems to prevent creditors from acting to force immediate bankruptcy or reorganization. This lengthens the effective maturity of the debt and makes it riskier. Creditors suffer, because $dP/dt > 0$, and stockholders gain.

There are many examples of these temptations at work. Leveraged buyouts (LBOs) provide examples of the effects of additional borrowing. Asquith and Wizman (1990) found that announcement of a leveraged buyout triggered an average loss in market value of 5.2% for bonds lacking covenant protection.[23] When RJR Nabisco's management proposed a LBO, the market value of the company's existing debt fell instantly by more that 10%. Alexander, Edwards and Ferri (2000) examine the returns of a large sample of junk bonds traded on Nasdaq. Junk-bond and common-stock returns should have opposite signs at the announcement of "wealth-transferring events", such as an impending LBO. They find evidence of negative correlation around such events.

Debt investors are of course aware of these temptations and try to write debt contracts accordingly. Debt covenants may restrict additional borrowing, limit dividend payouts or other distributions to stockholders, and provide that debt is immediately due and payable if other covenants are seriously violated. Smith and Warner (1979) provide

---

[23] At the time, investors were willing to buy the debt of supposedly blue-chip companies with minimal covenants. Asquith and Wizman (1990) found that the value of bonds with strong covenants actually increased when LBOs were announced. Marais, Schipper and Smith (1989) found insignificant negative price reactions for nonconvertible debt in a sample of buyouts from 1974 to 1985. This is surprising, since most issues' credit ratings were downgraded, and the average post-buyout debt ratio tripled.

a detailed analysis of debt contracts and covenants, and show how the contracts are designed to avoid indirect costs of financial distress.[24]

The recognition of the implications of potential conflicts of interest between lenders and stockholders was an important contribution to the trade-off theory. The conflicts of interest mean that the mere *threat* of default can generate agency costs, for example by deterring positive-NPV investment or shifting the firm to riskier strategies.

The agency costs of suboptimal investment and operating decisions are potentially much more serious than "workout" costs incurred post-default. The trade-off theory needs both types of costs to provide a credible counterweight to the present value of interest tax shields.

These agency costs also help to explain why growth firms tend to rely on equity. They have more to lose; the debt-overhang problem is no problem for a firm lacking valuable investment opportunities. Also, the value of those opportunities, which depends on *future* investment decisions, is lousy collateral for a loan today. Lenders are naturally averse to lending against the value of investments that haven't been made yet. (Would you lend today to a growth firm on the strength of its management's promise to undertake "all future investment projects with positive NPVs"? Even if the lender could identify positive NPVs, there would be no way to enforce such a contract.)

3.4. Other indirect costs of financial distress

The threat of default can have other adverse feedback effects on the value of the firm. Titman (1984) stresses the costs imposed by liquidation on customers, suppliers and employees.[25] When the value of a firm's product or service depends on the firm's continued existence – because of a need for spare parts or service, for example – then conservatively financed firms will have a competitive advantage.

Perhaps the most dramatic recent example is the impact of Enron's financial distress on the value of its energy-trading business. This business had the largest share of its market and significant competitive strengths (although Enron may have puffed up its profits and prospects). But trades can be executed only when counterparty risk – the risk that a trading partner will default – is acceptably low. Enron's trading volume fell precipitously once the company's debt rating fell below investment grade, and the trading business lost most of its value as a going concern. Enron's financing strategy also violated a key normative implication of the trade-off theory: if the value of the firm's assets and operations would be damaged severely in financial distress, reduce the odds of distress by reducing financial leverage.

There is another first-order reason why firms favor equity finance. Employees will shy from committing and specializing human capital to a firm threatened by default.

---

[24] The maturity and priority structures of corporate debt are also adapted to avoid costs of financial distress. See Barclay and Smith (1995a,b), for example.

[25] See also Cornell and Shapiro (1987) and Maksimovic and Titman (1991).

This factor is probably most important for high-tech growth firms. Human capital specialized to innovation will have few alternate uses if the innovating firm fails.

3.5. Evidence on costs of financial distress

It is difficult to distinguish costs of financial distress from the costs of the business setbacks that put the firm into distress. Andrade and Kaplan (1998) attack this problem by examining a sample of highly-leveraged transactions (HLTs, i.e., leveraged buyouts and restructurings). Most of their sample firms would have been financially healthy with normal financing. The firms started with unusually high leverage, however, so minor business setbacks were sufficient to trigger distress.

Andrade and Kaplan estimated costs of financial distress averaging 10 to 20% of firm value. These are not large effects, for two reasons. First, some of the costs may actually flow from the business setbacks that triggered distress. Estimated distress costs were negligible in a subsample of firms that encountered no evident adverse economic shocks. Second, a firm operating at normal debt ratios would be concerned with the *expected* consequences of additional borrowing, and would multiply the costs of distress by a small probability of distress.

HLTs were generally undertaken by established firms with ample operating cash flow and limited growth opportunities. Such firms' assets-in-place are likely to survive distress and reorganization – they are unlikely to be shut down or liquidated, for example. Andrade and Kaplan's results do not necessarily apply to firms with valuable intangible assets and growth opportunities. The value of such assets is fragile, particularly if the value depends on specialized human capital, which is likely to depart in conditions of financial distress.

Andrade and Kaplan also review previous research on financial distress and the bankruptcy process.

3.6. Leverage and product markets

Leverage could also affect firm value by changing the nature of competition in the market for the firm's products or services. If leverage is a competitive disadvantage, then the feedback effect of leverage on competitiveness is an additional cost of financial distress.

Chevalier (1995a,b) found that highly-leveraged supermarket chains competed less aggressively, to the advantage of the chains' more conservatively financed competitors. The announcement of a leveraged buyout (LBO) of a supermarket chain increased the stock prices of the chain's competitors. These competitors tended to expand later at the LBO chain's expense. Zingales (1998) found that highly-leveraged trucking companies invested less and were less likely to survive in a deregulated environment. Phillips (1995) and Kavenock and Phillips (1997) likewise find that highly-leveraged firms tend to invest less aggressively. These studies also suggest that highly-leveraged firms will charge higher prices if they can. But competitors with "deeper pockets" may take advantage of their highly-leveraged competitors by more intense price competition. In this case the highly-leveraged firms may have to follow suit.

Clearly there are interactions between financing and product markets. The empirical literature[26] so far suggests that highly-leveraged firms are "softer" competitors that will curtail investment and expansion. The choice of financial leverage should therefore depend on the firm's opportunities. A growth firm with valuable future investment opportunities should be a "hard" competitor, and should favor equity financing. A firm with limited opportunities that is tempted to over-invest should favor debt.

3.7. Evidence for the trade-off theory

The trade-off theory can be tested cross-sectionally, using proxies for tax status and the potential costs of financial distress. For example, the following proxies should be associated with low debt ratios: tax-loss carry-forwards; business risk, measured by the volatility of earnings or market value; intangible assets, measured by high expenditures on marketing and R&D (vs. tangible capital investment), and valuable future growth opportunities. Such proxies work reasonably well in cross-sectional tests. Important early papers include Auerbach (1985), Long and Malitz (1985), Titman and Wessels (1988) and Fischer, Heinkel and Zechner (1989).

Smith and Watts (1992) emphasize the empirical importance of the "investment opportunity set".[27] The more valuable a firm's future investment opportunities, the less it borrows today. I have mentioned two reasons why this makes theoretical sense. First, growth opportunities are intangible assets, which are likely to be damaged in distress or bankruptcy. Second, issuing risky debt today undermines the firm's incentives to invest in the future.

The value of future opportunities can be estimated by the ratio of the firm's market value to book value. (Market value includes the value of growth opportunities; book value is an estimate of the value of the firm's assets in place.) There is a strong inverse relationship between the market-to-book ratio and debt ratios, consistent with the casual observation that "growth firms borrow less". This inverse relationship is not confined to the USA – see Rajan and Zingales (1995) and Gul's study (1999) of growth opportunities and capital structure in Japan.

Financial research has now settled on a few general factors that seem to explain debt ratios cross sectionally. Large, safe firms with tangible assets[28] tend to borrow more

---

[26] Theory on this point is divided. Highly leveraged firms are softer competitors in some setups, harder competitors in others. Harris and Raviv (1991) review theory through 1990, and the papers cited above all discuss more recent theoretical work. See also Lambrecht (2001) and Chevalier and Scharfstein (1996).

[27] See also Barclay, Smith and Watts (1995), Barclay and Smith (1999), Gaver and Gaver (1993) and Goyal, Lehn and Racic (2002).

[28] Liquid assets should also enhance debt capacity and increase the target debt ratio – but only if creditors can be assured that the firm will retain those assets. Liquidity makes it easier to shift safe assets into risky ones. See Shleifer and Vishny (1992), Myers and Rajan (1998) and Morellec (2001).

than small, risky firms with mostly intangible assets. (Intangible assets are usually linked to expenditures on advertising and R&D.) Firms with high profitability and valuable growth opportunities tend to borrow less.[29] Most of these factors make sense under the trade-off theory. For example, intangible assets and growth opportunities are vulnerable in distress. Profitability could proxy for growth opportunities.

But the empirical case for the trade-off theory is not as strong as it looks. First, statistical results "consistent" with the trade-off theory can be consistent with other theories as well. I return to this point in Section 4.3. Second, there are too many examples of successful, highly profitable firms operating at low debt ratios. These firms are not "the exceptions that prove the rule", because studies of the determinants of actual debt ratios consistently find that the most profitable companies in a given industry tend to borrow the least.[30] For example, Wald (1999) found that profitability was "the single largest determinant of debt/asset ratios" in cross-sectional tests for the USA, UK, Germany, France and Japan. Booth et al. (2001) reached a similar conclusion for a sample of ten developing countries.

High profits mean low debt, and vice versa. But if managers can exploit valuable interest tax shields, as the trade-off theory predicts, we should observe exactly the opposite relationship. High profitability means that the firm has more taxable income to shield, and that the firm can service more debt without risking financial distress.

3.8. Target-adjustment models

The trade-off theory predicts a target debt ratio that depends on the potential value of interest tax shields and the consequences of financial distress. If immediate adjustment to the target is costly, the theory implies a target-adjustment model. The target is not observed directly, and would probably vary through time.

The simplest estimate of the target is the firm's average debt ratio over a sample period, although the target can also be estimated based on tax status, asset risk and other attributes of the firm. Successful early tests of target-adjustment models include Taggart (1977), Jalilvand and Harris (1984) and Auerbach (1985).

Hovakimian, Opler and Titman (2001) conducted a more extensive search for evidence of target-adjustment financing. First they regress debt-to-value ratios on firm size, industry and asset type (for example, tangible vs. intangible assets). The predicted ratio for each firm and year is taken as an estimate of the target ratio. Then the difference between this target and the firm's actual, start-of-year debt ratio is used, along with other variables, to predict whether the firm issues debt or equity. The difference between target and actual works as expected; the firm is more likely to

---

[29] See Harris and Raviv (1991) and Rajan and Zingales (1995).

[30] Myers (1984) stressed this point; see also Baskin (1989) and Fama and French (2002). Other studies are cited in Harris and Raviv's review article (1991). Rajan and Zingales (1995) confirm the negative correlation between profitability and leverage for the USA, Japan and Canada, although no significant correlations were found for France, Germany, Italy and Britain.

issue debt when it is below-target, for example. The probability of a debt issue is also higher for more profitable firms (profitability is taken as a measure of debt servicing capacity) and for firms with low market-to-book ratios (low ratios mean that growth opportunities are relatively unimportant). It appears that management acts to move the firm towards a target debt ratio, and that the target depends in reasonable ways on firm characteristics. But the difference between target and actual debt ratios did not explain the *amounts* of debt and equity issued.

Hovakimian, Opler and Titman also examined a sample of firms that returned capital to investors. Firms with debt ratios below target were more likely to repurchase shares; above-target firms were more likely to retire debt. The statistical performance of their regressions was better for this sample than for issuers, and the differences between firms' actual and target debt ratios explained the amounts of debt retired or equity repurchased. This is an interesting, but odd, finding: there is no a priori reason to expect the trade-off theory to work better for firms with excess capital than for firms with capital deficits.

3.9. Computational models

The trade-off model's testable implications are mostly qualitative. For example, the theory predicts that firms with valuable growth opportunities should borrow less, but not how much less. We can quantify one side of the trade-off, by estimating the present value of interest tax shields, but not the other side. The theory does not specify the probability of financial distress as a function of leverage, and it does not quantify the costs of financial distress, except to say that these costs are important.

"Computational" models seek to quantify both sides of the trade-off in a consistent valuation model. The valuation approach is based on option pricing theory, following Black and Scholes (1973), Merton (1974), Black and Cox (1976) and Brennan and Schwartz (1984). The advantages of computational models are stressed in Leland (1998).

Computational models are complex because value and cash flow evolve dynamically. Future investment and financing decisions typically interact because of conflicts of interest between creditors and stockholders. The model-builder must specify dividend payout rules, debt maturity and the rebalancing rule for debt as the value of the firm changes over time. Various parameters must also be specified. Then the model is checked, for example by comparing the computed credit spread – the difference between the computed bond yield and the risk-free interest rate – to spreads for actual bonds.

The payoff is a detailed description of the firm, suitable for numerical experiments. So far the results of these experiments are informative but not conclusive. Some experiments seem to confirm a long-standing criticism of the trade-off model, that at typical debt ratios the costs of financial distress come nowhere close to offsetting the value of additional interest tax shields. Mauer and Triantis (1994, p. 1253) conclude that "the impact of debt financing on the firm's investment and operating decisions is insignificant". Mello and Parsons (1992) estimate agency costs equal to about 4% of the face value of debt – not a large sum, but perhaps enough to deter some debt issues. Parrino and Weisbach (1999) conclude that distortions in investment due to risk shifting and underinvestment are small. A series of papers by Leland and co-authors consider taxes, agency costs of financing, default and credit risk. The latest model, in Goldstein, Ju and Leland (2001), generates optimal debt ratios and credit spreads that seem realistic. [31]

Computational models have evolved, and arbitrary limiting assumptions in early papers are gradually disappearing. I believe this is an important line of research.

4. The pecking-order theory

The pecking-order theory of Myers and Majluf (1984) and Myers (1984) starts with a firm with assets-in-place and a growth opportunity requiring additional equity financing. Myers and Majluf assume perfect financial markets, except for asymmetric information. Investors do not know the true value of either the existing assets or the new opportunity, so they cannot exactly value the shares issued to finance the new investment. Announcement of the stock issue could be good news for investors if it reveals a growth opportunity with positive NPV. It could also be bad news if managers are trying to issue overvalued shares.

Some firms will have *under*valued shares, however. Issuing shares at too low a price transfers value from existing shareholders to new investors. If managers act in the interest of existing shareholders, they will refuse to issue undervalued shares unless the transfer of value is more than offset by the growth opportunity's net present value (NPV).

Myers and Majluf derive an equilibrium in which firms can issue shares, but only at a marked-down price. Share price falls not because investors' demand for equity securities is inelastic, but because of information inferred from the decision to issue. It turns out that the bad news (about the value of assets in place) always outweighs the good news (about the positive-NPV investment). [32] Some good firms whose assets-in-place are *under*valued at the new price will decide not to issue even if it means passing by a positive-NPV opportunity.

The prediction that announcement of a stock issue will immediately drive down stock price was confirmed by several studies, including Asquith and Mullins (1986). The average fall in price is roughly 3%, that is, 3% of the pre-issue market capitalization of the firm. The price drops are much larger fractions of the amounts issued.

---

[31] See also Leland (1994, 1998) and Leland and Toft (1996).
[32] This result depends on Myers and Majluf's assumption that the firm will not undertake negative-NPV investments. See Cooney and Kalay (1993).

This price drop should not be interpreted as a transaction cost or compared to the underwriting spreads and other expenses of stock issues. On average, the companies that issue shares do so at a fair price.[33] However, the companies that decide to issue are, on average, worth less than the companies that hold back. Investors downgrade the prices of issuing firms accordingly.

The price drop at announcement should be greater where the information asymmetry (manager's information advantage over outside investors) is large. Dierkens (1991) confirms this using various proxies for information asymmetry. D'Mello and Ferris (2000) show that the price drop is greater for firms followed by few security analysts, and for firms with greater dispersion of analysts' earnings forecasts.

The price drop also depends on the value of growth opportunities vs. assets in place. According to the Myers–Majluf model, growth firms are more credible issuers. Investors' worries concentrate on the possible mis-valuation of assets in place. Several studies, including Pilotte (1992), Denis (1994) and Jung, Kim and Stulz (1996), find that the price impact of stock issue announcements is less for growth firms than for mature firms. In some cases, the average price impact for growth-firm samples is negligible.

4.1. Debt vs. equity in the pecking order

Now suppose the firm can issue either debt or equity to finance new investment. Debt has the prior claim on assets and earnings; equity is the residual claim. Investors in debt are therefore less exposed to errors in valuing the firm. The announcement of a debt issue should have a smaller downward impact on stock price than announcement of an equity issue. For investment-grade issues, where default risk is very small, the stock price impact should be negligible. Eckbo (1986) and Shyam-Sunder (1991) confirm this prediction.

Issuing debt minimizes the managers' information advantage. Optimistic managers, who believe their companies' shares are undervalued, will jump at the chance to issue debt rather than equity. Only pessimistic managers will want to issue equity – but who would buy it? If debt is an open alternative, then any attempt to sell shares will reveal that the shares are not a good buy. Therefore investors will spurn equity issues if debt is available on fair terms, and in equilibrium only debt will be issued. Equity issues will occur only when debt is costly, for example because the firm is already at a dangerously high debt ratio where managers and investors foresee costs of financial

---

[33] The companies that decide *not* to issue face a kind of transaction cost equal to the difference between the attainable issue price and the true value per share of their assets and growth opportunities.

distress.[34] In this case even optimistic managers may turn to the stock market for financing.

This leads to the pecking-order theory of capital structure:

(1) Firms prefer internal to external finance. (Information asymmetries are assumed relevant only for external financing.)[35]

(2) Dividends are "sticky", so that dividend cuts are not used to finance capital expenditure, and changes in cash requirements are not soaked up in short-run dividend changes. Changes in free cash flow (operating cash flow less investment) show up as changes in external financing.

(3) If external funds are required for capital investment, firms will issue the safest security first, that is, debt before equity. As the requirement for external financing increases, the firm will work down the pecking order, from safe to riskier debt and finally to equity as a last resort, when the firm is sufficiently threatened by financial distress. If internally generated cash flow exceeds capital investment, the firm works up the pecking order. Excess cash is used to pay down debt rather than repurchasing and retiring equity.[36]

(4) The firm's debt ratio therefore reflects its cumulative requirement for external financing.

The preference of public corporations for internal financing, and the relative infrequency of stock issues by established firms, have long been attributed to the separation of ownership and control, and the desire of managers to avoid the "discipline of capital markets". Myers and Majluf suggest a different explanation: market-value maximizing managers will avoid external equity financing if they have better information than outside investors and the investors are rational.

The pecking-order theory explains why the bulk of external financing comes from debt. It also explains why more profitable firms borrow less: not because their target debt ratio is low – in the pecking order they don't have a target – but because profitable firms have more internal financing available. Less profitable firms require more external financing, and consequently accumulate more debt.

---

[34] The decision to issue equity as a last resort can be modeled exactly as in Myers and Majluf (1984). In this setting, the "growth opportunity" is not a real investment, but an injection of equity to reduce the probability of financial distress. NPV is the reduction in the present value of the costs of financial distress. The firm has to trade off this NPV against the cost of issuing shares that may be undervalued. The decision to raise equity remains, on balance, a bad-news signal for investors.

[35] This assumption is questionable. See Myers and Majluf (1984, Section 4.1, pp. 210–214).

[36] The Myers–Majluf analysis works equally well (in theory) when the firm is distributing cash to investors. Information asymmetry leads to an equilibrium in which the firm is forced to pay down debt rather than repurchasing and retiring equity. See Shyam-Sunder and Myers (1999). However, the amount of cash returned to investors via stock repurchases has grown steadily. Stock repurchase programs are not as sticky as dividend payouts. See Jagannathan, Stephens and Weisbach (2000) and Guay and Harford (2000). Changes in repurchases may displace debt as the marginal source of financing for cash-cow firms. This would undermine the pecking order.

4.2. What's wrong with the pecking order as theory?

The pecking order assumes that managers act in the interest of *existing* shareholders, maximizing the value of existing shares. Myers and Majluf (1984) do not show why managers should care if a new stock issue is over- or undervalued, or why managers do not simply maximize the value of the entire firm, regardless of the division of value between existing and new shareholders. This policy would assure optimal capital investment decisions *and* make existing shareholders better off ex ante.

The pecking order is not derived from an explicit treatment of management incentives, as in Ross (1977). In Ross's signaling equilibrium, the design and parameters of the manager's compensation package drive the choice between debt and equity, and the firm's financing decision reveals the managers' information about the intrinsic value of the firm. Dybvig and Zender (1991) present examples of models in which managers have better information than investors, but managers' compensation schemes are fine-tuned to assure optimal capital investment decisions. In one of their setups, the announcement of a stock issue is bad news to investors, just as in the Myers–Majluf analysis. This setup does not generate the pecking order, however. Also, Persons (1994) questions whether shareholders or boards of directors could credibly commit to the optimal compensation schemes that Dybvig and Zender have in mind.

The pecking-order theory cannot explain why financing tactics are not developed to avoid the financing consequences of managers' superior information. For example, suppose that any special information available to the manager today will reach investors within the next year. Then the firm could issue "deferred equity" securities. For example, the firm could issue debt with a face value of $1000, to be repaid after one year by newly issued shares worth $1000 at the year-one stock price. [37] The manager cannot know today whether he or she will view the future price as too high or too low. Therefore issue of this deferred equity conveys no information. (The deferred equity is really debt payable in a particular currency, the firm's shares.) Thus the firm can pre-commit to issue equity with no adverse signal to investors. Why is this type of security not widespread? [38]

One final criticism: Myers and Majluf consider a very simple setting, where the firm's only financing choice is debt vs. equity. The pecking order does not necessarily hold in more complicating settings, for example when the firm also chooses between straight and convertible debt. [39]

---

[37] In other words, the debt will be converted to N shares, where N is not predetermined, but calculated as $N = 1000/P_1$, where P_1 is the stock price one year hence.

[38] PERCs (Preferred Equity Redemption Certificates), a special kind of convertible preferred stock, are in some ways similar to this deferred equity security, because they convert to a fixed dollar amount of the firm's stock if the stock price rises sufficiently. But otherwise PERCs convert to a fixed number of shares, thus leaving the downside risk to investors.

[39] See Brennan and Kraus (1987), Constantinides and Grundy (1989) and Noe (1988). See also Cadsby, Frank and Maksimovic (1990, 1998), who investigated the pecking order in experimental settings.

4.3. Pecking order vs. the trade-off theory – time-series tests

It's instructive to compare the time-series predictions of the pecking order and trade-off theories. The trade-off theory implies a target-adjustment model. The pecking-order theory says that the debt ratio depends on the firm's cumulative financial deficit – its cumulative requirement for external financing. Shyam-Sunder and Myers (1999) tested these time-series predictions on a panel of 157 firms from 1971 to 1989. They found statistically significant support for *both* the pecking order and a target-adjustment specification of the trade-off theory.

Shyam-Sunder and Myers questioned the statistical power of the target-adjustment specification, however. They calculated what each sample firm's annual debt ratios would have been if the firm had followed the pecking order exactly. They found that the target-adjustment specification worked just as well on these simulated financing decisions as on the real decisions. The trade-off theory, expressed as a target-adjustment model, was "consistent with" financing choices driven solely by the pecking order.

The pecking order generates mean-reverting debt ratios when capital investments are "lumpy" and positively serially correlated, and when free cash flow varies over the business cycle. Firms will tend to have strings of years with financial deficits, followed by strings of surpluses. Financing by the pecking order means that debt ratios increase in deficit years and fall in surplus years. The pecking-order debt ratios will therefore mean-revert, and the target-adjustment model will "explain" financing strategy.

This test was also run in reverse, by simulating firm's debt ratios on the assumption that they gradually adjust to a fixed target ratio. The pecking order was rejected totally on this simulated data. Thus Shyam-Sunder and Myers concluded that their test of the pecking order had statistical power relative to the trade-off-theory alternative, and that the pecking order was the best explanation of the financing behavior of the firms in their sample.[40]

This lesson about statistical power is general. It applies also to cross sectional tests of the trade-off theory. These tests look for statistically significant coefficients on proxies for the determinants of optimal debt ratios. Such results might support the theory if it were the only game in town. But the same results can be observed in a cross-section of firms whose financing decisions are driven solely by the pecking order or by some other theory.[41]

---

[40] Chirinko and Singha (2000) show that the time-series test used by Shyam-Sunder and Myers would lack power to reject the pecking order if the choice between debt and equity is determined not by a target-adjustment model, but by certain other rules.
[41] Shyam-Sunder and Myers (1999) also regressed the debt ratios generated by their pecking order simulations on some of the typical proxies used in cross-sectional tests of the trade-off theory. The coefficients on the proxies were plausible and significant.

4.4. Further tests of the trade-off and pecking-order theories

Frank and Goyal (2003) tested Shyam-Sunder and Myers' (1999) time-series specification for the pecking order on a much larger sample of firms from 1971 to 1998.[42] This specification worked reasonably well for large firms, particularly in the 1970s and 1980s. But Frank and Goyal show that financing behavior is more complicated than the simple pecking order predicts. For example, the coefficient on the financing deficit, which should be 1.0 in the simple pecking order, is at most .325 for the 1990s when estimated for their entire sample.[43] The performance of the pecking order degrades for smaller firms and for firms with data missing for some years.

The financing deficit has hardly any effect on debt issues for small, growth firms, which frequently rely on stock issues for external financing.[44] Frank and Goyal suggest that the pecking order should work especially well for this subsample, where the information asymmetries ought to be largest. But Myers and Majluf (1984) show that the most important asymmetries attach to assets in place. For example, firms with valuable growth opportunities, but minimal assets in place, should be credible issuers. In fact, small growth firms are more likely to issue stock than debt. When they announce a stock issue, the drop in stock price is small.[45]

Firms with few growth opportunities, relative to assets in place, should face the strongest pressures to follow the pecking order. Frank and Goyal find that the pecking order works best for large firms with moderate leverage.[46] But Jung, Kim and Stulz (1996) identify a class of low-growth firms that issue equity despite unused debt capacity and strong negative stock price reactions to the issue announcements. Such issues contradict the pecking order.

Frank and Goyal also find that variables motivated by the trade-off theory help explain changes in debt financing, even after accounting for changes in firms' financial deficits. Large firms with tangible assets borrow more, profitable firms with high market-book ratios borrow less.

Fama and French (2002) test the predictions of both trade-off and pecking-order models on a large panel of firms from 1965 to 1999. They also consider modified versions of the pecking order. As Myers (1984) notes, a firm with valuable future investment opportunities can take action immediately to assure that financing will

---

[42] Shyam-Sunder and Myers (1999) set out to compare the performance of target-adjustment models to simple expressions of the pecking order. They included only industrial firms with complete financial histories – no gaps in the data required for either model. This forced them to a relatively small sample of 157 firms.

[43] Frank and Goyal (2003, Table 4).

[44] Helwege and Liang (1996) follow a sample of firms after their initial public offerings. These firms did not follow the pecking order.

[45] See Jung, Kim and Stulz (1996) and Pilotte (1992). Denis (1994) finds no stock price drop at all, on average, for a subsample of small, high-growth firms that issue equity.

[46] Fama and French (2002) find that the pecking order works best for dividend-paying firms, which tend to be larger and more conservatively financed.

be available when needed. For example, if there is a window of opportunity when information asymmetries are small, it can make sense to issue shares immediately, violating the strict pecking order, in order to build financial slack for the future. This could explain why growth firms seek equity financing and keep leverage low.[47]

Both theories score some points in Fama and French's tests, but run into serious difficulties. The trade-off theory struggles to explain the strong inverse relationship of profitability and leverage. The pecking order struggles to explain the heavy reliance on equity issues by small growth firms. (Are all of these issues really undertaken to build up financial slack in windows of low information asymmetry?)

Baker and Wurgler (2002) find that issuing firms seem to "time" the market, issuing shares when their stock prices are high and turning to internal finance or debt when prices are low. Consistent pursuit of timing strategies would make debt ratios depend on paths of past stock prices as well as on requirements for external funds. Ritter (2003) calls this the "windows of opportunity" theory. If investors sometimes overprice issuing firms' shares, so that equity is truly cheap, then equity can move temporarily to the top of the pecking order. (There is evidence, summarized by Ritter, that stock issues are overpriced on average.)[48] Thus the windows of opportunity theory could absolve the pecking order of a major empirical shortcoming, provided that one is willing to assume systematic mispricing of new issues, at least in "hot" issue periods.

The reader may be forgiven some confusion at this point. It appears that both the trade-off and pecking-order theories are at work in real life. The economic factors that drive the theories – taxes, costs of financial distress and information asymmetries – clearly are important. Yet each theory stumbles when asked to explain the financing of certain classes of firms.

The stumbles should not be surprising. The theories are conditional, not general; each works better in some conditions than in others.[49] Further progress will require sharper predictions of these conditions. We also need better theory explaining how managers manage financing, acting as agents for shareholders.

5. Agency theories of capital structure

So far we have assumed that the interests of the firm's financial managers and its shareholders are perfectly aligned, and that financing decisions are in the shareholders'

---

[47] Minton and Wruck (2001) and Lemmon and Zender (2001) find that the most conservatively financed firms do appear to be stockpiling financial slack. See Korajczyk, Lucas and MacDonald (1991) for an analysis of information releases and the timing of equity issues.

[48] "Cheap" means that the price drop on announcement of a share issue is less than predicted by the Myers–Majluf (1984) model. If so, share issues are overpriced on average, and investors in these issues on average end up with substandard risk-adjusted rates of return.

[49] It is tempting to nest the theories, and to hope the data will tell us the relative impacts of taxes, distress costs and information asymmetries on financing. This will not work for cross sections or panels including a wide range of firm types. The data will be Delphic unless sharper hypotheses can be framed.

interest. As Jensen and Meckling (1976) argued, this assumption is implausible in theory and impossible in practice. Corporate managers, as agents for shareholders (the principals), will act in their own interests. They will seek private benefits, including higher-than-market salaries, perquisites, job security and, in extreme cases, direct capture of assets or cash flows. [50] They may make "entrenching investments", which adapt the firm's assets and operations to the managers' skills and knowledge, in order to increase the managers' bargaining power vs. investors. [51] Shareholders can discourage such value transfers by various mechanisms of monitoring and control, including supervision by independent directors and the threat of takeover. But these mechanisms are costly and subject to decreasing returns, so perfect monitoring is out of the question.

Managers' and investors' interests can also be aligned by design of compensation packages. Here again perfection is out of reach. First, the manager never bears the full costs that his or her actions impose on investors – unless, of course, the manager is also the owner. Second, there is no complete, verifiable measure of managers' performance. Investors would like to reward effort, commitment and good decisions, but these inputs are imperfectly observable. Even if good performance on these dimensions were observable by some informed monitor, the performance would not be verifiable. "Complete contracts" cannot be written. A contract offering a bonus for, say, "good decisions" is not enforceable, because the decisions could not be evaluated by a disinterested outsider or by a court of law.

If agency costs are taken seriously, then the trade-off and pecking-order theories seem naive. Each assumes that managers act solely in the interests of the firm's stockholders.

5.1. Jensen and Meckling's pecking order

One expects (or hopes) that principals and agents will arrange financing ex ante to minimize agency costs ex post. Jensen and Meckling (1976) consider the following trade-offs. Start with a firm owned entirely by its managers and employees. Agency costs should be minimal, because the costs of private benefits are internalized. If the firm subsequently needs external financing, debt is better than equity. With debt, the costs of private benefits stay internalized. Issuing "outside equity" would create agency costs, because the costs of private benefits are borne partly by the new stockholders, while the benefits are retained by the "inside" stockholders. As the amount of debt

---

[50] There can also be non-pecuniary private benefits, such as reputation or the personal satisfactions of running a corporate empire. Such benefits also generate agency costs if they tempt managers to make poor decisions.

[51] See Shleifer and Vishny (1989). Berger, Ofek and Yermack (1997) find an inverse relationship between leverage and several measures of managerial entrenchment. They also find that events that ought to reduce entrenchment generally lead to increased leverage. Garvey and Hanka (1999) find that legal changes that protect firms from takeovers lead to lower leverage.

expands, however, default risk increases, leading to conflicts between lenders and stockholders and costs of financial distress. These costs eventually force a shift to outside equity.

This is a pecking order, because the firm prefers internal to external finance, and prefers debt to outside equity until debt becomes so risky and costly that managers turn to outside equity as a last resort.

Jensen and Meckling's pecking order makes the most sense for smaller firms where managers and employees can own a large fraction of the firm's shares. It is less credible for larger companies that must seek outside equity. For most public companies, managers and employees do not have sufficient wealth to own more than a small fraction of the firm.[52] Separation of ownership and control is a fact of life, and attention must shift to mechanisms of control and to compensation and incentives, particularly the use of stock ownership or options to motivate managers.

Going public to raise outside equity also has advantages that can upset this agency-based pecking order. Public companies can use their shares as a currency to compensate managers – a currency whose value is determined not just by earnings from assets in place, but also by growth opportunities. Compensation by stock or options therefore gives incentives to create growth opportunities.

If outside equity is needed, the firm faces a choice between private equity, e.g., from venture-capital partnerships, and equity from public stock markets. Private equity investors face lower costs of monitoring, and thus should be the efficient source of equity financing in Jensen and Meckling's pecking order. But Myers (2000) and Burkhart, Gromb and Panunzi (1997) stress the importance of *not* giving equity investors too much power over managers or employees. Incentives for effort and risk-taking are weakened if shareholders can set compensation after the fact. Myers argues that growth firms "go public" in order to *reduce* the power of equity investors and to preserve incentives.

Jensen and Meckling's pecking order applies more generally in countries where outside investors are poorly protected. La Porta, Lopez-de-Silanes, Shleifer and Vishny (1997, 1998, 2000) find that weak institutional or legal protection for investors impedes external financing and forces corporations to rely mostly on inside equity and debt (usually bank) financing. An agency-based pecking order predicts this outcome when effective monitoring and control by outside equity investors is impossible or prohibitively costly. La Porta, Lopez-de-Silanes and Shleifer (1999), in a survey of 27 developed countries, find that few firms are widely held, except in a handful of countries with good shareholder protection. Most firms are controlled by families or governments.

---

[52] Some public companies' shares include concentrated block-holdings. The market value of such companies seems to increase with block size, other things equal. Very large blocks seem to depress value, however. See Morck, Shleifer and Vishny (1988).

5.2. Free cash flow, leveraged buyouts and restructurings

Jensen (1986, p. 323) later turned to a simpler idea, expressed in a brief but widely cited note: "The problem is how to motivate managers to disgorge the cash rather than investing it below the cost of capital or wasting it on organizational inefficiencies". The solution to this problem can, in some circumstances, be debt financing.

Debt is a contract that forces the firm to pay out cash. A high debt ratio can be dangerous, but it can also add value by putting the firm on a diet and curbing overinvestment. Stulz (1990) presents a model of how the diet works. He assumes that managers will always invest free cash flow, even in negative-NPV projects, unless the cash is required for debt service. The ideal level of debt (and debt service) leaves just enough cash to fund all – and only – positive-NPV projects. Thus leverage should depend on the investment opportunity set. Firms with valuable growth opportunities should choose low debt ratios to free up cash for expansion. Firms with limited growth opportunities should operate at high debt ratios to constrain management.

But what prevents the empire-building managers from (1) servicing previously issued debt, (2) raising more capital by selling shares, and (3) investing as they like? Perhaps the discipline comes from the threat of takeover, as in Zwiebel (1996). Linking top management's compensation to stock price (by stock options, for example) could also work. The announcement of a stock issue by a firm with limited growth opportunities should trigger an immediate drop in stock price. In fact leverage does appear to constrain investment. [53]

The LBOs of the 1980s were of course the classic examples of diet deals, in which debt ratios were set ahead of time to constrain investment (or force disinvestment). Here Jensen's and Stulz's arguments seem to apply exactly.

Contemporary accounts attributed various motives to the LBO organizers and investors: interest tax shields [Kaplan (1989)], artificially high junk bond prices [Kaplan and Stein (1993)], wealth transfer from existing bondholders, and attempts by raiders to capture value accruing to employees and other "stakeholders" [Shleifer and Summers (1988)]. There is some truth in each of these attributions, but with a decade's hindsight, it seems clear that the LBOs were first and foremost attempts to solve Jensen's free-cash-flow problem. They were shock therapy designed to cut back wasteful investment, force sale of underutilized assets, and to generate cash for investors.

Debt plays a similar role in leveraged restructurings, where a public firm all at once borrows a large fraction of the value of its assets and pays out the proceeds to stockholders. Wruck (1995) provides a fascinating case study of the leveraged restructuring at Sealed Air Corporation.

---

[53] See Lang, Ofek and Stulz (1996), Hanka (1998) and Peyer and Shivdasani (2001).

5.3. Is there a general free-cash-flow theory of capital structure?

Jensen's free-cash-flow problem is real. Many managers would like the freedom to overinvest and would prefer to operate at low debt ratios. There is no evidence that public corporations generally over-invest, however, or that debt issues generally add value by disciplining management. McConnell and Muscarella (1985) found that capital investments are generally viewed as good news, that is, positive-NPV, by investors. Shyam-Sunder (1991) and Eckbo (1986) found that announcements of debt issues had no significant effect on stock prices, even for junk debt issues, where the risk of default, and the pressure on managers to "disgorge cash", are high. [54, 55] Many of these debt issues may have been routine refinancings, however. Replacing one junk debt issue with another does not force management to disgorge any additional cash.

The free-cash-flow theory is best regarded as another conditional view of capital structure. The theory explains why cash-cow firms with few growth opportunities are candidates for LBOs or HLTs, and why small, growth firms are not. It may explain the higher debt ratios observed for large, mature firms. The higher the expected future costs of overinvestment, the greater the probability of a takeover followed by an increase in debt. Even unsuccessful takeovers may force a shift in financing, as in the leveraged restructurings of several major oil companies when threatened by takeover in the 1980s. [56] Some managers will voluntarily shift to high debt ratios, as in the Sealed Air case described by Wruck (1995).

But Jensen's (1986) free-cash-flow theory does not provide a principal-agent model of the incentives and actions of managers, except to say that they are prone to overinvest. It is really a theory about the consequences of high debt ratios in mature, cash-cow firms – and perhaps also a normative theory about how managers of such firms *should* arrange financing, given the financial objective of maximizing shareholder value.

6. What next?

Most research on corporate financing decisions considers the trade-off, pecking-order or free-cash-flow theories. My review necessarily concentrates on these theories.

---

[54] Pilotte (1992) does find negative announcement effects on the stock prices of firms issuing risky debt, but the price drops are much smaller than for equity issues.

[55] Several authors, starting with Masulis (1980) find that equity-for-debt exchange offers are bad news for investors (negative announcement effects) and debt-for-equity exchange offers good news. These effects are best interpreted as reactions to the repurchase or issue of equity, not to the issue or retirement of debt. Lie, Lie and McConnell (2001) find that equity-for-debt exchanges are undertaken by financially distressed firms. This is consistent with pecking-order theory, in which equity is issued as a last resort. See footnote 34 above.

[56] Safieddine and Titman (1999) find that leverage increases for targets of unsuccessful takeovers. The higher leverage can be part of the takeover defense, and may reflect the managers' perception of increased vulnerability to further takeover attacks.

There are convincing examples of all three theories at work. The economic problems and incentives that drive the theories – taxes, information and costs of agency and distress – show up clearly in financing tactics. Yet none of the theories gives a general explanation of financing strategy. They are plausible as conditional theories, but we have only a partial understanding of the conditions under which each theory, or some combination of the theories, works.

Zingales (2000) says that we need "new foundations" for corporate finance. The foundations will require a deeper understanding of the motives and behavior of managers and employees of the firm. I close with examples of research directed to this requirement.

6.1. Compensation and incentives

All of the standard theories of financing start by assuming that the manager pursues a simple objective. Managers' actual objectives depend on how they are rewarded for their actions.

Ross (1977) was first to show how financing choices could signal managers' inside information to investors. Suppose investors do not know how confident managers are about the future profitability and value of their firms. If managers' compensation is based in part on today's stock price, and if costs of financial distress make higher leverage a potentially costly signal, then a signaling equilibrium can be reached in which the more confident managers choose higher leverage. Firm value therefore increases with leverage because of information conveyed by financing. (MM's Proposition 1 would hold in other respects, however. For example, the cost of capital for real investment would be unaffected.)

Dybvig and Zender (1991) follow up with further examples showing how information asymmetry need not interfere with optimal real investment decisions, provided the manager's incentives are set optimally.

These points are important. Theorists should not make ad hoc assumptions about managers' objectives, particularly when those assumptions imply inefficiencies. There must be significant value gains from setting incentives optimally. But as yet there is no signaling or incentive-driven theory of capital structure that is meaningfully differentiated from the theories reviewed above. One reason, perhaps, is that the nature of optimal compensation for managers varies by firm type.

The first objective of compensation should be incentives for value-maximizing real investment and operating decisions. Decisions about the left-hand side of the balance sheet are more important than financing decisions for the value of the firm. The nature of efficient compensation schemes should vary from firm to firm, however. For example, one would expect growth firms to give more weight to stock price, mature firms more weight to current earnings. But compensation schemes focused on the left-hand side of the balance sheet may, as a by-product, create financing incentives that vary widely across firms. Researchers should consider how differences in managers' actual incentives lead to differences in financing.[57]

But we cannot fully understand financing choices just by writing down the CEO's utility function or the parameters of the CEO's compensation package. Most studies of capital structure focus on public corporations. These firms act as organizations, not individuals. They presumably act in the interests of a coalition of the managers or employees who make, or are affected by, investment and financing decisions. The firm acts to maximize the value of the current and future benefits flowing to this coalition.[58]

6.2. Human capital and financing

We are used to thinking of managers as the agents of stockholders. But managers and employees also invest their human capital. The investment comes in the form of personal risk-taking, sweat equity (working extra-hard for less than an outside wage) and by specialization of human capital to the firm. Of course the services of human capital can be withdrawn from the firm at any time.

A general financial theory of the firm would model the *co-investment* of human and financial capital.[59] A start has been made on such a theory, by research focused primarily on the conditions under which insiders can raise financing from outside investors when insiders can extract cash or private benefits after the investment is made. For example, Hart and Moore (1994, 1998) consider an entrepreneur who cannot commit to stay with a new venture or to work effectively in it. No contract can mandate the entrepreneur's participation and effort, and there is no way to verify whether cash flow is appropriately distributed or reinvested. But the venture requires a real asset in addition to human capital. The outside investors cannot reach the entrepreneur's human capital, but can take the asset and shut down the business. In fact that is their only property right.

Hart and Moore show that debt financing is optimal in this setting. Equity does not work. (If equity were issued, it would become the functional equivalent of debt. Outside investors can never extract more than the value of the real asset.) Thus the firm ends up at the bottom of Jensen and Meckling's (1976) pecking order, with a combination of inside equity – perhaps just the entrepreneur's human capital – and outside debt.

---

[57] An interesting recent paper by Lewellen (2002) estimates the risk-adjusted present values of compensation packages for top managers at nearly 2000 USA firms. She calculates how changes in leverage would have affected these values, thereby estimating the managers' incentives to issue or retire debt. These incentives predict financing choices. For example, firms are more likely to issue debt rather than equity when the volatility created by additional financial leverage would impose higher costs on risk-averse managers.

[58] See Treynor (1981), Donaldson (1984) and Myers (2000).

[59] The importance of co-investment by insiders and outside investors is stressed in Zingales (2000) and Myers (1999, 2000).

These and related papers[60] make no clear predictions about financing in practice, but they do put financing in a deeper and richer economic setting.[61] Three fundamental points emerge. First, when human capital is important to the firm, financing should be arranged to assure the humans' efficient participation. Second, even when managers and investors have all the same information, outside investors are not able to verify all relevant actions or outcomes in the firm. Contracts based on such outcomes or actions are not feasible. Third, because complete contracts cannot be written, financing must specify *control rights* as well as cash-flow rights.

Traditional capital structure theories focus on cash-flow rights, that is, the division of the value of the future cash flows generated by the firm. Modigliani and Miller (1958), for example, say that the division makes no difference. But securities are packages of cash-flow and control rights. Debt has fixed cash-flow rights and no control rights except in default. Equity has residual cash-flow rights and complete control rights so long as the firm does not default. Of course the exercise of control rights may be costly. For example, the dispersed stockholders of a public firm must overcome costs of collective action before their control rights can be exercised.

The study of capital structure in this richer economic setting is in infancy. Most work assumes inside equity – perhaps just the human capital contributed by the entrepreneur – and outside debt. There are only a handful of consistent models of outside equity, including Myers (2000) and Fluck (1998). These models must now be generalized to include debt vs. equity financing.[62]

6.3. Exporting capital-structure theory

The leading theories of financing all assume that firms have access to reasonably well-functioning capital markets and to modern financial institutions. This assumption is not always true. It may not hold for small, private firms in the USA. It clearly does not hold in many other countries. For example, in countries with limited public capital markets, firms may be forced to rely on bank debt. Levels of bank debt would reveal cumulative requirements for external financing. The debt ratio would not be a strategic choice, but an end result forced by market imperfections.

We are used to thinking of markets and institutions adapting to the financing needs and objectives of corporations. But in many countries adaptation is blocked by severe

---

[60] See also Diamond (1984), Bolton and Scharfstein (1990) and Aghion and Bolton (1992). Gale and Hellwig (1985) and Townsend (1979) analyze debt in a setting with costly state verification (outcomes can be verified if investors are willing to incur a cost to do so).

[61] See Hart (1995). Hart (2001) reviews research on financial contracting and relates it to research on the traditional theories of capital structure.

[62] Fluck (2001) presents a life-cycle model that distinguishes optimal financing of a startup from financing of an established firm. The startup relies primarily on equity, short-term debt or convertible debt. The established firm turns to retained earnings and long-term debt. Dybvig and Wang (2002) model the trade-off of debt vs. outside equity for an entrepreneur.

agency problems or by government restrictions. Nevertheless, public stock markets exist in nearly every country. Some companies are able to raise outside equity, even in emerging economies where protection for outside investors is poor.[63]

Most capital-structure theory was developed for public USA corporations. Even in that well-structured setting, no general theory of capital structure emerges. We have only conditional theories, and no definite specification of the conditions under which the theories work empirically. Export of the theories to emerging markets may therefore seem premature and foolhardy.

It depends on what "export" means. We can confidently identify the factors that drive financing: agency costs, information differences, distress costs and distorting taxes and regulations.[64] These factors should be stronger in emerging economies than "at home" in countries with well-developed financial markets and institutions. The impacts of these factors on financing choices should be more pronounced in emerging economies, and the chances for meaningful advances in understanding correspondingly greater. For example: if the object is testing or improving an agency theory of financing, it makes sense to investigate financing where agency problems are most severe.

Export of the *ideas* underlying the standard theories of optimal financing decisions should therefore be highly informative. Do not expect any simple, general theory, however. Financing is half of the field of corporate finance. If half of a broad field can be compressed into a simple equation or two, then the field itself cannot be very interesting. If this compression is in fact achieved, I will be sorely disappointed.

References

Aghion, P., and P. Bolton (1992), "An incomplete contracts approach to financial contracting", Review of Economic Studies 59:473–393.

Alexander, G.J., A.K. Edwards and M.G. Ferri (2000), "What does Nasdaq's high-yield bond market reveal about bondholder–stockholder conflicts?", Financial Management 29:23–39.

Andrade, G., and S.N. Kaplan (1998), "How costly is financial (not economic) distress? Evidence from highly leveraged transactions that became distressed", Journal of Finance 53:1443–1493.

Asquith, P., and D.W. Mullins Jr (1986), "Equity issues and offering dilution", Journal of Financial Economics 15:61–89.

Asquith, P., and T. Wizman (1990), "Event risk, covenants and bondholder risk in leveraged buyouts", Journal of Financial Economics 27:195–214.

[63] The staying power of such financing is questionable, however, when protection for outside investors is poor. For example, the East Asian financial crisis of 1997–1998 was most damaging to countries and companies with poor corporate governance. See Johnson, Boone, Breach and Friedman (2000), Mitton (2002) and Rajan and Zingales (1998).

[64] Booth et al. (2001), who examine a sample of firms in ten developing economies, find that debt ratios are correlated with most of the same factors that "work" in the USA and in other developed countries. For example, long-term debt ratios are lower for more profitable companies holding fewer tangible assets. This paper suggests that export of capital structure theories will be feasible, but does not distinguish the theories; it finds at least some evidence consistent with all of them.

Auerbach, A. (1985), "Real determinants of corporate leverage", in: B.M. Friedman, ed., Corporate Capital Structures in the United States (The University of Chicago Press, Chicago) pp. 301–324.

Baker, M., and J. Wurgler (2002), "Market timing and capital structure", Journal of Finance 57:1–32.

Barclay, M.J., and C.W. Smith Jr (1995a), "The maturity structure of corporate liabilities", Journal of Finance 50:899–917.

Barclay, M.J., and C.W. Smith Jr (1995b), "The priority structure of corporate liabilities", Journal of Finance 50:609–631.

Barclay, M.J., and C.W. Smith Jr (1999), "The capital structure puzzle: another look at the evidence", Journal of Applied Corporate Finance 12:8–20.

Barclay, M.J., C.W. Smith Jr and R.L. Watts (1995), "The determinants of corporate leverage and dividend policies", Journal of Applied Corporate Finance 7:4–19.

Baskin, J. (1989), "An empirical examination of the pecking order hypothesis", Financial Management 18:26–35.

Berger, P., E. Ofek and D. Yermack (1997), "Managerial entrenchment and capital structure decisions", Journal of Finance 52:1411–1438.

Bertrand, M., and A. Schoar (2002), "Managing with style: the effect of managers on firm policies", Working Paper (University of Chicago, IL; MIT, MA).

Black, F. (1986), "Noise", Journal of Finance 41:529–543.

Black, F. (1993), "Beta and return", Journal of Portfolio Management 20:8–18.

Black, F., and J.C. Cox (1976), "Valuing corporate securities: some effects of bond indenture provisions", Journal of Finance 31:351–367.

Black, F., and M. Scholes (1973), "The pricing of options and corporate liabilities", Journal of Political Economy 81:637–654.

Bolton, P., and D. Scharfstein (1990), "A theory of predation based on agency problems in financial contracting", American Economic Review 80:93–106.

Booth, L., V. Aivazian, A. Demirguc-Kunt and V. Maksimovic (2001), "Capital structures in developing countries", Journal of Finance 56:87–130.

Brealey, R.A., and S.C. Myers (2003), Principles of Corporate Finance, 7th Edition (Irwin/McGraw-Hill, Burr Ridge, IL).

Brennan, M., and A. Kraus (1987), "Efficient financing under asymmetric information", Journal of Finance 42:1225–1243.

Brennan, M., and E. Schwartz (1984), "Corporate income taxes, valuation and the problem of optimal capital structure", Journal of Business 51:103–114.

Burkhart, M., D. Gromb and F. Panunzi (1997), "Large shareholders, monitoring and the value of the firm", Quarterly Journal of Economics 112:693–728.

Cadsby, C.B., M. Frank and V. Maksimovic (1990), "Pooling, separating and semi-separating equilibria in financial markets", Review of Financial Studies 3:341–367.

Cadsby, C.B., M. Frank and V. Maksimovic (1998), "Equilibrium dominance in experimental financial markets", Review of Financial Studies 11:189–232.

Carow, K.A., G.R. Erwin and J.J. McConnell (1999), "Survey of U.S. corporate financing innovations: 1970–1997", Journal of Applied Corporate Finance 12:55–69.

Chevalier, J.A. (1995a), "Capital structure and product-market competition: empirical evidence from the supermarket industry", American Economic Review 58:415–435.

Chevalier, J.A. (1995b), "Do LBO supermarkets charge more? An empirical analysis of the effects of LBOs on supermarket pricing", Journal of Finance 50:1095–1112.

Chevalier, J.A., and D.S. Scharfstein (1996), "Capital-market imperfections and countercyclical markups: theory and evidence", American Economic Review 86:703–725.

Chirinko, R.S., and A.R. Singha (2000), "Testing static tradeoff against pecking order models of capital structure: a critical comment", Journal of Financial Economics 58:417–425.

Constantinides, G., and B. Grundy (1989), "Optimal investment with stock repurchase and financing as signals", Review of Financial Studies 2:445–466.

Cooney Jr, J.W., and A. Kalay (1993), "Positive information from equity issue announcements", Journal of Financial Economics 33:149–172.

Cornell, B., and A.C. Shapiro (1987), "Corporate stakeholders and corporate finance", Financial Management 16:5–14.

Denis, D.J. (1994), "Investment opportunities and the market reaction to equity offerings", Journal of Financial and Quantitative Analysis 29:159–177.

Diamond, D. (1984), "Financial intermediation and delegated monitoring", Review of Economic Studies 51:393–414.

Dierkens, N. (1991), "Information asymmetry and equity issues", Journal of Financial and Quantitative Analysis 26:181–199.

D'Mello, R., and S.P. Ferris (2000), "The information effects of analyst activity at the announcement of new equity issues", Financial Management 29:78–95.

Donaldson, G. (1984), Managing Corporate Wealth: The Operation of a Comprehensive Financial Goals System (Praeger, New York).

Dybvig, P.H., and Y. Wang (2002), "Debt and equity", Working Paper (Washington University in St. Louis).

Dybvig, P.H., and J.F. Zender (1991), "Capital structure and dividend irrelevance with asymmetric information", Review of Financial Studies 4:201–219.

Eckbo, E. (1986), "The valuation effects of corporate debt offerings", Journal of Financial Economics 15:119–152.

Fama, E.F. (1978), "The effects of a firm's financing and investment decisions on the welfare of its security holders", American Economic Review 68:272–284.

Fama, E.F., and K.R. French (1998), "Taxes, financing decisions, and firm value", Journal of Finance 53:819–843.

Fama, E.F., and K.R. French (2002), "Testing trade-off and pecking order predictions about dividends and debt", Review of Financial Studies 15:1–33.

Finnerty, J.D., and D.R. Emery (2002), "Corporate securities innovation: an update", Journal of Applied Finance 12:21–47.

Fischer, E.O., R. Heinkel and J. Zechner (1989), "Dynamic capital structure choice: theory and tests", Journal of Finance 44:19–40.

Fluck, Z. (1998), "Optimal financial contracting: debt vs. outside equity", Review of Financial Studies 11:383–418.

Fluck, Z. (2001), "Financial contracting in start-ups and ongoing firms: a life-cycle theory", Working Paper (Michigan State University).

Frank, M., and V. Goyal (2003), "Testing the pecking order theory of capital structure", Journal of Financial Economics 67:217–248.

Franks, J.R., and W.N. Torous (1994), "How shareholders and creditors fare in workouts and chapter 11 reorganizations", Journal of Financial Economics 35:349–370.

Gale, D., and M. Hellwig (1985), "Incentive-compatible debt contracts: the one-period problem", Review of Economic Studies 52:647–669.

Garvey, G.T., and G. Hanka (1999), "Capital structure and corporate control: the effect of antitakeover statutes on firm leverage", Journal of Finance 54:519–545.

Gaver, J.J., and K.M. Gaver (1993), "Additional evidence on the association between the investment opportunity set and corporate financing, dividend and compensation policies", Journal of Accounting and Economics 16:125–160.

Gilson, S.C. (1997), "Transactions costs and capital structure choice: evidence from financially distressed firms", Journal of Finance 52:161–196.

Goldstein, R., N. Ju and H. Leland (2001), "An EBIT-based model of dynamic capital structure", Journal of Business 74:483–512.

Goyal, V.K., K. Lehn and S. Racic (2002), "Growth opportunities and corporate debt policy: the case of the U.S. defense industry", Journal of Financial Economics 64:35–59.

Graham, J.R. (1996), "Debt and the marginal tax rate", Journal of Financial Economics 41:41–73.

Graham, J.R. (2000), "How big are the tax benefits of debt?", Journal of Finance 55:1901–1941.

Guay, W., and J. Harford (2000), "The cash-flow permanence and information content of dividend increases versus repurchases", Journal of Financial Economics 57:385–415.

Gul, F.A. (1999), "Growth opportunities, capital structure and dividend policies in Japan", Journal of Corporate Finance 5:141–168.

Hanka, G. (1998), "Debt and the terms of employment", Journal of Financial Economics 48:245–282.

Harris, M., and A. Raviv (1991), "The theory of capital structure", Journal of Finance 46:297–355.

Hart, O. (1995), Firms, Contracts and Capital Structure (Oxford University Press, Oxford, UK).

Hart, O. (2001), "Financial contracting", Journal of Economic Literature 34:1079–1100.

Hart, O., and J. Moore (1994), "A theory of debt based on the inalienability of human capital", Quarterly Journal of Economics 109:841–879.

Hart, O., and J. Moore (1998), "Default and renegotiation; a dynamic model of debt", Quarterly Journal of Economics 113:1–41.

Helwege, J., and N. Liang (1996), "Is there a pecking order? Evidence from a panel of IPO firms", Journal of Financial Economics 40:429–458.

Hovakimian, A., T. Opler and S. Titman (2001), "The debt-equity choice", Journal of Financial and Quantitative Analysis 36:1–24.

Irvine, P., and J. Rosenfeld (2000), "Raising capital using monthly income preferred stock: market reaction and implications for capital structure theory", Financial Management 29:5–20.

Jagannathan, M., C.P. Stephens and M.S. Weisbach (2000), "Financial flexibility and the choice between dividends and stock repurchases", Journal of Financial Economics 57:355–384.

Jalilvand, A., and R.S. Harris (1984), "Corporate behavior in adjusting to capital structure and dividend targets: an econometric study", Journal of Finance 39:127–145.

Jensen, M.C. (1986), "Agency costs of free cash flow, corporate finance and takeovers", American Economic Review 76:323–329.

Jensen, M.C., and W.H. Meckling (1976), "Theory of the firm: managerial behavior, agency costs and ownership structure", Journal of Financial Economics 3:305–360.

Johnson, S., P. Boone, A. Breach and E. Friedman (2000), "Corporate governance in the East Asian financial crisis", Journal of Financial Economics 58:141–186.

Jung, K., Y. Kim and R. Stulz (1996), "Timing, investment opportunities and the security issue decision", Journal of Financial Economics 42:159–185.

Kaplan, S.N. (1989), "Management buyouts: evidence on taxes as a source of value", Journal of Financial Economics 44:611–632.

Kaplan, S.N., and J. Stein (1993), "The evaluation of buyout structure and pricing (or, what went wrong in the 1980s)", Journal of Applied Corporate Finance 6:72–88.

Kavenock, D., and G.M. Phillips (1997), "Capital structure and product market behavior: an examination of plant exit and investment decisions", Review of Financial Studies 10:767–803.

Khanna, A., and J.J. McConnell (1998), "MIPS, QUIPS AND TOPrS: old wine in new bottles", Journal of Applied Corporate Finance 11:39–44.

Korajczyk, R.A., D. Lucas and R.L. MacDonald (1991), "The effect of information releases on the pricing and timing of equity issues", Review of Financial Studies 4:685–708.

La Porta, R., F. Lopez-de-Silanes, A. Shleifer and R.W. Vishny (1997), "Legal determinants of external finance", Journal of Finance 52:1131–1150.

La Porta, R., F. Lopez-de-Silanes, A. Shleifer and R.W. Vishny (1998), "Law and finance", Journal of Political Economy 106:1113–1155.

La Porta, R., F. Lopez-de-Silanes and A. Shleifer (1999), "Corporate ownership around the world", Journal of Finance 54:471–517.

La Porta, R., F. Lopez-de-Silanes, A. Shleifer and R.W. Vishny (2000), "Agency problems and dividend policies around the world", Journal of Finance 55:1–33.

Lambrecht, B.M. (2001), "The impact of debt financing on entry and exit in a duopoly", Review of Financial Studies 14:765–804.

Lang, L., E. Ofek and R.M. Stulz (1996), "Leverage, investment, and firm growth", Journal of Financial Economics 40:3–29.

Leland, H. (1994), "Corporate debt value, bond covenants, and optimal capital structure", Journal of Finance 49:1213–1252.

Leland, H.E. (1998), "Agency costs, risk management and capital structure", Journal of Finance 53: 1213–1244.

Leland, H.E., and K. Toft (1996), "Optimal capital structure, endogenous bankruptcy and the term structure of credit spreads", Journal of Finance 51:987–1019.

Lemmon, M.L., and J.F. Zender (2001), "Looking under the lamppost: an empirical examination of the determinants of capital structure", Working Paper (University of Utah).

Lerner, J. (2002), "Where does state street lead? A first look at finance patents, 1971–2000", Journal of Finance 57:901–930.

Lewellen, K. (2002), "Financing decisions when managers are risk averse", Working Paper (University of Rochester).

Lie, E., H.J. Lie and J.J. McConnell (2001), "Debt-reducing exchange offers", Journal of Corporate Finance 7:179–207.

Long, M.S., and I.B. Malitz (1985), "Investment patterns and financial leverage", in: B.M. Friedman, ed., Corporate Capital Structures in the United States (University of Chicago Press, Chicago) pp. 325–351.

MacKie-Mason, J.K. (1990), "Do taxes affect corporate financing decisions?", Journal of Finance 45:1471–1493.

Maksimovic, V., and G. Phillips (1998), "Efficiency of bankrupt firms and industry conditions: theory and evidence", Journal of Finance 53:1495–1532.

Maksimovic, V., and S. Titman (1991), "Financial policy and reputation for product quality", Review of Financial Studies 4:175–200.

Marais, L., K. Schipper and A. Smith (1989), "Wealth effects of going private for senior securities", Journal of Financial Economics 23:155–191.

Masulis, R.W. (1980), "The effects of capital structure change on security prices: a study of exchange offers", Journal of Financial Economics 8:139–178.

Mauer, D.C., and A.J. Triantis (1994), "Interactions of corporate financing and investment decisions: a dynamic framework", Journal of Finance 49:1253–1277.

McConnell, J.J., and C. Muscarella (1985), "Corporate capital expenditure decisions and the value of the firm", Journal of Financial Economics 14:399–422.

Mello, A., and J. Parsons (1992), "Measuring the agency cost of debt", Journal of Finance 47:1887–1904.

Merton, R. (1974), "On the pricing of corporate debt: the risk structure of interest rates", Journal of Finance 29:449–470.

Miles, J., and R. Ezzell (1980), "The weighted average cost of capital, perfect markets and project life: a clarification", Journal of Financial and Quantitative Analysis 15:719–730.

Miller, M.H. (1977), "Debt and taxes", Journal of Finance 32:261–276.

Miller, M.H. (1989), "The Modigliani–Miller propositions after thirty years", Journal of Applied Corporate Finance 2:6–18.

Miller, M.H., and F. Modigliani (1966), "Some estimates of the cost of capital to the electric utility industry, 1954–57", American Economic Review 56:333–391.

Minton, B.A., and K.H. Wruck (2001), "Financial conservatism: evidence on capital structure from low leverage firms", Working Paper (Ohio State University).

Mitton, T. (2002), "A cross-firm analysis of the impact of corporate governance on the East Asian financial crisis", Journal of Financial Economics 64:215–241.

Modigliani, F. (1982), "Debt, dividend policy, taxes, inflation and market valuation", Journal of Finance 37:255–273.

Modigliani, F., and M.H. Miller (1958), "The cost of capital, corporate finance, and the theory of investment", American Economic Review 48:261–297.

Modigliani, F., and M.H. Miller (1963), "Corporate income taxes and the cost of capital: a correction", American Economic Review 53:443–453.

Morck, R., A. Shleifer and R. Vishny (1988), "Management ownership and market valuation: an empirical analysis", Journal of Financial Economics 20:293–316.

Morellec, E. (2001), "Asset liquidity, capital structure, and secured debt", Journal of Financial Economics 61:173–206.

Myers, S.C. (1977), "Determinants of corporate borrowing", Journal of Financial Economics 5:147–175.

Myers, S.C. (1984), "The capital structure puzzle", Journal of Finance 39:575–592.

Myers, S.C. (1999), "Financial architecture", European Financial Management 5:133–141.

Myers, S.C. (2000), "Outside equity", Journal of Finance 55:1005–1037.

Myers, S.C. (2001), "Capital structure", Journal of Economic Perspectives 15:81–102.

Myers, S.C., and N.S. Majluf (1984), "Corporate financing and investment decisions when firms have information that investors do not have", Journal of Financial Economics 13:187–221.

Myers, S.C., and R. Rajan (1998), "The paradox of liquidity", Quarterly Journal of Economics 113: 733–771.

Myers, S.C., D.A. Dill and A.J. Bautista (1976), "Valuation of financial lease contracts", Journal of Finance 31:799–819.

Noe, T. (1988), "Capital structure and signaling game equilibria", Review of Financial Studies 1: 331–356.

Parrino, R., and M.S. Weisbach (1999), "Measuring investment distortions arising from stockholder–bondholder conflicts", Journal of Financial Economics 53:3–42.

Persons, J.C. (1994), "Renegotiation and the impossibility of optimal investment", Review of Financial Studies 7:419–449.

Persons, J.C., and V.A. Warther (1997), "Boom and bust patterns in the adoption of financial innovations", Review of Financial Studies 10:939–967.

Peyer, U.C., and A. Shivdasani (2001), "Leverage and internal capital markets: evidence from leveraged recapitalizations", Journal of Financial Economics 59:477–515.

Phillips, G.M. (1995), "Increased debt and industry product markets, an empirical analysis", Journal of Financial Economics 37:189–238.

Pilotte, E. (1992), "Growth opportunities and the stock price response to new financing", Journal of Business 65:371–395.

Pulvino, T.C. (1998), "Do asset fire sales exist: an empirical investigation of commercial aircraft transactions", Journal of Finance 53:939–978.

Rajan, R.G., and L. Zingales (1995), "What do we know about capital structure? Some evidence from international data", Journal of Finance 50:1421–1460.

Rajan, R.G., and L. Zingales (1998), "Which capitalism? Lessons from the East Asian Crisis", Journal of Applied Corporate Finance 11:40–48.

Ritter, J. (2003), "Investment banking and security issuance", in: G.M. Constantinides, M. Harris and R.M. Stulz, eds., Handbook of the Economics of Finance, Vol. 1A (Elsevier, Amsterdam) Chapter 5, this volume.

Ross, S.A. (1977), "The determination of financial structure: the incentive-signalling approach", Bell Journal of Economics 8:23–40.

Safieddine, A., and S. Titman (1999), "Leverage and corporate performance: evidence from unsuccessful takeovers", Journal of Finance 54:547–580.

Schallheim, J.S. (1994), Lease or Buy: Principles for Sound Decisionmaking (Harvard Business School Press, Boston, MA).

Shleifer, A., and L. Summers (1988), "Breach of trust in hostile takeovers", in: A.J. Auerbach, ed., Corporate Takeovers: Causes and Consequences (University of Chicago Press, Chicago, IL).

Shleifer, A., and R. Vishny (1989), "Management entrenchment: the case of manager-specific investments", Journal of Financial Economics 25:123–140.

Shleifer, A., and R. Vishny (1992), "Liquidation values and debt capacity: a market equilibrium approach", Journal of Finance 47:1343–1366.

Shyam-Sunder, L. (1991), "The stock price effect of risky versus safe debt", Journal of Financial and Quantitative Analysis 26:549–558.

Shyam-Sunder, L., and S.C. Myers (1999), "Testing static tradeoff against pecking order models of capital structure", Journal of Financial Economics 51:219–244.

Smith Jr, C.W., and J. Warner (1979), "On financial contracting: an analysis of bond covenants", Journal of Financial Economics 7:117–161.

Smith Jr, C.W., and R.L. Watts (1992), "The investment opportunity set and corporate financing, dividend and compensation policies", Journal of Financial Economics 32:263–292.

Stulz, R. (1990), "Managerial discretion and optimal financing policies", Journal of Financial Economics 26:3–27.

Taggart Jr, R.A. (1977), "A model of corporate financing decisions", Journal of Finance 32:1467–1484.

Taggart Jr, R.A. (1991), "Consistent valuation and cost of capital expressions with corporate and personal taxes", Financial Management 20:8–20.

Titman, S. (1984), "The effect of capital structure on a firm's liquidation decision", Journal of Financial Economics 13:137–151.

Titman, S. (2002), "The Modigliani and Miller theorem and the integration of financial markets", Financial Management 31:101–115.

Titman, S., and R. Wessels (1988), "The determinants of capital structure choice", Journal of Finance 43:1–19.

Townsend, R. (1979), "Optimal contracts and competitive markets with costly state verification", Journal of Economic Theory 21:265–293.

Treynor, J.L. (1981), "The financial objective in the widely held corporation", Financial Analysts Journal 37:68–71.

Tufano, P. (1989), "Financial innovation and first-mover advantages", Journal of Financial Economics 25:213–240.

Tufano, P. (1995), "Securities innovations: a historical and functional prospective", Journal of Applied Corporate Finance 7:90–102.

Wald, J. (1999), "How firm characteristics affect capital structure: an international comparison", Journal of Financial Research 22:161–187.

Warner, J.B. (1977), "Bankruptcy costs: some evidence", Journal of Finance 26:337–348.

Weiss, L.A. (1990), "Bankruptcy resolution: direct costs and violation of priority of claims", Journal of Financial Economics 27:285–314.

Weiss, L.A., and K.H. Wruck (1998), "Information problems, conflicts of interest, and asset stripping: chapter 11's failure in the case of Eastern Airlines", Journal of Financial Economics 48:55–97.

Wruck, K.H. (1995), "Financial policy as a catalyst for organizational change: Sealed Air's leveraged special dividend", Journal of Applied Corporate Finance 7:20–37.

Zingales, L. (1998), "Survival of the fittest or the fattest? Exit and financing in the trucking industry", Journal of Finance 53:905–938.

Zingales, L. (2000), "In search of new foundations", Journal of Finance 55:1623–1653.

Zwiebel, J. (1996), "Dynamic capital structure under managerial entrenchment", American Economic Review 86:1197–1215.

Chapter 5

INVESTMENT BANKING AND SECURITIES ISSUANCE

JAY R. RITTER*

University of Florida, Gainesville

Contents

* This chapter has benefited from comments from seminar participants at Emory University, the University of California at Davis, Korea University, Chung-Ang University (Korea), the Hong Kong University of Science and Technology, and City University of Hong Kong, and from Alon Brav, Hsuan-Chi Chen, Raghu Rau, René Stulz, Anand Vijh, Kent Womack, and Li-Anne Woo. The comments of Tim Loughran are particularly appreciated, as is research assistance from Donghang Zhang.

Handbook of the Economics of Finance, Edited by G.M. Constantinides, M. Harris and R. Stulz

Abstract

This chapter analyzes the securities issuance process, focusing on initial public offerings (IPOs) and seasoned equity offerings (SEOs). The IPO literature documents three empirical patterns: 1) short-run underpricing; 2) long-run underperformance (although this is contentious); and 3) extreme time-series fluctuations in volume and underpricing. While the chapter mainly focuses on evidence from the USA, evidence from other countries is generally consistent with the USA patterns. A large literature explaining the short-run underpricing of IPOs exists, with asymmetric information models predominating. The SEO literature documents 1) negative announcement effects; 2) the setting of offer prices at a discount from the market price; 3) long-run underperformance; and 4) large fluctuations in volume. In addition to long-run underperformance relative to other stocks, there is some evidence that issuers succeed at timing their equity offerings for periods when future market returns are low. When examining a large class of corporate financing activities, including equity offerings, convertible bond offerings, bond offerings, open market repurchases, stock- and cash-financed mergers and acquisitions, and dividend increases or decreases, several patterns emerge. In general, the announcement effects are negative for activities that provide cash to the firm, and positive for activities that pay cash out of the firm. Furthermore, the market generally underreacts, in that long-run abnormal returns are usually of the same sign as the announcement effect. In spite of the large expenditure of resources on analyst coverage, there is little academic work emphasizing the importance of the marketing of financial securities. Only recently have papers begun to focus on the corporate financing implications if firms face variations in the cost of external financing due to the mispricing of securities by the market.

Keywords

corporate finance, initial public offerings, seasoned equity offerings, underwriting, investment banking

JEL classification: G24, G32, G14

1. Introduction

1.1. Overview

This chapter analyzes the securities issuance process, largely taking the choice of what security to offer as given. Extensive attention is devoted to the controversies surrounding long-run returns on companies issuing equity, including both initial public offerings (IPOs) and seasoned equity offerings (SEOs). For IPOs, attention is also devoted to the mechanisms for selling IPOs, where considerable variation exists in global practices. Theories and evidence regarding the first-day returns on IPOs are also covered.

Most of this chapter is devoted to equity issues, even though fixed-income securities swamp equities in terms of the dollar value of issue volume. This is not because debt securities are unimportant, but because the pricing and distribution of fixed-income securities is generally much more straightforward. Specifically, credit risk is the main determinant of the relative yield on corporate bonds of a given maturity, and independent rating agencies such as Moody's provide credit ratings on bonds. In contrast, the payoffs on equities have substantial upside potential as well as downside risk, and are thus more sensitive to firm-specific information.

External financing is costly. When a firm decides to issue securities to the public, it almost always hires an intermediary, typically an investment banking firm. The issuing firm pays a commission, or gross spread, and receives the net proceeds when the securities are issued. In addition to the direct costs of issuing securities, an issuing firm that is already publicly traded frequently pays additional indirect costs through revaluations of its existing securities (the "announcement effect"). These indirect costs may, at times, be much larger than the direct costs. A major reason for writing this chapter is that the stock market's reaction to securities offerings conveys information about the firm's investment and financing activities. The interpretation of these reactions sheds light on broader issues such as market informational efficiency and the importance of adverse selection and moral hazard in corporate settings.

Investment banking firms are intermediaries that advise firms, distribute securities, and take principal positions. In the course of these activities, information is produced. Most investment banking firms are vertically integrated organizations that incorporate merger and acquisition (M&A) advisory services, capital raising services, securities trading and brokerage, and research coverage. Although there are distinctions, this chapter will use the terms investment bank, securities firm, and underwriter interchangeably. In Europe, universal banks have been permitted to perform both commercial and investment banking functions. In the USA, the Glass–Steagall Act separated commercial and investment banking functions from the 1930s to the 1990s. Commercial banks were permitted to take deposits from individuals that are guaranteed by the government (up to $100 000 per account-holder, as of 2003). In return for the government deposit guarantee, commercial banks were prohibited from certain activities, including taking equity positions in firms and underwriting corporate securities. The prohibition on underwriting securities was gradually relaxed, first for debt securities and then for equity securities. In 1999, the Glass–Steagall Act was finally repealed, although deposit insurance remains.

The key difference between commercial banks and investment banks in the corporate financing function is that commercial banks primarily act as long-term principals, making direct loans to borrowers, whereas investment banks primarily act as short-term principals. Since investment banks are selling to investors the securities that firms issue, the marketing of financial securities is important. This is a topic that has no reason for coverage in a Modigliani–Miller framework, where markets are perfect and there is no role for marketing. An important tool in the marketing of financial securities, especially equities, is research coverage (forecasts and recommendations) by security analysts. Since the investment banking firm providing research reports also underwrites offerings, this is referred to as "sell-side" coverage. There is a perception that analyst coverage has become more important over time, partly because for many industries (i.e., biotechnology and technology companies), historical accounting information is of limited use in discerning whether new products and services will create economic value added. At the end of 2000, the Securities and Exchange Commission's Regulation FD (fair disclosure) went into effect. This regulation may affect the role of analysts, for it requires that information that a corporation provides to analysts must be publicly disclosed to others as well.

This chapter updates and extends previous surveys of the investment banking and securities issuance literature, notably Smith (1986) on the capital acquisition process, Eckbo and Masulis (1995) on seasoned equity offerings (SEOs), and Ibbotson and Ritter (1995) and Jenkinson and Ljungqvist (2001) on initial public offerings (IPOs). For those interested in a comprehensive analysis of the literature on IPOs, the Jenkinson and Ljungqvist book goes into extensive detail. Ritter and Welch (2002) focus on the recent IPO literature, especially papers dealing with share allocations. Both the Smith survey and the Eckbo and Masulis survey are grounded in an equilibrium market efficiency framework, and neither discusses long-run performance issues. The Eckbo and Masulis survey has an extensive discussion of rights issues (equity issues where existing shareholders are given the right to purchase new shares at a fixed exercise price). Rights issues will not be covered here, partly because rights issues are not common in the USA and their use in other countries has been rapidly declining, and partly due to the excellent existing analysis. Many other topics in security issuance are mentioned in passing or not discussed at all. For example, will technology change the securities issuance process? Given the burgeoning literature on various aspects of security issuance, any coverage that is less than book-length must, unfortunately, be selective.

Many important issues in corporate finance and macroeconomics are driven by the assumption that external finance is costly. Examples include theories of conglomerates (internal versus external capital markets), the effects of monetary policy (bank "capital crunches" and the "bank lending channel" of monetary policy transmission), financial development and growth, and financial accelerator models of business cycles. Because this literature is discussed by Jeremy C. Stein in Chapter 2 in this volume, this chapter will not focus on these important issues. This chapter also is related to other topics in this volume, including Chapter 18 by Barberis and Thaler on behavioral finance and Chapter 15 by G.W. Schwert on anomalies and market efficiency.

This survey is somewhat USA-centric, largely reflecting the existing academic research literature. Although this is clearly a limitation, it is less of a limitation than it once was because capital markets are increasingly globally integrated, and USA institutional practices (in particular, book-building) and institutions are increasingly common throughout the world. As examples, Deutsche Bank's investment banking is headquartered in London; Credit Suisse First Boston, while nominally a Swiss firm, in 2000 was the lead manager on more IPOs in the USA than any other underwriter; and Goldman Sachs leads the league tables (market share tabulations) for M&A activity in Europe. Ritter (2003) provides a brief survey of the recent European IPO literature.

1.2.   A brief history of investment banking and securities regulation

Until the 1970s, almost all investment banking firms were private partnerships, generally with a limited capital base. When underwriting large securities offerings, these partnerships almost always formed underwriting syndicates, in order to meet regulatory capital requirements, distribute the securities, and share risk. Many investment banking firms had "relationships" with corporations. In the 1970s, the investment banking industry began to change to a more "transactional" form, where corporations use different investment bankers for different services, on an as-needed basis. Investment banking firms have grown in size and scope, largely through mergers, and most of the larger firms have converted to publicly traded stock companies. A reason for the increase in size of investment banking firms is the increased importance of information technology, with large fixed costs and low marginal costs. With their new-found large capital bases and distribution channels, the historical rationale for forming syndicates to distribute securities has largely disappeared. Consistent with this, the number of investment banking firms participating in a given syndicate has shrunk noticeably over the last few decades. A syndicate is composed of one or more managing underwriters and from zero to over one hundred other syndicate members. The lead manager does most of the work and receives most of the fees [Chen and Ritter (2000)]. All of the managers usually provide research coverage. Indeed, this is the major reason why syndicates still exist. Frequently, after a deal is completed, a "tombstone" advertisement listing the syndicate members is published.

As a consequence of distributing the shares in an initial public offering, the lead underwriter knows where the shares are placed, which gives a natural advantage for making a market later on, since the underwriter knows whom to call if there is an order imbalance [Ellis, Michaely and O'Hara (2000)]. Advice on acquisitions and follow-on stock offerings frequently follows as well. The underwriter almost always assigns an analyst to follow the company and provide research coverage. Thus, securities underwriting capabilities are combined with M&A advisory capabilities, as well as sales and trading capabilities. All of these activities are information-intensive activities. "Chinese walls", which are supposed to be as impregnable as the Great Wall of China, whereby proprietary information possessed in the M&A advisory function is not disclosed to stock traders, are supposed to exist. In the course of assisting in the issuance of securities, investment bankers perform "due diligence" investigations. In the M&A advisory role, they produce "fairness opinions". Investment bankers are thus putting their reputations on the line, certifying for investors that the terms of the deal are fair and that material information is reflected in the price [Chemmanur and Fulghieri (1994)]. [1]

In the USA, federal government regulation of securities markets is based upon a notion of *caveat emptor* (buyer beware) with full disclosure. The USA Securities and Exchange Commission (SEC) regulates securities markets. In addition, self-regulatory organizations such as the New York Stock Exchange and the National Association of Securities Dealers impose requirements on members, and the threat of class action lawsuits on behalf of investors constrains the actions of issuers and underwriters. Prospectuses are required to contain all material information, with specific requirements for the amount and form of accounting disclosures. In Europe, there is no prohibition on underwriters producing research reports immediately preceding a securities offering. In the USA, firms going public and their underwriters are prohibited from disclosing projections that are not in the prospectus during the "quiet period", starting before a firm announces its IPO and ending 40 calendar days after the offer. An exception to this is that limited oral disclosures may be made during "road show" presentations, where attendance is restricted to institutional investors. In 1999, the SEC started permitting certain qualified individual investors to have access to webcasts of the road show.

Typically, the managing underwriters issue research reports with "buy" or "strong buy" recommendations as soon as the quiet period ends. Michaely and Womack (1999) present evidence that sell-side analysts affiliated with managing underwriters face conflicts of interest. The conventional wisdom is that analysts have become "cheerleaders". The three reasons for this are that 1) they are dependent upon access to corporate managers for information; 2) their compensation is tied to whether their investment banking firm is chosen as a managing underwriter on equity or junk-bond offerings, or as an advisor on M&A deals; and 3) the institutional clients that pay attention to a report are likely to be long in the stock. In 2002, new rules were announced in an attempt to limit the conflicts of interest and alert investors to the conflicts.

On the front page of a prospectus, the offer price and underwriting discount (commission) are disclosed. The underwriter is prohibited from distributing any

---

[1] A due diligence investigation involves quizzing management to uncover material information, some of it proprietary in nature, that is relevant for valuation purposes. A fairness opinion is a formal statement that the terms of an M&A deal or leveraged buyout are reflective of "fair" market valuation, including appropriate control premiums or liquidity discounts.

securities at a price above the stated offer price, although if the issue fails to sell out at the offer price, the underwriter may sell at a lower price. Because the underwriter cannot directly gain from any price appreciation above the offer price on unsold securities, while bearing the full downside of any price fall, there is every incentive to fully distribute the securities offered.

Based on the logic of the efficient markets hypothesis, beginning in 1982 the SEC began permitting publicly traded firms meeting certain requirements (basically, large firms) to issue securities without distributing a prospectus. Instead, SEC Rule 415 states that by filing a letter with the SEC disclosing the intention of selling additional securities within the next two years, a firm can sell the securities whenever it wants. Existing disclosures, such as quarterly financial statements, are deemed to be sufficient information to investors. The securities can be taken off the shelf and sold, in what are known as "shelf" issues. In practice, shelf issues are commonly done for bond offerings. Before selling equity, however, many firms prefer to hire an investment banker and conduct a marketing campaign (the road show), complete with a prospectus. From 1984–1992 there were virtually no shelf equity offerings, but they have enjoyed a resurgence since then [Heron and Lie (2003)].

1.3.   The information conveyed by investment and financing activities

Smith's classic 1986 survey article *Investment Banking and the Capital Acquisition Process,* focused on announcement effects associated with securities offerings and other corporate actions. These transactions can be categorized on the basis of the leverage change and the implied cash flow change. For example, calling a convertible bond (forcing conversion into equity) decreases a firm's leverage and reduces its need for cash flow to meet interest payments, and repurchasing stock increases leverage and uses cash flow. The studies that he surveyed found that leverage-decreasing transactions on average are associated with negative announcement effects if new capital is raised (such as with equity issues). Leverage-increasing transactions on average are associated with positive announcement effects if no new capital is raised (such as with a share repurchase). As Smith pointed out, these patterns are difficult to reconcile with traditional tradeoff models of optimal capital structure. The patterns are consistent, however, with informational asymmetries and agency problems being of importance.

There are several problems with interpreting announcement effects. First, and most mechanically, in an efficient market the announcement effect will measure the difference between the post-announcement valuation and what was expected beforehand. If investors had a high likelihood of an announcement occurring beforehand, this updating element is small, and the announcement effect vastly underestimates the impact of the event. Second, any financing activity implicitly is associated with an investment activity, and any investment activity is implicitly associated with a financing activity. Corporate financing and investment actions invariably convey information about both of these activities, due to the identity that sources of funds = uses of funds. For example, if a firm raises external capital, the firm is implicitly conveying the information that internal funds will be insufficient to finance its activities (bad news). It is also conveying the information that it will be investing more than if it didn't finance externally. This may be good or bad news, depending upon the desirability of the investment. So the announcement effect depends upon the relative magnitude of multiple implicit and explicit pieces of information.

A substantial literature, dating back to the mid-1980s, documents that the market reacts negatively, on average, to the announcement of equity issues in the USA. Convertible bond issues generally are greeted with a moderate negative reaction. Bond offerings have slightly negative reactions, and share repurchases are greeted with positive announcement effects. In the last decade, researchers have examined the long-run performance of firms following these events. The long-run performance evidence shows that in general the market underreacts to the announcement.

Most of the literature on long-run performance has focused on *relative* performance, i.e., do issuing companies underperform a benchmark? Baker and Wurgler (2000), however, present empirical evidence that issuing firms display *market* timing ability. Using USA data on issues of debt and equity (IPOs and SEOs), they find that the fraction of external financing that is equity predicts the following calendar year's stock market return with greater reliability than either the market dividend yield or the market's market-to-book ratio. Baker and Wurgler's sample covers returns from 1928 to 1997. Interestingly, the fraction of equity issuance was highest in 1929, a year that included the October stock market crash. When the sample period is split in two, however, their results hold in both subperiods.

If firms can successfully time their equity offerings to take advantage of "windows of opportunity", they have a time-varying cost of external capital. How should this affect a firm's investment and financing policies? Stein (1996) addresses this important issue, and concludes that the normative answer depends upon the interaction of two assumptions. The first assumption is whether differences in the cost of external equity reflect misvaluations or differences in equilibrium expected returns. The second assumption is whether managers are trying to maximize short-run firm value or long-run firm value. If one assumes that a low expected return occurs because a stock is overvalued, then managers should issue stock but not invest in low return activities if they are focused on maximizing the wealth of long-term shareholders. On the other hand, if one assumes that low expected returns are rationally being forecast by investors, then a firm should issue stock and use a lower hurdle rate in choosing its investments, much as the neoclassical model of optimal investing and financing would recommend.

The remainder of this chapter discusses securities issuance. In Section 3, the short-run and long-run reactions to various corporate announcements will be summarized. In Section 4, initial public offerings will be analyzed in detail, with substantial focus on contractual mechanisms. But first, detailed attention is given to firms conducting seasoned equity offerings.

2. Seasoned equity offerings (SEOs)

When a firm that is already publicly traded sells additional stock, the new shares are perfect substitutes for the existing shares. For these transactions, the academic literature tends to use the term seasoned equity offering (SEO), as contrasted with an unseasoned equity offering, an IPO. Practitioners generally use the term follow-on offering, especially if the equity issue is within several years of the IPO. SEOs are also referred to as secondaries, although secondary offering is a term that can mean either a follow-on offering or shares being sold by existing shareholders, as opposed to a primary offer where the issuing firm is receiving the proceeds. (And on the subject of ambiguous terms, this chapter will use public ownership to mean stock that is traded in the market, rather than government ownership. Private ownership is used to mean non-traded stock, rather than being owned by the private sector).

2.1. Announcement effects

Numerous studies have documented that in the USA there is an announcement effect of -2%, on average, for SEOs. The most popular explanation among academics for this negative announcement effect is that of the Myers and Majluf (1984) adverse selection model. Myers and Majluf assume that management wants to maximize the wealth of its existing shareholders in the long run. At any point in time, however, the current market price may be too high or too low relative to management's private information about the value of assets in place. In other words, strong-form market inefficiency is being assumed. If management thinks that the current market price is too low, the firm will not issue undervalued stock, for doing so dilutes the fractional ownership of existing shareholders. If management thinks that the current stock price is too high, however, the firm will issue equity if debt financing is not an option. Rational investors, knowing this decision rule, therefore interpret an equity issue announcement as conveying management's opinion that the stock is overvalued, and the stock price falls. [2]

How this negative announcement effect should be interpreted is a subject of debate. If a firm is issuing shares equal to 20% of its existing shares, a downward revaluation of 2% for the existing shares is a dollar amount equal to 10% of the proceeds being raised. If this 2% drop is viewed as a cost of an equity issue, then external equity capital is very expensive. On the other hand, if this 2% drop would have occurred when the basis for management's opinion regarding firm value was disclosed in some other manner, then the downward revaluation is not a cost of the equity issue for long-term shareholders. It is a cost only to those shareholders who would have sold their shares in between the

---

[2] The Myers–Majluf predictions are very sensitive to the assumptions about the objective function of management, the portfolio rebalancing rules of investors, and the source of information asymmetries. Daniel and Titman (1995) discuss some of these issues in detail.

equity issue announcement and when the negative news would have otherwise been impounded into the share price. If this is the case, then the negative announcement effect is mainly a matter of indifference to a firm where long-term shareholder wealth maximization is the objective, and external equity is not inordinately costly.

As mentioned earlier, when a firm raises external equity capital, it not only conveys information about whether management thinks the firm is overvalued or not, but also suggests that something will be done with the funds raised. If the market interprets the equity issue as implying that a new positive net present value project will be undertaken, the announcement effect could be positive. On the other hand, if the market is concerned that the equity issue means that management will squander the funds on empire building, then the announcement effect could be interpreted as causally linked to the equity issue, in which case external equity is in fact very expensive. The rationale is that the additional equity resources are relaxing a constraint on management's tendency to engage in "empire-building", or growth for the sake of growth. In other words, agency problems between shareholders and managers are intensified.

A number of empirical studies have documented cross-sectional patterns in the equity issue announcement effect. In general, these results show that there is less of a negative reaction when a firm can convince the market that there is a good reason for issuing equity, and there is a more negative reaction when good motivations are not obvious. Jung, Kim and Stulz (1996) report that firms with a high q (market value-to-replacement cost), reflecting good investment opportunities, have an announcement effect that is insignificantly different from zero. Choe, Masulis and Nanda (1993) document that the announcement effect is less negative when the economy is in an expansionary segment of the business cycle, when there may be less adverse selection risk.

Korajczyk, Lucas and McDonald (1991) report that the announcement effect is less negative if it follows shortly after an earnings report, at which time there is presumed to be less asymmetric information. Houston and Ryngaert (1997) provide direct evidence that adverse selection concerns explain part of the negative announcement effect. They study bank mergers, where common stock is the dominant means of payment to the shareholders of target banks. Some merger agreements specify that the target shareholders will receive a fixed number of shares in the acquiring bank (a fixed ratio stock offer), and other merger agreements specify a variable number of shares that add up to a fixed dollar amount (a conditional stock offer). If target shareholders are concerned that the acquirer is offering overvalued stock, the conditional stock offer provides protection against price drops. Consistent with adverse selection concerns, the announcement effect is −3.3% for fixed ratio stock offers, but only −1.1% for conditional stock offers.

In general, studies find that larger issues have more negative effects. One problem with interpreting the relation between issue size and announcement effects is that if there is an unusually negative reaction, the issue size may be cut back by the time the deal is completed. Since existing empirical studies do not take this endogeneity into account, the empirical estimates of the effect of issue size on the announcement are subject to a simultaneous equations bias. This bias results in an underestimate of the magnitude of the effect of issue size on the stock price. Thus, academics undoubtedly underestimate the degree to which the demand curve for a stock is negatively sloped.

On the issue date, SEOs are, on average, sold at a discount of about 3% relative to the market price on the day prior to issuing [Corwin (2003), Mola and Loughran (2003)]. Mola and Loughran report that the size of this discount has grown over time, and that there has been an increasing tendency to set the offer price at an integer. For example, in recent years a stock trading at $31.75 would very likely be priced at $30.00 or $31.00, whereas in the 1980s it would have been more likely to be priced at $31.00 or $31.50.

2.2. Evidence on long-run performance

The long-run performance of SEOs has been the subject of a number of studies, all of which find that firms conducting SEOs typically have high returns in the year before issuing. For example, Loughran and Ritter (1995) report an average return in the year before issuing of 72%. During the five years after issuing, however, the returns are below normal. Partly this is due to "market timing", and partly it is due to abnormal performance relative to a benchmark. The conclusions regarding abnormal performance are hotly debated, and sensitive to the methodology employed and the sample used. Figure 1 illustrates the evidence regarding average annual returns in the five years after issuing. The numbers show that, for 7760 SEOs from 1970–2000, the average annual return in the five years after issuing is 10.8%. Nonissuing firms of the same size (market capitalization) have average annual returns of 14.4%. Therefore, relative to a size-matched benchmark, issuers underperform by 3.6% per year for five years.

Using a size benchmark, however, introduces a confounding effect. Issuing firms tend to be growth firms, and nonissuers tend to be value firms. Thus, in addition to comparing issuers with nonissuers, growth firms are being compared with value firms. To remove this confounding effect, Table 1 also reports the average annual returns on issuing firms and nonissuers matched by both size and book-to-market ("style" matching). In so doing, some issuers are lost because of missing book value information. Table 1 shows that when issuers are compared to style-matched nonissuers, the underperformance narrows slightly to 3.4% per year in the five years after issuing. Statistical significance levels are not reported in Table 1, because the large degree of overlap in post-issue returns among the sample greatly decreases the number of independent observations.

Inspection of Table 1 shows that issuers do not underperform in the first six months after issuing. This is probably due to a combination of momentum effects and a desire to avoid litigation by making sure that earnings numbers meet analyst forecasts in the first two quarters after issuing. Negative earnings surprises are rare immediately following an SEO [Korajczyk, Lucas and McDonald (1991)]. In the roughly two years after this six month honeymoon, however, there is very substantial underperformance,

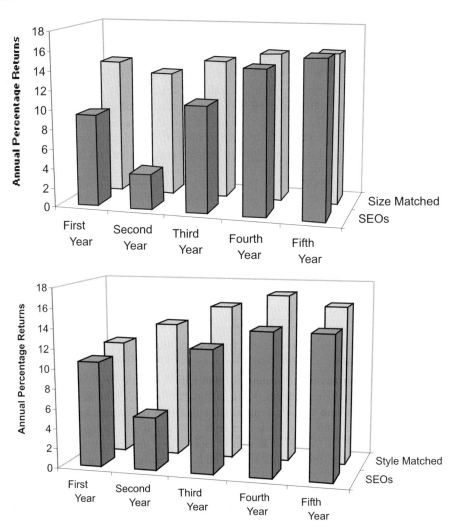

Fig. 1. Post-issue returns for firms conducting seasoned equity offerings (SEOs) in 1970–2000. The average annual return for each of the five years after issuing is shown for firms conducting SEOs and (top panel) size-matched nonissuing firms, and (bottom panel) style-matched nonissuing firms. The style matches are based upon size (market cap) and book-to-market matching. For each of the five post-issue years, the average annual return is calculated as an equally weighted average of the CRSP-listed issuers that are present at the beginning of the year. All matching firms have been CRSP-listed for at least five years at the time of the SEO with which they are matched, and have not conducted an SEO during this time. If an SEO is delisted before five years from the issue date, its annual return during the year of delisting is calculated by splicing in the CRSP value-weighted market return for the remainder of that year. Additional details are described in Table 1, where the numbers in this figure are reported. Returns are computed using CRSP returns ending on December 31, 2001.

Table 1

Mean percentage returns on SEOs from 1970–2000 during the first five years after issuing[a]

	1st 6 months	2nd 6 months	1st yr	2nd yr	3rd yr	4th yr	5th yr	Geometric mean yrs 1–5
SEO firms	6.7%	1.5%	9.4%	3.6%	10.9%	14.7%	15.9%	10.8%
Size-matched	6.1%	7.0%	14.0%	12.9%	14.4%	15.3%	15.5%	14.4%
Difference	0.6%	−5.5%	−4.6%	−9.3%	−3.5%	−0.6%	0.4%	−3.6%
Number	7502	7475	7504	7226	6603	5936	5188	7760
SEO firms	7.4%	2.2%	10.6%	5.3%	12.3%	14.2%	14.2%	11.3%
Style-matched	5.4%	5.6%	11.5%	13.6%	15.6%	16.9%	15.9%	14.7%
Difference	2.0%	−3.4%	−0.9%	−8.3%	−3.3%	−2.7%	−1.7%	−3.4%
Number	6638	6622	6638	6289	5711	5123	4448	6638

[a] All averages are equally weighted. For the first year, the returns are measured from the closing market price on the issue date until the 6th-month or one-year anniversary. All returns are equally weighted average returns for all seasoned equity offerings (SEOs) that are still traded on Nasdaq, the Amex, or the NYSE at the start of a period. If an issuing firm is delisted within an event year, its return for that year is calculated by compounding the CRSP value-weighted market index for the rest of the year. The matching firm is treated as if it delisted on the same date, and its return for the remainder of the year is calculated using the CRSP VW index. Thus, once an SEO is delisted, by construction there is no abnormal performance for the remainder of the year. For the size-matched returns, each SEO is matched with a nonissuing firm having the same market capitalization (using the closing market price on the first day of trading for the SEO, and the market capitalization at the end of the previous month for the matching firms). For the style-matched returns, each SEO is matched with a nonissuing firm in the same size decile (using NYSE firms only for determining the decile breakpoints) having the closest book-to-market ratio. For nonissuing firms, the Compustat-listed book value of equity for the most recent fiscal year ending at least four months prior to the SEO date is used, along with the market cap at the close of trading at month-end prior to the month of the SEO with which it is matched. Nonissuing firms are those that have been listed on the Amex–Nasdaq–NYSE for at least five years, without issuing equity for cash during that time. If a nonissuer subsequently issues equity, it is still used as the matching firm. If a nonissuer gets delisted prior to the delisting (or the 5th anniversary, or Dec. 31, 2001), the second-closest matching firm on the original SEO date is substituted, on a point-forward basis. For firms with multiple classes of stock outstanding, market cap is calculated based using only the class in the SEO for the SEO. For nonissuing firms, each class of stock is treated as if it is a separate firm. The sample size is 7760 SEOs from 1970–2000 when size-matching is used, excluding SEOs with an offer price of less than $5.00, ADRs, REITs, closed-end funds, and unit offers. All SEOs are listed on CRSP for at least 6 months, and after Nasdaq's inclusion, are listed within 6 months of going public. Returns are measured through December 31, 2001. For partial event-years that end on this date, the last partial year is deleted from the computations. In other words, for an SEO that issued on March 15, 2000, it's first-year return is included, but not the second-year return.

Table 2
Evidence on the long-run performance of SEOs, measured using buy-and-hold returns[a]

Study	Horizon, weighting[b]	Sample size	Sample period	Mean buy-and-hold return		Annualized difference
				SEOs	Matching	
USA data						
Mitchell & Stafford[c]	3 yr (EW)	4439	1961–1993	34.8%	45.0%	−2.7%
Eckbo, Masulis & Norli[d]	5 yr (EW)	3315	1964–1995	44.3%	67.5%	−4.8%
Jegadeesh[e]	5 yr (EW)	2992	1970–1993	59.4%	93.6%	−4.9%
Spiess & Affleck-Graves[f]	5 yr (EW)	1247	1975–1989	55.7%	98.1%	−6.1%
Brav, Geczy & Gompers[g]	5 yr (EW)	3775	1975–1992	57.6%	83.9%	−3.9%
Mitchell & Stafford[c]	3 yr (VW)	4439	1961–1993	41.1%	45.3%	−1.1%
Eckbo, Masulis & Norli[d]	5 yr (VW)	3315	1964–1995	51.6%	62.2%	−2.2%
Brav, Geczy & Gompers[g]	5 yr (VW)	3775	1975–1992	72.5%	97.5%	−3.4%
Japanese data						
Cai & Loughran[h]	5 yr (EW)	1389	1971–1992	74.1%	103.2%	−3.5%

continued on next page

as firm performance fails to live up to optimistic expectations. By year five, however, the abnormal returns are close to zero, suggesting that the underperformance does not persist forever.

Most of the empirical literature concerning the long-run performance of SEOs has used two procedures: buy-and-hold returns and 3-factor regressions. The results of studies using buy-and-hold returns with a style benchmark are reported in Table 2.[3]

Mitchell and Stafford have the lowest abnormal performance, which is presumably attributable to their sample being relatively intensive in utilities and SEOs listed on the New York Stock Exchange (NYSE) from the 1960s and early 1970s. Mitchell and Stafford (2000) report that the only issuers that underperform are small value firms. By contrast, Jegadeesh (2000) reports that it is growth firms among the issuers that

---

[3] Jegadeesh (2000) and Brav, Geczy and Gompers (2000) also adjust for momentum, in addition to size and book-to-market, with qualitatively unchanged results.

Table 2, notes

[a] The numbers reported in this table for matching firms are all based on size and book-to-market matching ("style" benchmarks). Most authors use buy-and-hold returns on individual stocks for their benchmarks, although some, such as Brav, Geczy and Gompers (2000), use portfolios and rebalance their benchmark monthly and then compound the monthly average returns. All of the benchmarks delete issuing firms from the universe of potential matches.

[b] EW is equally weighted, and VW is value weighted.

[c] For Mitchell and Stafford (2000, Table III) the compounded annual return difference of 2.7% assumes a 3.0 year mean holding period (they reinvest early delistings in an index). Their sample period is July 1961–December 1993 and they include utilities. The annualized difference is calculated as $[R_i^{\text{inverse}T} - R_b^{\text{inverse}T}] \times 100\%$ where R_i is the average gross buy-and-hold return on the issuing firms, R_b is the average gross compounded return on the benchmark, and inverse$T$ is the reciprocal of the average holding period length. For Mitchell and Stafford, R_i is 1.348, and the annualized difference is calculated as 1.348 to the 1/3 power minus 1.450 to the 1/3 power, and then converted to a percentage.

[d] Eckbo, Masulis and Norli (2000, Table 3, excluding utilities) truncate a firm's return if and when it conducts a subsequent SEO. The compounded difference in returns of 4.8% assumes a 3.5 year mean holding period.

[e] For Jegadeesh (2000, Table 2), a 4.5 year mean holding period is assumed, giving a compounded difference in returns of 4.8% per year for his sample period of 1977–1994, with returns truncated at Dec. 31, 1997.

[f] For Spiess and Affleck-Graves (1995, Table 3), a 4.5 year average holding period is assumed. They restrict their sample of SEOs to pure primary issues (offers where only the firm is selling shares), unlike the other studies, which include combination offers where both the firm and existing shareholders sell shares in the SEO.

[g] For Brav, Geczy and Gompers (2000, Table 3, Panel A), the compounded difference in annualized returns assumes a 4.5 year mean holding period. Their sample period is from 1975–1992, with returns ending on December 31, 1995, and includes utilities.

[h] For Cai and Loughran (1998, Table 2, Panel A), where Tokyo Stock Exchange-listed firms are used, the annualized difference is computed assuming a 5.0 year holding period, since very few of the sample firms delist early.

have the worst subsequent performance, and that large firms as well as small growth stocks underperform.

As discussed by Barber and Lyon (1997), Kothari and Warner (1997), Lyon, Barber and Tsai (1999), Brav (2000), and others, unbiased statistical significance levels are difficult to compute using buy-and-hold returns. Consequently, starting with Loughran and Ritter (1995), the long-run returns literature has commonly used 3-factor time-series regressions, introduced by Fama and French (1993), of the form

$$r_{pt} - r_{ft} = a + b(r_{mt} - r_{ft}) + s\text{SMB}_t + v\text{VMG}_t + e_{pt}, \tag{1}$$

where $r_{pt} - r_{ft}$ is the excess return over the risk-free rate on a portfolio in time period t, $r_{mt} - r_{ft}$ is the realization of the market risk premium in period t, SMB_t is the return on a portfolio of Small stocks Minus the return on a portfolio of Big stocks in period t, and VMG_t is the return on a portfolio of Value stocks Minus the return on a portfolio of Growth stocks in period t. Value and growth are measured using book-to-market ratios, and VMG is denoted HML in the literature (High book-to-market (value) Minus Low book-to-market (growth) stocks). The intercepts from these regressions are interpreted

Table 3
Equally weighted and value-weighted intercepts of Equation (1) on USA SEOs[a]

Studies	Sample size	Equally-weighted intercepts[b]	Value-weighted intercepts[b]
Mitchell and Stafford (2000, Table 9)[c], including utilities (July 1961–December 1993)	4911	−0.33 (−5.19)	−0.03 (−0.44)
Mitchell and Stafford (2000, Table 9)[c], excluding utilities (July 1961–December 1993)	3842	−0.37 (−5.58)	0.06 (0.77)
Eckbo, Masulis and Norli (2000, Table 10, Panel C), excluding utilities (March 1964–December 1997), Amex/NYSE only	1704	−0.12 (−0.65)	−0.17 (−1.12)
Eckbo, Masulis and Norli (2000, Table 10, Panel C), excluding utilities (February 1974–December 1997), Nasdaq only	2147	−0.42 (−2.37)	−0.12 (−0.19)
Jegadeesh (2000, Table IV)[d], (January 1975–December 1995)	2992	−0.45 (−5.07)	−0.33 (−2.84)
Loughran and Ritter (2000, Table 7)[e,g], (January 1973–December 1996)	6461	−0.47 (−5.42)	−0.32 (−3.00)
Loughran and Ritter (2000, Table 7)[e,g], purged (January 1973–December 1996)	6461	−0.61 (−6.08)	−0.35 (−3.38)
Brav, Geczy and Gompers (2000, Table 6)[f,g] (January 1976–December 1995)	4526	−0.37 (−4.81)	−0.14 (−1.36)
Brav, Geczy and Gompers (2000, Table 6)[f,g], purged (January 1976–December 1995)	4526	−0.40 (−4.65)	−0.17 (−1.63)

[a] A coefficient of −0.33 represents underperformance of 33 basis points per month, or −3.96% per year before compounding.
[b] *T*-statistics are in parentheses.
[c] Mitchell and Stafford use issuing firms from 1958–1993 and keep a firm in the portfolio for five years after issuing. Monthly returns from July 1961 through December 1993 are used in their regressions.
[d] Jegadeesh uses SEOs from 1970 to 1994, and keeps a firm in the portfolio for five years after issuing. The VW results that are reported for Jegadeesh are his EW "large firm" results.
[e] Loughran and Ritter use issuing firms from 1970–1996, and keep a firm in the portfolio for three years after issuing. They exclude utilities from their issuer portfolio.
[f] Brav, Geczy and Gompers use issuing firms from 1975–1992, and keep a firm in the portfolio for five years after issuing.
[g] The purged and unpurged numbers refer to whether the size and book-to-market factors are constructed exclusive (purged) or inclusive (unpurged) of firms that have issued equity within the prior five years.

as abnormal returns. In Table 3, the intercepts (and *t*-statistics) reported in various studies of abnormal performance following SEOs are listed.

Comparing the numbers in Tables 2 and 3, the results seem somewhat sensitive to what time period is examined, and what sample selection criteria are used. Evidence shows that SEOs from the heavy-volume period of 1970–1972 did very poorly in the bear market of 1973–1974, and failed to recover in the small stock rally of 1975–

1976. The Loughran and Ritter (1995, 2000) studies, as well as this chapter's Table 1, include these SEOs from the early 1970s in the post-issue returns, whereas Jegadeesh (2000), Eckbo, Masulis and Norli (2000), and Brav, Geczy and Gompers (2000) exclude them.[4] Thus, in January 1976, the Brav, Geczy, and Gompers issuing firm portfolio only includes issuing firms from 1975, whereas the Loughran and Ritter portfolio includes equity issuers from 1971–1975, including over 500 issuers listed, or subsequently listed, on Nasdaq. Issuing firms also did especially poorly during the bursting of the tech stock bubble in 2000. Thus, the different abnormal return estimates from various studies that are reported in Table 3, where the same methodology is used in every study, are largely due to differing sample periods. The Eckbo, Masulis and Norli finding of minimal abnormal returns after SEOs can partly be attributable to high returns on a small number of NYSE-listed issuing firms in the 1960s, which have a large impact on their conclusions, for these studies weight each period equally.[5]

This sensitivity of the performance results to the sample period used is not unique to issuing companies. Two of the best-known empirical patterns in finance are that growth stocks tend to underperform value stocks and that small firms outperform large firms [Fama and French (1992), Davis, Fama and French (2000)]. But if 1975–1982 is excluded, the "small firm" effect disappears, and if the sample period includes just 1983–1999, small firms underperform. In the 1990s, large growth firms had higher returns than any other style category. So just as the size and book-to-market effects vary across subperiods, it should be no surprise that the relative performance of issuing firms varies in different subperiods.

2.3. Reasons for underperformance

The evidence on the long-run performance of firms conducting SEOs is that issuing firms have relatively low returns in the 3–5 years after issuing. A number of

---

[4] Eckbo, Masulis and Norli (2000) exclude Nasdaq-listed issuers prior to 1974. Mitchell and Stafford (2000) exclude Nasdaq-listed issuers prior to 1973. Nasdaq started in February 1971, but CRSP does not start covering Nasdaq stocks until December 1972.

[5] Eckbo, Masulis and Norli (2000) find that large firms conducting SEOs in the 1960s subsequently outperformed a multifactor benchmark. Their sample excludes SEOs by Nasdaq firms prior to 1974, and includes only a small portion of Amex-NYSE issuers in the 1960s and early 1970s, apparently because their sample for this period required *Wall Street Journal* announcement dates when it was originally constructed. Their sample period is 32 years long (1964–1995), but over 80% of their sample is from the second half. In 1964–1979, 53% of their issuers are utilities, whereas in 1980–1995, only 13% are utilities. Because they do not include many SEOs from the 1960s, the portfolio for their multifactor regressions is frequently tiny when utility firms are excluded (Tables 6, 8, 9 and 10). For example, in November 1964, they have only four firms in the portfolio. In November 1965, the portfolio has increased to only ten firms, and a year after that, it has only 19 firms. In November 1967, only 23 firms are present. By contrast, some months in the 1980s and 1990s have close to 1000 firms in their issuer portfolio. While they adjust the standard errors for the resulting heteroscedasticity, the coefficient estimates weight each period equally.

Table 4
Multi-factor regressions[a] with an equally-weighted portfolio of USA SEOs, January 1973–December 2000

	a	b_t	b_{t-1}	s_t	v_t	R^2
(1)[b]	−0.52 (−2.84)	1.37 (34.65)				78.2%
(2)[b]	−0.60 (−3.28)	1.36 (35.16)	0.14 (3.60)			78.9%
(3)[b]	−0.52 (−5.53)	1.20 (53.43)		0.89 (30.87)	−0.01 (−0.36)	94.6%

[a] All regressions use 336 observations where the dependent variable is the monthly percentage return on a portfolio of SEOs that have gone public during the prior 36 months. A coefficient of −0.52 represents underperformance of 52 basis points per month, or −6.24% per year before compounding. The explanatory variables are described on p. 269.
[b] *T*-statistics are in parentheses.

explanations have been advanced for these low returns. These ideas also apply to IPOs, where the empirical evidence on long-run underperformance is discussed in Section 4 of this chapter.

One possibility is that the underperformance of issuing firms may be just a manifestation of a misspecified model for what the returns should have been. Fama (1998) refers to this as the "bad model" problem. Eckbo, Masulis and Norli (2000), for example, present evidence that a 6-factor asset-pricing model can explain the performance of issuing firms. They argue that the decreased leverage associated with an equity issue lowers the sensitivity of the stock price to inflation shocks, and the extra shares outstanding make the stock more liquid. In general, they argue that issuing firms have low risk as a result of the equity issue, and therefore should have low returns.

This raises the question of just how risky companies conducting SEOs really are. Fama–French (1993) 3-factor regressions typically find that SEOs have near-average systematic risk, a high sensitivity to the size factor, but a surprisingly modest sensitivity to the book-to-market factor. This presents a misleading picture, however.

Table 4 reports several single-factor and multifactor regressions. None of the factors are purged of issuing firms, so the intercepts underestimate the degree of abnormal performance. Row (1) reports a simple one-factor regression where the intercept is the "Jensen alpha". The intercept is a statistically significant negative 52 basis points per month. Row (2) includes a lagged market excess return, which is highly significant. Summing the contemporaneous and lagged betas [see Fama and French (1992) for another paper using this procedure] gives a systematic risk estimate of 1.50, which shows that SEOs expose investors to a high degree of market risk.

Row (3) of Table 4 reports Fama–French 3-factor regression coefficients. The estimate of systematic risk is 1.20, considerably lower than the 1.50 value of the summed betas in row (2). The reason for this difference is that the size factor catches some of the systematic risk. Small stocks tend to have higher betas than big stocks, so SMB tends to have a positive factor return in rising markets. In other words, SMB is not orthogonal to the market excess return. Indeed, if one runs regression (2) with

SMB as the *dependent* variable, the summed beta is 0.33. That is, small stocks expose an investor to a beta that is 0.33 higher than large stocks do. Since issuing firms tend to underrepresent the largest stocks, part of the high level of systematic risk that they expose an investor to is captured by the size effect.

Market efficiency requires that, if one uses the appropriate benchmark, there should be no abnormal returns on average after an event. As Loughran and Ritter (2000) point out, tests of market efficiency are always joint tests of a (theoretically motivated) model of market equilibrium and the existence of abnormal returns. Since matching by size and book-to-market is empirically motivated, rather than theoretically motivated, the abnormal returns reported in Tables 1–4 are not evidence for or against market efficiency. Still, it is hard to imagine that the relatively low post-issue returns on issuing firms can be attributed to low risk, since row (2) of Table 4 shows that issuing firms expose investors to a very high level of systematic risk.

Eckbo, Masulis and Norli (2000) argue that the decreased leverage after an equity issue lowers the systematic risk of equity issuers. Denis and Kadlec (1994), however, report that once various statistical biases are accounted for, there is no change in the equity beta for issuing firms, even though theoretically there should be a change if operating risk doesn't change. It is, however, entirely conceivable that lower leverage is more than offset by increased operating risk, if issuing companies embark on aggressive expansion plans with the money raised in an SEO.

Another possible explanation of the negative abnormal returns on issuers is that the findings are just due to chance, possibly because a few industries that had heavy issuance activity failed to live up to expectations. Although the sample sizes involve thousands of firms, the number of independent observations is considerably smaller. In Table 5 of Section 3, however, it is shown that over a wide variety of corporate financing-related events, there is a persistent pattern of underreaction. Thus, the chance explanation requires not only that SEOs just happened to underperform, but that underreaction just happened to occur in a large variety of other events.

Jung, Kim and Stulz (1996) examine a number of explanations for the decision to issue equity or debt. They interpret their evidence on debt and equity issues as consistent with an agency model. In particular, firms that issue equity when they could apparently issue debt have more negative announcement returns, the lower is their market-to-book ratio. The agency explanation is that managers will tend to squander corporate resources if given the opportunity, although this may not be intentional.

Another possibility is that investors and managers are systematically overoptimistic at the time of issue. After all, for most of the issuers, good things have been happening to the stock price in the year prior to issue. Issuers tend to be firms that have recently outperformed other firms in their industry, which in turn has outperformed the market, in a rising market. Profitability is increasing [Loughran and Ritter (1997)]. As Heaton (2002) notes, managers tend to be too optimistic, which then leads to a tendency to overinvest. Worse, competitors may be overinvesting, too, resulting in decreasing profit margins in the years after issuing. In general, managers of issuing firms act as if they are very confident about the prospects of their firms [Lee (1997)]. In their study of Tokyo Stock Exchange-listed firms conducting SEOs and convertible bond issues, Kang, Kim and Stulz (1999) report post-issue underperformance of the same magnitude as for the USA. The underperformance is present whether it is a private placement or a public issue. They interpret their evidence as consistent with the managerial overoptimism hypothesis.

Insight regarding whether investors are systematically disappointed in the post-issue performance of SEOs can be gained by examining the market reaction to earnings announcements. This has been done by Jegadeesh (2000) and Denis and Sarin (2001), who report that there are economically significant negative earnings announcement effects from the second quarter after the SEO until at least three years later. While this evidence does not identify the cause of the disappointment, it suggests that a misspecification of the model of expected returns is unlikely to be the sole cause of measured underperformance.

A less innocuous explanation for low post-issue returns is that issuing firms either intentionally or unintentionally manipulate their earnings prior to the SEO. Consistent with this hypothesis, the issuing firms that are most aggressive in their use of accruals to boost earnings have the worst subsequent performance [Rangan (1998) and Teoh, Welch and Wong (1998)].

In sum, the evidence suggests that both managers and investors are systematically too optimistic about the prospects of issuing firms when equity issues occur. If the market learns, this would predict that equity issue announcement effects should be more negative than they historically have been. There is no evidence, however, that this is occurring.

If firms are able to issue overvalued equity, the whole logic of the Myers and Majluf (1984) rationale for the reluctance of firms to issue equity is thrown into question. The Myers and Majluf model is based on the assumption that opportunities to issue overvalued equity are not present. Graham and Harvey (2001) present survey evidence from corporate executives that perceived misvaluations and recent stock price runups are among the most important determinants of the decision to issue equity. If firms can in fact issue overvalued equity, at least at certain times, then a new "windows of opportunity" model of capital structure is in need of development. Baker and Wurgler (2002) document that a firm's capital structure is strongly related to past market valuations, suggesting that capital structure is a cumulative outcome of past attempts to time the equity market.

3. Short-run and long-run reactions to corporate financing activities

Table 5 summarizes the empirical evidence on the short-run and long-run reaction to various corporate financing actions. This table is analogous to Table 1 in Fama (1998). The tables differ, however, in that Fama includes a variety of announcements having nothing to do with cash flows or corporate financing. [6] Underreaction is present when the abnormal returns in the announcement and post-announcement periods are the same. Overreaction occurs when the abnormal returns in the announcement period and the post-issue announcement period differ, and the announcement abnormal return is bigger in magnitude than the totality of the post-announcement abnormal returns. Misreaction occurs when the announcement and post-announcement returns are of opposite sign and the announcement effect is smaller than the totality of the post-announcement abnormal returns. Fama groups misreactions and overreactions together, and argues that the empirical evidence is as likely to show overreaction as underreaction.

The patterns in Table 5, however, show a tendency toward underreaction. That is, negative announcement effects tend to be followed by negative long-run abnormal returns, and positive announcement effects tend to be followed by positive long-run abnormal returns. This is true with USA SEOs, convertible bonds, bonds, open-market share repurchases, cash-financed acquisitions, and stock-financed acquisitions. The only apparent exceptions are Japanese SEOs, equity carveouts, private placements of equity, bank loans, and dividend decreases, where there are misreactions. There is no evidence of overreaction.

In general, the patterns suggest that corporate actions that use cash enhance shareholder value, and corporate actions that raise cash lower shareholder value. This pattern was first discussed by Smith (1986), but the magnitude of the effect is underestimated if one focuses only on announcement returns. The pattern is consistent with tendencies towards empire building by managers (investment in negative net present value projects) that are not fully anticipated by the market.

Kadiyala and Rau (2003) present evidence that significantly negative long-term abnormal returns are present only in subsamples of firms announcing after negative prior information (such as negative earnings surprises). Similarly, they report that long-run positive abnormal returns are present only in subsamples with prior positive information (such as positive earnings surprises). Thus, the assumption that the market efficiently impounds the information conveyed by a corporate financing action at the announcement must be called into question.

If the market is systematically underreacting to the information conveyed by corporate financing announcements, why don't arbitrageurs take advantage of the opportunity to make abnormal profits? As Shleifer and Vishny (1997) argue, "arbitrage" is in fact risky. As an example, think about the risks associated with shorting issuing firms, if one is of the opinion that firms that issue equity are overvalued. In the late 1990s, the firms that issued stock in the USA were

---

[6] Among the events that have been studied that are not corporate financing-related are insider trading, stock splits, and analyst buy and sell recommendations. Fama does not list all of these. Studies of these events have found underreaction. Studies that have found different signs for the announcement and long-term abnormal returns include those of listing changes (from Nasdaq to the NYSE, for instance) and proxy fights. Fama's table includes IPOs, classifying the first-day return as an announcement effect.

Table 5

Equally-weighted short-run and long-run reactions to corporate financing activities

Action	Study	Sample size	Sample period	Abnormal returns [a] Announcement effect	Annualized long-run performance
USA data					
Seasoned equity offerings [b]	Bayless and Chaplinsky	1884	1974–90	−2.3%	n.a.
	Heron and Lie	3658	1980–98	−2.5%	n.a.
	Clarke, Dunbar and Kahle	3092	1984–96	−1.7%	−5.5%
	Table 1 (p. 267)	6638	1970–00	n.a.	−3.4%
Equity carveouts [c]	Vijh (parent)	336	1980–97	+1.9%	n.a.
	Vijh (parent)	300	1981–95	n.a.	−1.9%
	Vijh (subsidiary)	628	1981–95	n.a.	+3.1%
Private placements of equity [d]	Hertzel et al.	591	1980–96	+2.4%	−8.2%
Convertible bonds [e]	Kim and Stulz	270	1970–87	−1.7%	n.a.
	Lee and Loughran	986	1975–90	n.a.	−3.9%
	Eckbo, Masulis and Norli	459	1964–95	n.a.	−2.8%
	Spiess and Affleck-Graves	400	1975–89	n.a.	−6.3%
	McLaughlin et al.	828	1980–93	n.a.	−3.1%
Investment grade	Lee and Loughran	247	1975–90	n.a.	−2.3%
Junk	Lee and Loughran	566	1975–90	n.a.	−5.2%
Bonds [f]	Jung, Kim and Stulz	276	1977–84	−0.1%	n.a.
	Howton, Howton and Perfect	937	1983–93	−0.5%	n.a.
	Eckbo, Masulis and Norli	981	1964–95	n.a.	−2.0%
	Spiess and Affleck-Graves	392	1975–89	n.a.	−1.9%
Bank loans [g]	Billett et al.	1306	1980–89	+0.6%	−7.9%
Open market repurchases [h]	Guay and Harford	1062	1981–93	+2.1%	n.a.
	Ikenberry et al.	1239	1980–90	+3.5%	+1.9%
	Mitchell and Stafford	2292	1961–93	n.a.	+3.4%

continued on next page

Table 5, *continued*

Action	Study	Sample size	Sample period	Abnormal returns[a] Announcement effect	Annualized long-run performance
M&A (acquirer)[i]					
Cash-financed	Travlos	100	1972–81	+0.2%	n.a.
	Loughran and Vijh	314	1970–89	n.a.	+2.4%
	Mitchell and Stafford	1039	1961–93	n.a.	+1.6%
Stock-financed	Travlos	60	1972–81	−1.5%	n.a.
	Loughran and Vijh	405	1970–89	n.a.	−3.5%
	Mitchell and Stafford	1029	1961–93	n.a.	−2.2%
Dividend changes[j]					
Decreases	Grullon et al.	677	1967–93	−3.7%	+1.7%
Substantial increases	Grullon et al.	3287	1967–93	+1.3%	+4.5%
	Guay and Harford	2943	1981–93	+1.2%	n.a.
International data[k]					
Japanese SEOs	Kang, Kim and Stulz	888	1980–88	+1.2%	−9.8%
ADR SEOs	Foerster and Karolyi	151	1982–96	n.a.	−3.2%

[a] n.a., not available. For announcement effects, a 2-day or 3-day window is typically reported. For long-run performance, the annualized difference is calculated as $[R_i^{inverseT} - R_b^{inverseT}] \times 100\%$ where R_i is the average gross buy-and-hold return on the issuing firms, R_b is the average gross compounded return on the benchmark, and $inverseT$ is the reciprocal of the average holding period length. For example, a 50% buy-and-hold return over 4.0 years is converted to an annualized 10.7% by taking 1.50 to the $\frac{1}{4}$ power, and then converting to a percentage return. Unless otherwise reported, for the long-run performance numbers, the benchmark is a size- and book-to-market matched (style-matched) sample.

[b] Bayless and Chaplinsky (1996, Table 1). Heron and Lie (2003, Table 2) using a weighted average of primary and mixed offerings. Clarke, Dunbar and Kahle (2001, Table 2) for announcement and long-run returns. They report a 3-year buy-and-hold abnormal return of −14.3%. Annualized abnormal returns have been calculated assuming a 2.7 year average holding period.

[c] Vijh (2002, Table 4) for announcement returns, and Vijh (1999, Table 4) for long-run returns. An equity carveout is an IPO of a subsidiary that remains partly owned by the parent corporation. For the long-run returns, the geometric means of the average annual excess return with respect to a style benchmark are used.

continued on next page

Table 5, notes

d Hertzel, Lemmon, Linck and Rees (2002, Tables I + II) use Amex, Nasdaq, and NYSE firms conducting private placements and report 3-year buy-and-hold returns. Annualized abnormal returns have been calculated assuming a 2.7 year average holding period.

e Kim and Stulz (1992, Table 3) for domestic issues. Lee and Loughran (1998, Tables 2 + 3) use Amex, Nasdaq, and NYSE issuers and report annual returns in the five post-issue years. For the investment grade/junk returns, where only buy-and-hold returns are reported, annualized returns have been calculated assuming a 4.5 year average holding period. Eckbo, Masulis and Norli (2000, Table 12) use Amex and NYSE issuers, and report 5-year buy-and-hold returns. A 4.0 year average holding period is assumed to annualize their buy-and-hold returns. Spiess and Affleck-Graves (1999, Table 3) use Amex, NYSE, and Nasdaq issuers, excluding utilities and financial institutions, and report 5-year buy-and-hold returns. A 4.5 year average holding period is assumed to calculated annualized returns. McLaughlin, Saffieddine and Vasudevan (1998, Table 5) report 3-year buy-and-hold returns. A 3.0 year average holding period is assumed to calculate annualized returns.

f Jung, Kim and Stulz (1996, Table 1) also report long-run returns, but only using a size benchmark. Howton, Howton and Perfect (1998, Table 2) where the day −1 and 0 abnormal returns are added. Lee and Loughran (1998, Table 2) use Amex, Nasdaq, and NYSE issuers, and report annual returns in the 5 post-issue years. Eckbo, Masulis and Norli (2000, Table 12) use Amex and NYSE issuers, and report 5-year buy-and-hold returns. A 4.0 year average holding period is assumed. Spiess and Affleck-Graves (1999, Table 3) use Amex, Nasdaq, and NYSE issuers, excluding utilities and financial institutions, and report 5-year buy-and-hold returns. A 4.5 year average holding period is assumed to calculate annualized returns. Billett, Flannery and Garfinkel (2001, Tables I + III) report 5-year buy-and-hold returns. A 4.5 year average holding period is assumed to calculate annualized returns.

g Guay and Harford (2000, Table 2) report announcement period returns. Ikenberry, Lakonishok and Vermaelen (1995, Table 2) for announcement effects, and Table 3 for annualized long-run performance. Mitchell and Stafford (2000, Table 4) report 3-year buy-and-hold returns. A 3.0 year holding period is assumed.

h Guay and Harford (2000, Table 2) report announcement period returns. Ikenberry, Lakonishok and Vermaelen (1995, Table 2) for announcement effects, and Table 3 for annualized long-run performance. Mitchell and Stafford (2000, Table 4) report 3-year buy-and-hold returns. A 3.0 year holding period is assumed.

i Mergers and acquisitions. Travlos (1987, Table III) uses a 2-day announcement return. Loughran and Vijh (1997, Table II) where their style-matched buy-and-hold returns have been annualized assuming a 4.5 year holding period. Mitchell and Stafford (2000, Table 2) report 3-year buy-and-hold returns. A 3.0 year holding period is assumed.

j Grullon, Michaely and Swaminathan (2002, Table 11) report 3-year buy-and-hold excess returns for Amex and NYSE firms changing their dividends. The raw buy-and-hold returns, supplied by the authors, have been annualized to compute the annual abnormal return. A 34-month average holding period has been assumed. The dividend increases are between 12.5% and 500%. Guay and Harford (2000, Table 2) report announcement period returns for Amex, Nasdaq, and NYSE firms. A substantial dividend increase is a bigger dividend increase than the prior year.

k Kang, Kim and Stulz (1999, Table 4, Panel B) report the difference in buy-and-hold returns ("excess returns") between issuers and style-matched nonissuers, after deleting the bottom and top 5% of excess returns. Annualized return differences have been computed by taking a weighted average of the private, public, and rights 5-year excess returns of −65.41%, assuming that the average buy-and-hold return for nonissuers was 100% and for issuers 34.59%. These buy-and-hold returns are then annualized, assuming a 4.5 year average holding period, and the difference in annualized returns is reported. The announcement return has N = 68 from Table 6. Foerster and Karolyi (2000, Table 3) report an average 36-month buy-and-hold return of 14.27%, and an average style-adjusted return of −10.97%, for foreign firms issuing American Depository Receipts (ADRs) in the USA for which a local market size and book-to-market matched firm was available.

disproportionately technology and telecommunications firms. From October 1998 to February 2000, these stocks greatly outperformed the market. Even if one hedged industry risk by going long in such firms as Hewlett-Packard, IBM, and AT&T, the issuing firms greatly outperformed the nonissuing firms by enormous amounts for month after month. Of course, in the long run the arbitrageur would have been right, as the issuing firms underperformed by an enormous amount in the two years beginning in March 2000. But few arbitrageurs have the ability to maintain their positions due to limited capital, and the limited patience of their investors, when they underperform by enormous amounts for month after month.

In empirical work examining the market reaction to corporate financing activities, it has been common to separate utilities and financial stocks from firms in other industries. The rationale has been that utilities were regulated, and many of their actions were highly predictable. Furthermore, in the 1970s utilities were tremendously overrepresented among firms raising external capital. Due to the deregulation of electrical and gas utilities in the late 1990s, and telecommunication firms in the 1980s, this industry segmentation presumably will not be done in future empirical work using samples from the late 1990s and later. In foreign markets, there were relatively few utilities that were not government owned before the 1990s, and thus few were publicly traded.

4. Initial public offerings (IPOs)

4.1. Overview

Ibbotson and Ritter (1995), Ritter (1998) and Ritter and Welch (2002) survey the IPO literature, focusing on three empirical patterns that have generated a large academic literature. These three patterns are i) short-run underpricing; ii) cycles in the number of IPOs and in the average first-day returns; and iii) long-run underperformance. This chapter will focus on several other aspects as well: why firms go public, mechanism design, the compensation of investment bankers and the role of analyst coverage, stabilization activities, and the variation in IPO volume across countries. Jenkinson and Ljungqvist (2001) cover these topics in book-length detail.

Pagano, Panetta and Zingales (1998) ask "Why do firms go public"? There are many tradeoffs, but the literature does not have a full model that can explain i) at what stage of a firm's lifecycle it is optimal to go public; and ii) why the volume of IPOs varies dramatically across time and across countries. In other words, private firms seem to face both life-cycle considerations and market-timing considerations in the decision of when to go public. The market-condition considerations can be viewed as time-varying relative costs of debt versus equity and private versus public funding costs.

When a firm goes public, its ownership structure changes, and as a public firm, the pre-issue shareholders are able to sell their shares (subject to regulations and lock-up provisions) in the future, allowing them to cash out if they so desire. Thus, undiversified portfolios become more liquid. Corporate control considerations are present, too [Zingales (1995)]. If a startup firm has been financed by venture capitalists, typically the VCs have at least partial control over the entrepreneurs. Black and Gilson (1998) argue that, by going public, the entrepreneurs are able to regain control as the VCs distribute the shares to the limited partners (the investors in the VC partnership). If a firm has a large "need" for external capital, public markets may be a cheaper source of funds because of the lack of a liquidity discount that investors in a private firm would demand [see Chemmanur and Fulghieri (1999)]. Alternatively, public market investors may be irrationally overoptimistic about an industry's prospects at some point. Firms take advantage of these "windows of opportunity" by issuing stock at these times [see Lerner (1994) for evidence on private vs. public financing in the biotech industry].

Because of the uncertainties about future cash flows, especially for young firms, the valuation of IPOs is difficult. Consequently, underwriters frequently use comparable firm multiples to come up with a preliminary price, or price range, to value a firm going public. The logic of comparable firm multiples is that if a similar firm sells at a price-to-earnings multiple of 20, and the firm going public has $2 million in earnings, then it should be valued at $40 million. In practice, underwriters typically use forecasts of the current or next year's numbers, rather than historical accounting numbers, in their multiples [Kim and Ritter (1999)]. Depending upon the industry, the multiples used include price-to-earnings, enterprise value-to-sales, enterprise value-to-EBITDA (earnings before interest, taxes, and depreciation and amortization), and industry-specific multiples. Enterprise value is defined as the market value of equity plus the book value of debt, representing unlevered firm value.

Purnanandam and Swaminathan (2002) examine the pricing of IPOs using comparable firms, and find that on average IPOs have an offer price 50% higher than predicted on the basis of industry peers. While this finding may be attributable to the higher expected growth of IPOs, their more interesting finding is that the more overpriced the IPO is relative to its comparables, the worse is the long-term performance.

In using comparable firm multiples, one factor that is typically not taken into account is the size of the public float. That is, if a scarcity premium exists, then the smaller the fraction of the shares outstanding that are not closely held, the higher the price should be. In other words, if the supply of shares to the public is smaller, the demand for the stock will result in a higher price. At this point, the academic literature is devoid of direct tests to see whether this is in fact a relevant valuation factor, although the negative stock returns when lockup provisions expire is consistent with the notion that the size of the public float does matter.

Given the fixed costs of going public and maintaining a liquid market, an IPO should be big enough so that there is sufficient liquidity in the public market. But the offer should be small enough so that the issuing firm does not raise more cash than it can profitably use. This leads to the concept of staged financing, as discussed by, among others, Mayers (1998). If an offer is too big there may be free cash flow problems, where funds are squandered. A closely related idea is the notion that abandonment options are valuable. That is, the optimal financing of a young firm with an uncertain future is to provide it with a limited amount of money at each stage of financing. As this money is about to run out, at each stage financiers can decide whether to provide more funds, and on what terms. If the firm's prospects continually live up to optimistic scenarios, the original shareholders can retain a larger percentage of the equity because subsequent rounds of financing are raised at ever-higher prices.

4.2. Short-run underpricing of IPOs

On average, the closing market price on the first day of trading of an IPO is higher than the offer price. In every country with a stock market, IPOs are underpriced. Table 6 reports the extent of underpricing for 38 countries. All of the average first-day returns weight each IPO equally. Thus, privatizations of state-owned enterprises with very large proceeds have less of an impact than if proceeds-weighted averages were reported.[7]

4.3. Alternative mechanisms for pricing and allocating securities

Loughran, Ritter and Rydqvist (1994) and Chowdhry and Sherman (1996) document that the average first-day return varies systematically with the mechanism used to price and distribute IPOs. The highest average first-day returns come in countries where government regulators impose formulas based on accounting information for setting the offer price, although the frequency of these constraints is declining. In general, the mechanisms used for pricing and allocating IPOs can be categorized as auctions, fixed-price offers, or book-building. Although different prices are sometimes paid by different investors (for example, sometimes individual investors pay less than institutional investors), uniform price mechanisms in which every investor pays the same price are most common.

In auctions, a market-clearing, or slightly below market-clearing, price is set after bids are submitted. Since there is little if any excess demand at the offer price, in general shares are allocated to all successful bidders. A fixed-price offer has the offer price set prior to requests for shares being submitted. If there is excess demand, shares are typically rationed on a pro rata or lottery basis, although frequently requests for large numbers of shares are cut back more than requests for moderate numbers. In other words, if there is discrimination in the allocation of shares, it is normally done solely on the basis of order size. Thus, there is no way for the underwriter to reward investors who provide information. In many countries, with a fixed-price offer investors must submit the money to purchase the requested shares, without knowing whether they will receive many shares. In Hong Kong, for example, the February 2000 offering of tom.com was oversubscribed by 66,900% (669 times the number of shares offered).

---

[7] Megginson and Netter (2001) provide references on the large number of studies concerning privatizations.

282   *J.R. Ritter*

Table 6
Average initial returns for 38 countries[a]

Country	Source[b]	Sample size	Time period	Average initial return
Australia	Lee, Taylor and Walter; Woo	381	1976–1995	12.1%
Austria	Aussenegg	76	1984–1999	6.5%
Belgium	Rogiers, Manigart and Ooghe; Manigart	86	1984–1999	14.6%
Brazil	Aggarwal, Leal and Hernandez	62	1979–1990	78.5%
Canada	Jog and Riding; Jog and Srivastava; Kryzanowski and Rakita	500	1971–1999	6.3%
Chile	Aggarwal, Leal and Hernandez; Celis and Maturana	55	1982–1997	8.8%
China	Datar and Mao; Gu and Qin (A shares)	432	1990–2000	256.9%
Denmark	Jakobsen and Sorensen	117	1984–1998	5.4%
Finland	Keloharju; Westerholm	99	1984–1997	10.1%
France	Husson and Jacquillat; Leleux and Muzyka; Paliard and Belletante; Derrien and Womack; Chahine	571	1983–2000	11.6%
Germany	Ljungqvist	407	1978–1999	27.7%
Greece	Kazantzis and Thomas	129	1987–1994	51.7%
Hong Kong	McGuinness; Zhao and Wu	334	1980–1996	15.9%
India	Krishnamurti and Kumar	98	1992–1993	35.3%
Indonesia	Hanafi	106	1989–1994	15.1%
Israel	Kandel, Sarig and Wohl; Amihud and Hauser	285	1990–1994	12.1%
Italy	Arosio, Giudici and Paleari	164	1985–2000	23.9%
Japan	Fukuda; Dawson and Hiraki; Hebner and Hiraki; Hamao, Packer, and Ritter; Kaneko and Pettway	1689	1970–2001	28.4%
Korea	Dhatt, Kim and Lim; Ihm; Choi and Heo	477	1980–1996	74.3%
Malaysia	Isa; Isa and Yong	401	1980–1998	104.1%
Mexico	Aggarwal, Leal and Hernandez	37	1987–1990	33.0%
Netherlands	Wessels; Eijgenhuijsen and Buijs; Ljungqvist, Jenkinson and Wilhelm	143	1982–1999	10.2%
New Zealand	Vos and Cheung; Camp and Munro	201	1979–1999	23.0%
Nigeria	Ikoku	63	1989–1993	19.1%
Norway	Emilsen, Pedersen and Saettern	68	1984–1996	12.5%
Philippines	Sullivan and Unite	104	1987–1997	22.7%

continued on next page

Table 6, *continued*

Country	Source[b]	Sample size	Time period	Average initial return
Poland	Aussenegg	149	1991–1998	35.6%
Portugal	Almeida and Duque	21	1992–1998	10.6%
Singapore	Lee, Taylor and Walter	128	1973–1992	31.4%
South Africa	Page and Reyneke	118	1980–1991	32.7%
Spain	Ansotegui and Fabregat	99	1986–1998	10.7%
Sweden	Rydqvist	251	1980–1994	34.1%
Switzerland	Kunz and Aggarwal	42	1983–1989	35.8%
Taiwan	Lin and Sheu; Liaw, Liu and Wei	293	1986–1998	31.1%
Thailand	Wethyavivorn and Koo-Smith; Lonkani and Tirapat	292	1987–1997	46.7%
Turkey	Kiymaz	138	1990–1996	13.6%
UK	Dimson; Levis; Ljungqvist	3122	1959–2001	17.4%
USA	Ibbotson, Sindelar and Ritter	14,840	1960–2001	18.4%

[a] Average initial returns are constructed in different manners from study to study, although all weight each IPO equally. In general, in countries where market prices are available immediately after offerings, the one-day raw return (offer price to close) is reported. In countries where there is a delay before unconstrained market prices are reported, market-adjusted returns over an interval of several weeks are reported.
[b] See references listed in Loughran, Ritter and Rydqvist (1994) and updated at http://bear.cba.ufl.edu/ritter/interntl.htm. Where more than one set of authors is listed as a source of information, a combined sample has been constructed.

In general, the longer the time that elapses between when a fixed offer price is set and trading begins, the higher is the average first-day return. Partly this is because the longer the time until completion, the higher is the probability that market conditions will deteriorate and the offering will fail. To reduce the probability of a failed offering, a lower offer price is set. Conditional on the offer succeeding, the expected underpricing is relatively high.

Book-building (also known as firm commitment in the USA) is a mechanism in which underwriters canvas potential buyers and then set an offer price. A key feature of book-building is that the underwriter has complete discretion in allocating shares. As part of the marketing campaign, a road show is usually conducted, in which management makes presentations in order to shift the demand schedule for the company's stock. These presentations are made either to groups of institutional investors or, for very important money managers such as Fidelity, in one-on-one meetings at the offices of the money managers. After stimulating demand, underwriters then try to set an offer price at which there is excess demand and allocate the securities to investors based upon various criteria. Historically, these criteria include attempting to allocate a portion to both institutional and individual investors. Institutional investors who might be expected to buy and hold the securities, based upon their existing portfolio holdings, would be favored. Also, investors who were willing to buy issues when demand was weak would be rewarded with favorable allocations when demand was strong [Cornelli and Goldreich (2001)]. This intertemporal pooling lessens the winner's curse problem (described below), and in equilibrium results in less underpricing than if shares were allocated on a pro rata basis when there is excess demand. There is a dark side to favoritism in the allocation of shares, however.

During the 1999–2000 internet bubble, the average first day return equaled an unprecedented 65% in the USA. During this period, IPOs were increasingly allocated as if they were the reward for providing profitable business to an underwriter. Indeed, in 1999, a number of USA underwriters began to allocate IPOs largely on the basis of commissions paid. In December 2000, *Wall Street Journal* articles [see Smith and Pulliam (2000)] revealed that some institutions were paying commissions of 50 cents per share (compared to a normal 5 cents) on trades of hundreds of thousands of shares in order to get IPOs. Furthermore, some underwriters were allocating shares in part on the basis of commitments to buy additional shares once the stock started trading, a practice known as "laddering" which is explicitly prohibited. Some of these practices have been going on for decades to some degree, but the incidence and magnitudes intensified as the amount of money left on the table exploded in 1999 and 2000 to roughly $30 billion in each year, as contrasted with numbers less than one-tenth that amount in most earlier years. Money left on the table is defined as the number of shares offered multiplied by the increase from the offer price on the first day of trading.

Auctions have been used in many countries, including France, Israel, Japan, Taiwan, and the USA, for pricing and allocating IPOs. In general, auctions have been associated with low, but positive, average first-day returns. These first-day returns are generally lower than when fixed-price offers or book-building is used, as illustrated in Table 7.

It is noteworthy that in Japan auctions continue to be permissible, but after book-building was permitted beginning in 1997, issuers have invariably chosen to use book-building instead. This is true not only for Japan, but for many other countries as well [Sherman (2001)]. In the USA, WRHambrecht and Co. introduced auctions for selling IPOs in 1999. After four years, their market share of IPOs is still below one percent. In France, Table 7 shows that the differences in first-day returns between the different procedures are not as striking as in Japan and Taiwan. This may partly reflect the endogeneity of the contract choice decision, since smaller offers are more likely to use auctions.

Biais and Faugeron (2002), Sherman (2001), and others argue that book-building is a superior mechanism for selling IPOs relative to auctions. Their argument is that book-building can be viewed as a dynamic auction conducted by underwriters, with the advantage that underwriters can use their discretion in allocating shares to reward regular investors who provide reliable information about valuation to the underwriters. However, they do not discuss the tradeoff with agency problems between underwriters

Table 7
Average initial returns on French, Japanese, and Taiwanese IPOs, by selling mechanism

Selling mechanism	Time period	Number of IPOs	Average first-day return
France [a]			
Fixed price	1992–1998	24	8.9%
Auctions	1992–1998	99	9.7%
Bookbuilding	1992–1998	135	16.9%
Japan [b]			
Fixed price	1970–1988	441	32.5%
Auctions	1989–1997	733	14.1%
Bookbuilding	1997–2000	368	43.7%
Taiwan [c]			
Fixed price	1986–1995	241	34.6%
Auctions	1995–1998	52	7.8%

[a] Derrien and Womack (2003, Table 1).
[b] Loughran, Ritter and Rydqvist (1994), Pettway and Kaneko (1996), Hamao, Packer and Ritter (2000) and Kaneko and Pettway (2003), including TSE, Nasdaq-Japan, Mothers, and OTC-listed IPOs.
[c] Lin and Sheu (1997) and Liaw, Liu and Wei (2000, Table VII). The Taiwanese auction average initial return is computed as the closing market price on the first day that price limits are not binding relative to the quantity-weighted average offer price in the discriminatory auction tranche, adjusted for market movements between the auction date and the date of the closing market price. In the IPOs, 50% of the shares are sold in a fixed price offering after the auction has been conducted. This tranche has an average market-adjusted first-day price gain of 22.3%.

and issuers. This tradeoff is analogous to the problem with high-powered compensation contracts for corporate executives: stock options may align the incentives of managers and shareholders, but self-dealing is a problem if a board of directors awards excessive numbers of stock options. At this point, the popularity of book-building relative to auctions has not been fully explained.

In addition to allowing underwriters to reward investors providing information, discretion in allocating shares has another potential use. Stoughton and Zechner (1998) and Mello and Parsons (1998) argue that giving underwriters discretion in allocating IPOs allows the creation of a block, where the blockholder has incentives to monitor the firm that atomistic shareholders do not have. This monitoring provides a positive externality for other shareholders in that firm value is increased due to lessened agency problems between management and shareholders. Brennan and Franks (1997), on the other hand, argue that management has a different objective function. If management values control, creating excess demand in the IPO allows shares to be allocated to atomistic shareholders, entrenching management. Booth and Chua (1996) argue that a large number of small shareholders has a different advantage. With more shareholders, there will be greater liquidity, and if the market values greater liquidity, then a higher share price will result. The empirical evidence suggests that underpricing is not used to allocate shares to a more dispersed investor clientele. Aggarwal, Prabhala and Puri (2002) present evidence that a larger fraction of shares are allocated to institutions when there is greater underpricing.

4.4. Explanations of underpricing

It is useful to think of the IPO process as a game involving three players: issuing firms, investment bankers, and investors. The objectives of the three players are quite different. A number of reasons for the short-run underpricing of IPOs have been advanced which give different weights to the objectives of the three players. In general, these reasons are not mutually exclusive, and their relative importance differs across countries, contractual mechanisms, and time.

4.4.1. Dynamic information acquisition

Investment bankers where book-building is used may underprice IPOs to induce regular investors to reveal information during the pre-selling period, which can then be used to assist in pricing the issue [Benveniste and Spindt (1989)]. Benveniste and Spindt present a model with both regular (informed) and occasional (uninformed) investors. The regular investors can be thought of as institutions, and the occasional investors as individuals. Each regular investor observes private information, which is not known to the issuing firm and its underwriter. Benveniste and Spindt solve a mechanism design problem, and show that state-contingent underpricing and discriminatory allocations are part of the optimal contract, both for a one-time sale and for repeat interactions. Their solution is pricing and allocation rules that closely resemble book-building, with regular investors given favorable allocations in hot issues. In order to induce regular investors to truthfully reveal their valuations, the investment banker compensates investors through underpricing. In order to induce truthful revelation for a given IPO, the investment banker must underprice issues for which favorable information is revealed by more than those for which unfavorable information is revealed. This leads to a prediction that there will only be a partial adjustment of the offer price relative to the file price range contained in the preliminary prospectus. In other words, those IPOs for which the offer price is revised upwards will be *more* underpriced than those for which the offer price is revised downwards. This pattern is in fact present in the data, as shown in Table 8.

4.4.2. Prospect theory

Perhaps the most puzzling aspect of the underpricing phenomenon is that in some circumstances issuers do not object to severe underpricing, even though pre-issue shareholders could have retained a larger fraction of the equity if the same amount

Table 8

IPOs categorized by the final offer price relative to the file price range [a,b], 1980–2001

Time period	IPOs (N)	Average first-day return	Mean first-day returns			% of First-day returns > 0		
			Below	Within	Above	Below	Within	Above
1980–1989	1971	7.4%	0.6%	7.8%	20.5%	32%	62%	88%
1990–1994	1632	11.2%	2.4%	10.8%	24.1%	49%	75%	93%
1995–1998	1752	18.1%	6.1%	13.8%	37.6%	59%	80%	97%
1999–2000	803	65.0%	7.9%	26.8%	119.0%	59%	77%	96%
2001	80	14.0%	7.2%	12.5%	31.4%	70%	83%	92%
1980–2001	6238	18.8%	3.3%	12.0%	52.7%	47%	72%	94%

[a] Ritter and Welch (2002, Tables I + III).
[b] IPOs are categorized by whether the offer price is below, within, or above the original file price range. For example, an IPO would be classified as within the original file price range of $10.00–$12.00 if its offer price is $12.00. Initial public offerings with an offer price below $5.00 per share, unit offers, ADRs, closed-end funds, REITs, bank and S&L IPOs, and those not listed by CRSP within six months of the offer date are excluded.

of money had been raised by selling fewer shares at a higher price. This was most apparent during the internet bubble of 1999 and early 2000, when over a dozen young USA companies agreed to offer prices that resulted in first-day returns exceeding three hundred percent. For example, Akamai Technologies sold 9 million shares at $26.00 per share and saw a first-day closing price of over $145 per share, leaving over $1 billion on the table. At the pricing meeting, their lead underwriter, Morgan Stanley, told the executives of the firm that a market price of over $100 was anticipated. Loughran and Ritter (2002) provide an explanation for this issuer complacency about severe underpricing using prospect theory.

Prospect theory, developed by Kahneman and Tversky (1979), is a descriptive theory of behavior that asserts that people focus on changes in their wealth, rather than the level of their wealth. Loughran and Ritter apply this to IPOs by noting that most of the money left on the table is by the minority of firms where the offer price is revised upwards during the book-building process, consistent with the numbers in Table 8. For these issuing firms, the executives are seeing a personal wealth increase relative to what they had expected based on the file price range, even as they agree to leave money on the table. Loughran and Ritter argue that the issuing firm's executives bargain less hard for a higher offer price in this circumstance than they otherwise do. Unlike the dynamic information acquisition explanation of conditional underpricing, prospect theory does not make a distinction between public information and private information. Thus, prospect theory can explain why offer prices do not fully adjust to market movements during the book-building period, a pattern documented by a number of authors.

Loughran and Ritter also provide an explanation for why underwriters prefer to underprice IPOs rather than charge higher gross spreads. They argue that issuers pay less attention to the opportunity cost of underpricing than the direct cost of gross spreads. If underwriters can allocate underpriced IPOs to buy-side clients who are competing for favorable allocations by overpaying for other services, part of the profits that investors receive on underpriced IPOs will wind up in the pockets of the underwriters.

Although Loughran and Ritter's application of prospect theory can rationalize why IPOs with unexpectedly strong demand are underpriced more, they do not explain why issuers choose underwriters with a history of severe underpricing in the first place. Presumably, the perceived importance of analyst coverage gives some prestigious underwriters the ability to attract issuers even though in the 1990s these underwriters underpriced offerings substantially. [See Rajan and Servaes (1997), Michaely and Womack (1999) and Bradley, Jordan and Ritter (2003) for evidence on IPOs and analyst recommendations].

4.4.3. Corruption

Loughran and Ritter (2003) argue that an agency problem between the decision makers at issuing firms (the top executives and venture capitalists) and other pre-issue shareholders (including the limited partners of venture capital firms) also contributes to a willingness to hire underwriters with a history of leaving large amounts of money on the table. While underpricing results in excessive dilution of all pre-issue shareholders, an underwriter with other hot IPOs to allocate can make side payments to the decision makers of an issuing firm. This is done by setting up a personal brokerage account for these individuals, and then allocating hot IPOs to these accounts, a practice known as "spinning". If shares are not allocated on a discretionary basis, the opportunity to give the decision makers preferential access is not present. This may account for part of the higher underpricing observed with book-building than with auctions that is documented in Table 7.

Table 8 shows that underpricing was much more severe in 1999–2000 than previously. Loughran and Ritter (2003) argue that underwriters competed for IPO business during this period partly through promising to allocate hot IPOs to the personal brokerage account of the chief executive of an issuing firm. The executive would be willing to hire an underwriter that was expected to underprice the firm's IPO because, in return, the executive would receive other hot IPOs. Consistent with this hypothesis, in August 2002, documents were released by the US House of Representatives Financial Services Committee showing that Salomon Smith Barney allocated hot IPOs to the chief executives of many telecommunications firms during 1996–2000. During this period, Salomon Smith Barney had a large market share of equity underwriting and M&A business in this industry.

4.4.4. The winner's curse

With fixed-price offers, potential investors face an adverse selection, or "winner's curse," problem. Since a more or less fixed number of shares are sold at a fixed offering price, rationing will result if demand is strong. Rationing in itself does not lead to underpricing, but if some investors are at an informational disadvantage relative to others, some investors will be worse off. If some investors are more likely to attempt to buy shares when an issue is underpriced, then the amount of excess demand will be higher when there is more underpricing. Other investors will be allocated a smaller fraction of the most desirable new issues, and a larger fraction of the least desirable new issues. They face a winner's curse: if they get all of the shares which they ask for, it is because the informed investors don't want the shares. Faced with this adverse selection problem, the less informed investors will only submit purchase orders if, on average, IPOs are underpriced sufficiently to compensate them for the bias in the allocation of new issues.

Numerous studies have attempted to test the winner's curse model, both for the USA and other countries. While the evidence is consistent with there being a winner's curse, other explanations of the underpricing phenomenon exist. Evidence from several countries indicates that while large investors (institutions) are better informed than small investors (individuals), the main winner's curse problem is not that institutions crowd out individuals in hot offerings. Instead, in hot offerings, strong institutional demand makes it difficult for any given institution to get shares, and strong individual demand makes it difficult for any given individual to get shares. Indeed, in Finland [Keloharju (1993)] and Singapore [Lee, Taylor and Walter (1999)], small investors are favored over large investors when there is strong excess demand. In general, with book-building, favoritism in the allocation of shares can be used to minimize the winner's curse problem. This can be accomplished by intertemporal pooling: buyers of deals with weak demand can be favored in allocations on other deals when there is strong demand.

4.4.5. Informational cascades

If potential investors pay attention not only to their own information about a new issue, but also to whether other investors are purchasing, bandwagon effects, or informational cascades, may develop [Welch (1992)]. If an investor sees that no one else wants to buy, he or she may decide not to buy even when in possession of favorable information. To prevent this from happening, an issuer may want to underprice an issue to induce the first few potential investors to buy, and induce a cascade in which all subsequent investors want to buy irrespective of their own information.

An interesting implication of the informational cascades explanation, in conjunction with the dynamic information acquisition hypothesis, is that positively sloped demand curves can result. In the market feedback hypothesis, the offering price is adjusted upwards if regular investors indicate positive information. Other investors, knowing that this will only be a partial adjustment, correctly infer that these offerings will be underpriced. These other investors will consequently want to purchase additional shares, resulting in a positively sloped demand curve. The flip side is also true: because investors realize that a cut in the offering price indicates weak demand from other investors, cutting the offer price might actually scare away potential investors. And if the price is cut too much, investors might start to wonder why the firm is so desperate for cash. Thus, an issuer faced with weak demand may find that cutting the offer price won't work, and its only alternative is to postpone the offering, and hope that market conditions improve.

4.4.6. Lawsuit avoidance

The frequency and severity of future class action lawsuits can be reduced by underpricing, since only investors who lose money are entitled to damages. Underpricing the IPO, however, is a very costly way of reducing the probability of a future lawsuit. Furthermore, other countries in which securities class actions are unknown, such as Finland, have just as much underpricing as in the USA. Hughes and Thakor (1992) model the necessary conditions under which underpricing would be an efficient method for avoiding lawsuits. Fear of lawsuits has been mentioned as one rationale for why internet IPOs were underpriced so much in 1999–2000. This explanation would have greater plausibility if the managing underwriters did not have their analysts issue "buy" or "strong buy" recommendations after the stock price went up by hundreds of percent once it started trading.

4.4.7. Signalling

Several signalling models [Allen and Faulhaber (1989), Grinblatt and Hwang (1989) and Welch (1989)] have formalized the notion that underpriced IPOs "leave a good taste" with investors, allowing the firms and insiders to sell shares in the future at a higher price than would otherwise be the case. In these models, issuing firms have private information about whether they have high or low values. They follow a dynamic issue strategy, in which the IPO will be followed by a seasoned offering. As Daniel and Titman (1995) point out, signalling by leaving money on the table in the IPO is a relatively inefficient way to signal. Thus, it is not clear that this will occur in equilibrium unless the strategy space is somehow restricted.

Furthermore, various empirical studies such as Michaely and Shaw (1994) find that the hypothesized relation between initial returns and subsequent seasoned new issues is not present, once one holds other variables constant, casting doubt on the empirical relevance of signalling as a reason for underpricing. One problem that the signaling stories have is the extreme swings in equity issuing volume. In order for it to be sensible for a firm to underprice its IPO in order to profit in an SEO, there must be some reasonable assurance that the "window" will be open when the firm wants to return to the market. Yet in some market environments, such as the late summer and early autumn of 1998, and all of 2001, equity issuance ground almost to a halt, irrespective of the merits of individual firms.

4.4.8. The IPO as a marketing event

Closely related to the signaling idea is the notion that publicity is generated by a high first-day return. This publicity could generate additional investor interest [Chemmanur

(1993) and Aggarwal, Krigman and Womack (2002)] or additional product market revenue from greater brand awareness [Demers and Lewellen (2003)]. Presumably the product market benefits would be greater for firms selling to consumers, which generates a cross-sectional prediction. One has to wonder how expensive this advertising is compared to traditional advertising venues. There is one piece of evidence, however, that is consistent with the IPO as a marketing event. Habib and Ljungqvist (2001) note that the smaller the fraction of the firm sold, the lower is the opportunity cost of a big first day runup. In 1999–2000, many of the internet IPOs with large first-day price jumps sold less than 20% of the shares in their IPOs.

4.4.9. Summary of explanations of new issues underpricing

In addition to the above explanations, there are other reasons for underpricing that may apply in some circumstances. All of the above explanations for new issues underpricing involve rational strategies by buyers. The quantitative importance of some of them, such as the dynamic information acquisition story and the winner's curse story, are lessened when one admits the possibility of intertemporal pooling. Several other explanations have also been proposed involving irrational strategies by investors. Any model implying that investors are willing to overpay at the time of the IPO also implies that there will be poor long-run performance.

Although their relative importance varies depending upon the institutional setup, all of the above explanations for the underpricing of IPOs have some element of truth to them. Furthermore, the underpricing phenomenon has persisted for decades, and in all countries, with no signs of its imminent demise. Indeed, during the internet bubble of 1999–2000, average first day returns rose to unprecedented levels in most of the developed capital markets. This suggests that the relative importance of different theories of underpricing has changed over time. It is possible that in the 1980s, when the average first-day return in the USA was 7%, the Benveniste and Spindt (1989) dynamic information acquisition model and Rock's (1986) winner's curse model can explain much of the underpricing. In the 1990s, when the average first-day return was much higher, behavioral and agency explanations of underpricing likely became more important. Studies of changes in underwriter market share [Beatty and Ritter (1986), Nanda and Yun (1997), Dunbar (2000)] find that underwriters whose IPOs experience negative returns on the first day generally lose market share. High first-day returns, however, generally don't show up in lost market share, although obviously there is a limit before issuers become upset [Krigman, Shaw and Womack (2001)]. Otherwise, underpricing would be even greater than it is.

4.5. Underwriter compensation

The direct compensation that underwriters receive for taking a firm public is primarily in the form of the underwriting discount, or gross spread. In the USA and most other countries, a firm selling securities to the public pays investment bankers both the buying and selling commissions, so that buyers do not have to pay commissions when buying a new issue. The conventional wisdom is that there are fixed costs of selling securities, so that economies of scale exist for issuing firms (see Lee, Lochhead, Ritter and Zhao (1996), although Altinkilic and Hansen (2000) caution that large offerings are typically conducted by established, easy-to-value firms). Logic would suggest that the gross spread should also be higher on riskier deals than safer deals. Chen and Ritter (2000), however, document that in the late 1990s, almost all IPOs raising between $20–80 million in the USA paid gross spreads of exactly 7.0%. Possible explanations for this clustering of gross spreads are a subject of debate. Issuing firms pay additional implicit costs in that IPOs are typically underpriced. Ljungqvist, Jenkinson and Wilhelm (2003) present evidence that for the IPOs of foreign firms, USA investment bankers charge higher direct fees, but leave less money on the table than non-USA underwriters.

Gande, Puri and Saunders (1999) provide evidence that commercial bank entry into underwriting debt issues has been associated with a reduction in gross spreads paid by issuing firms. There is no evidence that the same effect is occurring with IPOs, however. When one looks at the gross spreads paid on SEOs, economies of scale are evident, with considerable cross-sectional variation in the fees. Unlike IPOs, there is very little clustering in the gross spreads paid. Unlike the pattern with equity IPOs, where prestigious investment bankers charge the same gross spread as less prestigious underwriters, Livingston and Miller (2000) report that prestigious underwriters charge less on investment grade bond issues than do less prestigious underwriters.

4.6. Stabilization activities

Stabilization, or price support, activities are legally allowed manipulation practices at the time of securities offerings. In the USA, these practices are governed by the SEC's Regulation M. These practices include allowing underwriters to overallot securities, and then cover the resulting short position by retiring some of the securities and/or exercising an overallotment option (also known as a Green Shoe option, after the first IPO to use one). Almost all IPOs give the underwriter the option of selling up to an additional 15% shares. In about two-thirds of IPOs, this overallotment option is exercised in full. Penalty bids are also permitted, in which the lead underwriter will take back the commission from a broker whose client immediately resells ("flips") the securities that he or she has been allotted. This encourages the broker to allocate the securities to a buy-and-hold investor in the first place, and creates incentives to dissuade the client from selling in the market. Aggarwal (2003) and Loughran and Ritter (2003), among others, report that first-day trading volume is higher when there is strong demand.

Aggarwal (2000) reports that it is common for underwriters to sell up to 135% of an issue if weak aftermarket demand is expected. Since at most 115% of the issue can be sold, this commits the syndicate to covering their naked short position of 20%

of the offer size.[8] If strong aftermarket demand is expected, leading to a price rise, underwriters generally do not take a naked short position. Zhang (2003) offers a path dependency explanation for why underwriters allot extra shares to investors expressing an interest, rather than allowing them to satisfy their demand by buying shares in the aftermarket. He argues that investors are more likely to hold on to shares that they have been allocated, than to buy and hold these shares if they must buy them in the market.

4.7. Hot-issue markets

Ibbotson and Jaffe (1975) and subsequent authors have identified significant autocorrelation of both the monthly number of IPOs and the monthly average first-day returns on IPOs. Ibbotson and Jaffe define a hot issue market to be a month in which the average first-day return is higher than the median. Months of high average first-day returns tend to be followed by rising volume [Lowry and Schwert (2002)]. The autocorrelation of both volume and average first-day returns are high: for example, during the 1990s, Loughran and Ritter (2002) report that every month between March 1991 and August 1998 had an average first-day return of *below* 30%, whereas every month from November 1998 to March 2000 had an average first-day return of *above* 30%. (Each month had at least ten IPOs.) Furthermore, they report, as have previous authors, that the first-day returns are predictable based upon lagged market returns.

Loughran and Ritter's (2002) prospect theory argument that issuing firms don't object to underpricing when it occurs simultaneously with an unexpected increase in their wealth can explain part of the autocorrelation of first-day returns. Since offer prices do not fully respond to market movements during the book-building period, all of the IPOs that are in their book-building period when there is a market runup will have a higher expected first-day return.

As puzzling as the cycles in the monthly average first-day returns are, the extreme swings in the volume of IPOs are equally of interest. The IPO market seems to be hypersensitive to changes in market conditions. Rather than just lowering offer prices by 20% when the market drops by 20%, volume tends to dry up. SEO volume also experiences large changes.

In October 1996, 106 firms went public. During the four years from 1974 to 1977, a total of 93 firms went public in the USA, an average of about two per month. In contrast to this fifty-to-one ratio of monthly volume, aggregate corporate investment fluctuates by a factor of two-to-one. Lowry (2003) addresses why IPO volume fluctuates so much. She examines three hypotheses: changes in the adverse-selection costs of issuing

---

[8] The size of the naked short position that is permitted is determined by the Agreement Among Underwriters on each deal, rather than by any regulation. A common feature of the agreement is a 20% limit on the size of any naked short position.

equity, changes in the aggregate capital demands of private firms, and changes in the level of investor optimism. Lowry concludes that changes in aggregate capital demands and in investor optimism are the primary determinants of changes in IPO volume over time.

4.8. Market activity across countries

The volume of IPOs varies substantially from country to country. Pagano, Panetta and Zingales (1998) report that the industry market-to-book ratio is the single most important determinant of the decision to go public for Italian firms. Subrahmanyam and Titman (1999) argue that the ease of going public depends upon the costs of acquiring information in an economy. They argue that each publicly traded firm creates a positive externality by making it easier to value comparable firms. Benveniste, Busaba and Wilhelm (2002) also view information spillovers as an important reason for industry clustering in IPO volume. While information externalities are undoubtedly important, probably the biggest problem that less-developed countries have in developing functioning public capital markets is in the corporate governance area. In some countries, such as Brazil and Sweden, it is the norm that shares issued to the public have inferior voting rights. If investors rationally are concerned about their ability to receive a return on the capital that they are providing to issuing firms, the valuation that they are willing to pay will be constrained. It is not clear that an issuing firm can receive a higher valuation by making a credible commitment to promise better corporate governance in a country where corporate governance problems are severe. La Porta, Lopez-de-Silanes, Shleifer and Vishny (1997) report that the number of IPOs varies systematically across countries, with countries having a legal system based upon British common law having more IPOs. Holmen and Hogfeldt (2003) show that in Sweden firms typically issue shares with inferior voting rights in the IPO, and if the shares with superior voting rights are eventually sold, they are always sold as a block.

It should be noted that in the late 1990s, several trends were going on in the worldwide IPO market. First, industry sector became more important, irrespective of the country of headquarters. For instance, worldwide there was an internet stock price bubble in 1999 and early 2000, with high first-day returns everywhere. Second, all but the smallest IPOs in almost all countries increasingly used book-building, rather than alternative mechanisms for pricing and allocating IPOs [Sherman (2001)]. This convergence of issuing mechanisms is part of the general trend towards the integration of world capital markets. Large and moderate size deals now frequently have both a domestic and an international tranche. Third, in Europe tech stocks increasingly went public on Germany's Neuer Markt, even if they weren't from Germany. Easdaq and the various markets for growth companies (of which Germany's Neuer Markt was by far the largest) competed for new tech stock listings. The historical strong correlation between which country a company was from and where it listed has been breaking down, making it more difficult to assign IPOs to countries. Fourth, the new exchanges have changed the focus of listing requirements from accounting criteria such as profitability and assets to corporate governance and disclosure requirements. In Europe's traditional stock markets, a high level of disclosure has not been required. For example, Germany's Daimler Benz (now Daimler Chrysler) had never reported its cash reserves until it did so prior to seeking a joint listing on the NYSE in 1995. Fifth, for a variety of reasons, Europe's IPO market, relatively moribund for decades, came alive in the 1990s. For the first time in modern history, more European firms went public than American firms in both 1998 and 1999 [Jenkinson and Ljungqvist (2001)].

4.9. Long-run performance

When measuring the long-run abnormal returns on IPOs, the same performance measurement issues as with SEOs come up. As G.W. Schwert notes in his chapter in this Handbook, there is a tendency for anomalies to disappear once they have been identified. Whether this is because the original anomaly occurred by chance during some sample period, or because the market learns and begins to price securities differently, is unclear.

In Table 9, the annual returns on IPOs in the five years after issuing are reported, along with benchmark returns using either size or style matching. The style matches are based upon size (market cap) and book-to-market matching. The numbers reported in Table 9 are displayed in Figure 2. As first documented by Ritter (1991), Table 9 shows that IPOs have underperformed other firms of the same size by an average of 3.8% per year during the five years after issuing, not including the first-day return. When size- and book-to-market (style) matching is used, however, the underperformance shrinks to 2.2% per year for the IPOs. Thus, unlike SEOs, there is only modest evidence of underperformance once a style benchmark is used [Brav and Gompers (1997), Gompers and Lerner (2003)].

As shown by Brav, Geczy and Gompers (2000, Table 1), most IPOs fall in the extreme small growth category. Whether or not they issue, firms in this style category have had extremely low returns for the last several decades. As with SEOs, the tendency of IPO volume to be high near market peaks results in greater investment in IPOs prior to periods of low market returns. Lowry (2003) reports that high IPO volume is a reliable predictor of low equally weighted market returns during the following year. This pattern shows up in Figure 2, where the first year return on both the IPOs and their benchmarks tend to be lower than in subsequent years.

The relatively modest underperformance relative to a style benchmark shown in Table 9 and Figure 2 highlights the distinction between relative performance and absolute performance. IPOs do not dramatically underperform relative to a style benchmark, but firms apparently display some ability to time their IPOs for periods when future returns on small growth firms are low. Furthermore, the mystery of why small growth firms have such low returns on average remains unanswered. One unexplored area of research is the effect of market manipulation. The lowest returns are on the very smallest IPOs. These stocks are most likely to be taken public by

Table 9
Percentage returns on IPOs from 1970-2000 during the first five years after issuing[a]

	1st 6 months	2nd 6 months	1st yr	2nd yr	3rd yr	4th yr	5th yr	Geometric mean yrs 1–5
IPO firms	7.0%	−0.1%	7.0%	7.0%	10.4%	14.0%	12.6%	10.2%
Size-matched	4.7%	5.6%	10.4%	14.5%	15.1%	16.5%	13.4%	14.0%
Difference	2.3%	−5.7%	−3.4%	−7.5%	−4.7%	−2.5%	−0.8%	−3.8%
Number	7042	7023	7042	6839	5964	5175	4358	7437
IPO firms	7.4%	0.3%	7.8%	9.7%	11.3%	13.3%	10.6%	10.5%
Style-matched	2.5%	4.5%	7.9%	12.6%	14.4%	17.8%	11.2%	12.7%
Difference	4.9%	−4.2%	−0.1%	−2.9%	−3.1%	−4.5%	−0.6%	−2.2%
Number	6719	6702	6719	6371	5543	4772	3993	6834

[a] For the first year, the returns are measured from the closing market price on the first day of issue until the 6th-month or one-year anniversary. All returns are equally-weighted average returns for all IPOs that are still traded on Nasdaq, the Amex, or the NYSE at the start of a period. If an issuing firm is delisted within a year, its return for that year is calculated by compounding the CRSP value-weighted market index for the rest of the year. For the size-matched returns, each IPO is matched with a nonissuing firm having the same market capitalization (using the closing market price on the first day of trading for the IPO, and the market capitalization at the end of the previous month for the matching firms). For the (size and book-to-market) style-matched returns, each IPO is matched with a nonissuing firm in the same size decile (using NYSE firms only for determining the decile breakpoints) having the closest book-to-market ratio. For the IPOs, book-to-market ratios are calculated using the first recorded post-issue book value and the post-issue market cap calculated using the closing market price on the first CRSP-listed day of trading. For nonissuing firms, the Compustat-listed book value of equity for the most recent fiscal year ending at least four months prior to the IPO date is used, along with the market cap at the close of trading at month-end prior to the month of the IPO with which it is matched. Nonissuing firms are those that have been listed on the Amex–Nasdaq–NYSE for at least five years, without issuing equity for cash during that time. If a nonissuer subsequently issues equity, it is still used as the matching firm. If a nonissuer gets delisted prior to the delisting (or the fifth anniversary, or Dec. 31, 2001), the second-closest matching firm on the original IPO date is substituted, on a point-forward basis. For firms with multiple classes of stock outstanding, market cap is calculated using only the class in the IPO for the IPO. For nonissuing firms, each class of stock is treated as if it is a separate firm. The sample size is 7437 IPOs from January 1970–December 2000 when size-matching is used, excluding IPOs with an offer price of less than $5.00, ADRs, REITs, closed-end funds, and unit offers. All IPOs are listed on CRSP for at least 6 months, and after Nasdaq's inclusion, are listed within 6 months of going public. Returns are measured through December 31, 2001. For partial event-years that end on this date, the last partial year is deleted from the computations. In other words, for an IPO that issued on March 15, 2000, its first-year return is included, but not the second-year return.

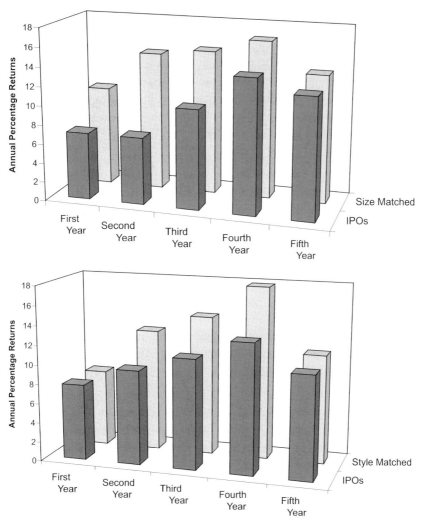

Fig. 2. Post-issue returns for firms conducting IPOs from 1970–2000, with returns through December 31, 2001. In the top panel, size-matched nonissuers use the nonissuing firm with the closest market capitalization as of the month-end prior to the IPO. In the bottom panel, style-matched nonissuers use the nonissuing firm in the market cap decile with the closest book-to-market ratio. The average annual percentage return for IPOs and matching nonissuing firms is shown for each of the five years after issuing. The data are described in Table 9. Nonissuers are CRSP-listed stocks that have not issued equity (IPO or SEO) is plotted during the prior five years, and have been listed on CRSP for at least five years. CRSP covers the common stock of domestic operating companies listed on the Amex, NYSE, and (after December 14, 1972) Nasdaq. Book-to-market for IPOs is measured using the post-issue book value and market cap at the close of trading on the first day. The first-year returns do not include the first day of trading. If an IPO is delisted before five years from the issue date, its annual return during the year of delisting is calculated by splicing in the CRSP value-weighted market return for the remainder of that year.

underwriters with regulatory problems, and these IPOs are least likely to be backed
by venture capitalists [Brav and Gompers (1997)]. Furthermore, there is little or no
institutional investor interest in these stocks.

When going public, IPOs almost always commit to a "lock-up period", whereby
insiders are prohibited from selling shares without the written permission of the lead
underwriter until a certain amount of time has passed. In recent years, the vast majority
of IPOs have lockup provisions of 180 days. Bradley, Jordan, Roten and Yi (2001),
Field and Hanka (2001) and Brav and Gompers (2003) document that, in the week that
the lockup expires, share prices fall approximately 2%. This is not an announcement
effect, in that the date that the lockup will end is known at the time of the IPO. Trading
costs (especially bid-ask spreads) probably prevent the implementation of a profitable
active trading rule to take advantage of this predictable price drop, but the drop would
appear to be a violation of market efficiency, even in its weakest form.

Further evidence that supply and demand shifts, unrelated to fundamentals, affect
the price of IPOs comes from price patterns at the end of the quiet period, 40 days after
an IPO starts trading. Bradley, Jordan and Ritter (2003) report average market-adjusted
returns of 3% in the week surrounding the end of the quiet period. For firms where
investment banks initiate analyst recommendations at this time, the average jump is
4%. For firms where there is no initiation of research coverage, the average market-
adjusted return is close to zero.

A number of reasons have been advanced for the low long-run returns on IPOs.
Probably the most plausible story is the argument of Miller (1977) and Morris (1996)
that with costly short-selling and heterogeneous beliefs among investors, the most
optimistic investors will determine the market price. As more information becomes
available about a firm over time, the divergence of beliefs will decrease, and the
marginal holder will no longer be as overoptimisitic. Also, as the public float increases
over time, the marginal holder will not be as extreme in his or her overoptimism. This
story is consistent with the patterns in the 1999–2000 internet bubble, where there
were extreme differences of opinion, costly short-selling, and small public floats on
many IPOs.

There is also clear evidence that some IPOs are overvalued relative to other firms at
the time of their IPO. There have been several internet "equity carveouts" where the
parent company retained a large ownership stake, the parent announced its intention to
distribute its shares in the subsidiary to shareholders, and yet the subsidiary's market
value exceeded the market value of the parent company [Lamont and Thaler (2003)]. In
all cases, eventually the subsidiary's stock price fell by the time the parent distributed
the remaining shares. In these situations, short-sellers had difficulty borrowing shares
immediately after the IPO.

Eckbo and Norli (2001) argue that IPOs have low returns because they actually have
low risk. Ritter and Welch (2002) compute the systematic risk of a portfolio of IPOs
including a lagged monthly market return (the summed beta approach used in Table 4
of this chapter for SEOs), and find a beta of 1.73 for IPOs, indicating a high exposure

to market risk. The high beta for IPOs is inconsistent with the hypothesis that IPOs have low returns because they have low risk.

A more subtle issue regarding the post-issue performance of IPOs is raised by Schultz (2003). He argues that, even if there is no ex ante abnormal performance expected, researchers conducting event studies are likely to find negative abnormal performance ex post. His logic can be summarized as follows. If, early in a sample period, IPOs underperform, there will be few IPOs in the future, and so the average performance will be weighted heavily towards the early IPOs that underperformed. If, instead, early in a sample period IPOs do well, there will be a lot more IPOs in the future. Thus, the average performance will place only a small weight on the early IPOs that outperformed. Because of this tendency, in studies that do not weight each time period equally, the expected performance is negative when all IPOs are weighted equally, even if ex ante there is no expected underperformance. Schultz refers to this problem as "pseudo market timing", and argues that it is relevant not just for IPOs, but for all endogenous corporate actions as reported in Table 5 of this chapter.

Time-series regressions that weight each period equally, such as the Fama–French 3-factor regressions reported in Tables 3 and 4 of this chapter, do not suffer from this pseudo market timing problem. Thus, while Schultz's argument is applicable for "fads" such as rollup IPOs [Brown, Dittmar and Servaes (2002)], it is not clear that it is quantitatively important for IPOs in general.

5. Summary

This chapter has surveyed the literature on investment banking and equity issuance. This survey is, by the necessity of space constraints, incomplete. It has focused on recent contributions to the academic literature, in that other surveys by Smith (1986), Eckbo and Masulis (1995), Ibbotson and Ritter (1995) and Jenkinson and Ljungqvist (2001) have done a comprehensive job of covering the earlier literature.

One of the most contentious empirical findings in the last decade concerns whether firms conducting IPOs and SEOs subsequently underperform relative to other similar non-issuing firms. Relative to size-matched firms, the answer is unambiguously yes. But since issuing firms tend to be small growth firms and non-issuers tend to be small value firms, the book-to-market effect is a confounding effect. When style (size and book-to-market) matching is used, IPOs underperform by only 2.2% per year, on average. With SEOs, on the other hand, economically significant underperformance of 3.4% per year is still present when a style benchmark is used. The reason for the difference in sensitivities is that the book-to-market effect is concentrated among very small firms (small growth firms, whether they are recent issuers or not, have extremely low stock returns, and small value firms have high returns). A high proportion of IPOs are very small growth firms, whereas SEOs are less concentrated in this extreme style category. Conclusions about underperformance are also affected by the sample period chosen and whether equal or value weighting is used.

An equally weighted portfolio of IPOs from January 1970–December 2000, purchased at the close on the day of offering and held for one year, gave investors an average annual return of 7.0% through December of 2001. An equally weighted portfolio of SEOs gave investors an average annual return of 9.4% through December of 2001. Yet, if one bought the S&P 500 at the beginning of 1970 and reinvested dividends, the compound annual return through December 2001 would have been 12.1%. Thus, the low returns on issuing firms partly reflect underperformance relative to a style benchmark, and partly a market-timing issue. Market-timing ability is manifested in the tendency for firms to issue after high market returns and before low market returns. Thus, investing an equal amount in each issuing firm tends to overweight periods with low market returns, and underweight periods with high market returns.

The volume of equity issues fluctuates dramatically from period to period. While explanations exist for the optimal time in a company's life cycle to go public, at this point there is no consensus on why market timing considerations appear to be so important. The number of companies going public also varies dramatically from country to country. Differences in corporate governance, laws and their enforcement, and culture explain much of the differences, but study of this important topic is still in its infancy.

In summary, in the 1980s and 1990s the number of firms around the world issuing equity increased dramatically. Not coincidentally, the academic literature related to securities issuance also exploded. Advances have been made in understanding the importance of contractual mechanism for determining the terms at which securities can be sold. There are, however, many unresolved issues remaining. In particular, even though there is abundant evidence that issuing firms face negatively-sloped demand curves for their shares, the marketing of financial securities is a relatively unexplored research area. Only recently have papers begun to focus on the corporate financing implications if firms face fluctuations in the cost of external financing due to the mispricing of securities by the market. Furthermore, the extreme underpricing of IPOs during the 1999–2000 internet bubble is unlikely to be explained by standard models based on information asymmetries.

References

Aggarwal, R. (2000), "Stabilization activities by underwriters after initial public offerings", Journal of Finance 55:1075–1103.

Aggarwal, R. (2003), "Allocation of initial public offerings and flipping activity", Journal of Financial Economics 68:111–135.

Aggarwal, R., L. Krigman and K. Womack (2002), "Strategic IPO underpricing, information momentum, and lockup expiration selling", Journal of Financial Economics 66:105–137.

Aggarwal, R., N. Prabhala and M. Puri (2002), "Institutional allocation in initial public offerings: empirical evidence", Journal of Finance 57:1421–1442.

Allen, F., and G. Faulhaber (1989), "Signalling by underpricing in the IPO market", Journal of Financial Economics 23:303–323.

Altinkilic, O., and R.S. Hansen (2000), "Are there economies of scale in underwriting fees? Evidence of rising external financing costs", Review of Financial Studies 13:191–218.

Baker, M., and J. Wurgler (2000), "The equity share in new issues and aggregate stock returns", Journal of Finance 55:2219–2257.

Baker, M., and J. Wurgler (2002), "Market timing and capital structure", Journal of Finance 57:1–32.

Barber, B.M., and J.D. Lyon (1997), "Detecting long-run abnormal stock returns: the empirical power and specification of test-statistics," Journal of Financial Economics 43:341–372.

Barberis, N., and R. Thaler (2003), "A survey of behavioral finance", in: G.M. Constantinides, M. Harris and R.M. Stulz, eds., Handbook of the Economics of Finance, Vol. 1B (Elsevier, Amsterdam) Chapter 18.

Bayless, M., and S. Chaplinsky (1996), "Is there a 'Window of Opportunity' for seasoned equity issuance?", Journal of Finance 51:253–278.

Beatty, R.P., and J.R. Ritter (1986), "Investment banking, reputation, and the underpricing of initial public offerings," Journal of Financial Economics 15:213–232.

Benveniste, L.M., and P.A. Spindt (1989), "How investment bankers determine the offer price and allocation of new issues", Journal of Financial Economics 24:343–361.

Benveniste, L.M., W. Busaba and W. Wilhelm (2002), "Information externalities and the role of underwriters in primary equity markets", Journal of Financial Intermediation 11:61–86.

Biais, B., and A.M. Faugeron (2002), "IPO auctions: English, Dutch, ... French and internet", Journal of Financial Intermediation 11:9–36.

Billett, M., M.J. Flannery and J.A. Garfinkel (2001), "The long-run performance of firms following loan announcements", Working Paper (University of Iowa; University of Florida).

Black, B.S., and R.J. Gilson (1998), "Venture capital and the structure of capital markets: banks versus stock markets", Journal of Financial Economics 47:243–277.

Booth, J., and L. Chua (1996), "Ownership dispersion, costly information, and IPO underpricing", Journal of Financial Economics 41:291–310.

Bradley, D., B. Jordan, I. Roten and H. Yi (2001), "Venture capital and lockup expiration: an empirical analysis", Journal of Financial Research 24:465–493.

Bradley, D., B. Jordan and J.R. Ritter (2003), "The quiet period goes out with a bang", Journal of Finance 58:1–36.

Brav, A. (2000), "Inference in long-horizon event studies: a bayesian approach with applications to initial public offerings", Journal of Finance 55:1979–2016.

Brav, A., and P. Gompers (1997), "Myth or reality? The long-run underperformance of initial public offerings: evidence from venture and nonventure capital-backed companies", Journal of Finance 52:1791–1821.

Brav, A., and P. Gompers (2003), "Insider trading subsequent to initial public offerings: evidence from expirations of lockup provisions", Review of Financial Studies 16:1–29.

Brav, A., C. Geczy and P. Gompers (2000), "Is the abnormal return following equity issuances anomalous?", Journal of Financial Economics 56:209–249.

Brennan, M., and J. Franks (1997), "Underpricing, ownership and control in initial public offerings of equity securities in the UK", Journal of Financial Economics 45:391–413.

Brown, K.C., A. Dittmar and H.J. Servaes (2002), "Why innovation fails: the case of roll-up IPOs", Working Paper (Indiana University).

Cai, J., and T. Loughran (1998), "The performance of Japanese seasoned equity offerings, 1971–1992", Pacific-Basin Finance Journal 6:395–425.

Chemmanur, T.J. (1993), "The pricing of initial public offerings: a dynamic model with information production", Journal of Finance 48:285–304.

Chemmanur, T.J., and P. Fulghieri (1994), "Investment bank reputation, information production, and financial intermediation", Journal of Finance 49:57–79.

Chemmanur, T.J., and P. Fulghieri (1999), "A theory of the going-public decision", Review of Financial Studies 12:249–279.

Chen, H.-C., and J.R. Ritter (2000), "The seven percent solution", Journal of Finance 55:1105–1131.

Choe, H., R. Masulis and V. Nanda (1993), "Common stock offerings across the business cycle: theory and evidence", Journal of Empirical Finance 1:3–31.

Chowdhry, B., and A.E. Sherman (1996), "The winner's curse and international methods of allocating initial public offerings", Pacific-Basin Finance Journal 4:15–30.

Clarke, J., C. Dunbar and K.M. Kahle (2001), "Long-run performance and insider trading in completed and canceled seasoned equity offerings", Journal of Financial and Quantitative Analysis 36:415–430.

Cornelli, F., and D. Goldreich (2001), "Bookbuilding and strategic allocation", Journal of Finance 56:2337–2369.

Corwin, S.A. (2003), "The determinants of underpricing for seasoned equity offers", Journal of Finance 58, forthcoming.

Daniel, K., and S. Titman (1995), "Financing investment under asymmetric information", in: R.A. Jarrow, V. Maksimovic and W.T. Ziemba, eds., Handbooks in Operations Research and Management Science, Vol. 9 (Elsevier, Amsterdam) Chapter 23.

Davis, J., E. Fama and K. French (2000), "Characteristics, covariances, and average returns: 1929–1997", Journal of Finance 55:389–406.

Demers, E., and K. Lewellen (2003), "The marketing role of IPOs: evidence from internet stocks", Journal of Financial Economics, forthcoming.

Denis, D.J., and G.B. Kadlec (1994), "Corporate events, trading activity, and the estimation of systematic risk: evidence from equity offerings and share repurchases", Journal of Finance 49:1787–1811.

Denis, D.J., and A. Sarin (2001), "Is the market surprised by poor earnings realizations following seasoned equity offerings?", Journal of Financial and Quantitative Analysis 36:169–193.

Derrien, F., and K.L. Womack (2003), "Auctions vs. bookbuilding and the control of underpricing in hot IPO markets", Review of Financial Studies 16:31–61.

Dunbar, C. (2000), "Factors affecting investment bank initial public offering market share", Journal of Financial Economics 55:3–41.

Eckbo, E., and R. Masulis (1995), "Seasoned equity offerings: a survey", in: R.A. Jarrow, V. Maksimovic and W.T. Ziemba, eds., Handbooks in Operations Research and Management Science, Vol. 9 (Elsevier, Amsterdam) Chapter 31.

Eckbo, E., and O. Norli (2001), "Leverage, liquidity, and long-run IPO returns", Working Paper (Dartmouth College, NH).

Eckbo, E., R. Masulis and O. Norli (2000), "Seasoned public offerings: resolution of the 'New Issues Puzzle' ", Journal of Financial Economics 56:251–291.

Ellis, K., R. Michaely and M. O'Hara (2000), "When the underwriter is the market maker: an examination of trading in the IPO aftermarket", Journal of Finance 55:1039–1074.

Fama, E.F. (1998), "Market efficiency, long-term returns, and behavioral finance", Journal of Financial Economics 49:283–306.

Fama, E.F., and K. French (1992), "The cross-section of expected stock returns", Journal of Finance 47:427–465.

Fama, E.F., and K. French (1993), "Common risk factors in the returns on bonds and stocks", Journal of Financial Economics 33:3–56.

Field, L.C., and G. Hanka (2001), "The expiration of IPO share lock-ups", Journal of Finance 56: 471–500.

Foerster, S.R., and G.A. Karolyi (2000), "The long-run performance of global equity offerings", Journal of Financial and Quantitative Analysis 35:499–528.

Gande, A., M. Puri and A. Saunders (1999), "Bank entry, competition, and the market for corporate securities underwriting", Journal of Financial Economics 54:165–195.

Gompers, P., and J. Lerner (2003), "The really long-term performance of initial public offerings: the pre-Nasdaq evidence", Journal of Finance, forthcoming.

Graham, J.R., and C.R. Harvey (2001), "The theory and practice of corporate finance: evidence from the field", Journal of Financial Economics 60:187–243.

Grinblatt, M., and C.-Y. Hwang (1989), "Signalling and the pricing of new issues", Journal of Finance 44:393–420.

Grullon, G., R. Michaely and B. Swaminathan (2002), "Are dividend changes a sign of firm maturity?", Journal of Business 75:387–424.

Guay, W., and J. Harford (2000), "The cash-flow permanence and information content of dividend increases versus share repurchases", Journal of Financial Economics 57:385–415.

Habib, M., and A. Ljungqvist (2001), "Underpricing and entrepreneurial wealth losses in IPOs: theory and evidence", Review of Financial Studies 14:433–458.

Hamao, Y., F. Packer and J. Ritter (2000), "Institutional affiliation and the role of venture capital: evidence from initial public offerings in Japan", Pacific-Basin Finance Journal 8:529–558.

Heaton, J.B. (2002), "Managerial optimism and corporate finance", Financial Management 31:33–45.

Heron, R.A., and E. Lie (2003), "A comparison of the motivations for and the information content of different types of equity offerings", Journal of Business, forthcoming.

Hertzel, M., M. Lemmon, J.S. Linck and L. Rees (2002), "Long-run performance following private placements of equity", Journal of Finance 57:2595–2617.

Holmen, M., and P. Hogfeldt (2003), "A law and finance analysis of initial public offerings", Working Paper (Stockholm University).

Houston, J.F., and M.D. Ryngaert (1997), "Equity issuance and adverse selection: a direct test using conditional stock offers", Journal of Finance 52:197–219.

Howton, S.D., S.W. Howton and S.B. Perfect (1998), "The market reaction to straight debt issues: the effects of free cash flow", Journal of Financial Research 21:219–228.

Hughes, P., and A. Thakor (1992), "Litigation risk, intermediation, and the underpricing of initial public offerings", Review of Financial Studies 5:709–742.

Ibbotson, R.G., and J.F. Jaffe (1975), " 'Hot issue' markets", Journal of Finance 30:1027–1042.

Ibbotson, R.G., and J.R. Ritter (1995), "Initial public offerings", in: R.A. Jarrow, V. Maksimovic and W.T. Ziemba, eds., Handbooks in Operations Research and Management Science, Vol. 9 (Elsevier, Amsterdam) Chapter 30.

Ikenberry, D., J. Lakonishok and T. Vermaelen (1995), "Market underreaction to open market share repurchases", Journal of Financial Economics 39:181–208.

Jegadeesh, N. (2000), "Long-run performance of seasoned equity offerings: benchmark errors and biases in expectations", Financial Management 29(3):5–30.

Jenkinson, T., and A. Ljungqvist (2001), Going Public: The Theory and Evidence on How Companies Raise Equity Finance, 2nd Edition (Oxford University Press).

Jung, K., Y.-C. Kim and R. Stulz (1996), "Managerial discretion, investment opportunities, and the security issue decision", Journal of Financial Economics 42:159–185.

Kadiyala, P., and R. Rau (2003), "Investor reaction to corporate event announcements: under-reaction or over-reaction?", Journal of Business, forthcoming.

Kahneman, D., and A. Tversky (1979), "Prospect theory: an analysis of decision under risk", Econometrica 47:263–291.

Kaneko, T., and R.H. Pettway (2003), "Auctions versus book-building of Japanese IPOs", Pacific-Basin Finance Journal, forthcoming.

Kang, J.-K., Y.-C. Kim and R. Stulz (1999), "The underreaction hypothesis and the new issue puzzle: evidence from Japan", Review of Financial Studies 12:519–534.

Keloharju, M. (1993), "The winner's curse, legal liability, and the long-run performance of initial public offerings", Journal of Financial Economics 34:251–277.

Kim, M., and J.R. Ritter (1999), "Valuing IPOs", Journal of Financial Economics 53:409–437.

Kim, Y.-C., and R. Stulz (1992), "Is there a global market for convertible bonds?", Journal of Business 65:75–91.

Korajczyk, R., D.J. Lucas and R.L. McDonald (1991), "The effect of information releases on the pricing and timing of equity issues", Review of Financial Studies 4:685–708.

Kothari, S.P., and J.B. Warner (1997), "Measuring long-horizon security price performance", Journal of Financial Economics 43:301–339.

Krigman, L., W. Shaw and K. Womack (2001), "Why do firms switch underwriters?" Journal of Financial Economics 60:245–284.

La Porta, R., F. Lopez-de-Silanes, A. Shleifer and R. Vishny (1997), "Legal determinants of external finance", Journal of Finance 52:1131–1150.

Lamont, O., and R. Thaler (2003), "Can the market add and subtract? Mispricing in tech stock carveouts", Journal of Political Economy 111:227–268.

Lee, I. (1997), "Do managers knowingly sell overvalued equity?", Journal of Finance 52:1439–1466.

Lee, I., and T. Loughran (1998), "Performance following convertible bond issuance", Journal of Corporate Finance 4:185–207.

Lee, I., S. Lochhead, J. Ritter and Q. Zhao (1996), "The costs of raising capital", Journal of Financial Research 19:59–74.

Lee, P.J., S.L. Taylor and T.S. Walter (1999), "IPO underpricing explanations: implications from investor application and allocation schedules", Journal of Financial and Quantitative Analysis 34:425–444.

Lerner, J. (1994), "Venture capitalists and the decision to go public", Journal of Financial Economics 35:293–316.

Liaw, G., Y.-J. Liu and K.C.J. Wei (2000), "On the demand elasticity of initial public offerings: an analysis of discriminatory auctions", Working Paper (Hong Kong University of Science and Technology).

Lin, T.H., and M. Sheu (1997), "The choice of underwriting contract in initial public offerings", Journal of Financial Studies 5:19–41.

Livingston, M., and R.E. Miller (2000), "Investment bank reputation and the underwriting of nonconvertible debt", Financial Management 29(2):21–34.

Ljungqvist, A., T. Jenkinson and W. Wilhelm (2003), "Global integration in primary equity markets: the role of U.S. banks and U.S. investors", Review of Financial Studies 16:63–99.

Loughran, T., and J.R. Ritter (1995), "The new issues puzzle", Journal of Finance 50:23–51.

Loughran, T., and J.R. Ritter (1997), "The operating performance of firms conducting seasoned equity offerings", Journal of Finance 52:1823–1850.

Loughran, T., and J.R. Ritter (2000), "Uniformly least powerful tests of market efficiency", Journal of Financial Economics 55:361–389.

Loughran, T., and J.R. Ritter (2002), "Why don't issuers get upset about leaving money on the table in IPOs?", Review of Financial Studies 15:413–443.

Loughran, T., and J.R. Ritter (2003), "Why has IPO underpricing changed over time?", Working Paper (University of Notre Dame; University of Florida).

Loughran, T., and A. Vijh (1997), "Do long-term shareholders benefit from corporate acquisitions?", Journal of Finance 52:1765–1790.

Loughran, T., J.R. Ritter and K. Rydqvist (1994), "Initial public offerings: international insights", Pacific-Basin Finance Journal 2:165–199.

Lowry, M. (2003), "Why does IPO volume fluctuate so much?" Journal of Financial Economics 67:3–40.

Lowry, M., and G.W. Schwert (2002), "IPO market cycles: bubbles or sequential learning?", Journal of Finance 57:1171–1200.

Lyon, J.D., B.M. Barber and C.-L. Tsai (1999), "Improved methods for tests of long-run abnormal stock returns", Journal of Finance 54:165–201.

Mayers, D. (1998), "Why firms issue convertible bonds: the matching of financial and real investment options", Journal of Financial Economics 47:55–82.

McLaughlin, R., A. Saffieddine and G.K. Vasudevan (1998), "The long-run performance of convertible debt issuers", Journal of Financial Research 21:373–388.

Megginson, W.L., and J.M. Netter (2001), "From state to market: a survey of empirical studies on privatization", Journal of Economic Literature 39:321–389.

Mello, A.S., and J.E. Parsons (1998), "Going public and the ownership structure of the firm", Journal of Financial Economics 49:79–109.

Michaely, R., and W.H. Shaw (1994), "The pricing of initial public offerings: tests of adverse-selection and signaling theories", Review of Financial Studies 7:279–319.

Michaely, R., and K.L. Womack (1999), "Conflict of interest and the credibility of underwriter analyst recommendations", Review of Financial Studies 12:653–686.

Miller, E.M. (1977), "Risk, uncertainty, and divergence of opinion", Journal of Finance 32:1151–1168.

Mitchell, M.L., and E. Stafford (2000), "Managerial decisions and long term stock price performance", Journal of Business 73:287–329.

Mola, S., and T. Loughran (2003), "Discounting and clustering in seasoned equity offering prices", Journal of Financial and Quantitative Analysis, forthcoming.

Morris, S. (1996), "Speculative investor behavior and learning", Quarterly Journal of Economics 111: 1111–1133.

Myers, S., and N. Majluf (1984), "Corporate financing and investment decisions when firms have information that investors do not have", Journal of Financial Economics 13:187–222.

Nanda, V., and Y. Yun (1997), "Reputation and financial intermediation: an empirical investigation of the impact of IPO mispricing on underwriter market value", Journal of Financial Intermediation 6:39–63.

Pagano, M., F. Panetta and L. Zingales (1998), "Why do firms go public? An empirical analysis", Journal of Finance 53:27–64.

Pettway, R.H., and T. Kaneko (1996), "The effects of removing price limits and introducing auctions upon short-term IPO returns: the case of Japanese IPOs", Pacific-Basin Finance Journal 4:241–258.

Purnanandam, A.K., and B. Swaminathan (2002), "Are IPOs underpriced?", Working Paper (Cornell University, NY).

Rajan, R., and H. Servaes (1997), "Analyst following of initial public offerings", Journal of Finance 52:507–529.

Rangan, S. (1998), "Earnings management and the performance of seasoned equity offerings", Journal of Financial Economics 50:101–122.

Ritter, J.R. (1991), "The long run performance of initial public offerings", Journal of Finance 46:3–27.

Ritter, J.R. (1998), "Initial public offerings", Contemporary Finance Digest 2(1):3–30.

Ritter, J.R. (2003), "Difference between European and American IPO markets", European Financial Management 9, forthcoming.

Ritter, J.R., and I. Welch (2002), "A review of IPO activity, pricing, and allocations", Journal of Finance 57:1795–1828.

Rock, K. (1986), "Why new issues are underpriced", Journal of Financial Economics 15:187–212.

Schultz, P. (2003), "Pseudo market timing and the long-run underperformance of IPOs", Journal of Finance 58:483–517.

Schwert, G.W. (2003), "Anomalies and market efficiency", in: G.M. Constantinides, M. Harris and R.M. Stulz, eds., Handbook of the Economics of Finance, Vol. 1B (Elsevier, Amsterdam) Chapter 15.

Sherman, A.E. (2001), "Global trends in IPO methods: book building vs. auctions", Working Paper (University of Notre Dame).

Shleifer, A., and R. Vishny (1997), "The limits of arbitrage", Journal of Finance 52:35–55.

Smith, C. (1986), "Investment banking and the capital acquisition process", Journal of Financial Economics 15:3–29.

Smith, R., and S. Pulliam (2000), "U.S. probes inflated commissions for hot IPOs", Wall Street Journal (December 7, 2000), p. C1.

Spiess, K., and J. Affleck-Graves (1995), "The long-run performance following seasoned equity issues", Journal of Financial Economics 38:243–267.

Spiess, K., and J. Affleck-Graves (1999), "The long-run performance of stock returns following debt offerings", Journal of Financial Economics 54:45–73.

Stein, J.C. (1996), "Rational capital budgeting in an irrational world", Journal of Business 69:429–455.

Stein, J.C. (2003), "Agency, information, and corporate investment", in: G.M. Constantinides, M. Harris and R.M. Stulz, eds., Handbook of the Economics of Finance, Vol. 1A (Elsevier, Amsterdam) Chapter 2, this volume.

Stoughton, N.M., and J. Zechner (1998), "IPO-mechanisms, monitoring and ownership structure", Journal of Financial Economics 49:45–77.

Subrahmanyam, A., and S. Titman (1999), "The going public decision and the development of financial markets", Journal of Finance 54:1045–1082.

Teoh, S.H., I. Welch and T.J. Wong (1998), "Earnings management and the post-issue underperformance in seasoned equity offerings", Journal of Financial Economics 50:63–99.

Travlos, N.G. (1987), "Corporate takeover bids, methods of payment, and bidding firms' stock returns", Journal of Finance 42:943–963.

Vijh, A.M. (1999), "Long-term returns from equity carveouts", Journal of Financial Economics 51: 273–308.

Vijh, A.M. (2002), "The positive announcement-period returns of equity carveouts: asymmetric information or divestiture gains?", Journal of Business 75:153–190.

Welch, I. (1989), "Seasoned offerings, imitation costs, and the underpricing of initial public offerings", Journal of Finance 44:421–449.

Welch, I. (1992), "Sequential sales, learning, and cascades", Journal of Finance 47:695–732.

Zhang, D. (2003), "Why do IPO underwriters allocate extra shares when they expect to buy them back?", Journal of Financial and Quantitative Analysis, forthcoming.

Zingales, L. (1995), "Insider ownership and the decision to go public", Review of Economic Studies 62:425–448.

Chapter 6

FINANCIAL INNOVATION

Harvard Business School, Boston

Contents

* I would like to thank René Stulz, Josh Lerner, Robert McLaughlin and Belén Villalonga for their very helpful comments, and Scott Sinawi for his able research assistance. This work was funded by the Division of Research of the Harvard Business School.

Handbook of the Economics of Finance, Edited by G.M. Constantinides, M. Harris and R. Stulz

Abstract

Although financial innovation has been an important part of the financial landscape throughout modern economic history, it has received relatively little attention in academia. This essay surveys the existing literature on financial innovation from the disciplines of financial economics, history, law, and industrial organization. I begin by defining financial innovation and discussing problems with creating taxonomies of financial innovations. I then discuss the explanations given for the extensive amount of financial innovation we observe both today and in history, which include: (a) completing inherently incomplete markets; (b) addressing persistent agency concerns and information asymmetries; (c) minimizing transaction, search or marketing costs; (d) responding to tax and regulatory forces; (e) responding to changes in economic conditions, in particular new or newly perceived risks; and (f) capitalizing on technological developments. I review work that studies the identity of innovators, the process of diffusion of innovation, and private benefits of innovation. I illustrate these general trends with a description of a sequence of innovations that show that repeated experimentation and failure characterize the evolutionary process. As difficult as it may be to measure the private benefits to innovators, it has proven even more problematic to conclusively model or measure the social welfare benefits of financial innovation, although one can point to specific innovations that appear to enhance welfare.

Keywords

financial innovation, capital markets, security design, financial institutions

JEL classification: G2 (G23, G24), O3 (O31)

1. Introduction

In Merton Miller's (1986) view on financial innovation, the period from the mid-1960s to mid-1980s was a unique one in American financial history. Looking backward, he rhetorically asked, "Can any twenty-year period in recorded history have witnessed even a tenth as much (financial innovation)"? Looking forward, he asked the question in Miller (1992), "Financial innovation: Another wave on the way"? Answering "No" to both questions, he concluded that the period was an extraordinary one in the history of financial innovation. However, with 20–20 hindsight, we can disagree with his assessment and answer the two questions somewhat differently.

History shows that financial innovation has been a critical and persistent part of the economic landscape over the past few centuries. In the years since Miller's 1986 piece, financial markets have continued to produce a multitude of new products, including many new forms of derivatives, alternative risk transfer products, exchange traded funds, and variants of tax-deductible equity. A longer view suggests that financial innovation – like innovation elsewhere in business – is an *ongoing* process whereby private parties experiment to try to differentiate their products and services, responding to both sudden and gradual changes in the economy. Surely, innovation ebbs and flows with some periods exhibiting bursts of activity and others witnessing a slackening or even backlash.[1] However, when seen from a distance, the Schumpeterian process of innovation – in this instance, financial innovation – is a regular ongoing part of a profit-maximizing economy.

In this review piece, I summarize the existing research on financial innovation and highlight the many areas where our knowledge is still very incomplete. The existing work, while fairly modest in scope relative to other topics covered in this volume, is spread over a wide range of fields: general-equilibrium analyses of the role for financial innovation; thought pieces proposing the reasons for innovation; legal and policy analyses of tax rules, regulation and innovation; studies of financial innovation in the industrial organization literature; clinical studies of individual innovations; and a handful of empirical studies of the process of innovation.[2] A number of books on the subject have been written, including Allen and Gale's (1994) comprehensive overview, and entire issues of journals have been devoted to the topic [e.g., *Journal of Economic Theory* (1995, Volume 65)]. The topic of financial innovation has been addressed by a

---

[1] For example, there have been numerous periods throughout the past centuries in which innovation flourished, failures took place, and public and regulatory sentiment led to temporary anti-innovation feelings. See Chancellor (1999). More recently, the failure of Enron has probably slowed the innovation of new forms of special purpose entities and off-balance sheet financing, although this chilling effect is unlikely to be permanent.

[2] In addition, there is a large variety of articles in the financial press as well as popular business books addressing the topic of financial innovation, typically from the perspective of how businesses can capitalize on them. For examples of popular book-length discussions of financial innovation, see Geanuracos and Millar (1991), Walmsley (1988) and Crawford and Sen (1996).

number of American Finance Association presidents, including Merton (1992, 1993, 1995), Miller (1986, 1991, 1992), Ross (1989) and Van Horne (1985), some in their Presidential Addresses. My goals in this short overview are to survey the breadth of the existing literature briefly, rather than treat one sub-area in detail, and to highlight open issues that researchers may find suitable for future work.

This piece is divided into five sections. Section 2 defines financial innovation and discusses the difficulty of creating a taxonomy of financial innovations. Section 3 discusses the explanations advanced for financial innovation. Section 4 discusses the identity of innovators. Section 5 discusses the implications of financial innovation on private and social wealth. Section 6 concludes with a brief discussion of new means of protecting the intellectual property of innovators and a review of the open issues in this field.

2. What is financial innovation?

Much of the theoretical and empirical work in financial economics considers a highly stylized world in which there are few types of securities (typically debt and equity) and maybe a handful of simple financial institutions (typically banks or exchanges). However, in reality there is a vast range of different financial products, many different types of financial institutions and a variety of processes that these institutions employ to do business. The literature on financial innovation attempts to catalog some of this variety, describe the reasons why we observe an ever-increasing diversity of practice, and assess the private and social implications of this activity.

"Innovate" is defined in *Webster's Collegiate Dictionary* as "to introduce as or *as if* new",[3] with the root of the word deriving from the Latin word "novus" or new. Economists use the word "innovation" in an expansive fashion to describe shocks to the economy (e.g., "monetary policy innovations") as well as the responses to these shocks (e.g., Eurodeposits). Broadly speaking, financial innovation is the act of creating and then popularizing new financial instruments as well as new financial technologies, institutions and markets. The "innovations" are sometimes divided into *product* or *process* innovation, with product innovations exemplified by new derivative contracts, new corporate securities or new forms of pooled investment products, and process improvements typified by new means of distributing securities, processing transactions, or pricing transactions. In practice, even this innocuous differentiation is not clear, as process and product innovation are often linked. The *processes* by which one creates a new index linked to college costs or invests to produce returns that replicate this index are hard to separate from a new indexed investment *product* that attempt to help parents save to pay for their children's education.

---

[3] Webster's Ninth New Collegiate Dictionary (1988).

Innovation includes the acts of invention (the ongoing research and development function) and diffusion (or adoption) of new products, services or ideas.[4] Invention is probably an overly generous term, in that most innovations are evolutionary adaptations of prior products. The lexicographer's addition of the phrase "as if" to the definition of innovation reflects one difficulty in any study of this phenomenon – almost nothing is completely "new" and the degree of newness or novelty is inherently subjective.[5] (Patent examiners charged with judging the novelty of inventions face this challenge routinely.)

One sub-branch of the literature on financial innovation has created lists or taxonomies of innovations. Given the breadth of possible innovations, this work tends to specialize in particular areas, such as securities innovations. For example, Finnerty (1988, 1992, 2001) has created a list of over 60 securities innovations, organized by broad type of instrument (debt, preferred stock, convertible securities, and common equities) and by the function served (reallocating risk, increasing liquidity, reducing agency costs, reducing transactions costs, reducing taxes or circumventing regulatory constraints). One investment bank published a guide to innovative international debt securities in the mid-1980s. This 64-page booklet did not describe individual innovations, but rather categorized the *characteristics* of the innovative securities along five dimensions (coupon, life, redemption proceeds, issue price and warrants).[6]

Neither innovation nor the impulse to categorize it are new activities. The 1934 edition of the investing classic, Benjamin Graham and David Dodd's *Security Analysis,* included an appendix entitled "A Partial List of Securities which Deviate from the Normal Patterns", which they introduced in this way:

> In assembling the material presented herewith it has not been our purpose to present a complete list of all types of securities which vary from the customary contractual arrangements between the issuing corporation and the holder. Such a list would extend the size of this volume beyond reasonable limits. We have, however, attempted to give a reasonably complete example of deviations from the standard patterns.

In the following 17 pages, they described 258 securities. Put in modern language, their list included pay-in-kind bonds, step-up bonds, putable bonds, bonds with stock dividends, zero coupon bonds, inflation-indexed bonds, a variety of exotic convertible and exchangeable bonds, 23 different types of warrants, voting bonds, non-voting shares, and a host of other instruments. Graham and Dodd's list is not an anomaly. A small literature on the history of financial innovation demonstrates that the creation of new financial products and processes has been an ongoing part of economies for

---

[4] See Rogers (1983) for a discussion of the adoption of innovations.

[5] Scholars in Industrial Organization sometimes differentiate between "drastic" and "incremental" innovations. Drastic innovations bring costs to a level below the corresponding monopoly price. See Tirole (1988, chapter 10).

[6] Other useful lists were drawn up by Tufano (1989, 1995), Matthews (1994) and Silber (1975).

at least the past four centuries, if not longer.[7] While many of these old innovations sound quite new even today, some have become extinct. For example, the "Million Adventure", described by Allen and Gale (1994, p. 13), raised one million pounds in 1694. The structure of this "lottery loan" innovation was a 16 year bond paying 10% with an added bonus – a lottery ticket which gave the holder a chance to share in an additional £40 000 per year for each of the next 16 years.

In preparing this chapter, I asked my research assistant to compile a complete list of security innovations so that I could update an estimate from the mid-80s that showed 20% of all new security issues used an "innovative" structure.[8] One place to begin this exercise was Thompson Financial Securities Data[9] (formerly Securities Data Corp. or SDC), a data vendor that tracks new public offerings of securities. He provided me with a list of 1836 unique "security codes" used from the early 1980s through early 2001, each purporting to be a different type of security. Some of the securities listed were nearly-identical products offered by banks trying to differentiate their wares from those of their competitors.[10] Others represented evolutionary improvements on earlier products. Perhaps a few were truly novel. Nevertheless, the length of the list represents a "normal" pattern of financial innovation, where a security is created, but then modified (and improved) slightly by each successive bank that offers it to its clients.

Even this list – if combed to eliminate false innovation – would severely underestimate the amount of financial innovation, as it only includes corporate securities. It excludes the tremendous innovation in exchange-traded derivatives, over-the-counter derivative contracts[11] (such as the credit derivatives, equity swaps, weather derivatives and exotic over-the-counter options), new insurance contracts (such as alternative risk transfer contracts or contingent equity contracts), and new investment management products (such as exchange traded funds or various schemes to allow investors to create the fractional-share portfolios of baskets of stocks).

The many different "lists" of financial innovations – even just security innovations – demonstrate the difficulty in categorizing new products. Lists organized by product name (like SDC's categorization) tend to be uninformative, because firms use names to differentiate similar products. Lists by "traditional labels" (e.g., legal or regulatory definitions of debt or equity, etc.) tend to be problematic, as innovations often

---

[7] For extended discussions, see Silber (1975), Allen and Gale (1994, Chapter 2) and Tufano (1995, 1997).
[8] The original estimate comes form Tufano (1989).
[9] Online service: www.tfsd.com.
[10] In the world of financial engineering, it is common to "reverse engineer" a new product, and offer a competing version of the innovation. These "knock-offs" are often very similar to the original product, while they bear a different service-mark.
[11] Duffie and Rahi (1995) cite the Wall Street Journal (June 14, 1994, p. C1) as stating there are over 1200 different types of derivative securities in use, although these journalistic calculations are somewhat suspect.

intentionally span across different traditional labels. Lists organized by product feature (e.g., maturity, redemption provisions, etc.) provide a great deal of information and highlight the component parts of each innovation, but do so at creating a classification system that has so many dimensions as to be unmanageable.

The alternative chosen by most academics writing about innovation has been to adopt a functional approach to classifying products. [12] Rather than group products by their names or features, authors categorize them by the functions they serve. Finnerty's taxonomy mentioned above does this, as does the Bank for International Settlements (1986). The BIS discusses the problems with creating taxonomies and concludes that the best scheme is a functional one. While there seems to be some agreement that the best categorization scheme is a functional one, it is less clear how to identify the particular functions.

3. Why do financial innovations arise? What functions do they serve?

If the world were free of all "imperfections" – such as taxes, regulation, information asymmetries, transaction costs, and moral hazard – and if markets were complete in the sense that existing securities spanned all states of nature, we could arrive at an M&M-like corollary regarding financial innovation. Financial innovations would benefit neither private parties nor society and would simply be neutral mutations. [13]

Against this backdrop, a sizeable body of literature attempts to understand how various "imperfections" (and changes in these imperfections) stimulate financial innovation. These *imperfections* prevent participants in the economy from efficiently obtaining the *functions* they need from the financial system. Generally, authors establish how financial innovations are optimal responses to various basic problem or opportunities, such as incomplete markets that prevent risk shifting or asymmetric information. Some of these analyses are "institution-free" in that they do not explicitly consider the role of innovators in the process, while other institutionally-grounded explanations study the parts played by financial institutions using innovation to compete.

What functions do innovations help us perform? Merton's (1993, 1995) functional decomposition identifies six functions delivered by financial systems: (1) moving funds across time and space; (2) the pooling of funds; (3) managing risk; (4) extracting

---

[12] While various authors have proposed functional classification schemes, the broader notion of using "function" as the means to understand financial systems has been advanced strongly by Merton (1992), and is developed in Crane et al. (1995).

[13] While the notion of neutral mutations has been long recognized in evolution, Miller (1977) used the term to describe a variety of financial decisions and financial innovations. While this term is normally used as a derogatory one, Miller is careful to note that the existence of seemingly neutral mutations can "permit the adaptation to new conditions to take place more quickly or surely" in response to real changes in the economy.

information to support decision-making; (5) addressing moral hazard and asymmetric information problems; and (6) facilitating the sale or purchase of goods and services through a payment system. Different writers use slightly different lists of functions, but there is much overlap in these descriptions. For example, Finnerty (1992) identifies a set of functions, two of which correspond closely to Merton's functions (reallocating risk and reducing agency costs), and a third ("increasing liquidity") which is an amalgam of Merton's movement of funds and pooling functions. The BIS (1986) has a slightly different scheme to identify the functions performed by innovation, focusing on the transfer of risks (both price and credit), the enhancement of liquidity, and the generation of funds to support enterprises (through credit and equity.) Each author strives to describe the functions in a parsimonious fashion, but it is probably fair to say that no commonly accepted and unique taxonomy of functions has been adopted. Even if it were to exist, no functional scheme could avoid the complication that a single innovation is likely to address multiple functions. For example, using Merton's functional scheme, asset securitization invokes at least three functions: it pools various future promises, modifies risk profiles through diversification, and moves funds across time and space.

If functions represent timeless demands put upon financial systems, then why do we observe innovation? Some authors adopt a static framework, where no attempt is made to explain the timing of the innovation. Other authors adopt a dynamic framework, where innovations reflect responses to changes in the environment, and the timing of the innovation mirrors this change. My discussion below summarizes most of the key arguments, and uses a combination of recent and historical examples to illustrate the points. [14]

3.1. Inherently incomplete markets stimulate innovation

In an incomplete market, not all states of nature can be spanned, and as a result, parties are not able to move funds freely across time and space, nor to manage risk. Duffie and Rahi (1995), in their introduction to a special issue of the *Journal of Economic Theory* on financial market innovation and security design, review the literature on market incompleteness and innovation. [15] This literature attempts to establish conditions under which innovation would occur in equilibrium. In summarizing a wide range of the literature they conclude:

> At this early stage, while there are several results providing conditions for the existence of equilibrium with innovation, the available theory has relatively few normative or predictive results. From a spanning point of view, we can guess that there are incentives to set up markets for securities for which there are no close substitutes, and which may be used to hedge substantive risks.

---

[14] Portions of this section are drawn from Tufano (1995).
[15] The survey of Duffie and Rahi (1995) describes a unified modeling framework to study the impact of innovation on risk-sharing and information aggregation.

This theoretical proposition is consistent with evidence of the pattern of innovation in exchange-traded contracts documented by Black (1986). She shows a relationship between a new contract's viability (measured by its trading volume) and its ability to complete markets (measured by its lack of correlation with large but uninsurable risks). Grinblatt and Longstaff (2000) study a different innovation (Treasury STRIPS or zero-coupon bonds). They find that investors create new STRIPS primarily to make markets more complete, a conclusion drawn from the observation that STRIPS are created when it would be most difficult to synthesize the discount bonds from existing coupon instruments.

Allen and Gale (1988) consider a particular form of market incompleteness – in the form of short sales restrictions – as motivation for innovation by parties seeking to share risk. They show it may be optimal for firms to offer multiple classes of claims ("breaking the firm into pieces") generating value from different investor preferences and needs ("selling the pieces to the clientele that values it most").

Cloaked in less academic language, the idea that innovation typically addresses the unmet preferences or needs of particular clienteles is reasonably well discussed in business practice. For example, one popular book describing the derivatives activities at a major bank [Partnoy (1997)] provides detail on relatively uncommon products designed for a small number of institutional investors.

3.2. Inherent agency concerns and information asymmetries stimulate innovation

Much of contracting theory (or the security design literature) explores how contracts can be written to better align the interests of different parties or to force the revelation of private information by managers. This extensive literature has been surveyed by Harris and Raviv (1989), and is also covered in Allen and Gale (1994, pp. 140–147). Persistent conflicts of interest between outside capital providers and self-interested managers, and asymmetric information between informed insiders and uniformed outsiders, leads to equilibria in which firms issue a multiplicity of securities. Most of this work deals with innovation in a fairly limited sense, explaining the existence of a few contracts like debt or equity, not scores of different types of corporate securities. However, Haugen and Senbett (1981) argue that incorporating embedded options into securities can mitigate moral hazard problems. This motive for innovation can possibly explain the embedded options in some innovative R&D financings [for a case study of these innovations, see Lerner and Tufano (1993) [16] and for an empirical analysis see Beatty, Berger and Magliolo (1995)]. In these structures, an R&D financing organization is set up with separate shareholders from the "parent", which retains all decision rights to the day-to-day activities of this separate organization. Attaching warrants exercisable into the stock of the "parent" of the R&D financing vehicles partially ameliorates the inherent conflicts of interest.

---

[16] This case study and others mentioned here are also in Mason, Merton, Perold and Tufano (1995).

Ross (1989) invokes agency issues to explain some financial innovations. He notes that agency considerations make borrowing costly or limited and, as a result, individuals contract with opaque financial institutions. When a shock (such as a change in taxes or regulation) occurs, financial intermediaries may find it efficient to sell off low-grade assets. Because outside investors cannot easily assess the value of these assets, the institutions turn to investment banks to place these securities with their network of clients. These investment banks innovate, creating new pools of these low-grade assets. Agency considerations interact with marketing costs to produce innovation.

Throughout history, information asymmetries have prompted a number of innovations. Throughout much of the 19th and early 20th century, firms disclosed very little credible financial information. Over time, market forces and governmental action materially increased the quantity and quality – and thus lowered the cost – of information about firms. Early innovations tended to substitute for (or economize on) the use of costly information, while later innovations capitalized on its lower cost. One of the earliest innovations, the nineteenth century practice of issuing assessable stock, provided some mechanisms to squeeze information from firms. An assessable shareholder committed to supply a certain amount of money to the firm, but doled out the cash to the firm in response to regular assessments. See Dewing (1919). Issuers of assessable common stock were forced to return to their investors regularly and make the case for continued commitment, because each investor held the option to fail to make the assessment and forfeit his interest. The 19th century firms' almost complete reliance on secured debt for debt financing [see Ripley cited in Baskin (1988, pp. 215–216)] may also be interpreted as a costly contracting choice that substituted for more precise monitoring prevented by inadequate disclosure.

Later 19th century innovations took advantage of the presence of cheaper and more reliable information. Later preferred stocks conditioned their holders' voting rights on firms' failure to comply with covenant terms [Johnson (1925) and Wilson (1930), both cited in Dewing (1934)]. These covenants, especially after 1900, were more likely to be tied to financial ratios, as were bond covenants keyed to working capital tests or asset maintenance tests [Dewing (1934)]. Finally, income bonds, popularized in the late 19th century, were completely linked to the availability of accounting information. These unsecured obligations required issuers to pay interest only if the firm earned positive accounting profits in the current period.[17] This early history shows how innovations were a response to information asymmetries. Certain innovations forced the revelation of information and others exploited the low cost information generated through other processes.

---

[17] Income bonds never took root, perhaps because they gave rise to a stream of litigation about firms' accounting earnings, which determined the issuer's responsibilities under the contract.

3.3. Transaction, search or marketing costs stimulate innovation

Merton (1989) discusses how the presence of transaction costs provides a critical role for financial intermediaries. Financial intermediaries permit households facing transaction costs to achieve their optimal consumption-investment program. Merton uses this argument to explain how equity swaps can be an efficient way to deliver returns to multinational investors. A similar explanation is invoked by McConnell and Schwartz (1992) who provide a clinical study of one particular innovation, LYONs (liquid yield option notes). A LYON is a callable, putable, convertible zero-coupon bond used by firms to raise financing. Lee Cole, the Options Marketing Manager at Merrill Lynch, noticed that retail investors tend to place most of their money in low-risk securities and then buy a series of call options. Merrill Lynch's LYONs allowed investors to replicate this payoff without having to incur the commission costs of rolling over their call option positions at least four times a year.

Many of the process innovations in payment systems technologies are aimed at lowering transaction costs. Automated Teller Machines (ATMs), smart cards, ACH technologies that permit easy transfers of funds, e-401k programs and many other new businesses are legitimate financial innovations that seek to dramatically lower the sheer costs of processing transactions. By some estimates, these innovations have the potential to lower the cost of transacting by a factor of over 100. For example, by one estimate, a teller-assisted transaction costs over $1.00 and the same transaction executed over the Internet would cost about $0.01.[18]

New businesses (some of which may not succeed) like Instinet, Open-IPO, Enron OnLine, Ebay, or the host of B-to-B exchanges are innovations that aimed at lowering the transaction costs faced by buyers and sellers. These transaction costs are search or marketing costs, which can include a variety of components – the sheer costs of identifying buyers and seller, information costs, and transaction costs of order processing. Ross's (1989) analysis of securitization keys off the expensive process of marketing in conjunction with agency considerations. Madan and Soubra (1991) examine how financial intermediaries attempt to maximize their revenues net of marketing costs, which leads them to design multiple products that appeal to wider sets of investors.

History shows that as marketing costs fall, financial innovations exploit the easier access to buyers and sellers of securities. For example, during World War I, the USA government instituted a massive program to fund its war-time efforts through selling small-denomination bonds to individual investors. Carosso (1970) describes the Liberty Loan program of 1917 which identified and educated a new clientele of retail investors:

> The Treasury immediately decided to mount an intensive nationwide sales effort. Advertisements and thousands of spokesmen emphasized the security, high yield, and probable appreciation of the

---

[18] The Economist, "Online Finance Survey" (May 20, 2000, p. 20).

new Liberty bonds. Established techniques were put aside. Instead of selling substantial amounts of large denominations for holding in relatively few hands, the government issued bonds in small denominations, utilized war saving stamps widely, and permitted installment payments. All the foregoing "new" departures were designed to appeal to individuals not considered potential investors since the Civil War days of Jay Cooke.

These activities by the federal government lowered the costs for the private sector to identify and educate new potential customers. After the war, innovations in the private sector took advantage of the lowered costs of raising funds from households. These innovations, tailored to meet the needs of small savers, included "baby bonds" sold in small denominations and securities sales on installment [Riegel (1920)].

3.4. Taxes and regulation stimulate innovation

While many authors have pointed out the link between taxes and innovation, Miller (1986) is often cited on this point: "The major impulses to successful innovations over the past twenty years have come, I am saddened to have to say, from regulation and taxes". The list of tax and regulatory induced products would include zero-coupon bonds, Eurodollar Eurobonds, various equity-linked structures used to monetize asset holdings without triggering immediate capital gains taxes, and trust preferred structures.[19]

If we think of taxes as a major "imperfection" added to the M&M world, then the search to maximize after-tax returns has arguably stimulated much innovation, and changes in tax law in turn stimulate even more innovation. For example, various equity-linked structures used by firms to monetize their holdings of stock permit these firms to delay paying capital gains taxes. These innovations decouple economic ownership or exposure from legal ownership (governance and tax implications). See Tufano (1996b) and Santangelo and Tufano (1997) for a case study of this type of innovation.

A number of legal scholars have written extensively on the relationship between laws and innovation, and have created a flourishing literature on this subject. They discuss how tax laws have both encouraged and discouraged innovation, analyzed the failures of the USA tax code for dealing with functionally-similar securities, suggested how to change the tax code to eliminate innovation, and given their opinions of the social welfare costs of tax-induced innovation.[20]

A century ago, taxes were a less visible force in the USA economy, yet they still played some role in the process of financial innovation. In the late 1920s, a few states (Delaware, New Jersey and New York) began to levy incorporation and transfer taxes based on the par value of firms' shares, and to assign par values of $100 to firms whose stock had zero par value. Corporations almost immediately reissued shares with small,

---

[19] For an example of this type of innovation for zero-coupon debt, see Fisher, Brick and Ng (1983).
[20] This is a very extensive literature. For representative papers, see Gergen and Schmitz (1997), Kollbrenner (1995), Warren (1993), Knoll (1997, 2001), Strnad (1994) and Schenk (1995).

but nonzero ($1–$5) par values [Hornberger (1933)]. Equipment trust certificates, by which a railroad leased cars from a manufacturer with financing provided by the certificates secured by the equipment, were more popular in states such as Pennsylvania that subjected bonds, but not the certificates, to income taxes [Dewing (1934)].

Changes in regulation are also credited with stimulating innovation. Kane (1986) identified what he calls the "regulatory dialectic" as a major source of innovation. Innovation responds to regulatory constraints, which in turn are adjusted in reaction to these innovations. Bank capital requirements are a good example of regulations that impose costs on the affected parties, who then use innovation to optimize in light of these constraints. Capital notes and certain preferred stocks that qualified as "capital" to bank regulators are examples of regulatory-induced innovation. Similarly, the early Eurobond market was motivated by regulatory concerns. By offering Eurodollar CDs, USA banks, led by Citicorp in 1966, sought to circumvent reserve requirements to stem the painful disintermediation they were experiencing.[21] Regulations limiting cross-border flows are sometimes credited with stimulating certain equity swaps, which enable foreign investors to hold an economic interest in equities they would find difficult to own.[22] The academic debate on regulation has taken many different forms: Whether regulation has stimulated or impeded innovation and whether regulation is "sensible" in light of innovation. See White (2000), Hu (1989), Pouncy (1998) and Russo and Vinciguerra (1991) for development of some of these themes. Emprical support for some of these claims is not as forceful as the arguments. For example, while regulation is considered a key driver of innovation, Jagtiani, Saunders and Udell (1995) fail to find that changes in capital requirements consistently affected the speed of adoption of certain innovations, like off-balance sheet products.

While ratings agencies are not governmentally-established regulators, they are a form of self-regulatory organization. Their rules have given rise to innovations. In particular, various forms of trust-preferred securities that seek to retain tax deductibility while being treated like equity from the perspective of ratings agencies are examples of innovation induced partially by ratings.

Court decisions, and the nature of the legal system, give rise to innovation. Throughout the late 19th century, the extreme business cycles experienced by the USA economy led to the massive failures of railroads and industrial firms. Security holders turned to the courts to enforce what they believed to be their legal rights, but judges set aside many "inviolable rights" to quickly reorganize the railroads. Specifically, super-senior "debtor-in-possession" financing was given priority above existing senior claimants, certain unsecured creditors were paid before secured creditors, and judges set "judicial" values for the claims of distressed firms. These legal innovations were

---

[21] Eurobond markets were also stimulated by related concerns, although more linked to tax considerations. See Kim and Stulz (1988).

[22] Regulation or lack of certain standard legal forms can also stymie innovation. For example, various laws have apparently slowed the growth of securitization in some European countries.

important stimuli for the adoption of contingent charge securities and voting trusts, which supplanted traditional creditors' rights with more direct means of monitoring and control. See Tufano (1997). In our own time, changes in the real and perceived legal and tax risk of various structured products may initially lead to reduced usage, but probably greater innovation over the medium to long term. Franks and Sussman (1999) argue that the nature of the "innovation regime" (whether driven by lenders and borrowers, or by judges and legislators) affects the nature of subsequent contract evolution and the amount of innovation.

Just as governmental or court rules can give rise to innovation, so too can religious prohibitions. The strong Islamic prohibition against interest has stimulated a number of alternative financing vehicles. Many of these innovations seem to respect the letter, but not the spirit, of the ban on interest, using sale-repurchase contracts to effectively deliver interest to lenders. For a discussion, see Vogel and Hayes (1998).

It may be more than semantics to comment that *legal engineering* has facilitated a range of new forms of contracting innovations. For example, the on-going quest for "tax-deductible equity" has largely been the product of *legal engineers* utilizing new ideas to develop securities whose cash payments are tax-deductible but which are treated like equity in the eyes of potential investors. McLaughlin (1999) discusses the relationship between legal engineering and financial innovation from the perspective of a practicing member of the legal bar.

3.5. Increasing globalization and perceptions of risk stimulate innovation

Most essays on financial innovation identify globalization and increasing volatility of financial markets as drivers of innovation. With greater globalization, firms, investors and governments are exposed to new risks (exchange rates or political risks), and innovations help them manage these risks. For example, a recent press report announced that the Interamerican Development Bank had created the first-ever instrument that incorporated a currency convertibility and transferability guarantee. In addition, globalization enables capital raisers to tap larger and more diverse populations of potential investors. A variety of innovations are attributed to attempts to meet the needs of specific investor clienteles. For example, one popular finance book describes a variety of innovative structures designed to appeal to particular Japanese insurance company investors, a form of cross-national regulatory arbitrage.

Some authors point to increasing volatility as a stimulus to innovation. For example, Smith, Smithson and Wilford (1990, p. 13), document the increase in the volatility of interest rates, exchange rates, and commodity prices, and draw a link between this increase in riskiness and financial innovation:

> Uncertainty in the global financial environment has caused many economic problems and disruptions, but it has also provided the impetus for financial innovation. Through financial innovation, the financial intermediaries were soon able to offer their customers products to manage or even exploit the new risks. Through this same innovation, financial institutions became even better able to evaluate and manage their own asset and liability processes.

They list a variety of innovations spawned by increasing volatility: foreign exchange futures, swaps, and options; interest-rate futures, swaps, options, and forwards; and commodity swaps, futures, and options. As a concrete example, the deregulation of natural gas in the USA suddenly exposed producers and consumers of gas to tremendous volatility. Drawing analogies to financial markets, gas marketers created (or adapted) a variety of new gas contracts, including Volumetric Production Payment contracts, cross-commodity swaps, and a line of branded price protection products. See Mason, Merton, Perold and Tufano (1995).

The volatility of exchange rates and inflation rates prompted earlier innovations. The period of World War I and its aftermath was characterized by high inflation uncertainty. "Stabilized" (inflation-indexed) bonds, which were introduced in 1925 with an issue by Rand-Kardex, linked interest and principal payments to the wholesale price index [Masson and Stratton (1938)]. This innovation, although apparently never popularized, was an explicit attempt to solve the problem of highly volatile prices. The instability of currency values prompted innovations regarding the medium of payment for bonds (currency-choice bonds). "Legal tender" bonds gave "the payer ... the option of paying in any kind of legal tender (gold, silver, or currency); they give to him the benefit of the cheaper form of currency" [Cleveland (1907)]. Non-USA issuers, facing the problems of "disordered or unstable monetary systems ... attempted to allay the fears of investors by various attempts to insure protection against depreciated currencies". These innovations included indexing payments to exchange rates and permitting investors to choose the form of the interest payment [Masson and Stratton (1938)]. Stabilized and currency-choice bonds show that volatility motivated innovations in the 1830–1930 period, just as it has spurred more recent innovation.

3.6. Technological shocks stimulate innovation

Shocks to technology are thought to provide a "supply-side" explanation for the timing of some innovations.[23] Advances in information technology support sophisticated pooling schemes that we observe in securitization. IT and improvements in telecommunications (more recently the Internet) have facilitated a number of innovations (not all successful), including new methods of underwriting securities (e.g., OpenIPO, a scheme to directly offer IPOs to investors without a traditional underwriting), new methods of assembling portfolios of stocks (folioFN, an innovation whereby investors could assemble portfolios of fractional shares), new markets for securities and new means of executing security transactions. White (2000) articulates this technological view of financial innovation.

New "intellectual technologies", i.e., derivative pricing models, are credited with stimulating the growth and popularization of a variety of new contracts. Many new

---

[23] Schmookler's (1967) classic work on innovation articulates a technological-driven view of broad classes of innovations.

forms of derivatives were made possible because business people could have some confidence in the methods of pricing and hedging the risks of these new contracts. Without the ideas developed by Black, Scholes, Merton, and many others, numerous developments in derivative products would probably never have occurred.

Various forms of innovations such as new risk-management systems and measures (such as Value-at-Risk based measures), on-line retirement planning services (like Financial Engines), and new valuation techniques (like real options) clearly were facilitated by both intellectual and information technology innovations. For example, the existence of lifetime portfolio choice models, developments in numerical analyses and simulation, hardware that enables faster processing, and the Internet are all elements that support (but may not ensure the success of) new businesses that seek to provide consumers with advice on their financial decisions.

3.6.1. A case study: No **one** explanation works

Let us consider a quarter century of innovation in one particular part of the investment management world, and how virtually every stimulus mentioned above played a role in a whole family of innovations.

In their 1974 piece, "From Theory to a New Financial Product", Black and Scholes describe the birth of a new product: "market funds", or what we call today index funds. Wells Fargo reportedly first offered a privately placed equally-weighted S&P 500 fund in 1971 (which apparently never caught on), and introduced a value-weighted fund in 1973.[24] Black and Scholes describe the challenges in bringing this product to market, which required Wells Fargo to navigate regulatory and tax issues, surmount systems processing requirements, and educate potential investors. What were the stimuli for this innovation? At one level, the introduction of index funds permitted investors to better manage their investment-consumption decisions – they "completed the market". These funds also were an economical solution to high transaction costs which would prevent most investors from creating a basket of securities that replicated the entire equity market. We must also acknowledge that these innovations were shaped by new technologies (both intellectual advancements such as portfolio theory as well as systems capabilities), were responses to tax and regulatory factors, and were driven by the presence of information asymmetries and transaction costs that made trading costly. Thus, this one innovation was the result of virtually every explanation advanced above. Attempts to distinguish which factor was *most* important seem pointless.

Later generations of indexed products (and futures contracts) followed, but moving ahead a later related development was exchange traded funds (EFT). EFTs essentially let investors trade the market index throughout the day.[25] Toronto Index Participations

---

[24] Vanguard's retail offering, the First Index Investment Trust, was introduced in 1976.

[25] Index futures also allow investors to buy and sell the market portfolio, although they take a different legal form, have different settling up features, and are not permissible investments for some investors. The Chicago Mercantile Exchange first offered a futures contract on the S&P 500 index in 1982.

(TIPS) in 1990, Leland O'Brian Rubinstein's SuperTrust in 1992, the American Stock Exchange's SPDRs (Standard and Poor's Depository Receipts) in 1993, and Merrill Lynch's HOLDRs in 1999 were steps in the evolutionary innovation process. Arguably, EFTs and HOLDRs were motivated by similar impulses as the index funds, but these innovations enhanced the functionality of the original innovation. They permitted investors to enjoy even lower transaction costs than many index funds and permit intraday trading, which facilitates speculation, arbitrage and risk management. These innovations were driven by regulation, in that they permit investors to short sell the index, which index funds do not, and avoid the uptick rule, which prescribes when an investor can short-sell a security. These products were also tax-motivated, in that they permitted investors to avoid potential tax liabilities resulting from the redemptions of other investors, and to "cherry pick" the timing of recognition of losses and gains on *individual* securities in the basket. The HOLDRS also reduced transaction costs by eliminating rebalancing, whose transaction costs (due to recognition of capital gains) can be material. [26]

The newest "generation" of products pushing this functionality to even greater levels are the "personal funds" that a few web-based firms are offering, such as folioFN. [27] These firms permitted investors to assemble baskets of stock in relatively small denominations, allowing investors to create and trade positions involving fractional shares. Like ETFs, these products permitted investors to assemble and trade baskets as well as enjoy certain tax-timing advantages while eliminating the overhang of capital gains triggered by mutual fund redemptions. This innovation takes us back to the days before the first "market portfolio" in that it makes it possible for investors to *directly* create the exposures that index funds and EFTS made possible. What accounts for this new innovation? At a functional level, this product represents another step in the line of products that enable investors to hold broad diversified baskets for consumption smoothing, risk management and speculation. Yet it is technology, embedded in improvements in information technologies, that permit personal funds to be technically feasible. Technology may enable these innovators to market these products via the web as well as execute transactions at low costs. One report noted that "It simply was impossible to consider such a strategy before the advent of the Internet, "This firm is a child of the Internet, [the founder] said". [28]

Market funds, index funds, ETFs, HOLDRs, personal funds – this family of innovations embodies just about every possible motive for innovation. All the innovations deliver a similar basic functionality, but successive innovations build upon

---

[26] For historical background on these products, see Gary Gastineau, "Exchange Traded Funds: An Introduction", Institutional Investor, Spring 2001. Also see the case studies of SuperTrust [Tufano and Kyrillos (1994)] and HOLDRS [Perold and Brown (2001)].

[27] Reportedly, the "fn" is apparently an abbreviation for financial innovation. See Eric Winig, "Virginia firm reinvents the stock market", Baltimore Business Journal (June 2, 2000, p. 23).

[28] Eric Winig, "Virginia firm reinvents the stock market", Baltimore Business Journal (June 2, 2000, p. 23).

each other. Each new generation attempts to lower the costs of transacting, be more tax efficient, and give investors increasing control over their decisions. This mini-history is a quick reminder of the evolutionary process of innovation. Along the way, some products died out (equal-weighted market funds or SuperTrust), some succeeded (index funds and ETFs) and some are too early to tell (personal funds). Individual innovations often fail, but even in their failure, they give subsequent innovators new information that can be used to develop the next generation of products. This role of failure in financial innovation is an important one. Given the relative ease of copying financial products, one firm's failure can be quickly exploited by a rival.

This evolutionary flavor reminds us that the innovation process is a dynamic one. Understanding these dynamics has been a long-standing topic among students of innovation, with research on patent races being well covered. [29] However, the easily imitated nature of financial innovation may not lend itself easily to these models. Merton (1992) characterizes the dynamics of innovation in the financial service world using a metaphor of "financial innovation spiral" in which one innovation begets the next. We see this in the sequence of innovations discussed above. We also see the spiral when we consider that the trading of standardized exchange-traded products facilitates the creation of custom-designed OTC products, which in turn stimulates even greater trading, lowering transaction costs and making possible even more new products. A variant of this concept would help explain how rival investment banks created a set of increasingly-improved preferred stocks that would maintain relatively constant principal values [Mason, Merton, Perold and Tufano (1995)], by copying and improving upon prior products. Persons and Warther (1997) model the innovation spiral in which adoption of innovations provides other participants with information about the profitability of innovation, creating waves of innovation and an S-curve shape of adoption.

4. Who innovates? The identities of and private returns to innovators

As Allen (2001) points out, much of financial economics act as if financial institutions do not exist. While this tendency has also characterized some of the literature on financial innovation, given the fairly applied nature of the field, writers have more explicitly dealt with the role of private parties and financial intermediaries as innovators. Duffie and Jackson (1989) consider the incentives of exchanges which lead them to offer one new contract rather than another. Ross (1989) explicitly incorporates a role for investment banks that maximize their own profits by coming up with innovative bundles of securities to lower marketing or search costs. Boot and Thakor (1997) model how different institutional structures might lead to different levels of innovation. They find that innovation would be lower in a universal banking system –

---

[29] See Reinganum (1989) for a review of this literature.

especially one with substantial market concentration – than in one in which commercial and investment banking were functionally separated. Essentially, greater competition among these private parties leads to increased innovation. Bhattacharyya and Nanda (2000) model the incentives for innovation within the investment banking industry. They find that banks with larger market shares will tend to innovate, as will banks whose client relationships are more sticky. Heinonen (1992) studies game-theoretic models of innovation, focusing on benefits on the costs of production (economies of scope) or on the costs of distribution (marketing).

There has been relatively little empirical work on the benefits accruing to financial innovators. Tufano (1989) and Carrow (1999) study the incentives of investment banks to innovate, focusing on the market shares they capture and the underwriting spreads they charge on new types of securities. Both studies find that innovators initially earn higher market shares than followers, even though imitation is rapid. The studies reach different conclusions about whether innovating investment banks charge higher underwriting spreads than do follower banks. Tufano found that underwriting spreads on the first offerings of innovations were not materially larger than those on later offerings, casting doubt on the notion that the primary profit from innovation comes from increased spreads. Carrow re-examined this question a decade later with a slightly different sample, incorporating additional variables into this analysis (underwriter prestige rankings and 14 dummy variables indicating specific features of the security). With this new specification, he finds that as the number of rivals increases, spreads do indeed decline. Neither of these studies looks at the many ways in which innovative bankers might profit by earning trading profits on aftermarket activities, increasing the likelihood of receiving subsequent business through enhanced reputation, increasing the quality of their own personnel leading to a higher quality staff, or, a matter of greater personal concern for the individuals involved, increasing their bonuses and career progression. All of these mechanisms for rewarding innovation are open questions for future research.

In some academic models, parties most constrained or inconvenienced by imperfections would be the most likely to innovate, as the shadow costs of releasing these constraints would be greatest for these firms. Silber (1975, 1983) articulates this constraint-based notion of innovation. This might suggest that the smallest, weakest firms, who face the most constraints, would be the most likely to innovate. In the broad field of innovation, this seems to be the case, with smaller firms thought to be more innovative.[30] There is some anecdotal evidence that supports this conclusion in financial services. Two upstart financial service firms – Vanguard and Drexel Burnham Lambert – substantially developed their businesses using a platform of innovative products (index funds and junk bonds), and a variety of e-Businesses attempted to create competitive advantage through innovation. However, this anecdotal observation is not consistently supported by the empirical data. At least for securities

---

[30] See Scherer and Ross (1990) for a review of the literature on this point.

innovations, larger, more financially secure investment banks have consistently been the
leading innovators [see Tufano (1989)]. Matthews (1994, chapter 13) adapts industrial-
organization models to show why there might be a self-reinforcing cycle between
innovation and market share, with larger firms innovating and thereby increasing their
size at the expense of their rivals. Whether large or small firms are the primary
innovators is still an open empirical question. Among issuers, it is difficult to argue that
the most constrained firms are the most innovative. Rather, a great deal of innovation
is directed at larger, well-established firms, as described by one banker: [31]

> The only way to reach large investment-grade companies is innovation. Such companies have
> ready access to every segment of the capital markets on attractive terms; we have to offer the
> better mousetrap. This inevitably leads to an array of products, often customized for individual
> issues.

Perhaps, smaller and weaker firms face a great number of constraints, and their
efforts are focused on addressing these constraints directly (e.g., communicating their
story to potential investors) rather than optimizing the form of capital. Larger firms
may have addressed these first-order imperfections and turned their attention to more
nuanced capital structuring issues and innovations. Among issuers, the question of
which firms innovate – and why – remains open.

Innovation includes not only inventing new products, but also the processes of the
diffusion or adoption of the inventions. Diffusion of innovations has long been studied
in the industrial-organization field [Molyneux and Shamroukh (1999) summarize the
industrial organizational literature on the adoption of innovations]. Empirical studies
of the adoption of financial innovations have focused on the introduction of automated
teller machines [Hannan and McDowell (1984, 1987) and Saloner and Shephard
(1995)], small business credit scoring [Akhavein, Frame and White (2001)], patents
[Lerner (2002)], off-balance sheet activities of banks [Molyneux and Shamroukh
(1996), Obay (2000)], junk-bond issuance [Molyneux and Shamroukh (1999)], and
corporate security innovations [Tufano (1989)]. The central question in much of this
literature is to determine which organizations adopt innovations and how quickly they
do so. While this literature is rich, much of it plays off of the question of whether
larger firms or smaller firms lead innovation, a long-standing debate. There is also
a "sociological" aspect to this research, in that it tries to understand the relative
importance of external stimuli versus internal factors (organizational characteristics
and competitive interactions among potential adopters). In many of these studies, it has
been the larger firms that have innovated more rapidly, for example, with larger banks
more quick to adopt credit scoring or larger investment banks faster to underwrite new
securities.

Bringing new securities to market requires the voluntary cooperation of both issuers
and investors. As a business proposition, innovation surely has the potential to enable

---

[31] E. Philip Jones, Head of Equity Linked Origination at Merrill Lynch and Co, in: "A market that feeds
on persistent innovation", Investment Dealers' Digest (May 22, 2000).

businesses to create value. This is the theme in a business book *The Power of Financial Innovation* by Geanuracos and Millar (1991), which studies 75 firms around the globe, showing "how the world's best-managed companies are ... putting the latest instruments to effective use". While some businesses will use innovation and profit, there is little systematic evidence of the benefits enjoyed by investors and issuers, and how they share any benefits of innovation. Preliminary evidence suggest that innovative investors in the 1970s and 1980s apparently endured greater risk than later investors (measured by variability of *ex post* holding period returns) and earned slightly higher returns for bearing these additional risks. However, whether the extra return is appropriate for the level of extra risk borne is difficult to ascertain in a small sample. [32]

There are several clinical studies of individual innovations that look at the wealth impacts of innovations. Nanda and Yun (1996) study poison puts in convertible bonds, and conclude that shareholders benefited from this innovation, perhaps at the expense of bondholders. Rogalski and Seward (1991) study foreign exchange currency warrants and find that their issuers apparently benefited from this innovation, although they find that investors substantially overpaid for this innovation. Jarrow and O'Hara (1989) find that purchasers of Primes and Scores (securities which carved the returns to individual stocks into different tranches) apparently overpaid for these products relative to the price of the stocks from which they were constructed. Jarrow and O'Hara note however that these products can serve valuable hedging demands for investors and in the presence of transaction costs may have benefited all parties.

As a general proposition, we have a great deal more to learn about the pricing of financial innovations and how benefits, if any, are shared among participants. This is a long standing research topic in industrial organization. See Tirole (1988, Chapter 10) for a discussion of the appropriation of the returns to innovation.

5. The impact of financial innovation on society

While most authors acknowledge that innovation has had both positive and negative impact on society, their conclusions regarding the *net* impact of financial innovation reflects a diversity of opinions. Merton (1992) stakes out one side of the argument: "Financial innovation is viewed as the "engine" driving the financial system towards its goal of improving the performance of what economists call the "real economy". Merton cites the USA national mortgage market, the development of international markets for financial derivatives and the growth of the mutual fund and investment industries as examples where innovation has produced enormous social welfare gains.

Others take the opposite viewpoint, sometimes employing literary license (and movie metaphors) to make the argument that innovation's benefits are less clear:

---

[32] See Tufano (1996a).

> Nothing is more dangerous than a good idea. That ominous generalization seems inescapable given the development of finance over the past 40 years. Time and again, business has seized upon a new idea – junk bonds, LBOs, derivatives – only to push it far past its sensible application to a seemingly inevitable disaster. If financial innovation is a gift, then the package ticks, and the donor is Alfred Hitchcock. [33]

> The phrase "financial engineer" suggests another profession, that of genetic engineer. Indeed, one legal scholar invoked the vision of derivatives inhabiting a financial Jurassic Park with the implication that financial engineers have the potential to create financial products that could end up destroying civilization. [34]

How do we research the question of the net social benefits of innovation? One "methodology" in the literature extrapolates from specific examples, like the mortgage market. For any one innovation, one can attempt to measure the impact of innovation. For example, researchers have attempted to measure the size of the gains from financial innovation in the mortgage market in the form of securitization and unbundling through the creation of collateralized mortgage obligations or CMOs. These papers conclude that innovation led to materially lower mortgage rates charged to borrowers. See Hendershott and Shilling (1989), Sirmans and Benjamin (1990) and Jameson, Dewan and Sirmans (1992). However, others are quick to identify contrary examples – the legal and policy literature has extended discussions of the "costs" of innovation that defer and evade taxation, giving rise to loss of tax revenues, loss of confidence in government, a sense of inequity, and extensive resources devoted to this activity which does not enhance social welfare. There are other arguments that innovation leads to complexity that in turn leads to bad business decisions and social costs.

One sustained attack on financial innovation is that specific innovations contribute to high levels of market volatility, and in particular, to outcomes like market crashes. For example, supporters of this argument point to examples like the impact of portfolio insurance trading on the stock market crash of 1987. Merton Miller's (1991) book *Financial Innovations and Market Volatility* is a sustained rebuttal to this argument. Miller refutes the contention that innovations have increased market volatility and then argues strongly that attempts to regulate innovation will be counterproductive, like those of King Canute trying to control the tides.

The derivatives market has been the site of battles between those who see innovation as a good or bad influence on social welfare. These discussions can quickly turn to very specific questions, such as "Do derivatives exacerbate emerging market crises"? [35]

Despite the best intentions of the authors on either side of these arguments, their studies cannot measure social welfare directly, nor can they benchmark the observed

---

[33] Terence P. Pare, "Today's hot concept, tomorrow's forest fire", Fortune (May 15, 1995, p. 197).

[34] Peter H. Huang, "A normative analysis of new financially engineered derivatives", Southern California Law Review, March 2000 (73 S. Cal. L. Rev 471). Huang was referring to Hu (1995) who used this term, but contrasted it with another image – of innovation permitting firms to hedge, producing "soothing, perfect hedges found in formal gardens".

[35] For a discussion of this topic, see the review piece by Garber (1999).

outcomes against those never observed. Furthermore, in light of the innovation spiral (where successful innovations beget others) and the evolutionary process (where many innovations fail), it is exceedingly difficult to identify the boundaries of a particular innovation, if one wanted to measure its costs.

Looking at the *ex post* impacts of *specific* financial innovations to judge the *ex ante* effects of an *innovative financial system* is a hopeless task. Seeking another way to approach the *ex ante* question, theorists have weighed into the discussion of the social welfare implications of financial innovation. In order to bring enough structure to the problem so as permit a meaningful discussion, they tend to focus on one particular aspect of innovation. Theorists studying the role of innovation in completing or spanning markets have made the most progress, and the surveys by Allen and Gale (1994) and Duffie and Rahi (1995) summarize the literature. Given that markets are incomplete, one might assume that innovation that gives participants greater freedom of choice (in terms of spanning) would enhance social welfare almost by definition, in the sense of being pareto-optimal. Unfortunately, this is not the case. For example, Elul (1995) studies the welfare effects of financial innovation in incomplete markets. Elul shows that the addition of a new security may have "almost arbitrary effects on agents' utilities". The introduction of a new security can "generically make all agents strictly worse off, or all agents strictly better off, or favor any group of agents over another".

Allen and Gale's (1994) comprehensive book puts together a set of their papers – but taken together, the results are discomforting. In a series of papers, they analyze the impact of short sale constraints on social welfare. In their 1988 paper, they show that if short selling is severely limited, innovation may enhance social welfare and is efficient. However, in their 1991 piece, in which they study the environment in which investors are allowed to undertake unlimited short sales, they find that financial innovation is not necessarily efficient. (Allen and Gale conclude that with unlimited short sales, even the concept of equilibrium is ill-defined). There are many more papers [see the reviews by Allen and Gale (1994) and Duffie and Rahi (1995)], but it is probably fair to say that the existing theoretical models are sufficiently stylized and sufficiently fragile so as to not permit sweeping generalizations to be made regarding the social welfare implications of financial innovation. This too remains an open issue in the literature. There may be an opportunity to apply advanced techniques from the "new" industrial organization literature to estimate supply and demand curves to estimate the social welfare impacts of financial innovation – if the necessary data can be found.

6. Issues on the horizon: patenting and intellectual property

In most businesses, innovators protect their property rights in a variety of ways: They can try to maintain their innovations as trade secrets, as Coca-Cola has done with its famous recipe. They can patent their inventions, then license them to partners or litigate to discourage infringement. They can attach proprietary labels (copyrights, trademarks, or servicemarks) to them, thereby branding them. They can attempt to capture first mover advantages – in the form of higher prices or greater market shares – by virtue of their innovation.

While financial innovators do put service marks on their products and benefit from some first mover advantages, the extent of financial innovation has been a bit of an intellectual property puzzle, because both trade secrecy and patenting were thought to be impossible means of protection. Secrecy is difficult for innovative securities, as investors and regulators typically demand disclosure of the terms of the offering. Secrecy is possible to a greater degree to protect process innovations, such as the pricing algorithms for exotic derivatives or information processing systems that would control the creation of new pooled security vehicles, such as collateralized products or personalized baskets of stocks. Until recently, patenting was considered infeasible, because the US Patent Office had historically taken a dim view of the patentability of most financial products. While there had been a few exceptions (e.g., Merrill Lynch's early patent on its process for Cash Management Accounts), financial innovations were considered "business processes" which were hard to patent.

However, Federal Circuit Court of Appeals decision in the case of *State Street Bank v. Signature Financial,* 47 U.S.P.Q.2d (BNA) 1596 (Fed. Cir. 1998), seemed to open the door for patents on financial products. Signature had developed a system for asset management that it called the Hub-and-Spokes system, in which a centrally-managed master fund (the hub) was distributed in a variety of institutionally-distinct forms (the spokes). Signature patented this system, and then sued State Street for using it. The Court of Appeals upheld Signature's patent, which was considered by some to be a watershed event in financial innovation, providing innovators with new means to protect their intellectual property. For a discussion, see Heaton (2000).

It is unclear whether the State Street decision will be construed narrowly or broadly, or whether it will have a substantial impact on business activity. However, as with any new development, this one is likely to invite additional research. Lerner (2002) has given us a first glimpse of the new phenomenon of financial patents, demonstrating the substantial increase in patenting activity, the failure of finance patents to give proper attribution to prior art, and the failure of many firms, individuals, and universities to seek protection for their ideas. The interested reader can browse the current set of applications and grants at www.uspto.gov/patft/index.html. Finance-related patents are being filed for a wide range of new products and processes, ranging from patents on Monte-Carlo valuation methods to "prepayment wristbands and computer debit systems". There is understandably some factual and legal disagreement over the validity of individual patents, in particular over the novelty of some of the patents in light of the substantial amount of prior (non-patented) prior art.

Academic research could help to understand whether patenting will encourage or discourage innovation, change the nature of financial innovation, encourage more innovation by smaller players, or change the competitive/cooperative interactions among financial service firms. In part, this yet-to-be completed work will simply build upon the extensive body of work in the industrial organization field on patenting.

However, trying to understand what – if anything – is different about the financial services industry, and the implications for protection of intellection property and the nature of competition, is likely to be a fertile area for future work.

7. Summary

The activity of financial innovation is large, but the literature on the topic is relatively sparse and spread out broadly among a number of fields. Unlike some other areas represented in this volume, where our profession had made a great deal of progress, the subject of financial innovation remains one in which our intellectual maps show vast uncharted – and potentially interesting – lands to be explored.

References

Akhavein, J., W.S. Frame and L.J. White (2001), "The diffusion of financial innovations: an examination of the adoption of small business credit scoring by large banking organizations", Unpublished Manuscript (Federal Reserve Bank of Atlanta) April 2001.

Allen, F. (2001), "Presidential address: do financial institutions matter?", Journal of Finance 56(4): 1165–1175.

Allen, F., and D. Gale (1988), "Optimal security design", Review of Financial Studies 1(3):229–263.

Allen, F., and D. Gale (1991), "Arbitrage, short sales and financial innovation", Econometrica 59(4): 1041–1068.

Allen, F., and D. Gale (1994), Financial Innovation and Risk Sharing (MIT Press, Cambridge, MA).

Bank for International Settlements (1986), "Recent innovations in international banking", Bank for International Settlements Report, April 1986 (Bank for International Settlements, Basel, Switzerland).

Baskin, J.B. (1988), "The development of corporate financial markets in Britain and the United States, 1600–1914", Business History Review 62:199–237.

Beatty, A., P.G. Berger and J. Magliolo (1995), "Motives for forming research & development financing organizations", Journal of Accounting and Economics 19(2–3):411–442.

Bhattacharyya, S., and V. Nanda (2000), "Client discretion, switching costs, and financial innovation", Review of Financial Studies 13(4):1101–1127.

Black, D.G. (1986), "Success and failure of futures contracts: theory and empirical evidence", Salomon Brothers Center for the Study of Financial Institutions Monograph Series in Finance and Economics 1986:1 (Graduate School of Business Administration, New York University).

Black, F., and M. Scholes (1974), "From theory to a new financial product", Journal of Finance 29(2):399–412.

Boot, A., and A. Thakor (1997), "Banking scope and financial innovation", Review of Financial Studies 10(4):1099–1131.

Carosso, V. (1970), Investment Banking in America: A History (Harvard University Press, Cambridge, MA).

Carrow, K.A. (1999), "Evidence of early-mover advantages in underwriting spreads", Journal of Financial Services Research 15(1):37–55.

Chancellor, E. (1999), Devil Take the Hindmost: A History of Financial Speculation (Farrar, Stras and Giroux, New York).

Cleveland, F.A. (1907), "Classification and description of bonds", Annals of the American Academy of Political and Social Sciences 30:621–631.

Crane, D., K. Froot, S. Mason, A. Perold, R. Merton, Z. Bodie, E. Sirri and P. Tufano (1995), Global Financial Systems: A Functional Perspective (Harvard Business School Press, Cambridge, MA).

Crawford, G., and B. Sen (1996), Derivatives for Decision Makers (Wiley, New York).

Dewing, A.S. (1919), The Financial Policy of Corporations (Ronald Press, New York).

Dewing, A.S. (1934), Study of Corporate Securities (Ronald Press, New York). This book quotes a number of unpublished and now-unavailable studies.

Duffie, D., and M.O. Jackson (1989), "Optimal innovation of futures contracts", Review of Financial Studies 2:275–296.

Duffie, D., and R. Rahi (1995), "Financial market innovation and security design: an introduction", Journal of Economic Theory 65:1–42.

Elul, R. (1995), "Welfare effects of financial innovation in incomplete market economies with several consumption goods", Journal of Economic Theory 65:43–78.

Finnerty, J.D. (1988), "Financial engineering in corporate finance: an overview", Financial Management 17:14–33.

Finnerty, J.D. (1992), "An overview of corporate securities innovation", Journal of Applied Corporate Finance 4(4):23–39.

Finnerty, J.D. (2001), Debt Management (Harvard Business School Press, Cambridge, MA).

Fisher, L., I. Brick and F. Ng (1983), "Tax incentives and financial innovation: the case of zero-coupon bonds and other deep discount corporate bonds", The Financial Review 18(4):292–305.

Franks, J., and O. Sussman (1999), "Financial innovations and corporate insolvency", Unpublished Manuscript (London Business School).

Garber, P. (1999), "Derivatives in international capital flows", in: M. Feldstein, ed., International Capital Flows (University of Chicago Press, Chicago) pp. 386–407.

Gastineau, G. (2001), "Exchange traded funds: an introduction", Journal of Portfolio Management (Spring):88–96.

Geanuracos, J., and B. Millar (1991), The Power of Financial Innovation (Harper Business, New York).

Gergen, M.P., and P. Schmitz (1997), "The influence of tax law on securities innovation in the U.S.: 1981–1997", Tax Law Review 52:119–197.

Graham, B., and D. Dodd (1934), Security Analysis (Whittlesey House, New York).

Grinblatt, M., and F.A. Longstaff (2000), "Financial innovation and the role of derivative securities: an empirical analysis of the Treasury STRIPS program", Journal of Finance 55(3):1415–1436.

Hannan, T., and J. McDowell (1984), "The determinants of technology adoption: the case of the banking firm", Rand Journal of Economics 15(Autumn):328–335.

Hannan, T., and J. McDowell (1987), "Rival precedence and the dynamics of technology adoption: an empirical analysis", Economica 54(May):155–171.

Harris, M., and A. Raviv (1989), "The design of securities", Journal of Financial Economics 24:255–287.

Haugen, R.A., and L.W. Senbett (1981), "Resolving the agency problems of external capital through options", Journal of Finance 36(3):629–647.

Heaton, J.B. (2000), "Patent law and financial engineering", Derivatives Quarterly 7(2):7–15.

Heinonen, T. (1992), "Financial innovation", Ph.D. Dissertation (Helsinki School of Economics, Finland).

Hendershott, P.H., and J.D. Shilling (1989), "The impact of agencies on conventional fixed-rate mortgage yields", Journal of Real Estate Finance and Economics 2:101–115.

Hornberger, D.J. (1933), "Accounting for no-par stocks during the depression", Accounting Review (March).

Hu, H.T.C. (1989), "Swaps, the modern process of financial innovation and the vulnerability of a regulatory paradigm", University of Pennsylvania Law Review 138:333–435.

Hu, H.T.C. (1995), "Hedging expectations: 'derivative reality' and the law and finance of the corporate objective", Texas Law Review 73:985–1040.

Huang, P. (2000), "A normative analysis of new financially engineered derivatives", Southern California Law Review 75:471–500.

Jagtiani, J., A. Saunders and G. Udell (1995), "The effect of bank capital requirements on bank off-balance sheet financial innovation", Journal of Banking and Finance 19:647–658.

Jameson, M., S. Dewan and C.F. Sirmans (1992), "Measuring welfare effects of 'unbundling' financial innovations: the case of Collateralized Mortgage Obligations", Journal of Urban Economics 31:1–13.

Jarrow, R., and M. O'Hara (1989), "Primes and scores: an essay on market imperfection", Journal of Finance 44:1263–1287.

Kane, E.J. (1986), "Technology and the regulation of financial markets," in: A. Saunders and L.J. White, eds., Technology and the Regulation of Financial Markets: Securities, Futures and Banking (Lexington Books, Lexington, MA) pp. 187–193.

Kim, Y., and R. Stulz (1988), "The Eurobond market and corporate financial policy: a test of the clientele hypothesis", Journal of Financial Economics 22(2):189–205.

Knoll, M.S. (1997), "Financial innovation, tax arbitrage and retrospective taxation: the problem with passive government lending", Tax Law Review 52(4):199–224.

Knoll, M.S. (2001), "Put-call parity and the law", Unpublished Manuscript (University of Pennsylvania Law School and The Wharton School, PA).

Kollbrenner, S.M. (1995), "Derivatives design and taxation", Virginia Tax Review 15:211–280.

Lerner, J. (2002), "Where does State Street lead? A first look at finance patents, 1971–2000", Journal of Finance 57(2):901–930.

Lerner, J., and P. Tufano (1993), "ALZA and Bio-Electrical Systems (A) Technological and financial innovation", Harvard Business School Case number 293-124 (Harvard Business School).

Madan, D., and B. Soubra (1991), "Design and marketing of financial products", Review of Financial Studies 4(2):361–384.

Mason, S., R. Merton, A. Perold and P. Tufano (1995), Cases in Financial Engineering: Applied Studies of Financial Innovation (Prentice Hall, Englewood Cliffs, NJ).

Masson, R.L., and S.S. Stratton (1938), Financial Instruments and Institutions: A Case Book (McGraw Hill Book Co., New York).

Matthews, J.O. (1994), Struggle and Survival on Wall Street (Oxford University Press, New York).

McConnell, J.J., and E.S. Schwartz (1992), "The origin of LYONS: a case study in financial innovation", Journal of Applied Corporate Finance 4(4):40–47.

McLaughlin, R. (1999), Over-the-Counter Derivative Products (McGraw Hill, New York).

Merton, R.C. (1989), "On the application of the continuous time theory of finance to financial intermediation and insurance", Geneva Papers on Risk and Insurance 14(July):225–262.

Merton, R.C. (1992), "Financial innovation and economic performance", Journal of Applied Corporate Finance 4(4):12–22.

Merton, R.C. (1993), "Operation and regulation in financial intermediation: a functional perspective", in: P. Englund, ed., Operation and Regulation of Financial Markets (The Economic Council, Stockholm).

Merton, R.C. (1995), "A functional perspective of financial intermediation", Financial Management 24(2):23–41.

Miller, M.H. (1977), "Debt and taxes", Journal of Finance 32:261–275.

Miller, M.H. (1986), "Financial innovation: the last twenty years and the next", Journal of Financial and Quantitative Analysis 21(4):459–471.

Miller, M.H. (1991), Financial Innovation and Market Volatility (Blackwell, Cambridge, MA).

Miller, M.H. (1992), "Financial innovation: achievements and prospects", Journal of Applied Corporate Finance 4:4–11.

Molyneux, P., and N. Shamroukh (1996), "Diffusion of financial innovations: the case of junk bonds and note issuance facilities", Journal of Money, Credit and Banking (August):502–526.

Molyneux, P., and N. Shamroukh (1999), Financial Innovation (Wiley, Chichester, UK).

Nanda, V., and Y. Yun (1996), "Financial innovation and investor wealth: a study of the poison put inconvertible bonds", Journal of Corporate Finance (3)1:1–22.

Obay, L. (2000), Financial Innovation in the Banking Industry: The Case of Asset Securitization (Garland Publishing, New York).

Partnoy, F. (1997), F.I.A.S.C.O. (W.W. Norton, New York).

Perold, A., and S. Brown (2001), "Merrill Lynch HOLDRS", Harvard Business School case 201-059 (Harvard Business School).

Persons, J.C., and V.A. Warther (1997), "Boom and bust patterns in the adoption of financial innovations", Review of Financial Studies 10(4):939–967.

Pouncy, C.R.P. (1998), "Contemporary financial innovation: orthodoxy and alternatives", Southern Methodist University Law Review 51:505–590.

Reinganum, J. (1989), "The timing of innovation: research, development and diffusion", in: R. Willig and R. Schmalensee, eds., The Handbook of Industrial Organization (Elsevier, Amsterdam) pp. 849–908.

Riegel, R. (1920), "The installment plan and the baby bond", Annals of the American Academy of Political and Social Sciences 88(March):169–176.

Rogalski, R.J., and J.K. Seward (1991), "Corporate issues of foreign currency exchange warrants", Journal of Financial Economics 30:347–366.

Rogers, E.M. (1983), The Diffusion of Innovations (Free Press, New York).

Ross, S.A. (1989), "Presidential addresss: institutional markets, financial marketing and financial innovation", Journal of Finance 44(3):541–556.

Russo, T.A., and M. Vinciguerra (1991), "Financial innovation and uncertain regulation: selected issues regarding new product development", Texas Law Review 69:1431–1538.

Saloner, G., and A. Shephard (1995), "Adoption of technologies with network effects: an empirical examination of the adoption of automated teller machines", Rand Journal of Economics 26(Autumn): 479–501.

Santangelo, R., and P. Tufano (1997), "Financial engineering and tax risk: the case of Times Mirror PEPS", HBS Note 297-056 (Harvard Business School).

Schenk, D.H. (1995), "Colloquium on financial instruments: foreward", New York University Tax Review 50:487–490.

Scherer, F.M., and D. Ross (1990), Industrial Market Structure and Economic Performance (Houghton-Mifflin, Boston).

Schmookler, J. (1967), Invention and Economic Growth (Harvard University Press, Cambridge, MA).

Silber, W. (1975), Financial Innovation (Lexington Books, Lexington, MA).

Silber, W. (1983), "The process of financial innovation", American Economic Review 73:89–95.

Sirmans, C.F., and J.D. Benjamin (1990), "Pricing fixed rate mortgages: some empirical evidence", Journal of Financial Services Research 4:191–202.

Smith, C., C. Smithson and D. Wilford (1990), Managing Financial Risk (Harper Business, New York).

Strnad, J. (1994), "Taxing new financial products: a conceptual framework", Stanford Law Review 436:569; 587–593.

Tirole, J. (1988), The Theory of Industrial Organization (MIT Press, Cambridge, MA).

Tufano, P. (1989), "Financial innovation and first mover advantages", Journal of Financial Economics 25:213–240.

Tufano, P. (1995), "Securities innovations: a historical and functional perspective", Journal of Applied Corporate Finance 7(4):90–113.

Tufano, P. (1996a), "Do fools rush in? Rewards to buying and selling the newest financial products", Unpublished Manuscript (Harvard Business School).

Tufano, P. (1996b), "Times Mirror Company PEPs Proposal Review", Harvard Business School case 296-089 (Harvard Business School).

Tufano, P. (1997), "Business failure, judicial intervention, and financial innovation: restructuring U.S. railroads in the nineteenth century", Business History Review (Spring):1–40.

Tufano, P., and B. Kyrillos (1994), "Leland O'Brien Rubinstein Associates, Inc.: SuperTrust", Harvard Business School case 294-050 (Harvard Business School).

Van Horne, J.C. (1985), "Of financial innovations and excesses", Journal of Finance 15:621–631.

Vogel, F.E., and S.L. Hayes III (1998), Islamic Law and Finance: Religion, Risk and Return (Kluwer Law International, The Hague, Netherlands).

Walmsley, J. (1988), The New Financial Instruments (John Wiley, New York).

Warren, A.C. (1993), "Financial contract innovation and income tax policy", Harvard Law Review 107:460–492.

White, L.J. (2000), "Technological change, financial innovation, and financial regulation in the U.S.: the challenge for public policy", in: P. Harker and S. Zenios, eds., Performance of Financial Institutions, (Cambridge University Press, Cambridge, UK) pp. 388–415.

Chapter 7

PAYOUT POLICY

FRANKLIN ALLEN[*]

University of Pennsylvania

RONI MICHAELY

Cornell University and IDC

Contents

[*] We are in debt to Gustavo Grullon for his insights and help on this project. We would like to thank Harry DeAngelo, Eric Lie, René Stulz and Jeff Wurgler for their comments and suggestions. We would also like to thank Meenakshi Sinha for her research assistance.

Handbook of the Economics of Finance, Edited by G.M. Constantinides, M. Harris and R. Stulz

Abstract

This paper surveys the literature on payout policy. We start out by discussing several stylized facts that are important to the development of any comprehensive payout policy framework. We then describe the Miller and Modigliani (1961) payout irrelevance proposition, and consider the effect of relaxing the assumptions on which it is based. We consider the role of taxes, asymmetric information, incomplete contracting possibilities, and transaction costs.

The tax-related literature on dividends explores the implications of differential taxes on dividends and capital gains on stocks' valuation and firms' propensity to pay out cash in the form of dividends. The issues investigated in this literature are of central importance to corporate finance and asset pricing. It is important to understand the degree to which investor taxes are impounded into security prices, which in turn can affect investment returns, the cost of capital, capital structure, investment spending, and governmental revenue collection. The overall empirical evidence on this issue appears to indicate that from a tax perspective, dividends should be minimized.

We review the theoretical as well as empirical literature on Signaling/Adverse Selection models and Agency models. The accumulated evidence indicates that changes in payout policies are not motivated by firms' desire to signal their true worth to the market. There is no evidence that firms that increase their dividends experience an unexpectedly high earnings or cash flow in subsequent periods. The literature does point out however, that changes in cash payments are negatively associated with firms' risk profile. This and other evidence seem to be consistent with the notion that both dividends and repurchases are paid when firms have excess cash flows in order to reduce potential overinvestment by management.

We also review the issue of the form of payout and the increased tendency to use open market share repurchases. Evidence suggests that the rise in the popularity of repurchases increases overall payout and increases firms' financial flexibility. It seems that young, risky firms prefer to use repurchases rather then dividends. We also observe that many large, established firms and those with more volatile earnings substitute repurchases for dividends. We believe that the choice of payout method and how payout policy interacts with capital-structure decisions (such as debt and equity issuance) are important questions and a promising field for further research.

Keywords

dividends, repurchases, payout policy, asymmetric information, agency problems, taxes

JEL classification: G30, G32, G35

1. Introduction

How much cash should firms give back to their shareholders? And what form should the payment take? Should corporations pay their shareholders through dividends or by repurchasing their shares, which is the least costly form of payout from a tax perspective? Firms must make these important decisions over and over again (some must be repeated and some need to be reevaluated each period), on a regular basis.

Because these decisions are dynamic they are labeled as *payout policy.* The word "policy" implies some consistency over time, and that payouts, and dividends in particular, do not simply evolve in an arbitrary and random manner. Much of the literature in the past forty years has attempted to find and explain the pattern in payout policies of corporations.

The money involved in these payout decisions is substantial. For example, in 1999 corporations spent more than $350b on dividends and repurchases and over $400b on liquidating dividends in the form of cash spent on mergers and acquisitions.[1]

Payout policy is important not only because of the amount of money involved and the repeated nature of the decision, but also because payout policy is closely related to, and interacts with, most of the financial and investment decisions firms make. Management and the board of directors must decide the level of dividends, what repurchases to make (the mirror image decision of equity issuance), the amount of financial slack the firm carries (which may be a non-trivial amount; for example, at the end of 1999, Microsoft held over $17b in financial slack), investment in real assets, mergers and acquisitions, and debt issuance. Since capital markets are neither perfect nor complete, all of these decisions interact with one another.

Understanding payout policy may also help us to better understand the other pieces in this puzzle. Theories of capital structure, mergers and acquisitions, asset pricing, and capital budgeting all rely on a view of how and why firms pay out cash.

Six empirical observations play an important role in discussions of payout policies:

(1) Large, established corporations typically pay out a significant percentage of their earnings in the form of dividends and repurchases.
(2) Historically, dividends have been the predominant form of payout. Share repurchases were relatively unimportant until the mid-1980s, but since then have become an important form of payment.
(3) Among firms traded on organized exchanges in the USA, the proportion of dividend-paying firms has been steadily declining. Since the beginning of the 1980s, most firms have initiated their cash payment to shareholders in the form of repurchases rather than dividends.
(4) Individuals in high tax brackets receive large amounts in cash dividends and pay substantial amounts of taxes on these dividends.

---

[1] Data on dividends and repurchases are from CRSP and Compustat. Data on cash M&A activity (for USA firms as acquirers only) is from SDC.

(5) Corporations smooth dividends relative to earnings. Repurchases are more volatile than dividends.
(6) The market reacts positively to announcements of repurchase and dividend increases, and negatively to announcements of dividend decreases.

The challenge to financial economists has been to develop a payout policy framework where firms maximize shareholders' wealth and investors maximize utility. In such a framework payout policy would function in a way that is consistent with these observations and is not rejected by empirical tests.

The seminal contribution to research on dividend policy is that of Miller and Modigliani (1961). Prior to their paper, most economists believed that the more dividends a firm paid, the more valuable the firm would be. This view was derived from an extension of the discounted dividends approach to firm valuation, which says that the value V_0 of the firm at date 0, if the first dividends are paid one period from now at date 1, is given by the formula:

$$V_0 = \sum_{t=1}^{\infty} \frac{D_t}{(1 + r_t)^t}, \tag{1}$$

where D_t = the dividends paid by the firm at the end of period t, and r_t = the investors' opportunity cost of capital for period t.

Gordon (1959) argued that investors' required rate of return r_t would increase with retention of earnings and increased investment. Although the future dividend stream would presumably be larger as a result of the increase in investment (i.e., D_t would grow faster), Gordon felt that higher r_t would overshadow this effect. The reason for the increase in r_t would be the greater uncertainty associated with the increased investment relative to the safety of the dividend.

Miller and Modigliani (1961) pointed out that this view of dividend policy is incomplete and they developed a rigorous framework for analyzing payout policy. They show that what really counts is the firm's investment policy. As long as investment policy doesn't change, altering the mix of retained earnings and payout will not affect firm's value. The Miller and Modigliani framework has formed the foundation of subsequent work on dividends and payout policy in general. It is important to note that their framework is rich enough to encompass both dividends and repurchases, as the only determinant of a firm's value is its investment policy.

The payout literature that followed the Miller and Modigliani article attempted to reconcile the indisputable logic of their dividend irrelevance theorem with the notion that both managers and markets care about payouts, and dividends in particular. The theoretical work on this issue suggests five possible imperfections that management should consider when it determines dividend policy:

(i) *Taxes.* If dividends are taxed more heavily than capital gains, and investors cannot use dynamic trading strategies to avoid this higher taxation, then minimizing dividends is optimal.

(ii) *Asymmetric information.* If managers know more about the true worth of their firm, dividends can be used to convey that information to the market, despite the costs associated with paying those dividends. (However, we note that with asymmetric information, dividends can also be viewed as bad news. Firms that pay dividends are the ones that have no positive NPV projects in which to invest).

(iii) *Incomplete contracts.* If contracts are incomplete or are not fully enforceable, equityholders may, under some circumstances, use dividends to discipline managers or to expropriate wealth from debtholders.

(iv) *Institutional constraints.* If various institutions avoid investing in non- or low-dividend-paying stocks because of legal restrictions, management may find that it is optimal to pay dividends despite the tax burden it imposes on individual investors.

(v) *Transaction costs.* If dividend payments minimize transaction costs to equityholders (either direct transaction costs or the effort of self control), then positive dividend payout may be optimal.

In Section 2 we elaborate further on some of the empirical observations about corporate payout policies. Section 3 reviews the Miller and Modigliani analysis. Subsequent sections recount the literature that has relaxed their assumptions in various ways.

2. Some empirical observations on payout policies

In the previous section we state six important empirical findings about corporate payout policies. Table 1 and Figure 1 illustrate the first observation that corporations pay out a substantial portion of their earnings. Table 1 shows that for USA industrial firms, dollar expenditures on both dividends and repurchases have increased over the years.

The table also illustrates the second empirical observation above. It shows that dividends have been the dominant form of payout in the early period, but that repurchases have become more and more important through the years. For example, during the 1970s the average dividend payout was 38% and the average repurchase payout was 3%. By the 1990s the average dividend payout was 58% and the average repurchase payout was 27%. From these numbers it appears that USA corporations paid out over 80% of their earnings to shareholders.[2] Clearly, payments to shareholders through dividends and repurchases represent a significant portion of corporate earnings. However, we note that these numbers are tilted towards large firms since we calculate payout as: $(\sum \text{Div}/ \sum \text{Earnings})$. In addition, aggregate earnings (i.e., the denominator) contain many negative earnings. This is especially true in the later period, when more and more small, not yet profitable, firms registered on Nasdaq. When we calculate payout for each firm and then average across firms (equal weighted)

---

[2] See also Dunsby (1993) and Allen and Michaely (1995).

Table 1
Aggregate cash distributions to equityholders[a,b]

Year	Number	EARN	MV	TP	DIV	REPO	TP/EARN	DIV/EARN	REPO/EARN	TP/MV	DIV/MV	REPO/MV
1972	2802	41437	803582	19121	17633	1488	46.1%	42.6%	3.6%	2.4%	2.2%	0.2%
1973	3107	57503	673974	23517	20470	3047	40.9%	35.6%	5.3%	3.5%	3.0%	0.5%
1974	3411	70139	500180	27508	25961	1547	39.2%	37.0%	2.2%	5.5%	5.2%	0.3%
1975	3573	65856	690795	28196	27389	807	42.8%	41.6%	1.2%	4.1%	4.0%	0.1%
1976	3600	84318	865569	33496	31917	1579	39.7%	37.9%	1.9%	3.9%	3.7%	0.2%
1977	3615	95147	825171	41768	38202	3566	43.9%	40.2%	3.7%	5.1%	4.6%	0.4%
1978	3536	106352	836025	44449	40193	4256	41.8%	37.8%	4.0%	5.3%	4.8%	0.5%
1979	3581	134988	999286	51525	46104	5421	38.2%	34.2%	4.0%	5.2%	4.6%	0.5%
1980	3868	136159	1306814	55978	50289	5689	41.1%	36.9%	4.2%	4.3%	3.8%	0.4%
1981	3972	132796	1143197	58064	51802	6262	43.7%	39.0%	4.7%	5.1%	4.5%	0.5%
1982	4574	103817	1313398	62294	52701	9593	60.0%	50.8%	9.2%	4.7%	4.0%	0.7%
1983	4461	130188	1648433	68282	59384	8899	52.4%	45.6%	6.8%	4.1%	3.6%	0.5%
1984	4686	151671	1554682	89327	61356	27971	58.9%	40.5%	18.4%	5.7%	3.9%	1.8%
1985	4721	141464	2082677	104606	71471	33136	73.9%	50.5%	23.4%	5.0%	3.4%	1.6%
1986	4719	133656	2436697	110569	74862	35707	82.7%	56.0%	26.7%	4.5%	3.1%	1.5%
1987	4908	185146	2581264	137014	84973	52041	74.0%	45.9%	28.1%	5.3%	3.3%	2.0%
1988	4895	220034	2878728	144980	96216	48765	65.9%	43.7%	22.2%	5.0%	3.3%	1.7%
1989	4804	227613	3610378	162795	107846	54949	71.5%	47.4%	24.1%	4.5%	3.0%	1.5%
1990	4781	213056	3331772	160245	113971	46275	75.2%	53.5%	21.7%	4.8%	3.4%	1.4%
1991	4780	168668	4255871	138124	115162	22962	81.9%	68.3%	13.6%	3.2%	2.7%	0.5%
1992	4934	171373	4385812	144268	110978	33289	84.2%	64.8%	19.4%	3.3%	2.5%	0.8%
1993	5120	209238	5155047	153834	117499	36334	73.5%	56.2%	17.4%	3.0%	2.3%	0.7%

continued on next page

Table 1, *continued*

Year	Number	EARN	MV	TP	DIV	REPO	TP/EARN	DIV/EARN	REPO/EARN	TP/MV	DIV/MV	REPO/MV
1994	5588	303578	5548638	183147	136645	46503	60.3%	45.0%	15.3%	3.3%	2.5%	0.8%
1995	5860	354987	7373933	221218	148889	72330	62.3%	41.9%	20.4%	3.0%	2.0%	1.0%
1996	6289	433290	9077805	276917	175109	101808	63.9%	40.4%	23.5%	3.1%	1.9%	1.1%
1997	6293	448572	11479240	321619	177777	143842	71.7%	39.6%	32.1%	2.8%	1.5%	1.3%
1998	5174	362827	11785621	349555	174067	175488	96.3%	48.0%	48.4%	3.0%	1.5%	1.5%

[a] Aggregate cash distributions to equityholders for a sample of USA firms, by year. The data sample consists of all firms on Compustat over the period 1972–1998 that have available information on the variables REPO, DIV, EARN, and MV. Abbreviations: REPO, expenditure on the purchase of common and preferred stocks (Compustat item 115) minus any reduction in the value (redemption value) of the net number of preferred shares outstanding (Compustat item 56); DIV, total dollar amount of dividends declared on the common stock (Compustat item 21); EARN, earnings before extraordinary items (Compustat item 18); MV, market value of common stock (Compustat item 24 × Compustat item 25); TP, average total payout (dividends plus repurchases) across firms for a given year. The data sample contains 121 973 firm–year observations and excludes banks, utilities, and insurance companies.

[b] Based on Table 1 of Grullon and Michaely (2002), "Dividends, share repurchases and the substitution hypothesis".

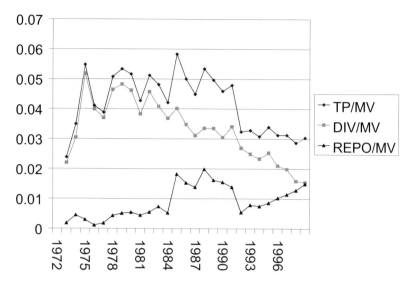

Fig. 1. Cash distributions to equityholders as a percentage of market value. This figure depicts the average total payout (dividends plus repurchases) yield, the average dividend yield, and the average repurchase yield (all relative to market value) for a sample of USA firms. The data sample consists of all firm–year observations on Compustat (Full-Coverage, Primary, Secondary, Tertiary, Research, and Back Files) over the period 1972–1998 that have positive earnings and have available information on the variables REPO, DIV, and MV. REPO is the expenditure on the purchase of common and preferred stocks (Compustat item 115) minus any reduction in the value (redemption value) of the net number of preferred shares outstanding (Compustat item 56). DIV is the total dollar amount of dividends declared on the common stock (Compustat item 21). MV is the market value of common stock (Compustat item 24 × Compustat item 25). The total payout is the sum of the dividend payout and the repurchase payout. The data sample contains 121 973 firm–year observations and excludes banks, utilities, and insurance companies. Based on data from Grullon and Michaely (2002), "Dividends, share repurchases and the substitution hypothesis".

the overall payout relative to earnings is around 25% [Grullon and Michaely (2002, Figure 1)].

To further illustrate the second observation, Figure 1 shows the evolution of dividend yield (total dividends over market value of equity), repurchase yield (repurchases over market value of equity) and payout yield (dividends plus repurchases over market value of equity) since the early 1970s. Whether we examine repurchases relative to earnings or to the market value of the firm, it is clear that repurchases as a payout method were not a factor until the mid-1980s. It is interesting that in the 1990s, firms' average total yield remained more or less constant while the dividend yield declined and the repurchase yield increased.

The third observation is that dividends are now being paid by fewer firms. As we can see in Figure 2, Fama and French (2001) show that the proportion of firms that pay dividends (among all CRSP-listed firms) has fallen dramatically over the years, regardless of their earnings level. Prior to the 1980s firms that initiated a cash payment

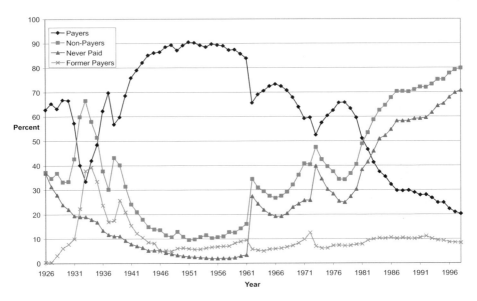

Fig. 2. Percent of all CRSP firms in different dividend groups. [Fama and French (2001, Figure 2),
"Disappearing dividends: changing firm characteristics or lower propensity to pay?"]

usually did so with dividends. But since the beginning of the 1980s, most firms have
initiated cash payments with repurchases. Figure 3 documents this observation for USA
industrial firms. We define a cash distribution initiation as the first time after 1972 that
a firm pays dividends and/or repurchases shares. Figure 3 shows that the proportion of
firms that initiated a cash distribution by using only share repurchases increased from
less than 27% in 1974 to more than 81% in 1998. Share repurchase programs have
now become the preferred method of payout among firms initiating cash distributions
to their equityholders. For earlier evidence on trend in repurchases see Bagwell and
Shoven (1989).

The fourth observation is that individuals pay substantial taxes on the large amounts
of dividends that they receive. We collected information from the Federal Reserve's
Flow of Funds Accounts for the United States, and from the IRS, SOI Bulletin
about total dividends paid and the amounts received by individuals and corporations
for the years 1973–1996. Table 2 presents the results. In most of the years in our
sample (1973–1996) individuals received more than 50% of the dividends paid out by
corporations. Moreover, most of these dividends were received by individuals in high
tax brackets (those with annual gross income over $50 000).

Peterson, Peterson and Ang (1985) conducted a study of the tax returns of
individuals in 1979. More than $33b of dividends were included in individuals' gross
income that year. The total of dividends paid out by corporations in 1979 was $57.7b,

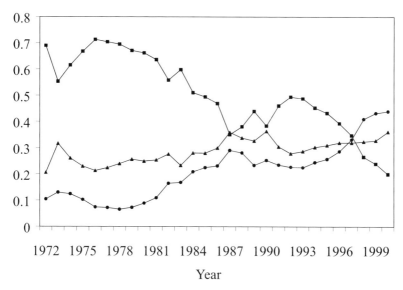

Fig. 3. Distribution of firms by payout method. This figure depicts the distribution of firms by payout method for a sample of USA firms. We determine the payout policy of a firm by observing the cash disbursements of the firm over a period of a year. The data sample consists of all firm–year observations on Compustat (Full-Coverage, Primary, Secondary, Tertiary, Research, and Back Files) over the period 1972–2000 that have available information on the following variables: REPO, DIV, EARN and MV. REPO is the expenditure on the purchase of common and preferred stocks (Compustat item 115) minus any reduction in the value (redemption value) of the net number of preferred shares outstanding (Compustat item 56). DIV is the total dollar amount of dividends declared on the common stock (Compustat item 21). EARN is the earnings before extraordinary items (Compustat item 18). MV is the market value of common stock (Compustat item 24 × Compustat item 25). The data sample contains 136 646 firm–year observations and excludes banks, utilities, and insurance companies. Squares, proportion of firms that payout only with dividends; triangles, proportion of firms that payout with dividends and repurchases; circles, proportion of firms that payout only with repurchases. [Grullon and Michaely (2002), "Dividends, share repurchases and the substitution hypothesis".]

so individuals received over two-thirds of that total. The average marginal tax rate on these dividends received by individuals (weighted by dividends received) was 40%.

The fact that individuals pay considerable taxes on dividends has been particularly important in the dividend debate, because there appears to be a substantial tax disadvantage to dividends compared to repurchases. Dividends are taxed as ordinary income. Share repurchases are taxed on a capital gains basis. Since the tax rate on capital gains has usually been lower than the tax rate on ordinary income, investors had an advantage if firms repurchased, rather than paid dividends. Even after the 1986 Tax Reform Act (TRA) when the tax rates on ordinary income and capital gains were equal for several years, there was a tax disadvantage to dividends because capital gains were only taxed on realization. In the 2001 tax code, long-term capital gains are lower than ordinary income for most individual investors. For example, an investor in the

Table 2
Cash dividends from the corporate to the private sector

Year	(1)[a]	(2)[b]	(3)[c]	(4)[d]	(5)[e]
1973	0.774	29.9	9.4	18.7 (62%)	42%
1974	0.740	33.2	13.8	20.8 (63%)	44%
1975	0.727	33	8.8	21.9 (66%)	45%
1976	0.741	39	11.9	24.5 (63%)	46%
1977	0.718	44.8	13.9	27.8 (62%)	47%
1978	0.696	50.8	13.3	30.2 (59%)	50%
1979	0.708	57.7	16.8	33.5 (58%)	53%
1980	0.710	64.1	18.6	43.6 (68%)	54%
1981	0.690	73.8	17.4	48.1 (65%)	52%
1982	0.653	76.2	18.15	52.1 (68%)	55%
1983	0.624	83.6	19.7	48.6 (58%)	56%
1984	0.600	91.0	21.2	48.6 (53%)	57%
1985	0.572	97.7	16.9	55.0 (56%)	58%
1986	0.592	106.3	15.1	61.6 (58%)	61%
1987	0.578	112.2	13.8	66.8 (59%)	57%
1988	0.617	129.6	15.1	77.3 (60%)	64%
1989	0.612	155	15.4	81.3 (52%)	66%
1990	0.617	165.6	13.4	80.2 (48%)	66%
1991	0.630	178.5	13.1	77.3 (43%)	66%
1992	0.620	185.5	13.1	77.9 (42%)	67%
1993	0.611	203.2	13.6	79.7 (39%)	65%
1994	0.585	234.9	13.2	82.4 (35%)	66%
1995	0.579	254.2	22.8	94.6 (37%)	71%
1996	0.543	297.7	16.3	104.2 (35%)	73%
1997	0.513	333.7	NA	NA	NA
1998	0.485	348.6	NA	NA	NA
1999	0.495	364.7	NA	NA	NA

[a] Share of corporate equity owned by individuals. Authors' calculation with data on market value of domestic corporations and the holding (at market value) of households, personal trust and estates. Source: Table L.213 from the Federal Reserve statistical release, Flow of Funds Accounts of the United States, March 2000.

[b] Total dividends paid by US corporations ($bln). From the Federal Reserve, Flow of Funds Accounts of the United States, Table f.7, March 2000.

[c] Dividends received by corporations. We include only dividends received from domestic corporations. Internal Revenue Service, SOI Bulletin, Corporations return, Table 2, various years.

[d] Dividends received by individuals (% of total div). Internal Revenue Service, SOI Bulletin, Individuals Tax Returns, Table 1.4, various years.

[e] Dividends received by individual with an adjusted gross income of over $50 000 relative to dividends received by all individual investors. Source: Internal Revenue Service, SOI Bulletin, Individuals Tax Returns, Table 1.4, various years.

highest marginal tax bracket pays 39.6% taxes on dividends and only 20% tax on long-term capital gains. Black (1976) calls the fact that corporations pay such large amounts of dividends despite the existence of another, relatively untaxed, payout method, the "dividend puzzle".

The fifth observation is that corporations smooth dividends. From Table 1, we can see that during the entire 1972–1998 period, aggregate dividends fell only twice (in 1992 and in 1998), and then only by very small amounts. On the other hand, aggregate earnings fell five times during the same time period and the drop was larger. Unlike dividends, repurchases are more volatile and more sensitive to economic conditions. During the recession in the early 1970s, firms cut repurchases. They did this again during the recession of the early 1990s. Overall, between 1972 and 1998, aggregate repurchases fell seven times.

Firms usually increase dividends gradually and rarely cut them. Table 3 shows the number of dividend increases and decreases for over 13 000 publicly held issues, for the years 1971 to 2001 (Moody's dividend records, 1999 and S&P's dividend book, 2001). In each year, the number of dividend cuts is much smaller than the number of dividend increases. For example, in 1999, there were 1763 dividend increases or initiations, but only 121 cuts or omissions.

In a classic study, Lintner (1956) showed that dividend-smoothing behavior was widespread. He started with over 600 listed companies and selected 28 to survey and interview. Lintner did not select these companies as a statistically representative sample, but chose them to encompass a wide range of different situations.

Lintner made a number of important observations concerning the dividend policies of these firms. The first is that firms are primarily concerned with the stability of dividends. Firms do not set dividends de novo each quarter. Instead, they first consider whether they need to make any changes from the existing rate. Only when they have decided a change is necessary do they consider how large it should be. Managers appear to believe strongly that the market puts a premium on firms with a stable dividend policy.

Second, Lintner observed that earnings were the most important determinant of any change in dividends. Management needed to explain to shareholders the reasons for its actions, and needed to base its explanations on simple and observable indicators. The level of earnings was the most important of these. Most companies appeared to have a target payout ratio; if there was a sudden unexpected increase in earnings, firms adjusted their dividends slowly. Firms were very reluctant to cut dividends.

Based on interviews of the 28 firms' management teams, Lintner reported a median target payout ratio of 50%. Despite the very small sample and the fact that the study was conducted nearly half a century ago, the target payout ratio is not far from what we present in Table 1 for all USA industrial firms over a much longer time period.

Lintner's third finding was that management set dividend policy first. Other policies were then adjusted, taking dividend policy as given. For example, if investment opportunities were abundant and the firm had insufficient internal funds, it would resort to outside funds.

Table 3
Comparative annual dividend changes 1971–1993 (based on data from approximately 13 200 publicly held issues)[a]

	Type of dividend change			
	Increase	Decrease	Resume	Omit
1971	794	155	106	215
1972	1301	96	124	111
1973	2292	55	154	95
1974	2529	100	162	225
1975	1713	215	116	297
1976	2672	78	133	153
1977	3090	92	135	168
1978	3354	65	127	144
1979	3054	70	85	115
1980	2483	127	82	122
1981	2513	136	82	226
1982	1805	322	97	319
1983	1807	68	57	109
1984	1562	71	32	138
1985	1497	95	46	198
1986	1587	71	54	107
1987	1702	65	40	117
1988	1683	80	42	152
1989	1312	137	39	255
1990	1072	188	48	264
1991	1314	139	55	145
1992	1333	131	53	146
1993	1635	87	75	106
1994	1826	59	52	77
1995	1882	49	51	73
1996	2171	50	37	80
1997	2139	46	24	49
1998	2047	84	17	61
1999	1701	62	38	83
2000	1438	69	32	75
2001	1244	117	17	70

[a] For data until 1982, Moody's Dividend Record; for data between 1983 and 2001, S&P dividend record.

Lintner suggested that the following model captured the most important elements of firms' dividend policies. For firm i,

$$D_{it}^* = \alpha_i E_{it}, \tag{2}$$

$$D_{it} - D_{i(t-1)} = a_i + c_i(D_{it}^* - D_{i(t-1)}) + u_{it}, \tag{3}$$

where, for firm i, D_{it}^* = desired dividend payment during period t; D_{it} = actual dividend payment during period t; α_i = target payout ratio; E_{it} = earnings of the firm during period t; a_i = a constant relating to dividend growth; c_i = partial adjustment factor; u_{it} = error term. This model was able to explain 85% of the dividend changes in his sample of companies.

Fama and Babiak (1968) undertook a comprehensive study of the Lintner model's performance, using data for 392 major industrial firms over the period 1946 through 1964. They also found the Lintner model performed well. Over the years, other studies have confirmed this.

The sixth observation is that the market usually reacts positively to announcements of increases in payouts and negatively to announcements of dividend decreases. This phenomenon has been documented by many studies, such as Pettit (1972), Charest (1978), Aharony and Swary (1980) and Michaely, Thaler and Womack (1995) for dividends, and by Ikenberry, Lakonishok and Vermaelen (1995) for repurchases. This evidence is consistent with managers knowing more than outside shareholders, and dividends and repurchases changes provide some information on future cash flows [e.g., Bhattacharya (1979), or Miller and Rock (1985), or about the cost of capital [Grullon, Michaely and Swaminathan (2002), Grullon and Michaely (2003)]. The evidence is also consistent with the notion that when contracts are incomplete, higher payouts can sometimes be used to align management's interest with that of shareholders', as suggested by Grossman and Hart (1980), Easterbrook (1984) and Jensen (1986).

3. The Miller–Modigliani dividend irrelevance proposition

Miller and Modigliani (1961) showed that in perfect and complete capital markets, a firm's dividend policy does not affect its value. The basic premise of their argument is that firm value is determined by choosing optimal investments. The net payout is the difference between earnings and investment, and is simply a residual. Because the net payout comprises dividends and share issues/repurchases, a firm can adjust its dividends to any level with an offsetting change in shares outstanding. From the perspective of investors, dividend policy is irrelevant, because any desired stream of payments can be replicated by appropriate purchases and sales of equity. Thus, investors will not pay a premium for any particular dividend policy.

To illustrate the argument behind the theorem, suppose there are perfect and complete capital markets (with no taxes). At date t, the value of the firm is

$V_t = $ present value of payouts,

where payouts include dividends and repurchases. For ease of exposition, we initially consider the case with two periods, t and $t+1$. At date t, a firm has
– earnings, E_t, (earned previously) on hand.
It must decide on
– the level of investment, I_t
– the level of dividends, D_t
– the amount of shares to be issued, ΔS_t (or repurchased if ΔS_t is negative).
The level of earnings at $t+1$, denoted $E_{t+1}(I_t, \theta_{t+1})$, depends on the level of investment I_t and a random variable θ_{t+1}. Since $t+1$ is the final date, all earnings are paid out at $t+1$. Given complete markets, let

$p_t(\theta_{t+1}) = $ time t price of consumption in state θ_{t+1}.

Then it follows that

$$V_t = D_t - \Delta S_t + \int p_t(\theta_{t+1}) E_{t+1}(I_t, \theta_{t+1}) \, d\theta_{t+1}. \tag{4}$$

The sources and uses of funds identity says that in the current period t:

$$E_t + \Delta S_t = I_t + D_t. \tag{5}$$

Using this to substitute for current payouts, $D_t - \Delta S_t$, gives

$$V_t = E_t - I_t + \int p_t(\theta_{t+1}) E_{t+1}(I_t, \theta_{t+1}) \, d\theta_{t+1}. \tag{6}$$

From Equation (6) we can immediately see the first insight from Miller and Modigliani's analysis. Since E_t is given, the only determinant of the value of the firm is current investment I_t.

This analysis can be extended to the case with more than two periods. Now

$$V_t = E_t - I_t + V_{t+1}, \tag{7}$$

where

$$V_{t+1} = E_{t+1}(I_t, \theta_{t+1}) - I_{t+1} + V_{t+2}, \tag{8}$$

and so on, recursively. It follows from this extension that it is only the sequence of investments $I_t, I_{t+1}, \ldots$ that is important in determining firm value. Firm value is maximized by making an appropriate choice of investment policy.

The second insight from the Miller–Modigliani analysis concerns the firm's dividend policy, which involves setting the value of D_t each period. Given that investment is chosen to maximize firm value, the firm's payout in period t, $D_t - \Delta S_t$, must be equal to the difference between earnings and investment, $E_t - I_t$. However, the level of dividends, D_t, can take any value, since the level of share issuance, ΔS_t, can always be set to offset this. It follows that dividend policy does not affect firm value at all. It is only investment policy that matters.

The analysis above implicitly assumes 100% equity financing. It can be extended to include debt financing. In this case management can finance dividends by using both debt and equity issues. This added degree of freedom does not affect the result. As with equity-financed dividends, no additional value is created by debt-financed dividends, since capital markets are perfect and complete so the amount of debt does not affect the total value of the firm.

The third and perhaps most important insight of Miller and Modigliani's analysis is that it identifies the situations in which dividend policy can affect firm value. It could matter, not because dividends are "safer" than capital gains, as was traditionally argued, but because one of the assumptions underlying the result is violated.

Perfect and complete capital markets have the following elements:

(1) No taxes.
(2) Symmetric information.
(3) Complete contracting possibilities.
(4) No transaction costs.
(5) Complete markets.

It is easy to see the role played by each of the above assumptions. The reason for Assumption 1 is clear. In the no-taxes case, it is irrelevant whether a firm pays out dividends or repurchases shares; what is important is $D_t - \Delta S_t$. If dividends and share repurchases are taxed differently, this is no longer the case. Suppose, for example, dividends are taxed at a higher rate than capital gains from share repurchases. Then it is optimal not to pay dividends, but instead to pay out any residual funds by repurchasing shares. In Section 5 we discuss the issues raised by relaxing Assumption 1.

Assumption 2 is that all participants (including the firms) have exactly the same information set. In practice, this is rarely the case. Managers are insiders and are likely to know more about the current and future prospects of the firm than outsiders. Dividends can reveal some information to outsiders about the value of the corporation. Moreover, insiders might even use dividends to deliberately change the market's perception about the firm's value. Again, dividend policy can affect firm value. Sections 6.1 and 7.1 consider the effect of asymmetric information.

The complete contracting possibilities specified in Assumption 3 mean that there is no agency problem between managers and security holders, for example. In this case, motivating the decisions of managers is possible through the use of enforceable contracts. Without complete contracting possibilities, dividend policy could, for example, help ensure that managers act in the interest of shareholders. A high payout ratio causes management to be more disciplined in the use of the firm's resources and consequently increase firm value. We cover these issues in Sections 6.2 and 7.2.

Assumption 4 concerns transaction costs. These come in a variety of forms. For example, firms can distribute cash through dividends and raise capital through equity issues. If flotation costs are significant, then every trip to the capital market will reduce the firm's value. This means changing dividend policy can change the value of the firm. By the same token, when investors sell securities and make decisions about such sales, the transaction costs that investors incur can also result in dividend policy affecting the value of the firm. Section 8 develops several transaction-cost-related theories of dividend policy.

Assumption 5 is that markets are complete. To illustrate why this is important, assume that because trading opportunities are limited, there are two groups with different marginal rates of substitution between current and future consumption. By adjusting its dividend policy, a firm might be able to increase its value by appealing to one of these groups. The literature has paid very little attention to explanations such as these for dividend policy. Nevertheless, these explanations could be important if some investors wish to buy stocks with a steady income stream, and markets are incomplete because of high transaction costs. Further analysis in this area might provide some insights into dividend policy.

Another issue that is central to our survey is the form of the payout. One area of significant growth in the literature is related to the role of repurchases as a form of payout, not only because repurchases have become more popular (Table 1), but also because of the research concerning the reasons for repurchases and the interrelation between dividends and repurchases. In Section 4 we define corporate payout, both conceptually and empirically. In Section 9 we review in detail the recent developments concerning repurchases.

4. How should we measure payout?

The Miller and Modigliani framework defines payout policy as the net payout to shareholders. However, most empirical work measures payout only by the amount of dividends the firms pay. Such studies do not consider repurchases. Neither do they factor in either net payout (accounting for capital raising activities) or cash spent on mergers and acquisitions.

If we wish to find out how much cash corporations pay out (relative to their earnings) at the aggregate level, we need to consider some of the aggregate measures, such as the one presented in Table 1, namely, aggregate dividends plus aggregate repurchases relative to aggregate earnings. But even this measure is incomplete. First, shareholders also receive cash payouts from corporations through mergers and acquisitions that are accomplished through cash transactions. That is, shareholders of the acquired firms receive a cash payment that can be viewed as a liquidating (or final) dividend.

Table 4
Mergers and acquisitions and capital raising activities by USA corporations[a]

Year	(1) Total M&A activity ($mln)	(2) Cash mergers (where USA firms are the target)	(3) IPOs proceeds ($mln)	(4) SEOs proceeds ($mln)	(5) Net payout from M&A and raising capital $(2-3-4)$
1977	191.8	191.8	221	382	−412
1978	8882	8086	225	305	7556
1979	7993	7589	398	247	6944
1980	17570	10417	1387	10901	−1871
1981	86098	59725	3114	10958	45653
1982	53426	27080	1339	14743	10998
1983	82757	30539	12460	26071	−7992
1984	151709	94029	3868	6032	84129
1985	169156	151999	8477	16493	127029
1986	193620	167028	22251	20430	124347
1987	185730	158662	23982	16613	118067
1988	310895	289377	23806	5941	259630
1989	235759	194966	13706	9332	171928
1990	143402	109427	10122	8998	90307
1991	106659	66778	25138	33749	7890
1992	130264	75957	39620	31866	4471
1993	203545	113186	57423	48995	6768
1994	307047	183956	33728	27487	122741
1995	462829	228104	30207	54176	143721
1996	544484	306812	50000	71222	185590
1997	819663	390359	44226	75409	270724
1998	1392997	410619	43721	70886	296012
1999	1021026	543324	71327	100048	371949

[a] Thompson Financial Securities Data.

Using data from SDC, Table 4 presents the magnitude of such payments. For each year we calculate the total dollar amount that was paid to USA corporations in all cash M&A deals. (Note that this figure is a lower bound, since it does not account for deals in which payment was partially in cash and partially in stocks). The amount is not trivial and it does vary by year. This type of liquidating dividend seems to have a significant weight in the aggregate payout of USA corporations. For example, in 1999, proceeds from cash M&As were more than the combined cash distributed to shareholders through dividends and repurchases combined.

Our next measure accounts not only for the outflow of funds from corporations to their shareholders, but also for the inflow of funds. Columns 3 and 4 in Table 4 present the dollar amount of capital raised by USA corporations through SEOs and IPOs. Column 5 reports the net amount (cash from M&As minus proceeds from IPOs and SEOs). It is clear that these are significant amounts. When we compare Tables 1 and 4, we see that in the last decade these amounts are as large as the cash payments through dividends and repurchases combined. We are also interested to see its impact on the overall aggregate payout. Clearly, in some years the aggregate payout is higher than after-tax earnings.

One can also define the aggregate payout as the total transfer of cash from the corporate sector to the private sector. This definition contains three elements: dividends paid to individual investors, repurchase of shares from individual investors, and net cash M&A activity where the proceeds are going to the private sector.

Using this definition and information from the *IRS Statistics of Income* and the *Federal Reserve Flow of Funds* publications, we can recalculate a rough measure of the total payout to the private sector over the years. We base this measure on the total dividends, repurchases, and cash M&A activity. We assume that the proportional holdings of each group (individuals, corporations and institutions) are the same for all firms in the economy.

In Table 2, we calculate the portion of shares held by individual investors (using information from Table L-312 from the *Federal Reserve Flow of Funds*).[3] Using this ratio, we can approximate the portion of repurchased shares and net cash M&As that went to the private sector. For example, in 1995, the private sector received $94b in dividends (see Table 2), $82b in cash M&As (57.9% of shares owned by individuals multiplied by $143b of net cash M&As, see Tables 2 and 4), and roughly $50b in repurchases (57.9% of shares owned by individuals multiplied by $72.3b of repurchases; see Tables 1 and 2). We note that out of total cash payments to the private sector of around $219b, less than half is through "formal" dividends. Table 5 presents the cash payout that goes to the private sector (dividends, repurchases, and net cash M&As) for the various years.

These issues have not received much attention in the literature. We believe they should. It is difficult to take a position on payout policy before we correctly measure it.

An equally interesting issue is to analyze the payout, its components, and the relation between payout and earnings at the firm level. For example, we think it would be interesting to investigate the type of firm that gives its shareholders liquidating dividends, and how such dividends relate to other types of payout. Analyzing the interaction between total payout, dividends, and the recent surge in repurchases would

---

[3] Total dividends are taken from Table F-7 (distribution of national income) of the Flow of Funds Accounts of the USA. The portion of dividends received by individuals is from Table 1 of the SOI Bulletin, Winter 1999–2000.

Table 5
Net total payout to individual investors

Year	(2)[a]	(3)[b]	(4)[c]	(5)[d]	(6)[e]	(7)[f]	(8)[g]
1977	0.718	−412	−296	3566	2560	27800	30065
1978	0.696	7556	5259	4256	2962	30200	38421
1979	0.708	6944	4916	5421	3838	33500	42254
1980	0.71	−1871	−1328	5689	4039	43600	46311
1981	0.69	45653	31501	6262	4321	48100	83921
1982	0.653	10998	7182	9593	6264	52100	65546
1983	0.624	−7992	−4987	8899	5553	48600	49166
1984	0.6	84129	50477	27971	16783	48600	115860
1985	0.572	127029	72661	33136	18954	55000	146614
1986	0.592	124347	73613	35707	21139	61600	156352
1987	0.578	118067	68243	52041	30080	66800	165122
1988	0.617	259630	160192	48765	30088	77300	267580
1989	0.612	171928	105220	54949	33629	81300	220149
1990	0.617	90307	55719	46275	28552	80200	164471
1991	0.63	7890	4971	22962	14466	77300	96737
1992	0.62	4471	2772	33289	20639	77900	101311
1993	0.611	6768	4135	36334	22200	79700	106035
1994	0.585	122741	71803	46503	27204	82400	181408
1995	0.579	143721	83214	72330	41879	94600	219694
1996	0.543	185590	100775	101808	55282	104200	260257
1997	0.513	270724	138881	143842	73791	NA	NA
1998	0.485	296012	143566	175488	85112	NA	NA
1999	0.495	371949	184115	202000	99990	NA	NA

[a] Portion held by individuals (from Table 2).
[b] Net payout from M&A and raising capital (from Table 4).
[c] Net M&A payout to individual investors (column 2×column 3).
[d] Amount repurchased (Table 1).
[e] Amount repurchased from individual investors (column 2×column 5).
[f] Dividends received by individuals (from Table 2).
[g] Net total payout to individual investors (columns 4 + 6 + 7).

also require information on individual firms' payout policies. But at the firm level, there may be another problem in the definition of payout relative to earnings, since a significant portion of firms have negative earnings. For these firms, it is not possible to define a total payout ratio, a repurchase payout ratio, or a dividend payout ratio.

Our discussion highlights several important points. First, in our opinion, the main issue is not whether one measure is better than another. Instead, we ask, what is the question that we are trying to answer? This question in turn should have an impact on which definition of payout we use.

The issue of how to define payout is also very relevant to the excess volatility literature. For example, Ackert and Smith (1993) showed that the results of variance-bound tests depend on how we measure cash distributions to shareholders. When they used only stated dividends, they found evidence of excess volatility. When the payout measure included share repurchase and takeover distributions as well, they did not find evidence of excess volatility. It is likely that using the net total payout to investors will add some variability to cash flows. It may also reduce even further the discrepancy between cash flow volatility and price volatility. In our opinion, this issue is worthy of further research.

Second, it is clear that most of the finance literature has analyzed the payout policy question using only the very narrow definition of dividend payout. Some studies have attempted to analyze repurchase payout. But with only a few exceptions, the literature does not cover the issue of total payout, its composition, and determination. This lacuna is understandable, given the fact that over many years, dividends were the most prominent form of payout. But this is not so anymore. Thus, to a great extent our review article reflects the current literature. We devote more space and put more emphasis on dividends relative to the other forms of payouts. We hope future research will explore the other aspects of payout policy and their implications.

5. Taxes

Much of the literature on payout policy focuses on the importance of taxes, and tries to reconcile several of the empirical observations discussed in our introduction. Firms pay out a large part of their earnings as dividends; many of the recipients are in high tax brackets. Firms did not traditionally use repurchases as a method of payout. The basic aim of the tax-related literature on dividends has been to investigate whether there is a tax effect: All else equal, we ask if firms that pay out high dividends are less valuable than firms that pay out low dividends.

Two basic ideas are important to understanding how to interpret the results of these investigations:
(1) Static clientele models:
    (i)   Different groups, or "clienteles", are taxed differently. Miller and Modigliani (1961) argued that firms have an incentive to supply stocks that minimize the taxes of each clientele. In equilibrium, no further possibilities for reducing taxes will exist and all firms will be equally priced.
    (ii) A particular case (labeled as the simple static model) is when all investors are taxed the same way, and capital gains are taxed less than dividend income. In this case, the optimal policy is not to pay dividends. Firms with high dividend yields would be worth less than equivalent firms with low dividend yields.

(2) Dynamic clientele model: If investors can trade through time, tax liabilities can be reduced even further. The dividend-paying stock will end up (just before the ex-dividend day) in the hands of those who are taxed the least when the dividend is received. Such trades will be reversed directly after the ex-day.

The empirical studies of dividend policy have tried to distinguish between the different versions of these models by attempting to identify one or more of the following:

(i)   Is there a tax effect so that low-dividend-paying stocks are more valuable than high dividend stocks?

(ii) Do static tax clienteles exist so that the marginal tax rates of high-dividend stockholders are lower than those of low-dividend stockholders?

(iii) Do dynamic tax clienteles exist so that there is a large volume around the ex-dividend day, and low-tax-rate investors actually receive the dividend?

This literature has traditionally been divided into CAPM-based studies and ex-dividend day studies. In our view, more insight is gained by comparing static to *dynamic* models. In the static models, investors trade only once. Thus, with the objective of minimizing taxes (keeping all else constant), investors must make a long-term decision about their holdings. The buy-and-hold CAPM studies, such as Litzenberger and Ramaswamy (1979) and Miller and Scholes (1982), fall into this category. The Elton and Gruber (1970) study is similar in that respect. Investors are allowed to trade only once, either on the cum-day or on the ex-day, but not on both. As we shall show, a static view is appropriate when transaction costs are exceedingly high, or when tax payments have been reduced to zero in the static clientele model.

In contrast, in dynamic models, investors are allowed to take different positions at different times. These models take into account risk, taxes, and transaction costs. Just before the ex-day, dividend-paying stocks can flow temporarily to the investors who value them the most.

5.1. Static models

First, we look at the special case in which all investors are taxed in the same way and the tax rate on dividend income is higher than the tax rate on capital gains income. In otherwise perfect capital markets, the optimal policy is to pay no dividends. Equityholders are better off receiving profits through repurchases or selling their shares so that they pay capital gains taxes rather than the higher taxes on dividends. Most USA corporations have not followed this scenario. For a long time, many firms have paid dividends regularly and have rarely repurchased their shares. On the face of it, this behavior is puzzling, especially if we believe that agents in the market place behave in a rational manner. The basic assumption of this simple static model is that for all investors there is a substantial tax disadvantage to dividends because they are taxed (heavily) as ordinary income, while share repurchases are taxed (lightly) as capital gains.

But even if the statutory tax rates on dividends and capital gains were equal (and usually, they have not been), from a tax perspective receiving unrealized capital gains is superior to dividend payments.

The first reason is that capital gains do not have to be realized immediately, and thus the associated tax can be postponed. An investor's ability to postpone may generate considerable value. Imagine a stock with an expected annual return of 15%, and an investor with a marginal tax rate of 20% on long-term capital gains. Say the investor has $1000 and an investment horizon of ten years, and consider whether she should realize gains at the end of each year or wait and realize all gains at the end of the tenth year. Under the first strategy, her final wealth would be $3106. Under the second strategy it would be $3436, a substantial difference.

Second, investors can choose when to realize capital gains (unlike dividends, for which they have no choice in the timing). In a more formal setting Constantinides (1984) showed that investors should be willing to pay for this option to delay capital gains realization, and labeled it the "tax timing option".

In reality, of course, not all investors are taxed as individuals. Many financial institutions, such as pension funds and endowments, do not pay taxes. They have no reason to prefer capital gains to dividends, or vice versa. Individuals hold stocks directly or indirectly, and so do corporations. One of the principal reasons corporations hold dividend-paying stocks as both a form of near-cash assets and as an investment is because under the USA tax code, a large fraction of intercorporate dividends are exempt from taxation, but intercorporate (or government) interest payments are not. Under the old tax code, only 15% of dividends, deemed taxable income, were taxed, so the effective tax rate on dividends received was 0.15×0.46 (marginal corporate tax rate) = 6.9%. But corporations had to pay the full amount of taxes on any realized gains. Under the current tax code, 30% of dividends are taxed. [4]

In a clientele model, taxpayers in different groups hold different types of assets, as illustrated in the stylized example below. Individuals hold low-dividend-payout stocks. Medium-dividend-payout firms are owned by people who can avoid taxes, or by tax-free institutions. Corporations own high-dividend-payout stocks. Firms must be indifferent between the three types of stock, or they would increase their value by issuing more of the type that they prefer.

---

[4] Prior to the 1986 Tax Reform Act (TRA), individual investors who held a stock for at least six months paid a lower tax on capital gains (20%) than on ordinary dividends (50%). The TRA eliminated all distinctions between capital gains and ordinary income. However, it is still possible to defer taxes on capital gains by not realizing the gains. Before the 1986 TRA, a corporation that held the stock of another corporation paid taxes on only 15% of the dividend. Therefore, the effective tax rate for dividend income was $0.15 \times 0.46 = 0.069$. After the TRA, the corporation income tax rate was reduced to 34%. The fraction of the dividend exempted from taxes was also reduced to 70%. The effective tax rate for dividend income was therefore increased to $0.3 \times 0.34 = 0.102$. In both time periods, the dividend exemption could be as high as 100% if the dividend-paying corporation was a wholly owned subsidiary of the dividend-receiving corporation.

Table 6
A clientele model example

	Dividend payout		
	High	Medium	Low
Before-tax earnings/share	$100	$100	$100
Payout policy:			
Dividends	$100	$50	$0
Capital gains	$0	$50	$100
After-tax payoff/share for group:			
(i) Individuals	$50	$65	$80
(ii) Corporations	$90	$77.5	$65
(iii) Institutions	$100	$100	$100
Equilibrium price/share	$1000	$1000	$1000

How are assets priced in this model? Since firms must be indifferent between the different types of assets, the assets must be priced so they are equally desirable. To show how this works, we use the following example.

Suppose there are three groups that hold stocks:
(i) Individuals who are in high tax brackets and pay high taxes on dividend-paying stocks. These investors are subject to a 50% tax rate on dividend income and a 20% tax rate on capital gains.
(ii) Corporations whose tax situation is such that they pay low taxes on stocks that pay dividends. Their tax rate on dividend income is 10% and 35% on capital gains.
(iii) Institutions that pay no taxes. Their opportunity cost of capital, determined by the return available in investment other than securities, is 10%.

Assume that these groups are risk neutral, so risk is not an issue. All that matters is the after-tax returns to the stocks. (We note that in this stylized market, a tax clientele is a result of both the risk neutrality assumption *and* the trading restrictions).

There are three types of stock. For simplicity, we assume that each stock has earnings per share of $100. The only difference between these shares is the form of payout. Table 6 describes the after-tax cash flow for each group if they held each type of stock.

In this example, individuals with high tax brackets will hold low-payout shares, corporations will hold the high-payout shares, and institutions will be prepared to hold all three. The asset holdings of these three groups are shown in Table 7.

To show why the shares must all have the same price, if the price of low-payout shares was $1050 and the prices of the high- and medium-payout stocks was $1000, what would happen? High- and medium-payout firms would have an incentive to change their dividend policies and increase the supply of low-payout stocks. This

Table 7
Asset holdings in the clientele model example

Group	Asset holdings
High tax bracket	Low-dividend-payout assets
Corporations	High-dividend-payout assets
Tax-free institutions	Any assets

change would put downward pressure on the price of low-payout stock. What amount of stock do investors demand? Individuals would still be prepared to buy the low-payout stock, since $80/$1050 = 7.62\%$, which is greater than the 6.5% ($65/$1000) they would obtain from holding medium-payout stocks, or the 5% ($50/$1000) they would obtain from holding high-payout stocks. What about institutions? They will not be prepared to hold low-payout stocks, since the return on them is $100/$1050 = 9.52\%$. This return is less than the 10% ($100/$1000) they can get on the other two stocks and the opportunity cost they obtain from holding foreign assets, so they will try to sell. Again, there is downward pressure on the price of low-payout stock. Therefore, the price must fall from $1050 to $1000 for equilibrium to be restored. A similar argument explains why the prices of other stocks are also $1000. Thus, in equilibrium, the price is independent of payout policy and dividend policy is irrelevant, as in the original Miller and Modigliani theory.[5]

Several studies have attempted to distinguish between the case of the static model in which everybody is taxed the same, and the static *clientele* model in which investors are taxed differently. Perhaps the easiest way to make the distinction is to investigate the relation between the marginal tax rates of stockholders and the amount of dividends paid.

Blume, Crockett and Friend (1974) found some evidence from survey data that there is a modest (inverse) relation between investors' tax brackets and the dividend yield of the stocks they hold. Lewellen, Stanley, Lease and Schlarbaum (1978), using individual investor data supplied by a brokerage firm, found very little evidence of this type of effect. Both studies indicate that investors in high tax brackets hold substantial amounts of dividend-paying stock.

Table 2 corroborates these findings for the last 30 years. It is evident that individuals in high tax brackets hold substantial amounts of dividend-paying stocks. There is no evidence that their dividend income relative to capital gains income is lower than that of investors in low tax brackets. According to the clientele theory, this phenomenon

---

[5] The equilibrium here is conceptually different from the one in Miller (1977). Miller presents an equilibrium in which there is a strict clientele. In the equilibrium here, potential arbitrage by institutions ensures one price for all stocks, regardless of their dividend policy. The existence of a strict tax-clientele is inconsistent with no-arbitrage. See also Blume (1980).

should not occur. For example, firms should be able to increase their value by switching from a policy of paying dividends to repurchasing shares.

Elton and Gruber (1970) sought to identify the relation between marginal tax rates and dividend yield by using ex-dividend date price data. They argued that when investors were about to sell a stock around its ex-dividend date, they would calculate whether they were better off selling just before it goes ex-dividend, or just after. If they sold before the stock went ex-dividend, they got a higher price. Their marginal tax liability was on the capital gain, represented by the difference between the two prices. If they sold just after, the price would have fallen because the dividend had been paid. They would receive the dividend plus this low price, and their marginal tax liability would be their personal tax rate times the dividend. In this setting, we can make a direct comparison between the market valuation of after-tax dividend dollars and after-tax capital gains dollars. In equilibrium, stocks must be priced so that individuals' marginal tax liabilities are the same for both strategies.

Assuming investors are risk neutral and there are no transaction costs, it is necessary that:

$$P_B - t_g(P_B - P_0) = \overline{P}_A - t_g(\overline{P}_A - P_0) + D(1 - t_d),\tag{9}$$

where P_B = stock price cum-dividend (the last day the stock is traded with the dividend); $\overline{P}_A$ = expected stock price on the ex-dividend day (the first day the stock is traded without the dividend); P_0 = stock price at initial purchase; D = dividend amount; t_g = personal tax rate on capital gains; t_d = personal tax rate on dividends. The left-hand side of Equation (9) represents the after-tax receipts the seller would receive if he sold the stock cum-dividend and had bought it originally for P_0. The right-hand side represents the expected net receipts from sale on the ex-dividend day. Rearranging,

$$\frac{P_B - \overline{P}_A}{D} = \frac{1 - t_d}{1 - t_g}.\tag{10}$$

If there are clienteles with different tax brackets, the tax rates implied by the ratio of the price change to the dividend will differ for stocks with different levels of dividends. The implied tax rate will be greater the higher the dividend yield, and, hence, the lower the tax bracket of investors. Elton and Gruber find strong evidence of a clientele effect that is consistent with this relation.

5.1.1. The role of risk

In the simplest versions of the theories presented above, risk has been ignored. In practice, because risk is likely to be of primary importance, it must be explicitly incorporated in the analysis.

As Long (1977) pointed out, there is an implicit assumption in the argument of a tax clientele that when there is risk, there are redundant securities in the market.

An investor can achieve the desired portfolio allocation in risk characteristics without regard to dividend yield. In other words, investors can create several identical portfolios in all aspects but dividend yield.

Keim (1985) presented evidence that stocks with different yields also have different risk characteristics. Zero-dividend-yield stocks and stocks with low dividend yields have significantly higher betas than do high-yield stocks. This finding implies that it may be a nontrivial task to choose the optimal risk-return tradeoff while ignoring dividend yield.

Depending on the precise assumptions made, some models that incorporate risk are similar to the simple static model, in that there is a tax effect and dividend policy affects value. On the other hand, other models are similar to the static clientele model in that there is no tax effect and dividend policy does not affect value. Therefore, most of the literature has focused on the issue of whether or not there is a tax effect.

Brennan (1970) was the first to develop an after-tax version of the CAPM. Litzenberger and Ramaswamy (1979, 1980) extend his model to incorporate borrowing and short-selling constraints. In both cases, the basic result is that for a given level of risk, the compensation for a higher dividend yield is positively related to the differential taxes between dividends and capital gains:

$$E(R_{it} - R_{ft}) = a_1 + a_2 \beta_{it} + a_3(d_{it} - R_{ft}).$$ (11)

Equation (11) describes the equilibrium relation between a security's expected return $E(R_{it})$, its expected dividend yield (d_{it}), and its systematic risk (β_{it}). Finding a significantly positive a_3 is interpreted as evidence of a tax effect. That is, two stocks with the same risk exposure (same beta) will have the same expected return only if they have the same dividend yield. Otherwise, the stock with the higher dividend yield will have a higher expected return to compensate for the higher tax burden associated with the dividend.

Several researchers have tested such a relation, including Black and Scholes (1974), Blume (1980), Morgan (1982), Poterba and Summers (1984), Keim (1985), Rosenberg and Marathe (1979), Miller and Scholes (1982), Chen, Grundy and Stambaugh (1990) and Kalay and Michaely (2000). The empirical results are mixed. Several of these studies find a positive yield coefficient, which they attribute to differential taxes.

Black and Scholes (1974) performed one of the earliest (and one of the most influential) tests. Using annual data, and a slightly different version of Equation (11), they tested the tax effect hypothesis:

$$\tilde{R}_i = \gamma_0 + [\tilde{R}_m - \gamma_0]\beta_i + \gamma_1(d_i - d_m)/d_m + \varepsilon_i, \quad i = 1, \ldots, N,$$ (12)

where $\tilde{R}_i$ = the rate of return on the ith portfolio; γ_0 = an intercept term that should be equal to the risk-free rate, R_f, based on the CAPM; $\tilde{R}_m$ = the rate of return on the market portfolio; β_i = the systematic risk of the ith portfolio; γ_1 = the dividend impact coefficient; d_i = the dividend yield on the ith portfolio, which is measured as the sum of dividends paid during the previous year divided by the end-of-year stock price; d_m = the dividend yield on the market portfolio measured over the prior 12 months; ε_i = the error term.

To test the tax effect, Black and Scholes formed portfolios of stocks and used a long-run estimate of dividend yield (the sum of prior-year dividends divided by year-end price). Their null hypothesis was that the dividend-yield coefficient is not significantly different from zero. This hypothesis cannot be rejected for the entire time period (1936 through 1966) or for any of the ten-year subperiods. Black and Scholes concluded that "... it is not possible to demonstrate that the expected returns on high yield common stocks differ from the expected return on low yield common stocks either before or after taxes".

In a series of studies, Litzenberger and Ramaswamy (1979, 1980, 1982) re-examined this issue.[6] Their experimental design differs from that of Black and Scholes (1974) in several important aspects. They use individual instead of grouped data, and they correct for the error in variables problems in the beta estimation by using maximum likelihood procedures. Perhaps most important, they classify stock into yield classes by using a monthly definition of dividend yield, rather than a long-term dividend yield definition as in Black and Scholes (1974).

The Litzenberger and Ramaswamy experiment involves three steps. First, they estimate the systematic risk of each stock for each one of the test months. The estimation uses the market model regression. Formally,

$$R_{it} - R_{ft} = a_{it} + \beta_{it}(R_{mj} - R_{fj}) + \varepsilon_{it} \quad j = t - 60, \ldots, t - 1, \tag{13}$$

where R_{mj} is the return on the market portfolio during period j; R_{ij} is the rate of return on stock i during period j; β_{it} is the estimated beta for stock i for period t; the riskless rate of interest during period t is R_{ft}; and ε_{it} is a noise term. The second stage uses the estimated beta for stock i during month t, β_{it}, and an estimate of stock i's expected dividend yield for month t, d_{it}, as independent variables in the following cross-sectional regression for month t:

$$R_{it} - R_{ft} = a_{1t} + a_{2t}\beta_{it} + a_{3t}(d_{it} - R_{ft}) + \varepsilon_i \quad i = 1 \ldots N. \tag{14}$$

The experiment requires an ex-ante estimate of the test month dividend yield. They obtain the estimate of expected dividend yield for month t from past observations. For cases in which the dividends are announced at month $t - 1$, the estimate is d_t/p_{t-1}.

When the announcement and ex-date occur in month t, Litzenberger and Ramaswamy had to estimate the market's time t expected dividend as of the end of month $t - 1$. The estimate they chose was the last dividend paid during the previous

---

[6] The econometric technique used by Litzenberger and Ramaswamy to correct for the errors in variables problem represents a significant contribution to the empirical asset pricing literature. However, we do not review it here, given the focus of this chapter.

12 months. If no dividends were paid during this period, they assumed that the expected dividend was zero.

They repeated the second step for every month included in the period 1936 to 1977. They estimated β_{it+1} by using the previous 60 months of data. They provided an updated estimate of the expected dividend yield for each stock for each one of the test months.

This sequence of cross-sectional regressions results in a time series of a_{3t}'s. The estimate of a_3 is the mean of this series. They compute the standard error of the estimate from the time series of the a_{3t}'s in a straightforward manner. Litzenberger and Ramaswamy (1979, 1980) found that a_3 was positive and significantly different from zero. Using MLE and GLS procedures, Litzenberger and Ramaswamy corrected for the error in variables and heteroskedasticity problems presented in the data. However, the empirical regularity they documented – a positive and statistically significant dividend yield coefficient – was not sensitive to which method they used. The various procedures yielded similar estimated coefficients with minor differences in the significance level. Litzenberger and Ramaswamy interpreted their finding as consistent with Brennan's (1970) after-tax CAPM. That is, the positive dividend yield coefficient was evidence of a dividend tax effect.

Miller and Scholes (1982) argue that the positive yield coefficient found by Litzenberger and Ramaswamy was not a manifestation of a tax effect, but an artifact of two information biases. First, Litzenberger and Ramaswamy's estimate of the next-month dividend yield could be correlated with month t information. Of the firms paying dividends, about 40% announced and paid the dividend (i.e., the ex-dividend day) in the same month. Using the Litzenberger and Ramaswamy yield definition assumes that the ex-dividend month is known a priori even for ex-months in which dividends were not declared in advance.

Second, Litzenberger and Ramaswamy ignored the potential effect of dividend omission announcements. An omission announcement, which is associated with bad news, will tend to bias upward the dividend yield coefficient, since it reduces the return of the zero yield group. The effect of these informational biases is the center of the debate between Litzenberger and Ramaswamy (1982) and Miller and Scholes (1982).

Miller and Scholes showed that when they included only dividends declared in advance in the sample, or when they defined the dividend yield as the dividend yield in month $t-12$, the yield coefficient was statistically insignificant. Based on these results, Miller and Scholes attributed the Litzenberger and Ramaswamy results to information, rather than tax effects.

Responding to this criticism, Litzenberger and Ramaswamy (1982) constructed a dividend-yield variable that incorporated only such information as investors could possess at the time. Their sample contained only stocks that either declared in month $t-1$ and paid in month t, or stocks that paid in month $t-1$ and therefore were not likely to repay in the current month. Using the "information-free" sample, Litzenberger and Ramaswamy found the yield coefficient was positive and significant. Miller and Scholes remained unconvinced.

To resolve the informational issue, Kalay and Michaely (2000) performed the Litzenberger and Ramaswamy experiment on weekly data, excluding all weeks containing both the announcement and ex-day (3.4% of the sample). They also excluded all weeks containing dividend omission announcements. Nevertheless, they found a positive and significant yield coefficient, implying that information is not the driving force behind the Litzenberger and Ramaswamy result. The question still remains whether the positive yield coefficient found by Litzenberger and Ramaswamy can be attributed to taxes. Kalay and Michaely (2000) argue that the single-period model derived by Brennan (1970) and Litzenberger and Ramaswamy (1979) predicts *cross-sectional* return variation as a function of dividend yield. In contrast, the Litzenberger and Ramaswamy test of Brennan's model is inadvertently designed to discover whether the ex-dividend period offers unusually large risk-adjusted returns (i.e., time-series return variation).

Litzenberger and Ramaswamy classified stocks as dividend-paying stocks only during the ex-dividend months. For example, they classify a stock that pays quarterly dividends to the zero dividend yield group in two thirds of the months. Therefore, when Litzenberger and Ramaswamy find a significant positive dividend yield coefficient in a Fama–Macbeth type test, it is not clear how to interpret these findings. Are their findings due to cross-sectional differences in dividend yield, which can then be interpreted as evidence consistent with the Brennan model, or are their results evidence of time-series variations in return between dividend-paying and non-dividend paying months? In other words, can we conclude from the Litzenberger and Ramaswamy results that higher-dividend-yield stocks show larger long-run (e.g., annual) risk-adjusted pretax returns (hereafter, cross-sectional return variations)? Or, do their results merely point out that stocks experience higher risk-adjusted pretax returns during their ex-month (hereafter, time-series return variations), and tell us little about the relation between long-run pretax risk-adjusted returns and yields? Time-series return variation, per se, is not evidence of a tax effect.

Since most stocks pay dividends quarterly, trying to avoid dividend income involves realizing short-term capital gains. Under USA tax laws, short-term capital gains are taxed as ordinary income. Thus, even though a long-term investor prefers long-term capital gains to dividend income, he or she does not require a larger pretax risk-adjusted return during only the ex-dividend period. Therefore, the implications of the Brennan model, combined with the USA tax code, is that differences in tax rates between dividend income and long-term capital gains income should result in cross-sectional return variation. As do other studies (such as the ex-day studies), Kalay and Michaely find strong evidence of time-series return variation around the ex-day period. However, there is no evidence of cross-section return variation. This result does not support the Brennan's and Litzenberger and Ramaswamy's buy-and-hold models.

Another potential problem is whether some omitted risk factors (other than beta) that are correlated with dividend yield, rather than taxes, can explain the positive yield coefficient. As a first indication of the potential importance of some omitted risk factors, Miller and Scholes (1982) demonstrated that when the reciprocal of price, $(1/P)$, is incorporated in the regression equation instead of the dividend yield, (D/P), its coefficient is still positive and significant. This issue was thoroughly investigated by Chen, Grundy and Stambaugh (1990). Categorizing all dividend-paying stocks into 20 portfolios according to size and yield, they found that when they used a single risk factor, large firms with high dividend yield were the only ones to experience a positive yield coefficient; and when they used two risk factor models, the yield coefficient was significant for only one of the 20 portfolios.

As also suggested by Miller and Scholes (1982) and Hess (1983), Chen, Grundy and Stambaugh (1990) presented evidence that dividend yield and risk measures were cross-sectionally correlated. When they allowed the risk measures to vary, they found that the yield coefficient was positive but insignificant. Chen, Grundy, and Stambaugh showed that the positive association between yield and their portfolios' returns could be explained by a time-varying risk premium that was correlated with yield. Thus, they concluded that there was no reliable relation between cross-sectional variation in returns and dividend yield that is a consequence of a tax penalty.

Fama and French (1993) offer an interesting insight that is relevant to this issue. They argue that the yield coefficient might capture factors other than taxes, and that those other factors might affect assets' returns. They then show that when using the three-factor model, there is no trace of different intercepts among portfolios with different dividend yields.

Summing up, a growing body of evidence shows that within static, single-period equilibrium models, there is no convincing evidence of a significant cross-sectional relation between stocks' returns and their dividend yields. Perhaps a more promising avenue for investigating this issue is to examine a model that allows for dynamic trading around the ex-dividend day.

5.2. Dynamic models

An important development in the literature on taxes and dividends was the realization that investors could trade dynamically to reduce their tax liability. The first paper to emphasize this aspect was that of Miller and Scholes (1978). They argued that there were a number of dynamic strategies that allowed investors to avoid taxes, and that in perfect capital markets all taxes could be avoided. This observation brings us back to the case in which dividend policy is irrelevant. However, in practice, the transaction costs of pursuing these strategies appear to be too high to make them empirically significant.

An area where dynamic strategies appear to be more empirically relevant is trading around the ex-date. A number of studies, starting with Kalay (1982a), have studied the implications of this strategy. We look at both types of approach.

5.2.1. Dynamic tax avoidance strategies

Miller and Scholes (1978) suggested an ingenious strategy for avoiding taxes. By borrowing and investing the proceeds with tax-free institutions, such as insurance companies or pension funds, investors could create an interest deduction that allowed them to avoid taxes. Since there were assets that were held to offset the borrowing, the position could be closed out at an appropriate point.

Several other dynamic tax avoidance strategies were suggested by Stiglitz (1983). If individuals can easily "launder" dividends so they do not have to pay taxes on them, then essentially, we are back in a Miller and Modigliani world, and dividend policy is irrelevant.

However, there is little evidence that investors are actually using this or other such strategies. Peterson, Peterson and Ang (1985) showed that individual investors' marginal tax on dividend income has been about double the marginal tax rate they pay on capital gains income. This evidence does not support a widespread use of tax avoidance strategies of the type described by Miller and Scholes. Rather, it suggests that the transaction costs of such strategies are too high to be useful to investors.

5.2.2. Dynamic ex-dividend day strategies

Several studies have considered dynamic trading strategies around the ex-dividend day. The basic idea is that investors can change their trading patterns around the ex-dividend day to capture or avoid the upcoming dividend. Kalay (1982a) argued that in a risk-neutral world, without any restrictions or imperfections such as transaction costs, dynamic arbitrage could eliminate a tax effect in prices. Traders with the same tax rate on dividends and capital gains will buy the stock before it goes ex-dividend and sell it just after. Without risk or transaction costs, the arbitrage will ensure that the price drop is equal to the dividend, i.e.,

$$\frac{P_B - \overline{P}_A}{D} = 1. \tag{15}$$

If there are transaction costs, and no price uncertainty, then $(P_B - \overline{P}_A)/D$ must lie within a range around one. This range will be larger the greater are transaction costs. However, Kalay (1982a) did not explicitly account for the risk involved in the ex-day trading.

The framework used by Michaely and Vila (1995) describes the ex-day price formation within a dynamic equilibrium framework in which, because of taxes, agents have a heterogeneous valuation of a publicly traded asset. The intuition behind their model is that an investor equates the marginal benefit of trading that arises from being more heavily invested in the dividend-paying stock with the marginal cost that arises from the deviation from optimal risk sharing.

Agents trade because they have heterogeneous valuation of dividends relative to capital gains (on an after-tax basis). This framework incorporates short-term, corporate, and individual investors' desire to trade around the ex-dividend day. The model explicitly accounts for the risk involved in the trade, and concludes that it is not arbitrage, but equilibrium, that determines prices and volume. In other words, the

existence of risk precludes pure arbitrage opportunities and prices are determined in
equilibrium. Consequently, no trader will attempt to take an unlimited position in the
stock, regardless of his or her tax preference.

The model illustrates that although two-period models like those of Brennan (1970)
or Litzenberger and Ramaswamy (1979) adequately describe the effect of taxes on
portfolio holdings in a static equilibrium, they mask a qualitative difference between
models of financial markets with and without taxation, namely, optimal tax-induced
trading. Because of the dynamic nature of the Michaely and Vila model, it is possible
to derive volume and price behavior implications. As it turns out, they can extract the
second moment of the heterogeneity distribution (i.e., the dispersion in the after-tax
valuation of dividends) from the trading volume around the ex-day.

Using this framework, it is possible to show that in equilibrium, the expected
price drop in relation to the dividend reflects the average preference of *all* traders,
weighted by their risk tolerance and wealth, and the risk involved in the ex-dividend
day transaction:

$$E(Pr) = \frac{P_c - E(P_e|P_c)}{D} = \overline{\alpha} - \frac{X(\sigma_e^2/K)}{D},$$ (16)

where $E(Pr) =$ is the expected price drop in relation to the dividend amount (hereafter,
"the premium"); P_c = the cum-day price; P_e = the ex-day price; D = the dividend
amount; σ_e^2 = the ex-day variance; K = the after-tax weighted average of investors'
risk tolerance; X = the supply of securities; $\alpha_i = \frac{1-T_d^i}{1-T_g^i}$ = the relative tax preference
of dividend relative to capital gains; $\overline{\alpha} = \frac{\sum_{i=1}^{N} k_i \alpha_i}{\sum k_i}$ = the average of investors tax
preferences (α_i) weighted by their risk tolerance (k_i).

As it turns out, unless a perfect tax clientele exists in which different groups
hold different stocks rather than just different quantities of the same stock, it is
not possible to infer tax rates from price alone. However, we can infer the cross-
sectional distribution of tax rates by using both price and volume data. By observing
the premium alone, we can infer only the weighted-average relative tax rates, not the
entire distribution of tax rates for the trading population. Michaely and Vila (1995)
show that the second moment of the distribution could be extracted from the volume
behavior on the ex-dividend day.[7]

This point can be illustrated by the following example. Assume that there are three
groups of traders in the marketplace with a marginal rate of substitution between
dividends and capital gains income of 0.75, 1.0, and 1.25, respectively. Assume further
that the average price drop relative to the dividend amount is one. Using the standard

[7] Boyd and Jagannathan (1994) provide a model in which proportional transactions costs faced by
different classes of traders induce a non-linear relationship between ex-day price movement and dividend
yield.

analysis, we can conclude that the second group dominates the ex-dividend day price determination.

However, this conclusion might not be valid. For example, suppose that half of the traders are from the first group and half are from the third group, and both have the same effect on prices. This market composition will also result in a relative price drop equal to the dividend amount. The only way to distinguish between the two scenarios is by incorporating volume into the analysis. In the first case, there are no gains from trade, and therefore no excess volume on the ex-dividend day. In the second case, there are gains from trade, excess volume is observed, and the particular equilibrium point is at a relative price drop equal to one. The model allows the researcher to distinguish between such cases.

$$AV = \tfrac{1}{2}\{D\sum_{i=1}^{N}\left|(\alpha^i - \overline{\alpha})(K^i/\sigma^2)\right|\}, \tag{17}$$

where AV is the abnormal trading volume on the ex-dividend day.

This framework also incorporates the Elton and Gruber (1970) and Kalay (1982a) analyses in Equation (17). Both analyses assume an arbitrage framework in the sense that the last term in Equation (17) is zero, i.e., there is no risk involved in the trade. Elton and Gruber assume that for some exogenous reason (e.g., transaction costs), the only trade around the ex-day will be done by investors within the same tax clientele group. In other words, if there is a perfect holding clientele and all trading is done intra-group, then the relative price drop will reflect the marginal value of dividends relative to capital gains. (Note that in this scenario, the marginal and the weighted average values are the same). In this case there are two reasons why there will be no abnormal trading volume around the ex-dividend day. First, since all trades are within the same clientele group, all relevant traders value the dividend equally, and there are no gains from trade. Second, there are no incentives for investors within the clientele group to delay or accelerate trades because of the upcoming dividends as, for example, suggested by Grundy (1985). In other words, Elton and Gruber suggest that taxes affect price, but do not locally affect investors' behavior [no extra trading, as in Equation (17)]. Kalay takes the opposite view. Taxes affect behavior but not prices, i.e., through their trading the arbitrageurs will ensure that the price drop equals the dividend amount. Since Kalay uses the arbitrage framework, he can show that short-term investors may take an unlimited position in the stock as long as the expected price drop is not equal to the dividend amount.

Tests of these propositions have taken several forms. Most studies examine the price behavior and infer investors' preferences and behavior from prices. With only a few exceptions [Grundy (1985), Lakonishok and Vermaelen (1986), Michaely and Vila (1995, 1996), and Michaely and Murgia (1995)], researchers have devoted much less attention to a direct examination by using volume to determine the effect of differential taxes on investors' trading behavior. Researchers have almost always found that the average price drop between the cum- and the ex-day is lower than the dividend amount [see Elton and Gruber (1970), Kalay (1982a), Eades, Hess and Kim (1984), and Poterba and Summers (1984), among others]. [8] For example, Eades, Hess and Kim (1984) find an excess return of 0.142% on the ex-dividend day and a cumulative excess return of 0.334% in the ten days surrounding the ex-day (day −5 to day +5, relative to the ex-dividend day). The positive abnormal return before the ex-day and the negative excess return after the ex-day indicate that investors who prefer dividends start to accumulate the stock several days before the event (its timing is known in advance). Likewise, the negative return after the event supports the notion that investors' selling after the ex-day is more gradual than we would predict in perfect markets.

Many of these studies also find that the average premium increases with dividend yield [see, for example, Elton and Gruber (1970), Kalay (1982a), Lakonishok and Vermaelen (1986) and Boyd and Jagannathan (1994)]. This finding is consistent with tax clienteles. (The tax clientele we allude to can be either a holding clientele or a trading clientele. Only examination of trading volume can separate the two). Corporations, which prefer dividends over capital gains, and tax free institutions, which are indifferent to the form of payment, hold high-yield stocks. The ex-day premium reflects those preferences. Eades, Hess and Kim's (1984) findings of a premium greater than one for preferred stock is also consistent with this idea. That is, this group of stocks pays a high dividend yield, and the dominant traders of these stocks (at least around the ex-day) are the corporate traders, who prefer dividends.

Another way to examine the effect of taxes on ex-day price behavior is to examine the effect of tax changes. If taxes affect investors' decisions on buying or selling stocks around the ex-day, a change in the relative taxation of dividends to capital gains should affect prices. Poterba and Summers (1984) looked at the British market before and after tax changes and found evidence that indicated a tax effect. Barclay (1987) compared the ex-day price behavior prior to the introduction of federal taxes in 1913 with its behavior in the years 1962 to 1985. He found that the average premium was not significantly different from one before the enactment of the federal taxes, and significantly below one after. Barclay concluded that the higher taxes on dividends after 1913 caused investors to discount their value.

Michaely (1991) examined the effect of the 1986 Tax Reform Act (TRA) on ex-day stock price behavior. The 1986 TRA eliminated the preferential tax rates for long-term capital gains that had been adopted in 1921; dividend income and realized capital gains were taxed equally after the reform. If taxes are at work, we would expect the premium to be closer to one after the 1986 TRA. (The premium is defined as the price difference between the ex-day and the cum day, relative to the amount of dividend paid). Surprisingly, this was not the case. The average premium, both before and after the TRA, was not lower than one. Comparing his results to the Elton and Gruber study, which used data from the 1960s, Michaely concludes that the change in the

---

[8] For international evidence, see Kato and Loewenstein (1995) for the Japanese market, Lakonishok and Vermaelen (1983) for the Canadian market, and Michaely and Murgia (1995) for the Italian market.

Table 8
Ex-dividend day premium[a]

Period	Mean premium	S.D.	Z Value	% above One	Fisher test
1966–67	0.838	1.44	−7.23	46.1	−4.94
1986	1.054	1.32	2.32	49.9	−0.03
1987	1.028	1.229	1.33	50.7	0.80
1988	0.998	0.821	0.168	NA	NA

[a] This table presents the average premiums (price drop relative to dividend paid) for three time periods. The first period, 1966 and 1967, is in Elton and Gruber (1970) and Kalay (1982a); the second, third, and fourth periods, 1986, 1987, and 1988, are the periods before the implementation of the 1986 TRA, the transition year, and after the implementation of the 1986 TRA, respectively. We adjust premiums to the overall market movements using the OLS market model. Premiums are corrected for heteroskedasticity. Results are taken from Michaely (1991). The null hypothesis is that the mean premium equals one.

relative pricing of dividends between the 1960s and the 1980s was not because of taxes, but perhaps, because of the change in weights of the various trading groups. Facing lower transaction costs in the equity, options, and futures markets, institutional and corporate investors seem to trade more around the ex-day in the latter period. Thus, their preferences have a greater effect on the price formation. These results are summarized in Table 8.

Although in static models, such as Brennan (1970) or Elton and Gruber (1970), transaction costs can be safely ignored (since investors trade only once), in the dynamic models they are potentially much more important. If investors trade in and out of stocks because of taxes, the multiple rounds of trades could result in a nontrivial cost of transacting. Disregarding risk, Kalay (1982a) showed that the "arbitrage" by the short-term traders would take place as long as the level of transaction costs was low enough. Indeed, Karpoff and Walkling (1988, 1990) showed that excess returns were lower for stocks with lower transaction costs. This is especially pronounced for stocks with high dividend yields, both on the NYSE/Amex and for Nasdaq stocks. In other words, corporations and short-term traders have a greater effect on the ex-day prices of stocks with lower levels of transaction costs.

When the risk involved in the ex-day trading is accounted for, the effect of transaction costs on trading is not as straightforward. Michaely, Vila and Wang (1996) developed a formal model that incorporated the effect of both transaction costs and risk on ex-day prices and trading. As expected, they predicted that transaction costs would reduce the volume of trade.

More interesting is the interaction between transaction costs and risk. First, with or without transaction costs, risk reduces volume. However, unlike price, volume is negatively affected by the level of idiosyncratic risk. As the level of transaction costs increases, systematic risk negatively affects the volume of trade. The reason is simple. Without transaction costs, investors can afford to hedge all of the systematic risk. In the presence of transaction costs, the systematic risk is not completely hedged; therefore it affects the amount of trading.

Empirical evidence supports these results. Grundy (1985), Lakonishok and Vermaelen (1986), and Michaely and Vila (1996) show that the abnormal volume on and around the ex-day is significant. This evidence indicates that a perfect tax clientele where investors hold strictly different stocks, does not exist. (In a perfect clientele, no ex-day trading will take place, because each clientele group will strictly hold only stocks with the dividend yield appropriate to its type). Moreover, the evidence questions the idea that the marginal tax rate can be inferred from prices alone.

Michaely and Vila (1996) show that both risk and transaction costs affect volume. They demonstrate that stocks with lower transaction costs experience higher abnormal volume, and that the differences are substantial. For example, between 1988 and 1990, stocks with a low average bid-ask spread experienced an abnormal trading volume of 556% compared with an abnormal trading volume of 78% for high-spread stocks. The differences were even larger when they looked at only stocks with high dividend yields, where the incentives to trade are larger. Moreover, they find that idiosyncratic risk significantly affects trading volume and that market risk has a greater effect (negative) on trading volume when the level of transaction costs is higher.

Some of these effects are captured in the following regression analysis:

$$
\text{CAV}_i = 1.89 + 63.17 \left(\tfrac{D}{P}\right)_i - 0.49\tfrac{\sigma_i}{\sigma_m} - 0.37\beta_i + 0.134\text{SIZE}
$$
$$
\quad\;\;(15.8)\;(8.5) \qquad\qquad (-18.2)\;(-9.3)\quad(5.7),
$$

(18)

where CAV_i is the cumulative abnormal volume in the 11 days around the ex-dividend day; $(D/P)_i$ is the stock's dividend yield, calculated as the dividend amount relative to the cum-day price; σ_i/σ_m is the idiosyncratic risk scaled by the market risk during the same time period; β_i is the systematic risk; and SIZE is the market value of equity, which is used as a proxy for the cross-sectional variation in transaction costs. t-Statistics are reported in parentheses.

Both the idiosyncratic risk and the systematic risk are negative (and significant). The idiosyncratic risk is about 35% higher (in absolute value) than the beta risk coefficient. The fact that both risk factors are significant indicates that investors do not hedge all of their risk exposure. If they did, the beta coefficient would have been zero. The reason for the incomplete hedging is transaction costs.

Koski and Michaely (2000) report that ex-day trading volume increases more in orders of magnitude when traders are able to arrange the cum-day/ex-day trading using non-standard settlement days. That is, by virtually eliminating the risk exposure and reducing transaction costs, volume increases significantly.

Koski and Michaely (2000) examine very large block trades around the ex-day. Block trades involve a large purchase and subsequent sale of the dividend-paying stock within minutes (with a different settlement day for each transaction). These trades are done through bilateral bargaining between the two parties involved, usually Japanese insurance companies on the buying side and a USA institution on the selling side.

This procedure substantially reduces the risk exposure (and transaction costs) relative to "conventional" dividend-capture trading. [9]

As discussed earlier, examining prices alone may mask investors' tax preferences and the trading motives that are related to taxes. Kalay (1982a) and Eades, Hess and Kim (1984), and more recently Bali and Hite (1998) and Frank and Jagannathan (1998), have raised two additional obstacles in interpreting the ex-day price drop as evidence that differential taxes affect prices and trading behavior. First, that discreteness in prices may cause a bias in measuring the ex-day price drop relative to the dividend. (Until recently, the minimum tick size was one eighth in the USA.) These studies, and those by Dubofsky (1992) and Bali and Hite (1998), show that this bias may cause the average price drop to be less than the dividend amount. Second, that the high correlation between dividend yield and the dollar amount of dividend paid (high yield stocks tend to be stocks that pay large dividends) can also result in an association between relative price drop and dividend yields¾the very same evidence that many studies have attributed to dividend clienteles. Eades, Hess and Kim (1984) and Frank and Jagannathan (1998) present supporting evidence. Frank and Jagannathan find that the average price drop is less than the dividend in Hong Kong, where dividends and capital gains are not taxed. Eades, Hess and Kim (1984) find that the average price drop is less than the dividend for non-taxable distributions in the USA. This collective evidence seems to indicate that institutional factors such as tick size play a role in the determination of the ex-day prices.

However, in light of the results of other studies, the conclusion that the entire ex-day price anomaly is driven by the tick size is unlikely. For example, Barclay (1987) finds that prior to the introduction of the income tax in the USA, the average ex-day price drop was equal to the dividend amount, despite the fact that even then, prices were quoted in discrete multiples. Michaely (1991) also finds that the average price drop around the 1986 TRA was essentially equal to the dividend amount (see Table 8). Again, also during this time period, prices were quoted in one-eighth increments.

Green and Rydqvist (1999) conducted an experiment relevant to this issue using data on Swedish lottery bonds. Taxes in the lottery bond market lead investors to prefer cash to capital gains. Some of the friction identified in the literature, such as price discreteness, would work in the opposite way. In addition, the activity of arbitrageurs is not an issue. Green and Rydqvist find that both the price drop around the ex-day and volume behavior around this event reflects the relative tax advantage of the cash distribution. Their findings support the interpretation of the ex-day price behavior as tax-motivated and that this behavior cannot be attributed to market frictions.

The information on volume behavior in the USA [Lakonishok and Vermaelen (1986), Michaely and Vila (1996)] and other countries such as Italy [Michaely

---

[9] Michaely and Murgia (1995) show that the trading volume of both block trades and non-block trades (on the Milan stock exchange) increases substantially for stocks with high dividend yield and low transaction costs. Their findings support the notion that low transaction costs enhance ex-day trading.

and Murgia (1995)], Japan [Kato and Loewenstein (1995)] and Sweden [Green and Rydqvist (1999)] also clearly indicates that there is abnormal activity around the ex-dividend day. The evidence also shows that the trading activity is positively related to the magnitude of the dividend and negatively related to the level of transaction costs and risk. The evidence is consistent with the notion that this trading activity is related to differential taxes.

5.3. Dividends and taxes – conclusions

Differential taxes affect both prices (at least around the ex-dividend day) and investors' trading decisions. In most periods examined, the average price drop is less than the dividend paid, implying a negative effect on value. The entire price behavior cannot be attributed to measurement errors or market frictions. However, it is also rather clear that market imperfections such as transaction costs, the inability to fully hedge, and price discreteness inhibit tax-motivated trading. Absent these imperfections, it is possible that no trace of the tax effect would show up in the pricing data. So, while in perfect and complete capital markets dividends may not affect value, this relation is much less clear in incomplete markets with transaction costs. The theory and some of the empirical evidence indicate that taxes do matter, and that dividends reduce value when risk cannot be fully hedged and transactions are costly.

Overall, the evidence from the ex-day studies appears to indicate that from a tax perspective, dividends should be minimized. The volume of trade around these events is much higher than usual, indicating that the shares change hands from one investor' group to the other. This evidence tells us that taxes affect behavior.

The facts also indicate that a pure dividend-related tax clientele does not exist. First, there is clear evidence for intergroup ex-day trading that is motivated by taxes. It is also apparent that ex-day trading volume increases as the degree of tax heterogeneity among investors increases. This evidence suggests that as the benefits of trading increase, so does trading volume. Second, direct examination of individuals' tax returns indicates that throughout most of the period 1973–1999, individuals in high tax brackets receive substantial amounts of taxable dividends, which refutes the tax clientele argument. Third, there is no evidence that dividend changes indicate any significant clientele shift, as we would expect if dividend clienteles did exist.

One way of looking for evidence of clientele shifts is to see whether the turnover rate for firms that initiate or omit dividends shows a marked change following the announcement. Richardson, Sefcik and Thompson (1986) do this for 192 firms that initiated dividends. They concluded that the volume response is primarily in response to the news contained in the initiation announcement rather than to a clientele shift. Michaely, Thaler and Womack (1995) examined the turnover of both initiating and omitting firms. They concluded that the relatively minor increase in volume around the event and the absence of an increase in the six months thereafter was too low to be consistent with a significant clientele shift.

Michaely, Thaler and Womack also directly investigated whether the share of institutional ownership changed after dividend omission. For the 182 firms with available data, they found that the average institutional ownership was 30% in the three years prior to the omission and was 30.9% after. This evidence further supports the impression that dividend changes do not produce dramatic changes in ownership.

However, Brav and Heaton (1998) find a drop in institutional ownership around dividend omissions after the ERISA regulations took effect in 1974. Binay (2001) examines both initiations and omissions and reports a significant drop in institutional ownership after omissions and an increase in institutional ownership after initiations. Perez-Gonzalez (2000) looks at changes in firms' dividend policy as a result of tax reforms. He finds that dividend policy is much more affected by the tax reform when the largest shareholder is an individual than it is when the largest shareholder is an institution or when there is no large shareholder. Finally, Del Guercio (1996) examines the role of dividends in the portfolio selection of institutions. She finds that after controlling for several other factors such as market capitalization, liquidity, risk, and S&P ranking, dividend yield has no power in explaining banks' portfolio choice, and is a negative indicator in mutual funds' portfolio choice. Overall, her evidence indicates that the prudent man rule has a role in portfolio selection but that dividends do not play a major role in it.

In light of the above discussion, perhaps it is less surprising that tests of the static models with taxes have not been successful. These tests cannot accommodate dynamic trading strategies, which seem to be important in this context. In addition, time-varying risk may result in spurious positive yield coefficients [Chen, Grundy and Stambaugh (1990)] and missing pricing factors can also result in a positive yield coefficient [Fama and French (1993)]. As Naranjo, Nimalendran and Ryngaert (1998) show, even when they do find a dividend yield effect, it is difficult to attribute it to taxes, since it does not vary with relative taxation and is absent in large-cap stocks. Indeed, the ex-dividend day studies that account for these effects have been more successful in identifying the extent to which taxes affect prices and traders' behavior.

6. Asymmetric information and incomplete contracts – theory

6.1. Signaling and adverse selection models

Capital markets are imperfect, but not just because individuals and corporations have to pay taxes. Another potentially important imperfection relates to the information structure: if insiders have better information about the firm's future cash flows, many researchers suggest that dividends might convey information about the firm's prospects: dividends might convey information not previously known to the market, or they may be used as a costly signal to change market perceptions concerning future earnings prospects.

Using the sources and uses of funds identity, and assuming the firm's investment is known, dividend announcements may convey information about current earnings (and maybe even about future earnings, if earnings are serially correlated) even in the absence of any signaling motive. Since investment is known, dividends are then the residual. Thus, larger-than-expected dividends imply higher earnings. Since the market does not know the current level of earnings, higher-than-anticipated earnings would lead to a positive stock price increase. (When we talk about dividends in this context, what we really mean is net dividends. We define these in Section 4 as dividends plus repurchases minus equity issues). This interpretation of dividend announcements is not new and originated with Miller and Modigliani (1961) and later to the more formal argument in Miller and Rock (1985).

However, it was not until the late 1970s and early 1980s that any signaling models were developed. The best known are those of Bhattacharya (1979), Miller and Rock (1985) and John and Williams (1985). The basic intuitive idea in all these models is that firms adjust dividends to signal their prospects. A rise in dividends typically signals that the firm will do better, and a decrease suggests that it will do worse. These theories may explain why firms pay out so much of their earnings as dividends. Thus, they are consistent with the first empirical observation.

However, in this context one of the central questions that arises is why firms use dividends, and not share repurchases or some other less costly means of signaling, to convey their prospects to investors.

Bhattacharya (1979) used a two-period model in which the firm's managers act in the original shareholders' interests. At time zero, the managers invest in a project. The managers know the expected profitability of this investment, but investors do not. At this time, the managers also "commit" to a dividend policy. At time 1, the project generates a payoff that is used to pay the dividends committed to at time zero. A crucial assumption of the model is that if the payoff is insufficient to cover the dividends, the firm must resort to outside financing and incur transaction costs in doing so.

At time zero, the managers can signal that the firm's project is good by committing to a large dividend at time 1. If a firm does indeed have a good project, it will usually be able to pay the dividend without resorting to outside financing and therefore will not have to bear the associated transaction costs. In equilibrium, it is not worthwhile for a firm with a bad project to do this, because it will have to resort to outside financing more often and thus will have to bear higher transaction costs. If the dividends are high enough, these extra costs will more than offset the advantage gained from the higher price received at time 1. Since the critical trade-off in the model is between the transaction costs incurred by committing to a large dividend and the price paid at time 1, it follows that similar results hold when the dividends are taxed.

Just after the dividends are paid, the firm is sold to a new group of shareholders, which receives the payoff generated by the project at time 2. The payoffs in the two periods are independent and identically distributed. The price that the new shareholders are prepared to pay at time 1 depends on their beliefs concerning the profitability of the project. Bhattacharya's model was a significant step forward. It is consistent with the observation that firms pay dividends even when these are taxed. However, Bhattacharya's model has been criticized on the grounds that it does not explain why firms use dividends to signal their prospects. It would seem that firms could signal better if they used share repurchases instead of dividends. This way of signaling would result in the same tradeoff between the transaction costs of resorting to outside financing and the amount received when the firm is sold, but it would result in lower personal taxes than when dividends are used.

Bhattacharya's model, like many dividend signaling models, has the feature that dividends and share repurchases are perfect substitutes for one another. It does not matter whether the "good" firm signals its value through repurchasing shares or paying dividends, because the end result will be the same: the payout increases the chances that the firm will need outside financing that is costly. Therefore, one of the implications of these models is that dividends and repurchases are perfect substitutes, an issue we return to in a later section.

Bhattacharya's model reveals both the strengths and weaknesses of the dividend signaling literature. Its main strength is that it is able to explain the positive market reaction to dividend increases and to announcements of share repurchases. The explanation is based on an intuitive notion that dividends tell us something about the firm's future prospects. The model is internally consistent and assumes that both investors and management behave in a rational manner.

However, like many such models, several of its assumptions are subject to some criticism. For example, why would a management care so much about the stock price next period? Why is its horizon so short that it is willing to "burn money" (in the form of a payout) just to increase the value of the firm now, especially when the true value will be revealed next period? It is also not clear from this model why firms smooth dividends. Finally, why should a firm use dividends (or repurchases) to signal? It would be more dramatic to burn the money in the middle of Wall Street, and it might even be cheaper.

The dissatisfaction with early models led to the development of a number of alternative signaling theories. Miller and Rock (1985) also constructed a two-period model. In their model, at time zero firms invest in a project, the profitability of which cannot be observed by investors. At time 1, the project produces earnings and the firm uses these to finance its dividend payment and its new investment. Investors cannot observe either earnings or the new level of investment. An important assumption in the Miller and Rock model is that some shareholders want to sell their holdings in the firm at time 1, and that this factor enters managers' investment and payout decisions.

At time 2, the firm's investments again produce earnings. A critical assumption of the model is that the firm's earnings are correlated through time. This setting implies that the firm has an incentive to make shareholders believe that the earnings at time 1 are high so that the shareholders who sell will receive a high price. Since both earnings and investment are unobservable, a bad firm can pretend to have high earnings by cutting its investment and paying out high dividends instead. A good firm must pay a level of dividends that is sufficiently high to make it unattractive for bad firms to reduce their investment enough to achieve the same level.

The Miller and Rock theory has a number of attractive features. The basic story, that firms shave investment to make dividends higher and signal high earnings, is entirely plausible. Unlike the Bhattacharya (1979) model, the Miller and rock theory does not rely on assumptions that are difficult to interpret, such as firms being able to commit to a dividend level.

What are its weaknesses? It is vulnerable to the standard criticism of signaling models that we discuss above. It is not clear that if taxes are introduced, dividends remain the best form of signal. It appears that share repurchases could again achieve the same objective, but at a lower cost.

In Bhattacharya (1979), the dissipative cost that allowed signaling to occur was the transaction cost of having to resort to outside financing. In Miller and Rock (1985), the dissipative costs arise from the distortion in the firm's investment decision. John and Williams (1985) present a model in which taxes *are* the dissipative cost. The theory thus meets the criticism that the same signal could be achieved at a lower cost if the firm were to repurchase shares instead. So while the Miller and Rock and the Bhattacharya models imply that dividends and repurchases are perfect substitutes, the John and Williams model implies that dividends and repurchases are not at all related. A firm cannot achieve its objective of higher valuation by substituting a dollar of dividends for a dollar of capital gains.

What is the reasoning behind this result? Like other models, John and Williams's starting point is the assumption that shareholders in a firm have liquidity needs that they must meet by selling some of their shares. The firm's managers act in the interest of the original shareholders and know the true value of the firm. Outside investors do not. If the firm is undervalued when the shareholders must meet their liquidity needs, then these shareholders would be selling at a price below the true value. However, suppose the firm pays a dividend, which is taxed. If outside investors take this as a good signal, then the share price will rise. Shareholders will have to sell less equity to meet their liquidity needs and will maintain a higher proportionate share in the firm.

Why is it that bad firms do not find it worthwhile to imitate good ones? When dividends are paid, it is costly to shareholders because they must pay taxes on them. But there are two benefits. First, shareholders receive a higher price for the shares that are sold. Second, and more importantly, these shareholders retain a higher proportionate share in the firm. If the firm is actually undervalued, this higher proportionate share is valuable to the shareholder. If the managers' information is bad and the firm is overvalued, the opposite is true. It is this difference that allows separation. If dividends are costly enough, only firms that are actually good will benefit enough from the higher proportionate share to make it worthwhile bearing the cost of the taxes on the dividends.

John and Williams's model thus avoids the objection to most signaling theories of dividends. Firms do not repurchase shares to avoid taxes, because it is precisely the cost of the taxes that makes dividends desirable. This is clearly an important innovation.

What are the weaknesses of the John and Williams' theory? In terms of assumptions, they take it as a given that shareholders must meet their liquidity needs by selling their shares. They rule out the use of debt, either by the firm or the shareholders themselves. We could ask why the firm does not borrow and use the proceeds to repurchase its shares. Again, doing so would meet the liquidity needs of investors and would only be worthwhile if the firm's shares were undervalued. It should be possible to signal the firm's value costlessly by repurchasing shares and thus increasing the proportionate share held by the firm. The Ross (1977) study shows that borrowing serves as a credible signal. Even if, for some reason, corporate borrowing is not possible, an alternative is for the investors to borrow on their personal accounts instead of selling shares. Again, this would allow them to meet their liquidity needs without incurring the cost of signaling.

It is also not obvious that the John and Williams model's empirical implications support dividend smoothing. The best way to extend the model over a longer time is not entirely clear. If firms' prospects do not change over time, then once a firm has signaled its type, no further dividend payments will be necessary and payouts can be made through share repurchases. If firms' prospects are constantly changing, which seems more plausible, and if dividends signal these, we would expect that dividends will also constantly change. This prediction of the model is difficult to reconcile with the observation that corporations smooth dividends, and in many cases do not alter them at all for long periods of time. We can also make the same criticism of the other signaling models. After the Miller and Rock (1985) and John and Williams (1985) papers, a number of other theories with multiple signals were developed. Ambarish, John and Williams (1987) constructed a single-period model with dividends, investment, and stock repurchases. Williams (1988) developed a multi-period model with these elements and showed that in the efficient signaling equilibrium, firms typically pay dividends, choose their investments in risky assets to maximize net present value, and issue new stock. Constantinides and Grundy (1989) focused on the interaction between investment decisions and repurchase and financing decisions in a signaling equilibrium. With investment fixed, a straight bond issue cannot act as a signal, but a convertible bond issue can. When investment is chosen optimally rather than being fixed, this is no longer true; a straight bond issue can act as a signal.

Bernheim (1991) also provided a theory of dividends in which signaling occurs because dividends are taxed more heavily than repurchases. In his model, the firm controls the amount of taxes paid by varying the proportion of the total payout that is in the form of dividends, rather than repurchases. A good firm can choose the optimal amount of taxes to provide the signal. As with the John and Williams model, Bernheim's model does not provide a good explanation of dividend smoothing.

Allen, Bernardo and Welch (2000) took a different approach to dividend signaling. As in the previous models, dividends are a signal of good news (i.e., undervaluation). However, in their model firms pay dividends because they are interested in attracting a better-informed clientele. Untaxed institutions such as pension funds and mutual funds are the primary holders of dividend-paying stocks because they are a tax-disadvantaged payout method for other potential stockholders.

Another reason for institutions to hold dividend-paying stocks is the restrictions in institutional charters, such as the "prudent man" rules that make it more difficult for many institutions to purchase stocks that pay either no dividends or low dividends. According to Allen, Bernardo and Welch (2000), the reason good firms like institutions to hold their stock is that these stockholders are better informed and have a relative advantage in detecting high firm quality. Low-quality firms do not have the incentive to mimic, since they do not wish their true worth to be revealed.

Thus, taxable dividends are desirable because they allow firms' management to signal the good quality of their firms. Paying dividends increases the chance that institutions will detect the firm's quality.

Another interesting feature of the Allen, Bernardo, and Welch model is that it does accommodate dividend smoothing. Firms that pay dividends are unlikely to reduce the amount of the dividend, because their clientele (institutions) are precisely the kind of investors that will punish them for it. Thus, they keep dividends relatively smooth.

As in the John and Williams model, the Allen, Bernardo, and Welch model involves a different role for dividends and repurchases. They are not substitutes. In fact, firms with more asymmetric information and firms with more severe agency problems will use dividends rather than repurchases.

Kumar (1988) provided a theory of dividend smoothing. In his model, the managers who make the investment decision know the true productivity type of the firm but the outside investors do not. Also, because they are less diversified the managers want to invest less than the outside investors. Managers will try to achieve lower investment by underreporting the firm's productivity type.

Kumar shows that there cannot be a fully revealing equilibrium in which dividends perfectly signal productivity. If there were such an equilibrium, shareholders could deduce the firm's true productivity type. However, this is inconsistent with managers underreporting.

A coarse signaling equilibrium can exist, though. Within an interval of productivity, Kumar shows that it is optimal for the different types of firm to cluster at a corresponding dividend level. This theory is consistent with smoothing, because small changes in productivity will not usually move a firm outside the interval, so its dividend will not change. Unfortunately, this theory does not explain why share repurchases, which are taxed less, are not used instead of dividends. Kang and Kumar (1991) have looked at the empirical relation between firm productivity and the frequency of dividend changes. Their results are consistent with Kumar's analysis.

The signaling models discussed here are important contributions. They are also intuitively appealing. Firms that pay dividends, and especially firms that increase their dividends, are firms that are undervalued by the market. Thus, the most important prediction that is common to all of these models is that dividends convey good news about the firm's future cash flows.

The majority of the theoretical (and empirical) research has assumed that firms use dividend changes to signal changes in future earnings or cash flows. But given the less than enthusiastic empirical endorsement this prediction has received (as we describe in the next section), we might want to consider another possibility, that increases in dividends convey information about changes in risk rather than about growth in future cash flows.

By definition, the fundamental news about a firm must be about either its cash flows or its discount rates (risk characteristics). If the good news in a dividend increase is not about (expected) increases in future cash flow, then it might concern a decline in (systematic) risk.

Current dividend-signaling models have very little to say about the relation between dividend changes and risk changes. Grullon, Michaely and Swaminathan (2002) present an alternative explanation, which they refer to as the "maturity hypothesis". They propose that there are several elements that contribute to firms becoming mature. As firms mature, their investment opportunity set shrinks, resulting in a decline in their future profitability. But perhaps the most important consequence of a firm becoming mature is a change in its (systematic) risk characteristics, specifically, a decline in risk. The decline in risk most likely occurs because the firm's assets in place have become less risky and/or the firm has fewer growth opportunities available. Finally, the decline in investment opportunities generates an increase in free cash flows, leading to an increase in dividends. Thus, a dividend increase indicates that a firm has matured.

According to the maturity hypothesis, firms increase dividends when growth opportunities decline, which leads to a decrease in the firm's systematic risk and profitability. How, then, should the market react to a dividend increase? The dividend increase clearly contains at least two pieces of news. The good news is that the risk has decreased, and the bad news is that profits are going to decline. The positive market reaction implies that news about risk dominates news about profitability. Another possibility is that because of agency considerations, investors treat dividend increases as good news, in spite of the declining profitability. For instance, if investors expect managers to squander the firm's wealth by overinvesting, then a dividend increase suggests that managers are likely to act more responsibly. Thus, in addition to the good news conveyed about a risk reduction, investors might interpret a dividend increase as good news per se (they reduce the overinvestment problem), and the stock price would rise. Modeling the dynamic relation between firms' dividend policy, investment opportunities, and cost of capital is still an unexplored path that could yield valuable new insights into the determination of corporate payout policy.

6.2. Incomplete contracts – agency models

If we relax the assumption of complete (and fully enforceable) contracts, we realize that a firm is more than just a "black box". The different forces that operate within a firm can, at different points in time, pull it in different directions, and the interests of different groups within a firm may conflict. The three groups that are most likely to be affected the most by a firm's dividend policy are stockholders, management, and bondholders.

The first conflict of interest that could affect dividend policy is between management and stockholders. As suggested by Jensen and Meckling (1976), managers of a publicly held firm could allocate resources to activities that benefit them, but that are not in the shareholders' best interest. These activities can range from lavish expenses on corporate jets to unjustifiable acquisitions and expansions. In other words, too much cash in the firm may result in overinvestment.

Grossman and Hart (1980), Easterbrook (1984) and Jensen (1986) have suggested a partial solution to this problem. If equityholders can minimize the cash that management controls, they can make it much harder for management to go on (unmonitored) spending sprees. The less discretionary cash that management has, the harder it is for them to invest in negative NPV projects. One way to take unnecessary cash from the firm is to increase the level of payout.

We note that these theories suggest a significant departure from the original Miller and Modigliani assumption in that payout policy and investment policy are interrelated. Paying out cash would increase firm value by reducing potential overinvestments.

Cash payouts make an appealing argument, and as we will show, it also receives significant empirical support. But payouts also have several shortcomings. First, if managers want to overinvest, either to increase their power base by acquiring more firms, or simply to spend more on jets and hunting trips, what is the mechanism that will force them to commit to an action that will prevent them from doing so? Or is it the board of directors that forces them to change their payout policy? If so, what is the information structure and the enforcement mechanism between the board of directors and the management that allows the board to set the appropriate dividend policy ex-ante, but not to monitor management's actions ex-post? Put another way, if the board (which we assume is independent of the management and cares about shareholders' best interests – a very strong assumption indeed) knows that management overinvests, why can't it monitor it better?

Several authors, most notably Zwiebel (1996), Fluck (1999) and Myers (2000), address this issue in the context of capital structure, but the basic insight for payout policy is straightforward. It must be in management's self-interest to maintain positive payout ex-post. In contrast to the standard free cash flow stories, management voluntarily commits to pay out cash because of constant potential threat of some (limited) disciplinary actions. This is also the notion that the Allen, Bernardo and Welch (2000) paper brings to the payout policy issue. Their paper highlights the role of large outsider shareholders' constant monitoring role.

Another question asks why firms pay out in the form of dividends and not share repurchases, since the latter are a cheaper way to take money out of management hands. A related question is why monitor through payout and not debt? As Grossman and Hart (1980) and Jensen (1986) argue, a more effective mechanism to achieve this goal is to increase the level of debt. It is harder for management to renege on a debt commitment relative to a dividend commitment. This argument can also be applied to the choice of dividends versus repurchases. If we take as given the empirical observation that the market strongly dislikes dividend reductions and that management is therefore reluctant to reduce dividends, then dividends represent a more effective mechanism than repurchases to impose discipline.

Third, although the agency story offers a palatable explanation for dividend increases, it is much less so for dividend decreases. Firms increase their dividends when they have free cash flow, and the positive market reaction to the dividend announcement happens because the market realizes that now management will have to be more disciplined in its action. But what about dividend cuts? One possibility is that management cuts dividends when cash flow, and hence free cash flow, has fallen. Another possibility is that management (or the board) cuts dividends when there are good investments, so the cut should also be greeted positively by the market. Needless to say, this does not happen. In this case, the good investments could be financed by debt.

The earlier work of Shleifer and Vishny (1986) and the more recent work by Allen, Bernardo and Welch (2000) provides a framework that can overcome the first two problems (management incentive to pre-commit and dividends as opposed to repurchases). Building on the work of Grossman and Hart (1980), Shleifer and Vishny (1986) suggested that because of conflict of interest, management should be monitored, and this monitoring must be done by large shareholders. The presence of such shareholders increases the value of the firm because of the monitoring role they play, and because they help facilitate takeover activities (even if they are not involved). Thus, the board has an incentive to induce major shareholders to take a position in the firm, especially if the firm is likely to have excess cash.

Given the favorable tax treatment of dividends by some large shareholders such as corporations, it is possible that dividends are paid to attract this type of clientele. Allen, Bernardo and Welch (2000) extend this analysis and show that a favorable tax rate for institutions relative to individuals is enough for those large shareholders to prefer dividend-paying stocks. This observation is important, since now the analysis can encompass not only corporations (as in Shleifer and Vishny), but also various types of tax-free institutions.

This clientele will increase the value to all shareholders, including individual shareholders, since it monitors the management and thereby increases the firm's value. Whether indeed large shareholders are attracted to firms that pay dividends and much less to firms that repurchase their shares is an unresolved empirical issue that is worth pursuing. [10]

The second conflict of interest that may be affected by payout policy is between stockholders and bondholders. As Myers (1977) and Jensen and Meckling (1976) have argued, there are some situations in which equityholders might try to expropriate

---

[10] Based on potential conflict of interest between outside shareholders and the minority shareholders who manage the firm, Fluck (1999) presents an interesting idea in which the more effective outsiders are in disciplining management, the more they receive in dividends. Thus, the better outsiders are at monitoring, either because of the resources they devote to it or because of their fractional ownership, more of the profits will be distributed to shareholders.

wealth from debtholders. This wealth expropriation could come in the form of excessive (and unanticipated) dividend payments. Shareholders can reduce investments and thereby increase dividends (investment-financed dividends), or they can raise debt to finance the dividends (debt-financed dividends). In both cases, if debtholders do not anticipate the shareholders' action, then the market value of debt will go down and the market value of equity will rise.

To summarize, in this section we presented two views of why dividends are paid. The first view is that dividends convey good news. The alternative view is that dividends are in themselves good news because they resolve agency problems. In the next section we review the corresponding empirical literature.

7. Empirical evidence

7.1. Asymmetric information and signaling models

In their original paper, Miller and Modigliani suggested that if management's expectations of future earnings affects their decisions about current dividend payouts, then changes in dividends will convey information to the market about future earnings. This notion has been labeled as "the information content of dividends". As discussed earlier, this notion has been formalized in two ways: In the first, dividends are used as an ex-ante signal of future cash flow as, for example, in Bhattacharya (1979). In the second, dividends provide information about earnings as a description of the sources and uses of funds identity as, for example, in Miller and Rock (1985). The second alternative can be interpreted as saying that the fact that dividends convey information does not necessarily imply that they are being used as a signal. This distinction may be subtle, but it is crucially important in interpreting the empirical tests as supporting the signaling theory. Most, if not all, of the empirical tests we are aware of cannot help us to distinguish between these two alternatives.

The information/signaling hypotheses contain three important implications that have been tested empirically:
(i)   Dividend changes should be followed by subsequent earnings changes in the same direction.
(ii) Unanticipated dividend changes should be accompanied by stock-price changes in the same direction.
(iii) Unanticipated changes in dividends should be followed by revisions in the market's expectations of future earnings in the same direction as the dividend change.

It is important to note that all of the above implications are necessary, but not sufficient, conditions for dividend signaling. The condition that earnings changes will follow dividend changes is the most basic. If this condition is not met, we can conclude that dividends do not have even the potential to convey information – at least not about future cash flows, – let alone to signal.

Most of the empirical literature has concentrated on the second implication, that unexpected dividends changes are associated with price changes in the same direction. Therefore, we start our review by describing the empirical findings on the association between dividend changes and price changes. For example, Pettit (1972) showed that a significant price increase follows announcements of dividend increases, and a significant price drop follows announcements of dividend decreases. Aharony and Swary (1980) showed that these price changes hold even after they controlled for contemporaneous earnings announcements. Using a comprehensive sample of dividend changes of at least 10% over the period 1967–1993, Grullon, Michaely and Swaminathan (2002) found that the average abnormal return to dividend increases was 1.34% (a median of 0.95%) and the average abnormal market reaction to dividend decreases was −3.71% (a median of −2.05%).

Table 9 describes some of the characteristics of firms that change their dividends. Both dividend-increasing and decreasing firms are larger than the typical NYSE/Amex firm. During the last four decades (the sample is from 1963 to 1998), the average dividend-increasing firm has a dividend yield of 3.74% before the dividend increase and the average dividend-decreasing firm has a dividend yield of 3.29% prior to the dividend decrease. The change in dividend is greater (in absolute terms) for firms that decrease their dividends (−44.8% compared to 31.1%), but the frequency of a decrease is smaller (1358 compared to 6284).

Studies by Asquith and Mullins (1983) (dividend initiations), Healy and Palepu (1988) and Michaely, Thaler and Womack (1995) (dividend initiations and omissions) focused on extreme changes in dividend policy. Their research showed that the market reacts quite severely to those announcements. The average excess return is 3.4% for initiation and −7% for omissions.

It seems that the market has an asymmetric response to dividend increases and decreases (and for initiations and omissions), which implies that lowering dividends carries more informational content than increasing dividends, perhaps because reductions are more unusual, or because reductions are of greater magnitude. Michaely, Thaler and Womack (1995) examined this issue and found that when they controlled for the change in yield, the announcement of an omission had a larger impact on prices than did an announcement of an initiation. They also reported that the effect of a unit change in yield (say, a 1% change in yield) had a greater effect on prices for initiations than it did for omissions. The price impact may explain, to some extent, why managers are so reluctant to cut dividends.

There seems to be general agreement that:
(1) Dividend changes are associated with changes in stock price of the same sign around the dividend change announcement.
(2) The immediate price reaction is related to the magnitude of the dividend.
(3) The price reaction is not symmetric for increases and reductions of dividends. Announcements of reductions per se have a larger price impact than announcements of increases.

Table 9
Firm characteristics of dividend-changing firms [a,b]

	Mean	Std.	Median
Dividend increases (6,284 obs.)			
CHGDIV %	30.1	29.3	22.2
CAR %	1.34	4.33	0.95
SIZE	1,185.1	3,796.1	195.9
RSIZE	8.1	2.1	9
PRICE	29.60	24.23	24.50
DY %	3.74	2.09	3.46
Dividend decreases (1358 obs.)			
CHGDIV %	−44.8	16.4	−45.9
CAR %	−3.71	6.89	−2.05
SIZE	757.4	2,489.4	148.0
RSIZE	7.7	2.4	8
PRICE	26.31	25.31	18.50
DY %	3.29	2.19	2.87

[a] This table reports the firm characteristics for a sample of firms that change their cash dividends over the period 1967–1993. To be included in the sample, the observation must satisfy the following criteria: 1) the firm's financial data is available on CRSP and Compustat; 2) the cash dividend announcement is not accompanied by other non-dividend events; 3) only quarterly cash dividends are considered; 4) cash dividend changes that are less than 10% or greater than 500% are excluded; 5) cash dividend initiations and omissions are excluded; 6) the last cash dividend payment is paid within 90 days prior to the announcement of the cash dividend change. CHGDIV is the percentage change in the cash dividend payment, CAR is the three-day cumulative NYSE/Amex value-weighted abnormal return around the dividend announcement, SIZE is the market value of equity at the time of the announcement of the cash dividend change, RSIZE is the size decile ranking relative to the entire sample of firms on CRSP, PRICE is the average price, and DY is the dividend yield at the time of the announcement of the cash dividend change.
[b] Source: Grullon, Michaely and Swaminathan (2002), "Are dividend changes a sign of firm maturity"?

Prices can tell us not only about the immediate market reaction to the dividend change, but also how the market perceived dividend-changing firms before the dividend change occurred and whether the market absorbed the information contained in the dividend change. It is clear that dividend-increasing firms have done well prior to the announcement and dividend-decreasing firms have not done as well. For example, for the period 1947–1967 Charest (1978) found an abnormal performance of around 4% in the year prior to the dividend increase month and a negative 12% for the dividend decreasing firms. Benartzi, Michaely and Thaler (1997) documented an average 8.6% abnormal return in the year prior to a dividend increase and −28% for firms that decreased dividends. For dividend initiations and omissions, the magnitude of the pre-announcement price movement was even more pronounced [Michaely, Thaler and Womack (1995)].

What is perhaps more interesting and important, from both the corporate finance and the market efficiency perspectives, is the post-dividend-change performance. Charest (1978) found a 4% abnormal return in the two years after dividend increase announcements and a negative 8% for dividend-decreasing firms. Using the Fama–French three-factor model Grullon, Michaely and Swaminathan (2002) reported a three-year abnormal return of 8.3% for dividend increases, which is significant. They did not detect any abnormal performance for dividend-decreasing firms. Not surprisingly, the post-dividend abnormal performance was even more pronounced for initiations and omissions. Michaely, Thaler and Womack (1995) reported a market-adjusted return of almost 25% in the three years after initiations and a negative abnormal return of 15% in the three years after omissions.

The post-dividend announcement drift is both encouraging and disturbing from the signaling-theory perspective. It is encouraging because it is consistent with the implication that dividend changes have some useful informational content. It is disturbing because it implies that even if firms try to signal through dividends, the market does not "get it" – or at least it does not get the full extent of the signal. Otherwise, the entire price reaction would have happened right after the announcement. The fact that the market doesn't get it (better future earnings or cash flows) is problematic, since the models described above rely on the rationality assumption. Investors and firms use the information at their disposal in the best possible way. The long-term drift does not support this assumption. In other words, if investors do not understand the signal, there is no incentive for those firms to use a costly signal.

Our next step is to examine the fundamental implication of the signaling models – that dividend changes and future earnings changes move in the same direction. Watts (1973) was among the first to test the proposition that the knowledge of current dividends improves the predictions of future earnings, over and above knowledge of current and past earnings. Using 310 firms with complete dividends and earnings information for the years 1946–67, and annual definitions of dividends and earnings, Watts tested whether earnings in year $t + 1$ could be explained by the current (year t) and past (year $t - 1$) levels of dividend and earnings. For each firm in the sample, Watts estimated the current and past dividend coefficients (while controlling for earnings). Although he found that the average dividend coefficients across firms were positive, the average t-statistic was very low. In fact, only the top 10% of the coefficients were marginally significant. Using changes in levels yielded similar results. He concluded that: "... in general, if there is any information in dividends, it is very small".

Gonedes (1978) reached a similar conclusion. Penman (1983) also finds that after controlling for management's future earnings forecast, there was not much information conveyed by dividend changes themselves. Interestingly, Penman also reports that many firms with improved future earnings did not adjust their dividends accordingly.

Somewhat more in line with the theory are Healy and Palepu's (1988) results. For their sample of 131 firms that initiated dividend payments, earnings had increased rapidly in the past and continued to increase for the following two years. However, for their sample of 172 firms that omitted a dividend payment, the results were the opposite of what signaling theory predicts. Earnings declined in the year in which the omission announcement took place, but then improved significantly in the next several years. For a sample of 35 firms that increased their dividends by more than 20%, Brickley (1983) found a significant earnings increase in the year of and the year after the dividend increase.

Perhaps we can attribute the somewhat mixed results on the relation between current changes in dividends and future changes in earnings to the limited number of firms used in most of these studies. Another factor that makes the task difficult is knowing how to model unexpected earnings.

Using a large number of firms and events over the period 1979–1991 and several definitions of earnings innovations, Benartzi, Michaely and Thaler (1997) investigate the relation between dividend changes and future changes in earnings. They measure earnings changes relative to the industry average changes in earnings that they adjusted for earnings momentum and for mean reversion in earnings. Two robust results emerge. First, there is a very strong lagged and contemporaneous correlation between dividend changes and earnings changes. When dividends are increased earnings *have* gone up. There is no evidence of a positive relation between dividend changes and future earnings changes. In the two years following the dividend increase, earnings changes were unrelated to the sign and magnitude of the dividend change.

The results were strong but perverse for dividend decreases. Like Healy and Palepu (1988), Benartzi, Michaely and Thaler (1997) find a clear pattern of earnings increase in the two years following the dividend cut. Using a sample of firms that changed their dividends by more than 10%, Grullon, Michaely and Swaminathan (2002) confirmed these results. They show that not only do future earnings not continue to increase, but that the level of firms' profitability decreases in the years following announcement of dividend increases. Figure 4 presents these results. The figure shows that firms move from a period of increasing ROA before the dividend increase to a period of declining ROA after the dividend increase.

Nissim and Ziv (2001) offer yet another look at this problem. They attempt to explain future innovation in earnings by the change in dividend, like Benartzi, Michaely and Thaler (1997). They argue that a good control for mean reversion is the ratio of earnings to the book value of equity (ROE) and add it as an additional explanatory variable. They advocate the inclusion of ROE to improve the model of expected earnings, and to fix what they call an "omitted correlated variables". Rather than adopting the natural convention of assigning a dividend change to the year in which it actually takes place, Nissim and Ziv change this convention by assigning dividend changes that occur in the first quarter of year $t + 1$ to year t. Since we know that dividends are very good predictor of past and current earnings, this change is bound to strengthen the association between dividend changes and earnings growth in year 1. Indeed using this methodology, the dividend coefficient is significant in about 50% of the cases when next year's earning is the dependent variable. When using the

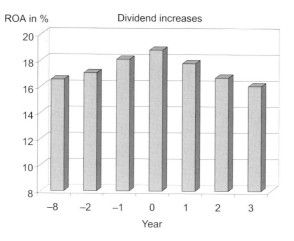

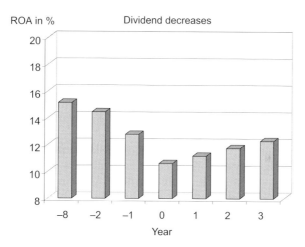

Fig. 4. Level of return of assets. This figure depicts the level of return on assets (ROA) based on operating income before depreciation (Compustat annual item 13) for a sample of firms that change their dividends over the period 1967–1993. Year 0 is the year in which the dividend change was announced. The data have been winsorized at the first and 99th percentiles. [Grullon, Michaely and Swaminathan (2002), "Are dividend changes a sign of firm maturity"?]

more conventional methodology, it is significant in only 25% of the years. When using several independent variables in addition to ROE, Benartzi, Michaely and Thaler (1997) do not find any significant relation between current changes in dividends and future changes in earnings.

Using the Fama and French (2000) modified partial adjustment model to control for the predictable component of future earnings changes based on lagged earnings levels and changes, Grullon, Michaely, Benartzi and Thaler (2003) re-examine the relation between dividends and earnings changes. Fama and French explicitly model the time-series of earnings in a way that captures the empirical fact that earnings changes are more mean-reverting in the tails. They show that their model explains the evolution of earnings much better than a model with a uniform rate of mean reversion. We have thus adopted their methods to investigate this problem.[11] The model is the following:

$$
\begin{aligned}
\frac{E_\tau - E_{\tau-1}}{B_{-1}} &= \beta_0 + \beta_1 \mathrm{R\Delta DIV}_0 \\
&\quad + \left(\gamma_1 + \gamma_2 \mathrm{NDFED}_0 + \gamma_3 \mathrm{NDFED}_0^* \mathrm{DFE}_0 + \gamma_4 \mathrm{PDFED}_0^* \mathrm{DFE}_0\right)^* \mathrm{DFE}_0 \\
&\quad + \left(\lambda_1 + \lambda_2 \mathrm{NCED}_0 + \lambda_3 \mathrm{NCED}_0^* \mathrm{CE}_0 + \lambda_4 \mathrm{PCED}_0^* \mathrm{CE}_0\right)^* \mathrm{CE}_0 + \varepsilon_\tau.
\end{aligned}
$$
(19)

In this equation DFE_0 is equal to $\mathrm{ROE}_0 - E[\mathrm{ROE}_0]$, where $E[\mathrm{ROE}_0]$ is the fitted value from the cross-sectional regression of ROE_0 on the log of total assets in year -1, the market-to-book ratio of equity in year -1, and ROE_{-1}. CE_0 is equal to $(E_0 - E_{-1})/B_{-1}$. NDFED_0 (PDFED_0) is a dummy variable that takes the value of 1 if DFE_0 is negative (positive) and 0 otherwise, and NCED_0 (PCED_0) is a dummy variable that takes the value of 1 if CE_0 is negative (positive) and 0 otherwise. As discussed in Fama and French (2000), the dummy variables and squared terms in Equation 19 are included to capture the fact that large changes in earnings revert faster than small changes and that negative changes revert faster than positive changes. It is important to control for these non-linearities in the behavior of earnings because assuming linearity when the true functional form is non-linear has the same consequences as leaving out relevant independent variables.

The Grullon, Michaely, Benartzi and Thaler (2003) estimation of Equation 19 is presented in Table 10. They find no evidence that dividend changes contain information about future earnings growth. The coefficient for RΔDIV is not statistically different from zero when either year 1 earnings changes or year 2 earnings changes are the dependent variables. Furthermore, even for predictions of first year earnings growth, the coefficient for the dividend change is significant at the 10% level in only 4 out of the 34 years of the sample. For year 2 earnings it is significantly positive at the 10% level in just 5 out of the 34 years. As documented in previous studies, this evidence suggests that dividend changes are very unreliable predictors of future earnings.

The overall accumulated evidence does not support the assertion that dividend changes convey information about future earnings. Miller (1987) summarized the empirical findings this way: "... dividends are better described as lagging earnings than as leading earnings". Maybe, as Miller and Rock (1985) suggested, dividends convey information about current earnings through the sources and uses of funds identity, not because of signaling. At the minimum, the empirical findings on the long-term price drift and the lack of positive association between dividend changes and future changes in earnings raise serious questions about the validity of the dividend

---

[11] See Fama and French (2000) for a detailed discussion of this econometric model.

Table 10
Regressions of raw earnings changes on dividend changes using the Fama and French approach to predict expected earnings (see Equation 19) [a,b]

Year		β_1	Adjusted-R^2
$\tau = 1$	Mean	0.005	22.5%
	T-statistic	0.56	
	% of $t(\beta_i) > 1.65$	11.8%	
$\tau = 2$	Mean	0.011	9.7%
	T-statistic	1.13	
	% of $t(\beta_i) > 1.65$	12.1%	

[a] This table reports estimates of regressions relating raw-earnings changes to dividend changes. We use the Fama–MacBeth procedure to estimate the regression coefficients. In the first stage, we estimate cross-sectional regression coefficients each year using all the observations in that year. In the second-stage, we compute time-series means and t-statistics of the cross-sectional regression coefficients. The t-statistics are adjusted for autocorrelation and reported in parentheses. a, b, and c denote significantly different from zero at the 1%, 5%, and 10% level, respectively.
[b] Source: Grullon, Michaely, Benartzi and Thaler (2003), "Dividend changes do not signal changes in future profitability".

signaling models. If firms are sending a signal through dividends, it is not a signal about future growth in earnings or cash flows, and the market doesn't get the message. Why would firms waste money by paying a costly dividend to send a signal that investors do not receive?

In an interesting paper, DeAngelo, DeAngelo and Skinner (1996) examined 145 firms whose annual earnings growth declined in year zero, after at least nine years of consecutive earnings growth. Thus, year zero represented the first earnings decline in many years. Their test focused on the year zero dividend decision, which could have conveyed a lot of information to outsiders by helping the market to assess whether the decline in earnings was permanent or transitory. DeAngelo, DeAngelo and Skinner found no evidence that favorable dividend decisions (i.e., dividend increases) represented a reliable signal of superior future earnings performance. There was no evidence of positive future earnings surprises (and even some indications of negative earnings surprises) for the 99 firms that increased their dividends. Not only did the dividend-increasing firms not experience positive earnings surprises in subsequent years in absolute terms, their earnings performance was no better than those firms that did not change their dividend. Overall, there was no evidence that dividends had provided a useful signal about future earnings.

None of us know for sure what market expectations are, either about prices or about earnings. But in the case of earnings, we can test for changes in market expectations by looking at the earnings estimates of Wall Street's analysts. This is how we can test the third implication of the information/signaling theories, that unanticipated changes in dividends should be followed by revisions in the market's expectations of future earnings in the same direction as the dividend change. Ofer and Siegel (1987) used 781 dividend change events to examine how analysts change their forecast about the *current* year earnings in response to the dividend changes. Consistent with the positive association between dividend changes and actual changes in concurrent year earnings (the year of the dividend change), Ofer and Siegel found that analysts revised their current year earnings forecast by an amount that was positively related to the size of the announced dividend change. They also provided evidence that their revision was positively correlated with the market reaction to the announced dividend.

Most of the empirical research centers on the necessary conditions (price reaction, subsequent earnings and changes in earnings expectations) for dividend signaling. The outcome, as we have shown, is not encouraging. Several papers looked at the sufficient conditions for dividend signaling, most notably at taxes. Recall that tax-based dividend signaling theories are based on the idea that dividends are more costly than repurchases, and that managers intentionally use this costly device to signal information to the market.

Bernheim and Wantz (1995) investigated the market reaction to dividend changes during different tax regimes. In periods when the relative taxes on dividends are higher than taxes on capital gains, the signaling hypothesis implies that the market reaction to dividend increases should be stronger, because it is more costly to pay dividends. Since it is more expensive to signal, the signals are more revealing for those who choose to use them. The free cash flow hypothesis makes the opposite prediction. Since it is more expensive to pay dividends and the benefit presumably does not change, when the taxes on dividends are relatively higher, the market should react less favorably to dividend increases. Bernheim and Wantz's results are consistent with the dividend-signaling hypothesis. In periods of higher relative taxes on dividends, the market reaction to dividend payments is more favorable.

However, applying nonparametric techniques that account for the nonlinear properties common to many of the dividend-signaling models in an experiment similar to Bernheim and Wantz (1995), Bernhardt, Robertson and Farrow (1994) did not find evidence to support the tax-based signaling models. Furthermore, using data from six years before and six years after the Tax Reform Act of 1986, Grullon and Michaely (2001) found that the market responded much more positively to dividend increases when dividend taxation was lower (after the tax change), a finding that is inconsistent with tax-based signaling theories.

Amihud and Murgia (1997) examine dividend policy in Germany, where dividends are not tax disadvantaged and in fact dividend taxation is lower than capital gains taxation for most classes of investors. In this setting, the tax-based models [such as John and Williams (1985), Bernheim (1991) and Allen, Bernardo and Welch (2000)] predict that dividend changes should not have any informational value. Thus, we should not observe a price reaction around changes in dividends. However, Amihud and Murgia (1997) find that dividend changes in Germany generated a stock price

Table 11

Average stock price before and after the dividend-increase announcement, the change in the firm cost of capital (using the Fama–French three-factor model), the change in the average dividend payment, and the implied change in growth; the implied change in growth is imputed from the Gordon growth model

	Before the dividend change	After the dividend change	Comments
Actual average share prices	$29.6	$30	We calculate the price of $30 based on an average market reaction of 1.43%)
Discount rates	13.2%	12.2%	We calculate the discount rate based on Fama–French 3-factor models and a riskless rate of 5
Average dividend	$1.1 (Table 1)	$1.4	The average increase in dividend is 30% (Table 1)
Implied growth rate	9.48%	7.48%	

reaction that was very similar to what other researchers have found in the USA. This finding is not consistent with the theory.

Grullon, Michaely and Swaminathan (2002) examined the relation between changes in dividend policy and changes in the risk and growth characteristics of the firm. Their sample comprised 7642 dividend changes announced between 1968 and 1993. Using the Fama–French three-factor model or the CAPM, they found that firms that increased dividends experienced a significant decline in their systematic risk, but firms that decreased dividends experienced a significant increase in systematic risk. Firms that increased dividends also experienced a significant decline in their return on assets, which indicates a decline in systematic risk. Capital expenditures of firms that increased dividends stayed the same and the levels of cash and short-term investments on their balance sheets declined.

Moreover, Grullon, Michaely and Swaminathan found that the greater the subsequent decline in risk, the more positive was the market reaction to the announced dividend. Thus, changes in risk, conditional on changes in profitability, begin to provide an explanation for the price reaction to dividend announcements.

Using the Gordon growth model and the actual changes in risk and dividends, Table 11 illustrates the relations between the risk reduction, the reduction in growth, and the price reaction to the announced dividend. The table shows that the average stock price prior to the announcement is $29.6, and the average market reaction is 1.34%, implying a post-announcement price of $30. Grullon, Michaely and Swaminathan (2002) further reported a decline in the equity cost of capital from an average of 13.2% in the years before the dividend change to 12.2% in the years after the dividend change. Now, using the Gordon growth model, we can calculate the implied change in growth. We find that because of the decline in risk, a growth rate decline of even 20% (from 9.48% to 7.48%) is still consistent with a positive market reaction.

In summary, the empirical evidence provides a strong *prima facie* case against the traditional dividend signaling models. First, the relation between dividend changes and subsequent earnings changes are the opposite of what the theory predicts, so if firms signal, the signal is not about future growth in earnings or cash flows. Second, the market doesn't "get" the signal. There is a significant price drift in subsequent years. (However, there is a change in the dividend-changing firms' risk profile, and that the change is related both to the dividend and to subsequent performance.) Third, a cross-sectional examination strongly indicates that it is the large and profitable firms and those firms with less information asymmetries that pay the vast majority of dividends.

7.2. Agency models

Since most agency models are not as structured as the signaling models, it is difficult to derive precise empirical implications. According to the free-cash-flow models what should happen to earnings after a dividend increase? The answer is ambiguous. If the board of directors decides to increase the dividend after management has already invested in some negative NPV projects, then, since the payment of dividends prevents management from continuing to invest in "bad" projects, we should expect earnings and profitability to increase. However, if the board decides on dividends before management has the chance to overinvest, then it is difficult to say how future earnings will be relative to past earnings. If dividends increase around the time the firms face declines in investment opportunities, then even a decline in profitability is consistent with the free-cash-flow hypothesis.

A clearer implication of the free-cash-flow hypothesis is that the overinvestment problem is likely to be more pronounced in stable, cash-rich companies in mature industries without many growth opportunities. Lang and Litzenberger (1989) exploited this feature to test the free-cash-flow hypothesis, and to contrast it with the information-signaling hypothesis. The basic idea is that, according to the free cash flow hypothesis, an increase in dividends should have a greater (positive) price impact for firms that overinvest than for firms that do not. Empirically, they identified overinvesting firms as ones with Tobin's Q less than unity. When they examined only dividend changes that were greater than 10% (in absolute value), they found that for dividend-increase announcements, firms with Q less than one experienced a larger price appreciation than firms with Q greater than one. For dividend-decrease announcements, firms with Q lower than one showed a more dramatic price drop. The greater effect (in absolute value) of dividend changes on firms with lower Q is consistent with the free-cash-flow hypothesis. On the other hand, the information-signaling hypothesis would have predicted a symmetric effect regardless of the ratio of market value to replacement value.

Yoon and Starks (1995) repeated the Lang and Litzenberger experiment over a longer time period. They found that the reaction to dividend decreases was the same for high and low Tobin's-Q firms. The fact that the market reacts negatively to dividend decrease announcements by the value-maximizing (high Q) firms is not consistent with the free-cash-flow hypothesis.

Like Lang and Litzenberger (1989), Yoon and Starks found a differential reaction to announcements of divided increases. However, when they controlled for other factors, such as the level of dividend yield, firm size, and the magnitude of the change in the dividend yield (through a regression analysis), Yoon and Starks found a symmetric reaction to dividend changes (both increases and decreases) between high and low Tobin's Q firms. Again, this evidence is not consistent with the free-cash-flow hypotheses.

Grullon, Michaely and Swaminathan's findings of declining return on assets, cash levels, and capital expenditures in the years after large dividend increases suggest that firms that anticipate a declining investment opportunity set are the ones that are likely to increase dividends. This is consistent with the free-cash-flow hypothesis. Lie (2000) thoroughly investigated the relation between excess funds and firms' payout policies and found that dividend-increasing (or repurchase) firms had cash in excess of peer firms in their industry. He also showed that the market reaction to the announcement of special dividends (and repurchases) was positively related to the firm's amount of excess cash and negatively related to the firm's investment opportunity set as measured by Tobin's Q. These results are consistent with the idea that limiting potential overinvestment through cash distribution, especially for firms that have limited investment opportunities, enhances shareholder wealth.

Christie and Nanda (1994) examined the reaction of stocks to President Roosevelt's unexpected announcement in 1936 of taxes on undistributed corporate profits. The new tax increased the attractiveness of dividends relative to retained earnings. According to the free-cash-flow hypothesis, firms would now have had more incentive to reduce retained earnings and thereby reduce potential overinvestment problems, since it had become less expensive (in relative terms) to dispense of those cash flows. This effect would have been particularly pronounced for firms that were more susceptible to agency costs. Christie and Nanda (1994) found that share prices rose in response to the announcement of the tax change, consistent with the notion that paying dividends may alleviate some free cash flow problems. They also found that firms that were more likely to suffer from free cash flow problems experienced a more positive price reaction to the announcement.

The ability to monitor and the rights of outside shareholders differs across countries, and by implication the potential severity of conflicts of interests will also differ. La Porta, Lopez-De Silanes, Shleifer and Vishny (2000) examined the relation between investors' protection and dividend policy across 33 countries. They tested two hypotheses. The first was that when investors were better able to monitor and enforce their objectives on management (countries with higher investors' protection), they would also pressure management to disgorge more cash. The second hypothesis was that because of market forces (e.g., management wants to maintain the ability to raise more cash in the capital markets or wants to maintain a high stock price for other reasons), management would actually pay high dividends in those countries where investors' protection was not high. [12]

La Porta et al. (2000) found that firms in countries with better investor protection made higher dividend payouts than did firms in countries with lower investor protection. Moreover, in countries with more legal protection, high-growth firms had lower payout ratios. This finding supports the idea that investors use their legal power to force dividends when growth prospects are low. That is, an effective legal system provides investors with the opportunity to reduce agency costs by forcing managers to pay out cash. There is no support for the notion that managers have the incentive to "do it on their own".

The results of La Porta et al. (2000) indicate that without enforcement, management does not have a strong incentive to "convey its quality" through payout policy. There is also no evidence that in countries with low investor protection, management will voluntarily commit itself to pay out higher dividends and to be monitored more frequently by the market.

Before concluding this section we discuss the empirical evidence on the relation between the potential shareholder–debtholder conflict of interest and dividend policy.

Handjinicolaou and Kalay (1984) examined the effect of dividend-change announcements on both bond and equities prices. If dividend changes are driven by equityholders' desire to extract wealth from debtholders, then an increase in dividends should have a positive impact on stock prices (which we know it does), and a negative impact on bond prices. The reverse should be true for dividend decreases. The alternative hypothesis, that dividends are a consequence of asymmetric information or that they resolve free cash flow problems, implies that bond prices should move in the same direction as equity prices. Handjinicolaou and Kalay found that bond prices dropped significantly at the announcement of dividend decreases, and did not change significantly at dividend-increase announcements. These results do not lend support to the wealth expropriation hypothesis. [13]

Myers (1977) and Jensen and Meckling (1976) suggested that both equityholders and bondholders may a priori agree on restricting dividends. Indeed, most bond covenants contain constraints that limit both investment- and debt-financed dividends.

Kalay (1982b) examined these constraints and found that firms held significantly more cash (or cash equivalents) than the minimum they needed to hold, according to the bond covenants. We can interpret Kalay's finding as a reverse wealth transfer. That is, if debt were priced under the assumption that only the minimum cash would be

---

[12] The notion that in countries where investors' protection is low, firms would pay higher dividends is also consistent with many of the signaling models. In countries with low protection, the degree of asymmetric information is likely to be higher, and hence the desire to pay dividends by high-quality firms should be higher as well.

[13] The asymmetry in the bond price reaction may be explained by several factors. Among them is the fact that dividend decreases are larger in absolute value than dividend increases, and therefore have a more significant impact on both bond and stock prices.

held by the corporation, then a positive reservoir would increase the market value of debt at the expense of equityholders.

In hindsight, this is not too surprising. We should not expect that large, established firms, which are likely to have to come back to the well and seek more debt financing at some point in the future, are going to relinquish their reputation for a small gain at the expense of bondholders. We can readily see how a one-time wealth transfer from existing bondholders to equityholders may result in a long-term loss because of the increase in the cost of capital. When would the problem arise? In precisely those cases where there is a great probability that the firm's time horizon is short, e.g., the firm is in financial distress, or is about to be taken private. DeAngelo and DeAngelo (1990) found evidence that was consistent with this assertion. They showed that firms in financial distress were reluctant to cut their dividends. In these cases, not cutting dividends may constitute a significant wealth transfer from debtholders to equityholders. This is still an open question that is worth further consideration. [14]

8. Transaction costs and other explanations

Under certain circumstances, it is possible that investors would prefer dividends despite the tax disadvantage of dividends relative to capital gains.

The first explanation of why firms pay dividends has to do with the "prudent man" laws. These laws and regulations are intended to protect small investors from agents (pension funds, for example) that do not invest in their interest. Private trusts, acting under the Prudent Man Investment Act, are the most constrained fiduciaries. Pension funds are governed by the ERISA, which is less restrictive than the Prudent Man Rule. Lastly, mutual funds are supervised by the SEC according to the Investment Company Act of 1940, which is less restrictive than either the common law (for bank trusts) or ERISA (for pension funds). [See Del Guercio (1996) for information about the various laws and regulation described here].

Del Guercio (1996) presented evidence indicating that the Prudent Man Rule affects investment decisions. Bank managers significantly tilt the composition of their portfolios that are viewed by the courts as being subject to the Prudent Man Rule. Mutual funds do not. Bank trusts weight their portfolios towards S&P stocks and towards stocks that are ranked A+ (the highest ranking based on earnings and dividend history). Mutual funds load their portfolios the other way, towards lower rank stocks. We find it interesting that there is no difference between the portfolios' composition of bank trusts (mainly trusts of wealthy individuals, which are highly taxed) and bank pension funds (nontaxable entities). Both types of portfolio are weighted more towards S&P stocks and on stocks that are ranked A+.

---

[14] DeAngelo and DeAngelo (1990) allude to another link between conflict of interest and dividend policy. They report that some dividend reductions are intended to enhance the firm's bargaining position regarding labor negotiations.

Del Guercio went a step further. Using a regression analysis, she examined the role of dividends in the portfolio selection of institutions and found that after controlling for several other factors, such as market capitalization, liquidity, risk, and S&P ranking, dividend yield had no power to explain banks' portfolio choices, and had negative explanatory power in mutual funds portfolio choice.

Overall, the evidence indicates that the Prudent Man Rule has a role in portfolio selection, but that dividends do not play a major role (if any). This evidence is also consistent with the information presented in Table 2, which indicates that dividend taxation is not an issue in portfolio selection, not even for highly taxed investors.

A second motive for paying dividends is based on a transaction costs argument. If investors want a steady flow of income from their capital investment (say, for consumption reasons), then it is possible that dividend payments would be the cheapest way to achieve this goal. This result may hold if the cost of the alternative (i.e., to sell a portion of the holdings and receive capital gains) involves nontrivial costs. These costs might be the actual transaction costs for selling the shares, which can be quite high for retail investors, or they could represent the time and effort spent on these transactions.

However, this argument does not seem to be supported by the time-series evidence on transaction costs, nor by stock ownership. First, through the years, and especially after the switch to negotiated commissions in May 1975, the transaction costs of buying and selling shares have been substantially reduced. This reduction should have resulted in lower demand for dividends, as the alternative became cheaper. The evidence in Table 1 does not support this prediction. We do not observe a reduction in dividend payments that is related to the change in transaction costs.

Second, this argument particularly applies to individual small investors who do not hold many shares. Hence, the cost of transacting may be higher. But the role of small investors in the market place has been shrinking. The overall level of dividends in the economy has not been reduced accordingly.

Third, if this effect is in fact substantial, it should lead to an optimal dividend policy at the aggregate level. However, as Black and Scholes (1974) argued, firms will adjust their dividend policy such that the demand for dividends by this clientele is fulfilled. Thus, in equilibrium, any specific firm should be indifferent to dividend policy. So, while this explanation can account for positive payouts despite the adverse tax consequences, it cannot explain why, in equilibrium, firms care about the level of dividends paid.

Shefrin and Statman (1984) suggested a third explanation as to why investors may prefer dividend-paying stocks. Rather than developing an economic model based on maximizing behavior, they eliminated the maximizing assumptions that are the cornerstone of neoclassical economics, and which we have maintained throughout. Instead, Shefrin and Statman developed a theory of dividends based on several recent theories of investors' behavior. The basic idea is that even if the eventual cash received is the same, there is a significant difference in whether it comes in the form of dividends or as share repurchases. In other words, the form of cash flow is important for psychological reasons.

We illustrate Shefrin and Statman's approach with one of the theories they develop, based on Thaler and Shefrin's (1981) theory of self-control. Thaler and Shefrin suggested that people have difficulties behaving rationally when they want to do something but have problems doing so. Examples that illustrate this suggestion are the prevalence of smoking clinics, credit counselors, diet clubs, and substance-abuse groups. Individuals wish to deny themselves a present indulgence, but find that they yield to temptation. Thaler and Shefrin represented this conflict in a principal-agent form. The principal is the individual's internal planner, which expresses consistent long-run preferences. However, the responsibility for carrying out the individual's action lies not with the planner, but with the doer, the agent.

There are two ways the planner can control the agent. The first is will power. The problem is that this causes disutility. The second is to avoid situations in which will power must be used. This avoidance is accomplished by adopting rules of behavior that make it unnecessary for people to question what they are doing most of the time.

Shefrin and Statman suggested that by having money in the form of dividends rather than capital gains, people avoid having to make decisions about how much to consume. Thus, they avoid letting the agent in them behave opportunistically. They postulated that the benefit of doing this was sufficient to offset the taxes on dividends.

As with the transaction costs story, the self-control explanation can account for an aggregate positive payout policy, but not for an individual firm optimal payout policy. That is, in equilibrium, firms will adjust their dividend policy such that the marginal firm is indifferent to the level of dividend paid out. Thus, neither the transaction costs explanation nor the behavioral explanation can account for the positive price reaction to dividend increases and the negative price reaction to dividend decreases. Nevertheless, this explanation is innovative and intriguing.

We also note that this explanation relies heavily on the effect that individual investors have on market prices. The need for a steady stream of cash flows combined with significant transaction costs (the transaction costs story) may adequately describe the actions of small retail investors, but may not hold when applied to corporate and institutional investors. Likewise, using self-control as an explanation for why firms pay dividends is more persuasive when individual investors are the dominant force in the marketplace. As the evidence in Table 1 indicates, the level of dividend payout did not decrease through time. This evidence does not support the self-control and transaction costs explanations.

However, Long's (1978) study of Citizens Utilities (CU) is illuminating. CU stocks are an almost perfect medium for examining the effect of dividend policy on prices. The reason is that from 1955 until 1989, this company had two types of common stocks that differed only in their dividend policy. Series A stock paid a stock dividend and

Series B stock paid a cash dividend.[15] The company's charter required that the stock dividend on Series A stock be of equal value with Series B cash dividends. However, in practice, the board of directors chose stock dividends that averaged 10% higher than the cash dividends. Even without taxes, we would expect the price ratio of Series A stock to Series B stock to be equal to the dividend ratio, i.e., to 1.1. Long found that the price ratio was consistently below 1.1 in the period considered. This price ratio implies a preference for cash dividends over stock dividends despite the tax penalty.

Poterba (1986) revisited the Citizens Utilities case. For the period 1976–84, he found that the price ratio and the dividend ratios were comparable: the average price ratio was 1.134 and the average dividend ratio was 1.122. This evidence implies indifference between dividend and capital gains income. Poterba also examined the ex-dividend day behavior of CU for the period 1965–84, and found that the average ex-day price decline was less than the dividend payment. This evidence supports the ex-dividend day studies discussed previously. It is hard to reconcile the ex-day evidence of the CU stocks with the relative prices of the two stocks on ordinary days.

Hubbard and Michaely (1997) examined the relative prices of these two stocks after the passage of the 1986 TRA. Because the 1986 TRA substantially reduced the advantage of receiving stock dividends rather than cash dividends, they hypothesized that the price ratio should decrease. Indeed, they found that during 1986, the price ratio was considerably lower than in the previous years. However, in the years 1987 through 1989, the price ratio rose and stayed consistently above the dividend ratio.

It seems that the evidence from the price behavior of Citizens Utilities deepens the dividend mystery, rather than enlightening us. It is difficult to know just how to interpret it.

There is another rationale for paying dividends, but it is not consistent with efficient markets. If managers know more about their firm than the market does and they can time their equity issues decisions to periods when their firm is highly overvalued, then a positive payout is optimal. That is, if investors prefer constant cash flow and managers can sell additional equity when it is overvalued, then investors will be better off receiving a steady stream of dividends and leaving the timing of the sales to the firm. However, in efficient markets, outside investors will realize that when a firm sells its securities, it implies that the firm is overvalued (see Myers and Majluf (1984), for example), and its price (post announcement) will reflect this fact. In such a case, current equityholders are not better off, even if the managers know more about the firm's value than the market does. The attempt to raise equity will result in a reduction in the existing equity's value. The new shares will be sold at fair value, which renders dividend policy irrelevant.

---

[15] CU received a special IRS ruling so that for tax purposes, the Series A stock dividends would be taxed in the same way as proportionate stock dividends are treated for firms having only one series of common stock outstanding. The special ruling expired in 1990.

A growing number of studies are presenting evidence that is not consistent with the market rationality described above. Their evidence is consistent with the notion that managers can time the market [e.g., Baker and Wurgler (2000)]; and that the market underreacts to some financial policy decisions, such as seasoned equity issues [Loughran and Ritter (1995)], Initial Public Offerings [Ritter (1991) and Michaely and Shaw (1994)], and repurchases [Ikenberry, Lakonishok and Vermaelen (1995)]. We know that announcements of seasoned equity issues are associated with a price decline [e.g., Masulis and Korwar (1986)], and share repurchases announcements are associated with price increases [e.g., Vermaelen (1981)]. However, these studies go further by showing that a significant price movement in the same direction continues several years after the event.

Moreover, the post-dividend announcement drift [Charest (1978), Michaely, Thaler and Womack (1995), Benartzi, Michaely and Thaler (1997)] may be a result of investor behavior that is less than fully rational. This drift can be explained to some extent by the fact that dividend changes indicate changes in the denominator (risk profile) rather than in the numerator (cash flows), and thus are harder to detect. Grullon, Michaely and Swaminathan (2002) find that the long-term drift is negatively related to future changes in risk. The greater the decline in risk, the larger the drift. Thus, in the long run, prices increase with a decline in risk. This price behavior indicates a securities market in which investors only gradually learn the full implications of a dividend change for a firm's future profitability and systematic risk. Hence, we could argue that paying dividends is the optimal policy so that investors do not have to sell their stock when it is below its (true?) market value.

The literature on dividend policy is plentiful. Due to a lack of space, we cannot cover the many contributions in detail. However, one approach that has received considerable attention in the economics literature, but not in the finance literature, was developed by King (1977), Auerbach (1979) and Bradford (1981). The assumption in this framework is that the prohibition on repurchasing shares is binding, and paying dividends is the only way firms can distribute cash to investors. The market value of corporate assets is therefore equal to the present value of the after-tax dividends firms are expected to pay. Because dividend taxes are capitalized into share values, firms are indifferent on the margin between policies of retaining earnings or paying dividends. Thus, the model supports the idea that firms pay out a significant portion of corporate earnings as dividends. However, this theory fails to explain the market reaction to dividend announcements that was the starting point of many of the other theories. This theory has also not received much attention in the finance literature because of its assumption that dividends are the only way the firm can pay out money to shareholders.[16]

This assumption is appropriate in some countries, such as the UK, where repurchases have historically been illegal. It is less appropriate for the USA. Nonetheless, the

[16] Some models have been criticized on the grounds that they implicitly assume that dividends cannot be financed by equity or debt issues. See Hasbrouck and Friend (1984) and Sarig (1984).

use of open-market share repurchases in the USA was not common until 1983, perhaps because of some legal restrictions. For example, the risk of violating the antimanipulative provisions of the Securities Exchange Act (SEA) of 1934 deterred most corporations from repurchasing shares. After the SEC adopted a safe-harbor rule (Rule 10b-18) in 1982 that guaranteed that, under certain conditions, the SEC would not file manipulation charges against companies that repurchased shares on the open market, repurchase activity experienced an upward structural shift.

9. Repurchases

Today, repurchases represent a significant portion of total USA corporate payouts (Figure 1). In the last several years, the dollar amount of repurchases has been virtually equal to that of cash dividends. Not only has the amount of repurchases increased, but also the number of firms that repurchase has increased dramatically.

The phenomenon of the decline in the number of firms that pay dividends [Fama and French (2001), Grullon and Michaely (2002)] might be directly related to the trend we see in repurchases. These trends represent a significant departure from historical patterns in repurchase and dividend policies of corporations.

9.1. The mechanics and some stylized facts

Firms repurchase their shares through three main vehicles: (1) open-market share repurchase, (2) fixed-price tender offer, and (3) Dutch auction. Repurchased shares can either be retired or be counted as part of the firm's treasury stock. In any case, those shares lose their voting rights and rights to cash flows.

In an open-market share repurchase, the firm buys back some of its shares in the open market. Historically, regulatory bodies in many countries frowned on this practice, since it might make it possible for corporations to manipulate the price of their shares. Indeed, there are still many countries where share repurchases are not allowed and many other countries, such as Japan and Germany, that have only recently relaxed the restrictions on repurchases.

In the USA, share repurchase activity is governed by the antimanipulative provisions of the Securities Exchange Act of 1934. These provisions exposed repurchasing firms (and anyone else involved in the repurchase activity, such as investment banks) to the possibility of triggering an SEC investigation and being charged with illegal market manipulation. This risk seemed to deter firms from purchasing their shares. Conscious of this problem, the SEC started to design guidelines for corporations on how to carry out share repurchase programs without raising suspicions of manipulative behavior. As part of the deregulation wave of the early 1980s, the SEC approved a legislation to regulate open market share repurchases. In 1982, the SEC adopted Rule 10b–18, which provides a safe-harbor for repurchasing firms against the anti-manipulative provisions of the Securities Exchange Act of 1934.[17] Specifically, Rule 10b-18 was adopted in order to establish guidelines for repurchasing shares on the open market without violating Sections 9(a) (2) or 10(b) of the SEA of 1934.[18] In general, Rule 10b-18 requires that firms repurchasing shares on the open market should publicly announce the repurchase program, only use one broker or dealer on any single day, avoid trading on an up tick or during the last half-hour before the closing of the market, and limit the daily volume of purchases to a specified amount.

In a fixed-price tender offer, the corporation, through an investment bank, offers to purchase a portion of its share at a prespecified price. The tender offer includes the number of shares sought and the duration of the offer. However, the firm usually reserves the right to increase the number of shares repurchased if the tender offer is oversubscribed, and/or to buy shares from the tendering shareholders on a pro-rata basis. If the offer is not fully subscribed, the company has the right to either buy the shares tendered or to cancel the offer altogether.

In a Dutch auction, the firm specifies the number of shares to be purchased and the price range for the repurchase. Each interested shareholder submits a proposal containing a price and the number of shares to be tendered. The firm aggregates all the offers and finds the minimum price at which it can buy the prespecified number of shares. This price is paid to all tendering shareholders, even if they submitted a lower price.

Table 12 shows that open-market repurchases are by far the most popular method of repurchase. For example, in 1998 open market repurchases accounted for over 95% of the dollar value of shares repurchased. The relative importance of Dutch auctions and tender offers, was significantly higher in the 1980s. The introduction of Rule 10b-18 and the consequent rise in the popularity of open-market share repurchases have made the other methods much less important. Therefore, in this section we concentrate on open market share repurchases.[19]

In practice, fixed-price tender offers and Dutch auctions are likely to be used when a corporation wishes to tender a large amount of its outstanding shares in a short period of time, typically around 15% [see for example Vermaelen (1981), Comment

---

[17] 47 Fed Reg. 53333 (November 26, 1982).

[18] Section 9(a) (2) establishes that it will be illegal "... to effect, alone or with one or more other persons, a series of transactions in any security registered on a national securities exchange creating actual or apparent active trading in such security, or raising or depressing the price of such security, for the purpose of inducing the purchase or sale of such securities by others". Section 10(b) establishes that it will be unlawful "... to use or employ, in connection with the purchase or sale of any security registered on a national securities exchange or any security not so registered, any manipulative or deceptive or contrivance in contravention of such rules and regulations as the Commission may prescribe as necessary or appropriate in the public interest or for the protection of investors".

[19] Another type of share repurchase is a targeted stock repurchase, in which the firm offers to buy stocks from a subset of shareholders. For example, a "greenmail agreement" is a type of targeted stock repurchase from (usually) one large shareholder. Greenmail is typically used in conjunction with takeover threats and is used to a much lesser extent than those described above.

Table 12
The use of Dutch auctions, tender offers and open-market share repurchases through time [a]

Dutch auctions			Tender offers			Open market		
year	Cases	$(mln)	year	Cases	$(mln)	year	Cases	$(mln)
1980	–	–	1980	1	5	1980	86	1,429
1981	–	–	1981	44	1,329	1981	95	3,013
1982	–	–	1982	40	1,164	1982	129	3,112
1983	–	–	1983	40	1,352	1983	53	2,278
1984	1	9	1984	67	10,517	1984	236	14,910
1985	6	1,123	1985	36	13,352	1985	159	22,786
1986	11	2,332	1986	20	5,492	1986	219	28,417
1987	9	1,502	1987	42	4,764	1987	132	34,787
1988	21	7,695	1988	32	3,826	1988	276	33,150
1989	22	5,044	1989	49	1,939	1989	499	62,873
1990	10	1,933	1990	41	3,463	1990	778	39,733
1991	4	739	1991	51	4,715	1991	282	16,139
1992	7	1,638	1992	37	1,488	1992	447	32,635
1993	5	1,291	1993	51	1,094	1993	461	35,000
1994	10	925	1994	52	2,796	1994	824	71,036
1995	8	969	1995	40	542	1995	851	81,591
1996	22	2,774	1996	37	2,562	1996	1111	157,917
1997	30	5,442	1997	35	2,552	1997	967	163,688
1998	20	2,640	1998	13	4,364	1998	1537	215,012
1999	19	3,817	1999	21	1,790	1999	1212	137,015

[a] Source: Grullon and Ikenberry (2000), "What do we know about stock repurchase?"

and Jarrell (1991) and Bagwell (1992)]. The duration of such programs is usually about one month. Open-market repurchases are often used to repurchase smaller portions of outstanding shares, with firms repurchasing an average of 6% of the shares [Ikenberry, Lakonishok and Vermaelen (1995), Grullon and Michaely (2002)]. The duration of open-market repurchases is much longer. Stephens and Weisbach (1998) report that firms complete their open-market repurchase program in about three years.

The average announcement price effect of an open-market share repurchase program is around 3% and the market reaction is positively related to the portion of shares outstanding sought [Ikenberry, Lakonishok and Vermaelen (1995), Grullon and Michaely (2002)]. Vermaelen (1981) and Ikenberry, Lakonishok and Vermaelen (1995) report a decrease in stock price that is similar in magnitude in the month prior to the announcement. Comment and Jarrell (1991) report an abnormal price reaction of around 12% for fixed-price offers and around 8% for Dutch auction repurchases.

Using more than 1200 open market repurchases announced between 1980 and 1990, Ikenberry, Lakonishok and Vermaelen (1995) investigated the long-term performance of repurchasing stocks in the four-year repurchase period. They found that repurchasing firms' stock outperformed the market by an average of about 12% over the four-year period. They were particularly interested to find that most of the drift was concentrated in "value" stocks (high book-to-market stocks). Those stocks exhibited an abnormal return of 45% in the four years following the repurchase announcement!

9.2. Theories of repurchases

The positive market reaction to repurchase announcements, and the fact that just like dividends, the firms pay out cash, makes it easier to see why many of the dividend theories apply to repurchases as well. For example, we can seamlessly apply the Miller and Rock (1985) or the Bhattacharya (1979) signaling models to repurchases. At the cost of shaving investments firms pay out cash to signal quality (Miller and Rock) or the need for external costly financing (Bhattacharya). The free-cash-flow models can also work as easily with repurchases as with dividends. Models that are based on relative taxation [such as John and Williams (1985) or Allen, Bernardo and Welch (2000)] or those studies that posit that dividends are a better signaling device do not assume (or imply) that repurchases and dividends are perfect substitutes.

Before turning our attention to the substitutability of dividends and repurchases, we review some of the work that explains why firms repurchase their shares in isolation.

Vermaelen (1984) used a standard signaling model in which managers were more informed than outside investors about future profitability. He showed that repurchasing shares could be used as a credible signal to convey this information. It is costly for bad firms to mimic because managers hold a portion of the firm and do not tender. Thus, if the firm buys overpriced shares and managers do not participate, the value of their fractional share decreases. Vermaelen's study also explains why the market reaction increases with the portion of shares sought as it increases the credibility of the signal.

Another oft-mentioned reason for buybacks relates to takeover battles. By buying back stocks from investors who value them the least, the firm makes any potential takeover more expensive by increasing the price the acquirer will have to pay to gain control [Bagwell (1991), Stulz (1988)]. The larger the fractional ownership controlled by the management, the higher the likely premium in case of a takeover. This motive might play a role in fixed-price tender offers and Dutch auctions, in which firms repurchase a large fraction of shares over a short period. Although important in their own right, these types of repurchase represent a very small fraction (see Table 12) relative to open market repurchases. They do not appear to be a major factor from an overall payout policy perspective.

Repurchases can also reduce the free-cash-flow problem and mitigate conflicts of interest between outside shareholders and management. If a firm has too much cash (beyond what it can invest in positive NPV projects), then repurchasing its shares is a fast and tax-effective way to give the cash back to its shareholders. Moreover, buying back shares (and assuming management has some equity, either in stocks or through stock options) increases the relative ownership of management and decreases potential conflicts of interest by better aligning management interests with outside shareholders' interests [as in Jensen and Meckling (1976)].

9.3. Repurchases compared to dividends

Since dividend distributions are associated with a heavier tax burden, why not signal or resolve agency problems only through repurchases? One answer is institutional constraints. As we noted earlier, in many countries repurchases were prohibited. In the USA, they were limited because of regulations that subjected the firm to manipulation charges. Nevertheless, open-market repurchases were done prior to 1983, before the introduction of Rule 10b-18 (though on a much smaller scale), and dividends continue to be a major vehicle to distribute cash even now, nearly 20 years after the implementation of Rule 10b-18. Some researchers have argued that if firms were to start repurchasing shares on a regular basis, they would be challenged by the IRS. This is another institutional constraint, but to the best of our knowledge this has not happened yet. We are not aware of any case in which the IRS has taxed a repurchase as ordinary income on the grounds that it is a dividend in disguise, despite the fact that a significant number of firms repurchase on a regular basis. Therefore, institutional constraints cannot be the entire story.

Several researchers have attempted to explain this puzzle from a theoretical perspective. Ofer and Thakor (1987) presented a model in which firms could signal their value through two mechanisms, paying dividends or repurchasing their shares. There are two types of cost associated with these signals. First, by paying out cash, firms expose themselves to the possibility of having to resort to outside financing, which is more expensive than generating internal capital. Whether a firm pays dividends or repurchases its shares, it will be subject to this cost because these actions deplete its internal capital. The second cost, which is unique to repurchases, is that relative to dividends, repurchases reduce managers' risk. If a firm pays dividends, which are prorated, the manager has a portion of his wealth in cash. In the case of repurchases, since she typically does not tender her shares, her portfolio is riskier. Thus, the signaling costs through repurchases are higher. It immediately follows that if future prospects of the firms are much higher than perceived by the market, then the managers will use repurchases. If the discrepancy is not that severe, managers will use dividends. In other words, repurchases are a stronger signal.

Barclay and Smith (1988) and Brennan and Thakor (1990) provided a different explanation as to why so many firms rely so heavily on dividends rather than repurchases. The crux of their arguments is that a portion of the firm's cost of capital is a function of the adverse selection costs [see Amihud and Mendelson (1986) and Easley, Hvidkjaer and O'Hara (2002)]. When a firm announces a repurchase program, the cost to the uninformed investors of adverse selection increases. When some shareholders are better informed than others about the prospects of the firm, they will be able to take advantage of this information. They will bid for stock when it is worth more than the tender price, but will not bid when it is worth less. Uninformed buyers will receive only a portion of their order when the stock is undervalued, but will receive the entire amount when it is overvalued. This adverse selection means that they are at a disadvantage in a share repurchase. When money is paid out in the form of dividends, the informed and the uninformed receive a pro rata amount, so there is no adverse selection. As a result, uninformed shareholders prefer dividends to repurchases. Further, this preference will persist even if dividends are taxed more heavily than repurchases, provided the tax disadvantage is not too large. On the other hand, the informed will prefer repurchases because this allows them to profit at the expense of the uninformed.

Brennan and Thakor (1990) argue that the method of disbursement chosen by firms will be determined by a majority vote of the shareholders. If the uninformed have more votes than the informed, firms will use dividends, but if the informed predominate, firms will choose repurchases. When there is a fixed cost of obtaining information, the number of informed depends on the distribution of shareholdings and the amount paid out. For a given payout, investors with large holdings will have an incentive to become informed. When a small amount is paid out, only the investors with the largest holdings will become informed; most shareholders will remain uninformed and will prefer dividends. When a larger amount is paid out, more shareholders become informed, so the firm may choose repurchases.

We note that this model has exactly the opposite prediction to Allen, Bernardo and Welch (2000) on the relation between large (and presumably informed) shareholders and payout policy. In this model, larger shareholders favor repurchases. In Allen et al., large shareholders prefer dividends. It is still an open question as to which one of these predictions holds empirically.

The Brennan and Thakor model is an intriguing explanation of the preference that firms appear to have for dividends. It answers the question of why firms prefer to use dividends even though dividends are taxed more heavily. Unlike the John and Williams' theory, the Brennan and Thankor model supports the idea that dividends are smoothed.

However, their model is not above criticism. First, the range of tax rates for which dividends are preferred to repurchases because of adverse selection is usually small. To explain the predominance of dividends, we must use another argument that relies on shareholders being homogeneous. For tax rates above the level at which adverse selection can explain the preference for dividends, everybody will tender in a repurchase, so it will be pro rata. But this universal tendering clearly does not occur. Second, if superior information is the motive for repurchases, it is surprising that management almost never tenders its shares. Presumably, they are the ones with the best information. Another criticism is that if adverse selection were a serious problem, firms could gather the relevant information and publicly announce it. Nevertheless,

Brennan and Thakor's theory sheds new light on the choice between dividends and repurchases.

Chowdhry and Nanda (1994) and Lucas and McDonald (1998) also considered models in which there is a tax disadvantage to dividends and an adverse selection cost to repurchases. In their models, managers are better informed than are shareholders. Their models show how payout policy depends on whether managers think the firm is over- or undervalued relative to the current market valuation. Both models provide interesting insights into the advantages and disadvantages of dividends and repurchases. However, the stability and smoothing of dividends is difficult to explain in this framework unless firms remain undervalued or overvalued relative to their market value through time.

9.4. Empirical evidence

The market usually reacts positively to an announcement of any type of share repurchase. The extent of the reaction is positively related to the size of the repurchase program and negatively related to the market value of the firm. Despite the positive reaction, many studies have found that the market does not comprehend the full extent of the information contained in the announcement, given the long-term post-announcement drift. The drift is particularly pronounced in high book-to-market stocks [for open-market share repurchases, see Ikenberry, Lakonishok and Vermaelen (1995)]. Vermaelen (1981), Comment and Jarrell (1991), Ikenberry, Lakonishok and Vermaelen (1995), and others document a negative abnormal return in the months leading to the (open market) repurchase announcement, a finding that suggests that firms time the repurchase announcement to when the stock is more undervalued.

A subtler issue concerns the number of shares that have actually been repurchased and the duration of the program. A firm is under no obligation to repurchase all of the shares it seeks. The announcement merely serves to inform investors of its intentions. If there is a significant discrepancy between the announced and the actual number of shares repurchased, this discrepancy can affect the long-term reaction in the years after the announcement. Just as important, when we wish to examine the relation between repurchases and other types of payout such as dividends, or to relate actual repurchases to performance, we must measure the actual repurchases as accurately as possible.

9.4.1. How to measure share repurchase activity?

Using 450 open-market repurchase programs announced between 1981 and 1990, Stephens and Weisbach (1998) suggest several measures of repurchases.
(1) The change in number of shares outstanding as reported on the CRSP or Compustat databases.
A potential problem with this measure is that if a firm repurchases shares and simultaneously distributes shares (either to the public or to employees), this measure will understate the actual amount of repurchase.

(2) The net dollar spent on repurchases as reported in the firm's cash flow statement.
If we want to analyze the dollar amount spent on repurchases, this measure is probably
the best one to use. If we wish to compute the number of shares repurchased, we must
convert the dollar number that is reported in the cash flow statement to number of
stocks repurchased. However, doing so creates a difficulty, since we do not know the
purchase price. We can use the average trading price over the period as a proxy for
the purchase price. Another possible shortcoming of this measure is that it includes
purchases of not only common stocks, but also other type of stocks such as preferred
stocks. However, repurchases of securities other than common stocks represent only a
very small portion of firms' repurchase activity.
(3) The change in Treasury stock (also reported on Compustat).
However, this measure can be problematic, since firms often retire the shares they
repurchase. Thus, while the number of shares outstanding decreases, the number of
Treasury shares does not change. In addition, if a firm repurchases shares and at the
same time distributes shares, say in lieu of stock options, there is no change in Treasury
stock, despite the repurchase activity. This factor may represent a significant problem,
given the recent popularity of stock options as a method of compensation.

For example, imagine a firm that repurchases 1000 shares, say for $10000, and
then a few months later turns around and give these shares to its CEO as part
of her compensation. The firm is involved in two distinct actions. The first is a
financing action (repurchasing shares), and the second is an investment decision
(paying the manager). If we try to analyze the impact of a financing decision, holding
all else constant, especially holding investment constant, this measure of repurchase
is inadequate.

The problem is even more severe if we try to compare repurchases and dividend
decisions. Say, our firm pays a total dividend of $10000, instead of repurchasing its
shares. At the same time, it also issues shares and gives them to the manager. In the
first case (when the firm repurchases its shares in the open market and the researcher is
using Treasury shares to measure repurchases), we would record no repurchase activity.
But in the second case (pay a dividend and issue shares), we would record a $10000
dividend. But in reality, assuming away taxes, both routes are exactly identical. Our
firm pays $10000 to shareholders and gives $10000 worth of stock to the manager.

In summary, measuring repurchases through the change in Treasury stock is likely to
yield the most biased measure of repurchases. It can bundle investment and financing
decisions (as discussed above), it combines other overlapping distributions, and it does
not account for the fact that many firms retire the stocks they repurchase rather than
putting them into Treasury stock. Stephens and Weisbach (1998) find that this measure
is substantially different from the other measures they use. They show that the first
two measures yield similar results in the measurement of share repurchases, while the
Treasury-stock method yields estimates that are lower than the other two methods by
about 60%.

Which method should we use? We recommend using the cash flow spent on
repurchases, and trying to account for any changes in the shares outstanding. This

measure is likely to yield the least biased estimate of the actual dollar amount spent on repurchases.

Given these measures of actual repurchases, we can address the issue of how long it takes firms to complete their announced stock repurchase program. Stephens and Weisbach (1998) reported that approximately 82% of the programs were completed within three years. More than half of the firms completed their announced repurchase program, but one tenth of the firms repurchased less than 5% of their announced intentions. The authors also showed that the initial market reaction to share repurchases was positively related to the actual share repurchase activity in the two years after the announcement. Firms that repurchased more, experienced a larger positive price effect at the announcement. However, the announcement effect was not related to the announced quantity of share repurchase.

Stephens and Weisbach (1998) also showed that the actual amount of repurchase in a given quarter was related to the firm's cash flow level. Using a Tobit model, they showed that the decision to repurchase was positively related to both the level of expected cash and unexpected cash. They also showed that the actual repurchase activity was negatively related to the equity return in the previous quarter: the more negative the return was in quarter $t - 1$, the more likely the firm was to engage in repurchase activity in quarter t.

9.4.2. Empirical tests of repurchase theories

So repurchases are positively greeted by the market, they are preceded by bad performance, and some (mainly value stocks) are followed by positive abnormal price performance. All of these attributes are consistent with both the asymmetric information/signaling and the free cash flow theories as the main motive behind the decision to repurchase. But, as with dividends, there are two possibilities. The positive price impact of the announcement can be because repurchases are good news (i.e., they lead to better investment decisions because management has less cash to squander), or repurchases can convey good news (i.e., they do not change investment decisions, but they merely convey that the firm's future growth in cash flows are under-valued). The negative price performance in the months before the announcement and the positive price performance in the years after also support both explanations. The stock price might have increased either because the market did not comprehend the full extent of the undervaluation, or because it did not incorporate the extent of the better investment decisions by management after the repurchase.

Thus, to determine the dominant force behind the decision to repurchase, we must look elsewhere. We begin with Vermaelen (1981). Using a number of fixed-price tender offers over the period 1962–1977, Vermaelen documented a significant increase in earnings per share in the years following fixed-price repurchases. Using 122 observations from a similar period, Dann, Masulis and Mayers (1991) confirmed Vermaelen's findings. They also showed that the initial market reaction was positively related to subsequent increases in earnings. Although a decline in cash flows (or earnings) in the years after fixed-price tender offers will lead to a rejection of the information/signaling hypothesis, these studies found that an increase in earnings was consistent with the information/signaling hypothesis.

However, in a detailed investigation of 242 fixed-price tender offers, Nohel and Tarhan (1998) showed that the entire improvement in earnings documented in previous studies could be attributed to firms with high book-to-market. That is, to low-growth value firms. Furthermore, they showed that firms involved in tender offers did not increase their capital expenditure, and in fact that the improvement in operating performance of the high book-to-market firms was positively related to asset sales. This finding was inconsistent with the signaling model. They interpreted their evidence as supporting the notion that fixed-price tender offer, and the market reaction to them, is motivated by free cash-flow considerations rather then signaling.

The earnings pattern after open-market share repurchases shows an even more consistent lack of improvement than those after fixed-price tender offers. Grullon and Michaely (2003) examined a comprehensive sample of 2735 open-market share repurchases in the period 1980–2000. They reported a decline in the level of profitability (measured by ROA) in the three years after the year in which the repurchase was announced.[20] They also reported decline in capital expenditures and cash reserves for those firms. (Using a different sample, Jagannathan and Stephens (2001) reach similar conclusions). Overall, it seems that earnings performance subsequent to open-market repurchase programs and earnings performance after large changes in dividends have a very similar pattern.

The risk profile of firms changes in conjunction with open-market share repurchases – just as it changes after dividend increases. Grullon and Michaely (2003) found that beta declined in the year after the announcement. The cost of capital in the three years after open-market repurchases declined significantly from an average of 16.3% before the repurchase to 13.7% after.[21]

The evidence of declining earnings, a reduction in capital expenditures and cash reserves, and a decline in risk is not consistent with the traditional signaling stories. It is consistent with the notion that when investment opportunities shrink and there is less need for capital expenditures in the future, firms increase their payout to shareholders, either through dividends or through open-market share repurchases. Thus, when a firm is in a different stage of its life cycle, its investment opportunities change, and consequently its risk profile and need for cash changes as well. This change in turn

---

[20] Using a sample of 185 open-market share repurchases over the period 1978–1986, Bartov (1991) reported mixed results on the relation between earnings changes and repurchases. In the year after the open-market repurchase, those firms' earnings were significantly worse then the control sample. In the year after that, they were significantly better. These mixed results might be attributable to the small sample size.

[21] Other studies found a similar phenomenon with fixed-price tender offers. See Dann, Masulis and Mayers (1991), Hertzel and Jain (1991) and Nohel and Tarhan (1998). These studies showed that the market reaction to the offer is positively related to the subsequent decline in risk.

affects it payout policy, because it increases dividends, repurchases or both. (It is still an open question what determines the form of payout a firm chooses to use.)

Some of the evidence in Ikenberry, Lakonishok and Vermaelen (1995)[22] also supports this notion. They reported that the largest price appreciation in the years after the repurchase occurred for those firms that were most likely to benefit from disposing of cash. Those firms with high book-to-market ratio were the firms that had less need for future capital expenditure and were more likely to encounter free cash-flow problems.

This is not to say that perceived undervaluation does not play a role at least in the timing of the repurchase programs. Many of the studies cited above show that there is a clear tendency for firms to repurchase shares after a decline in stock price, which suggests that management repurchases shares when they think the stock is undervalued. An extreme example is the heavy wave of share repurchases immediately after the stock market crash of October 1987.

In addition, Ikenberry, Lakonishok and Vermaelen (2000) provided evidence that in value stocks and small cap stocks, management bought more shares when the price dropped and fewer shares when the price rose. What is clear from their evidence is that this undervaluation is not related to future earnings growth. It may happen because of changes in the risk profile of the firm that are not impounded in market price. It might be that for value stocks that have not performed well in the past, investors are more reluctant to believe that these firms will turn around, cut capital expenditure, reduce the amount of cash reserves, and reap the benefits of reductions in free cash flows. Hence, ex-post, those stocks outperform their peers when information about the realization of these issues starts to appear in the market place.

Miller and McConnell (1995) studied adverse selection as a motive for repurchases by examining one of the direct implications of Barclay and Smith's (1988) conjecture and the Brennan and Thakor (1990) model. These theories argued that corporations relied on dividends rather than repurchases because of adverse selection problems. When a firm announces a share repurchase program, the uninformed market participants, particularly the market makers, should assume that they are more likely to trade with informed traders. Hence, in response to this signal, the bid-ask spread should widen. Using daily closing quotes around 152 open market share repurchase programs, Miller and McConnell found no evidence of an increase in bid-ask spread that they could associate with repurchases. There was no evidence that firms were deterred from engaging in open market share repurchase programs because of the adverse effect of such programs on market liquidity or on the firm's cost of capital. Moreover, Grullon and Ikenberry (2000) presented evidence that share repurchase programs enhanced liquidity, rather than reducing it.

---

[22] Ikenberry, Lakonishok and Vermaelen (2000) reported similar results for Canadian open-market repurchases.

The empirical evidence indicates that repurchase activity is motivated by several factors. Firms with more cash than they need for operation (excess cash) are more likely to repurchase their shares. Lower-growth firms are more likely to repurchase shares, because their investment opportunities shrink. Researchers find evidence that both the announcement of repurchases and the actual repurchase activity is more pronounced at times when firms experience downward price pressure. There is no evidence that adverse selection in the market place is a reason for repurchases, nor is there any evidence that the market's underestimation of future cash flows or growth in earnings (or cash flows) are a motive in management's decision to repurchase. In fact, the evidence shows that repurchasing firms experience a reduction in operating performance, have excess cash, and invest less in the years after the repurchase announcement, and that their risk is significantly lower in the post-announcement years.

It is also clear that the market does not incorporate the entire news contained in the repurchase announcement, be it about risk reduction, reduction in agency costs, or some other misvaluation. The market underreaction is particularly pronounced for value stocks.

9.4.3. Some empirical evidence on dividends compared to share repurchases

Equipped with the measures of actual repurchases that we discussed above, researchers were able to examine the issue of how dividend and repurchase policies interact. It was also possible to consider whether firms view these methods as substitutes.

Many of the theories discussed above have implications to whether repurchases and dividends are substitutes, or if they are used for different objectives altogether, which would indicate that there is no relation between dividends and repurchase policies.

Theories that address the issue of total payout policy, such as Miller and Rock (1985) or Bhattacharya (1979), and which make no distinction between dividends and repurchases, imply that these two payout policies are perfect substitutes. Other theories, which rely on differential taxation, such as those by John and Williams (1985) and Allen, Bernardo and Welch (2000), imply that these two payout policies are distinctly different and that there cannot be direct substitution between the two.

The agency theories also imply substitution, but the substitution is not perfect. On the one hand, both repurchases and dividend payments take money out of management's hands and thereby reduce potential abuses. On the other hand, dividends act as a stronger commitment device, because management is more committed to maintaining a stable dividend policy than a stable repurchase policy [see Lintner (1956)]. Thus, it is possible that management might distribute temporary excess cash through repurchases and more permanent excess cash through dividends.

There is another reason why managers may have an incentive to pay fewer dividends and distribute more of the cash in the form of repurchases. This is the growing popularity of stock options, and especially of executive stock options. Stock options can affect the form of payment for at least two reasons. First, since these options are typically not protected against dividends, managers (who own stock options) have an incentive to repurchase shares with the available cash rather than pay it out in the form of dividends. Second, many market analysts center their stock valuation on EPS numbers. Since the exercise of stock options dilutes EPS numbers, both the boards of directors and top management may decide to repurchase more shares to prevent dilution.[23] Thus, stock options can lead to the substitution of dividends for repurchases.

We could argue that by definition, dividends and repurchases are perfect substitutes. A firm can either pay dividends or repurchase its shares. If, and only if, total payout is held constant is this statement correct. But we already know that all else is not constant. Firms can change the amount of cash kept in the firm, they can alter the amount of cash that goes to investments, and they can change the amount of cash that they raise from other sources, such as debt or equity.

Therefore, another way to pose the question is to ask what has happened to total corporate payout since repurchases have become so popular. Have dividends been reduced correspondingly so that total payout remains at a constant level? Or has total payout increased? Whether the increased popularity of repurchases increased corporate payout can be critically important to corporations, investors, and policy makers alike. The answer to this question has significant implications concerning corporate reinvestment rates, resource allocation, and the role of taxes in corporations' decisions. But despite its importance, only recently has the issue begun to receive attention from financial economists.

An analogous question has been recently debated in the public finance literature. The issue is the impact of 401k and IRA programs on USA saving rates, where 401k is the equivalent of repurchase programs and the total saving rates is analogous to total payout. Has the introduction of these saving programs increased savings rates, or has it merely caused a shift from one saving vehicle to another? (See Poterba, Venti and Wise (1996) for an excellent review of this issue).

In both cases (saving rates and payout rates), the key impediment to determining the impact of IRAs on saving and repurchases on payouts is agents' heterogeneity. Some corporations pay cash (mostly, the mature firms) and some corporations (those firms with growth opportunities) do not pay out cash to shareholders. Those that do pay tend to pay more in both forms. Thus, one of the main challenges for such an investigation is to control for this heterogeneity in various ways.

In Table 1 and in Figure 1 we presented the pattern of dividends, repurchases, and total payout of USA industrial corporations through time relative to total corporate

---

[23] We do not to argue that this reason is rational (or irrational). It seems to be the case however, that this is a driving force behind many corporate financial decisions. For example, both authors of this chapter have heard on numerous occasions that one of the important yardsticks of mergers to be consummated is its impact on EPS. Managers are very reluctant to enter into a merger or an acquisition that dilutes EPS. Likewise, the impact of repurchases on EPS is also often mentioned. See also the discussion in Dunbar (2001) of how British institutional investors impose dilution constraints on management.

earnings and relative to the corporations' market value. The table shows that relative to total earnings, total payout has increased through time. It also shows that dividend payout did not decrease, despite the surge in repurchases. However, when we scale the cash payout by market value (Figure 1), the opposite picture emerges. Dividend yield has been going down through the years and repurchase yield has been going up. At least through the 1990s, there is no change in the total payout yield.

However, the aggregate data may mask a qualitative difference across firms. For example, there could be some firms that never paid dividends and have recently started to pay out cash in the form of repurchases. At the same time, firms that have been paying dividends might have continued to do so.

To address the interaction between repurchase and dividend policy, Grullon and Michaely (2002) examined this relation at the individual-firm level as well. Their test relies on Lintner's (1956) analysis of how firms determine their dividend policy. Lintner observed that firms' dividend change decisions were a function of their targeted payout ratio and the speed of adjustment of current dividends to the target ratio. Using this model, Grullon and Michaely calculated the expected dividend payment for a firm based on its past dividend behavior, and determined whether actual dividend payments were above or below the expected dividend payment. That way, they were able to observe whether a firm was deviating from its past dividend policy. If the use of repurchases increased payout and did not affect dividend policy, then there would not be any relation between the dividend forecast error from the Lintner model and repurchase activity. Grullon and Michaely defined the dividend-forecast error as:

$$\text{ERROR}_{t,i} = \frac{\Delta\text{DIV}_{t,i} - (\beta_{1,i} + \beta_{2,i}\text{EARN}_{t,i} + \beta_{3,i}\text{DIV}_{t-1,i})}{\text{MV}_{t-1,i}},$$

where $\Delta\text{DIV}_{t,i}$ is the actual change in dividends at time t; $\text{EARN}_{t,i}$ is the earnings at time t; $\text{DIV}_{t-1,i}$ is the dividend level at $t-1$; and $\text{MV}_{t-1,i}$ is the market value of equity at time $t-1$. The coefficients $\beta_{2,i}$ and $\beta_{3,i}$ are the parameters of earnings and lagged dividends from Lintner's (1956) model, respectively, that have been estimated over the pre-forecast period, 1972–1991. By scaling by the firm market value of equity, they were able to directly compare the forecast error to the repurchase and dividend yields.

However, if repurchase activity reduces dividend payout, then the test should have result in a negative correlation between the dividend forecast error (actual minus expected) and share repurchase activity. In other words, finding a negative correlation between these two variables would indicate that share repurchases have been partially financed with potential dividend increases.

Their empirical evidence indicates that the dividend forecast error is negatively correlated with the share-repurchase yield. The forecast error becomes more negative (monotonically) as the share repurchase yield increases. That is, as firms repurchase more, the actual dividend is lower than the expected dividend.

They confirmed this result by a cross-sectional regression of the dividend-forecast error on the repurchase yield (controlling for size, the return on assets, the volatility of return on assets, and nonoperating income). The results indicate that the repurchase yield has a negative effect on the dividend forecast error even after controlling for firm characteristics.

In summary, the evidence suggests that dividend-paying firms have been substituting dividends with share repurchases, but the rate of substitution is not one (i.e., they are not perfect substitutes). This finding supports the idea that share-repurchase policy and dividend-policy are interrelated.

But what types of firms use, and under which circumstances would managers decide to use, repurchases and/or dividends? We do not yet have the complete picture, but some recent research gives us some idea.

The first issue is the relation between stock-option programs and payout policy. Incentive compensation such as stock options could affect total payout if it aligns management incentive with those of shareholders, and therefore induces management not to invest in value-destroying projects and pay more to shareholders. Thus, incentive compensation may increase total payout. Additionally, as suggested before, managers with stock options, which are not dividend-protected, will be motivated to shift the form of payout from dividends to repurchases.

Using a large sample of 1100 nonfinancial firms during the period 1993–1997, Fenn and Liang (2001) reported a negative relation between stock-option plans and dividends, a finding that supports the notion that the use of managerial incentive plans reduces managers' incentive to pay dividends. Moreover, their cross-sectional regression results indicated that (1) dividend payout was negatively related to the magnitude of stock-option plans; (2) repurchase payout was positively related to the magnitude of stock-option plans; and (3) total payout was negatively related to the magnitude of stock-option plans. The reduction in total payout was larger than the increase in repurchases.

Using a sample of 324 firms that announce a change in payout policy in 1993, Jolls (1998) found a positive relation between the repurchase decision and the magnitude of the executive stock-option plan.

Weisbenner (2000) extended these studies. He asked if the group holding the stock options (the firm's employees or management) made a difference on payout choice. A priori, we would expect it to do so. If mainly nonexecutive employees hold stock options, then the dividend protection is less of a factor (assuming management does not maximize employees' wealth). The dilution factor is still important, since it affects everyone who holds the stock, not just the employees. Thus, in the case of nonexecutive stock option plans we would expect an increase in repurchase activity but no reduction in dividends. If executives hold stock options, then we should expect both a reduction in dividends and an increase in repurchase activity.

Weisbenner (2000) found empirical support for these hypotheses. The overall size of a firm's stock option program had a significant influence on the firm's repurchase policy (presumably in an attempt to prevent dilution). Stock-option programs are also related to the firm's propensity to reduce retained earnings. Second, the larger the executives' holding of stock options, the more likely the firm was to reduce dividends and to retain more of its earnings (presumably an outcome of managers' incentive not to pay dividends).

The studies discussed above show an important link between compensation, and executive compensation in particular, and the form of payout. As the extent of stock option programs increase, firms tend to use more repurchases and to reduce retained earnings. When more of these stock option programs are directed towards top management, dividends also tend to be reduced.

Jagannathan, Stephens and Weisbach (2000) found another important link between firm's characteristics and payout policy. As with Lintner's model, the authors hypothesized that dividends were more of a permanent commitment than were share repurchases. Hence, dividends were more likely to be paid out of permanent earnings and repurchases were more likely to be used as a way to distribute temporary cash flows. The empirical implication of this hypothesis is that firms that experience higher cash flow variability tend to use repurchases while firms with lower cash flow variability tend to use dividends.

Using a large sample of repurchase and dividend change events, Jagannathan, Stephens and Weisbach (2000) found that firms that repurchased their shares had a higher variability of operating income relative to firms that only increased dividends, or to firms that increased their dividend and repurchased their shares. Not surprisingly, they found that firms that did not pay cash had the highest cash flow variability of all. Using a Logit model, they showed that higher cash flow variability and higher nonoperating cash flow (two measures of temporary earnings) increased the likelihood of repurchases relative to dividends. As had earlier studies, they also found that although dividends appeared to be paid out of permanent earnings, there was no evidence of earnings improvements following dividend increases.

Lie's (2001) results also pointed in the same direction. He found that tender offers were more likely to occur when firms had excess cash on their balance sheet (a temporary build-up of cash), and dividends were more likely to increase with excess cash on the income statement (presumably a permanent increase in cash flow).

Overall, the evidence indicates that at least in cross-sectional tests, firms that use stock options more intensely are more likely to use share repurchases. The evidence also associates firms that only repurchase with firms that are riskier (relative to those who pay dividends and those who do both). There is also some evidence that the increase in popularity of repurchases might be related to changes in regulation. The extent to which these variables can explain the dramatic increase in repurchases and the more moderate increase in overall payout is still an open question.

9.5. Summary

Open-market repurchases have become a dominant form of payout. Given the economic climate and the deregulation of repurchasing shares around the world, we believe that the phenomenon is here to stay. Repurchases are likely to remain a dominant form of payout from corporations to their shareholders. As researchers, we do not yet have a clear grasp on how firms decide among the various forms of payouts, and in particular, how they decide on whether to pay cash in the form of dividends or share repurchases. Nor do we know how the decision affects their retained earnings and their investment decisions.

The empirical evidence starts to give us some directions. It seems that young, risky firms prefer to use repurchases rather then dividends, though we do not fully understand what determines the choice. We observe that many large, established firms have substituted repurchases for dividends. That is not to say that those firms have necessarily cut the nominal dividends, but they have increased dividends at a much lower rate than before. Instead, they have been paying more money to shareholders through repurchases. We see that those firms with more volatile earnings tend to substitute more often. But again, we do not have a firm understanding of what determines that choice. Finally, we ask how repurchases and payout policy as a whole interact with capital structure decisions (such as debt and equity issuance). We believe that these are very important questions and a promising field for further research.

10. Concluding remarks

There are a number of important empirical regularities concerning firms' payout policy. The first is that the mid-1980s represented a watershed. Earlier, dividends constituted the vast majority of corporate payouts. They grew at an average of about 15% per year. Dividend yields over the long run remained fairly constant. There were repurchases, but they represented only a small fraction of payouts.

Since the mid 1980s, repurchases have become increasingly important. Dividends have continued to increase in absolute terms, but at an average rate of 6% rather than 15% a year. Instead of increasing dividends, companies have been much more willing to increase the absolute payout by increasing repurchases. Repurchases have grown steadily and are now about the same level of magnitude as dividends. The result of these changes is that in the last decade or so, dividend yield has fallen significantly from 3% to 1.5%, but the yield resulting from the combination of dividends and repurchases has remained fairly constant at 3%.

At the level of the individual firm there are a number of interesting regularities. Although dividends have decreased in relative importance and firms are much more willing to switch to repurchases, dividends are still important in absolute terms. Firms seem reluctant to cut dividends. However, firms that have never paid dividends do not seem to regard them as a necessity. Over the years, firms that initiate payments do so increasingly through repurchases. In the last five years, about 75% of initiating firms have used this method of payout.

Another important aspect of the comparison between dividends and repurchases is that both have similar effects in terms of the sign of the impact. Initiation of dividends, dividend increases, or repurchases are all taken as good news by the market.

The difference is that repurchases are larger in size relative to dividend increases or initiations, and their impact on prices is more pronounced.

Although these empirical regularities seem clear and provide a guide for how managers should behave, our understanding of why firms behave in this way is, to say the least, limited. This is the case despite the enormous effort that has been invested in the topic of payout policy over the years. It is possible to tell a story, but it is by no means clear that it is anything more than a story.

If we go back over a century or more, there seem to be obvious advantages to paying dividends. Information was sparse and any firm that could consistently pay out dividends was signaling that it had long-term earning potential. Firms that constantly repurchased and intervened in the market for their shares may well have been suspected of manipulating the stock price. Moreover, for individuals to sell shares was an expensive business in terms of direct transaction costs. Extensive insider trading and other similar abuses meant that, in terms of adverse selection, there was also a significant short-term cost from selling. This environment established a convention that paying dividends was good and cutting dividends was bad.

The change in the laws concerning repurchases and stock-price manipulation in 1982 meant that repurchases could be used without risk and made them an acceptable alternative. However, since cutting dividends is perceived as a bad signal, at least in the short run, firms are not willing to replace dividends with repurchases even though repurchases have tax advantages. However, as payout is increased, repurchases can be increasingly used.

The other piece of the payout puzzle is that total payout yield in terms of dividends and repurchases has remained fairly constant at least for the last ten years. One possible explanation for this is a signaling story. The market treats increases in dividends and repurchases as good news. In theory, this reaction could be because increases are interpreted as signals of future operating performance. However, there is evidence that increases in payout are not followed by improved operating performance, thus rejecting this explanation. An alternative interpretation is that the market is relieved that managers will no longer acquire cash that can be squandered, and this is why an increase in payout leads to a higher share price.

Of course, all of this argument ignores many important factors, but it is an example of one explanation for the patterns that are observed in the data. Much work remains to be done.

So far, our discussion here has focused on dividends and repurchases. But there is a third component of payout that has been largely ignored in the literature, and that is the cash payments for securities acquired in M&A transactions. The precise amount paid out in this way is difficult to measure exactly. However, the data we have gathered that does allow us to establish a lower bound suggests that over the last decade, such payments have been around $240b per year, or over 50% of aggregate payout if we also include dividends and repurchases. Measuring and understanding this component of payout policy is an important task for future research.

At this stage, we cannot recommend an optimal payout policy. However, we can make several general (and, admittedly, somewhat speculative) suggestions:

(1) Following the example of the last decade, repurchases should be used much more frequently than they have been. Investment and repurchase policies should be coordinated to avoid the transaction costs of financing. When there are positive NPV investments, repurchases should be avoided. In years where NPV investment opportunities are low, unneeded cash should be paid out by repurchasing shares.

(2) To the greatest extent possible, firms that have a high degree of information asymmetry and large growth opportunities should avoid paying dividends. The significant costs associated with raising equity capital for these firms makes payment of dividends even more costly. Stated differently, in periods when a firm faces many good investment opportunities, a dividend reduction might not be such a bad idea.

(3) Given the restrictive dividend-related covenants and the fact that firms interact with bondholders more than once, the use of dividends to extract wealth from debtholders should be avoided. Most times, it does not work. Even when it does, the long-run result can be detrimental to equityholders. (There is no evidence that management follow this strategy in practice.)

(4) We cannot think of a good reason why most USA firms pay dividends on a quarterly basis instead of on an annual basis. Longer intervals between payments would allow investors that are interested in long-term capital gains to sell the stock before the ex-day, avoid paying tax on the dividend, and maintain the long-term tax status of the stock. Such a schedule would also allow corporations who might be interested in dividend income to minimize transaction costs and deviation from optimal asset allocation while capturing the dividend. Finally, it would save the dividend-paying corporation administrative and mailing costs associated with dividend payments.

(5) Avoid costly "signals". Hopefully, the firm is going to stay alive for a long time. Managers can find cheaper and more persuasive ways to credibly convey the company's true worth to the market.

(6) The difference in taxes between dividends and capital gains makes high-yield stocks less attractive to individual investors in high tax brackets. Such investors should try to hold an otherwise identical portfolio with low-yield stocks.

Other people might disagree with these suggestions. However, until our understanding of the subject is improved, they represent a logical way for managers and investors to proceed. Much more empirical and theoretical research on the subject of payout is required before a consensus can be reached.

References

Ackert, L., and B. Smith (1993), "Stock price volatility, ordinary dividends, and other cash flows to shareholders", Journal of Finance 48(4):1147–1160.

Aharony, J., and I. Swary (1980), "Quarterly dividend and earnings announcements and stockholders' returns: an empirical analysis", Journal of Finance 35(1):1–12.

Allen, F., and R. Michaely (1995), "Dividend policy", in: R. Jarrow, V. Maksimovic and W.T. Ziemba, eds., Handbook in Operations Research and Management Science, Vol. 9 (Elsevier, Amsterdam).

Allen, F., A. Bernardo and I. Welch (2000), "A theory of dividends based on tax clientele", Journal of Finance 55(6):2499–2536.

Ambarish, R., K. John and J. Williams (1987), "Efficient signaling with dividends and investments", Journal of Finance 42(2):321–343.

Amihud, Y., and H. Mendelson (1986), "Asset pricing and bid-ask spread", Journal of Financial Economics 17:223–250.

Amihud, Y., and M. Murgia (1997), "Dividends, taxes, and signaling: evidence from Germany", Journal of Finance 52(1):397–408.

Asquith, P., and D.W. Mullins Jr (1983), "The impact of initiating dividend payments on shareholders' wealth", Journal of Business 56(1):77–96.

Auerbach, A.J. (1979), "Wealth maximization and the cost of capital", Quarterly Journal of Economics v93(3):433–446.

Bagwell, L. (1992), "Dutch auction repurchases: an analysis of shareholder heterogeneity", Journal of Finance 47(1):71–105.

Bagwell, L.S. (1991), "Shareholder heterogeneity: evidence and implications", American Economic Review 81(2):218–221.

Bagwell, L.S., and J. Shoven (1989), "Cash distributions to shareholders", Journal of Economic Perspectives 3(3):129–140.

Baker, M., and J. Wurgler (2000), "The equity share in new issues and aggregate stock returns", The Journal of Finance 55:2219–2257.

Bali, R., and G. Hite (1998), "Ex-dividend day stock price behavior: discreteness or tax-induced clientele?", Journal of Financial Economics 47:127–159.

Barclay, M. (1987), "Dividends, taxes, and common stock prices: the ex-dividend day behavior of common stock prices before the income tax", Journal of Financial Economics 14:31–44.

Barclay, M.J., and C.W. Smith Jr (1988), "Corporate payout policy: cash dividends versus open-market repurchases", Journal of Financial Economics 22(1):61–82.

Bartov, E. (1991), "Open-market stock repurchase as signals for earnings and risk changes", Journal of Accounting and Economics 14:275–294.

Benartzi, S., R. Michaely and R. Thaler (1997), "Do changes in dividends signal the future or the past?", Journal of Finance 52(3):1007–1043.

Bernhardt, D., J.F. Robertson and R. Farrow (1994), "Testing dividend signaling models", Working Paper (Queen's University, Ontario, Canada).

Bernheim, D. (1991), "Tax policy and the dividend puzzle", Rand Journal of Economics 22:455–476.

Bernheim, D., and A. Wantz (1995), "A tax-based test of the dividend signaling hypothesis", American Economic Review 85(3):532–551.

Bhattacharya, S. (1979), "Imperfect information, dividend policy, and 'the bird in the hand' fallacy", Bell Journal of Economics 10(1):259–270.

Binay, M. (2001), "Do dividend clienteles exist? Institutional investor reaction to dividend events", Working Paper (University of Texas, Austin).

Black, F. (1976), "The dividend puzzle", Journal of Portfolio Management 2:5–8.

Black, F., and M. Scholes (1974), "The effects of dividend yield and dividend policy on common stock prices and returns", Journal of Financial Economics 1:1–22.

Blume, M.E. (1980), "Stock return and dividend yield: some more evidence", Review of Economics and Statistics 62:567–577.

Blume, M.E., J. Crockett and I. Friend (1974), "Stock ownership in the United States: characteristics and trends", Survey of Current Business, pp. 16–40.

Boyd, J., and R. Jagannathan (1994), "Ex-dividend price behavior of common stocks: fitting some pieces of the puzzle", Review of Financial Studies 7(4):711–741.

Bradford, D.F. (1981), "The incidence and allocation effects of a tax on corporate distributions", Journal of Public Economics 15:1–22.

Brav, A., and J.B. Heaton (1998), "Did ERISA's prudent man rule change the pricing of dividend omitting firms?", Working Paper (Duke University, NC).

Brennan, M.J. (1970), "Taxes, market valuation and financial policy", National Tax Journal 23:417–429.

Brennan, M.J., and A.V. Thakor (1990), "Shareholder preferences and dividend policy", Journal of Finance 45(4):993–1019.

Brickley, J. (1983), "Shareholders wealth, information signaling, and the specially designated dividend: an empirical study", Journal of Financial Economics 12:187–209.

Charest, G. (1978), "Dividend information, stock returns and market efficiency – II", Journal of Financial Economics 6:297–330.

Chen, N.F., B. Grundy and R.F. Stambaugh (1990), "Changing risk, changing risk premiums, and dividend yield effects", Journal of Business 63:S51-S70.

Chowdhry, B., and V. Nanda (1994), "Repurchase premia as a reason for dividends: a dynamic model of corporate payout policies", Review of Financial Studies 7:321–350.

Christie, W., and V. Nanda (1994), "Free cash flow, shareholder value, and the undistributed profits tax of 1936 and 1937", Journal of Finance 49(5):1727–1754.

Comment, R., and G. Jarrell (1991), "The relative power of Dutch-Auction and fixed-priced self-tender offers and open market share repurchases", Journal of Finance 46(4):1243–1271.

Constantinides, G.M. (1984), "Optimal stock trading with personal taxes", Journal of Financial Economics 13:65–89.

Constantinides, G.M., and B.D. Grundy (1989), "Optimal investment with stock repurchase and financing as signals", Review of Financial Studies 2(4):445–466.

Dann, L., R. Masulis and D. Mayers (1991), "Repurchase tender offers and earning information", Journal of Accounting and Economics 14:217–251.

DeAngelo, H., and L. DeAngelo (1990), "Dividend policy and financial distress: an empirical investigation of troubled NYSE firms", Journal of Finance 45(5):1415–1431.

DeAngelo, H., L. DeAngelo and D. Skinner (1996), "Reversal of fortune, dividend signaling and the disappearance of sustained earnings growth", Journal of Financial Economics 40:341–371.

Del Guercio, D. (1996), "The distorting effect of the prudent-man laws on institutional equity investments", Journal of Financial Economics 40:31–62.

Dubofsky, D.A. (1992), "A market microstructure explanation of ex-day abnormal returns", Financial Management (Winter):32–43.

Dunbar, N. (2001), "UK firms consider option scheme", Risk Magazine (March), p. 14.

Dunsby, A. (1993), "Share repurchases and corporate distributions: an empirical study", Working Paper (University of Pennsylvania).

Eades, K., P. Hess and H.E. Kim (1984), "On interpreting security returns during the ex-dividend period", Journal of Financial Economics 13:3–34.

Easley, D., S. Hvidkjaer and M. O'Hara (2002), "Is information risk a determinant of asset returns?", Journal of Finance 57:2185–2221.

Easterbrook, F.H. (1984), "Two agency-cost explanations of dividends", American Economic Review 74(4):650–659.

Elton, E., and M. Gruber (1970), "Marginal stockholders' tax rates and the clientele effect", Review of Economics and Statistics 52:68–74.

Fama, E., and K. French (2000), "Forecasting profitability and earnings", Journal of Business 73: 161–175.

Fama, E., and K. French (2001), "Disappearing dividends: changing firm characteristics or lower propensity to pay?", Journal of Financial Economics 60:3–43.

Fama, E.F., and H. Babiak (1968), "Dividend policy: an empirical analysis", Journal of the American Statistical Association 63(324):1132–1161.

Fama, E.F., and K.R. French (1993), "Common risk factors in the returns on stocks and bonds", Journal of Financial Economics 33:3–56.

Fama, E.F., and J.D. Macbeth (1973), "Risk, return and equilibrium: empirical tests", Journal of Political Economy 81:607–636.

Federal Reserve Statistical Release (2000), Flow of Funds Accounts of the United States, Federal Reserve Statistical Release (Board of Governors of the Federal Reserve System, Washington DC).

Fenn, G., and N. Liang (2001), "Corporate payout policy and managerial stock incentives", Journal of Financial Economics 60:45–72.

Fluck, Z. (1999), "The dynamics of the manager–shareholder conflict", Review of Financial Studies 12(2):379–404.

Frank, M., and R. Jagannathan (1998), "Why do stock prices drop by less than the value of the dividend? Evidence from a country without taxes", Journal of Financial Economics 47:161–188.

Gonedes, N.J. (1978), "Corporate signaling, external accounting, and capital market equilibrium: evidence on dividends, income, and extraordinary items", Journal of Accounting Research 16(1):26–79.

Gordon, M. (1959), "Dividends, earnings and stock prices", Review of Economics and Statistics 41: 99–105.

Green, R., and K. Rydqvist (1999), "Ex-day behavior with dividend preference and limitation to short-term arbitrage: the case of Swedish lottery bonds", Journal of Financial Economics 53:145–187.

Grossman, S.J., and O.D. Hart (1980), "Takeover bids, the free-rider problem, and the theory of the corporation", Bell Journal of Economics 11:42–54.

Grullon, G., and D. Ikenberry (2000), "What do know about stock repurchase?", Journal of Applied Corporate Finance 13:31–51.

Grullon, G., and R. Michaely (2001), "Asymmetric information, agency conflicts and the impact of taxation on the market reaction to dividend changes", Working Paper (Cornell University, Ithaca, NY).

Grullon, G., and R. Michaely (2002), "Dividends, share repurchases and the substitution hypothesis", The Journal of Finance 62(4):1649–1684.

Grullon, G., and R. Michaely (2003), "The information content of share repurchase programs", The Journal of Finance, forthcoming.

Grullon, G., R. Michaely and B. Swaminathan (2002), "Are dividend changes a sign of firm maturity?", The Journal of Business 75:387–424.

Grullon, G., R. Michaely, S. Benartzi and R. Thaler (2003), "Dividend changes do not signal changes in future profitability", Working Paper (Cornell University, NY).

Grundy, B. (1985), "Trading volume and stock returns around ex-dividend dates", Working Paper (University of Chicago, Chicago, IL).

Handjinicolaou, G., and A. Kalay (1984), "Wealth redistributions or changes in firm value: an analysis of returns to bondholders and the stockholders around dividend announcements", Journal of Financial Economics 13(1):35–63.

Hasbrouck, J., and I. Friend (1984), "Why do companies pay dividends?: Comment", American Economic Review 74:1137–1141.

Healy, P.M., and K.G. Palepu (1988), "Earnings information conveyed by dividend initiations and omissions", Journal of Financial Economics 21(2):149–176.

Hertzel, M., and P. Jain (1991), "Earnings and risk changes around stock repurchase tender offers", Journal of Accounting and Economics 14:252–274.

Hess, P.J. (1983), "Test of price effects in the pricing of financial assets", Journal of Business 56: 537–554.

Hubbard, J., and R. Michaely (1997), "Do investors ignore dividend taxation? A re-examination of the Citizen Utilities case", Journal of Financial and Quantitative Analysis 32(1):117–135.

Ikenberry, D., J. Lakonishok and T. Vermaelen (1995), "Market underreaction to open market share repurchases", Journal of Financial Economics 39:181–208.

Ikenberry, D., J. Lakonishok and T. Vermaelen (2000), "Share repurchases in Canada: performance and strategic trading", Journal of Finance 55:2373–2397.

Internal Revenue Service (various years), SOI Bulletin (Department of Treasury).

Jagannathan, M., and C.P. Stephens (2001), "Motives for open market share repurchases: under-valuation, earnings signaling or free cash flow", Working Paper (University of Missouri, Columbia).

Jagannathan, M., C.P. Stephens and M.S. Weisbach (2000), "Financial flexibility and the choice between dividends and stock repurchases", Journal of Financial Economics 57:355–384.

Jensen, M.C. (1986), "Agency costs of free cash flow, corporate finance, and takeovers", American Economic Review 76(2):323–329.

Jensen, M.C., and W.H. Meckling (1976), "Theory of the firm: managerial behavior, agency costs and ownership structure", Journal of Financial Economics 3(4):305–360.

John, K., and J. Williams (1985), "Dividends, dilution, and taxes: a signaling equilibrium", Journal of Finance 40(4):1053–1070.

Jolls, C. (1998), "The role of incentive compensation in explaining the stock repurchase puzzle", Working Paper (Harvard Law School).

Kalay, A. (1982a), "The ex-dividend day behavior of stock prices: a re-examination of the clientele effect", Journal of Finance 37:1059–1070.

Kalay, A. (1982b), "Stockholder–bondholder conflict and dividend constraint", Journal of Financial Economics 14:423–449.

Kalay, A., and R. Michaely (2000), "Dividends and taxes: a reexamination", Financial Management 29(2):55–75.

Kang, S.H., and P. Kumar (1991), "Determinants of dividend smoothing: Evidence from dividend changes", Working Paper (Carnegie Mellon University, PA).

Karpoff, J.M., and R.A. Walkling (1988), "Short-term trading around ex-dividend days: additional evidence", Journal of Financial Economics 21(2):291–298.

Karpoff, J.M., and R.A. Walkling (1990), "Dividend capture in NASDAQ stocks", Journal of Financial Economics 28(1/2):39–66.

Kato, K., and U. Loewenstein (1995), "The ex-dividend-day behavior of stock prices: the case of Japan", Review of Financial Studies 8:817–847.

Keim, D. (1985), "Dividend yields and stock returns: implications of abnormal January returns", Journal of Financial Economics 14:473–489.

King, M. (1977), Public Policy and the Corporation (Chapman and Hall, London).

Koski, J., and R. Michaely (2000), "Prices, liquidity and the information content of trades", Review of Financial Studies 13(3):659–696.

Kumar, P. (1988), "Shareholder–manager conflict and the information content of dividends", Review of Financial Studies 1(2):111–136.

La Porta, R., F. Lopez-De Silanes, A. Shleifer and R. Vishny (2000), "Agency problems and dividend policy around the world", Journal of Finance 55:1–33.

Lakonishok, J., and T. Vermaelen (1983), "Tax reform and the ex-dividend day behavior", Journal of Finance 38:1157–1179.

Lakonishok, J., and T. Vermaelen (1986), "Tax induced trading around ex-dividend dates", Journal of Financial Economics 16:287–319.

Lang, L.H.P., and R.H. Litzenberger (1989), "Dividend announcements: cash flow signaling vs. free cash flow hypothesis", Journal of Financial Economics 24(1):181–192.

Lewellen, W.G., K.L. Stanley, R.C. Lease and G.G. Schlarbaum (1978), "Some direct evidence on the dividend clientele phenomenon", Journal of Finance 33(5):1385–1399.

Lie, E. (2000), "Excess funds and the agency problems: an empirical study of incremental disbursements", Review of Financial Studies 13(1):219–248.

Lie, E. (2001), "Financial flexibility and the corporate payout policy", Working Paper (College of William and Mary, VA).

Lintner, J. (1956), "Distribution of incomes of corporations among dividends, retained earnings, and taxes", American Economic Review 46(2):97–113.

Litzenberger, R., and K. Ramaswamy (1979), "The effects of personal taxes and dividends on capital asset prices: theory and empirical evidence", Journal of Financial Economics 7:163–195.

Litzenberger, R., and K. Ramaswamy (1980), "Dividends, short selling restrictions, tax induced investor clientele and market equilibrium", Journal of Finance 35:469–482.

Litzenberger, R., and K. Ramaswamy (1982), "The effects of dividends on common stock prices: tax effects or information effects?", Journal of Finance 37:429–443.

Long, J.B. (1977), "Efficient portfolio choice with differential taxation of dividend and capital gains", Journal of Financial Economics 5:25–53.

Long Jr, J.B. (1978), "The market valuation of cash dividends: a case to consider", Journal of Financial Economics 6(2/3):235–264.

Loughran, T., and J. Ritter (1995), "The new issues puzzle", Journal of Finance 50(1):23–51.

Lucas, D.J., and R.L. McDonald (1998), "Shareholder heterogeneity, adverse selection, and payout policy", Journal of Financial and Quantitative Analysis 33(2):233–253.

Masulis, R.W., and A.N. Korwar (1986), "Seasoned equity offerings: an empirical investigation", Journal of Financial Economics 15(1/2):91–118.

Michaely, R. (1991), "Ex-dividend day stock price behavior: the case of the 1986 Tax Reform Act", Journal of Finance 46:845–860.

Michaely, R., and M. Murgia (1995), "The effect of tax heterogeneity on prices and volume around the ex-dividend day: evidence from the Milan stock exchange", Review of Financial Studies 8:369–399.

Michaely, R., and W.H. Shaw (1994), "The pricing of initial public offerings: tests of the adverse selection and signaling theories", Review of Financial Studies 7(2):279–319.

Michaely, R., and J.-L. Vila (1995), "Investors' heterogeneity, prices and volume around the ex-dividend day", Journal of Financial and Quantitative Analysis 30:171–198.

Michaely, R., and J.-L. Vila (1996), "Trading volume with private valuations: evidence from the ex-dividend day", Review of Financial Studies 9(2):471–510.

Michaely, R., R.H. Thaler and K. Womack (1995), "Price reactions to dividend initiations and omissions: overreaction or drift?", Journal of Finance 50(2):573–608.

Michaely, R., J.-L. Vila and J. Wang (1996), "A model of trading volume with tax-induced heterogeneous valuation and transaction costs", Journal of Financial Intermediation 5:471–510.

Miller, J., and J. McConnell (1995), "Open-market share repurchase programs and bid-ask spreads on the NYSE: implications for corporate payout policy", Journal of Financial and Quantitative Analysis 30(3):365–382.

Miller, M. (1977), "Debt and taxes", The Journal of Finance 32(2):261–275.

Miller, M. (1987), "The information content of dividends", in: J. Bossons, R. Dornbush and S. Fischer, eds., Macroeconomics: Essays in Honor of Franco Modigliani (MIT Press, Cambridge, MA) pp. 37–61.

Miller, M., and F. Modigliani (1961), "Dividend policy, growth and the valuation of shares", Journal of Business 34:411–433.

Miller, M., and K. Rock (1985), "Dividend policy under asymmetric information", Journal of Finance 40(4):1031–1051.

Miller, M., and M. Scholes (1978), "Dividends and taxes", Journal of Financial Economics 6:333–264.

Miller, M., and M. Scholes (1982), "Dividends and taxes: empirical evidence", Journal of Political Economy 90:1118–1141.

Moody's dividend record (various years) (Mergert FIS, Inc., New York).

Morgan, I.G. (1982), "Dividends and capital asset prices", Journal of Finance 37:1071–1086.

Myers, S.C. (1977), "Determinants of corporate borrowing", Journal of Financial Economics 5(2): 147–175.

Myers, S.C. (2000), "Outside equity", Journal of Finance 55(3):1005–1038.

Myers, S.C., and N.S. Majluf (1984), "Corporate financing and investment decisions when firms have information that investors do not have", Journal of Financial Economics 13(2):187–221.

Naranjo, A., M. Nimalendran and M. Ryngaert (1998), "Stock returns, dividend yield and taxes", Journal of Finance 53(6):2029–2057.

Nissim, D., and A. Ziv (2001), "Dividend changes and future profitability", Journal of Finance 61(6): 2111–2134.

Nohel, T., and V. Tarhan (1998), "Share repurchases and firm performance: new evidence on the agency costs of free cash flow", Journal of Financial Economics 49:187–222.

Ofer, A.R., and D.R. Siegel (1987), "Corporate financial policy, information, and market expectations: an empirical investigation of dividends", Journal of Finance 42(4):889–911.

Ofer, A.R., and A.V. Thakor (1987), "A theory of stock price responses to alternative corporate cash disbursement methods: stock repurchases and dividends", Journal of Finance 42(2):365–394.

Penman, S.H. (1983), "The predictive content of earnings forecasts and dividends", Journal of Finance 38(4):1181–1199.

Perez-Gonzalez, F. (2000), "Large shareholders and dividends: evidence from U.S. tax reforms", Working Paper (Harvard University).

Peterson, P., D. Peterson and J. Ang (1985), "Direct evidence on the marginal rate of taxation on dividend income", Journal of Financial Economics 14:267–282.

Pettit, R.R. (1972), "Dividend announcements, security performance, and capital market efficiency", Journal of Finance 27(5):993–1007.

Poterba, J. (1986), "The market valuation of cash dividends: the citizens utilities case reconsidered", Journal of Financial Economics 15:395–406.

Poterba, J., and L.H. Summers (1984), "New evidence that taxes affect the valuation of dividends", Journal of Finance 39:1397–1415.

Poterba, J., S. Venti and D. Wise (1996), "How retirement saving programs increase saving. Reconciling the evidence", Journal of Economic Perspectives 10(4):91–112.

Richardson, G., S. Sefcik and R. Thompson (1986), "A test of dividend irrelevance using volume reactions to a change in dividend policy", Journal of Financial Economics 17:313–333.

Ritter, J.R. (1991), "The long run performance of initial public offerings", Journal of Finance 46(1):3–28.

Rosenberg, B., and V. Marathe (1979), "Tests of capital asset pricing hypotheses", Research in Finance 1:115–224.

Ross, S.A. (1977), "The determination of financial structure: the incentive signalling approach", Bell Journal of Economics, pp. 13–40.

Sarig, O. (1984), "Why do companies pay dividends?: Comment", American Economic Review 74:1142.

Shefrin, H.M., and M. Statman (1984), "Explaining investor preference for cash dividends", Journal of Financial Economics 13(2):253–282.

Shleifer, A., and R. Vishny (1986), "Large shareholders and corporate control", Journal of Political Economy 94(3):461–488.

Standard and Poor's Dividend Record (various years) (Standard and Poor's Corporation, New York).

Stephens, C., and M. Weisbach (1998), "Actual share reacquisitions in open market repurchases programs", Journal of Finance 53(1):313–333.

Stiglitz, J.E. (1983), "Some aspects of the taxation of capital gains", Journal of Public Economics 21:257–296.

Stulz, R. (1988), "Managerial control of voting rights: financing policies and the market for corporate control", Journal of Financial Economics 20(1–2):25–54.

Thaler, R.H., and H.M. Shefrin (1981), "An economic theory of self-control", Journal of Political Economy 89(2):392–406.

Vermaelen, T. (1981), "Common stock repurchases and market signaling: an empirical study", Journal of Financial Economics 9(2):138–183.

Vermaelen, T. (1984), "Repurchase tender offers, signalling and managerial incentives", Journal of Financial and Quantitative Analysis 19:163–181.

Watts, R. (1973), "The information content of dividends", Journal of Business 46(2):191–211.

Weisbenner, S. (2000), "Corporate share repurchase in the mid-1990s: What role do stock options play", Working Paper (MIT, MA).

Williams, J. (1988), "Efficient signaling with dividends, investment, and stock repurchases", Journal of Finance 43(3):737–747.

Yoon, P.S., and L. Starks (1995), "Signaling, investment opportunities, and dividend announcements", Review of Financial Studies 8(4):995–1018.

Zwiebel, J. (1996), "Dynamic capital structure under managerial entrenchment", American Economic Review 86(5):1197–1215.

Chapter 8

FINANCIAL INTERMEDIATION

The Wharton School, University of Pennsylvania, and NBER

Carlson School of Management, University of Minnesota

Contents

Abstract	432
Keywords	432
1. Introduction	433
2. The existence of financial intermediaries	437
2.1. Empirical evidence on bank uniqueness	437
2.2. Banks as delegated monitors	440
2.3. Banks as information producers	444
2.4. Banks as consumption smoothers	448
2.5. Banks as liquidity providers	453
2.6. Banks as commitment mechanisms	456
2.7. Empirical tests of bank-existence theories	458
2.8. Bonds versus loans	459
2.9. Banks versus stock markets	461
3. Interactions between banks and borrowers	462
3.1. Dynamic relationships and the pros and cons of bank monitoring	463
3.2. Monitoring and loan structure	469
3.3. Beyond lending: equity stakes, board seats, and monitoring	474
3.4. Banking sector structure and lending	479
3.5. Credit cycles and the effect of bank funding on lending	490
4. Banking panics and the stability of banking systems	494
4.1. Definitions of banking panics and the relation of panics to the business cycle	495
4.2. Panics and the industrial organization of the banking industry	499
4.3. Private bank coalitions	501
4.4. Are banks inherently flawed institutions?	503
4.5. Information-based theories of panics	505
4.6. Other panic theories	507
4.7. Tests of panic theories	508
4.8. The banking crises during the Great Depression	511

Handbook of the Economics of Finance, Edited by G.M. Constantinides, M. Harris and R. Stulz

Abstract

The savings/investment process in capitalist economies is organized around bank-like financial intermediaries ("banks"), making them a central institution of economic growth. These intermediaries borrow from consumer/savers and lend to companies that need resources for investment. In contrast, in capital markets investors contract directly with firms, creating marketable securities. The prices of these securities are observable, while financial intermediaries are opaque. Why are banks so pervasive? What are their roles? Are banks inherently unstable? Must the government regulate them? In this chapter we survey the last 15 years' of theoretical and empirical research on these issues

We begin with theories and evidence on the uniqueness of banks. Key issues include monitoring or evaluating borrowers, providing liquidity, combining lending and liquidity provision as a commitment mechanism, and the coexistence of banks and markets. We then examine interaction between banks and borrowers in more detail, focusing on the pros and cons of dynamic bank–borrower relationships, the relationship between loan structure and monitoring, and between banking sector structure and monitoring, "credit cycles" and capital constraints, and the role of "non-traditional" bank activities such as equity investment.

We then turn to research on banking panics and the stability of the banking system, focusing on the incidence of banking panics internationally and historically, the causes of panics, the role of bank coalitions in forestalling panics, and whether banks are inherently flawed. This leads to questions concerning government regulation of banks. Here, we focus on possible moral hazard problems emanating from deposit insurance and on the roles of bank corporate governance and capital requirements. We conclude with a summary of our current understanding and directions for future research.

Keywords

financial intermediation, external finance, saving–investment process, monitoring, loans, securitization, deposit insurance, credit rationing

JEL classification: G2, G21, E22, E53

1. Introduction

Financial intermediation is a pervasive feature of all of the world's economies. But, as Franklin Allen (2001) observed in his AFA Presidential Address, there is a widespread view that financial intermediaries can be ignored because they have no real effects. They are a veil. They do not affect asset prices or the allocation of resources. As evidence of this view, Allen pointed out that the millennium issue of the Journal of Finance contained surveys of asset pricing, continuous time finance, and corporate finance, but did not survey financial intermediation. Here we take the view that the savings-investment process, the workings of capital markets, corporate finance decisions, and consumer portfolio choices cannot be understood without studying financial intermediaries.

Why are financial intermediaries important? One reason is that the overwhelming proportion of every dollar financed externally comes from banks. Table 1, from Mayer (1990), is based on national flow-of-funds data. The numbers are percentages, so in the USA for example, 24.4% of firm investment was financed with bank loans during the 1970–1985 period. Bank loans are the predominant source of external funding in all the countries. In none of the countries are capital markets a significant source of financing. Equity markets are insignificant. In other words, if finance department staffing reflected how firms actually finance themselves, roughly 25% of the faculty would be researchers in financial intermediation and the rest would study internal capital markets.

Table 1
Net financing of nonfinancial enterprises[a] (%), 1970–1985

	Canada	Finland	France	Germany	Italy	Japan	UK	USA
Retentions	76.4	64.4	61.4	70.9	51.9	57.9	102.4	85.9
Capital transfers	0.0	0.2	2.0	8.6	7.7	0.0	4.1	0.0
Short-term securities	−0.8	3.7	−0.1	−0.1	−1.3	NA	1.7	0.4
Loans	15.2	28.1	37.3	12.1	27.7	50.4	7.6	24.4
Trade credit	−4.4	−1.4	−0.6	−2.1	0.0	−11.2	−1.1	−1.4
Bonds	8.5	2.8	1.6	−1.0	1.6	2.1	−1.1	11.6
Shares	2.5	−0.1	6.3	0.6	8.2	4.6	−3.3	1.1
Other	1.3	7.4	−1.4	10.9	1.0	−3.8	3.2	−16.9
Statistical adjustment	1.2	−5.0	−6.4	0.0	3.2	NA	−13.4	−5.1
Total	99.9	100.1	100.1	99.9	100.0	100.0	100.1	100.0

[a] Source: Mayer (1990) based on OECD Financial Statistics. See Mayer (1990) for details.

As the main source of external funding, banks play important roles in corporate governance, especially during periods of firm distress and bankruptcy. The idea that banks "monitor" firms is one of the central explanations for the role of bank loans in corporate finance. Bank loan covenants can act as trip wires signaling to the bank that it can and should intervene into the affairs of the firm. Unlike bonds, bank loans tend not to be dispersed across many investors. This facilitates intervention and renegotiation of capital structures. Bankers are often on company boards of directors. Banks are also important in producing liquidity by, for example, backing commercial paper with loan commitments or standby letters of credit.

Consumers use bank demand deposits as a medium of exchange, that is, writing checks, using credit cards, holding savings accounts, visiting automatic teller machines, and so on. Demand deposits are securities with special features. They can be denominated in any amount; they can be put to the bank at par (i.e., redeemed at face value) in exchange for currency. These features allow demand deposits to act as a medium of exchange. But, the banking system must then "clear" these obligations. Clearing links the activities of banks in clearinghouses. In addition, the fact that consumers can withdraw their funds at any time has, led to banking panics in some countries, historically, and in many countries more recently.

Banking systems seem fragile. Between 1980 and 1995, thirty-five countries experienced banking crises, periods in which their banking systems essentially stopped functioning and these economies entered recessions [see Demirgüç-Kunt, Detragiache and Gupta (2000) and Caprio and Klingebiel (1996)]. Because bank loans are the main source of external financing for firms, if the banking system is weakened, there appear to be significant real effects [e.g., see Bernanke (1983), Gibson (1995), Peek and Rosengren (1997, 2000)]. The relationship between bank health and business cycles is at the root of widespread government policies concerning bank regulation and supervision, deposit insurance, capital requirements, the lender-of-last-resort role of the central bank, and so on. Clearly, the design of public policies depends on our understanding of the problems with intermediaries. Even without a collapse of the banking system, a credit crunch has sometimes been alleged to occur when banks tighten lending, possible due to their own inability to obtain financing. Also, the transmission mechanism of monetary policy may be through the banking system.

Basically, financial intermediation is the root institution in the savings-investment process. Ignoring it would seem to be done at the risk of irrelevance. So, the viewpoint of this paper is that financial intermediaries are not a veil, but rather the contrary. In this paper, we survey the results of recent academic research on financial intermediation.

In the last fifteen years, researchers have made significant progress in understanding the roles of financial intermediaries. These advances are not only theoretical. Despite a lack of data as rich as stock market prices, significant empirical work on intermediaries has been done. All of this work has contributed to a deeper appreciation of the role of banks in the savings-investment process and corporate finance, of the issues in crises associated with financial intermediation, and of the functioning of government regulation of intermediation. We concentrate on research addressing why bank-like financial intermediaries exist, and the implications for their stability. By bank-like financial intermediaries, we mean firms with the following characteristics:
(1) They borrow from one group of agents and lend to another group of agents.

(2) The borrowing and lending groups are large, suggesting diversification on each side of the balance sheet.

(3) The claims issued to borrowers and to lenders have different state contingent payoffs.

The terms "borrow" and "lend" mean that the contracts involved are debt contracts. So, to be more specific, financial intermediaries lend to large numbers of consumers and firms using debt contracts and they borrow from large numbers of agents using debt contracts as well. A significant portion of the borrowing on the liability side is in the form of demand deposits, securities that have the important property of being a medium of exchange. The goal of intermediation theory is to explain why these financial intermediaries exist, that is, why there are firms with the above characteristics.

Others have cited additional important characteristics of bank-like financial intermediaries, but in our view these seem less important. For example, the maturity of the loan contracts is typically longer than the maturity of the debt on the liability side of the balance sheet, but that is essentially the third point above. Also, Boyd and Prescott (1986) assert that financial intermediaries lend to agents whose information set may be different from their own, in particular, would-be borrowers have private information concerning their own credit risk. Although this suggests a clear role for intermediaries, it is not clear that this is a necessary condition.

Empirical observation is the basis for the statement that intermediaries involve large number of agents on each side of the balance sheet and also for the view that the nature of the securities issued to borrowers and lenders are different. On the liability side of the balance sheet, intermediaries often issue a particular security to households, demand deposits, securities that serve as a medium of exchange. On the asset side of the balance sheet, bank loans are not the same as corporate bonds. Moreover, the structure of the bank loans does not mirror the bank's obligations in the form of deposits. Financial intermediaries with the above characteristics correspond most closely to commercial banks, savings and loans, and similar institutions. But, securitization vehicles and conduits also satisfy the above definition, blurring the distinction between intermediated finance and direct finance, a topic we return to below.

There are a number of issues in studying intermediation that are perhaps unique, compared to other areas of finance. First, there are issues of data. While governments often collect an enormous amount of data about banks, for example, in the USA there are the *Call Reports* that provide a massive amount of accounting information about commercial banks, there is a lack of price data. Thus, unlike other areas of finance, there is an almost embarrassing lack of essential information, prices of loans, of secondary loan sales, and so on. Researchers have been creative in finding data, however, as we discuss below. Other periods of history have also been intensively studied. Apparently, more so than other areas of finance, research in financial intermediation is intimately linked with economic history. In addition, other countries offer rich laboratories as banking systems vary across countries to a significant degree.

Second, in the study of financial intermediation, institutions, regulations, and laws are important. Banking systems have been influenced by laws and regulations for hundreds of years and it is difficult to make progress on many issues without understanding the enormous variation in banking system structures across countries and time, which is due to these laws and regulations. This is most apparent in the variety of industrial organization of banking systems around the world and through history. This variation is just beginning to be exploited by researchers and seems a likely area for further work.

Finally, intermediation is in such a constant state of flux that it is not much of an exaggeration to say that many researchers in financial intermediation do not realize that they are engaged in economic history. It is a challenge to determine whether there are important features of intermediation that remain constant across time, or whether intermediation is being fundamentally altered by securitization, loan sales, credit derivatives, and other recent innovations.

The paper proceeds as follows. We begin in Section 2 by discussing evidence on the uniqueness of banks and theories that seek to motivate the existence and structure of these financial intermediaries. Key issues include monitoring or evaluating borrowers, providing consumption smoothing and other types of liquidity, combining lending and liquidity provision as a commitment mechanism, and the coexistence of banks and markets.

In Section 3 we focus on the specifics of interaction between banks and borrowers. Key issues include the pros and cons of dynamic bank–borrower relationships, the relationship between loan structure and monitoring and between banking sector structure and monitoring, "credit cycles" and capital constraints, and the role of "non-traditional" bank activities such as equity investment.

In Section 4 we focus on banking panics and the stability of the banking system. Key issues include evidence on the incidence of banking panics internationally and historically, the causes of panics, the role of bank coalitions in forestalling panics, whether banks are inherently flawed. Section 5 concerns bank regulation, deposit insurance, and bank capital requirements. Government intervention into banking is a fairly recent phenomenon, but has come to be a widely accepted role because of concerns about moral hazard problems emanating from deposit insurance. The paradigm of moral hazard is reviewed, with particular focus on the empirical evidence. Corporate governance in banks, capital requirements for banks, and other issues are also reviewed.

Finally, in Section 6 we summarize where all of this research leaves us, both in terms of our present understanding and in terms of directions for the future.

2. The existence of financial intermediaries

The most basic question with regard to financial intermediaries is: why do they exist? This question is related to the theory of the firm because a financial intermediary is a firm, perhaps a special kind of firm, but nevertheless a firm. Organization of economic activity within a firm occurs when that organizational form dominates trade in a market. In the case of the savings-investment process, households with resources to invest could go to capital markets and buy securities issued directly by firms, in which case there is no intermediation. To say the same thing a different way, nonfinancial firms need not borrow from banks; they can approach investors directly in capital markets. Nevertheless, as mentioned in the Introduction, most new external finance to firms does not occur this way. Instead, it occurs through bank-like intermediation, in which households buy securities issued by intermediaries who in turn invest the money by lending it to borrowers. Again, the obligations of firms and the claims ultimately owned by investors are not the same securities; intermediaries transform claims. The existence of such intermediaries implies that direct contact in capital markets between households and firms is dominated. "Why is this?" is the central question for the theory of intermediation.

Bank-like intermediaries are pervasive, but this may not require much explanation. On the liability side, demand deposits appear to be a unique kind of security, but originally this may have been due to regulation. Today, money market mutual funds may be good substitutes for demand deposits. On the asset side, intermediaries may simply be passive portfolio managers, that is, there may be nothing special about bank loans relative to corporate bonds. This is the view articulated by Fama (1980). Similarly, Black (1975) sees nothing special about bank loans. Therefore, we begin with an overview of the empirical evidence, which suggests that there is indeed something that needs explanation.

2.1. Empirical evidence on bank uniqueness

What do banks do that cannot be accomplished in the capital markets through direct contracting between investors and firms? There is empirical evidence that banks are special. Some of this evidence also attempts to discriminate between some of the explanations for the existence of financial intermediaries, discussed below.

To determine whether bank assets or liabilities are special relative to alternatives, Fama (1985) and James (1987) examine the incidence of the implicit tax due to reserve requirements. Their argument is as follows. Over time, USA banks have been required to hold reserves against various kinds of liabilities. In particular, if banks must hold reserves against the issuance of certificates of deposit (CDs), then for each dollar of CDs issued, the bank can invest less than a dollar. The reserve requirement acts like a tax. Therefore, in the absence of any special service provided by bank assets or bank liabilities, bank CDs should be eliminated by nonbank alternatives. This is because either bank borrowers or bank depositors must bear the tax. Since CDs have

Table 2
Stock price response to announcements of corporate security offerings [a]

Type of security offering	Two-day abnormal return [b]
Common stock	−3.14% (155)
Preferred stock	−0.19% (28)
Convertible preferred stock	−1.44% [c] (53)
Straight bonds	−0.26% (248)
Convertible bonds	−2.07% [c] (73)
Private placement of debt	−91.0% (37)
Bank loans	1.93% [c] (80)

[a] Source: Smith (1986) and James (1987).
[b] Sample size in parentheses.
[c] Indicates significantly different from zero.

not been eliminated, some party involved with the bank is willing to bear the tax. Who is this party? Fama finds no significant difference between the yields on CDs and the yields on commercial paper and bankers acceptances. CD holders do not bear the reserve requirement tax and he therefore concludes that bank loans are special. James revisits the issue and looks at yield changes around changes in reserve requirements and reaches the same conclusion as Fama.

Another kind of evidence comes from event studies of the announcement of loan agreements between firms and banks. Studying a sample of 207 announcements of new agreements and renewals of existing agreements, James (1987) finds a significantly positive announcement effect. This contrasts with non-positive responses to the announcements of other types of securities being issued in capital markets [see James (1987) for the references to the other studies]. Mikkelson and Partch (1986) also look at the abnormal returns around the announcements of different types of security offerings and also find a positive response to bank loans. [1] Table 2 provides a summary of the basic set of results. There are two main conclusions to be drawn. First, bank loans are the only instance where there is a significant positive abnormal return upon announcement. Second, equity and equity-related instruments have significantly negative abnormal returns. James (1987, p. 234) concludes, "... banks provide some special service not available from other lenders".

The results of James are quite dramatic and many researchers followed up on them. Lummer and McConnell (1989) distinguish between new bank loan agreements and revisions to agreements already in place. Further, they classify announcements

[1] Slovin, Sushka and Hudson (1988) find significantly positive announcement abnormal returns associated with the announcement of standby letters of credit. Preece and Mullineaux (1989) find that the reaction to loan agreements with insurance companies is similar to that for bank loan agreements. Also, see Mullineaux and Preece (1996).

concerning existing agreements into announcements containing positive information and those containing negative information. This classification is based on whether the terms of the agreement (maturity, interest rate, dollar value, covenants) are revised favorably or unfavorably (some have both favorable revisions in some dimensions and unfavorable revision in others). They find no abnormal return to announcement of new agreements. Favorable renewals have significantly positive abnormal returns, while negative renewals have significantly negative abnormal returns. The strongest negative response comes when the bank initiates a loan cancellation. The strongest positive response is associated with loan renewals where there was previously public information suggesting the loan was in trouble. The results of Lummer and McConnell suggest that the bank is not producing information upon first contact with a borrower. Rather, the bank either learns information later or takes action later, and this is revealed when a loan is renewed or restructured. The results are consistent with the view that a continuing relationship with a bank can signal changes in value to capital markets.

Best and Zhang (1993) confirm Lummer and McConnell (1989). But, with a revised definition of "new" loans, Billet, Flannery and Garfinkel (1995) find no significant differences between initiation of loans and loan renewals. Slovin, Johnson and Glascock (1992) and Hadlock and James (2000) also find no differences.

Slovin, Sushka and Polonchek (1993) look at an interesting implication of the result that bank loans are somehow different than other securities. If loans are special, in some sense, then when a borrower's bank fails, does that adversely affect that borrower? To address this they examine share price responses of bank borrowers' shares upon the announcement of the failure of their bank, Continental Illinois. If banks are simply passive investors, and their loans are indistinguishable from bonds, then when there is a bank failure, borrowers simply go elsewhere to borrow funds. However, if there is a "customer relationship", then banks acquire private information about their borrowers and the bank's failure would mean that this intangible asset is destroyed, causing borrowers losses. Slovin, Sushka and Polonchek (1993) find that Continental Illinois borrowers incurred significantly negative abnormal returns (−4.2% annually) during the bank's impending failure. This evidence is consistent with bank relationships being important, an issue discussed further below. Bernanke (1983) essentially argues that crisis in the USA banking system during the Great Depression can be viewed in the same way, causing real adverse effects for borrowers. Gibson (1995) studying the effects of the health of Japanese banks finds that investment is 30% lower by firms that have a Japanese bank that is weak.

Another area in which banks appear to be different from bondholders' concerns reorganization of firms in financial distress, though this depends on the characteristics of the particular sample studied. Gilson, John and Lang (1990) find that the likelihood of a successful debt restructuring by a firm in distress is positively related to the extent of that firm's reliance on bank borrowing. The interpretation is that it is easier to renegotiate with a single bank, or small number of banks, than it is with a large number of dispersed bondholders, in which case there are free rider problems. However, Asquith, Gertner and Scharfstein (1994) and James (1995), find that for firms with public debt outstanding, banks rarely make unilateral concessions to distressed firms. Franks and Torous (1994) study 45 distressed exchanges and 37 Chapter 11 reorganizations during the period 1983 to 1988. Unlike Gilson, John and Lang (1990), Franks and Torous find that firms that successfully complete exchange offers do not owe significantly more of their long-term debt to banks. Franks and Torous' firms all have publicly traded debt and tend to be larger than the firms in the Gilson, Lang, and John sample. James (1996) partially reconciles some of these conflicting results. He finds that the higher the proportion of total debt held by the bank, the higher the likelihood the bank debt will be impaired, and so the higher the likelihood it participates in the restructuring. Banks do not act unilaterally when the firm has significant public debt outstanding because banks, as senior lenders, would be transferring wealth to the public debt holders in these cases.

In other countries, banks interact with borrowers in different ways than in the USA. Such examples offer another type of evidence on the ability of banks to provide valuable services that cannot be replicated in capital markets. Hoshi, Kashyap and Scharfstein (1990a,b, 1991) find that Japanese firms in keiretsu, that is, firms with close ties to banks, are less liquidity constrained compared to firms without such ties. Also, firms with close ties are able to invest more when they are financially distressed, suggesting the importance of a bank relationship. In Germany, Gorton and Schmid (2000) find that bank equity ownership improves the performance of firms. Also, see Fohlin (1998). We review more evidence on "bank relationships" in Section 3 below.

We conclude that financial intermediaries are producing services that are not easily replicated in capital markets. We turn now to the major theories that have been put forth as explanations for the existence of financial intermediation. These theories are not mutually exclusive.

2.2. Banks as delegated monitors

Diamond (1984) offered the first coherent explanation for the existence of financial intermediaries.[2] Diamond's intermediaries "monitor" borrowers. Since monitoring is costly, it is efficient to delegate the task to a specialized agent, the bank. The notion of monitoring borrowers has become an influential idea, which subsequent researchers have further developed.

Not only do Diamond's intermediaries contain most of the important elements of a theory of intermediation, discussed above, but he also identifies and solves a fundamental problem at the root of intermediation theory. That problem concerns the fact that whatever problem the intermediary solves to add value with respect to borrowers would seem to imply that lenders to the intermediary would face the same problem with respect to their lending to the intermediary. In Diamond (1984), the

---

[2] For reasons of space, we do not survey the previous transaction-cost-based literature. For surveys of this literature, see Benston (1976) and Baltensperger (1980).

intermediary "monitors" borrowers on behalf of investors who lend to the intermediary. But, then it would appear that the lenders to the intermediary have to "monitor" the intermediary itself. How is this problem, which has come to be known as the "monitoring the monitor" problem, solved? Diamond (1984) was the first to recognize and then solve this problem.

In Diamond (1984) borrowers must be "monitored" because there is an ex post information asymmetry in that lenders do not know how much the firm has produced. Only the individual borrower observes the realized output of his project, so contracts cannot be made contingent on the output. Consequently, a lender is at a disadvantage because the borrower will not honor ex ante promises to pay unless there is an incentive to do so. The first possibility Diamond considers to solve this contracting problem is the possibility of relying on a contract that imposes nonpecuniary penalties on the borrower if his payment is not at least a certain minimum. This contract is costly because such penalties are imposed in equilibrium, reducing the utility of borrowers. If, instead, the lender had available an information production technology, then the information asymmetry could be overcome by application of this technology, at a cost. Perhaps this would be cheaper, and hence more efficient, than imposing nonpecuniary penalties. Diamond termed production of information about the borrower's realized output, at a cost, "monitoring".

The notion of "monitoring" in Diamond (1984) appears inspired by Townsend (1979), but there is a critical difference. In Townsend the lender must bear a cost to determine whether the borrower has the resources to repay the loan or not, a decision made after the borrower's project output has been realized and after a payment has been offered to the lender. That is, in Townsend, the decision by a lender to monitor a borrower is made *after* the entrepreneur has made a payment to the lender; it is contingent on the amount of the payment. Hence, it is known as "costly state verification". In Diamond, however, monitoring is not state contingent and the cost must always be borne because, in Diamond, the monitoring cost must be incurred *before* the output realization of the borrower's project is known to anyone.

This difference between Townsend and Diamond, with respect to monitoring, leads to another difference. In Townsend, the costly state verification problem motivates the form of the contract between a borrower and lender: it is a debt contract [since random monitoring is assumed away; see Boyd and Smith (1994)]. In Diamond, the optimal contract between the borrower and the lender is a debt contract in the absence of monitoring, but once monitoring is introduced, the optimal contract is undetermined. It is feasible for the contract to be an equity contract, for example. On the one hand, this does not matter for Diamond's basic argument, but, on the other hand, it seems potentially important for understanding why agents trading in markets cannot replicate the function of the intermediary, as we discuss further below.

The monitoring solution may dominate the contract that imposes nonpecuniary penalties, but it raises another problem. If a single borrower has many lenders, then each lender will have to bear the cost of monitoring, which in turn will lead to duplication of monitoring costs or free riding problems among individual lenders. This raises the prospect of a third solution. If the task of monitoring were delegated to a single agent, free riding and duplication of monitoring costs problems could potentially be eliminated. But if the lenders were to delegate the task of monitoring, then the same problem would still exist, but at one step removed. That is, the individual lenders would then face the task of monitoring the agent delegated to monitor the borrower(s). This is the problem of "monitoring the monitor". Diamond (1984) presents the first coherent theory of banking that solves the problem of monitoring the monitor.

To be more precise, the problem of "monitoring the monitor" is this: lenders to the intermediary can reduce monitoring costs if the costs of monitoring the intermediary are lower than the costs of lenders lending directly to borrowers and directly incurring the monitoring costs. Diamond's fundamental result is to show that as an intermediary grows large, it can commit to a payment to depositors that can only be honored if, in fact, the intermediary has monitored as it promised. If not, then the intermediary incurs nonpecuniary penalties, interpreted by Diamond as bankruptcy costs or loss of reputation.

To see the argument, we follow Williamson's (1986) presentation of the Diamond result; unlike Diamond, it does not rely on precise contractual specification of nonpecuniary penalties, which is rarely seen in practice. Williamson's monitoring technology follows Townsend, so Diamond's result does not depend on the timing of monitoring (that is, whether it is state contingent or not). A brief outline of the essential part of the Williamson model is as follows. Borrowers need resources to invest in their projects. They invest K units of endowment at date 0 and receive $K\tilde{w}$ at date 1, where $\tilde{w}$ is a random variable distributed according to the density $f(w)$. As shown by Gale and Hellwig (1985), the optimal contract between the borrower and a lender is a debt contract. At date 1 borrower j has a realized return of w_j per unit invested. Borrower j pays the lending intermediary a gross rate of return $\bar{R}$ in a state, w_j, where there is no monitoring and $R(w_j)$ when there is monitoring. Define the set $B = \{w_j : R(w_j) < \bar{R}\}$ and $B^c = \{w_j : R(w_j) \leqslant \bar{R}\}$. Finally, let r denote the certain market return, required by risk-neutral investors.

When the intermediary has m borrowers, each investing K, then the total return to the intermediary (before compensating depositors) is:

$$\pi_m = K \sum_{j=1}^{m} \min\{R(w_j), \bar{R}\}.$$

By the strong law of large numbers:

$$p \lim_{m \to \infty} \frac{1}{mK} \pi_m = \int_B R(w_j)\, dw_j + \int_{B^c} f(w_j)\, dw_j.$$

Consequently, since the intermediary's return must be at least the market return, r, if the following inequality holds:

$$\int_B R(w_j) f(w_j)\, dw_j + \bar{R} \int_{B^c} f(w_j)\, dw_j - \frac{c}{K} \int_B f(w_j)\, dw_j \geqslant r,$$

then, as the intermediary grows large, it can guarantee a certain return of r to its depositors.

If the intermediary is finite sized, that is, it lends to a finite number of borrowers, then depositors must monitor the intermediary to ensure that the intermediary, in turn, is monitoring the borrowers. Since monitoring is costly, and given the certain market return that must be obtained, the depositors must be compensated for these monitoring costs by the intermediary. Compensating the depositors for monitoring costs incurred, lowers the profitability (utility) of the intermediary. However, the central result of Diamond (1984) applies here, namely, that the depositors need not monitor an infinitely large intermediary because such a firm can achieve r with probability one. In the limit, depositors do not need to monitor the intermediary. The "monitoring the monitor" problem is solved by diversification.

One might object that, in practice, financial intermediaries are not infinitely diversified, and some credit risk is not diversifiable; also, it seems likely that a depositor finds it more difficult to monitor a large bank than to monitor a small bank. Krasa and Villamil (1992, 1993) address these concerns. Suppose we modify Williamson (1986) by assuming that larger banks' returns are more costly to verify. If loan returns are stochastically independent of one another, Krasa and Villamil (1992) apply the Large Deviation Principle to show that, so long as a depositor's cost of monitoring doesn't increase exponentially with bank size, the expected costs of monitoring a sufficiently large bank go to zero. Moreover, they show through examples that even relatively small banks (e.g., 32 loans) get enough gains from diversification to dominate direct lending. If some loan risk is systematic, the chance of bank failure is bounded away from zero as bank size grows [Krasa and Villamil (1993)]. In this case, since the cost of monitoring banks that fail is increasing in bank size, there is a bank size past which the increase in monitoring costs dominates marginal benefits from additional diversification. Moreover, this optimal size diminishes as the systematic component of loan risk increases.

Winton (1995a) addresses another issue, namely the role of bank capital. Suppose that the banker invests his own funds in the bank as "inside" equity capital. Being junior, such equity absorbs losses first, reducing the probability with which the bank defaults and depositors must monitor. Thus, bank capital is another mechanism for implementing delegated monitoring. Since the bankers' capital is fixed, it will be most helpful for smaller banks; also, the relative importance of capital versus diversification increases as more loan risk is systematic.[3]

Of course, Diamond (1984) does not explain all the characteristics of intermediaries. But, he elegantly explains the existence of intermediaries, in particular, as coalitions, of borrowers and lenders, which dominate the alternative of direct investment by investors in securities issued by firms. The securities market fails in the sense that

---

[3] Winton (1995b) shows that further reductions in monitoring costs are possible if a class of "outside" equity holders is created, who are junior to depositors but senior to the banker.

intermediation, centralization of the task of monitoring, is a lower cost solution to the ex post information asymmetry between borrowers and lenders. Diversification is critical to intermediation providing a lower cost solution because diversification is critical to reducing the monitoring the monitor problem. The textbook idea that individual investors can diversify nonsystematic risk on their own does not take into account the role diversification plays in allowing an intermediary to be monitored costlessly (in the limit).

Other papers that study banks as delegated monitors include Gorton and Haubrich (1987) and Seward (1990).

2.3. Banks as information producers

If information about investment opportunities is not free, then economic agents may find it worthwhile to produce such information. There will be an inefficient duplication of information production costs if multiple agents choose to produce the same information. Alternatively, a smaller number of agents could produce the information, becoming informed, and then sell the information to the uninformed agents. This, however, introduces the "reliability problem" originally identified by Hirshleifer (1971): it may be impossible for the information producer to credibly ensure that he has, in fact, produced the valuable information.

A related problem concerns resale of the information. If an information producer could credibly produce valuable information, and then sell it to another agent, then there is no way to prevent the second agent from selling it to a third agent, and so on. In other words, purchasers of the information can sell or share the information with others without necessarily diminishing its usefulness to themselves. This is known as the "appropriability problem". The returns to producing the information could not all be captured by the information producer, possibly making the production of information uneconomic [see Grossman and Stiglitz (1980)]. The resale and appropriability problems in information production can motivate the existence of an intermediary.

Leland and Pyle (1977) were the first to suggest that an intermediary could overcome the reliability problem. The intermediary can credibly produce information by investing its wealth in assets about which it claims to have produced valuable information. The starting point for Leland and Pyle (1977) is a single entrepreneur who has private information about an investment opportunity, but who has insufficient resources to undertake the investment. Since outside investors do not observe the entrepreneur's private information, there is an adverse selection problem. Leland and Pyle show that the entrepreneur's private information can be signaled by the fraction of equity in the project that the entrepreneur retrains, while he sells the remaining fraction to outside investors.[4] At the end of their paper, Leland and Pyle suggest that financial

---

[4] See also Kihlstrom and Mathews (1990) and Duffie and Demarzo (1999).

intermediaries might efficiently solve the reliability and appropriability problems inherent in information production by issuing securities and using the proceeds to invest in a portfolio of securities about which the intermediary has become privately informed. After deriving his delegated monitoring model, Diamond (1984) also derives a Leland and Pyle model in which diversification lowers the intermediary's signaling costs compared to the entrepreneur's costs.

Following Leland and Pyle, a number of papers, notably Campbell and Kracaw (1980), also argued that financial intermediaries might exist to produce information about potential investments, information that could not be efficiently produced in securities markets. Campbell and Kracaw (1980) show that appropriability and reliability problems can be eliminated if the information producer has a sufficient minimum amount of wealth to risk if he does not produce the information. To risk his own money requires that the intermediary actually invest on behalf of other agents. The paper, however, that most fully articulates the argument that coalitions of agents should form to produce information ex ante about potential investments is Boyd and Prescott (1986).

The underlying problem faced by agents in Boyd and Prescott (1986) is an information asymmetry that occurs prior to contracting and investing, resulting in an adverse selection problem. Agents are of different types and this information is private to each agent. Each agent, however, is endowed with a technology to evaluate projects, that is, the technology can determine agent type. Ex ante information production can alleviate the adverse selection problem. This can be done in a market context, where an agent evaluates his own project, and then issues securities to investors that promise specified returns. Or, a coalition of agents can offer investors a claim on group returns. Financial intermediaries are coalitions of agents that evaluate projects, invest in those determined to be high-value projects, and share the returns from the portfolio of projects.

More specifically, the outline of the model is as follows. Agents live for two periods. Each agent is endowed with a project of unknown type (good or bad). Agents know their own type, so there is no opportunity to enter into contracts before knowing their types. Each project type can have a high or low return (good projects are more likely to realize the high return). An agent can expend his endowment either on producing information about a single project's type or as an investment in a single project, his own if he has not evaluated it or another agent's project. If a project is evaluated, then a noisy signal of true project type is received. Project evaluation and investment are publicly observable and verifiable, as are project returns, evaluation results, consumption outcomes, and contract terms.

An efficient outcome invests in as many good projects as possible. But, the difficulty in accomplishing this is that bad-type agents will want to mimic good-type agents, claiming that they are good, promising the same high return to investors as the good-type agents, and then hoping that their project realizes the high return. Indeed, there is such a securities market equilibrium, but it is one in which some bad-type projects are evaluated, by mimicking agents. This is inefficient.

The alternative is the financial intermediary coalition. The model is one of mechanism design. One interpretation of how to implement the equilibrium with the coalition (given by Boyd and Prescott) is as follows. Coalition members deliver their endowments to the coalition prior to investment. These endowments are used for project evaluation. Depositors are other agents who turn over their endowments to the coalition in exchange for a promised amount of consumption. The depositors give the coalition the right to invest in their project and to receive the entire project output, if the coalition desires. Project owners are promised very high returns if evaluation reveals a good project and if the realized return is high. Otherwise, depositors are promised an amount of consumption which is more than a bad-type agent could achieve on his own, but less than the promised amount for projects with a good evaluation and high realized returns. Members of the coalition are residual claimants and share profits equally.

The coalition's sharing rules induce truthful revelation of agent type. The coalition then evaluates good-type projects and funds each of these projects with a good evaluation. It uses the remaining proceeds to fund bad-type projects without evaluation. This is the critical point. The promised returns separate types, and since good types are relatively scarce, the coalition ends up funding some bad-type projects, but it does not waste resources evaluating those projects. This is why it dominates the securities market.

The intermediary dominates the securities market because the intermediary coalition can induce agents to truthfully reveal their type and this cannot be achieved in the securities market. Truthful revelation allows the coalition to avoid inefficiently evaluating some bad-type projects. The reason is that, by conditioning returns on the coalition's portfolio returns, rather than on the returns of a single project, the coalition can offer higher returns to bad-type agents, so they will participate in the coalition. The relative proportions of good-types and bad-types are also important. In particular, good-type agents must be scarce. Note also that it is important that a coalition be large because a small coalition may end up with so many good-type projects that they cannot all be funded. In the population, good-type projects are relatively scarce and this must be reflected in coalition membership. Thus, as in Diamond (1984), size of the coalition is critical for the argument.

The equilibrium concept in Boyd and Prescott is based on the core of an economy. That is, an allocation is an equilibrium if no large coalition of agents, with specified fractions of agent types, can achieve a different allocation, satisfying resource, consumption, incentive and other constraints, and make at least some agent type better off without reducing any other type's utility. Deviating coalitions are not allowed to attract higher than population proportions of type-i agents unless it makes them strictly better off. Although the solution of the model is standard in that it relies on the revelation principal, the equilibrium concept is less common in the finance and financial contracting literature. This may account for why this paper has not led to a successor literature in banking per se; instead, it has been more influential in macroeconomics, where the equilibrium concept has been taken up, though see the discussion of Williamson (1988), below.

Boyd and Prescott's intermediary has the characteristics of bank-like intermediaries identified in the introduction. Other researchers have pursued solutions to the problems of reliability and appropriability of valuable private information, but these other solutions do not involve bank-like intermediation. Two settings in particular have been examined. The first considers delegated portfolio management, i.e., a setting where a fund manager may claim to have superior information or superior ability and offers to invest on behalf of investors. The second considers the sale of valuable information about investments when the information producer does not invest on behalf of investors. A theory of intermediation must distinguish between firms that sell information, like rating agencies, firms that are delegated portfolio managers, like mutual funds or hedge funds, and bank-like financial intermediaries.

At the level of casual empiricism there are identifiable differences between these types of arrangements. A bank-like intermediary does not sell information that it produces. Rather, as in Boyd and Prescott, it uses the information internally to improve the returns to coalition members. This is very different from the case of a firm that sells information to investors, like a rating agency. Firms selling information face problems of reliability and appropriability, but they do not lend money. Purchasers of the information may lend in reliance on the information purchased, but they are then directly lending, not via an intermediary. A portfolio manager, claiming to have superior information, accepts investments from one set of agents and then uses the proceeds to invest in securities. This seems very similar to a bank-like intermediary. One difference is that the claims held by the investors do not have different state contingent payoffs than the payoff on the portfolio of claims chosen by the portfolio manager; essentially, the investors and the portfolio manager all hold equity claims in the portfolio.

In Bhattacharya and Pfleiderer's (1985) model, investors want to hire portfolio managers, but there are two sources of private information that make this difficult. First, investors must hire a manager from pool of managers with heterogeneous abilities. A manager or agent has the ability to receive an informative signal about the risky asset (there is also a riskless asset). Once a manager has been hired, he must be induced to truthfully reveal the signal he has received. However, once the principal has designed the contract and hired a manager, the manager/agent's only role is to transmit the information to the principal. There is no portfolio management by the manager/agent since the principal can directly invest using the information supplied by the manager/agent. There is no intermediary (nor do Bhattacharya and Pfleiderer claim that there is; the purposes of their paper are different).

Allen (1990) presents a model that distinguishes conditions under which information is sold to agents who then use the information to make investments from the case where the buyers of the information then act as intermediaries and resell the information. Essentially, reselling the information allows more of the value of the information to be captured. Because the initial information seller must distinguish himself from potential uniformed mimics, he faces a number of constraints. These constraints limit the amount of profit he can take in from selling the information. This is the basis for information resellers to enter the market; they find it profitable to resell the information rather than use it as a basis for their own investments because they can capture more of the value of the information. Here there is a type of intermediation: there are agents who buy information and then resell it. But, these agents do not invest on behalf of others.

Ramakrishnan and Thakor (1984) consider a setting in which firms issuing new shares to the public can hire an agent to produce information about their quality. Information production requires a costly, and unobservable, effort, so the information producer would like to avoid this cost if he can do so without being detected. There is an ex post noisy indicator of the information producer's effort choice, so compensation for information production can be linked to this indicator. Because information producers are risk averse, they would prefer to avoid the risk that the noise in the indicator prevents them from obtaining compensation for their efforts. The main point of Ramakrishnan and Thakor is that this risk is mitigated if one infinitely large intermediary is formed since this diversifies the risk associated with the effort indicator. The large intermediary is formed when information producers can costlessly monitor each other's efforts. [Millon and Thakor (1985) extend the analysis to the case where the internal monitoring is costly]. Ramakrishnan and Thakor's intermediary, however, does not accept funds for investment. Rather, it is a pure information seller. In this regard, also see Lizzeri (1999).

In general, the differences in settings where some agents would like valuable, but costly, information produced for investment purposes are subtle. In many models there is no need for the information seller to actually accept the funds that will be invested on the basis of the superior information. In Bhattacharya and Pfleiderer, Allen, and Ramakrishnan and Thakor, the information producer sells the information to investors, but does not need to actually invest the funds of the investors. In Boyd and Prescott the intermediary accepts deposits, produces information, and invests in projects based on the information produced. Only by conditioning the returns on the portfolio that is produced by the coalition can truthful revelation be induced.

A potentially important aspect of information production by banks concerns whether the information is produced upon first contact with the borrower or is instead learned through repeated interaction with the borrower over time. Another strand of the literature on banks as information producers argues that banks acquire (private) information over time through repeatedly lending to a borrower. The acquisition of this private information over time is known as a "customer relationship" and is discussed in Section 3 below.

2.4. Banks as consumption smoothers

Bryant (1980) and Diamond and Dybvig (1983) develop a role for bank liabilities, without stressing any particular features of bank assets. Bank liabilities do not function as a transactions medium. Rather, banks are vehicles for consumption smoothing; they offer insurance against shocks to a consumer's consumption path.

The Diamond and Dybvig model assumes that the payoffs from the available investment opportunities are inconsistent with the possible consumption paths desired by consumers. In particular, consumers have random consumption needs, and satisfying these needs may require them to prematurely end investments unless they save via intermediation so that they can to some extent diversify these consumption shocks. The model offers a view of the liability side of banking; the right to withdraw from the bank, prematurely ending investment in order to satisfy sudden consumption needs, corresponds with notions of how demand deposits actually work. The model also focuses on banking panics, a separate topic that we discuss in Section 4 below.

The outlines of the Diamond and Dybvig model are as follows. There are three dates 0, 1 and 2, and a single good. The available technology allows one unit of investment to be transformed over two periods into $R > 1$ units at the final date. If this investment is interrupted at the interim date, then it just returns the initial one unit. Importantly, the long-term investment only realizes a return over the initial investment if it reaches fruition at date 2. All consumers are identical initially, at date 0, but each faces a privately observable, uninsurable risk with regard to their preferences. At date 1, each consumer learns whether he cares only about consumption at date 1, an "early consumer", or only about consumption at date 2, a "late consumer". The problem is evident: consumers would like to insure themselves against the bad luck of being an early consumer. Without being able to write such insurance contracts, because consumer type is not observable, early consumers can do no better than consuming their single unit of endowment, which was invested in the investment technology but which is liquidated early. The lucky late consumers consume $R > 1$.

Diamond and Dybvig (1983) argue that a bank can provide insurance against the risk of being an early consumer. Basically, a bank works as follows. At date 0 the bank opens and accepts "deposits" of endowment. The bank promises a fixed claim of r_1 per unit deposited will be paid out to consumers who withdraw at date 1. The return on a deposit that is not withdrawn at date 1, but is withdrawn at date 2, depends on how much was withdrawn at date 1. Suppose the fraction of consumers who will turn out to be early consumers is fixed and known. Then Diamond and Dybvig show that the return of r_1 can be set to the amount that an early consumer would achieve if there were complete insurance markets. So the bank can support the full-information risk-sharing equilibrium.

The Diamond and Dybvig model has important features of intermediaries and the real world environment. First, it incorporates the idea that consumers have uncertain preferences for expenditure streams, producing a demand for liquid assets. Furthermore, the modeling representation of this uncertainty, the technique of early and late consumers, has been very influential in its own right. Uncertainty about preferences for expenditure streams leads to the bank offering claims that look like demand deposits. This is combined with a second important feature, namely, real investment projects are irreversible, or at least costly to restart once stopped.

A third important feature of the model is the idea that individual consumers have private information about the realization of their type, the realization of their preferred consumption stream. There is no credible way to truthfully reveal this information.

We now turn to some details about why insurance or securities markets cannot provide consumption smoothing or insurance against the risk of uncertain preferences for expenditure streams. In Diamond and Dybvig, an intermediary that issues demand deposits allows greater risk sharing than autarky. Diamond and Dybvig assume that demand deposits cannot be traded and do not consider other securities markets. Their model assumes a sequential service constraint, that is, a first-come-first-served ruled under which at date 1 the bank honors claims to withdraw in the order in which they are received until the bank runs out of resources to honor the claims. The remaining consumers seeking to withdraw receive nothing and the bank fails. We discuss models that motivate the sequential service constraint in Section 4 below. Here, we simply note that the idea it attempts to capture is that consumers cannot coordinate to go to any securities market at the same time to trade; they are busy doing other things such as shopping, eating, sleeping, working, etc. Thus, Diamond and Dybvig's assumptions that demand deposits cannot be traded and that no other securities markets are open are not completely without foundation.

This point is important because Jacklin (1987) and Haubrich and King (1990) argue that the existence of Diamond and Dybvig intermediaries requires the restriction that consumers only have nontraded demand deposits available to them. Jacklin (1987) begins by asking, why does a securities market fail in the Diamond and Dybvig model? In order to highlight the importance of trading restrictions and preferences for Diamond and Dybvig's result that intermediation is the best insurance arrangement, he proposes an alternative arrangement that uses traded securities. Suppose that there are firms in Diamond and Dybvig that own the two-period production technology. Each firm raises capital by issuing dividend-paying shares at date 0. Consumers buy the shares, entitling them to set the production policy and to set dividend policy about the amount paid out to share owners at date 1. The "dividends" on Jacklin's equity are set to smooth income in exactly the desired way; they are not just pass-throughs from the firms. Shareholders of record at date 0 receive the dividend at date 1 and then can sell the share in a share market at date 1. At date 1 consumers learn their preferred consumption streams. Early consumers will want sell their shares ex dividend to late consumers. Jacklin shows that the social optimum obtains with this share market in place. Thus, the bank cannot do any better.

Jacklin goes on to show that the result that the intermediary cannot improve upon trading dividend-paying shares is not true in general. Recall that, in Diamond and Dybvig, some consumers find that they must consume early; it is all or nothing. If instead preferences are smooth, so that one type of consumer will learn that he has a stronger preference for earlier consumption than the other type, then it can happen that demand deposits dominate traded equity shares, but only under certain conditions. Furthermore, if demand deposits can be traded, then optimal risk sharing does not occur regardless of preferences. Finally, Jacklin argues that, if new assets can be introduced, individuals will deviate from either the demand deposit arrangement or from the economy with traded dividend-paying shares. These points lead Jacklin to conclude that the Diamond and Dybvig "demand-deposit" intermediary can only exist if trading restrictions limit consumers to the type of demand deposits that Diamond and Dybvig model. This highlights the importance of the sequential service constraint and its interpretation.

Haubrich and King (1990) revisit in detail the issue of financial intermediation in settings where agents are subject to privately observable income shocks. Their main conclusions are similar to Jacklin (1987), namely, that "demand deposits *uniquely* provide insurance only if there are restrictions on financial side exchanges, which may be interpreted as exclusivity provisions or regulations on security markets. If these restrictions cannot be implemented, then our environment does not rationalize banks" (p. 362; emphasis in original). They also make the useful distinction between two separate issues. One is the fact that the available investment technology is illiquid in the sense that no return is earned if the two-period investment is ended early. The other is that risk averse consumers with privately observable income shocks have a demand for insurance. They argue that a securities market is as good as banks in providing liquidity. In their model, the bank's comparative advantage is in providing insurance against private income shocks rather than providing liquidity per se, but that advantage still depends on trading restrictions.

Hellwig (1994) and von Thadden (1998) examine how banks function when additional considerations are introduced into Diamond and Dybvig's structure. Hellwig shows that if market returns at the interim (early-consumption) date are subject to systematic "interest-rate shocks", banks optimally do not provide insurance against such interest rate risk. Von Thadden shows that if depositors can join outside coalitions that engage in market activity, banks' ability to provide insurance is severely curtailed, and banks are more constrained as long-term investment opportunities are more reversible. Intuitively, ex ante insurance makes the return to holding deposits at the interim date deviate from returns available by directly investing, allowing arbitrage.

Diamond (1997) responds to Jacklin (1987), Haubrich and King (1990), Hellwig (1994), and von Thadden (1998) in a model with both banks and a securities market in which (by assumption) only a limited subset of agents participate in the market. The main focus of the paper is on the interactions between bank provision of "liquidity" and the depth of the market. As more agents participate in the securities market, banks are less able to provide additional liquidity.

Allen and Gale (1997) introduce a different smoothing role for financial inter-mediaries, namely, that they are unique in providing a mechanism for smoothing intertemporal intergenerational risks. Allen and Gale study the standard overlapping (risk averse) generations model with two assets, a risky asset in fixed supply and a safe asset that can be accumulated over time.[5] The risky asset lasts forever and pays out a random dividend each period. The safe asset consists of a storage technology. First, consider the market equilibrium in this economy. Perhaps counterintuitively, the safe asset is not a useful hedge against the uncertainty generated by the risky asset. Because the risky asset's returns are independently and identically distributed in any period, a representative young agent solves the same decision problem at any date. Old agents supply the risky asset inelastically, so the equilibrium price of the risky asset is constant and nonstochastic. Because the dividend is nonnegative, the safe asset is dominated and is not held in equilibrium.

This market equilibrium is in contrast with the portfolio allocation that would occur for an infinitely lived agent facing the same investment opportunities. Such an individual can self-insure against low dividend periods by holding a buffer stock of precautionary savings in the form of the safe asset. Intuitively, when the dividend is high, the individual saves some of the dividend for a "rainy day" when the dividend is low. In the overlapping generations setting, a social planner can make a Pareto improvement by following the same type of rule.

The market equilibrium in the overlapping generations model cannot achieve the allocation that the social planner could achieve because private agents cannot trade before they are born, while the social planner can, in effect, trade at all dates. In particular, the social planner trades ex ante, that is, before the realization of the path of dividends. A representative young agent, however, is born into a world where the dividend has just been realized. There is no willingness to implement insurance once the state is known. For example, suppose the dividend just realized is low. Then, the social planner would like to implement a transfer from the young to the old, to smooth their income. On the other hand, if the dividend just realized is high, then the social planner would like to transfer some of that to the current young. Some excess may be saved for the next period. These transfers insure that each generation receives the expected utility targeted by the social planner.

It is well known that markets are incomplete in overlapping generations models, but the point made by Allen and Gale is that a long-lived financial intermediary may be the institutional mechanism to provide for this intertemporal smoothing. The intermediary would hold all the assets and offer a deposit contract to each generation. After accumulating large reserves, the intermediary offers (almost) all generations a constant return on deposits, independent of the actual dividend realizations. How such an institution would be set up initially, and how it would be maintained when some agents will have incentives to renege on the arrangement, are not clear. Allen and Gale loosely interpret the institution as corresponding to German universal banks.

Consumption insurance that implements smooth patterns of intertemporal consumption plans is at the center of the model of consumer behavior of neoclassical economics.

[5] Freeman (1988) and Qi (1994) introduce Diamond and Dybvig banks into an overlapping generations model, but do not consider intertemporal smoothing of risk.

Another central notion concerns the use of "money" to facilitate exchange. The search models of money or models with cash-in-advance constraints attempt to explain why "money" exists. The notion of banks as consumption-smoothing institutions attempts to wed these two ideas. Bank liabilities are seen as claims that facilitate consumption smoothing. But, there is no notion of exchange in the model, no sense in which transactions are taking place where bank "money" is being used to facilitate the smoothing. Instead, agents are essentially isolated from each other; there is no trade with other agents where "money" buys goods. Rather agents fear missing out on long-term investment opportunities because of possible shocks to their preferences. Agents trade only with the bank.

2.5. Banks as liquidity providers

Bank liabilities function as a medium of exchange. This basic observation leads to ideas and models concerning "liquidity" that are quite distinct and perhaps more natural than viewing bank liabilities as allowing consumption smoothing. A medium of exchange is a set of claims or securities that can be offered to other agents in exchange for goods. Such claims can dominate barter and may dominate government-supplied money. What are the advantages of privately-produced trading claims to be a medium of exchange? One class of these models considers settings where agents cannot contract and trade with each other due their inability to meet at a single location. Without "money" they must barter, and this is clearly inefficient. This generates a need for a payments system, essentially a trading center or bank that can produce and net claims. A second notion of liquidity is related to the information properties of claims that are privately produced as a medium of exchange. The focus is on reducing trading losses that agents who need to consume face when other traders with private information seek to use this information to make trading profits. Yet a third notion of liquidity uses a setting where moral hazard problems limit firms' ability to borrow to meet unexpected investment needs. Because moral hazard limits the effectiveness of transactions between firms with excess liquidity and firms that need liquidity, a bank that provides contingent liquidity to those that need it can dominate a decentralized market.

The first view of banks as liquidity providers concerns the role of banks in the payments system. Freeman (1996a,b) models an environment where agents are spatially separated and the timing of transactions is such that they cannot simultaneously trade at a central location. The problem in the model is that some agents, buyers, wish to consume goods from other agents, but have no goods that the buyers want to offer these sellers in exchange. Nor do buyers have any money, though later at another location they will be able to sell their goods in exchange for money. So, buyers issue i.o.u.'s – promises to pay at the central location next period with fiat money – to the sellers. Fiat money is used to settle the debts, but money and private debt coexist. Now, at the central clearing location it may happen that all creditors and debtors arrive simultaneously, in which case clearing occurs directly. If arrival is not simultaneous, however, settling can take place through a clearinghouse. The clearinghouse accepts money in payment of i.o.u.'s and pays off i.o.u.'s presented. However, if creditors arrive first, then the clearinghouse must have some means of paying them before the debtors arrive. A basic point of Freeman is develop the notion of the clearinghouse issuing its own i.o.u.'s, bank notes for example, that can circulate and be redeemed for fiat money later.

Green (1997) builds on the Freeman model, arguing that a clearinghouse "netting by novation" can also achieve the efficiency gain in Freeman's model. In the same vein, McAndrews and Roberds (1999) model the efficiency gains from introducing banks that allow for centralized netting of claims. A bank can lend to firms via overdrafts. The firms are willing to accept payment in bank funds since the income funds can be used to repay the overdraft loan. Banks can provide "liquidity" to the extent that the payments they are requested to make are offsetting. Williamson (1992) also presents a model in which fiat money and private bank "money" coexist in equilibrium. Cavalcanti and Wallace (1999) study a random-matching model in which some agents, called banks, can produce information about the trading histories of other agents, called nonbanks. The equilibrium is one in which the banks issue and redeem private bank notes.

In these models, banks issue private money to facilitate their role in clearing transactions. This is related to the historical experiences during which banks actually did issue their own private money, notably during the American Free Banking Era, 1838–1863. During this period hundreds of different banks' monies circulated. Early economic historians and monetary theorists viewed the experience as a failure, arguing that it was marked by "wildcat banking" which justified a role for the government in the provision of a fiat currency. Following earlier work by Rockoff (1974, 1975), Rolnick and Weber (1982, 1983, 1984, 1988) reexamine failure rates over the cross section of states with different banking regimes and conclude that the period was not marked by such episodes. Gorton (1996, 1999) analyzes the prices of private bank notes and concludes that the market for banknotes worked well in pricing the risk of bank failure and in preventing wildcatting. Some experiences of Illinois, New York and Wisconsin during the Free Banking period are studied by Economopoulos (1988, 1990).

The pricing of free bank notes raises another issue concerning the production of liquidity. When offered a bank liability in exchange for goods, the seller of goods must recognize the risk that the bank can fail before the liability is honored. If some agents have private information about the likelihood of bank failure, they may be able to benefit from this when trading bank liabilities. An important property of a medium of exchange may well be that there is little or no such risk; that is, the value of the medium of exchange is independent of such considerations. But then it must be riskless in the sense that its value does not depend on the likelihood of the bank failing. This intuition is developed in the second view of liquidity, exemplified by Gorton and Pennacchi (1990).

Gorton and Pennacchi (1990) begin with a common assumption of financial market models, namely the existence of "noise traders" or "liquidity traders". Kyle (1985) originally introduced these traders as a reduced-form modeling device, following Grossman and Stiglitz (1980). These models do not explicitly examine the motives of these noise traders; instead, they are posited to conveniently trade and lose money, making it profitable for other traders to undertake costly information production. Implicitly, these models seem to assume larger settings in which agents face cash-in-advance constraints and suffer shocks to income or preferences, causing them to sell securities. These models assume symmetrically that there are also noise traders who have sudden urges to buy securities, though it is less clear what the source of this urge is exactly. Intuitively, these traders either sell securities at too low a price or buy securities at too high a price because they are uninformed and the prices at which securities are traded are not fully revealing.

Gorton and Pennacchi (1990) observe that these noise traders should recognize their problem, namely, that they lose money when they trade securities with better-informed traders. Consequently, they should demand securities with the property that when they are traded it is not possible for insiders to benefit at the expense of less informed traders. Thus, a security is said to be "liquid" if uninformed traders can sell it (unexpectedly) without a loss to more informed traders. The higher the variance of the value of a security, the greater the potential losses to insiders when uninformed traders must sell. If securities could be valued independently of information known only to the informed traders, then these securities would be highly desirable for trading purposes. Gorton and Pennacchi (1990) argue that splitting the cash flows of an underlying portfolio to create debt and equity can create such "liquid" securities, namely the debt. If the debt is riskless, then there can be no information advantage that other agents could possess. Uninformed agents with unexpected needs to sell securities can sell these securities to satisfy their liquidity needs. Financial intermediaries are the natural entities to create such securities, as they hold diversified portfolios of assets. Consequently, their debt should be used for transactions purposes.

Holmstrom and Tirole (1998) provide another rationale for intermediaries based on a third notion of "liquidity." They begin by deriving a demand for "liquidity" that emanates from firms rather than consumers. There are three dates in their model, 0, 1 and 2. At date 0 the entrepreneur running the firm raises outside financing. At date 1 there is a "liquidity shock" requiring the entrepreneur to invest more in the project if it is to obtain a return at date 2. After the realization of the liquidity shock, the decision to continue or not is made, followed by the entrepreneur's effort choice. If the project is continued, then an outcome is realized at date 2 and contract payments are made. Because there is a moral hazard problem in inducing the entrepreneur to expend effort, outside investors cannot be promised the full social value of the investment. The firm raises less financing than the first-best social optimum. If the firm can store the initial resources, then it faces a dilemma. It can reduce the amount it invests at date 0, to have an amount to hedge against a liquidity shock. Or, it can invest more at date 0, but then have less on hand if it needs more at date 1.

Now, suppose there is no storage and no aggregate uncertainty. The only way to transfer value across time is to use claims issued by firms. In general equilibrium, some firms will need resources at date 1 and some will not. A second-best arrangement would allow firms with large needs for resources at date 1 to utilize the market value of those firms with low needs at date 1. How would this actually work? A firm with a liquidity shock at date 1 cannot meet its needs by selling claims at date 1; it is too late to do that. Could the firm instead hedge against an adverse liquidity shock at date 1 by buying claims on other firms at date 0, and then selling those claims at date 1? There are two problems with this arrangement. First, if the moral hazard problem is severe enough, then a market in firm claims will not supply enough "liquidity". Second, there is an inefficient distribution of liquid assets (the claims that can be sold at date 1 by firms needing resources). Firms without adverse liquidity shocks end up holding claims at date 1 that they do not need.

An intermediary can provide liquidity by issuing claims to investors at date 0 on its value at date 2. At date 0 it contracts with each firm to provide a line of credit at date 1. The maximum credit line is incentive compatible with the entrepreneur making an effort.[6] Unlike claims in the financial market, which cannot be made contingent on a firm's liquidity shock, firms only draw on the credit line at date 1 to the extent that they need resources. If there is aggregate uncertainty, then this arrangement may not work, and there can be a role for a government bond market.

Both Gorton and Pennacchi (1990) and Holmstrom and Tirole (1998) have intermediaries creating securities that have desirable state contingent payoffs. In Gorton and Pennacchi, the bank creates demand deposits whose value does not depend on the state of the world. This security is in demand because its value is not state contingent and, therefore, uninformed traders will not lose to better-informed traders who know the state of the world. In Holmström and Tirole, the intermediary creates a security, the credit line, which is valuable because it is state contingent; it is only drawn on when a firm needs resources at the interim date. Capital market securities issued by firms cannot replicate this state-contingent payoff.

2.6. Banks as commitment mechanisms

An important question concerns why illiquid bank assets are financed by demand deposits that allow consumers to arrive and demand liquidation of those illiquid assets. Calomiris and Kahn (1991) and Flannery (1994) link the fragility of bank capital structures to the role of banks. These authors begin with the assumption that banks are somewhat opaque institutions, more so than nonfinancial firms. Evidence for this opaqueness compared to nonfinancial firms can be found, for example, in Slovin, Sushka and Polonchek (1992) and Morgan (2000). Calomiris and Kahn (1991) argue that bank demand deposits include the right to withdraw at anytime at par along

---

[6] Because the entrepreneur pays a fee at date 0 for the credit line, he can borrow at a lower rate at date 1 than if he issued securities at date 1. This lower rate leads to greater effort for any amount of borrowing.

with a sequential service constraint in order to control the risk taking activities of bankers. If information about the banker's decisions must be produced at a cost, then individual depositors who expend resources to produce the information will get into line to withdraw at the bank first. Because the sequential service constraint is a first-come-first-served rule, it rewards those depositors in line first, and so information-producing depositors will recover more than other depositors. This argument was the first to suggest that banks' capital structures are deliberately made fragile so as to commit to not engaging in certain activities. From this viewpoint, fragility is a positive attribute of banks. Jean-Baptiste (1999) also argues that the instantly callable feature of demand deposits is necessary as a device to discipline bankers.

Flannery (1994) makes a related argument. He argues that bank creditors cannot effectively control bank asset substitution because of the ease of flexibly altering the bank portfolio, but they can estimate a bank's riskiness at any point in time. To control bankers, short-term debt is used because changes in bank risk will be reflected in financing costs. Again, the basic point is that the capital structure of banks is designed to be fragile, so that it functions as a commitment mechanism. Flannery and Sorescu (1996) show empirically that bank debt prices do reflect bank risk.

Diamond and Rajan (2001a,b) use this idea that fragility is a commitment device to construct a model of bank-like financial intermediation. In their model, entrepreneurs need to raise money from outside investors to finance their projects. The specific abilities of the entrepreneur are important for the project to generate high cash flows; that is, if the entrepreneur refuses to work, then the project is worth less when someone else runs it. Moreover, the entrepreneur cannot commit to stay with the project. A lender, however, can build a relationship by lending to entrepreneur and learning about the project. If this relationship lender "liquidates" the project by separating the entrepreneur from the project, then the project is worth less than it would be worth with the entrepreneur, but more than if it is run by someone other than the relationship lender.

Because the entrepreneur cannot commit to stay with the asset, Diamond and Rajan say that the asset is "illiquid." This "illiquidity" makes it possible for the entrepreneur to hold up the relationship lender. Because potential relationship lenders anticipate this holdup problem, the amount that the entrepreneur can borrow is limited. Lenders also have problems because they may face a realized liquidity shock at an interim date. If a relationship lender needed cash at the interim date, the project would have to be sold to a non-relationship investor in whose hands it is worth even less. The prospect of such a shock makes relationship lending expensive, if not prohibitive.

The consequences of this chain of illiquidity could be mitigated if the relationship lender could borrow against the full value of the loan when faced with a liquidity shock. But this requires that the relationship lender commit to not separate from the project in the future. Diamond and Rajan argue that a bank can achieve such a commitment by designing a fragile capital structure, as follows. If the relationship lender issues demand deposits that are subject to collective action problems among the depositors, then if the relationship lender threatens to withdraw from the project, depositors will run the bank and the relationship lender will receive no rents.

As Diamond and Rajan note, this fragile structure is not first-best if banks face undiversifiable liquidity shocks. In this case, runs may occur because of high liquidity demand rather than because of bank moral hazard. Diamond and Rajan (2000) use this problem to motivate the existence and optimal level of bank equity capital. We return to this point in Section 3 below.

2.7. Empirical tests of bank-existence theories

Theories of the existence of bank-like financial intermediaries link banks' activities on the asset side of their balance sheets with the unique liabilities that banks issue on the liability side of their balance sheets. Such a link is important for establishing what it is that banks do that cannot be replicated in capital markets. As we have seen, these arguments take two linked forms. First, the banks' balance sheet structure may ensure that the bank has incentive to act as delegated monitor or information producer. Second, by virtue of holding a diversified portfolio of loans, banks are in the best position to create riskless trading securities, namely, demand deposits.

Two papers, in particular, construct empirical tests of hypotheses about links between the two sides of bank balance sheets. Berlin and Mester (1999) look for a link between bank market power in deposits markets and the types of loan contracts that the bank enters into with borrowers.[7] "Core deposits" are those deposits, demand deposits and savings deposits, which are mostly interest rate inelastic. To the extent that a bank has such core deposits, it can safely engage in long-term contracts with borrowers; in particular, it can smooth loan rates. Using a large sample of loans from the Federal Reserve's Survey of Terms of Bank Lending to Business, they find that banks that are more heavily funded through core deposits do provide borrowers with smoother loan rates in response to aggregate shocks.

Kashyap, Rajan and Stein (2002) empirically analyze the link between loan commitments and demand deposits. While demand deposits are liabilities and loan commitments are assets, the two securities both commit the bank to potentially meet demands for cash. That is, depositors may withdraw their deposits and borrowers may draw on their loan commitments. To be prepared for such contingencies, each of these security types requires the bank to hold liquidity. As long as the demands for cash on loan commitments and on deposits are not perfectly correlated, there are economies of scale to holding cash against both types of contingencies. They find that banks make more loan commitments than other types of intermediaries and that, within the banking sector, banks with high ratios of transaction deposit to total deposits also have high ratios of loan commitments to total loans.

---

[7] Hannan and Berger (1991) and Neumark and Sharpe (1992) provide evidence of bank monopoly power in the retail deposit market.

The dramatic increase in loan sales constitutes a challenge, both theoretically and empirically, to arguments concerning bank existence. In a loan sale, the cash flows from a loan on a bank's balance sheet are sold to investors in the capital markets, through issuance of a new security (a secondary loan participation). This seems paradoxical: the borrowing firm could have issued a security directly to the same investor in the capital markets without going to the bank, and yet chose to borrow from a bank. The above arguments for the existence of financial intermediation imply that the bank loan should not be resold because if it can be resold there is no incentive for the bank to screen ex ante or monitor ex post. Gorton and Pennacchi (1995) explore these issues empirically, testing for the presence of incentive-compatible arrangements that could explain loan sales. One of their main findings is that the bank keeps a portion of the cash flows that is consistent with maintaining incentives. The idea is that the bank faces the same incentives as it would have had the entire loan been kept on its balance sheet. There are now a number of papers on this subject, but the basic paradox of loan sales remains unexplained. Indeed, the paradox is somewhat deepened to the extent that banks can transfer the credit risk of their loans to third parties via credit default swaps. Market participants seem to rely on banks' incentives to maintain their reputations for monitoring, but the efficacy of this mechanism is largely unexplored.

2.8. Bonds versus loans

If banks monitor borrowers in ways that cannot be accomplished by dispersed bondholders, or produce information that capital markets investors cannot produce, then how can bonds and loans coexist?[8] Why don't loans dominate bonds? This poses the question of the existence of bank loans in a different light. A number of authors have addressed this issue, attempting to differentiate between bonds and loans, in terms of their characteristics, but also in such a way that firms will demand both.

Detragiache (1994) presents a model in which firms use both bonds and loans. Bonds (or synonymously "public debt") cannot be renegotiated, while loans (synonymously "private debt") can be costlessly renegotiated. Loans are senior to bonds. Equity holders face an asset substitution problem at the initial date, and renegotiation with the bank or liquidation may occur at the interim date. In renegotiation only the senior lender, the bank, can forgive debt, so bank debt has a clear advantage. But bonds also have a role. The payoff to equity is decreasing in the amount of bonds and this helps to limit the incentive to engage in asset substitution at the interim date. Renegotiation allows equity to capture some surplus at the interim date, even if creditors are not satisfied, so risky projects can become attractive. But, if some debt is owed to creditors with whom it is impossible to renegotiate, equity's payoff is reduced and the incentive to engage in asset substitution is mitigated.

---

[8] The idea that dispersed lenders cannot renegotiate effectively compared to a single lender, like a bank, is commonly assumed. Bolton and Scharfstein (1996) provide the theoretical foundation for this notion.

In Diamond (1991), new borrowers, i.e., young firms, borrow from banks initially. Then later, based on the credit record established while being monitored by a bank, the firm can issue bonds. There are three types of borrowers. Two of these types are fixed at either Good (G) or Bad (B) while the third can choose between Bad and Good (BG). Type refers to the value of the firm's project so that if the investors knew the firm's type, its debt would be priced accordingly. Over time, investors or the bank can learn the type of the firms with a fixed type by observing whether there has been a default. Diamond (1989), with the same model, shows that, over time, a surviving BG type has a "reputation" that is consistent with being a G type, and this makes the cost of funding so low that it always chooses the Good project. In Diamond (1991) reputation effects eliminate the need for future monitoring so G types can issue bonds. Also, B types cannot benefit from monitoring, so they issue bonds that are appropriately priced. The BG types borrow from banks, which then monitor them. This result explains the coexistence of bonds and loans, but not for the same firm.

In Bolton and Freixas (2000) bank loans are valuable to firms because, unlike bonds, bank loans can be renegotiated. The problem, however, is that bank capital is costly, which makes bank loans costly relative to bonds. Firms trade off the benefits of bank loans against the cost. Cantillo (1998) also considers the cost of banks in determining the choice between loans and bonds. Outside investors lend to firms but can only verify the firms realized returns at a cost, which is necessary if there is a default on the debt. Thus, the set-up is one of costly state verification following Townsend (1979). Banks, however, are better at performing the costly state verification; banks take less time to verify than do nonbank lenders. Nevertheless, banks do not dominate nonbank lenders because they too are firms, so their returns also require costly state verification. The more banks lend, for a given amount of equity, the more likely that consumers financing the bank will have to expend costs to verify the state of the bank. Again, this causes firms that are more likely to be in financial distress to choose bank loans, whereas firms that are less likely to be in financial distress choose direct lending.

Chemmanur and Fulghieri (1994) take a different approach. They assume that some firms are more likely to be in financial distress than others. Firm type is private information. Banks are valuable to these firms if they will commit more resources to evaluating firm type in financial distress. Banks can develop a reputation for doing this. Then firms with a high likelihood of needing a bank select banks that are more committed to adding value to distressed firms because of their reputation. Firms that have a low likelihood of being in financial distress issue bonds because they do not want to pool with the riskier firms. Banks are of high and low cost types in terms of their ability to evaluate firms. The game is repeated so that over time firms learn about bank type, corresponding to a "reputation."

Cantillo and Wright (2000) empirically investigate two large panel data sets of firms to investigate the choice of firms between bonds and loans. Their evidence is consistent with their model, in which large firms that are less likely to need banks as monitors and reorganizers in the event of financial distress issue bonds. Smaller firms rely more heavily on bank loans. These determinants of choice of lender are most important during downturns.

In the papers just discussed, firms generally choose between bank loans and bonds but do not mix the two. In Section 3, we return to this issue in more detail and discuss two extensions – papers that focus on the optimal mix of bank loans and bonds, and papers that explore differences in the contractual features of these two funding sources.

2.9. Banks versus stock markets

The fact that some economies are more bank-dependent and have small or almost nonexistent stock markets raises the question of how these savings and investment organizations differ. Research on the roles of banks has been discussed above. But what function do stock markets perform? Do stock markets perform the same functions as banks, so that banks and stock markets are substitute institutions? These questions are implicitly posed by studies of Germany, for example, where the economy appears to be very successful, but where historically the economy has been organized around banks.[9] Little research has been done on these questions. In part, more economic history research is needed, but perhaps surprisingly it is also not so clear what role the stock market really performs.

Dow and Gorton (1997) present a model of the stock market in which stock prices serve two roles. First, informative stock prices can lead to efficient executive compensation. But stock prices are only informative if some traders are willing to trade on their information about projects that the firm is considering undertaking. Thus, informative stock prices have a second role: the firm can use information from stock prices in making capital budgeting decisions. In this way, the stock market performs both a screening role for projects and a monitoring role in the sense of performance-sensitive compensation. But Dow and Gorton show that a bank can also perform these roles, suggesting that banks and stock markets are alternative institutions in the savings/investment process.

By contrast, Allen (1993) and Allen and Gale (1999) argue that banks and stock markets are fundamentally different in the way that they process information. Stock markets can aggregate diverse opinions, particularly about new technologies, while banks are inherently conservative. The prediction is that stock market-based economies will embrace new technologies, while bank-based economies will be less dynamic. This appears consistent with casual observations about venture capital, and raises interesting questions about the differences between banks and venture capital.[10]

Baliga and Polak (2001) address the question of why financial systems with banks and with bonds arise and persist. They argue that an important distinction between the

---

[9] The distinction between bank-based systems and stock-market-based systems is not as stark as it is usually presented. In the case of Germany, for example, see Fohlin (1999).

[10] See also Boot and Thakor (1997).

German and Anglo-Saxon financial systems concerns not the distinction between banks and stock markets, but between bank loans and bonds. They ignore equity because equity finance was unimportant quantitatively at the start of the industrial revolution, the period that they have in mind for their model. Their model is one of moral hazard on the part of borrowers. If a borrower is monitored (bank finance), then the first best outcome can be enforced, but at a cost. If the borrower is not monitored (bonds), then only a second best outcome can be achieved, but there is no monitoring cost. There are multiple equilibria that can be Pareto-ranked. Interestingly, the Anglo–Saxon system can only persist if it is efficient, but the economy can get stuck in an inefficient German system.

Levine (2000) and Levine and Zervos (1998) are examples of the latest empirical research to explore questions about bank-based systems and stock market-based systems. The general conclusion of this literature is that the level of financial development is more critical than the relative dominance of banks or stock markets. Nevertheless, these papers focus on questions of overall economic growth rather than cross-sectional effects on different industries or firms. Differential effects such as those predicted by Allen (1993) or Allen and Gale (1999) remain largely unexamined.

3. Interactions between banks and borrowers

As discussed in the previous section, one view of banks as intermediaries focuses on their role as delegated monitors or evaluators of borrowers that hold loans as a way of making their monitoring credible. To make this basic point, however, initial models of delegated monitoring abstracted from a number of realistic complications. In terms of interaction between borrower and lender, monitoring or evaluation is a one-time affair, behavior is fixed ex ante by contract, and optimal loan contracts are quite simple. In terms of interaction among lenders, borrowers use only one lender, and if competition among lenders is modeled at all, it is assumed that there are infinite numbers of perfectly diversified intermediaries offering identical terms.

Reality is much more complex. Loan contracts often include many pages of terms and conditions ("covenants"), and some banks hold equity claims on borrowers. Terms are often selectively enforced or renegotiated as bank and borrower interact repeatedly over time. Borrowers often obtain financing from multiple sources: even small firms may have trade creditors, and larger firms often use several bank lenders or mix bank finance with funding from dispersed investors. Indeed, many loan terms govern relations between the bank and other claimants. Banks are rarely perfectly diversified and face varying degrees of competition.

In what follows, we survey research on these issues. In order to narrow the field, we emphasize work that has appeared since the beginning of the 1990s; for a survey of some of the earlier work, see Bhattacharya and Thakor (1993). Moreover, we emphasize papers that focus on monitored finance – that is, papers in which some lenders have access to information that the investing public does not have. Because work on banks as underwriters has largely focused on potential conflicts of interest between banks and investors rather than its impact on bank borrowers per se, we reserve this topic for our discussion of regulation in Section 5 below. For reasons of space, we also abstract from work on how bank lenders may influence borrowers' industry structure. [11]

3.1. Dynamic relationships and the pros and cons of bank monitoring

As noted above, early papers on delegated monitoring focused on one-time interaction between banks and borrowers and emphasized the savings from having a single investor monitor. Subsequent research has shown that a dynamic setting introduces additional pluses and minuses to delegated monitoring. On the plus side, long-term relationships between banks and borrowers allow for improved outcomes through implicit contracts enforced by concerns for reputation or future rents. On the minus side, a credible long-term relationship leaves bank and borrower locked in to one another, so the borrower may exploit the bank, the bank may exploit the borrower, or the borrower may find itself without needed funding if the bank suffers difficulties from the rest of its business. If these problems are severe, it may be better to forgo delegated monitoring entirely and rely instead on "arm's-length" finance from dispersed investors.

One of the first papers to recognize the potential gains from long-term interaction between banks and borrowers is Haubrich (1989). In single-period delegated monitoring models, there is some probability each period that the borrower will do poorly enough that the bank must monitor. Haubrich's insight is that, in a repeated relationship between bank and borrower, the bank can simply keep track of reports from the borrower and penalize the borrower if too many reports are bad. If both the bank and borrower are sufficiently patient (have discount rates close to zero), the threat of being penalized and losing funding access in the future is sufficient to make the borrower report truthfully, sparing the bank the need to monitor more closely. This is true even if the reports are not verifiable in a court of law – the relationship is sustained by a tacit ("implicit") agreement. To the extent that reviewing and tracking reports is still costly, there is still a gain to having a single bank lender rather than multiple lenders.

Boot, Greenbaum and Thakor (1993) suggest another way in which long-term relationships and implicit contracting may reduce costs compared to explicit, completely specified contracts. They start with the observation that many bank-borrower arrangements give banks a great deal of flexibility: for example, credit lines often have clauses which let the bank renege on the credit line if the borrower's situation undergoes a "material adverse change". Since many of these lines are used to back

---

[11] Examples include how cross-shareholdings or board seats between firms and banks affect tradeoffs between improved industry coordination on the one hand [e.g., Da Rin and Hellmann (1996)] and harmful anticompetitive effects on the other hand [e.g., Cantillo (1998), Adams (1999), Arping (2001)]. Other papers on how banks influence borrowers' industry structure include Maksimovic (1990), Yosha (1995), Bhattacharya and Chiesa (1995), Kanatas and Qi (2001) and Stomper (2001).

commercial paper borrowings and are meant to be used when the borrower is having trouble refinancing its commercial paper, it is not clear why borrowers pay fees for such a credit line – and yet they do.

The key insight of Boot et al. is that if the bank committed to honor the credit line no matter what, it might be forced to make good on its commitment in situations where its overall situation was weak, further weakening its financial position. The "material-adverse-change" clause allows the bank to renege in such situations. Nevertheless, the bank does not wish to renege all the time – if it did, market participants would not pay for its credit lines, hurting its future profits. By putting its reputation on the line, the bank is able to offer a product that lets it renege when its current situation is so severe that the hit to its reputation and future profits is less costly than honoring the commitment now. Of course, if this arrangement is to work, the bank must be sufficiently patient and must have future rents or quasi-rents that are sufficiently attractive; an increase in competition among banks would reduce such rents and jeopardize such implicit contracting.

There is some evidence that bank relationships do help borrowers through implicit contracting. Petersen and Rajan (1994) find that small firms that have been with their bank for a longer time (controlling for firm age) have greater access to credit, especially if they rely on a single bank rather than multiple banks. Berger and Udell (1995) find that a longer bank relationship (again controlling for firm age) lowers interest rates and collateral requirements on loan commitments. As noted in Section 2, Hoshi, Kashyap and Scharfstein (1990a,b, 1991) find that Japanese firms that are members of a *keiretsu* face lower costs of financial distress than those faced by non-member firms. Elsas and Krahnen (1998) find that troubled German firms are more likely to get additional financing if they have a "main bank" (*hausbank*) relationship. [12]

Petersen and Rajan (1995) suggest yet another way in which long-term relationships can benefit borrowers. Suppose that banks do not initially know which borrowers are good and which are bad, but do learn this over time as the firm establishes a track record for itself. Initially, firms can also unobservably choose projects with higher risk but lower returns, and their incentive to do so increases in the interest rate they are charged. If banks compete actively for loans, the rate they charge initially will reflect average credit quality, which may in turn be so high that even good firms choose risky projects, which in turn may lead to credit rationing [as per Stiglitz and Weiss (1981)]. By contrast, if banks have some market power, then they can choose a lower rate initially, knowing that they can make up any losses by earning monopoly rents on good firms in the future; this in turn may reduce initial risk-shifting incentives and thus initial credit rationing.

Petersen and Rajan test their theory by regressing the rates that small businesses pay on their loans against a number of controls for firm risk and the Herfindahl

[12] See also the references and discussion in Berger and Udell's (1998) review article on small firm finance.

index of the local banking market. Consistent with their theory, in highly concentrated banking markets, young firms are more likely to receive bank finance, and the rate of interest that firms pay declines more slowly over time, allowing banks to earn rents on survivors. [13]

The common theme of these papers is that long-term relationships increase contracting flexibility. Since the theoretic models rely on future rents or quasi-rents to maintain incentive compatibility, it follows that if increased competition among banks decreases rents, such competition should also undermine relationships. This in turn suggests a possible drawback to relationships: since bank-borrower relationships implicitly rely on lack of competition, they create an environment where the borrower is exposed to the bank's weakness or outright exploitative behavior, and vice versa.

The first paper to focus on the drawbacks of bank–borrower relationships is Sharpe (1990), who shows that a bank's monitoring activity may give it informational rents which in turn may distort borrower behavior. To see this, consider a firm's "inside" bank (one that already has a lending relationship with the firm). Based on the relationship, the inside bank will have some idea of the firm's eventual chance of success ("credit quality"); by contrast, banks that do not have a relationship with the firm ("outside banks") have not monitored and are thus relatively uninformed about the firm's credit quality. If outside banks were to offer rates that reflected average credit quality, only below-average firms would switch, and the outside banks would lose money on average. To protect themselves from this "Winner's Curse", these banks offer higher rates. This in turn lets the inside bank charge higher rates, letting it earn informational rents on above-average quality firms. [14] Higher borrowing rates discourage investment by good firms with established bank relationships. Moreover, even if initial competition for unattached borrowers causes banks to compete away these subsequent rents, this gives too much capital to firms that are unproven.

Rajan (1992) takes this analysis further in several ways. Unlike Sharpe, he explicitly models agency problems between a firm and its investors that may make delegated

---

[13] In related work, Fischer (2000) finds that German firms in more concentrated banking markets are less credit-constrained and transfer more information to their lender; also, banks provide more liquidity if they have received such information. Bonaccorsi di Patti and Dell'Ariccia (2001) examine the impact of local bank concentration on rates of firm creation in Italy. They find that less competitive banking markets have lower rates of firm creation on average, but the opposite is true in industries with low fixed assets, which they argue proxies for high asymmetric information. At a "macro" level, Cetorelli and Gambera (2001) examine how cross-country differences in banking sector concentration affects different industries' growth rates. They find that more concentrated banking sectors lower average growth rates, but do increase the growth rates of industries that have very high external finance needs.

[14] Strictly speaking, Sharpe's analysis of the Winner's Curse is incorrect, since he assumes that a pure strategy equilibrium in rate-setting exists. Broecker's (1990) analysis of bidding by multiple banks with private signals of borrower quality suggests that the equilibrium should involve mixed strategies (randomized rate-setting); this holds in Rajan's (1992) setting, and von Thadden (2003) shows that this holds in Sharpe's setting as well. Nevertheless, the informed bank does earn positive rents on average, so Sharpe's basic intuition is correct.

monitoring attractive. Specifically, a firm's eventual chance of success is determined by the unobservable costly effort of its entrepreneur. After this initial exertion of effort, an interim private and unverifiable signal reveals whether the firm will be successful or not; if not, it is efficient to liquidate the firm promptly rather than let it continue. If a single investor ("bank") holds the firm's debt, it also sees this signal, but free-rider problems are assumed to rule this out when investors are dispersed ("arm's-length finance").

First, if the bank holds short-term debt, it can threaten to liquidate the firm regardless of the interim signal, triggering renegotiation of the loan. If the bank's bargaining power in renegotiation is high, it can hold up the entrepreneur for a high share of any surplus; knowing this will happen, the entrepreneur underinvests in effort. Long-term bank debt removes the hold-up problem by removing the bank's ability to threaten to liquidate the borrower. The *borrower* can still initiate negotiations if liquidation is efficient, capturing a share of any liquidation proceeds. The drawback to this arrangement is that, ex ante, the borrower's incentive to put effort into assuring good future outcomes is reduced, since the borrower effectively gets some insurance against bad outcomes that lead to liquidation. If the bank has a lot of bargaining power, long-term bank debt is better: renegotiations favor the bank, so short-term debt would lead to excessively high rents whereas long-term debt gives the borrower little insurance against liquidation. When bank bargaining power is low, the opposite is true.

Second, Rajan considers the incentive effects of arm's-length finance from dispersed lenders. Since arm's-length lenders are poorly informed, their decisions to renew loans or demand immediate repayment forcing liquidation are not efficient. Moreover, since they will charge a rate to protect themselves from inefficient continuation/liquidation decisions, the borrower's initial investment decisions may also be distorted. Nevertheless, for intermediate levels of bank bargaining power, arm's-length finance may dominate both types of bank finance.

Finally, Rajan endogenizes bargaining power by allowing for interim competition between an "inside" bank, which has monitored and knows the firm's situation, and uninformed "outside" banks. As in Sharpe (1990), the "Winner's Curse" lets the inside bank earn rents on average; the greater the information advantage, the greater the rents and thus the bank's effective bargaining power. If a firm's chance of success ("quality") is high, the inside bank's information advantage is small, and there is little difference between bank finance and arm's-length finance. At intermediate quality levels, bank finance dominates, while at lower quality levels, the informed bank's information advantage is so high that the benefits of efficient liquidation are outweighed by the bank's high rents and the entrepreneur's consequent underinvestment in effort.

Dinc (2000) examines how such informational rents affect banks' ability to sustain implicit relationship lending arrangements. In his model, it is ex ante efficient for bank lenders to commit to rescue firms that are distressed but not outright failures; however, because much of the benefits from such rescues flow to the entrepreneur, it is not in a bank's interest ex post to rescue the firm. Although the bank can be compensated by giving it higher payments when the firm is successful, in one-shot arm's-length lending, the bank always reneges on rescues ex post. In a repeated-game setting, so long as banks do not discount future profits too much, they may be able to establish reputations for rescuing distressed firms and so capture relationship rents. Such implicit contracting is impossible if too few banks compete: informational monopoly lets the lender set its rate so high that any additional gains to maintaining a good reputation are too small to prevent reneging. On the other hand, if too many banks compete, rents from maintaining a good reputation are reduced, and once again banks renege.[15] Thus, relationship lending can only be sustained for an intermediate number of banks.

As noted by Detragiache, Garella and Guiso (2000), another implication of the "Winner's Curse" is that firms that rely on a bank may be hurt if that bank faces financial distress. Intuitively, a distressed bank may have difficulty supplying its good borrowers with sufficient credit for their needs. If instead these borrowers try to switch to new banks, the "Winner's Curse" problem will be especially severe because the inside bank's mix of loans is known to be worse than average. As a result, good borrowers of a distressed bank may find that additional financing is very expensive or perhaps even nonexistent.

In Section 2, we noted that Slovin, Sushka and Polonchek (1993) find evidence that Continental Illinois Bank's near-failure in 1984 had a significant negative impact on firms for whom Continental was the main bank. Moreover, since their results focus on firms with *some* access to public markets (those with publicly-traded stock), it seems likely that smaller firms without such access were hit even harder. Kang and Stulz (2000) find similar effects when examining how Japan's long-drawn banking crisis of the 1990s affected firms that were dependent on bank finance.

By themselves, these findings do not prove that bank relationships are wholly bad; after all, before the banks in these samples got into trouble, they may have been critical in funding their relationship borrowers. Nevertheless, to the extent that a relationship with a single bank leads to possible hold-up problems or overexposure to that bank's risk, firms may wish to establish multiple bank relationships, breaking a single bank's information monopoly and diversifying exposure to any one bank's risk.[16] Jean-Baptiste (2001) shows how multiple relationships mitigate the hold-up problem. Detragiache, Garella and Guiso (2000) examine the diversification argument. They find that, when asymmetric information concerns are high, firms opt for multiple banks; the risk of being denied funding if the firm relies on a single bank that gets into trouble

---

[15] A key difference between Rajan (1992) and Dinc (2000) is that, in Rajan, only the inside bank has private information, so it alone earns informational rents; in Dinc, all competing banks get (costless) private signals, and in equilibrium they earn positive informational rents that decline with the number of banks.

[16] Carletti (2000) shows that having multiple banks has the drawback of decreasing each bank's incentive to monitor; however, total monitoring may increase if monitoring costs are sufficiently convex in monitoring intensity.

is too great. Similarly, the number of relationships should increase as bank fragility increases.[17]

Empirical tests of the number of bank relationships per firm yield mixed results. For example, using data on Italian firms, Detragiache et al. generally find support for their model's predictions: if bank liquidity shocks are high or bank size is low, firms are more likely to opt for multiple banks and more likely to have more relationships once they go to multiple banks. By contrast, Foglia, Laviola and Reedtz (1998) examine Italian data and find that multiple bank relationships tend to be associated with greater borrower risk; however, they do not control for bank fragility. Similarly, Farinha and Santos (2002) examine Portuguese data and find that firms with greater growth opportunities, less liquidity, or greater bank dependence are more likely to switch to multiple bank relationships, all of which is consistent with reducing hold-up problems. Ongena and Smith (2000a,b) examine how the number of bank relationships per firm varies across different countries. They find that, for low levels of bank fragility (measured by credit rating), the number of relationships per firm decreases as fragility increases, but the relationship does become positive at higher levels of bank fragility; however, they do not control for firm risk.

A final piece of evidence comes from Houston and James (1996), who examine the mix of bank debt and public (i.e., arm's-length) debt for a sample of publicly-traded USA firms. To the extent the hold-up problem of Sharpe (1990) and Rajan (1992) is significant, it is likely to be most costly for firms that have many growth opportunities that need funding, and so these firms should use more public debt. Conversely, if the hold-up problem is not an issue, the advantages of relationship lending should make bank debt more attractive for firms with greater growth opportunities. Houston and James find that firms with a single bank relationship tend to rely less on bank debt as growth opportunities are higher, but the opposite is true for firms with multiple bank relationships. This is consistent with the notion that having multiple bank relationships mitigates the hold-up problem.[18]

In sum, theory and evidence both suggest pros and cons to bank–borrower relationships. Benefits include increased flexibility and access to funding; drawbacks include hold-up problems and negative spillovers from bank fragility. Which of these is dominant depends critically on both the nature of the borrowing firm and the nature of the banks that the firm has access to. Increased competition among banks tends to undermine relationships, but too much monopoly power may have the same effect.

---

[17] If the probability of bank liquidity problems is very high, however, firms switching banks face *less* of an adverse selection problem: outside banks know that the firm is more likely to switch because its old bank had problems rather than because the firm is a "lemon". Thus, for high bank fragility, single banking may again dominate.

[18] For further references on the pros and cons of bank relationships, see the survey by Boot (2000).

3.2. Monitoring and loan structure

The papers just discussed generally assume that a firm is funded either by one bank or by many dispersed lenders with loans of the same size, that a single bank lender costlessly monitors whereas dispersed lenders do not, and that any debt has a simple structure. We now discuss research that has focused on these missing details: how bank monitoring interacts with loan features and a borrower's overall financial structure.

As noted at the beginning of this section, bank loans are often quite complex, and the terms are often renegotiated over time. Moreover, if one compares bank loans and other privately-held debt with publicly-held bonds and notes, privately-held debt typically has more covenants and other terms and is much more likely to be renegotiated than publicly-held debt. These general facts make sense if banks are to be delegated monitors; after all, complex covenants are only useful if the lender observes whether these have been violated, and dispersed lenders will lead to duplication of effort and free-riding problems in monitoring. Similarly, renegotiation is likely to be inefficient if lenders are poorly-informed or dispersed ("arm's-length" lending); again, see Bolton and Scharfstein (1996).

These ideas have led to a more dynamic view of loan features. In the old view, best represented by Smith and Warner (1979), covenants and repayment schedules simply prevent borrowers from exploiting lenders. For example, a borrower may shift into a riskier line of business, capturing any increased upside over and above the promised payments on the debt while using limited liability to share any increased downside with the lender ("risk-shifting" or "asset-substitution"); a covenant forbidding change of business focus prevents this. In the new view, covenants and repayment schedules are tripwires which give an informed lender the right to threaten the borrower with default, after which renegotiation can occur. In our example, a lender faced with a borrower's proposal to change to a riskier line of business can make several choices. If the change is a reaction to deteriorating conditions, and the firm's assets are best used elsewhere, the lender can force default and liquidation. If the change is truly the best option, the bank can simply increase the interest rate to reflect increased risk, and perhaps tighten other terms to prevent any increased chance of future exploitation.

Berlin and Mester (1992) are among the first to model these issues [though see Berlin and Loeys (1988)]. They show that the ability to renegotiate covenants can substantially improve their usefulness, because renegotiation allows the use of unverifiable information that the borrower and lender may have. If the borrower's actual situation is poor, the borrower can comply with the covenant, eschewing exploitative behavior and preventing default. If the borrower's actual situation is good, so that violating the covenant is actually good for overall firm value, the borrower can violate the covenant knowing that it will be in the lender's interest to renegotiate rather than allow default and associated costs to occur. As a result, in settings where lenders are concentrated (so that the lenders have more incentive to be informed and renegotiation is easier), covenants can be set more stringently, improving overall firm value on an ex ante basis. Since the value of allowing renegotiation increases with the ex ante risk of the borrower, private debt contracts should be more prevalent among riskier borrowers.

Berlin and Mester's work has some weaknesses. First, renegotiation is possible only when the covenant is tripped, so it is possible that the firm may actually be in trouble based on unverifiable information and yet its covenants are not violated. In such a case, a loan with short-term maturity would be better, since the bank could use all information (verifiable or not) in deciding whether to renew the loan or instead call for immediate repayment, triggering default. Second, the bank observes the borrower's condition at no cost, abstracting from the need to provide the bank with incentives to monitor. Subsequent research has addressed both issues.[19]

One problem with a short-term loan is the hold-up problem of Sharpe (1990) and Rajan (1992); indeed, Rajan shows that a severe hold-up problem may make long-term bank debt attractive. One can then think of long-term debt with covenants as a happy medium: unlike pure long-term debt, this gives the bank *some* power to force renegotiation, but this power is limited to cases where verifiable information suggests that the firm is likely to be in trouble.

Rajan and Winton (1995) highlight another possible disadvantage of short-term loans: paradoxically, by restricting the bank's power to call for repayment, long-term debt with covenants may increase the bank's incentive to monitor in the first place. Suppose that a firm has a number of claimants besides the bank (trade creditors, shareholders, etc.). Two signals of the firm's condition are available: a free but noisy public signal, and a costly but more precise private signal that is only partially verifiable. If the public signal is not too noisy, a bank that holds short-term debt may prefer to rely on this signal; the bank would bear the entire cost of the private signal, but the benefits of more efficient continuation/liquidation decisions would accrue to all claimants. By allowing the bank to call the loan only when costly verifiable information suggests that the firm is in trouble, long-term debt with covenants forces the bank to observe the private signal. Of course, if the public signal is very imprecise (as for very young firms), even a bank with short-term debt will monitor; conversely, if the public signal is very precise, costly monitoring is unnecessary, and the firm can rely on publicly-held arm's-length debt. These results are consistent with the fact that firms that rely on long-term privately-placed debt tend to be larger and older than firms that rely on relatively short-term bank debt, whereas both types of firms tend to be smaller than firms that issue public debt.

Gorton and Kahn (2000) explore a different aspect of the dynamic nature of bank loans. Suppose that an entrepreneur who borrows money may engage in two forms of moral hazard: as in Rajan (1992), he may continue the firm when liquidation is

---

[19] A more technical issue is that Berlin and Mester focus on the case where the verifiable information in covenants is almost perfectly correlated with the firm's actual (unverifiable) situation, ruling out comparative statics on the relative precision of verifiable information.

more efficient, and he may also choose to increase the firm's risk in continuation even though this increase in risk is costly. There are situations where it is better to forgive some of the debt so as to deter additional risk-shifting rather than forcing liquidation, but this requires that the debt be held by a single lender so as to allow renegotiation. Even with a single bank lender, short-term debt may lead to excessive liquidation, and so it may be better to give the bank long-term debt with limited ability to call the loan early. The upshot is that, for bank debt, initial terms are not set to price default risk but rather are set to efficiently balance bargaining power in later renegotiation, and renegotiated interest rates may not be monotonic in firm risk.

Yet another strand of research has focused on how the need for bank monitoring affects the mix of bank debt and public debt and the allocation of maturity or seniority between these two groups of creditors. One early paper on this topic is Besanko and Kanatas (1993). As in Rajan (1992), entrepreneurs require outside financing, which then reduces their incentive to exert effort. A bank can force the entrepreneur to exert effort ("monitor") at a cost that is increasing in the effort level desired, but such monitoring is not contractible. Since the bank chooses monitoring levels without considering the entrepreneur's cost of effort, it is optimal to use some public debt as a way of reducing the bank's claim on the firm and thus its incentive to monitor excessively.

Besanko and Kanatas say little about the relative priority or maturity of bank and public creditors. A starting point for this topic can be found in the work of Diamond (1993a,b) and Berglof and von Thadden (1994). In these papers, splitting a firm's financing into a short-term senior component and a long-term junior component creates a credible threat of liquidation: the firm's value in liquidation may be enough to satisfy short-term senior debtholders even if junior claimants would prefer to let the firm continue. An appropriate mix of short-term senior debt and long-term junior debt balances credible liquidation *threats* against *actual* inefficient liquidation in a way that either forces the firm to avoid risk-shifting (Berglof and von Thadden) or minimizes the firm's total cost of capital (Diamond).

Although Diamond (1993b) argues that an active monitor should hold short-term senior debt and focus on deciding when to liquidate the firm, none of these papers explicitly analyze monitoring incentives. It is not immediately clear that active monitors should be senior; if a senior secured creditor's claim is safe regardless of what happens to the firm, the creditor will have no incentive to monitor. Models of costly state verification such as Winton (1995b) suggest that the investor with greatest monitoring skills or lowest costs should be most junior and thus monitor more often, and indeed, venture capital and other private equity funds hold relatively junior claims and monitor intensively.

On the other hand, bank loans are often secured, hence senior to other debt. If banks are active monitors, it follows that their security cannot make them completely safe. Rajan and Winton (1995) show that giving the bank collateral can improve monitoring incentives if the collateral's value is sensitive to inefficient continuation of the firm's current business strategy. In this case, the bank must monitor the firm's situation so that it can use the threat of calling the loan to force the firm to adopt a more conservative policy or even outright liquidation so as to preserve the value of the bank's collateral. Examples of collateral with this feature include inventory and accounts receivable, both of which may suffer drastic declines in value if the borrowing firm continues to run its operations inefficiently. By contrast, a loan secured by real estate whose value was independent of the firm's operations would give the bank little incentive to monitor. [20]

Although Rajan and Winton explore a mechanism where the bank's taking of additional collateral signals to public creditors that the borrower is in trouble, they do not examine the implications that this has for the optimal mix of public versus private debt. Repullo and Suarez (1998) focus on this mix in a somewhat simpler setting. An entrepreneur borrows money now and exerts costly effort that increases his firm's chance of eventual success; if it does not succeed, the firm is worth zero. If the firm is liquidated at an interim date, proceeds are less than the initial investment amount, but this may still be better than letting the firm continue if initial effort is too low and the chance of failure is high. For a fixed cost, an investor can commit to monitor the entrepreneur's effort choice at this interim date.

If liquidation values are low or the entrepreneur has sufficient investable wealth, uninformed finance (arm's length debt or equity) is optimal. If liquidation values are high relative to the entrepreneur's wealth, it is optimal to have a single investor (bank) monitor and hold short-term debt, forcing liquidation if the entrepreneur does not exert enough effort. For intermediate levels, however, giving the bank all of the firm's debt does not achieve first-best effort: if the entrepreneur deviates slightly from this effort level, the bank's share of future proceeds in success is high enough that it prefers to let the firm continue rather than forcing liquidation. In this case, giving junior debt to arm's length investors restores the credibility of the bank's liquidation threat by shrinking the bank's share of future proceeds relative to its senior claim on liquidation proceeds. As liquidation value falls, the optimal mix of debt shifts towards public (junior) debt and away from private (senior) debt.

A weakness with this model is that it requires that the bank can commit to monitoring. Without commitment, the bank would not monitor if it knew that the entrepreneur would choose first-best effort for sure, and this lack of monitoring would in turn reduce the entrepreneur's effort incentives. Park (2000) examines monitoring choice when commitment is impossible. He shows that it is optimal to give the bank senior debt that is *not* fully collateralized, so that the bank is somewhat impaired when it forces interim liquidation. This gives the bank an incentive to monitor so that it only liquidates when liquidation is efficient. Even so, subject to this incentive constraint, it is best to use as little senior bank debt as possible; otherwise, as in Repullo and Suarez (1998), the liquidation threat is less credible. Note the contrast with the results

---

[20] Along similar lines, Manove, Padilla and Pagano (2001) show that if entrepreneurs have sufficiently high low-risk collateral, similar considerations undermine banks' incentives to screen good entrepreneurial projects from bad ones.

of Besanko and Kanatas (1993). In Besanko and Kanatas, monitoring automatically forces the entrepreneur to exert effort, and the problem with too much bank debt is excessive monitoring. In Park, monitoring only forces effort through the liquidation threat, and too much bank debt undermines efficient liquidation.

Longhofer and Santos (2000) provide another motivation for making banks senior to other creditors, one that combines monitoring incentives with active benefits from relationship lending. For relationship lending to have value, the bank must have incentive not only to monitor the borrowing firm's situation but also to help the firm when times are bad but the firm is essentially sound, which is just when uninformed investors are unwilling to lend more money. If the bank had a junior claim, it might not be willing to advance the firm *additional* money in bad times. This is a version of the underinvestment problem of Myers (1977): in bad times, even senior creditors' claims may be somewhat risky, in which case some of the benefit from the bank's additional investment flows to the senior creditors. If the bank is senior, it internalizes this benefit and is willing to lend in bad times.

These theories of public and private debt are consistent with a number of stylized facts: bank loans tend to be secured and relatively short-term, public debt is more likely to be subordinated or relatively long-term, etc. Nevertheless, there has been relatively little empirical work on the detailed implications of these theories. As noted in Section 2, James (1995, 1996) finds that, for firms in financial distress, banks generally do not make concessions unless public debt holders do, and banks typically make fewer concessions than public debt holders. This is consistent with the view that banks hold more senior claims and are tougher negotiators than public, more junior debt holders.

Other empirical work has focused on how the mix of public debt and bank debt varies with firm characteristics. As noted above, Houston and James (1996) find that firms that rely on a single bank use more public debt as growth opportunities are larger, which is consistent with the view that firms with lower tangible assets (and thus liquidation value) should use more public debt. Although Houston and James find that the opposite relationship holds for firms with multiple banks, they note that multiple banks are a step in the direction of public, diffusely-held debt. Johnson (1997) finds that the proportion of firm debt held by banks is greater as the firm has a lower market to book value ratio, which again is consistent with a positive link between public debt and growth opportunities. He also finds that smaller and younger firms use more bank debt, consistent with the notion that banks focus on firms with relatively greater information costs. In a study of initial public debt offerings, Datta et al. (2000) find that the negative average stock price response to these offerings is mitigated for firms with higher growth opportunities. Since such offerings reduce the fraction of financing provided by bank debt, this too is consistent with the notion that firms with fewer tangible assets should use more public debt. On the other hand, one could argue that this is simply a case where having well-known positive NPV projects mitigates the "lemons"-type announcement effect of issuing securities.

The upshot is that many of the complexities found in actual loan contracts – seniority, collateral, covenants – can be motivated as mechanisms for fine-tuning the bank's monitoring and control incentives as a function of firm characteristics. The same applies to the mix of (concentrated) bank debt and (diffuse) public debt.

3.3. Beyond lending: equity stakes, board seats, and monitoring

Thus far, we have assumed that banks only make loans, i.e., they do not hold equity. Although this is generally the case in the USA, other countries have allowed banks to hold equity, Japan and Germany being well-known examples. Moreover, as James (1995) shows, USA banks have been allowed to take equity as a consequence of loan restructuring, and in many cases they hold these stakes for a considerable time after the restructuring. Banks may also gain power over firms by proxy voting of shares that the banks hold in trust.[21] Finally, even in the United States, bank officers may sit on the board of directors of firms to which they lend. In this subsection, we discuss research on how a bank's relationship with a borrower is affected by having the bank hold shares, vote proxies, or occupy board seats.

At first glance, allowing banks to hold equity has several potential advantages. In a discussion piece, Stiglitz (1985) argues that, although institutional shareholders might have goals more aligned with value-maximization, their shareholdings are usually too small to give them much direct control. By contrast, banks have a lever of control that an institution holding 1% of a firm's shares does not have – namely, the ability to refuse to renew loans. Since lenders get at most a fixed payment (interest plus principle), they care little about a firm's upside and much more about its downside. To the extent they exercise control over management, they will focus on avoiding bad outcomes; moreover, for large firms with extremely low chances of default, banks may simply do nothing. If banks hold significant equity stakes along with their loans, then they would care more about maximizing overall firm value.

John, John and Saunders (1994) examine this issue in a simple model of firm risk-taking. If a bank's loan covenants give it effective veto power over the borrower's choice of project risk, then allowing bank holdings of equity does improve the efficiency of the borrower's risk choice; the intuition is precisely that of Stiglitz. The downside is that, because all else equal equity is riskier than debt, and because the firm chooses a higher (albeit more efficient) level of risk, holding equity increases the bank's overall portfolio risk. Thus, allowing banks to hold equity may exacerbate costs linked to bank failure.[22]

---

[21] Although voting shares held in trust is typically associated with German banks [see Gorton and Schmid (2000)], Haubrich and Santos (2002) show that modern-day USA bank trust departments also have significant voting powers.
[22] On the other hand, if the bank is a relatively passive investor, John, John, and Saunders show that letting the bank hold equity is more likely to *reduce* the risk of both the firm and the bank. The intuition follows Green (1984). If the bank holds only debt, the firm's controlling shareholders engage in some

Mahrt-Smith (2000) shows that bank holdings of equity have another advantage: they can reduce the hold-up problem analyzed in Rajan (1992). In Mahrt-Smith's model, a firm that has already received funds from an informed inside bank needs financing for additional investment. As in Rajan, the Winner's Curse faced by outside banks gives the inside bank informational rents which in turn distort the firm's investment decisions. If the inside bank holds both debt and equity, then any debt that outside banks provide is senior to the inside bank's equity claim. The more the inside bank's claim consists of equity, the more senior and so the less risky are the outside banks' claims. Less risk means less sensitivity to information, diminishing the Winner's Curse problem faced by the outside banks. Thus, having the inside bank hold equity reduces the informational rent earned by that bank. The caveat is that, as in Jensen and Meckling (1976), greater use of external equity finance reduces the amount of effort that the firm's owner exerts, and so there is a cost to having the firm's inside bank hold equity. Because the ability to reduce the outside bank's risk is tied to the firm's need for additional funds, bank equity holdings are most attractive for financing firms with high growth potential.

Berlin, John and Saunders (1996) focus on how a bank's shareholdings in a firm affect potential collusion between the bank and the firm against the interests of other nonequity stakeholders. Bank debt is assumed to be senior to the stakeholders' claims, and the firm and the bank observe an interim signal of the firm's situation, whereas the stakeholders do not. If the signal is good and the firm is really healthy, the firm and the bank may collude to convince stakeholders that the firm is distressed and concessions are required from creditors; these unnecessary concessions boost the firm's profits. The bank finds this attractive only if its equity share of the increase in profits offsets the concessions it must make on its debt. This puts a cap on the optimal amount of equity the bank can hold. On the other hand, if the firm is really distressed and concessions are required to prevent costly bankruptcy, the bank and the firm may collude to convince the stakeholders that the firm is healthy. This is a problem when deadweight bankruptcy costs are small, so that the bank prefers its senior claim on net bankruptcy proceeds to making concessions. In this case, having the bank hold some equity subordinates part of its claim to the stakeholders and rules out the bank's incentive to collude.

One caveat to Mahrt-Smith (2000) and Berlin, John and Saunders (1996) is that subordinating the bank's loans accomplishes the same ends as having the bank hold equity. Indeed, in Mahrt-Smith's model, subordinated debt dominates equity because it does not cause under-exertion of effort by the firm's owner. Berlin, John, and Saunders suggest that the bank may not be able to credibly subordinate its debt claim because it could always take additional collateral when the firm's position begins to deteriorate.

---

risk-shifting, so firm risk and thus the bank's loan risk are inefficiently high. Equity lets the bank share in the firm's upside potential, diminishing the controlling shareholders' gains from risk-shifting. Santos (1999) pursues the implications that this has for optimal regulation, and finds that regulation restricting bank equity holdings is either not binding or inefficient.

This would be most applicable to firms with many collateralizable assets. All else equal, such firms also tend to have lower bankruptcy costs, so this is consistent with their prediction that bank equity holdings are most useful for firms with small bankruptcy costs.

A more far-reaching objection to these models is that, even in countries where banks are permitted to hold equity, bank portfolios overwhelmingly favor loans over shareholdings. Santos (1998) finds that, as of year-end 1995, bank shares and equity participations were less than five percent of bank assets in a number of developed countries, including the G7. Germany, Japan, and Switzerland topped the list with shareholdings at 4.8%, 4.6%, and 4.9% of total bank assets, respectively.[23] Large banks in these countries had somewhat greater shareholdings, but even in Germany (the highest), shareholdings for large banks were only 6.3% of assets. Moreover, Mahrt-Smith and Berlin, John, and Saunders motivate bank shareholdings as a way to resolve frictions between a well-informed inside bank and uninformed outsiders, yet there is evidence that bank shareholdings tend to focus on the shares of large, publicly-traded firms, where such information asymmetries should be smallest. For example, Saunders and Walter (1994) report that, in 1989, German banks as a group held only .6% of all industrial firms' shares, but roughly 5% of the top 100 firms' shares. Thus, there must be some countervailing friction that weighs against bank shareholdings in general and bank shareholdings in smaller firms in particular.

Winton (2001) motivates these patterns as responses to banks' liquidity considerations. When a bank seeks funding to meet unexpected withdrawals, loan takedowns, and so forth, there is some chance that this funding must be explicitly or implicitly backed by the bank's claims on firms that it monitors. These are precisely the assets on which the bank has more information than its providers of funds have, giving rise to an adverse selection problem. In equilibrium, the bank prefers to let some liquidity needs go unmet, creating liquidity costs. Because, all else equal, equity is more risky, hence more exposed to inside information, than debt, the bank can minimize adverse selection costs by holding debt rather than equity. Of course, the bank can hold *some* equity without having a high chance that it will have to use these assets as backing for funding, but the bulk of its claims on firms that it monitors should be debt. Similarly, because the bank's information advantage is smallest for large, publicly-traded firms, holding equity in these firms leads to fewer adverse selection costs. Finally, to the extent that larger banks are better diversified against individual customer liquidity needs, they are less likely to face very severe liquidity needs, so they are able to hold more equity as a fraction of assets.

Thus far, our discussion has focused on the impact of bank shareholdings in terms of cash flow rights: Stiglitz, Mahrt-Smith, and Berlin, John, and Saunders emphasize

---

[23] Because these numbers include equity investments in financial firms, some of which may be unconsolidated affiliates, Santos' numbers may overstate the extent of bank shareholdings in unaffiliated firms.

shares' junior status and their claim to the firm's potential upside, and Winton focuses on the higher risk and thus information-sensitivity that these features create. Shares' voting rights provide banks with control rights over and above those associated with bank loans, and a bank with a significant equity stake in a firm may be pivotal in proxy or takeover contests. Such control rights can be amplified beyond the bank's actual shareholdings if it uses stock pyramids to concentrate its voting power, or if it can exercise the votes of shares that it holds in trust for investors. Moreover, whether through shareholdings or through their role as lenders, banks may use their influence to win seats on a firm's board of directors. We conclude this segment with a discussion of research on these issues.

There has been relatively little theoretical research on how the additional control rights possible through shares or board seats affect optimal contracting between a bank and its borrower. By contrast, such modeling is very common in work on venture capital, where, in contrast to bank loans, contracts typically provide far more control rights and far more upside via equity or conversion features.[24] Although there has been little work on the circumstances in which venture capital financing dominates traditional bank lending, von Thadden (1995) is a partial exception: he does not explicitly model debt versus equity lending contracts, but he does show that giving delegated monitors significant control rights and claims on a firm's cash flow "upside" is optimal in circumstances that resemble venture capital.

In von Thadden's model, an entrepreneur chooses between short- and long-term projects. Interim returns reveal information about the project's innate quality, and this is the *only* information about project quality that the entrepreneur and arm's-length investors receive. There are cases where long-term projects are ex ante optimal, yet the firm has a high chance of poor interim returns and should be liquidated if these occur. Short-term arm's-length finance implements such liquidation, but it may cause the entrepreneur to myopically prefer the short-term project, which has a higher chance of good interim returns. By monitoring at a cost, a "bank" can get clearer information on the firm's eventual chance of success, avoiding inefficient liquidation based on interim returns alone and achieving first-best results. The contract that implements the first-best outcome is a long-term contract that gives the "bank" total control over project continuation but requires that the bank compensate the entrepreneur whenever the interim return is poor, even if the project is then liquidated.

There are two critical ways in which this model differs from "standard" models of bank control such as Rajan (1992). First, the "bank" can learn information that even the entrepreneur does not have. Second, monitoring is optimal for projects that are very likely to be (optimally) liquidated, yet have a very small chance of producing very high returns. It follows that the "bank" gets most of its return in unlikely but very high return states. Both features resemble venture capital settings: the venture capitalist

[24] For further discussion of venture capital contracting, see Sahlman (1990) and Kaplan and Strömberg (2001).

typically has more financial and general business expertise than the entrepreneur, and most target firms do poorly and are terminated but a few offset this by doing very well. Nevertheless, von Thadden does not model the "bank's" incentives to monitor, nor does he allow for intermediate levels of monitoring that would correspond to bank lenders being less informed than venture capitalists but better informed than arm's-length investors. The choice between bank loans and venture capital remains largely unmodeled.

Empirical work on bank control rights through shareholdings and board seats typically focuses on two competing hypotheses. On the one hand, it is possible that these additional control rights enhance bank's ability to control firm agency problems in a positive way. On the other hand, because a bank's shareholdings are typically small relative to its loans to and other dealings with a firm, the bank may emphasize policies that help it at the expense of shareholders as a group.[25]

Findings depend critically on the economic and institutional environment in which banks operate. Examining German banks in 1975 and 1986, Gorton and Schmid (2000) find that banks use their shareholdings and board representation to improve firm performance. They find little evidence that banks use their voting powers for shares held in trust, whether for good or bad. Gorton and Schmid also find that banks' use of control is more beneficial than that of a nonblank blockholder. This suggests that bank blockholders are less likely to emphasize private benefits that harm shareholder value, perhaps because banks' "private benefits" take the form of loans, which do benefit from improved firm performance. Similar results are found by Kaplan and Minton (1994), who find that Japanese banks are more likely to get seats on a firm's board following poor performance by the firm, and that turnover of incumbent top executives increases in the year of the appointment. On the other hand, Weinstein and Yafeh (1998) and Morck, Nakamura and Shivdasani (2000) find that Japanese firms with a main bank relationship tend to have lower growth and profitability and pay higher interest rates than firms without such relationships, and the effects tend to rise with the fraction of shares held by the main bank. Although the results on growth might be due to selection bias (banks prefer to hold more shares in more stable firms), the results on interest expense suggest that banks are not entirely innocent of pursuing private benefits of control.

By contrast with these results, Kroszner and Strahan (2001a,b) find that USA banks are more likely to sit on the boards of firms that are large and stable, have high proportions of tangible assets, and rely little on short-term financing. Although these firms are more likely to borrow from a bank that has seats on their board than from other banks, this does not seem to alter loan terms: the terms do not differ significantly from those of loans that the same bank makes to similar firms whose board it does

---

[25] This is a variant of the corporate governance concern that shareholders with more voting power than cash-flow rights tend to pursue private benefits of control rather than enhancement of shareholder value. See the discussion and references in Chapter 1 by Becht, Bolton and Roell in this volume.

not sit on. Kroszner and Strahan interpret this as evidence that USA legal doctrines such as equitable subordination and lender liability discourage banks from sitting on boards of firms that have high expected costs of financial distress, and from sitting on boards of informationally-opaque firms where conflicts of interest might be easier to hide, hence more tempting.[26] Also, see Gilson (1990).

3.4. Banking sector structure and lending

We now turn to research on how banking sector structure interacts with banks' role as delegated monitors of borrowing firms. This research largely falls into two broad and overlapping areas: the role of scale economies or diseconomies in monitoring, and the role of economies of scope in monitoring.

Much of the literature on scale economies in monitoring focuses on the role of diversification. In the early work on delegated monitoring discussed in Section 2, a better-diversified bank is better able to resolve the agency concerns of its own investors, giving it a funding advantage. Since fixed costs of monitoring or evaluating borrowers are at the heart of these models, it follows that, rather than diversifying by making smaller loans to more borrowers, it is cheaper to diversify by keeping loan size fixed and lending to more borrowers. For this reason, larger banks should find it cheaper to diversify than small banks, giving them an efficiency advantage.

The early papers did not go much beyond this insight. In Diamond (1984), a single bank is examined in isolation; in Boyd and Prescott (1986) or Williamson (1986), infinite numbers of perfectly diversified banks compete perfectly. Also, all of these papers assumed that all loans are stochastically independent of one another, and that the marginal cost of monitoring additional loans is constant, so that infinitely-diversified banks offer depositors risk-free investments. In reality, there are only finite numbers of different borrowers, default risk across loans is partly systematic (defaults rise in recessions), and larger banks may face various diseconomies of scale. All of these issues have been the focus of later research into banking sector structure.

Yanelle (1989, 1997) and Winton (1995a, 1997) focus on how the finiteness of the economy affects equilibrium banking sector structure. As Yanelle (1989) notes, one immediate problem is that when finite numbers of banks compete for finite numbers of depositors and borrowers, the paradigm of perfect Bertrand (price) competition is not reasonable. To see why, suppose that two banks are competing; one offers a lower lending rate than the other, but the bank with the higher rate has offered a higher rate on its deposits and is expected to capture the deposit market. All else equal, a borrower

---

[26] Under equitable subordination, a bank that is found to have exercised managerial control over and above what any arm's length lender might do may have all its claims subordinated to those of other creditors. Lender liability allows creditors to sue the bank if it has exercised such control. Berlin and Mester (2001) show that these features can be an optimal way of getting a large investor to both monitor and try to assure good outcomes for the firm as a whole – if a court finds that the investor misused its private information and control rights, it is subordinated and so penalized.

that chooses the bank with lower lending rates might find itself at a bank without any funds to lend. If everyone expects this to be the case, the bank with higher rates may end up capturing the market.

A related feature of these models is the existence of multiple equilibria. This is due to "adoption externalities", where a depositor's or borrower's utility from a given bank's offered rates depends on how many other depositors and borrowers plan to use that bank. To see this, suppose that two banks compete and offer the same deposit and lending rates. If the market splits (the classic Bertrand outcome), both banks will have equal size and diversification. Now suppose instead that a number of depositors "switch" from the first bank to the second, and that several borrowers at the first bank anticipate this and also switch so as to get funding. If this occurs, the second bank is better diversified than the first, and to the extent that the second bank is now less likely to fail, its depositors are better off. Anticipating this, more depositors (and thus firms) may also want to switch to the second bank. Thus, if agents can coordinate, one bank should dominate. On the other hand, if they cannot coordinate, the market-splitting outcome is also possible.[27] These adoption externalities mean that agents' beliefs about how other agents will react to a given set of bank rates have dramatic effects on equilibrium outcomes, leading to multiple equilibria.

Winton (1995a) looks at bank structure when agents can freely become investors, banks, or firms, after which banks compete for deposits and loans simultaneously. There are usually multiple equilibria, so without coordination there is no guarantee that the most efficient outcome will emerge. If a single bank is most efficient and regulators charter one bank to attain this, the monopoly bank might exploit its power so greatly that direct lending without banks is preferable. This is least likely to be a problem when monitoring costs are high; intuitively, this is when direct lending is most likely to cause credit rationing [Williamson (1986)] or even autarky, so that the reduction in monitoring costs through delegation to the monopoly bank is most attractive.[28]

Both Yanelle (1997) and Winton (1997) address the problem of multiple equilibria in models where numbers of firms and investors are fixed exogenously. Yanelle (1997) assumes that fixed numbers of banks compete for each side of the market sequentially, and applies game-theoretic equilibrium refinements such as coalition-proofness and evolutionary stability. Outcomes depend on which side of the market "moves" first. When banks compete for loans first, multiple banks can coexist and earn positive profits in equilibrium. The coalition-proof equilibrium has the maximum feasible number of banks coexisting and earning zero profits, but this is not evolutionarily stable, so refinements do not yield clear predictions. If instead banks compete first for deposits, the coalition-proof outcome is evolutionarily stable. In it, heavy competition

---

[27] Since a single depositor's wealth cannot finance an entire firm, switching by a single depositor does not increase a bank's effective lending capacity, and market-splitting is a Nash Equilibrium.

[28] Yosha (1997) also examines tradeoffs between diversification and competition, but his focus is on Cournot competition among risk-sharing intermediaries that resemble mutual funds more than banks.

for deposits makes both deposit and lending rates Walrasian levels. At most one bank is active, capturing the market and earning zero profits. Since higher deposit rates increase banks' chance of default and associated costs, it is possible that direct lending is preferable to delegated monitoring, in which case banks compete themselves out of existence.[29]

Rather than use "standard" single-period equilibrium refinements, Winton (1997) examines which investor beliefs are most plausible at different stages of a banking system's development. Early on, banks are not yet well established, and investors can only coordinate on banks via the rates that banks offer. Here, free entry tends to the maximal number of small, fragile banks. Although a larger, better-diversified bank that pays somewhat lower deposit rates would be best, the only way for banks to achieve this profitably is to lower their rate from the competitive equilibrium – a move that is unlikely to attract depositors to an untried bank. Over time, some banks fail, and investor beliefs begin to focus on the survivors in the sense that, all else equal, they expect the survivors will maintain their market shares. This creates an endogenous barrier to entry: expecting incumbent banks to be better diversified than new entrants, depositors are willing to accept lower deposit rates from incumbents. Barriers to entry and smaller numbers of surviving banks both promote collusive outcomes.[30] Evidence from this history of relatively unregulated banking regimes is consistent with these conclusions.

Up to this point, our discussion has assumed that a larger, better-diversified bank is always potentially more efficient than a smaller, less-diversified bank. There are several reasons why this may not be true. As noted in Section 2, Krasa and Villamil (1992, 1993) show that the combination of increasing costs for monitoring larger banks and nondiversifiable risk lead to an optimal bank size; Winton (1995a) shows that a banker's own limited capital can reduce expected costs of monitoring, which is most beneficial for smaller banks. Cerasi and Daltung (2000) focus on a third possibility, which is that the marginal cost for monitoring additional loans may be increasing. Again, the motivation stems from an individual banker's limited resources. Because any one banker has limited time and attention, his or her cost of monitoring additional loans increases with the number of loans already being monitored. Even if the bank creates a hierarchy of bankers monitoring other bankers, greater size should lead to more layers of monitoring and thus higher costs per loan. Since the diversification benefit from an additional loan diminishes as bank size grows, this cost structure leads to a finite

---

[29] The difference between the "loans-first" and "deposits-first" results is caused by Yanelle's assumption that deposits are in excess supply. Winton (1997) focuses on competition for deposits when loans are in excess supply, and gets results similar to Yanelle's "loans-first" case.

[30] Deposit insurance reduces this barrier to entry, since depositors will no longer care as much (if at all) about a bank's chance of failure. Applying deposit insurance early on leads to even greater entry, fragmentation, and fragility, but fairly-priced insurance applied to a system that is already concentrated can be beneficial: by threatening incumbents with entry, deposit insurance can reduce their ability to sustain collusion.

optimal bank size. Although Cerasi and Daltung focus on the case where loans are stochastically independent, it is clear that any systematic loan risk will reinforce the effect of their scale diseconomy.

Another objection to these models is that, whereas they all assume that diversification is a passive function of bank size, in practice, diversification is to some extent a choice variable. For example, in 1982, Continental Illinois was one of the ten largest banks in the USA, yet roughly 20% of its loan portfolio was in the energy sector – a fact that proved nearly fatal when oil prices dropped precipitously that year. To the extent that depositors cannot observe loan concentrations in timely fashion, banks may be tempted to choose a more concentrated and risky portfolio than depositors initially expected: shareholders gain from increased upside, while increased downside is shared with depositors because of limited liability. In a single-period setting where depositors cannot observe bank portfolio choice before risk is resolved, Hellwig (1998) shows that the bank will concentrate risk as much as possible. Even though depositors anticipate this and charge a higher rate as compensation, some diversification benefits are lost; indeed, if all funds can be concentrated on a single (large) borrower, delegated monitoring is completely undermined.

In a more dynamic setting, matters are less stark. As Marcus (1984) first showed, future rents or quasi-rents reduce a bank's incentive to take on more risk now, since higher risk means a greater chance of failure and loss of future value. Besanko and Thakor (1993) embed this in a model that combines active choice of diversification across two loan sectors with future relationship rents along the lines of Petersen and Rajan (1995). If bank competition increases, banks earn lower relationship rents and generally have more incentive to concentrate their portfolios.[31]

Winton (1999) suggests that risk-shifting via loan concentration per se may not be the biggest problem in banking in developed economies. If loans are relatively illiquid and it is difficult to change loan concentrations very quickly, investors are able to get *some* information about loan concentrations and adjust deposit rates accordingly before the loans mature and the outcome of risk shifting is realized. This gives banks some ability to commit to diversification strategies: loan concentrations will be detected before the bank can exploit depositors, so more "virtuous" strategies will be rewarded with lower deposit rates, and vice versa. By contrast, loan monitoring is more difficult to observe in a timely fashion, which may let a bank shift risk simply by not monitoring its loans.

This possibility does not arise in the previous papers on diversification because they model monitoring as ex post costly state verification that can be committed to up front. As we have seen, a more realistic view is that the bank must have incentives to monitor, and monitoring is useful because it lets the bank intervene before matters deteriorate

---

[31] Strictly speaking, Besanko and Thakor assume that bank deposits have flat-rate government insurance. Nevertheless, as Hellwig's (1998) analysis shows, even with risk-sensitive deposit rates or insurance premiums, banks would have incentive to engage in risk shifting if there were no future rents at stake.

too greatly – it is proactive. In other words, monitoring must be done ex ante and it is mostly of use when a borrower is in bad shape ex post. Similarly, banks' ex ante screening activities [e.g., Boyd and Prescott (1986)] seek to avoid making bad loans. In both cases, the emphasis is on avoiding or ameliorating bad outcomes. This is in contrast to most nonfinancial firms, where firms' actions may also seek to improve good outcomes. Loans have limited upside, and the emphasis is on avoiding downside.

It follows that a bank that does not monitor saves the cost of monitoring but makes bad outcomes worse or more likely. Since credit risk is correlated across loans in a given sector, the ex post gains from monitoring are greatest when a loan sector is in a downturn. If the chance of troubled loans is very low when the sector is doing well (as for many commercial loans), not monitoring loans is a form of risk shifting. In good times, the bank saves monitoring costs and does not have many more defaults; in bad times, the bank is more likely to fail, leaving its debtholders with much of the worse performance. In this case, diversifying across sectors can improve monitoring incentives; diversification reduces the dispersion of the bank's loan returns (monitored or no), decreasing the gains to risk shifting. On the other hand, if the risk of troubled loans is so high in good times that monitoring pays for itself even then (as might be the case for credit card loans), monitoring incentives are strong even if the bank focuses on a single sector.[32] Winton argues that this may be one reason why Continental Illinois' focus on "Rust-Belt" and energy sector commercial loans was accompanied by lack of monitoring and eventual failure, whereas specialized credit card banks such as CapitalOne or MBNA had strong monitoring skills and cultures that withstood repeated sector downturns in the 1990s.

Since diversification is in part a matter of choice as well as a passive function of size, it follows that the decision to diversify rather than specialize will depend on the presence of scope economies as well as scale economies. The role of scope economies in monitoring and bank sector structure began with models of spatial differentiation, where transportation or other distance costs give local banks an advantage over more distant rivals. As Besanko and Thakor (1992) note, "local" advantage in the lending market need not be geographic; a bank with a lending focus on one industry or sector may be more effective in making loans to that sector than rivals whose focus is somewhat different.[33]

---

[32] If there are deadweight costs to bank failure (such as ex post verification), diversification may still be attractive, but it is also possible that diversification can actually *increase* the bank's chance of failure for plausible levels of leverage. This occurs because loan returns are highly skewed to the left: there is a high chance loans pay off in full, and a low chance that they are troubled and produce losses. If losses in a sector downturn are high but the chance of a downturn is sufficiently low, a diversified bank may fail if any sector it is exposed to has a downturn, whereas a specialized (one-sector) bank only fails if its sector has a downturn.

[33] There is a great deal of evidence that the pricing of small loans and retail deposits does in fact vary regionally within the USA; see for example Petersen and Rajan (1995) and Neumark and Sharpe (1992).

Both Besanko and Thakor (1992) and Gehrig (1995) use spatial models to examine the impact of increased entry on overall welfare and bank risk. In both papers, banks, firms, and depositors are located equidistantly around a "circular" economy of constant size. In Besanko and Thakor, an exogenous increase in the number of banks increases competition for both deposits and loans, making depositors and firms better off and bank shareholders worse off. The increase in deposit rates also increases the amount of deposits in the system and reduces bank capital ratios, increasing banks' chance of failure. Gehrig improves on this analysis in two ways. First, he endogenizes entry, and shows that entry can be either excessive or insufficient relative to the social optimum. Second, whereas Besanko and Thakor assume that downturns affect all locations at once, Gehrig assumes that downturns hit an economic region of random size and location. Since larger banks are less likely to have their whole portfolio suffer a negative shock, they are less likely to fail. Increased entry tends to increase the risk of bank failure by shrinking bank size, and so increased incidence of regional shocks make entry less attractive, all else equal.

Matutes and Vives (1996) use a simpler spatial model to examine the impact of deposit insurance on bank competition and diversification. Two banks compete for deposits, which they then invest; depositors face distance costs, and larger banks are less likely to fail. As in Yanelle (1989, 1997) and Winton (1995a, 1997), there are multiple equilibria. Deposit insurance eliminates multiple equilibria and increases the supply of deposits, but increases the probability of bank failure and associated costs. The positive effects tend to dominate negative effects when uninsured banks would be local monopolies (some depositors don't use either bank); the opposite is true when uninsured banks would serve the entire market and compete directly.

Another approach to scope economies focuses on explicit information differentials between banks that are competing for the same borrowers. The first paper to address this is Broecker (1990). He shows that when banks get imperfectly-correlated binary signals about a borrower's quality, whichever bank gets the borrower's business knows that other banks were likely to have received more negative signals – a version of the "Winner's Curse." As there are more banks bidding for a given pool of borrowers, the equilibrium probability that *some* bank will accept a given borrower increases, and so the average quality of actual loans goes down. Riordan (1993) takes this a step further by examining continuous signals. He finds that, as the number of banks increases, banks apply more conservative acceptance standards, but the overall percentage of bad loans granted still increases.

We have already seen another implication of the Winner's Curse in the work of Sharpe (1990), Rajan (1992), and von Thadden (forthcoming): banks that are better informed about a given borrower have a comparative advantage over uninformed banks, enabling them to earn rents. Dell'Ariccia, Friedman and Marquez (1999), Marquez (2002), and Dell'Ariccia (2001) explore how this affects banking sector structure. In Dell'Ariccia et al. (1999), two banks compete, first offering rates to all firms that they do not have relationships with, then offering rates to their existing customer bases. The Winner's Curse gives each bank an advantage over its existing customers that are in good shape. Because Dell'Ariccia et al. assume that banks cannot distinguish between naturally unattached firms and "lemons" that have left their existing bank, the bank with smaller customer base faces relatively more adverse selection when competing for new business. As a result, the smaller bank breaks even on new business, and the larger bank earns higher overall profits. Moreover, if a third bank with no market share tries to enter the market, it loses money in equilibrium; the Winner's Curse is a barrier to entry. Marquez (2002) shows that entry is easier as borrower turnover is higher (so that the pool of unattached firms has relatively fewer "lemons") or as entrants' ability to screen is higher. Dell'Ariccia (2001) endogenizes entry and market shares by incorporating a spatial setting in which firms face "distance" costs of borrowing. He shows that the equilibrium number of banks under free entry decreases as information asymmetries increase; intuitively, this worsens the Winner's Curse problem faced by entrants.

Since informational rents can lead to ex ante effort distortions as per Rajan (1992), it might be welfare improving if banks could commit to share their information. In fact, credit bureaus provide just this function and are becoming widespread. Pagano and Jappelli (1993) show that lenders' incentives to join such an information-sharing arrangement are greater as there is more borrower heterogeneity, as borrowers are more mobile, and as the lending market is larger – all of which tend to increase adverse selection problems. Padilla and Pagano (1997) show that such information sharing intensifies competition by reducing Winner's-Curse effects, reducing effort distortions as well. Nevertheless, the higher effort makes lenders better off, so it is possible that banks participate despite the loss of potential rents. In addition, when default information is shared, borrowers may further increase their efforts so as to avoid defaulting and being labeled a bad credit risk [Padilla and Pagano (2000)].[34]

In these papers, a bank's screening ability is innate and any signals that it receives are free. Some recent work has sought to endogenize banks' screening or monitoring ability. Thakor (1996) and Ruckes (1998) endogenize the probability with which banks engage in costly screening, and focus on how this interacts with macroeconomic conditions. We will return to their work in the next subsection. Gehrig (1998) examines the impact of integrating two previously separate monopoly banking markets when banks can choose their costly screening technologies' Type I and Type II error probabilities. Although integration may increase rate competition in a beneficial way, entry may be blocked as in Dell'Ariccia et al. (1999); if so, each bank focuses exclusively on its "home" market. Also, in some cases, integration reduces banks' investment in screening, reducing overall welfare.

---

[34] Gehrig and Stenbacka (2001) raise an important caveat to these results. Just as in switching-cost models in the industrial organization literature, the prospect of future information rents can make banks compete heavily ex ante for borrowers. By reducing future rents and thus current competition for unattached borrowers, information sharing may actually increase bank collusion and reduce social welfare.

Boot and Thakor (2000) focus on banks' decision to invest in expertise that differentiates them from their competitors. Firms can get "transaction" loans in which the bank simply lends and takes borrower quality (default chance) as given, or "relationship" loans in which the bank monitors at a cost and has some chance of improving the return of firms that would otherwise fail. Because relationship loans are assumed to be a differentiated product, increases in competition between banks undermine rents on transaction loans relatively more than rents on relationship loans. As a result, banks invest less in relationship expertise, but more of their loans are relationship loans.[35]

In Boot and Thakor (2000), both interbank competition and relationship expertise are modeled in reduced form. Hauswald and Marquez (2000) endogenize these features and get a richer set of implications for bank strategy choice. In their model, banks are spatially differentiated and can make unscreened "transaction" loans or make screened "relationship" loans. Screening ability deteriorates as the "distance" between bank and borrower increases. Banks can improve their screening ability by investing in "sector" expertise that is location-specific or in "transferable" expertise that reduces the negative effects of distance. As in Boot and Thakor (2000), as costs of entry decline and more banks enter, transaction lending decreases and relationship lending increases; however, banks invest less in transferable expertise and more in sector-specific expertise. Thus, greater entry makes banks compete less heavily in peripheral lending markets, freeing up resources which are used to bolster their position in their core lending markets.[36]

Because all of these models of differential information focus exclusively on expected loan returns, they ignore how differential information affects bank risk. Winton (1999) addresses this issue. Just as effective monitoring or screening reduces the potential downside of loans, weaker or monitoring or screening skills exacerbate this downside. As a result, a bank diversifying into sectors where it lacks expertise faces greater downside risk from this sector, offsetting the potential benefits of risk diversification. Moreover, this increased downside risk can undermine the bank's incentive to monitor not only loans in the new sector but in the bank's core sector as well. Indeed, a number of well-known large banks that aggressively diversified during the 1980s found themselves with poor loan performance in many sectors, Citicorp being a case in point.

The general thrust of these theoretical papers on banking sector structure and monitoring is that the assumption that perfectly-diversified-and-perfectly-competitive

---

[35] Boot and Thakor also allow firms to access the capital market at a cost that decreases in borrower quality. A decrease in this cost has the opposite effect as an increase in interbank competition: bank lending rents and the total number of bank loans fall, reducing entry into banking; this makes relationship expertise *more* attractive.

[36] In a related vein, Almazan (2002) examines banks' specialization decisions in a spatial model, where monitoring is more expensive the further a borrower is from the bank. Because capital improves bank monitoring incentives, capital and "expertise" (distance from a borrower) are substitutes, and high capital banks have greater market share.

banks form quickly and efficiently is overstated. Even if diversification offers scale economies, competitive forces may lead to high entry and fragmentation in the early stages of a banking system. Diseconomies of scale and informational economies of scope make slower diversification or even a strategy of specialization attractive. To the extent that a bank does want to expand, the results on Winners-Curse-type barriers to entry suggest two strategies. One is to focus on lending types or sectors where the entrant bank has the least disadvantage relative to incumbents; an example is Citicorp's successful expansion of credit card lending in East Asia in the 1990s, which exploited Citicorp's technological advantages vis-à-vis local banks in credit scoring and information systems. [37] An alternative strategy is to acquire banks that are already established in unfamiliar sectors, effectively buying lending expertise; drawbacks are that the acquiring bank may find itself buying *banks* that are "lemons," and the acquiring bank may find it harder to monitor its lenders in such unfamiliar sectors.

There are many empirical papers on these issues, mostly focusing on the impact of bank size and diversification on lending and loan portfolio risk. This in turn is somewhat subsumed in the even larger literature on bank efficiency. Rather than survey the efficiency literature in detail, we present highlights here, and refer the interested reader to the surveys by Berger and Mester (1997) and Berger, Demsetz and Strahan (1999). Essentially, throughout the 1980s, studies tended to find few significant scale economies in banking past banks of moderate size; however, more recent studies [such as Berger and Mester (1997)] *have* found significant scale economies for banks of sizes as high as $25 billion. One possibility is that advances in technology have led to significant advantages for large banks; a case in point is credit card operations, which benefit from specialized expertise in credit scoring, account servicing, and customer information retrieval. A second possibility, which we explore below, is that larger banks are better diversified and can invest more of their assets in risky loans rather than safer but less profitable cash and government securities.

That larger USA banks *do* take on more risk is beyond doubt; see e.g., Boyd and Graham (1991), Chong (1991), Akhavein, Berger and Humphrey (1997), Demsetz and Strahan (1997) and Hughes, Lang, Mester and Moon (1999). Whether or not this is wholly due to greater risk-bearing capacity or to exploitation of deposit insurance and "too-big-to-fail" is less clear. Boyd and Graham (1991) present evidence that, in the 1970s and 1980s, a higher percentage of large banks failed than of small banks, suggesting that banks may have gone beyond the exploitation of scale economies of diversification. Examining publicly-traded USA banks during 1980–1993, Demsetz and Strahan (1997) find that larger banks' stock returns have less firm-specific risk, and that banks that are more diversified (both by loan sector and by geographic region) have lower firm-specific risk. Nevertheless, up through 1991, larger banks' total stock return variance was no less than that of smaller banks, suggesting that larger banks took on more risk to offset diversification advantages. Hughes et al. (1999) estimate

---

[37] Dell'Ariccia and Marquez (2001b) provide a theoretical model of such behavior.

a structural model of the decisions of risk-averse bank managers. They find that geographically-diversified banks gain both in efficiency and in reduced "insolvency risk" (standard deviation of return on equity normalized by expected gross return on equity). Together with Demsetz and Strahan's results, this may indicate a reduction in large bank's risk-taking behavior in the 1990s. On the other hand, Winton (1999) notes that bank loan portfolio risk is highly-skewed to the left, with losses peaking during infrequent downturns. Thus, risk measures such as variance which work well for normal distributions may not perfectly capture bank failure risk, especially if the sample does not include a major downturn.

Another focus of the bank-size literature has been whether larger banks are less likely to lend to small firms. There are several overlapping motivations here. One focuses on diseconomies of monitoring more loans, as per Cerasi and Daltung (2000); if this is true, larger banks may prefer to focus their lending on large firms, since this requires fewer loans per dollar of assets. Since larger firms tend to be better diversified than smaller firms in the same industry, this need not reduce overall diversification very much, and saves on costs. An alternative argument is that large organizations favor the use of "hard" information; this may favor lending to large firms, since more information is publicly-available for them. Finally, large firms may prefer large banks simply because the level and complexity of their financial needs is beyond the capacities of a small bank or small group of small banks.

Again, a full discussion of the literature is beyond the scope of our paper, so we report highlights and refer the reader to Berger, Demsetz and Strahan (1999) for references not otherwise given. The general finding is that large banks focus more on larger firms, and small banks on small firms. Thus, a number of USA studies find that small loans are a smaller fraction of total assets at large banks than at small banks. Berger and Udell (1995) find that small firm loans at large banks have significantly lower rates and collateral requirements than those at small banks. Since a number of studies suggest that higher collateral goes along with more risky borrowers, this is consistent with the idea that large banks focus more on relatively safe, "transparent" small firms, while small banks take on the riskier, "opaque" small firms which require greater monitoring. Most USA studies find that mergers among larger banks reduce small business lending; Sapienza (2002) finds similar results following mergers of Italian banks. Conversely, recent studies of *de novo* USA banks find that these small banks focus more on small loans than do established banks of similar size, which is consistent with entry aimed at filling the financial needs of small firms that have been abandoned by large-bank mergers.

We now turn to empirical evidence for scope economies linked to geographic or sector focus. Generally, in contrast to the findings for expansion within the USA, there is evidence of geographic barriers to entry when banks expand internationally. This makes sense, since international cultural, legal, and informational differences are much greater than regional differences within the USA. Berger, DeYoung, Genay and Udell (2000) survey this literature, and provide a more comprehensive test by examining the efficiency of banks from a number of countries in five different "home" countries

(France, Germany, Spain, UK, USA). Home country banks are generally more efficient than foreign banks, but when the foreign bank is from the USA, matters are usually reversed. Berger et al. interpret this as evidence that at least some USA banks are simply superior and able to more than overcome geographical barriers to entry. On the other hand, the sample may have been relatively favorable for foreign expansion: the "home" countries are relatively advanced economies, where informational barriers may be relatively less severe, and the sample period is from the mid-1990s, a relatively recession-free period. [38]

Acharya, Hasan and Saunders (2001) examine the impact of commercial loan diversification on the profitability and risk of Italian banks. Consistent with models of specialization advantages, they find that diversification across industries reduces average returns and increases levels of doubtful or nonperforming loans. The effect of geographic diversification is mixed. Although such diversification generally hurts returns, for banks whose loans have moderate levels of risk, it actually improves returns slightly and reduces risk. This is consistent with the model of Winton (1999), which suggests that diversification is most likely to improve monitoring incentives when loans have moderate levels of risk.

Indirect evidence for economies of scope and specialization advantages is provided by DeLong (2001), who finds that stock market reaction (bidder plus acquirer) to mergers between USA banks is only positive for mergers between banks with similar sector focus or geographic scope. This is consistent with the bulk of research on nonfinancial mergers from the 1980s on, which find that focusing mergers add value whereas diversifying mergers tend to destroy value.

Finally, there is evidence that Winner's-Curse effects can be significant. Shaffer (1998) finds that, consistent with Broecker (1990) and Riordan (1993), loan loss rates are higher in local USA markets with more banks. He also finds that, during every year from three to nine years after founding, *de novo* banks have loan loss rates that are significantly worse than those of the average bank. Since *de novo* banks are required to have experienced bank management and are often started by an existing bank holding company, Shaffer argues that this is due to the Winner's Curse rather than lack of basic lending skills.

To summarize, research on the industrial organization of the bank lending sector suggests caveats to the initial models of delegated monitoring. Because of inherent adoption externalities, laissez-faire banking need not quickly lead to a competitive, well-diversified banking sector. Informational problems such as the Winner's Curse can compound this problem by creating endogenous barriers to entry; conversely, scope economies tied to specialized monitoring expertise may make "well-diversified" loan portfolios suboptimal.

---

[38] At a more micro level, Berger, Klapper and Udell (2001) examine lending in Argentina and find that smaller borrowers are less likely to borrow from foreign banks, especially those headquartered outside Latin America. Since smaller borrowers tend to be more "opaque", this is consistent with cultural and informational barriers to entry.

3.5. Credit cycles and the effect of bank funding on lending

The papers we have discussed so far in this section typically focus on microeconomic concerns such as the nature of interactions between bank and borrower or the structure of the banking sector. We now briefly discuss work that focuses on how such microeconomic concerns can interact with macroeconomic business conditions. Given the vast literature on this subject, our approach is selective, aiming at key points and a few illustrative papers. This also leads us to a discussion of papers that examine the interaction between a bank's funding and lending activities, since some have argued that this is a critical source of business cycle effects.

The basic issue concerns the fact that banks change their lending standards over the business cycle. Asea and Blomberg (1998) study a very large panel data (two million loans) set of loan contract terms on commercial and industrial loans. They estimate a Markov switching panel model and find that banks change their lending standards over the cycle; they become tight in recessions and lax during upturns. Lown and Morgan (2001) study the Federal Reserve's Survey of Senior Loan Officers, which asks a sample of large banks about whether their lending standards have become higher or lower. They also find evidence of cyclical behavior in lending standards. Also, see Schreft and Owens (1991) and Weinberg (1995).

In principle, effects can flow both from business conditions to bank lending decisions and vice versa. Worsening business conditions will clearly increase the risk of many potential borrowers, making banks more conservative (the "credit risk channel"). To the extent that bank borrowers tend to be smaller and riskier than firms that access public debt markets, bank-dependent borrowers may be hit harder by higher interest rates or worsening business conditions, and bank lending may fall further than public debt borrowings. Conversely, if banks are an important source of funds for firms and consumers, bank-specific shocks that make banks more conservative will reduce borrowers' ability to invest or consume, and again this will hit bank-dependent borrowers hardest ("bank lending channel"). Thus, the evidence that the ratio of bank loans to public debt drops more when monetary policy is tight [see e.g., Kashyap, Stein and Wilcox (1993)] is consistent with both models.

Since it seems likely that both channels occur in practice, and that there is feedback between them, we will ignore the perennial debate in the macroeconomic literature on which of these channels is more important than the other. Instead, we will discuss models that illustrate how these two effects come about and empirical evidence on these effects.

The simplest view of how worsening business conditions affect bank lending is that of Bernanke and Gertler (1989, 1990): worsening business conditions hurt borrowers' net worth, increasing agency costs that lenders such as banks face. Since loans are less attractive, fewer loans are made, and rates on any loans that are made are higher to compensate for higher costs of distress. Thus, the presence of agency costs exacerbates business cycles.

Although Bernanke and Gertler focus on the monitoring view of bank lending, Ruckes (1998) shows that similar results obtain when competing banks screen potential borrowers. Intuitively, screening does two things: it avoids making a bad loan, and (if the borrower is good) the screening bank has an information advantage over rivals that have not screened that borrower. When times are good, the chance of bad borrowers is low and any information rents are small, so banks do not screen intensively. As the proportion of bad borrowers grows, banks at first screen more intensively; eventually, however, there are so many bad borrowers that banks screen few borrowers and make few loans. These endogenous screening effects make lending contract and expand more than it would in the absence of differential information.

Whereas Bernanke and Gertler and Ruckes assume that banks are out to maximize loan value, Rajan (1994) motivates credit cycles through an agency problem between bank managers and their investors. Suppose bank managers vary in their lending ability: only poorly-run banks have bad loans in expansions, but all banks have bad loans in recessions. In expansions, poorly-skilled managers have incentives to renew bad loans so as to hide their incompetence; in recessions, they liquidate bad loans because good banks can also have bad loans, so liquidation does not send a signal of their ability. The upshot is that banks have overly loose lending standards during expansions. One caveat to this argument is that it assumes that the relative difference in loan quality between poorly-run banks and well-run banks is highest in expansions. It seems more likely that normal recessions create more difficulties for weaker borrowers, which should then hit poorly-run banks harder than well-run banks.

By focusing on problems within banks, Rajan's work is also a step in the direction of "bank lending channel" models, which focus on how problems at banks can then spill over to their borrowers and thus the entire economy. This literature has two major strands: papers that focus on how a bank's net worth (its level of equity capital) affects its lending behavior, and papers that focus on how adverse selection and other funding costs affect a bank's ability to make loans. Since capital constraints would not be an issue if banks could raise additional equity at no cost, and costs related to adverse selection are a significant part of the costs of raising additional equity, the two strands are interrelated. We begin with bank capital effects.

Thakor (1996) examines how changes in risk-based capital requirements affect bank lending decisions when it is costly to screen borrowers. Because equity capital is assumed to be more expensive than deposits, an increase in risk-based capital requirements makes loans less attractive on the margin relative to risk-free securities. As a result, higher capital requirements tend to reduce banks' willingness to screen and thus to lend. Conversely, banks that are more constrained by capital requirements are less likely to lend than are their less-constrained rivals.

Holmstrom and Tirole (1997) obtain similar results in a model of agency costs between borrowers and lenders. Firms are more likely to engage in risk-shifting as their net worth declines. Banks can prevent this via monitoring, but because banks borrow money from other investors, they too may engage in risk-shifting by not monitoring. As in Thakor (1996), banks with more capital monitor borrowers more intensively, allowing banks to credibly lend more. Thus, the link between capital shocks and lending depends critically on whether the net worth of nonfinancial firms or of banks is most affected.[39]

Whereas Thakor and Holmstrom and Tirole assume that bank managers are fully aligned with their shareholders' interests, Besanko and Kanatas (1996) distinguish between insider shareholders and external shareholders. Raising external equity capital dilutes bank insiders' incentives to monitor loans – another variant of the Jensen and Meckling (1976) agency problem between managers and outside shareholders. In some cases, the reduction in monitoring more than offsets the additional "cushion" against bank failure that the additional capital provides; thus, higher bank capital requirements can sometimes increase the risk of bank failures. Although these results are striking, they seem most applicable to small banks, where issuing additional equity can substantially dilute top management's stake in the bank. In a large bank such as Citigroup, even a relatively small stock or option-based stake can leave management with significant risk in absolute terms, and it seems less likely that issuing equity will significantly affect top management's incentive to monitor loans effectively.

Diamond and Rajan (2000) also incorporate external equity capital, using their "bank fragility" model (see Section 2) as a base. Recall that, in their model, short-term deposits limit the rents a bank manager can extract, but bank failure is costly because the bank manager's expertise is lost. Because it is junior to deposits, external equity cushions the bank against costly failure; however, shareholders have a weaker bargaining position than depositors and allow the bank manager to appropriate rents when the bank does not fail. It follows that, as the probability of good loan returns increases, the optimal level of bank capital falls. Also, because banks that are more capital-constrained face a greater risk of failure, their threat to liquidate borrowers is more credible, and they liquidate cash-constrained borrowers more often. By contrast, capital-constrained banks may find that their ability to extract cash now out of cash-rich borrowers is weakened, depending on the relationship between the firm's current cash flows, its liquidation value now, and its liquidation value in the future.

Diamond and Rajan's results are heavily influenced by their use of a Hart and Moore (1998) "incomplete contracts" setting, where everything is observable but only liquidation values are verifiable. Thus, "good loan returns" are linked to high firm liquidation values rather than high firm cash flows per se. As we have argued, banks may have private information that outside investors do not have. Also, in developed

---

[39] In a related paper, Covitz and Heitfeld (1999) examine the link between bank market power and bank lending rates. When bank incentives to risk-shift are weak (i.e., banks are well-capitalized or have large future rents at stake), but firm incentives to risk-shift are strong, monopoly banks charge lower rates than competitive banks. The intuition is that lower rates reduce firm risk-taking incentives, but when bank competition increases, borrowers have more influence on equilibrium rates, and they prefer high rates so that banks prefer to "go along for the ride" on risk-shifting rather than engage in costly monitoring and liquidation. Conversely, when risk-shifting incentives are reversed, monopoly rates are higher than competitive rates.

economies such as the USA or Japan, banks may be able to attach borrower cash flows. In this case, a capital-constrained bank may have incentive to squeeze cash out of small borrowers without much access to alternative funding sources; conversely, the bank may let a large, cash-constrained borrower with low liquidation value continue in the hope that its cash flows recover before outside investors realize the extent of the bank's (or the firm's) problems. Indeed, anecdotal evidence from Japan during the 1990s is suggestive of this sort of behavior. Thus, Diamond and Rajan's results may be most applicable to economies where legal and institutional safeguards are less advanced.

Note that all four of these papers suggest that higher bank capital tends to increase lending, but whether this is good or bad depends on whether or not bank managers are aligned with bank shareholders. In Thakor (1996) and in Holmstrom and Tirole (1997), higher capital improves banks' monitoring incentives and thus the quantity of loans banks can credibly make. In Besanko and Kanatas (1996) and Diamond and Rajan (2000), higher capital loosens banks' lending standards, but this has either a bad (Besanko and Kanatas) or mixed (Diamond and Rajan) impact on credit quality.

A large empirical literature has examined the link between bank capital and lending. Much of this work stems from the debate over whether implementation of the 1988 Basel Accord's capital standards caused a "credit crunch" in the USA. Sharpe (1995) surveys this literature and finds that, overall, evidence suggests that bank profitability has a positive effect on loan growth, whereas loan losses have a significant negative effect on loan growth.[40] To the extent that higher profits increase capital and higher losses decrease it, this is consistent with banks cutting back lending when capital is low, but it is also consistent with banks cutting back lending when low profits or high losses suggest that loans will be less profitable going forward. In a more recent study, Beatty and Gron (2001) estimate a structural model of USA banks' simultaneous choice of asset growth and capital growth during the period from 1986 to 1995. They find that, for banks whose capital to assets ratio is in the bottom decile, increases in capital go with higher risk-weighted asset growth or higher initial levels of risk-weighted assets, and vice versa. (Risk-weighted assets weight loans most heavily.) For other banks, these relationships are less significant.

Several studies have examined firm-specific effects of bank capital levels. Thakor (1996) finds evidence that announcement of a bank loan commitment causes the borrower's stock price to increase significantly, which is consistent with bank screening activity. For the largest quartile of loan commitments as a fraction of bank capital, the increase is greater when the bank's capital is lower, which is consistent with such banks being more choosy about making large loans. Hubbard, Kuttner and Palia (2002) find that banks with weaker capital levels charge borrowers higher rates, even controlling for borrower risk characteristics. The effect is significant only for borrowers that are small and unrated, or whose loans are priced over prime, all of which proxy for firms with high informational switching costs.

---

[40] Empirical papers on the "credit crunch" are discussed in detail in a later section.

The picture painted by these findings is most consistent with Thakor (1996) and Holmstrom and Tirole (1997): as capital levels fall, banks become more conservative. The findings of Hubbard et al. (2002) suggest that informational frictions as in Rajan (1992) are also important. The caveat is that these findings all come from recent studies of USA banks. As noted above, in other countries, different institutional settings may favor models where bank moral hazard becomes more severe as capital falls. We return to the issue of bank moral hazard in Section 4 below.

We now turn to papers that examine how adverse selection costs affect bank lending behavior. In these models, banks' private information about their loan portfolios leads them to face adverse selection costs when they seek funds by selling loans or by issuing uninsured liabilities or equity. Stein (1998) shows that, on the margin, these costs lead banks to prefer to fund loans by either selling off liquid securities that they hold or else issuing insured deposits. Tighter monetary policy reduces bank reserves and thus the amount of insured deposits banks can have. Since uninsured liabilities involve adverse selection costs, banks that have fewer liquid securities to draw on for cash cut back on lending. To the extent that smaller banks are less diversified across loans, their private information about loans matters more and they face greater adverse selection costs; thus, such banks should cut back lending more. Kashyap and Stein (2000) find evidence of such behavior: during monetary contractions, small banks with lower securities holdings do cut back on lending significantly more than their more liquid rivals. Ostergaard (2001) examines how lending at the USA state level and finds that loan supply in states with many small banks depends positively on banks' internal cash flows, whereas this is not true for states with few small banks. [41]

To sum up, there are a number of models that suggest that banks' monitoring or screening incentives can intensify credit cycles, both through changes in the external lending environment and through changes in banks' internal capital and funding situations. Empirical evidence from the USA suggests that negative shocks to bank capital have effects over and above any worsening of borrowers' conditions and that these effects are strongest for low-capital banks. Similarly, costs associated with non-core deposit funding also constrain bank lending, with the effects being strongest for small banks.

4. Banking panics and the stability of banking systems

A key question about financial intermediaries is whether they are inherently unstable, that is, prone to banking panics? Some researchers believe that a theoretical model of the existence of financial intermediaries must simultaneously be a model of panics;

---

[41] Bolton and Freixas (2000) and Gorton and Winton (2000) model another implication of adverse selection costs. In downturns, bank loans are more risky because borrowers' chance of default is higher. This increases adverse-selection costs associated with equity or uninsured liability funding, again making banks more conservative about making additional loans. We return to these issues in Section IV below.

banks and panics are inherently intertwined and models should reflect this. Whether this is the correct view or not clearly is at the root of public policies towards banks. In this section we first review the historical evidence on the experience of banking systems with respect to panics. This experience is quite heterogeneous, even though all these systems have banks offering the same asset and liability contracts. We also review the international experience with private bank coalitions. Private bank coalitions are a widespread feature of banking systems, though their roles vary greatly. In some systems they act as lenders-of-last-resort, while in others they are much less important. A great deal of research has been conducted on the economic history of various banking systems in different countries and different periods. Theories of banking panics should be seen in light of this research. We then review the theoretical models that have been proposed as explanations of banking panics. In the final subsection we briefly review the literature on bank regulation, including deposit insurance and capital requirements.

4.1. Definitions of banking panics and the relation of panics to the business cycle

A great deal of confusion surrounds the notion of a banking panic. One problem is the definition. There is a fairly broad range of phenomena that some researchers seem to have in mind. These are described by a number of terms, such as "financial crisis", "contagion", "banking crisis", "bank run", and "banking panic", that are somewhat unclear. Many of the events being referred to are situations in which banking systems are weakened due to shocks, but nothing happened corresponding to a banking panic, as defined below. It is not that such broader phenomena are uninteresting or unimportant. The issue is first of all what exactly happened in these "crises" and then secondly whether such events are inherently related to the structure of bank contracts and bank capital structures. Another problem is researchers' narrow focus on the USA experience and, in particular, the Great Depression in the USA. Many theorists cite Sprague (1910) as providing a description of the phenomenon they are interested in explaining and then proceed to develop a theory. Indeed, Sprague does describe USA panics, but those experiences appear to be somewhat special, compared to the experiences of most other countries.

With respect to a definition of a panic, it is difficult to be precise. It is tempting to define a panic in terms of an increase in the currency/deposit ratio, but because of bank suspensions of convertibility this is not accurate. Also, depending on the period over which the decline is defined, there can be large increases in this ratio without a panic having occurred. For these reasons precise definitions have not been used. Bernanke and James (1991), for example, express skepticism about this approach. Instead, definitions rely on a reading of the historical literature. Calomiris and Gorton (1991) define a banking panic as an event in which bank depositors at all or many banks in the banking system suddenly demand that banks convert their debt claims into cash, to such an extent that banks suspend convertibility. In other words, if the depositors of a *single* bank suddenly demand cash in exchange for their deposits, this is not system-wide event. It may be called a "run", but it is not a *banking panic*. In reality, however, panics in the USA tended to spread spatially and suspension happened in some cities before other cities, and sometimes not at all. Such considerations make precise definitions hard. A similar definition is given by Wicker (1996, p. 17):

> ... we define a banking panic to be an exogenous shock whose origins can be found in any sudden unanticipated revision of expectations of deposit loss accomplished by an attempt to substitute currency for checkable deposits, a situation usually described as a run on the banks. A general loss of depositor confidence distinguishes a banking panic from other episodes of bank failures. A transfer of deposits from weak to strong banks during a bank run without any change in the public's preference for currency does not qualify.

These definitions have in common the feature that a panic is a systemic event in which consumers want to hold currency in exchange for their demand deposits. The structure of the banking contract allows such withdrawals from banks by consumers, and these withdrawals, or attempted withdrawals, is the precipitating event. [42]

Applying the definition to Pre-Federal Reserve history in the USA is not easy. Calomiris and Gorton (1991) identify six panics in the USA prior to 1865, seven during the National Banking Era, and finally the Great Depression (discussed below). Table 3 shows the business cycle chronology and the dates of the panics in the USA during the National Banking Era. Prior to the National Banking Era, there were panics in 1814, 1819, 1837, 1839, 1857, and 1861 [see Calomiris and Gorton (1991)]. After the National Banking Era ends, with the founding of the Federal Reserve System in 1914, there were the panics associated with the Great Depression. Sprague (1910) labels 1873, 1893, and 1907 as major panics. Kemmerer (1910) identifies six major panics and fifteen minor panics between 1890 and 1908. Kemmerer's major panics include 1873, 1893, and 1907, but he adds 1899, 1901, and 1903. Wicker (2000) agrees on 1873, 1893, and 1907, and calls 1884 and 1890 "incipient" panics. The point is that there is no consensus about the events that should be called "panics" in the USA prior to the founding of the Federal Reserve System. While there are common elements, corresponding to the definition, each episode has some unique features. There are important papers on some individual panic episodes, e.g., Wicker (1980), Donaldson (1993), Moen and Tallman (1992), Calomiris and Schweikart (1991) and White (1984). Wicker (2000) details each of the USA episodes.

Definitions of other crisis phenomena abound. An older literature links problems with the banking system to broader events and the business cycle, e.g., Fisher (1932), but is not specific about the details. Similarly, Bordo (1986) lists what he describes as "key elements of a financial crisis". One of the key elements listed is "bank runs precipitated by ... threats to solvency" (p. 191). But, there are many other elements listed as well suggesting a link between panics and the macroeconomy. Grossman (1994) argues that historically "banking crises" included one of three elements: (1) a

---

[42] Many authors have discussed definitions of "banking crisis". See, for example, Grossman (1994) and Bernanke and James (1991).

Table 3
Banking panics during the USA national banking era[a]

NBER cycle peak–trough	Panic date	Change in the currency-to-deposits ratio[b] (%)	Change in pig-iron production[c] (%)	Loss per deposit ($)	% Nat'l bank failures (N)
Oct. 1873–Mar. 1879	Sept. 1873	14.53	−51.0	0.021	2.8 (56)
Mar. 1882–May 1885	Jun. 1884	8.8	−14.0	0.008	0.9 (19)
Mar. 1887–Apr. 1888	No panic	3.0	−9.0	0.005	0.4 (12)
Jul. 1890–May 1891	Nov. 1890	9.0	−34.0	0.001	0.4 (14)
Jan. 1893–Jun. 1894	May 1893	16.0	−29.0	0.017	1.9 (74)
Dec. 1895–Jun. 1897	Oct. 1896	14.3	−4.0	0.012	1.6 (60)
Jun. 1899–Dec. 1900	No panic	2.78	−6.7	0.001	0.3 (12)
Sept. 1902–Aug. 1904	No panic	−4.13	−8.7	0.001	0.6 (28)
May 1907–Jun. 1908	Oct. 1907	11.45	−46.5	0.001	0.3 (20)
Jan. 1910–Jan. 1912	No panic	−2.64	−21.7	0.0002	0.1 (10)
Jan. 1913–Dec. 1914	Aug. 1914	10.39	−47.1	0.001	0.4 (28)

[a] Source: Gorton (1988).
[b] Percentage change in the ratio at the panic date from the previous year's average.
[c] Measured from peak to trough.

high proportion of banks failed; (2) an especially large or important bank failed; or finally, (3) that government intervention prevented the failures associated with (1) or (2). There are many other examples of attempts at definitions. For the most part, the same events are identified.

There are some notable features to Table 3. First, the table shows the proximity of the panic to the last business cycle peak. The timing of the panics in the USA prior to the National Banking Era is similar; see Calomiris and Gorton (1991). The percentage change in pig-iron production is a measure of real economic activity. As might be expected, the currency deposit ratio rises sharply in a panic. Remarkably, the losses on deposits and the fraction of (national) banks failing during panics are very small. This is due to the activity of private bank clearinghouses, discussed below. It is, however, worth emphasizing that the actual historical experience of panics, small losses on deposits and few bank failures, seems at odds with the widely-held view of panics, mostly based on the experience of the Great Depression in the USA.

In the twenty-five year period following World War II banking crises all but disappeared. Bordo and Eichengreen (1999) find only one banking crisis between 1945 and 1971 in their sample of twenty-one industrial and emerging market countries. In the 1980s and 1990s, however, the International Monetary Fund counts 54 crises in member countries between 1975 and 1997, and the World Bank lists a larger number [see IMF (1998), and Caprio and Klingebiel (1996) for World Bank estimates]. In the case of recent international banking "crises" it seems difficult, at least so far, to determine whether these events are panics or whether the banking systems suffered severe losses due to macroeconomic shocks. Five recent studies, for example, all offer different definitions of a "banking crisis". [See Caprio and Klingebiel (1996), Demirgüç-Kunt and Detragiache (1998), Dziobek and Pazarbasioglu (1997), Kaminsky and Reinhart (1999) and Lindgren, Garcia and Saal (1996)]. Caprio and Klingebiel (1996) is the root study for many of the lists of crises. Basically, their definition focuses on loan losses and the extent to which the net worth of the banking industry has eroded. If most or all of the capital in the banking system is gone, then there is a crisis.

It is clear that there are situations in which a banking system faces a common shock of sufficient magnitude to bring the soundness of the banking system into question. For example, the USA savings and loan debacle of the 1980s [see e.g., Brumbaugh (1988), Kane (1989), Barth (1991) and White (1991)], and the current situation of the Japanese banking system, were caused by deregulation [see Hoshi and Kashyap (1999)]. These events may be called "crises", but there were no banking panics involved. A systemic shock to the banking system, whether it is part of a broader macroeconomic downturn or exchange rate shock, or a shock specific to the financial sector, do not obviously call into question the contractual design of financial intermediation. Nevertheless, these crises raise a number of issues about banks, which are discussed further below.

Despite the large number of "crises" it seems that bank panics and bank runs (on individual banks, but not systemic) have been relatively rare. But, this is due to a rather narrow definition of "panic". Recent history suggests that "panic" and "bank crisis" are rather difficult to distinguish, and certainly more research is needed. Lindgren, Garcia and Saal (1996) provide the most extensive study; they analyze all IMF member countries from 1980 to 1995. By their definition 133 member countries of the 180 members experienced "crises" or significant problems in the banking sector during the period. [43] Their analysis then focuses more specifically on 34 countries (19 developing economies, eight transition economies, and seven developed economies). They single out 36 cases of banking crises. In this sample there were seven cases of panic. The study highlights the difficulties in distinguishing "panics" from other phenomena. Indeed, unlike 19th century America, banking "crises" or "panics" may well be more complicated now by depositor beliefs about implicit or explicit deposit insurance. Thus, although it is tempting to say that the definition of a "banking panic" is ultimately an empirical matter, the phenomena of interest are very complicated and seem likely to vary for many reasons, not the least of which is data availability, making any definition problematic. Nevertheless, some important empirical regularity has been found. We turn next to this evidence.

---

[43] Lindgren, Garcia and Saal (1996) define a "crisis" as a situation where a large group of financial intermediaries have liabilities exceeding the market value of their assets, and the economy experiences bank runs or significant withdrawals, some financial firms collapse, and there is government intervention. If the banking system is unsound, but there is no crisis, it is termed a "significant problem".

It appears that there is an important business cycle component to the timing of panics. Gorton (1988), studying USA panics, provides evidence that panics come at or near business cycle peaks (see Table 3). Mishkin (1991) summarizing the findings of his study states that "with one exception in 1873, financial panics always occurred after the onset of a recession" (p. 96). Also, see Donaldson (1992a). In the recent international context Demirgüç-Kunt and Detragiache (1998) study a large cross section of countries during the period 1981–1994 and also find that banking crises are more likely to occur with the onset of recession. Lindgren, Garcia and Saal (1996) also find that banking crises of the modern era are related to the business cycle.

In terms of USA history, a seasonal factor in the timing of panics is noted by Andrew (1907), Kemmerer (1910), Miron (1986), Canova (1991) and Donaldson (1992a), among others, though Calomiris and Gorton (1991) and Wicker (2000), among others, dispute the evidence. All these studies focus on the USA experience. While the timing of panics is, broadly speaking, clear, it is not clear that seasonal money demand shocks *caused* panics. At root the problem is that there are a small number of panic observations. Miron (1986) and Canova (1991) focus on interest rate movements and the inelastic supply of money in the period before the Federal Reserve System. Miron attributes the deceased occurrence of financial crises after 1914 to Federal Reserve activities, because the Fed essentially smoothed out seasonal interest rate movements. Canova argues that the decline in the seasonal pattern of interest rates to Fed activity has been overemphasized. Miron, Mankiw and Weil (1987) and Barsky, Mankiw, Miron and Weil (1988) also compare the pre-Fed period with the post-Fed period with respect to interest rate behavior.

4.2. Panics and the industrial organization of the banking industry

Another stylized fact about banking panics is summarized by Calomiris (1993a, p. 21):

> International comparisons of the incidence and costs of banking panics and bank failures, and comparisons across regulatory regimes within the USA, clearly document differences in banking instability associated with different regulatory regimes. The central lesson of these studies is that instability is associated with some historical examples of banking that had common institutional characteristics; it is not an intrinsic problem with banking per se ... the single most important factor in banking instability has been the organization of the banking industry.

That the industrial organization of the banking industry is a critical determinant of the propensity for an economy to experience panics has been confirmed in a large literature on the historical and international experience of banking panics. Bordo (1985, 1986), Calomiris and Gorton (1991) and Calomiris (1993a) survey much of this literature and provide some new evidence on the causes of panics.

Calomiris (1993a) examined Scotland, England, Canada, Australia and the USA. Bordo (1986) studies the experiences of six countries (USA, UK, Canada, Sweden, Germany and France) over the period 1870 to 1933. One of his conclusions is that most severe cyclical contractions in all the countries are associated with stock market crises, but not with banking panics, except for the USA. He notes that: "In contrast with the USA experience, the five other countries in the same period developed nationwide branch banking systems consolidating into a very few large banks" (p. 230). Bordo (1985) surveys banking and securities market panics in six countries from 1870 to 1933 and concludes that: "the USA experienced panics in a period when they were a historical curiosity in other countries" (p. 73). Grossman (1994) examines the experience of Britain, Canada, and ten other countries during the Great Depression to determine the causes of the "exceptional stability" exhibited by their banking systems. He considers three possible explanations: the structure of the banking system, macroeconomic policy and performance, and the behavior of the lender of last resort. He concludes that banking stability is the product of exchange-rate policy and banking structure.

Cross section variation in the USA is also interesting because some states allowed branch banking and some states did not. In the USA, states that allowed branching experienced lower failure rates in the 1920s [see Bremer (1935) and White (1983, 1984)]. Studying this cross section of state experience, Calomiris (1990) reaches the same conclusion about the importance of branching: "States that allowed branch banking saw much lower failure rates, reflecting the unusually high survivability of branching banks ... From 1921 to 1929 only 37 branching banks failed in the USA, almost all of which operated only one or two branches. Branching failures were only 4% of branch-banking facilities, almost an order of magnitude less than the failure rate of unit banks for this period" (p. 291). Wheelock (1992a) compares the experiences of banks in different states during the 1920s in the USA and finds that states that allowed branch banking had fewer failures. Also, see Wheelock (1995). Calomiris (1993a) reviews more evidence. [44]

The importance of industrial organization of the banking system for the incidence of panics is illustrated by a comparison of the USA experience with the Canadian experience, which has been the focus of research by a number of scholars. The economies are similar and close in proximity, but Canada is a system that historically has consisted of a small number of highly branched banks, in contrast to the American system of many banks that are not branched across state lines, and sometimes not even within the state. Haubrich (1990), Bordo, Rockoff and Redish (1994, 1995) and White (1984), among others, have studied the two systems. The contrast in experience is dramatic, as summarized by Bordo, Rockoff and Redish (1994): "There is an immediate and important difference between the Canadian and USA banking systems. The Canadian experience has been one of considerable stability. There has been only one major bank failure sine World War I, and there were no failures during the Great Depression. In contrast, the American system has been characterized by a number of periods of instability. Rates of bank failures were high in the 1920s, and of

---

[44] Carlson (2001) empirically examines USA banks during the 1920s and argues that branched banks were *less* likely to survive because they held riskier portfolios.

course the entire system collapsed during the 1930s" (p. 325). Similarly, White (1984) writes: "In Canada, from 1920 to 1929, only one bank failed. The contraction of the banking industry was carried out by the remaining banks reducing the number of their offices by 13.2%. This was very near the 9.8% decline in the USA ... In spite of the many similarities with the USA, there were no bank failures in Canada during the years 1929–1933. The number of bank offices fell by another 10.4%, reflecting the shocked state of the economy; yet this was far fewer than the 34.5% of all bank offices permanently closed in the USA" (p. 132).[45]

4.3. Private bank coalitions

Bank coalitions, formal and informal, are an essential part of the industrial organization of the banking system. The existence or nonexistence of coalitions, the extent of their activity, and their interaction with the government are related to the likelihood of panic and to the resolution of panics if they do occur.

Banks are involved with each other because of the clearing of their liabilities. Banks mutually hold claims on each other because of their depositors writing checks and the banks need mechanisms for efficiently netting these claims. Historically, this led to the establishment of clearinghouses, joint associations of banks that had the purposes of organizing the netting of interbank claims. But these coalitions developed into institutions with many more functions. And, more generally, other types of coalitions, sometimes less formal, sometimes organized around a single large bank or even the government's central bank, seem to characterize the banking systems of many countries in many different historical periods. The extent to which these private bank coalitions exist, or existed historically, seems related to the industrial organization of the banking system and the incidence of bank panics.

The USA experience with banking panics appears to be an outlier in that it experienced fairly regular panics during the 19th century when few other economies did, as discussed above. Until the last few years, there have been a very large number of rather small, undiversified banks in the USA. The research cited above suggests that these two facts are linked. USA banking history has also been intertwined with the development of the private clearinghouse system. Clearinghouses are private associations of banks that formed in major cities, spreading out across the country during the 19th century. On the USA clearinghouse system see Andrew (1908), Cannon (1910), Gorton (1984, 1985a), Gorton and Mullineaux (1987), Timberlake (1984), Sprague (1910), Moen and Tallman (2000) and Wicker (2000), among others.

---

[45] An alternative point of view about the Canadian experience during the Great Depression is that of Kryzanowski and Roberts (1993) who argue that all of the major banks in Canada were insolvent during the Great Depression, but that there was no banking crisis because of implicit support from the government. This viewpoint is disputed by Carr, Mathewson and Quigley (1995). Also, see Kryzanowski and Roberts' (1999) rejoinder.

The USA clearinghouse system developed over the course of the 19th century. In particular, the clearinghouses developed methods for coping with banking panics. At first the clearinghouse organized a method of pooling or equalizing reserves. Wicker (2000) argues that such action prevented panics in 1860 and 1861. By the end of the century they had invented a method of turning illiquid loan portfolios into private hand-to-hand money that could be handed out to depositors in exchange for their demand deposits during times of panic. This money, called "clearinghouse loan certificates," originated in the interbank clearing system as a way to economize on cash during a panic. During a banking panic member banks were allowed to apply to a clearinghouse committee, submitting assets as collateral in exchange for certificates. If the committee approved the assets, then certificates would be issued only up to a percentage of the face value of the assets. The bank borrowing against its illiquid assets would have to pay interest on the certificates to the clearinghouse. The certificates could then be used to honor interbank obligations where they replaced cash, which instead could be used to pay out to depositors. The clearinghouse loan certificate process is the origin of the discount window (and is described in detail in the above cited sources), and serves the same function. Notably, the loan certificates were the joint obligations of the clearinghouse member banks; the risk of member banks defaulting was shared by allocating member liabilities in proportion to member bank capital. Thus, the certificates implemented a risk-sharing device, where the members jointly assumed the risk that individual member banks would fail. In this way, a depositor who was fearful that his particular bank might fail was able to insure against this event by trading his claim on the individual bank for a claim on the portfolio of banks in the clearinghouse. This was the origin of deposit insurance. In order for this to work, the clearinghouses in the USA developed bank examination and supervision methods, as well as reporting systems for bank information to be made public on a regular basis.

During the Panics of 1873, 1893, and 1907 the clearinghouse loan certificate process was extended, in increasingly sophisticated ways. In particular, the clearinghouse loan certificates were issued directly to the banks' depositors, in exchange for demand deposits, in denominations corresponding to currency. The amount of private money issued during times of panic was substantial. During the Panic of 1893 about $100 million of clearinghouse hand-to-hand money was issued (2.5% of the money stock). During the Panic of 1907, about $500 million was issued (4.5% of the money stock) [see Gorton (1985a)]. If the depositors would accept the certificates as money, then the banks' illiquid loan portfolios would be directly monetized.

The USA clearinghouse system was not the only private central bank-like institution. Before the USA Civil War, coincident with the beginnings of the clearinghouse system, the Suffolk Bank of Massachusetts was the focal point of a clearing system and acted as a lender-of-last-resort during the Panic of 1837. The Suffolk banking system operated in New England from 1825 to 1858 and was the first region-wide clearing system in the USA. The Suffolk system was unique in using a net clearing system [see Rolnick, Smith and Weber (1998) and Rolnick and Weber (1998)]. Rolnick, Smith and Weber (1998) argue that during the Panic of 1837 the Suffolk Bank essentially acted as a lender-of-last-resort. Also, see Mullineaux (1987), Calomiris and Kahn (1996), Rolnick, Smith and Weber (1998), Rolnick and Weber (1998) and Bodenhorn (2002).

Bank coalitions are also not unique to the USA, though the extent of their activities varies enormously across countries. Most countries did not experience banking panics as frequently as the USA, but there are many examples of bank coalitions forming on occasion in other countries as well. For example, the Clearing House of Montreal was maintained by the Canadian Bankers' Association and, according to Watts (1972), was officially recognized in 1901 "as an agency for the supervision and control of certain activities of the banks" (p. 18). According to Bordo and Redish (1987) "the Bank of Montreal (founded in 1817) emerged very early as the government's bank performing many central bank functions. However, the Bank of Montreal never evolved into a full-fledged central bank as did the Bank of England (or the government's bank in other countries) perhaps because of the rivalry of other large Canadian banks (for example the Royal Bank)". See Watts (1972), Haubrich (1990) and Breckenridge (1910).

The pattern of the Bank of Montreal (and earlier precursors like the Suffolk Bank) in which the bank coalition is centered on one large bank, is quite common. Another common feature is the cooperation of a (perhaps, informal) coalition of banks with the government to rescue a bank in trouble or stem a panic. For example, major Canadian banks joined with the Canadian government to attempt a rescue of the Canadian Commercial Bank in March 1985. See Jayanti, Whyte and Do (1993). Similarly, in Germany the Bankhaus Herstatt was closed June 26, 1974. There was no statutory deposit insurance scheme in Germany, but the West German Federal Association of banks used $7.8 million in insurance to cover the losses [see Beck (2002)].

4.4. Are banks inherently flawed institutions?

Diamond and Dybvig (1983), reviewed above, is the most important paper on banking panics. Recall that this model combines preference shocks for early or late consumption with investment opportunities that are long-term. The model becomes one of banking panics with the additional assumption that depositors face a first-come-first-served rule, that is, a sequential service constraint. The assumption of this rule, combined with the irreversibility of long-term investment, means that if all agents decide to withdraw at the interim date, then those in front of the line will receive more than those at the end of the line. Consequently, a panic corresponds to an equilibrium in which agents believe, for whatever reasons, that other agents are intending to withdraw their deposits at the interim date. Such beliefs are self-fulfilling because the best response to the belief that other agents are intending to withdraw is to withdraw oneself. As Wallace (1988) points out, without the assumption of sequential service the model does not generate panics.

The theory of banking panics in Diamond and Dybvig intuitively corresponds to what many view as an irrational element of banking panics. The theory articulates the view that banks are inherently unstable arrangements. The theory is silent on the issue of what kinds of events would cause agents to have beliefs that other agents are going to withdraw their deposits; the events are "sunspots".[46] So, it is not testable; see Gorton (1988). Moreover, the "sunspots" have to concern all banks in a banking system, in order to generate a system-wide panic, rather than a run on a single bank. The theory is consistent with the cross-country variation in panic incidence only in the trivial sense that some countries have had system-wide sunspots, while other have not.

As an explanation of panics, the theory amounts to the assertion that the sequential service constraint is an inherent feature of reality. This is clearly unsatisfying in the sense that the underlying reality that would give rise to the sequential service constraint is not modeled. Recognizing this several researchers have tried to address this shortcoming.

Wallace (1988) presents a model that rationalizes the existence of the sequential service constraint. He assumes the basic Diamond and Dybvig set-up where consumers' preferences are such that they need to have assets that can be "cashed" at optional times and where long-term investments are irreversible. They key new assumption is that consumers are isolated in the sense that they cannot coordinate their withdrawals or the amounts the bank will give each of them upon withdrawal. Consumers know where the bank is located and so they can go withdraw. But, their isolation means that at random times they will withdraw and there is no possibility for coordination. Sequential service is an outcome of the assumption that people are isolated from each other at the interim date, the date at which they learn their preferences for early or late consumption. As Wallace explains the assumption "... is consistent with the notion that people hold liquid assets because they may find themselves impatient to spend when they do not have access to asset markets, in which they can sell any asset at its usual price". Wallace shows that the details of the model have implications for Diamond and Dybvig's arguments about deposit insurance.

In Wallace's formulation, following Diamond and Dybvig, bank liabilities do not circulate as a medium of exchange. Instead, when a consumer learns that he has preferences for early consumption, he withdraws from the bank to satisfy those needs. There is no purchase of consumption goods using bank liabilities as money. In the model, the bank is, in effect, also the store. But, in cash-in-advance type models or search-theoretic models, consumers buy goods with bank liabilities without any need to return to the bank to withdraw. This is the essence of a medium of exchange. And that is how bank notes and bank deposits work. While consumption smoothing, and the demand for consumption insurance, are likely important features of reality, it is not clear that consumption smoothing is really a meaningful sense in which bank liabilities are a medium of exchange.

Calomiris and Kahn (1991) rationalize sequential service as an optimal contractual response to depositors being uninformed about the value of their bank's assets. This

---

[46] Postlewaite and Vives (1987) modify the Diamond and Dybvig model so that runs are an equilibrium phenomena, though see the comments of Jacklin (1989).

information can be produced, but at a cost. As discussed above, Calomiris and Kahn (1991) assume that information about the banker's decisions must be produced at a cost. Individual depositors who expend resources to produce the information will get into line to withdraw at the bank first. The sequential service constraint, i.e., a first-come–first-served rule, rewards those depositors in line first, so the information-producing depositors will recover more than other depositors. [As noted above, Jean-Baptiste (1999) is also relevant here].

Green and Lin (1999, 2000) critique the Diamond and Dybvig model. They argue that the Diamond and Dybvig deposit contract is one of the feasible arrangements in the environment of their model. They argue that there are other arrangements that implement an efficient allocation without bank runs. In particular, agents are allowed to send messages of their type, i.e., their consumption timing preferences, to the bank. It turns out that truth-telling is a strictly dominant strategy. Green and Lin do not argue that their contracts are necessarily realistic, but that "Our results imply that environmental features from which Diamond and Dybvig's model abstracts are crucial to a full understanding of banking instability".

Reflecting its importance in the literature, there have been many extensions of the Diamond and Dybvig model. Goldstein and Pauzner (1999) is an important one. They address some of the more fundamental problems with the multiplicity of equilibria in Diamond and Dybvig's model. Agents, for example, do not consider the possibility of a run at the initial date when they deposit in the bank, so the subsequent date is not part of a rational expectations equilibrium. As a result, it is not clear that the deposit contract is optimal. Since there is no theory of selection from the multiplicity of equilibria, the theory is empirically vacuous. Goldstein and Pauzner modify the Diamond and Dybvig model by assuming that consumers do not have common knowledge about the fundamentals; rather they only obtain private signals. A private signal provides information about the final payoff on the bank's portfolio. But, the signal, though private, allows an agent to draw inferences about what signals other agents received. If an agent receives a high signal, the agent believes that other agents are likely to have obtained high signals as well. In this environment, there is a unique equilibrium and the probability of a bank panic is related to news about fundamentals and to the promised payoff on the demand deposit. Morris and Shin (2001)'s set-up is similar.

4.5. Information-based theories of panics

Another view of panics sees them as rational events where depositors are essentially reacting to new information that is not bank-specific. The basic idea is that depositors learn some information that is relevant for assessing the risk of their bank, but is not specific to any particular bank; it is macroeconomic information. Nevertheless, the macroeconomic information is negative, i.e., a recession is looming, and risk averse depositors, revising their assessment of bank risk, may rationally decide to withdraw their deposits. In other words, there is consumption smoothing because the consumers realize that a recession is coming and consequently will need draw down their saving. They withdraw from their bank because they want to avoid losing their savings during the recession. Gorton (1985b), Chari and Jagannathan (1988), Jacklin and Bhattacharya (1988), Alonso (1996), Allen and Gale (1998) and Gorton and Huang (2001) all have versions of this basic story.

In Gorton's (1985b) model, bank portfolios are subject to both idiosyncratic shocks and economy-wide shocks, but only the latter are observable by depositors.[47] Depositors update their beliefs about the state of bank portfolios based on the economy-wide shocks. Sometimes they seek to withdraw their deposits, a panic, because of fears that the banking system has a low quality portfolio, although they do not know whether their individual bank is in such a situation or not. Banks suspend convertibility to communicate information to depositors. In the model of Jacklin and Bhattacharya (1988) the bank cannot observe the true liquidity needs of depositors (i.e., depositor type) while depositors do not observe the quality of bank assets. A unique (i.e., there are not multiple equilibria) bank run occurs when some of the depositors receive bad news about the realized state of the bank assets. In Chari and Jagannathan (1988) the proportion of depositors wanting to consume early and the state of bank assets is also stochastic. Depositors can observe the initial size of the line of depositors at the bank and act conditional on this observation. The line may be especially long because some depositors received news that the bank's asset portfolio is in a bad state. But, this can be confused with a high proportion of early consumers. Thus, sometimes runs result in liquidating banks that do not have low quality asset portfolios.

Allen and Gale (1998) modify Diamond and Dybvig's model so that panics are related to the business cycle, rather than unexplainable events caused by "sunspots". The two important modifications are, first, that there is aggregate uncertainty about the value of the long-term assets held by banks. This assumption is introduced to link panics to business cycles, modeled as this aggregate risk. Second, the assumption of sequential service is dropped, as unrealistic. Consumers face consumption risk, as in Diamond and Dybvig. They can, however, observe a signal, a "leading indicator", that perfectly predicts the realization of the payoff on the long-term asset, but is not contractible. First best risk sharing can be achieved if contracts could be written on this signal. With noncontingent deposit contracts, but with the signal observable, panics can implement first best risk sharing when there is no cost to early withdrawal. Roughly speaking this is because when the long-term asset is worth zero, the bank's remaining investment is shared equally among the depositors because there is no sequential service. If there is a cost to early withdrawal, then the panic is inefficient and there is a role for the government.

An important difficulty with the information-based view of panics is that it views the problem as inherent in the banking system, like Diamond and Dybvig. Gorton

---

[47] Gorton assumes that banks exist and he assumes the structure of the contracts.

and Huang (2001) present an information-based explanation, with the same basic source of confusion between aggregate and idiosyncratic shocks as the above theories, but in the context of the industrial organization of the banking system. In addition to the asymmetric information setting, bankers may engage in moral hazard if their bank is in a low state. So, depositors must monitor banks. In their model, a panic is a manifestation of depositors monitoring their banks by withdrawing. But, only in systems of many small banks does the panic lead to banks being liquidated. Systems of large banks are monitored via withdrawals, but not panics. This is consistent with, for example, the comparison between the USA and Canadian experiences. Gorton and Huang's main result is to show how a coalition resembling a clearinghouse endogenously arises.

4.6. Other panic theories

There are a number of papers that study banking panics in the context of the entire banking system. These are models that focus on interdependencies between banks, either through interbank lending or through interbank clearing systems. The first of these was Bhattacharya and Gale (1987) who extend the Diamond and Dybvig model to examine the effects of preference shocks when there are many banks. Each individual bank faces uncertain liquidity demands, but there are many banks and there is no aggregate uncertainty. Bhattacharya and Gale show that when banks meet unanticipated demands for liquidity by borrowing in the interbank market, there is a free rider problem so that banks under invest in liquid assets. The basic result is that an unregulated interbank market for resources can be improved upon by a central bank that offers restricted opportunities to borrow and lend. Allen and Gale (2000) focus on the transmission of a shock in one location to other locations, suggesting that "contagion" is an important feature of financial crises. Other papers that examine crises and interbank links include Smith (1984, 1991), Donaldson (1992b), Champ, Smith and Williamson (1996) and Rochet and Tirole (1996), among others.

Williamson (1988) is a quite different model of panics. It is a multi-period extension of Boyd and Prescott (1986). His agents are risk neutral so there is no demand for consumption-smoothing insurance, but they do have random preferences and there are both a long-term and a short-term investment opportunity. With decentralized trade there is a possible lemons problem in that agents selling high quality capital cannot distinguish themselves from those selling low quality capital. Banks are large coalition of agents that overcome this information problem. However, the bank must allow for early withdrawals due to the random preferences of the depositors, so it issues demand deposits. The bank can achieve an allocation that is strictly preferred to the decentralized capital markets allocation by all agents in some states of the world. But, in other states of the world agents are indifferent between the two allocations. In states where agents are indifferent, the bank may dissolve. Williamson interprets this as a bank failure or collapse of the banking system.

4.7. Tests of panic theories

On the basis of the stylized facts about cross-country banking history, reviewed above, it would seem straightforward to observe that banks are not fundamentally flawed institutions. In fact, it does not seem to be an exaggeration to say that most of the theoretical work on panics has been motivated by the USA experience, which has then been incorrectly generalized. Panics simply are not a feature of most economies that have banks. The world is more complicated; industrial organization seems to be at the center of the incidence of panics. Not surprisingly, therefore, almost all the empirical work on panics has been on the USA experience. Until bank "crises" around the world in the last ten years, there simply has not been much else to study. Clearly, from the point of view of public policy and the design of bank regulation and central bank lender-of-last-resort activity it is important to distinguish between the two views of banking panics outlined above, if only because policies should be in place that are workable in economies where the banking system is susceptible to panics.

With regard to testing, a major difficulty is that Diamond and Dybvig (1983) is not a testable theory, since any observed a phenomenon is consistent with "sunspots". Instead, empirical investigations of panics have focused on the timing of panics in the USA, checking for patterns that would be consistent with the information-based theories of panics. Importantly then, there are no formal tests that have been conducted that test one hypothesis against any particular alternative. Rather, there has been a variety of empirical work studying the times series behavior of the deposit–currency ratio, interest rates, and other variables, as well as studies of individual panic episodes. Empirical investigations include Gorton (1988), Donaldson (1992a), Mishkin (1991), Park (1991), Calomiris and Gorton (1991) and Calomiris and Mason (2002a,b). Wicker (1980, 1996, 2000), Donaldson (1993), Moen and Tallman (1992, 2000), Calomiris and Schweikart (1991) and White (1984) are also relevant.

Gorton (1988) argues that demand deposits are risky, like other securities, and that depositor behavior should correspond to consumption smoothing behavior based on the aggregate information available to them at the time. The basic idea is that when depositors receive information forecasting a recession they know that they will be dissaving, drawing down their bank accounts. But, their banks are more likely to fail during recessions, so they withdraw in advance to avoid such losses. Empirically Gorton analyzes the period 1863–1914 (and also the Great Depression) and shows that the post Civil War period behavior of the deposit–currency ratio displays the hypothesized timing. In fact, on every single occasion that a leading indicator of recession crosses a threshold, there is a recession. The basic conclusion is that there is nothing special about panic dates compared to nonpanic dates in terms of the behavior of the deposit–currency ratio. While the "sunspots" theory cannot be rejected, the conclusion is that if there are "sunspots" they must be consistent with estimated reduced for description of the deposit–currency ratio.

Donaldson (1992a) revisits the issues raised by Gorton (1988) using weekly data, compared to Gorton who used data from the *Call Reports,* reported five times a year.

Donaldson confirms that there are periods that predictably (from the point of view of an econometrician) correspond to instances when panics are more likely to occur, but that the exact starting dates during such periods are unpredictable. One interpretation of his results is that, although panics do tend to occur at business cycle peaks, there is some unknown triggering event that is not predictable, perhaps a "sunspot", but the data are not fine enough to say anything further.

Calomiris and Gorton (1991) first examine whether pre-panic periods were unusual. That is, do measures of seasonal flows of reserves and deposits show any evidence of tightness or shocks? There is no such evidence. The onset of panics is after the money flows associated with planting and harvesting. However, measures of real economic activity, in particular, the liabilities of failed businesses do decline. Also, stock prices declines did precede panics. Calomiris and Gorton write: "if one posits that the simultaneous violations of thresholds for percentages of real stock price decline and commercial failure increase are sufficient for panic, one can predict panics perfectly" (p. 144). Second, Calomiris and Gorton analyze bank liquidations and deposits losses during and after panics. Basically, there is no evidence of banks failing due to the panic. Rather, weak banks, by pre-panic measures, fail. Finally, Calomiris and Gorton look at sufficient condition for panics to end. The basic point here is that availability of liquidity to satisfy depositor demands does not seem to end panics, with the availability of the discount window during the Great Depression being the outstanding example. Rather, panics end when information becomes available, information typically produced by clearinghouses or the government about which banks are weak.

Mishkin (1991) also studies the National Banking Era in the USA, as well as the Great Depression. He focuses on the timing of events and financial variables to distinguish between the monetarist and asymmetric information-based views of bank panics.[48] For example, an observation that interest rate spreads widen and stock market prices decline just prior to the panic, rather than a disruption in the financial markets following the panic, is viewed as evidence in favor of the information theory. Mishkin analyses each panic episode in USA history starting with the Panic of 1857 and concludes that "the asymmetric information approach to financial crises explains the timing of patterns in the data and many feature of these crises which are otherwise hard to explain" (p. 104). Mishkin's evidence is consistent with that of Gorton and Donaldson.

If asymmetric information is at the root of panics, then panics should end when depositors receive credible information about individual bank shocks. Park (1991)

---

[48] Some tests of theories of panics have focused, in part, on discriminating between the monetarist views of crises, associated with Friedman and Schwartz (1963) and the information-based theories, discussed above. Monetarists do not propose a theory of panics, but note that panics reduce the money supply since withdrawals decrease the money multiplier. Thus, monetarists propose a central bank that acts as a lender-of-last-resort. However, if panics are due to asymmetric information, then monetary policy alone cannot eliminate panics or mitigate their effects.

argues that empirically the evidence suggest that panics in the USA did end when information about banks was provided to the public. He focuses on the actions of private bank clearinghouses and the government in providing credible information and concludes: "this empirical finding confirms the crucial link between bank-specific information and bank panics" (p. 285). Calomiris and Mason (1997) study the June 1932 bank panic in Chicago. They compare the attributes of banks that failed during that event to those that did not fail. They conclude that: "the failures during the panic reflected the relative weakness of failing banks in the face of a common asset value shock rather than contagion" (p. 881). "Private cooperation by the Chicago clearing house banks appears to have been instrumental in preventing the failure of at least one solvent bank during the panic" (p. 864). Other papers on the Great Depression are discussed below.

Demirgüç-Kunt and Detragiache (1998) study banking crises in a large sample of countries internationally during the period 1981–1994.[49] Their basic results "reveal strong evidence that the emergence of banking crises is associated with a deteriorated macroeconomic environment. Particularly, low GDP growth, high real interest rates, and high inflation significantly increase the likelihood of systemic problems in our sample; thus crises do not appear to be solely driven by self-fulfilling expectations as in Diamond and Dybvig (1983). This is consistent with the evidence presented in Gorton (1988) on determinants of bank runs in the USA during the 18th century" (p. 3–4). While this study is the only study of an international cross section of countries, and therefore is unique, it did not include any variables that might capture cross section variation in the industrial organization of the banking system, which the studies reviewed above suggest would be important. However, the study does include a dummy variable for the presence of explicit deposit insurance and an index of the quality of law enforcement. The presence of explicit deposit insurance significantly increases the likelihood of a banking crisis, while the "law and order" index shows that more "lawful" countries are less likely to have a crisis.

It should be emphasized that none of the above work constitutes a test in a statistical sense. While the evidence is suggestive, the basic finding that panics are associated with business cycle downturns does not rule out any theory of panics. In fact, in the Goldstein and Pauzner (1999) and Morris and Shin (2001) extensions of Diamond and Dybvig, the business cycle timing is completely consistent with the self-fulfilling nature of a panic. Morris and Shin write of their extension that: "The theory suggests that depositors will indeed withdraw their money when the perceived riskiness of deposits crosses a threshold value. But, nevertheless, the banking panic is self-fulfilling in the sense that individual investors only withdraw because they expect others to do so" (pp. 14–15).

---

[49] The sample ranges from sixty five to forty five countries in different regression, depending on data availability.

In fascinating recent research Kelley and Ó Gráda (2000) and Ó Gráda and White (2001) study the patterns of withdrawals from a single bank, the Emigrant Savings Industrial Bank, during bank runs in 1854 and 1857. Study at this level of detail can address questions concerning whether depositors respond to a signal that causes them to all crowd at once at the bank, or whether the run builds up slowly. Do rich or poor, less sophisticated or uninformed, line up first? And so on. Kelley and Ó Gráda (2000) find that in 1854 the bank panic followed ethnic patterns, particularly within the Irish community. Ó Gráda and White (2001) document time patterns in withdrawals (or account closings). There are responses to bad news, but there are elements of contagion as well. Moreover, the patterns are different in 1854 and 1857. In 1857, unlike 1854, the run was led by business leaders and apparently sophisticated agents, followed by less informed depositors.

What is more important, however, is to keep in mind that, while to date it has not been possible to discriminate between panic theories with data, it is clear that the prima facie evidence is against theories that inherently intertwine banks and panics. The previous evidence about the industrial organization of the banking system strongly suggests that, at least historically, there is no necessary link between banks and panics.

4.8. The banking crises during the Great Depression

The Great Depression was a momentous event, resulting in vast institutional change in the USA, and casting a shadow over the discipline of economics. In the case of USA banking, the Great Depression led to enormous change. Deposit insurance was enacted, and the Glass–Steagall Act, separating commercial banking from investment banking, was also passed in response to this event. Much has been written on the Great Depression [e.g., Kindleberger (1973), Temin (1989), Eichengreen (1992), Bordo, Goldin and White (1998) and James (2001)] and we do not survey this vast literature here. Even the literature more narrowly focused on banking and financial factors during the Great Depression is large. Our focus is only on issues concerning the experience of banks, and banking systems, during the Great Depression, to the extent that these can be separated from other issues. Understanding the experience of banks during the Great Depression is important because much of bank regulatory policy emanates from this experience, rather than from the earlier panic experience. But, the Great Depression was a very different banking crisis than the earlier episodes in the USA.

The panics during the Great Depression in the USA were certainly different from the previous episodes in terms of the extent of bank failures and losses on deposits. In the USA more than nine thousand banks failed during the Great Depression, between 1930 and 1933. That amounts to about one third of the total number of banks in existence at the end of 1929. In previous panics, the numbers of banks failing were miniscule, as shown in Table 3. Internationally, there was a variety of experience with regard to bank failure and system collapse. While the experience in much of Europe was similar to that in the USA, in that banking systems did collapse [e.g., see Beyen (1951), James (1986) and Kindleberger (1973)], many countries experienced the Great Depression without banking crises (e.g., the UK, Canada, Czechoslovakia, Denmark, Lithuania, Holland and Sweden). The international cross section variation with regard to banking crises during the Great Depression, and the magnitude of the failures in the USA are puzzles. The experience of Canada, discussed above, is an important example of an economy that had a dramatically different experience than the USA. We begin with the international experience and then turn to the USA.

Bernanke and James (1991) use annual data on twenty-four countries to study banking crises during the 1920s and 1930s. They construct a chronology of banking crises during the interwar period and focus on the links between the gold standard, banking crises, and real economic activity. The cite the industrial organization of the banking system as a significant factor in explaining which countries experienced banking panics during this period. In terms of the shock causing panics in those countries whose banking systems were prone to panics, they observe that there "were virtually no serious banking panics in any country after abandonment of the gold standard ... " (p. 53), suggesting that deflation was the important shock. Another important point they make concerns the real effects of severe banking problems. They argue that countries that experienced panics had deeper depressions than countries that did not experience panics. Bordo (1986), Calomiris (1993a) and Grossman (1994), all mentioned above, also focus on the cross-section variation of banking experiences internationally. Grossman (1994), like Bernanke and James, finds that a combination of macroeconomic policy and banking structure can explain much of the cross section experience in banking crisis. He rules out, as an explanation, lender-of-last-resort behavior of central banks.

Indeed, central banks were relatively new and inexperienced at dealing with bank crises, with the exception of the Bank of England. The Great Depression is a turning point in the history of central banking. According to Capie (1997), there were only eighteen central banks at the beginning of the 20th century. By 1950 there were 59 central banks and by 1990 there were 161. At the beginning of the 20th century, the U.S. Federal Reserve System was not yet established; this would occur in 1914. The Bank of Canada came into being *after* the Great Depression, in 1934. Prior to the 20th century central banks were established as institutions with monopoly rights over money issuance. But, if a critical element of central banking is the function of lender-of-last-resort, then these institutions generally did not become central banks until later, typically during the 20th century – after the Great Depression.

Although the Federal Reserve System came into existence in 1914, and so there was a central bank with a discount window in existence during the Great Depression, there was no deposit insurance. Prior to the Federal Reserve being enacted there was the private system of clearinghouses that did provide a form of deposit insurance. And after 1934 there is explicit government-provided deposit insurance. However, during the period 1914–1934, there is no deposit insurance in the USA, either private or public. Although during the Great Depression there were various points at which the government together with the clearinghouses attempted to act, nothing came of this.[50] Clearinghouses acquiesced to the Federal Reserve, but the Federal Reserve did not play the role that clearinghouses had played in earlier episodes. This accounts for much of how the panics of the Great Depression in the USA differed from earlier panics.

Unlike the earlier episodes in the USA, during the Great Depression there was not a single panic near the business cycle peak, but rather a series of panics coming after the peak. What would have happened had the Federal Reserve system not come into existence and, instead, the clearinghouse system had continued? Gorton (1988) constructs a counterfactual, based on estimated structural equations and argues that if the private clearinghouse system in existence prior to 1914 had been in existence during the Great Depression (and there had been no Federal Reserve system), then there would have been a panic in December 1929 (and also in June 1920).[51]. Instead of one quarter to one third of the banks failing, Gorton estimates that less than 1% would have failed had the private clearinghouse system been in place. Instead of a single panic during the Great Depression there was a series of panics, extending over a period of time. In fact, it is a matter of dispute which episodes really constituted panics. The dates in question are periods in which there were numerous bank failures; November 1930 to January 1931, April to August 1931, September and October 1931, and February and March 1933. Friedman and Schwartz (1963) were the first to argue that these were four separate national banking panics during the Great Depression. This has been disputed, as we discuss below. The difficulty is not just the matter of the definition of what is a "panic", but also that these episodes were different than previous USA Panics in another way, emphasized by Wicker (1996), namely, that the center of the panic was not the money market in New York City. Rather, the initial banking problems were region specific. Wicker (1996, p. 98): "There is no discernible pattern in the diffusion of the crisis from certain regional centers to the periphery. One reason for the absence of such a pattern is the fact that the panic did not at any time engulf any of the largest banks of Philadelphia, Pittsburgh, and Chicago. Exactly how the loss of confidence spread across the twelve Federal Reserve Districts is still a matter requiring explanation".

The fact that the panics were more regional, at least they originated outside New York City, has led to disputes among researchers about which of the four events identified by Friedman and Schwartz really were national panics. It has also complicated efforts to test hypotheses about the causes of panics during the Great Depression. The debate over the origins of the panics in the Great Depression echoes the debates about whether panics are irrational contagion or information-based. The

---

[50] In 1930 the Federal Reserve Bank of New York and the New York Clearinghouse Association attempted to arrange a rescue of the Bank of the United States, but the plan failed [see Wicker (1996)]. Later, in 1933 there was a proposal to issue clearinghouse loan certificates to the public, but this also failed [see Wicker (1996)].

[51] The fact that there was no panic in 1920 was also significant because the 1920s saw significant numbers of banks fail in the USA. See Alston, Grove and Wheelock (1994).

fact that rural areas play a role has led to consideration of the fall in agricultural income as an important factor. In a famous quotation, Friedman and Schwartz (1963, p. 308) put it this way: "In November 1930 . . . a crop of bank failures, particularly in Missouri, Indiana, Illinois, Iowa, Arkansas, and North Carolina, led to widespread attempts to convert demand and time deposits into currency . . . a contagion of fear spread among depositors starting from agricultural areas, which had experienced the heaviest impact of bank failures in the twenties. But such contagion knows no geographical limits". In contrast to this view of contagion emanating from agricultural problems, Temin (1976) argued that sharp declines in the value of bank asset portfolios caused bank failures. He constructed proxies for the quality of bank portfolios using traded bond prices and performed annual cross section regressions, attempting to explain the pattern of bank failures. Wicker (1980) presents a third point of view, arguing that the collapse in November 1930 of Caldwell and Company of Nashville, Tennessee was the shock setting off the panic, rather than declines in bank asset values or agricultural incomes.

A number of other authors have contributed to the subsequent debate, attempting to shed light on the three interpretations. The main innovation has been more detailed bank-level data. White (1984) studies USA national banks during four years, 1929–1932. For each of these years, the failed banks are matched with a stratified random sample of non-failing banks based on similar assets and geographical location. White then uses financial ratios to try to discriminate between failed and nonfailed banks, using logit regression. He argues that his results show that Temin and Friedman and Schwartz are not really in conflict. Bank failures are explained by shocks causing agricultural distress, leaving banks with poorly performing loans. Thies and Gerlowski (1993) revisit White's analysis a bit differently and confirm his findings. Calomiris and Mason (2002a) construct an even more detailed data set to analyze the causes of bank failure during the Great Depression. Their measures of fundamentals include attributes of individual banks, as well as proxies for local, regional, and national economic shocks. They find no evidence of contagion-like effects for the first three of the Friedman and Schwartz panics, but in the last episode this does not appear to be the case. Hamilton (1985) also examines the Panic of 1930 and the interpretations of Friedman and Schwartz, Temin, Wicker and White. Hamilton presents a fairly nuanced view, concluding that "The banking panic of 1930 . . . had no single cause, and none of the various interpretations of the panic's causes – poor loans and investments made in the twenties, the Caldwell failure, or falling cotton prices – can fully account for the rise in the number of failures and for the shift in the states and regions afflicted with banking difficulties. The wave of failures can be explained by the combined effect of the overextended condition of the failed banks, the Caldwell shock, and the deteriorating agricultural conditions" (p. 607).

There is also controversy concerning the effects of the collapse of the banking system during the Great Depression. Friedman and Schwartz (1963) argue that the collapse of the banking system was only important because if meant a major decline in the supply of money, via the money multiplier when depositors withdrew currency. Temin (1976) sees the collapse of the banking system as a result of real shocks and that even without the banking crisis "the overall story of the Great Depression would not have been much different" (p. 9–10). Bernanke (1983) initiated a revision of the debate when he introduced another interpretation of the events. He argues that "the financial crises of 1930–1933 affected the macroeconomy by reducing the quality of certain financial services, primarily credit intermediation" (p. 263). In other words, banks perform a real allocative role, which is important for the functioning of the economy. Without banks, due a collapse of the banking system, output will decline because banks can no longer allocate capital to firms. Bernanke works in the general econometric framework of unanticipated money causing changes in real output (the rate of growth of industrial production), introduced by Barro (1978). His first finding is that declines in money are not quantitatively large enough to explain the output declines of 1930–1933. He then includes proxies for the effects of declines in intermediation services, for example, the real deposits of failing banks and the liabilities of failing businesses. These and other proxies improve the explanatory power of the output equation, strongly suggesting his interpretation.

Bernanke's paper has been very influential and generated a number of responses. Temin (1989) argued that firms which were more reliant on bank loans, namely smaller firms, should suffer the most when the banking system collapses. His analysis is based on dividing industries into bank-reliant ones and non-bank-reliant ones. He finds no pattern, arguing that Bernanke is wrong. Hunter (1982), however, provides more detailed analysis based on firm level characteristics and does find that small firms were affected differently. Also see the discussion in Calomiris (1993b). Another critique of Bernanke is that of Rockoff (1993) who argues that Bernanke's results are not robust to how money is defined. He constructs a measure of money that takes into account the fact that deposits in banks that have suspended convertibility are not "money" in the same sense as deposits in other banks. When this measure of money is used, Rockoff finds that the nonmonetary proxy variables are not important in the specification. Essentially, Rockoff argues that any times series variable with a spike during 1929–1933 will have statistical significance. Calomiris and Mason (2002b), in preliminary work, attempt to examine the issues at a much disaggregated level, asking whether indicators of local banks' conditions can explain cross section variation in state income.

Bernanke's original paper discusses the Canadian experience during the Great Depression, since it provides such a contrast to that of the USA suggesting that a more careful study of Canada would be valuable. Haubrich (1990) provides such a study. In Canada, there were no panics and no banking crises, though the number of branches declines from 4049 to 3640 between 1929 and 1933.[52] Essentially, Haubrich follows

---

[52] As noted above, Kryzanowski and Roberts (1993, 1999) claim that all of the large Canadian banks were insolvent during the 1930s and that the only reason that there was not a banking crisis was that there was implicitly complete deposit insurance provided by the government. This view is disputed by Carr, Mathewson and Quigley (1995).

Bernanke's path, but studies Canada. He also looks at cross industry comparisons. He finds that measures of financial distress have no economic or statistical significance. His interpretation is that the real effects are due to crisis or panic. The banking system can contract because the demand for loans declines, but real effects only occur when the supply of loans contracts due to crisis. This interpretation is disputed by Calomiris (1993b).

4.9. Contagion

"Contagion" is the idea that some event can cause a chain reaction or domino effect among banks. For example, when one bank (or possibly a nonfinancial firm) fails, this, it is argued, can cause depositors at other banks to withdraw their deposits. Alternatively, when one bank becomes insolvent this can cause other banks to become insolvent because of a chain of "illiquidity" stretching through the interbank market. So, one view of "contagion" is that it refers to "interdependence" among banks, more so than nonfinancial firms. In Bhattacharya and Gale (1987) or Allen and Gale (2000), as well as the other papers mentioned above, banks are interdependent so shocks to one or a few banks may have an impact on other banks. This type of shock transmission mechanism is also prominent in discussions of the risks in the payments system. For example, Flannery (1996) develops a model in which banks become wary of lending to other banks, although most banks are in fact solvent. At root, the interbank loan market creates an interdependence that can propagate shocks through the banking system. Another view of "contagion" is informational. Banks are opaque institutions, so that information about a single institution might rationally or irrationally lead to a revision of beliefs about the value of other institutions.

There are a variety of ways of testing contagion hypotheses. Calomiris and Mason (1997) look for informational contagion effects. They adopt the empirical strategy of comparing the ex ante attributes of banks that failed during the Chicago panic of June 1932 with those that did not fail. If banks that failed were just as strong as those that survived, then this would be evidence in favor of confusion on the part of depositors. If banks that failed were weaker, then runs on individual banks were not purely random; weaker banks were run on and then failed. They find that weaker banks did fail, and interpret their evidence as being inconsistent with contagion. Rather, there is evidence that while depositors were somewhat confused about the states of individual banks, only the weakest banks were forced into insolvency.[53] Though Calomiris and Mason also point to Chicago clearinghouse as the institution that facilitated this. Their study shows that weak banks failed in the panics while the strong survived. So, the panic did not cause ex ante stronger banks to fail. But, is it is not clear that this is a statement

---

[53] Esbitt (1986) examined Chicago banks that failed in 1931 and shows that they were plagued by poor management.

about the causes of the panic. The panic may have been caused by some version of "contagion," but in the end only weak banks failed.

Other studies of contagion have been event studies that examined the abnormal return on bank stocks when a bank fails, in the post-WW II USA economy. For example, Aharony and Swary (1983) look at the stock reactions to three large bank failures in the 1970s. They found that other banks' stock prices did not respond. Similar studies include Aharony and Swary (1996), Swary (1986) and Wall and Peterson (1990). Basically, the empirical results support the idea that the stock market prices respond to new information, rather than to contagion caused by interbank linkages or irrationality. Kaufman (1994) reviews more of these studies.[54] Event studies test a number of joint hypotheses which makes them difficult to interpret. Chief among these problems is the fact that large USA banks are viewed as being "too-big-to-fail." This is the implicit government policy of rescuing large banks, possibly preventing their failure to the benefit of shareholders. O'Hara and Shaw (1990) find positive announcement effects to encouraging government announcements concerning too-big-to-fail, suggesting that big-bank shareholders benefit from this policy. Consequently, there may be detectable contagion effects to a large bank failure were it not for the too-big-to-fail doctrine.

Furfine (2001) analyzes the interbank market by analyzing all individual U.S. federal funds transactions during 1998, a year during which Russia defaulted on its sovereign debt and the hedge fund Long-Term Capital Management (LTCM) was rescued by the private sector. These transactions allow Furfine to trace any chain reaction or domino effect and allow him to identify whether banks, as a group, became fearful of transacting with other banks. Furfine (2001) finds that interest rates did not move from their level intended by the Fed, and that interest rate variability was not really affected by the crises with Russia and LTCM. Aggregate volume in the fed funds market rose in the second half of 1998, during the crises. Credit spreads in the interbank market did not increase, but were often narrower. Finally, individual banks borrowers at least as much during the crises as before. Furfine's results are the strongest results against contagion effects in the interbank market, but these results too are possibly a function of the too-big-to-fail policy of the USA government.

There are a large number of studies that examine banking crises in emerging markets in the 1980s and 1990s, arguing that some of these events seem to have elements of contagion. [Karolyi and Stulz review the literature on international contagion in this handbook; see Chapter 16]. While definitions of "contagion" vary considerably, one view of "contagion" is that it is the transmission of real shocks from country to country due to trade links, financial links, or "fear". Some studies of recent crises provide

---

[54] Saunders and Wilson (1996) study deposit flows in a sample of failed and healthy banks over the period 1929–1933 in the USA. They find evidence of contagion for 1930–1932, but not in 1929 or 1933. However, during 1930–1932, failing-bank deposit outflows exceeded those at a matched control sample of nonfailing banks suggesting that there were informed depositors who distinguished among ex ante failing and nonfailing banks.

evidence that banks were an important transmission mechanism of shocks, possibly accounting for phenomena labeled "contagion". Peek and Rosengren (1997, 2000) see banks as a transmission mechanism, but do not think of it as contagion. Kho, Lee and Stulz (2000) examine the impact of crises and bailouts in emerging market countries on USA bank stock prices. Their main finding is that banks without exposure to the country in question are not adversely affected, while those with exposure are affected. Bailouts benefited banks with large exposures.

More generally, Kaminsky and Reinhart (1999, 2000) identify three channels that may transmit shocks from one country to another: bank lending, liquidity, and trade. Their empirical work is based on forming clusters of countries based on measures of these three channels. They then show that these clusters are regional, a possible source of transmission of shocks. In the case of bank lending they distinguish a cluster of countries that borrows from Japanese banks and one which borrows from USA banks. Their main result is that the probability of crisis, conditional on crisis having happened in a certain banking cluster, tends to be higher than the unconditional probability of crisis. However, the clusters associated with each channel overlap so much that it is hard to argue that the common bank lender channel has really been isolated from the other channels. In a similar vein, Caramazza, Ricci and Salgado (1999) using BIS data define a "common bank lender" for each crisis as the country that lent the most to the first country in crisis in each of the major crises, using a sample of 41 emerging markets. For example, in the Mexican crisis the common bank lender is the USA. Their main result is that countries that experienced crises were more reliant on a common lender than other countries. Van Rijckeghem and Weder (1999, 2000) also investigate the idea that international banks are a major channel for the transmission of shocks. Studies in this area are relatively new, but seem promising.

5. Bank regulation, deposit insurance, capital requirements

Government provision of deposit insurance and government intervention into banking markets, including bank supervision and examination, limitations on bank activities, capital requirements, charter requirements and entry restrictions, closure rules, and other rules for banks, are now widespread around the globe. The rationale for deposit insurance and bank regulation is the argument that banks are inherently flawed institutions, being prone to harmful banking panics. Consequently, the government should provide deposit insurance and regulate bank risk taking. Moreover, once deposit insurance has been adopted, there is a further need for government intervention via bank regulation because of the incentive of banks to take additional risks once they have (underpriced) government deposit insurance [see Buser, Chen and Kane (1981)].

Most of the vast literature on bank regulation is within this paradigm of panics, deposit insurance, and moral hazard. In general, the literature on bank regulation, and related issues, assumes the need for deposit insurance and government regulation and focuses on the implications of moral hazard problems for the design of bank regulation. There is an associated empirical literature that has attempted to uncover evidence that moral hazard is a problem in banking systems with insured deposits. The empirical literature, while covering a variety of topics, has not been particularly successful at finding evidence of moral hazard problems, despite its dominance as a theory of bank behavior and bank regulation. We start, however, with a discussion of the origins of bank regulation and deposit insurance. This is an important topic because the government provision of deposit insurance, and the associated bank regulation, is a quite recent phenomenon.

5.1. The origins of government bank regulation and government deposit insurance

If banks are inherently unstable institutions, prone to panics, then government regulation is perhaps justified, in the form of government deposit insurance, capital requirements, and bank supervision and examination. However, as discussed above, most countries did not have banking panics, or, if they did, panics were infrequent. Why then are government deposit insurance schemes and bank regulation so widespread? Part of the answer is that they were not widespread until recently, reflecting policy advice based on the paradigm of panics, deposit insurance, and moral hazard.

Bank regulation and deposit insurance have their origins in the private arrangements among banks, as described above in the discussion of bank clearinghouses and other private bank coalitions, and theoretically by Gorton and Huang (2001). Governments took over these insurance schemes and regulations fairly recently, although in the USA there were various earlier deposit insurance arrangements sponsored by state governments [see White (1983), Calomiris (1990) and Wheelock (1992b)]. The first formal nationwide government deposit insurance system in the world was established in the USA in 1934. Other countries did not follow the USA lead, even those that had experienced the depression of the 1930s. It was not until after World War II that countries around the globe began to adopt deposit insurance. For example, Canada did not adopt deposit insurance until 1967. Figure 2 (p. 525) shows the number of explicit national deposit insurance programs in countries around the world.[55] In 1980 only 16 countries had explicit deposit insurance programs; by 1999, 68 countries had such programs [see Kyei (1995), Garcia (1999) and Demirgüç-Kunt and Sobaci (2000)]. Two thirds of the deposit insurance programs in the world have been established in the last fifteen years. Widespread banking crises during the 1980s and 1990s were the proximate cause of the spread of government deposit insurance.

Not only is deposit insurance recent, it has been hard to explain why it was adopted in the first place. In the USA, the federal deposit insurance legislation was originally supported by all but the largest banks, but was widely viewed by others as special interest legislation, a subsidy for banks. Even with the collapse of the banking

---

[55] Demirgüç-Kunt and Detragiache (2000) and Garcia (1999) detail the variation in the schemes adopted around the world.

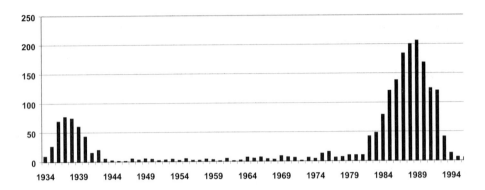

Fig. 1. Number of bank failures in the USA. Source: FDIC.

system during the Great Depression, the Roosevelt administration, the bank regulatory agencies, and large banks opposed the legislation. See Flood (1992) and White (1998). In fact, looking at USA history, White (1998) concludes that: "There is no ready model to explain the growth and spread of federal insurance of intermediaries" (p. 87–89). Kane and Wilson (1998) do address this issue, arguing that as banks grew in size, their shareholder bases became wider, undermining the efficiency of double liability for bank stock. Federal deposit insurance, in their view, restored depositor confidence in because the government undertook the task of monitoring bank managers.

That deposit insurance and capital requirements are recent developments is consistent with the above observations that instability is not inherent in banking, that most banking systems do not have problems with banking panics; the USA experience is an outlier. Since 1934, when deposit insurance came into being, most of the USA banking experience has been quiescent. Figure 1 shows the number of bank failures in the USA since 1934. The figure strongly suggests that deposit insurance per se is not subject to moral hazard. For fifty years the banking industry in the USA was a rather quiet industry, with few failures and little academic attention. It appears that there was a regime switch in the mid-1980s. We return to this issue below.

5.2. Deposit insurance and moral hazard

Moral hazard is the idea that bank shareholders have an incentive to take advantage of under-priced deposit insurance by engaging in riskier actions than they would otherwise. The idea that equity holders want to increase risk, at the expense of bondholders, applies to all situations where there is limited liability (and under the standard Black–Scholes assumptions). This is the observation that, viewing equity as a call option on the value of the firm, option values are increasing in volatility. In other words, the equity holders do not care if the payoffs are low because of limited liability, but they will benefit if the payoffs are high. This idea is commonly described as "gambling for resurrection" or "playing the lottery". Moral hazard has been viewed as being of particular relevance to banking because government deposit insurance premia are not (explicitly) based on the riskiness of the bank. Moreover, the argument is that banks are regulated, in part, to prevent them from engaging in moral hazard. The usual view, however, is that the equity holders will engage in risk-increasing strategies only when bank capital is low or nonexistent. This view implicitly reflects the idea that there are some institutional and contractual constraints on equity holders, but that these constraints lose their force when equity value is low. It has never been clear what these constraints actually are, or why they lose their force at low equity values.

A starting point for considering the moral hazard issue concerns whether deposit insurance premia are (implicitly) set to reflect the risk of individual banks. If insurance premia are fairly priced, then the incentives to engage in moral hazard are the same as in nonfinancial firms and, presumably it is prevented in the same way. Using stock price data and an option-based approach, Marcus and Shaked (1984) found that the vast majority of large banks are overcharged for deposit insurance. Pennacchi (1987), also using an option-based approach, finds that nearly all the banks in his sample were overcharged. These results suggest that the bank regulators or corporate governance mechanisms exert control over banks to limit their risk-taking so that they are effectively being overcharged even with flat rate premia. Also, see Ronn and Verma (1986). Federal Deposit Insurance Corporation (2000) discusses a variety of risk-based pricing methods.

Buser, Chen and Kane (1981) and Marcus (1984) raise an important issue with the standard moral hazard argument. In order to enter the banking industry, a charter from the government is required, that is, a license to take deposits and make loans. The charter is not a transferable asset and it is lost if the bank fails. Charters are in limited supply because the government, in most countries, does not allow free entry into banking. The existence of a valuable charter alters the bank's risk-taking behavior, compared to the standard argument. Rather than engage in risk-increasing activities when the value of their equity is low, shareholders want to protect the bank from failing because they do not want to lose the valuable charter. Loss of the charter is a large bankruptcy cost. As Marcus (1984, p. 565) put it "... the traditional view of bank finance in the presence of FDIC insurance is overly simplistic in that it ignores the effects of potential bankruptcy costs".

The pattern of bank failures shown in Figure 1 may be understandable based on the value of commercial bank charters. What changed? Essentially, the story is that prior to the 1980s banks were partially protected from competition. They often had local monopolies in deposit markets [see Hannan and Berger (1991) and Neumark and Sharpe (1992)]; there was no competition from money market mutual funds and there are interest rate ceilings. In other words, the charter values of banks were high. Keeley (1990) was the first to link Marcus' theoretical insight to the empirical world of banking in the mid-1980s. Keeley (1990) uses Tobin's q as a measure of market power or charters in banking. [Also, see Saunders and Wilson (2001)]. For example, banks that have a local monopoly on deposits can issue deposits at below-market rates, and this will be reflected in the bank's stock price. He finds "that [Tobin's] q appears to be useful proxy for market power and that banks with greater market power hold more capital and pay lower rates on CD's" (p. 1186). Keeley's interpretation of banking in the 1980s is that increased competition in banking reduced charter values, causing banks to increase risk in response. Demsetz, Saidenberg and Strahan (1996) also conclude that banks with high charter values operate more safely than other banks. Keeley's argument is consistent with moral hazard being operative when commercial bank charter values are low. We return to Keeley's argument below.

The bulk of the empirical work aimed at testing the moral hazard hypothesis as applied to financial intermediaries analyzes the behavior of insolvent or poorly capitalized USA savings and loan institutions, "thrifts", during the 1980s. The S&L crisis would appear to be a good testing ground for the moral hazard hypothesis. A series of exogenous interest rate shocks in late 1979 and early 1980, and the deregulation of deposit rates, caused large numbers of thrifts to lose significant amounts of equity. Essentially, deregulation reduced the value of thrift charters while interest rate shocks almost simultaneously reduced their equity value. Between January 1980 and December 1988, nearly 1200 thrifts failed, though not all were actually closed, later described as a policy of regulatory "forbearance", which makes for an even more interesting testing ground for moral hazard. Brumbaugh (1988), Kane (1989), Kormendi et al. (1989), Barth (1991) and White (1991), among others, provide background on the thrift crisis.

The first type of tests for the presence of moral hazard in the thrift industry focused on comparing the behavior of insolvent thrifts with those of solvent counterparts. For example, Barth, Bartholomew and Bradley (1990) find that failed thrifts had disproportionately high concentrations of commercial mortgages, real estate loans, and direct equity investments, compared to the average thrift. DeGennaro, Lang and Thomson (1993) study the investment strategies of the 300 largest thrifts to post capital deficiencies in 1979. The institutions of this group that subsequently failed followed "higher-growth investment strategies" than did those that returned to health. Benston (1985) analyzed a matched sample of solvent and insolvent thrifts. Between January 1, 1980 and August 31, 1985, 202 thrifts failed. Each of these thrifts was matched to two nonfailing thrifts, two just smaller and two just larger. Benston's study is fairly exhaustive and he finds that failed thrifts were different from their nonfailed peers in some interesting ways. For example, failed thrifts had significantly higher ratios of foreclosed mortgages to total loans. However, a main finding is that growth by a thrift does not appear to be motivated by financial weakness, contrary to the moral hazard/deposit insurance argument. Other also pursue the empirical strategy of a matched sample of failed and nonfailed thrifts. For example, Barth and Bradley (1989) also pursue this empirical strategy. Rudolph and Hamdan (1988) use financial ratios to try to discriminate between failed and solvent thrifts in the post-deregulation period (i.e., after the Depository Institutions Deregulation and Monetary Control Act of 1980 and the Garn–St. Germain Act of 1982). Brewer (1995) look at changes in thrifts' stock prices in response to changes in the mix of asset investments. These studies and other are reviewed by Benston, Carhill and Olasov (1991).

A related approach is to look at changes in thrift behavior following major legislation to see whether solvent and insolvent thrifts responded differently. The Depository Institutions Deregulation and monetary Control Act of 1980 and the Garn–St. Germain Depository Institutions Act of 1982 allowed thrifts to invest in previously forbidden assets. McKenzie, Cole and Brown (1992) estimate the average returns on various types of thrift investments for the years ending June 30, 1987 and June 30, 1988. In particular, they estimate the returns on traditional thrift assets and on the new, nontraditional, investments. Returns on nontraditional assets are estimated to be lower than on traditional assets, but in particular, the results are more pronounced at capital deficient thrifts. This can be interpreted as evidence that thrifts with low capital were engaging in moral hazard. However, as the authors note, there are a number of other explanations consistent with the finding. First, thrifts that were about to fail may have already sold the more liquid traditional assets, biasing the estimates of returns. Second, nontraditional assets may be easier to use to engage in fraud or "looting," a hypothesis distinct from moral hazard, as discussed below. Third, regulators were more inclined not to close insolvent thrifts with traditional portfolios.

These approaches to testing for moral hazard are fraught with difficulties. There is no question that failed thrifts are different than solvent thrifts; this is true by definition, since they failed and the others did not. And it is not surprising that the failed thrifts have many common characteristics; they engaged in similar types of investments and those investments did not do well. But, it is not clear that these observations have anything to do with moral hazard. For example, if a thrift is not successful investing in traditional asset categories, for whatever reasons, it may invest in new asset classes allowed by deregulation. If there is a negative exogenous shock to this new asset class, and the thrift subsequently is closed, it may have nothing to do with moral hazard. But, this outcome must be distinguished from the case where the thrift, seeing that its net worth is negative invests in the new asset class because the new assets are viewed ex ante as being very risky.

In addition to the problems mentioned above, another problem involves ensuring that the risk-taking behavior is caused by insolvency, rather than the other way around. This issue is related to the use of accounting data, which almost all of the studies rely on. Benston, Carhill and Olasov (1991) discuss the accounting issues, and then go on to base their analysis on estimates of market values. These authors "conclude that insolvent thrifts did not expand more rapidly than did solvent thrifts and, in general, did not take greater risks" (p. 379). Brickley and James (1986) also avoid the accounting issues by looking at the response of stock prices to changes in Federal Savings and Loan Insurance Corporation closure policy. They find that the response is as if access to underpriced federal deposit insurance is a valuable option, but it is not clear that there is moral hazard. According to standard option theory, call options are more valuable if the maturity is extended, ceteris paribus.

Another interesting experiment concerns the U.S. Comptroller of the Currency's announcement, in 1984, that the eleven largest U.S. banking firms were "too big to fail" (TBTF), implying they would receive de facto 100% deposit insurance. Did this encourage risk-taking? O'Hara and Shaw (1990) investigate the effect on bank equity of the Comptroller of the Currency's announcement using event study methodology. They find positive wealth effects accruing to TBTF banks, with corresponding negative effects accruing to non-TBTF banks. Boyd and Gertler (1994) study the poor performance of banks in the 1980s in a statistical study controlling for location, asset size remains a significant factor in poor performance of large banks. They find that the poor performance of the USA banking industry in the 1980s was due mainly to the risk-taking of the largest banks and interpret this as risk-taking that was encouraged by the USA government's too-big-to-fail policy. Also, see Black, Collins, Robinson and Schweitzer (1997). De Nicolo (2001) shows that the link between bank size and risk extends beyond the USA. He examines banks in 21 industrialized countries during 1988–1998 and finds that larger banks have lower charter values (as measured by Tobin's q ratio) and higher risk of insolvency.

Some authors have attempted to address the shortcomings of studies based on the thrift crisis by examining historical situations where some institutions are covered by insurance, while other similar institutions are not. Wheelock (1992b), Wheelock and Kumbhakar (1995) and Wheelock and Wilson (1995) looked at individual banks in Kansas that participated in a state deposit insurance program in the 1920s, on a voluntary basis. Banks that chose insurance coverage took additional risks. Calomiris (1990) finds that deposit insurance in the early 1900s increased bank risk-taking, more so for states with mandatory insurance than for states with voluntary insurance. Grossman (1992), examining thrifts in the 1930s, found that thrifts entering the voluntary federal insurance program did take on more risks than uninsured thrifts after several years.

Demirgüç-Kunt and Detragiache (2000) analyze international evidence. They estimate the probability of a systemic banking crisis in a panel of 61 countries over the period 1980–1997. This is the period when most countries adopted deposit insurance; see Figure 2.[56] About 40 banking crises are identified in the panel and for about half the observations a deposit insurance system was present. The main result is that a dummy variable for the presence of deposit insurance is positive and significant. Refining this by distinguishing different types of deposit systems shows that explicit deposit insurance is associated with higher likelihood of crisis. As the authors point out, one possibility for the association between deposit insurance and bank crises is that economies with fragile banking systems tend to adopt deposit insurance. An instrumental variable approach to this issue shows deposit insurance to still be associated with crisis. The authors conclude that "explicit deposit insurance tends to be detrimental to bank stability" (p. 22).

---

[56] Years in which banking crises were occurring were excluded.

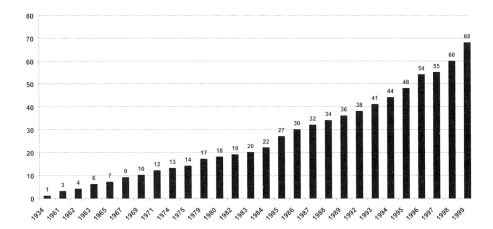

Fig. 2. Number of explicit deposit insurance schemes in the world. Source: Demirgüç-Kunt and Sobaci (2000).

The international evidence of Demirgüç-Kunt and Detragiache raises another issue. The moral hazard argument is the idea that equity holders are motivated to take on risk inefficiently in the hopes that there is a state of the world that could be realized in the future in which their equity would be positively valued. But, Akerlof and Romer (1993) point out that much of what is claimed to be evidence of moral hazard, in fact, appears to be behavior in which there is NO state of the world in which equity would be positively valued. Rather, it is "looting," that is, the equity holders are simply illegally stealing from the institution. Akerlof and Romer attempt to estimate the extent of looting during the USA S&L crisis and present a range of estimates that would account for a large fraction of the government clean-up costs. The argument is also applied to the banking systems of emerging markets. As Akerlof and Romer write: "... it is a safe bet that many developing countries that have far less sophisticated and honest regulatory mechanisms than those that exist in the USA will be victimized by financial market fraud as their financial markets develop" (p. 59). An important question concerns whether this type of fraud is increased when deposit insurance is adopted.

Returning to the USA S&L crisis, there is little dispute that if the government had closed thrifts faster, then the costs of resolving the insolvencies would have been lower. But, closure policies are somewhat complicated by the constraints the government may face. The government may optimally not want to close banks or thrifts and instead engage in a kind of moral hazard itself. See Gorton and Winton (2000). Acharya and Dreyfus (1989) and Mailith and Mester (1994) also analyze government closure policies for financial intermediaries. If there had been no deposit insurance for USA savings and loan institutions, then there would likely have been a generalized panic

shock that had the same detrimental effect on equity capital that occurred with thrifts. Competition increased in banking, and over a protracted period of time commercial banks failed. The question is: Who made the decision to engage risky investments, equity holders or bank managers?

Gorton and Rosen (1995) empirically analyze whether the risk-taking identified by Keeley is explained by shareholders making the decisions, i.e., moral hazard, or by managers. They look at the relationship between risk-taking and the ownership structure in banks. The banking environment of the late 1980s was not the usual environment. It was a competitive environment where opportunities were shrinking. In such an environment, managers may resist shrinking their banks through merger, acquisition, or directly by making fewer loans. But, equity value is not yet low. As charter values decline, shareholders prefer to exit the industry and redeploy their resources in investments with higher returns. But, to the extent that managers are entrenched, this could mean that their careers as bankers are over in many cases, as the industry is shrinking. In a shrinking industry, managers and equity holders have different incentives, and they are different than they would be in a growing industry.

Which group, managers or equity holders, make decisions depends sensitively on the relative sizes of the equity holdings of the managers versus the outside equity concentrations. At one extreme, the manager is the owner if he owns all the equity. At the other extreme, the manger may have no equity and face a large outside block holder who is in control. But, more likely combinations involve a manager with a small amount of equity in a bank where all the other shareholders are dispersed or there is a group of outside block holders. In these cases, a manager may not have enough equity to care as much about his pecuniary returns as he does about his private benefits of control, but his equity holding may be large enough for him to exert control. Because the other shareholders are dispersed, he is effectively entrenched and can attempt keep the size of his bank from decreasing in the shrinking industry. These issues mean that the sought after relationship is potentially nonlinear. This turns out to be very important empirically. Gorton and Rosen find that the managerial hypothesis is empirically more important than the moral hazard hypothesis, which can be rejected, in explaining risk-taking by banks.

The relations between managers' equity holdings and the ownership structure of the outside shareholders, i.e., the extent to which there are blocks, makes the relationship between control and risk taking potentially highly nonlinear. Gorton and Rosen use semiparametric methods to tests for the nonlinearities. Saunders, Strock and Travlos (1990) estimate a linear relation between managerial stock holdings and the stock price volatility of their bank holding company over the period 1978–1985 and find a positive relation. Demsetz, Saidenberg and Strahan (1997) use piecewise linear regression. They find that risk increases with the shareholdings of managers, but only for banks with relatively low charter value. The sample period is 1991–1995.

The structure of ownership and risk taking has also been investigated in the thrift industry. Cebenoyan, Cooperman and Register (1995) analyze balance sheet measures of risk for samples of thrifts in 1988 and 1991. Independent variables include the holdings of insiders, and this variable squared, and a measure of the percentage of equity held by institutional investors. They find that "S&Ls with a high concentration of managerial stock ownership exhibit greater risk-taking behavior than other S&Ls in 1988, a period of regulatory leniency and forbearance on S&L closures, but lower risk-taking behavior in 1991, a period of regulatory stringency and nonforbearance" (p. 63). These results are confirmed in Cebenoyan, Cooperman and Register (1999) over the period 1986 to 1995 with the same quadratic term included for insider holdings.

5.4. Bank capital requirements

Like deposit insurance, bank capital requirements, or at least, explicit capital requirements, are also a recent development. In the USA, the Banking Act of 1933 required that bank regulators consider the "adequacy of the capital structure". In the 1950s, the Federal Reserve mandated capital levels on the basis of a formula based on amounts to be held against different asset categories. This was dropped in the 1970s. But it seems that no attempt was made to enforce explicit capital requirements until 1982 [see Morgan (1992) and Baer and McElravey (1992)]. Risk-based capital requirements became effective in the USA in 1991 with the passage of Federal Deposit Insurance Corporation Improvement Act, which explicitly required regulators to enforce capital requirements. The Basle Accord, reached on July 12, 1988, was a regulatory agreement among the G-10 countries, together with Switzerland and Luxembourg, which specified risk-based capital requirements.

Intuitively, bank capital reduces the likelihood of bank failure. So, if banks are riskier than socially desirable, why not require that they hold more capital? What is the cost of such a policy? For nonfinancial firms equity finance is costly because of asymmetric information, the explanation developed by Myers and Majluf (1984). Wansley and Dhillon (1989) and Polonchek, Slovin and Sushka (1989) find that the announcement of common stock issuances by commercial banks in the USA results in a significant negative stock price reaction, though the reaction is smaller, on average, than for industrial firms. This is somewhat surprising because banks are generally viewed as more opaque institutions than nonfinancial firms. Cornett and Tehranian (1994) may provide some of the answer. They document that the stock price reaction to a voluntary equity issuance is significantly more negative than those associated with an involuntary issuance taken to satisfy capital requirements.[57] But, these results do not address other issues concerning bank capital, to which we now turn.

The recent attention to bank capital requirements seems ironic, as Benveniste, Boyd and Greenbaum (1991) point out. They observe that in the USA there has been a

---

[57] Wagster (1996) studies the wealth effects to shareholders of stocks of banks in Canada, Germany, Japan, the Netherlands, Switzerland, UK, and USA, due to announcements of eighteen important events leading up the Basle Accord, starting on September 11, 1985 and ending on March 28, 1990. The main result is that only shareholders of Japanese banks experienced significant wealth effects for all eighteen events. Moreover, the cumulative gain was a positive 31.63%.

century-long secular decline in bank capital ratios, until about forty years ago. Prior to 1850 about 50% of bank assets were financed with capital. By the turn of the century the fraction financed by capital had shrunk to less than 20%. It was about 14% in 1929 and just over 6% at the end of World War II. Since then bank capital rose a small amount from the mid-1940s through the mid-1960s, then declined through the mid-1970s, and rose thereafter. In 1986, total capital was 6.8%, the same as it was in 1950. When first implemented, the Basle Accord called for a minimum capital of 7.25% of total assets by the end of 1990 (of which at lest half was to be "core capital") and at least 8.0% of assets by the end of 1992 (again with at least half in core capital). [58] During the late 1980s and through the 1990s USA bank holding companies increased their capital ratios to the highest levels in 50 years. See Saunders and Wilson (1999) and Flannery and Rangan (2001). However, the nation's largest banks lost about one fourth of their market capitalization in the third quarter of 1998, coinciding with the Russian crisis and the Long-Term Capital Management debacle. Hovakimian and Kane (2000) argue empirically that neither the market nor regulators prevented large banks from shifting risk to the government deposit insurance safety net.

These trends raise a number of questions. Why was there such a long downward trend? Why has it been reversed? Why did regulators (and academics) start focusing on capital requirements? What are the trends in other countries? Most of these questions have not been studied. Benveniste, Boyd and Greenbaum (1991) interpret bank charter value (monopoly rents) as a hidden source of capital that began to dissipate in the late 1970s and 1980s, as discussed above. Flannery and Rangan (2001) argue that the increase in capital ratios in the last fifteen years is due to market forces disciplining banks. This argument contrasts with earlier views that banks always held the minimum amount of required capital, and that increases in capital ratios imposed costs on banks, and possibly on borrowers through a "credit crunch".

If there are significant costs to raising bank capital, government-imposed capital requirements can have real effects. Banks may choose to exit the industry rather than satisfy the requirements. Such "exit" may occur through a reduction in bank loans rather than a reduction in bank assets per se. In such an event, otherwise worthy borrowers would not obtain bank loans. There would be a "credit crunch" due to capital requirements. Shortly after the Basle Accord in 1988, USA banks reduced their investments in commercial loans and increased the investments in government securities. More specifically, the share of total bank assets composed of commercial and industrial loans fell from about 22.5% in 1989 to less than 16% in 1994. At the same time, the share of assets invested in government securities increased from just over 15% to almost 25%. See Keeton (1994) and Furfine (2001). This period has been identified as a "credit crunch", which refers to the possibility that banks were reluctant to lend to worthy loan applicants because of capital requirements.

---

[58] "Core capital" includes common equity and minority interests in consolidated subsidiaries, but excludes loan loss reserves.

In fact, the credit crunch, broadly outlined above, could be due to a number of nonmutually exclusive factors. Banks may have voluntarily and autonomously reduced their risk appetites. Regulators may have become tougher, causing the loan contraction. The Basle Accord, because of its risk-sensitive measures of capital, may have encouraged banks to reallocate their assets towards government securities. Finally, aside from the risk-sensitive nature of the capital requirements, the level of the required capital (to assets ratio) may have caused the reallocation. These factors are all supply-related. But, since there was a recession during the early 1990s, the decline in lending may have been demand-related. As noted above in Section 3, a large empirical literature has searched for evidence of a supply-related credit crunch. The basic approach is to regress bank loan growth on measures of bank capital and control variables. Versions of this regression have been studied by Bernanke and Lown (1991), Hall (1993), Berger and Udell (1994), Haubrich and Wachtel (1993), Hancock and Wilcox (1994), Brinkman and Horvitz (1995), Peek and Rosengren (1995) and Beatty and Gron (2001). With different sample periods, slightly different econometric specifications, different definitions of capital adequacy, and so on, it is not surprising that the results are mixed. Other researchers have tested whether bank supervisors or regulators become tougher during recessions, causing or contributing to a credit crunch. See, for example, Bizer (1993), Wagster (1999), Furfine (2001) and Berger, Kyle and Scalise (2001). Although there is some evidence that bank capital does affect bank lending, the studies have a difficult time distinguishing loan demand shifts from loan supply shifts, leaving the question of the relative importance of different effects unanswered.

While we discussed bank-capital models generally above, there are other papers focusing on the effects of increasing regulatory capital on bank risk taking. Flannery (1989), Furlong and Keeley (1989, 1990) and Kim and Santomero (1988) are examples of partial equilibrium models that examine the relationship between bank leverage and risk-taking. Because these papers are partial equilibrium, the issue of whether there is anything peculiar about banks raising capital is not addressed. Gennotte and Pyle (1991) is more general equilibrium. Gorton and Winton (2000) present a general equilibrium of bank capital in which there is a social cost to increasing bank capital requirements, as well as a benefit. The benefits are clear; nontransferable charter value, which is also socially beneficial, is protected more with higher capital ratios. But, there is a unique cost to forcing banks to raise capital, namely, they can supply fewer deposits in general equilibrium. Deposits are in demand for the reasons put forth by Gorton and Pennacchi (1990); they provide a way for uniformed agents to transact. In this context, the government never imposes binding capital requirements because it is not socially optimal for bank equity holders to exit the industry, resulting in a smaller banking industry.

5.5. Other issues

There are many other regulatory issues that have been studied. In this subsection, we mention a few of the more important or more interesting issues.

The Glass–Steagall Act, passed in the USA in the aftermath of the Great Depression, separated commercial banking from investment banking, ostensibly because of conflicts-of-interest in undertaking lending activity and underwriting activity. While this is no longer the case under current USA law (due to changes that culminated in the passage of the Financial Services Modernization Act of 1999), the question whether such separation is socially desirable remains of interest. If banks produce private information in their lending activity, might they have an incentive to only underwrite their poor-quality borrowers? Such questions have been addressed by Ang and Richardson (1994), Gande, Puri, Saunders and Walter (1997), Kroszner and Rajan (1994, 1997), Puri (1994, 1996), Gande, Puri and Saunders (1999), Yasuda (1999) and Schenone (2001), among others. An open issue is the way in which these joint activities affect bank relationships with borrowers and borrower corporate governance.

Market discipline of banks refers to the extent to which market participants can determine when and which banks are riskier, and impound this information into asset prices. To the extent that market participants are better able to perform this role, there is less need for government oversight. A large literature has investigated this question. For example, Flannery and Sorescu (1996) consider the extent to which bank subordinated debt prices reflect the riskiness of banks. Berger, Davies and Flannery (2000) compare the information in market security prices to the information produced by bank supervisors. See Flannery (2001) for a discussion.

Another interesting regulatory issue concerns the behavior of the regulators. Kane (1990) focuses on the incentives of regulators during the resolution of insolvent thrifts in the USA. According to Kane, the Resolution Trust Corporation, the government agency charged with liquidating insolvent thrifts, was inefficient due to the agency problem of the government wanting to avoid recognizing losses that would be borne by the government insurance fund. Dell'Ariccia and Marquez (2001a) analyze competition among regulators when there are externalities across national markets. Competition can result in lower regulatory standards.

6. Conclusion

We have surveyed the major themes and major developments in research in financial intermediation over the last two decades, or so. There are many related topics that we have not covered. For example, the roles of banks in economic growth, and the role of banks in the transmission of monetary policy, are large subjects that we have not touched on at all. Other topics have been only briefly examined. Nevertheless we hope the reader is convinced of the progress made in understanding financial intermediation. Despite this progress there are still major questions. Some of these are:

(1) Why do banking crises and banking panics persist? Most theories of banking panics seem inconsistent with the facts put forth by economic historians. The view that banks are inherently unstable seems based on a misreading of USA financial history. Overall, it seems that the question of whether banking is inherently unstable or not remains unresolved.

(2) Recent experience in emerging markets again raises the issue stability of banking systems. Why are emerging markets experiencing banking panics and crises? Are these crises fundamentally different than earlier historic episodes? Is the basic problem corruption, bad regulations, moral hazard, or some combination?

(3) What features of the industrial organization of banking systems make the banks in the system more prone to panics? Are these features consistent with the usual model of competition? In other words, if a few large banks are not panic prone, are they prone to being monopolists?

(4) On a related note, how does the industrial organization of the bank lending sector interact with banks' funding and capital structures? Empirically, how does bank-funding structure affect the structure of the bank's loans and loan portfolio?

(5) The basic paradigm of bank regulation, namely, moral hazard emanating from mispriced deposit insurance, may have outlived its usefulness, if it was ever relevant. It is clear that in the USA this has not been a problem since the inception of deposit insurance, nor has clear-cut evidence been produced for the existence of this problem. Corporate governance issues in intermediaries and the intersection of governance and alleged incentives for moral hazard have yet to be fully explored. What is the rationale for government intervention into banking markets?

(6) Is corporate governance in banks fundamentally different than nonbanks?

(7) Why are deposit insurance and capital requirements such recent developments, especially if their efficacy is as claimed?

(8) The differences between loans and bonds seem clear, but questions remain. The existence of loan sales complicates the distinctions that have been made theoretically. The existence of vulture investors, who act like state-contingent banks, buying up blocks of bonds in distressed firms and then actively participating in restructuring, also complicates the distinction. Finally, despite the large literature on potential conflicts of interest, there has been little work on how bank lending and bank underwriting activities jointly affect the corporate governance of bank borrowers.

(9) Our survey has focused on the traditional "bank-like" model of monitored finance. There are other forms of monitored finance, such as venture capital. What determines the choice between these different structures? Are these differences driven by the type of firm that seeks financing, or by financing structure of the intermediary?

(10) Most models of banking assume that banks and borrowers are perfectly rational. How can insights from the growing field of behavioral finance change our understanding of banks? This question is only just starting to receive attention. [59]

(11) Why are bank liabilities used as media of exchange, but not the liabilities of nonbanks? Why can't demand deposits be traded without being cleared through the banking system? These questions remain largely unexplored.

(12) How have loan sales, credit derivatives, commercial paper conduits, collateralized loan obligations, and other recent financial innovations, affected banking?

(13) Are banks and stock markets substitutes? Is there a meaningful distinction between of "bank-based" systems and "stock-market-based" systems? What are the welfare implications of "bank-based" systems versus "stock-market-based" systems?

References

Acharya, S., and J.-P. Dreyfus (1989), "Optimal bank reorganization policies and the pricing of federal deposit insurance", Journal of Finance 44:1313–1333.

Acharya, V., I. Hasan and A. Saunders (2001), "The effects of focus and diversification: evidence from individual bank loan portfolios", Working Paper (London Business School).

Adams, M. (1999), "Cross holdings in Germany", Journal of Institutional and Theoretical Economics 155:80–109.

Aharony, J., and I. Swary (1983), "Contagion effects of bank failures: evidence from capital markets", Journal of Business 56:302–322.

Aharony, J., and I. Swary (1996), "Additional evidence on the information-based contagion effects of bank failures", Journal of Banking and Finance 20:57–69.

Akerlof, G., and P. Romer (1993), "Looting: the economic underworld of bankruptcy for profit", Brookings Papers on Economic Activity 2:1–73.

Akhavein, J., A. Berger and D. Humphrey (1997), "The effects of megamergers on efficiency and prices: evidence from a bank profit function", Review of Industrial Organization 12(1):95–139.

Allen, F. (1990), "The market for information and the origin of financial intermediation", Journal of Financial Intermediation 1:3–30.

Allen, F. (1993), "Stock markets and resource allocation", in: C. Mayer and X. Vives, eds., Capital Markets and Financial Intermediation (Cambridge University Press) pp. 81–104.

Allen, F. (2001), "Presidential address: do financial institutions matter?", Journal of Finance 56:1165–1175.

Allen, F., and D. Gale (1997), "Financial markets, intermediaries, and intertemporal smoothing", Journal of Political Economy 105(3):523–546.

Allen, F., and D. Gale (1998), "Optimal financial crises", Journal of Finance 53:1245–1284.

Allen, F., and D. Gale (1999), "Diversity of opinion and financing new technologies", Journal of Financial Intermediation 8:68–89.

---

[59] Manove and Padilla (1999) examine how the presence of overly optimistic entrepreneurs complicates bank lending decisions; under competition, banks may be insufficiently conservative, reducing investment efficiency. Coval and Thakor (2001) show how rational agents may endogenously choose to become intermediaries between overly optimistic agents, who become entrepreneurs, and overly pessimistic agents, who become depositors.

Allen, F., and D. Gale (2000), "Financial contagion", Journal of Political Economy 108:1–33.

Almazan, A. (2002), "A model of competition in banking: bank capital vs. expertise", Journal of Financial Intermediation 11(1):87–121.

Alonso, I. (1996), "On avoiding bank runs", Journal of Monetary Economics 37:73–87.

Alston, L.J., W.A. Grove and D. Wheelock (1994), "Why do banks fail? Evidence from the 1920s", Explorations in Economic History 31:409–431.

Andrew, A.P. (1907), "The influence of crops upon business in America", Quarterly Journal of Economics 20:323–353.

Andrew, A.P. (1908), "Substitutes for cash in the panic of 1907", Quarterly Journal of Economics 22:497–516.

Ang, J.S., and T. Richardson (1994), "The underwriting experience of commercial bank affiliates prior to the Glass–Steagall Act: a re-examination of evidence for passage of the Act", Journal of Banking and Finance 18:351–395.

Arping, S. (2001), "Banking, commerce, and antitrust", Working Paper (University of Lausanne, Switzerland).

Asea, P., and B. Blomberg (1998), "Lending cycles", Journal of Econometrics 83:89–128.

Asquith, P., R. Gertner and D. Scharfstein (1994), "Anatomy of financial distress: an examination of junk bond issuers", Quarterly Journal of Economics 109:625–634.

Baer, H., and J. McElravey (1992), "The changing impact of capital requirements on bank growth: 1975 to 1991", Working Paper (Federal Reserve Bank of Chicago).

Baliga, S., and B. Polak (2001), "The emergence and persistence of the Anglo-Saxon and German financial systems", Working Paper (Department of Economics, Yale University, CT).

Baltensperger, E. (1980), "Alternative approaches to the theory of the banking firm", Journal of Monetary Economics 6:1–37.

Barro, J., and R. Barro (1990), "Pay, performance and turnover of bank CEOs", Journal of Labor Economics 8:448–481.

Barro, R. (1978), "Unanticipated money, output, and the price level in the United States", Journal of Political Economy 86:549–580.

Barsky, R., G. Mankiw, J. Miron and D. Weil (1988), "The world wide change in the behavior of interest rates and prices in 1914", European Economic Review 32:1136–1154.

Barth, J., and M. Bradley (1989), "Thrift deregulation and federal deposit insurance", Journal of Financial Services Research 2:231–259.

Barth, J., P.F. Bartholomew and M.G. Bradley (1990), "Determinants of thrift resolution costs", Journal of Finance 45:731–754.

Barth, J.R. (1991), The Great Savings and Loan Debacle (American Enterprise Institute, Washington, DC).

Beatty, A., and A. Gron (2001), "Capital, portfolio, and growth: bank behavior under risk-based capital guidelines", Journal of Financial Services Research 20(1):5–31.

Beck, T. (2002), "Deposit insurance as a private club: the case of Germany", Quarterly Review of Economics and Finance 42:701–719.

Benston, G. (1976), "A transaction cost approach to the theory of financial intermediation", Journal of Finance 31:215–231.

Benston, G. (1985), "An analysis of the causes of savings and loan association failures", Monograph Series in Finance and Economics, Monograph 1985-4/5 (New York University Graduate School of Business, Salomon Brothers Center for the Study of Financial Institutions).

Benston, G., M. Carhill and B. Olasov (1991), "The failure and survival of thrifts: evidence from the Southeast", in: G. Hubbard, ed., Financial Markets and Financial Crises (University of Chicago Press, Chicago) pp. 305-384.

Benveniste, L., J. Boyd and S. Greenbaum (1991), "Bank capital regulation", Osaka Economic Papers 40:210–226.

Berger, A., and L. Mester (1997), "Inside the black box: what explains differences in the efficiencies of financial institutions?" Journal of Banking and Finance 21(7):895–947.

Berger, A., R. Demsetz and P. Strahan (1999), "The consolidation of the financial services industry: causes, consequences, and implications for the future", Journal of Banking and Finance 23(2–4):135–194.

Berger, A., S. Davies and M. Flannery (2000), "Comparing market and regulatory assessments of bank performance: who knows what when?", Journal of Money, Credit and Banking 32:641–667.

Berger, A., R. DeYoung, H. Genay and G. Udell (2000), "Globalization of financial institutions: evidence from cross-border banking performance", Brookings-Wharton Papers on Financial Services 3:23–125.

Berger, A., L. Klapper and G. Udell (2001), "The ability of banks to lend to informationally opaque small businesses", Working Paper (Federal Reserve Board of Governors, Washington DC).

Berger, A., M. Kyle and J. Scalise (2001), "Did U.S. bank supervisors get tougher during the credit crunch? Did they get easier during the banking boom? Did it matter for bank lending?", in: F. Mishkin, ed., Prudential Supervision: What Works and What Doesn't (University of Chicago Press).

Berger, A.N., and G. Udell (1994), "Did risk-based capital allocate bank credit and cause a 'credit crunch' in the U.S.?", Journal of Money, Credit and Banking 26:585–628.

Berger, A.N., and G. Udell (1995), "Relationship lending and lines of credit in small firm finance", Journal of Business 68:351–382.

Berger, A.N., and G. Udell (1998), "The economics of small business finance: the roles of private equity and debt markets in the financial growth cycle", Journal of Banking and Finance 22:613–673.

Berglof, E., and E.-L. von Thadden (1994), "Short-term versus long-term interests: capital structure with multiple investors", Quarterly Journal of Economics 109(4):1055–1084.

Berlin, M., and J. Loeys (1988), "Bond covenants and delegated monitoring", Journal of Finance 43:397–412.

Berlin, M., and L. Mester (1992), "Debt covenants and renegotiation", Journal of Financial Intermediation 2:95–133.

Berlin, M., and L. Mester (1999), "Deposits and relationship lending", Review of Financial Studies 12(3):579–607.

Berlin, M., and L. Mester (2001), "Lender liability and large investors", Journal of Financial Intermediation 10(2):108–137.

Berlin, M., K. John and A. Saunders (1996), "Bank equity stakes in borrowing firms and financial distress", Review of Financial Studies 9(3):889–919.

Bernanke, B. (1983), "Nonmonetary effects of the financial crisis in the propagation of the Great Depression", American Economic Review 73:257–276.

Bernanke, B., and M. Gertler (1989), "Agency costs, net worth, and business fluctuations", American Economic Review 79(1):14–31.

Bernanke, B., and M. Gertler (1990), "Financial fragility and economic performance", Quarterly Journal of Economics 105(1):87–114.

Bernanke, B., and H. James (1991), "The gold standard, deflation, and financial crisis in the great depression: an international comparison", in: R.G. Hubbard, ed., Financial Markets and Financial Crises (University of Chicago Press, Chicago) pp. 33–68.

Bernanke, B., and C. Lown (1991), "The credit crunch", Brookings Papers on Economic Activity 2:205–247.

Besanko, D., and G. Kanatas (1993), "Credit market equilibrium with bank monitoring and moral hazard", Review of Financial Studies 6(1):213–232.

Besanko, D., and G. Kanatas (1996), "The regulation of bank capital: do capital standards promote bank safety?" Journal of Financial Intermediation 5(2):160–183.

Besanko, D., and A. Thakor (1992), "Banking deregulation: allocational consequences of relaxing entry barriers", Journal of Banking and Finance 16(5):909–932.

Besanko, D., and A. Thakor (1993), "Banking, deposit insurance and bank portfolio", in: C. Mayer and X. Vives, eds., Capital Markets and Financial Intermediation (Cambridge University Press, Cambridge, UK) pp. 292–319.

Best, R., and H. Zhang (1993), "Alternative information sources and the information content of bank loans", Journal of Finance 48:1507–1522.

Beyen, J.W. (1951), Money in a Maelstrom (MacMillan, New York).

Bhattacharya, S., and G. Chiesa (1995), "Proprietary information, financial intermediation, and research incentives", Journal of Financial Intermediation 4(4):328–357.

Bhattacharya, S., and D. Gale (1987), "Preference shocks, liquidity and central bank policy", in: W.A. Barnett and K. Singleton, eds., New Approaches to Monetary Economics (Cambridge University Press, Cambridge, UK) pp. 69–88.

Bhattacharya, S., and P. Pfleiderer (1985), "Delegated portfolio management", Journal of Economic Theory 36:1–25.

Bhattacharya, S., and A. Thakor (1993), "Contemporary banking theory", Journal of Financial Intermediation 3:2–50.

Billet, M., M. Flannery and J. Garfinkel (1995), "The effect of lender identity on a firm's equity return", Journal of Finance 50:699–718.

Bizer, D. (1993), "Regulatory discretion and the credit crunch", Working Paper (U.S. Securities and Exchange Commission).

Black, F. (1975), "Bank fund management in an efficient market", Journal of Financial Economics 2:323–339.

Black, H.A., M.C. Collins, B.L. Robinson and R.L. Schweitzer (1997), "Changes in market perception of riskiness: the case of too-big-to-fail", Journal of Financial Research 20:389–406.

Bodenhorn, H. (2002), "Making the little guy pay: payments system networks, cross-subsidization, and the collapse of the Suffolk system", Journal of Economic History 62:147–169.

Bolton, P., and X. Freixas (2000), "Equity, bonds, and bank debt: capital structure and financial market equilibrium under asymmetric information", Journal of Political Economy 108:324–351.

Bolton, P., and D.S. Scharfstein (1996), "Optimal debt structure and the number of creditors", Journal of Political Economy 104(1):1–25.

Bonaccorsi di Patti, E., and G. Dell'Ariccia (2001), "Bank competition and firm creation", Working Paper (Bank of Italy Research Department, Rome, Italy).

Boot, A. (2000), "Relationship banking: what do we know?" Journal of Financial Intermediation 9(1): 7–25.

Boot, A., and A. Thakor (1997), "Financial system architecture", Review of Financial Studies 10(3): 693–733.

Boot, A., and A. Thakor (2000), "Can relationship banking survive competition?" Journal of Finance 55(2):679–713.

Boot, A., S. Greenbaum and A. Thakor (1993), "Reputation and discretion in financial contracting", American Economic Review 83(5):1165–1183.

Bordo, M. (1985), "The impact and international transmission of financial crises: some historical evidence, 1870–1933", Revista di Storia Economica 2:41–78.

Bordo, M. (1986), "Financial crises, banking crises, stock market crashes and the money supply: some international evidence, 1870–1933", in: F. Capie and G. Wood, eds., Financial Crises and the World Banking System (Macmillan, London) pp. 190–248.

Bordo, M., and B. Eichengreen (1999), "Is our international financial environment unusually crisis prone?", in: D. Gruen and L. Gower, eds., Capital Flows and the International Financial System (Reserve Bank of Australia, Sydney) pp. 18–75.

Bordo, M., and A. Redish (1987), "Why did the Bank of Canada emerge in 1935?", Journal of Economic History 47:405–417.

Bordo, M., H. Rockoff and A. Redish (1994), "The U.S. banking system from a Northern exposure: stability versus efficiency", Journal of Economic History 54:325–341.

Bordo, M., H. Rockoff and A. Redish (1995), "A comparison of the stability and efficiency of the Canadian and American banking systems, 1870–1925", NBER Historical Working Paper 67 (NBER, Cambridge, MA).

Bordo, M., C. Goldin and E. White, eds (1998), The Defining Moment: The Great Depression and the American Economy in the Twentieth Century (University of Chicago Press, Chicago).

Boyd, J., and S. Graham (1991), "Investigating the banking consolidation trend", Federal Reserve Bank of Minneapolis Quarterly Review 15(2):3–15.

Boyd, J., and E. Prescott (1986), "Financial intermediary coalitions", Journal of Economic Theory 38:211–232.

Boyd, J., and B. Smith (1994), "How good are standard debt contracts? Stochastic versus nonstochastic monitoring in a costly state verification environment", Journal of Business 67:539–561.

Boyd, J.H., and M. Gertler (1994), "The role of large banks in the recent U.S. banking crisis", Federal Reserve Bank of Minneapolis Quarterly Review 18:2–21.

Breckenridge, R.M. (1910), The History of Banking in Canada. National Monetary Commission, 61st Congress, 2nd Session, Document 332 (Government Printing Office, Washington DC).

Bremer, C.D. (1935), American Bank Failures (Columbia University Press, New York).

Brewer, E. (1995), "The impact of deposit insurance on S&L shareholders' risk/return trade-offs", Journal of Financial Services Research 9:65–89.

Brickley, J., and C. James (1986), "Access to deposit insurance, insolvency rules and the stock returns of financial institutions", Journal of Financial Economics 16:345–371.

Brickley, J., and C. James (1987), "The takeover market, corporate board composition, and ownership structure: the case of banking", Journal of Law and Economics 35:161–180.

Brinkman, E.J., and P.M. Horvitz (1995), "Risk-based capital standards and the credit crunch", Journal of Money, Credit and Banking 27:848–863.

Broecker, T. (1990), "Credit-worthiness tests and interbank competition", Econometrica 58:429–452.

Brumbaugh, R.D. (1988), Thrifts Under Siege (Ballinger Publishing Company, Cambridge, MA).

Bryant, J. (1980), "A model of reserves, bank runs, and deposit insurance", Journal of Banking and Finance 4:335–344.

Buser, S., A. Chen and E. Kane (1981), "Federal deposit insurance, regulatory policy, and optimal bank capital", Journal of Finance 35:51–60.

Calomiris, C. (1990), "Is deposit insurance necessary? A historical perspective", Journal of Economic History 50:283–295.

Calomiris, C. (1993a), "Regulation, industrial structure, and instability in U.S. banking: an historical perspective", in: M. Klausner and L. White, eds., Structural Change in Banking (Business One Irwin, Homewood, IL) pp. 19–116.

Calomiris, C. (1993b), "Financial factors in the Great Depression", Journal of Economic Perspectives 7:61–85.

Calomiris, C., and G. Gorton (1991), "The origins of banking panics: models, facts, and bank regulation", in: G. Hubbard, ed., Financial Markets and Financial Crises (University of Chicago Press, Chicago) pp. 109–173.

Calomiris, C., and C. Kahn (1991), "The role of demandable debt in structuring optimal banking arrangements", American Economic Review 81:497–513.

Calomiris, C., and C. Kahn (1996), "The efficiency of self-regulated payments systems: learning from the Suffolk system", Journal of Money, Credit and Banking 28:766–797.

Calomiris, C., and J. Mason (1997), "Contagion and bank failures during the Great Depression: the Chicago banking panic of June 1932", American Economic Review 87:863–884.

Calomiris, C., and J. Mason (2002a), "Fundamentals, panics and bank distress during the Great Depression", American Economic Review, forthcoming.

Calomiris, C., and J. Mason (2002b), "Consequences of bank distress during the Great Depression", American Economic Review, forthcoming.

Calomiris, C., and L. Schweikart (1991), "The panic of 1857: origins, transmission, and containment", Journal of Economic History 51:807–834.

Campbell, T., and W. Kracaw (1980), "Information production, market signaling and the theory of financial intermediation", Journal of Finance 35:863–881.

Cannella, A., D. Fraser and D.S. Lee (1995), "Firm failure and managerial labor markets: evidence from Texas banking", Journal of Financial Economics 38:185–210.

Cannon, J.G. (1910), Clearing Houses. National Monetary Commission, 61st Congress, 2nd Session, Senate Document 491 (Government Printing Office, Washington DC).

Canova, F. (1991), "The sources of financial crises: pre and post fed evidence", International Economic Review 32:689–713.

Cantillo, M. (1998), "The rise and fall of bank control in the United States: 1890–1939", American Economic Review 88(5):1077–1093.

Cantillo, M., and J. Wright (2000), "How do firms choose their lenders? An empirical investigation", Review of Financial Studies 13:155–189.

Capie, F. (1997), "The evolution of central banking", in: G. Caprio and D. Vittas, eds., Reforming Financial Systems (Cambridge University Press, Cambridge, UK).

Caprio, G., and D. Klingebiel (1996), "Bank insolvencies: cross-country experience", World Bank Policy Research Working Paper 1620 (World Bank, Washington, DC).

Caramazza, F., L. Ricci and R. Salgado (1999), "International financial contagion", Background Paper to the World Economic Outlook, May 1999 (IMF, Washington, DC) pp. 66–87.

Carletti, E. (2000), "The structure of bank relationships, endogenous monitoring and loan rates", Working Paper (University of Mannheim, Germany).

Carlson, M. (2001), "Are branch banks better survivors? Evidence from the Depression Era", Finance and Economics Discussion Series 2001-51 (Board of Governors of the Federal Reserve System, Washington DC).

Carr, J., F. Mathewson and N. Quigley (1995), "Stability in the absence of deposit insurance: the Canadian banking system, 1890–1966", Journal of Money, Credit and Banking 27:1137–1158.

Cavalcanti, R., and N. Wallace (1999), "Inside and outside money as alternative media of exchange", Journal of Money, Credit and Banking 31(3, Part 2):443–457.

Cebenoyan, A.S., E. Cooperman and C. Register (1995), "Deregulation, reregulation, equity ownership, and S&L risk-taking", Financial Management 24:63–75.

Cebenoyan, A.S., E. Cooperman and C. Register (1999), "Ownership structure, charter value, and risk-taking behavior for thrifts", Financial Management 28:43–60.

Cerasi, V., and S. Daltung (2000), "The optimal size of a bank: costs and benefits of diversification", European Economic Review 44(9):1701–1726.

Cetorelli, N., and M. Gambera (2001), "Banking market structure, financial dependence and growth: international evidence from industry data", Journal of Finance 56(2):617–648.

Champ, B., B. Smith and S. Williamson (1996), "Currency elasticity and banking panics: theory and evidence", Canadian Journal of Economics 29:828–864.

Chari, V.V., and R. Jagannathan (1988), "Banking panics, information, and rational expectations equilibrium", Journal of Finance 43:749–763.

Chemmanur, T., and P. Fulghieri (1994), "Reputation, renegotiation and the choice between bank loans and publicly traded debt", Review of Financial Studies 7:475–506.

Chong, B.S. (1991), "The effects of interstate banking on commercial banks' risk and profitability", Review of Economics and Statistics 73(1):78–84.

Cornett, M., and H. Tehranian (1994), "An examination of voluntary versus involuntary security issuances by commercial banks", Journal of Financial Economics 35:99–122.

Coval, J., and A. Thakor (2001), "Financial intermediation as a beliefs-bridge between optimists and pessimists", Working Paper (University of Michigan Business School).

Covitz, D., and E. Heitfeld (1999), "Monitoring, moral hazard, and market power: a model of bank lending", Working Paper (Federal Reserve Board of Governors).

Crawford, A., J. Ezzell and J. Miles (1995), "Bank CEO pay–performance relations and the effects of deregulation", Journal of Business 68:231–256.

Da Rin, M., and T. Hellmann (1996), "Banks as catalysts for industrialization", Graduate School of Business Research Paper 1398 (Stanford University, CA).

Datta, S., M. Iskandar-Datta and A. Patel (2000), "Some evidence on the uniqueness of initial public debt offerings", Journal of Finance 55(2):715–743.

De Nicolo, G. (2001), "Size, charter value and risk in banking: an international perspective", Working Paper (International Monetary Fund, Washington, DC).

DeGennaro, R.P., L. Lang and J.B. Thomson (1993), "Troubled savings and loan institutions: turnaround strategies under insolvency", Financial Management (Autumn), pp. 163–175.

Dell'Ariccia, G. (2001), "Asymmetric information and the structure of the banking industry", European Economic Review 45:1957–1980.

Dell'Ariccia, G., and R. Marquez (2001a), "Competition among regulators and credit market integration", Working Paper (University of Maryland).

Dell'Ariccia, G., and R. Marquez (2001b), "Flight to quality of captivity? Information and credit allocation", Working Paper (University of Maryland).

Dell'Ariccia, G., E. Friedman and R. Marquez (1999), "Adverse selection as a barrier to entry in the banking industry", RAND Journal of Economics 30(3):515–534.

DeLong, G. (2001), "Stockholder gains from focusing versus diversifying bank mergers", Journal of Financial Economics 59(2):221–252.

Demirgüç-Kunt, A., and E. Detragiache (1998), "The determinants of banking crises: evidence from developed and developing countries", IMF Staff Papers 45(1).

Demirgüç-Kunt, A., and E. Detragiache (2000), "Does deposit insurance increase banking system stability? An empirical investigation", Working Paper (International Monetary Fund, Washington, DC).

Demirgüç-Kunt, A., and T. Sobaci (2000), "Deposit insurance around the world: a data base", Mimeo (World Bank, Washington, DC).

Demirgüç-Kunt, A., E. Detragiache and P. Gupta (2000), "Inside the crisis: an empirical analysis of banking systems in distress", Working Paper (World Bank, Washington, DC).

Demsetz, R., and P. Strahan (1997), "Diversification, size, and risk at bank holding companies", Journal of Money, Credit, and Banking 29(3):300–313.

Demsetz, R., M. Saidenberg and P. Strahan (1996), "Banks with something to lose: the disciplinary role of franchise value", Economic Policy Review 2:1–14.

Demsetz, R., M. Saidenberg and P. Strahan (1997), "Agency problems and risk taking in banks", Working Paper (Federal Reserve Bank of New York).

Detragiache, E. (1994), "Public versus private borrowing: a theory with implications for bankruptcy reform", Journal of Financial Intermediation 3:327–354.

Detragiache, E., P. Garella and L. Guiso (2000), "Multiple versus single banking relationships: theory and evidence", Journal of Finance 55(3):1133–1161.

Diamond, D. (1984), "Financial intermediation and delegated monitoring", Review of Economic Studies 51:393–414.

Diamond, D. (1989), "Reputation acquisition in debt markets", Journal of Political Economy 97:828–862.

Diamond, D. (1991), "Monitoring and reputation: the choice between bank loans and directly placed debt", Journal of Political Economy 99:689–721.

Diamond, D. (1997), "Liquidity, banks, and markets", Journal of Political Economy 105:928–956.

Diamond, D., and P. Dybvig (1983), "Bank runs, deposit insurance, and liquidity", Journal of Political Economy 91:401–419.

Diamond, D., and R. Rajan (2000), "A theory of bank capital", Journal of Finance 55:2431–2465.

Diamond, D., and R. Rajan (2001a), "Liquidity risk, liquidity creation and financial fragility: a theory of banking", Journal of Political Economy 109:2431–2465.

Diamond, D., and R. Rajan (2001b), "Banks and liquidity", American Economic Review Papers and Proceedings 91:422–425.

Diamond, D.W. (1993a), "Seniority and maturity of debt contracts", Journal of Financial Economics 33(3):341–368.

Diamond, D.W. (1993b), "Bank loan maturity and priority when borrowers can refinance", in: C. Mayer and X. Vives, eds., Capital Markets and Financial Intermediation (Cambridge University Press, Cambridge, UK) pp. 46–68.

Dinc, S. (2000), "Bank reputation, bank commitment, and the effects of competition in credit markets", Review of Financial Studies 13(3):781–812.

Donaldson, R.G. (1992a), "Sources of panics: evidence from the weekly data", Journal of Monetary Economics 30:277–305.

Donaldson, R.G. (1992b), "Costly liquidation, interbank trade, bank runs, and panics", Journal of Financial Intermediation 2:59–85.

Donaldson, R.G. (1993), "Financing banking crises: lessons from the panic of 1907", Journal of Monetary Economics 31:69–95.

Dow, J., and G. Gorton (1997), "Stock market efficiency and economic efficiency: is there a connection?", Journal of Finance 52:1087–1129.

Duffie, D., and P. Demarzo (1999), "A liquidity-based model of security design", Econometrica 67: 65–99.

Dziobek, C., and C. Pazarbasioglu (1997), "Lessons from systemic bank restructuring: a survey of 24 countries", IMF Working Paper 97-161 (IMF, Washington, DC).

Economopoulos, A.J. (1988), "Illinois free banking experience", Journal of Money, Credit, and Banking 20(2):249–264.

Economopoulos, A.J. (1990), "Free banking failures in New York and Wisconsin: a portfolio analysis", Exploration in Economic History 27:421–441.

Eichengreen, B. (1992), Golden Fetters: The Gold Standard and the Great Depression, 1919–1939 (Oxford University Press, New York).

Elsas, R., and J.P. Krahnen (1998), "Is relationship lending special? Evidence from credit-file data in Germany", Journal of Banking and Finance 22:1283–1316.

Esbitt, M. (1986), "Bank portfolios and bank failures during the Great Depression: Chicago", Journal of European History 46:455–462.

Fama, E. (1980), "Banking and the theory of finance", Journal of Monetary Economics 10:10–19.

Fama, E. (1985), "What's different about banks?", Journal of Monetary Economics 17:239–249.

Farinha, L., and J. Santos (2002), "Switching from single to multiple bank lending relationships: determinants and implications", Journal of Financial Intermediation 11:124–151.

Federal Deposit Insurance Corporation (2000), Options Paper (Federal Deposit Insurance Corporation, Washington DC).

Fischer, K.-H. (2000), "Acquisition of information in loan markets and bank market power – an empirical investigation", Working Paper (J.W. Goethe University, Germany).

Fisher, I. (1932), Booms and Depressions (Adelphi, New York).

Flannery, M. (1989), "Capital requirements and insured banks' choice of individual loan default risk", Journal of Monetary Economics 24:235–258.

Flannery, M. (1994), "Debt maturity and the deadweight cost of leverage: optimally financing banking firms", American Economic Review 84:320–331.

Flannery, M. (1996), "Financial crises, payments system problems, and discount window lending", Journal of Money, Credit and Banking 28:804–824.

Flannery, M. (2001), "The faces of market discipline", Journal of Financial Services Research 20: 107–119.

Flannery, M., and K. Rangan (2001), "Market forces at work in the banking industry: evidence from the capital buildup of the 1990s", Working Paper (University of Florida).

Flannery, M., and S. Sorescu (1996), "Evidence of bank market discipline in subordinated debenture yields: 1983–1991", Journal of Finance 51:1347–1377.

Flood, M.D. (1992), "The great deposit insurance debate", Federal Reserve Bank of St. Louis Review 74:51–77.

Foglia, A., S. Laviola and P. Reedtz (1998), "Multiple banking relationships and the fragility of corporate borrowers", Journal of Banking and Finance 22:1441–1456.

Fohlin, C. (1998), "Relationship banking, liquidity, and investment in the german industrialization", Journal of Finance 53:1737–1758.

Fohlin, C. (1999), "Universal banking in pre-World War I Germany: model or myth?", Explorations in Economic History 36:305–343.

Franks, J., and W. Torous (1994), "A comparison of financial recontracting in distressed exchanges and Chapter 11 reorganizations", Journal of Financial Economics 35:349–370.

Freeman, S. (1988), "Banks as the provision of liquidity", Journal of Business 61:45–64.

Freeman, S. (1996a), "The payments system, liquidity, and rediscounting", American Economic Review 86:1126–1138.

Freeman, S. (1996b), "Clearinghouse banks and banknote over-issue", Journal of Monetary Economics 38:101–115.

Friedman, M., and A.J. Schwartz (1963), A Monetary History of the United States, 1867–1960 (National Bureau of Economic Research, New York).

Furfine, C. (2001), "Bank portfolio allocation: the impact of capital requirements, regulatory monitoring, and economic conditions", Journal of Financial Services Research 20:33–56.

Furlong, F., and M. Keeley (1989), "Capital regulation and bank risk-taking: a note", Journal of Banking and Finance 13:883–891.

Furlong, F., and M. Keeley (1990), "A reexamination of mean-variance analysis of bank capital regulation", Journal of Banking and Finance 14:69–84.

Gale, D., and M. Hellwig (1985), "Incentive-compatible debt contracts: the one-period problem", Review of Economic Studies 52(4):647–663.

Gande, A., M. Puri, A. Saunders and I. Walter (1997), "Bank underwriting of debt securities: modern evidence", Review of Financial Studies 10:1175–1202.

Gande, A., M. Puri and A. Saunders (1999), "Bank entry, competition and the market for corporate securities underwriting", Journal of Financial Economics 54:165–195.

Garcia, G. (1999), "Deposit insurance: a survey of actual and best practices", IMF Working Paper 96/83 (IMF, Washington, DC).

Gehrig, T. (1995), "Excessive risks and banking regulation", Working Paper (University of Basel, Switzerland).

Gehrig, T. (1998), "Screening, cross-border banking, and the allocation of credit", Research in Economics 52(4):387–407.

Gehrig, T., and R. Stenbacka (2001), "Information sharing in banking: a collusive device?" CEPR Discussion Paper 2911 (CEPR, UK).

Gennotte, G., and D. Pyle (1991), "Capital controls and bank risk", Journal of Banking and Finance 15:805–824.

Gibson, M. (1995), "Can bank health affect investment? Evidence from Japan", Journal of Business 68:281–308.

Gilson, S. (1990), "Bankruptcy, boards, banks, and blockholders: evidence on changes in corporate ownership and control when firms default", Journal of Financial Economics 27:355–388.

Gilson, S., K. John and L. Lang (1990), "Troubled debt restructurings: an empirical study of private reorganization of firms in default", Journal of Financial Economics 27:315–353.

Goldstein, I., and A. Pauzner (1999), "Demand deposit contracts and the probability of runs", Mimeo (Eitan Berglas School of Economics, Tel Aviv University).

Gorton, G. (1984), "Private bank clearinghouses and the origins of central banking", Business Review of the Federal Reserve Bank of Philadelphia 1(January, February):3–12.

Gorton, G. (1985a), "Clearinghouses and the origin of central banking in the U.S", Journal of Economic History 45:277–283.

Gorton, G. (1985b), "Bank suspension of convertibility", Journal of Monetary Economics 15:177–193.

Gorton, G. (1988), "Banking panics and business cycles", Oxford Economic Papers 40:751–781.

Gorton, G. (1996), "Reputation formation in early bank note markets", Journal of Political Economy 104:346–397.

Gorton, G. (1999), "Pricing free bank notes", Journal of Monetary Economics 44:33–64.

Gorton, G., and J. Haubrich (1987), "Bank deregulation, credit markets, and the control of capital", Carnegie-Rochester Conference Series on Public Policy 26:289–334.

Gorton, G., and L. Huang (2001), "Bank panics and the endogeneity of central banking", Mimeo (Wharton School, University of Pennsylvania).

Gorton, G., and J. Kahn (2000), "The design of bank loan contracts", Review of Financial Studies 13:331–354.

Gorton, G., and D. Mullineaux (1987), "The joint production of confidence: endogenous regulation and the 19th century commercial bank clearinghouse", Journal of Money, Credit, and Banking 19:457–468.

Gorton, G., and G. Pennacchi (1990), "Financial intermediaries and liquidity creation", Journal of Finance 45:49–72.

Gorton, G., and G. Pennacchi (1995), "Bank and loan sales: marketing non-marketable assets", Journal of Monetary Economics 35:389–411.

Gorton, G., and R. Rosen (1995), "Corporate control, portfolio choice, and the decline of banking", Journal of Finance 50:1377–1420.

Gorton, G., and F. Schmid (2000), Universal banking and the performance of German firms", Journal of Financial Economics 58(1–2):29–80.

Gorton, G., and A. Winton (2000), "Liquidity provision, bank capital, and the macroeconomy", Working Paper (University of Minnesota).

Green, E. (1997), "Money and debt in the structure of payments", Bank of Japan Monetary and Economic Studies 15:63–87.

Green, E., and P. Lin (1999), "Implementing efficient allocations in a model of financial intermediation", Working Paper 92 (Centre for Public Policy Studies, Lingnan University, Hong Kong).

Green, E., and P. Lin (2000), "Diamond and Dybvig's classic theory of financial intermediation: what's missing?", Federal Reserve Bank of Minneapolis Quarterly Review 24:3–13.

Green, R.C. (1984), "Investment incentives, debt, and warrants", Journal of Financial Economics 13(1): 115–136.

Grossman, R. (1992), "Deposit insurance, regulation, and moral hazard in the thrift industry: evidence from the 1930's", American Economic Review 82:800–822.

Grossman, R. (1994), "The shoe that didn't drop: explaining banking stability during the Great Depression", Journal of Economic History 54:654–682.

Grossman, S., and J. Stiglitz (1980), "On the impossibility of informationally efficient markets", American Economic Review 61:393–408.

Hadlock, C., and C. James (2000), "Bank lending and the menu of financing options", Mimeo (University of Florida).

Hall, B. (1993), "How has the Basel Accord affected bank portfolios?", Journal of the Japanese and International Economies 7:408–440.

Hamilton, D.E. (1985), "The causes of the banking panic of 1930: another view", Journal of Southern History 51:581–608.

Hancock, D., and J.A. Wilcox (1994), "Bank capital and the credit crunch: the roles of risk-weighted and unweighted capital regulation", Journal of the American Real Estate and Urban Economics Association 22:59–94.

Hannan, T., and A. Berger (1991), "The rigidity of prices: evidence form the banking sector", American Economic Review 81:938–945.

Hart, O., and J. Moore (1998), "Default and renegotiation: a dynamic model of debt", Quarterly Journal of Economics 113(1):1–41.

Haubrich, J. (1989), "Financial intermediation, delegated monitoring, and long-term relationships", Journal of Banking and Finance 13:9–20.

Haubrich, J. (1990), "Nonmonetary effects of financial crises: lessons from the Great Depression in Canada", Journal of Monetary Economics 25:223–252.

Haubrich, J., and R. King (1990), "Banking and insurance", Journal of Monetary Economics 26: 361–386.

Haubrich, J., and J. Santos (2002), "Alternative forms of mixing banking and commerce: evidence from American history", Working Paper (Federal Reserve Bank of New York).

Haubrich, J., and P. Wachtel (1993), "Capital requirements and shifts in commercial bank portfolios", Federal Reserve Bank of Cleveland Economic Review 29:2–15.

Hauswald, R., and R. Marquez (2000), "Competition and strategic focus in lending relationships", Working Paper (University of Maryland).

Hellwig, M. (1994), "Liquidity provision, banking, and the allocation of interest rate risk", European Economic Review 38(7):1363–1389.

Hellwig, M. (1998), "Allowing for risk choices in Diamond's 'Financial Intermediation as Delegated Monitoring' ", Discussion Paper 98-04 (Sonderforschungsbereich 504, University of Mannheim, Germany).

Hirshleifer, J. (1971), "The private and social value of information and the reward to inventive activity", American Economic Review 61:561–574.

Holmstrom, B., and J. Tirole (1997), "Financial intermediation, loanable funds, and the real sector", Quarterly Journal of Economics 112:663–691.

Holmstrom, B., and J. Tirole (1998), "Private and public supply of liquidity", Journal of Political Economy 106:1–40.

Hoshi, T., and A. Kashyap (1999), "The Japanese banking crisis: where did it come from and how will it end?", NBER Macroeconomics Annual (NBER, Cambridge, MA).

Hoshi, T., A. Kashyap and D. Scharfstein (1990a), "Bank monitoring and investment: evidence from the changing structure of Japanese corporate banking relationships", in: R.G. Hubbard, ed., Asymmetric Information, Corporate Finance and Investment (University of Chicago Press, Chicago, IL) pp. 105–126.

Hoshi, T., A. Kashyap and D. Scharfstein (1990b), "The role of banks in reducing the costs of financial distress in Japan", Journal of Financial Economics 27:67–88.

Hoshi, T., A. Kashyap and D. Scharfstein (1991), "Corporate structure, liquidity and investment: evidence from Japanese industrial groups", Quarterly Journal of Economics 106:33–60.

Houston, J., and C. James (1993), "Management and organizational changes in banking: a comparison of regulatory intervention with private creditor actions in nonbank firms", Carnegie-Rochester Conference Series in Public Policy 38:143–178.

Houston, J., and C. James (1995), "CEO compensation and bank risk: is compensation in banking structured to promote risk taking?", Journal of Monetary Economics 36:405–431.

Houston, J., and C. James (1996), "Bank information monopolies and the mix of private and public debt claims", Journal of Finance 51(5):1863–1889.

Hovakimian, A., and E. Kane (2000), "Effectiveness of capital regulation at U.S. commerical banks, 1985–1994", Journal of Finance 55:451–468.

Hubbard, G., and D. Palia (1995), "Executive pay and performance: evidence from the U.S. banking industry", Journal of Financial Economics 39:105–130.

Hubbard, R.G., K. Kuttner and D. Palia (2002), "Are there 'bank effects' in borrower's costs of funds? Evidence from a matched sample of borrowers and banks", Journal of Business 75:559–582.

Hughes, J., W. Lang, L. Mester and C.-G. Moon (1999), "The dollars and sense of bank consolidation", Journal of Banking and Finance 23(2–4):291–324.

Hunter, H.M. (1982), "The role of business liquidity during the Great Depression and afterwards: differences between large and small firms", Journal of Economic History 42:883–902.

International Monetary Fund (1998), "Financial crises: characteristics and indicators of vulnerability", World Economic Outlook (May):74–97.

Jacklin, C. (1987), "Demand deposits, trading restrictions, and risk-sharing", in: E. Prescott and N. Wallace, eds., Contractual Arrangements for Intertemporal Trade (University of Minnesota Press, Minneapolis, MN) pp. 26–47.

Jacklin, C. (1989), "Banks and risk-sharing: instabilities and coordination", in: S. Bhattacharya and G. Constantinides, eds., Financial Markets and Incomplete Information (Rowan and Littlefield, Maryland) pp. 317–327.

Jacklin, C., and S. Bhattacharya (1988), "Distinguishing panics and information-based bank runs: welfare and policy implications", Journal of Political Economy 96:568–592.

James, C. (1984), "An analysis of the effect of state acquisition laws on managerial efficiency: the case of the bank holding company acquisitions", Journal of Law and Economics 27:211–226.

James, C. (1987), "Some evidence on the uniqueness of bank loans", Journal of Financial Economics 19:217–233.

James, C. (1995), "When do banks take equity? An analysis of bank loan restructurings and the role of public debt", Review of Financial Studies 8:1209–1234.

James, C. (1996), "Bank debt restructurings and the composition of exchange offers in financial distress", Journal of Finance 51:711–727.

James, H. (1986), The German Slump: Politics and Economics, 1924–1936 (Oxford University Press).

James, H. (2001), The End of Globalization: Lessons from the Great Depression (Harvard University Press).

Jayanti, S.V., A.M. Whyte and A.Q. Do (1993), "Bank failures and contagion effects: evidence from Britain, Canada and Germany", Working Paper (Cleveland State University).

Jean-Baptiste, E. (1999), "Demand deposits as an incentive mechanism", Mimeo (Wharton School, University of Pennsylvania).

Jean-Baptiste, E. (2001), "Information monopoly and commitment in intermediary-firm relationships", Working Paper (Graduate School of Business, Columbia University).

Jensen, M., and W. Meckling (1976), "Theory of the firm: managerial behavior, agency costs and ownership structure", Journal of Financial Economics 3(4):305–360.

John, K., T. John and A. Saunders (1994), "Universal banking and firm risk-taking", Journal of Banking and Finance 18:307–323.

Johnson, S. (1997), "An empirical analysis of the determinants of corporate debt ownership structure", Journal of Financial and Quantitative Analysis 32(1):47–69.

Kaminsky, G., and C. Reinhart (1999), "The twin crises: the causes of banking and balance of payments crises", American Economic Review 89:473–500.

Kaminsky, G., and C. Reinhart (2000), "On crises, contagion, and confusion", Journal of International Economics 51:145–168.

Kanatas, G., and J. Qi (2001), "Imperfect competition, agency, and financing decisions", Journal of Business 74(2):307–338.

Kane, E. (1990), "Principal agent problems in S&L salvage", Journal of Finance 45:755–764.

Kane, E., and B. Wilson (1998), "A contracting theory interpretation of the origins of federal deposit insurance", Journal of Money, Credit and Banking 30:573–595.

Kane, E.J. (1989), The S & L Mess: How Did it Happen? (Urban Institute Press, Washington, DC).

Kang, J.-K., and R. Stulz (2000), "Do banking shocks affect borrowing firm performance? An analysis of the Japanese experience", Journal of Business 73(1):1–23.

Kaplan, S., and B. Minton (1994), "Appointments of outsiders to Japanese boards: determinants and implications for managers", Journal of Financial Economics 36(2):225–258.

Kaplan, S., and P. Strömberg (2001), "Venture capitalists as principals: contracting, screening, and monitoring", American Economic Review 91(2):426–430.

Kashyap, A., and J. Stein (2000), "What do a million observations on banks say about the transmission of monetary policy?" American Economic Review 90(3):407–428.

Kashyap, A., J. Stein and D. Wilcox (1993), "Monetary policy and credit conditions: evidence from the composition of external finance", American Economic Review 83:78–98.

Kashyap, A., R. Rajan and J. Stein (2002), "Banks as liquidity providers: an explanation for the coexistence of lending and deposit-taking", Journal of Finance 57:33–73.

Kaufman, G. (1994), "Bank contagion: a review of the theory and evidence", Journal of Financial Services Research 8:123–150.

Keeley, M.C. (1990), "Deposit insurance, risk, and market power in banking", American Economic Review 80:1183–1200.

Keeton, W. (1994), "Causes of the recent increase in bank security holdings", Federal Reserve Bank of Kansas City Economic Review (2nd Quarter):45–57.

Kelley, M., and C. Ó Gráda (2000), "Market contagion: evidence from the panics of 1854 and 1857", American Economic Review 90(5):1110–1124.

Kemmerer, E.W. (1910), "Seasonal variations in the relative demand for money and capital in the United States", National Monetary Commission, 61st Cong., 2nd sess., Senate Doc. 588 (Government Printing Office, Washington, DC).

Kho, B.-C., D. Lee and R. Stulz (2000), "U.S. banks, crises, and bailouts: from Mexico to LTCM", American Economic Review 90:28–31.

Kihlstrom, R., and S. Mathews (1990), "Managerial incentives in an entrepreneurial stock market model", Journal of Financial Intermediation 1:57–79.

Kim, D., and A. Santomero (1988), "Risk in banking and capital regulation", Journal of Finance 43:1219–1233.

Kindleberger, C. (1973), The World in Depression (University of California Press, Berkeley).

Kormendi, R., V. Bernard, S.C. Pirrong and E. Snyder (1989), Crisis Resolution in the Thrift Industry (Kluwer Academic Publishers, Boston).

Krasa, S., and A. Villamil (1992), "Monitoring the monitor: an incentive structure for a financial intermediary", Journal of Economic Theory 57:197–221.

Krasa, S., and A. Villamil (1993), "A theory of optimal bank size", Oxford Economic Papers 44: 725–749.

Kroszner, R., and R. Rajan (1994), "Is the Glass–Steagall Act justified? A study of the United States experience with universal banking before 1933", American Economic Review 84:810–832.

Kroszner, R., and R. Rajan (1997), "Organizational structure and credibility: evidence from commercial bank activities before the Glass–Steagall Act", Journal of Monetary Economics 39:475–516.

Kroszner, R., and P. Strahan (2001a), "Bankers on boards: monitoring, conflicts of interest, and lender liability", Journal of Financial Economics 62:415–452.

Kroszner, R., and P. Strahan (2001b), "Throwing good money after bad? Board connections and conflicts in bank lending", Working Paper (University of Chicago).

Kryzanowski, L., and G.S. Roberts (1993), "Canadian banking solvency, 1922–1940", Journal of Money, Credit and Banking 25:361–376.

Kryzanowski, L., and G.S. Roberts (1999), "Perspectives on Canadian banking insolvency during the 1930s", Journal of Money, Credit and Banking 31:130–136.

Kyei, A. (1995), "Deposit protection arrangements: a survey", IMF Working Paper 95/134 (International Monetary Fund, Washington, DC).

Kyle, A.S. (1985), "Continuous auctions and insider trading", Econometrica 53:1335–1355.

Leland, H., and D. Pyle (1977), "Information asymmetries, financial structure, and financial intermediation", Journal of Finance 32:371–387.

Levine, R. (2000), "Bank-based or market-based financial systems: which is better?", Mimeo (University of Minnesota).

Levine, R., and S. Zervos (1998), "Stock markets, banks and economic growth", American Economic Review 88:537–558.

Lindgren, C.-J., G. Garcia and M. Saal (1996), Bank Soundness and Macroeconomic Policy (International Monetary Fund, Washington, DC).

Lizzeri, A. (1999), "Information revelation and certification intermediaries", Rand Journal of Economics 30:214–231.

Longhofer, S., and J. Santos (2000), "The importance of bank seniority for relationship lending", Journal of Financial Intermediation 9(1):57–89.

Lown, C., and D. Morgan (2001), "The credit cycle and the business cycle: new findings using the survey of senior loan officers", Working Paper (Federal Reserve Bank of New York).

Lummer, S., and J. McConnell (1989), "Further evidence on the bank lending process and the capital market responses to bank loan agreements", Journal of Financial Economics 25:99–122.

Mahrt-Smith, J. (2000), "Should banks own equity? A corporate finance perspective", Working Paper (London Business School).

Mailith, G., and L. Mester (1994), "A positive analysis of bank closure", Journal of Financial Intermediation 3:272–299.

Maksimovic, V. (1990), "Product market imperfections and loan commitments", Journal of Finance 45(5):1641–1653.

Manove, M., and J. Padilla (1999), "Banking (conservatively) with optimists", RAND Journal of Economics 30(2):324–350.

Manove, M., J. Padilla and M. Pagano (2001), "Collateral versus project screening: a model of lazy banks", RAND Journal of Economics 32(4):726–744.

Marcus, A. (1984), "Deregulation and bank financial policy", Journal of Banking and Finance 8: 557–565.

Marcus, A., and I. Shaked (1984), "The valuation of FDIC deposit insurance using option pricing estimates", Journal of Money, Credit and Banking 16:446–460.

Marquez, R. (2002), "Competition, adverse selection, and information dispersion in the banking industry", Review of Financial Studies 15:901–926.

Matutes, C., and X. Vives (1996), "Competition for deposits, fragility, and insurance", Journal of Financial Intermediation 5(2):184–216.

Mayer, C. (1990), "Financial systems, corporate finance, and economic development", in: G. Hubbard, ed., Asymmetric Information, Corporate Finance, and Investment (University of Chicago Press, Chicago).

McAndrews, J., and W. Roberds (1999), "Payment intermediation and the origins of banking", Working Paper 99-11 (Federal Reserve Bank of Atlanta).

McKenzie, J., R. Cole and R. Brown (1992), "Moral hazard, portfolio allocation, and asset returns for thrift institutions", Journal of Financial Services Research 5:315–339.

Mikkelson, W., and M. Partch (1986), "Valuation effects of security offerings and the issuance process", Journal of Financial Economics 15:31–60.

Millon, M., and A. Thakor (1985), "Moral hazard and information sharing: a model of information gathering agencies", Journal of Finance 40:1403–1422.

Miron, J., G. Mankiw and D. Weil (1987), "The adjustment of expectations to a change in regime: a study of the founding of the Federal Reserve", American Economic Review 77:358–374.

Miron, J.A. (1986), "Financial panics, the seasonality of the nominal interest rate, and the founding of the Fed", American Economic Review 76:125–140.

Mishkin, F. (1991), "Asymmetric information and financial crises: a historical perspective", in: G. Hubbard, ed., Financial Markets and Financial Crises (University of Chicago Press, Chicago) pp. 69–108.

Moen, J., and E. Tallman (1992), "The bank panic of 1907: the role of trust companies", Journal of Economic History 52:611–630.

Moen, J., and E. Tallman (2000), "Clearinghouse membership and deposit contraction during the panic of 1907", Journal of Economic History 60:145–163.

Morck, R., A. Shleifer and R. Vishny (1989), "Alternative mechanisms for corporate control", American Economic Review 79:842–852.

Morck, R., M. Nakamura and A. Shivdasani (2000), "Banks, ownership structure, and firm value in Japan", Journal of Business 73(4):539–567.

Morgan, D. (2000), "Rating banks: risk and uncertainty in an opaque industry", Staff Report 105 (Federal Reserve Bank of New York).

Morgan, G. (1992), "Capital adequacy", in: P. Newman, M. Milgate and J. Eatwell, eds., The New Palgrave Dictionary of Money and Finance (Macmillan Press).

Morris, S., and H.S. Shin (2001), "Rethinking multiple equilibria in macroeconomic modeling", in: B. Bernanke and K. Rogoff, eds., NBER Macroeconomics Annual (MIT Press, Cambridge, MA) pp. 139–161.

Mullineaux, D. (1987), "Competitive monies and the Suffolk system: a contractual perspective", Southern Economic Journal 53:884–898.

Mullineaux, D., and D. Preece (1996), "Monitoring, loan renegotiability, and firm value: the role of lending syndicates", Journal of Banking and Finance 20:577–593.

Myers, S. (1977), "The determinants of corporate borrowing", Journal of Financial Economics 5: 147–175.

Myers, S., and N. Majluf (1984), "Corporate financing and investment decisions when firms have information that investors do not have", Journal of Financial Economics 13:187–221.

Neumark, D., and S.A. Sharpe (1992), "Market structure and the nature of price rigidity: evidence from the market for consumer deposits", Quarterly Journal of Economics 107(2):657–680.

Ó Gráda, C., and E.N. White (2001), "Who panics during panics? Evidence from a nineteenth century savings bank", Working Paper (Rutgers University, NJ).

O'Hara, M., and W. Shaw (1990), "Deposit insurance and wealth effects: the value of being 'too big to fail' ", Journal of Finance 45:1587–1600.

Ongena, S., and D.C. Smith (2000a), "What determines the number of bank relationships? Cross-country evidence", Journal of Financial Intermediation 9(1):26–56.

Ongena, S., and D.C. Smith (2000b), "The duration of bank relationships", Journal of Financial Economics 61:449–475.

Ostergaard, C. (2001), "External financing costs and banks' loan supply: does the structure of the bank sector matter?" Working Paper (Norwegian School of Management, Sandvika, Norway).

Padilla, A.J., and M. Pagano (1997), "Endogenous communication among lenders and entrepreneurial incentives", Review of Financial Studies 10(1):205–236.

Padilla, A.J., and M. Pagano (2000), "Sharing default information as a borrower discipline device", European Economic Review 44:1951–1980.

Pagano, M., and T. Jappelli (1993), "Information sharing in credit markets", Journal of Finance 48: 1693–1718.

Park, C. (2000), "Monitoring and structure of debt contracts", Journal of Finance 55(5):2157–2195.

Park, S. (1991), "Bank failure contagion in historical perspective", Journal of Monetary Economics 28:271–286.

Peek, J., and E. Rosengren (1995), "The capital crunch: neither a borrower nor a lender be", Journal of Money, Credit and Banking 27:625–638.

Peek, J., and E. Rosengren (1997), "The international transmission of financial shocks: the case of Japan", American Economic Review 87(4):495–505.

Peek, J., and E. Rosengren (2000), "Collateral damage: effects of the Japanese bank crisis on real economic activity in the United States", American Economic Review 87(4):30–45.

Pennacchi, G. (1987), "A reexamination of the over- (or under-)pricing of deposit insurance", Journal of Money, Credit and Banking 19:340–360.

Petersen, M., and R. Rajan (1994), "The benefits of lending relationships: evidence from small business data", Journal of Finance 49:3–37.

Petersen, M., and R. Rajan (1995), "The effect of credit market competition on lending relationships", Quarterly Journal of Economics 110:407–443.

Polonchek, J., M. Slovin and M. Sushka (1989), "Valuation effects of commercial bank securities offerings: a test of the information hypothesis", Journal of Banking and Finance 13:443–461.

Postlewaite, A., and X. Vives (1987), "Bank runs as an equilibrium phenomenon", Journal of Political Economy 95:485–491.

Preece, D., and D. Mullineaux (1989), "The nonuniquenss of bank loans", Mimeo (University of Kentucky, Lexington, KY).

Prowse, S. (1995), "Alternative methods of corporate control of commercial banks", Federal Reserve Bank of Dallas Economic Review, 3rd Quarter, pp. 24–36.

Puri, M. (1994), "The long-term default performance of bank underwritten security issues", Journal of Banking and Finance 18:397–418.

Puri, M. (1996), "Commercial banks in investment banking: conflict of interest or certification role?", Journal of Financial Economics 40:373–401.

Qi, J. (1994), "Bank liquidity and stability in an overlapping generations model", Review of Financial Studies 7:389–417.

Rajan, R. (1992), "Insiders and outsiders: the choice between informed and arm's-length debt", Journal of Finance 47:1367–1400.

Rajan, R. (1994), "Why bank credit policies fluctuate: a theory and some evidence", Quarterly Journal of Economics 109(2):399–441.

Rajan, R., and A. Winton (1995), "Covenants and collateral as incentives to monitor", Journal of Finance 50(4):1113–1146.

Ramakrishnan, R.T.S., and A. Thakor (1984), "Information reliability and a theory of financial intermediation", Review of Economic Studies 51:415–432.

Repullo, R., and J. Suarez (1998), "Monitoring, liquidation, and security design", Review of Financial Studies 11(1):163–187.

Riordan, M. (1993), "Competition and bank performance: a theoretical perspective", in: C. Mayer and X. Vives, eds., Capital Markets and Financial Intermediation (Cambridge University Press, Cambridge, UK) pp. 328–343.

Rochet, J.-C., and J. Tirole (1996), "Interbank lending and systemic risk", Journal of Money, Credit and Banking 28:733–762.

Rockoff, H. (1974), "The free banking era: a reinterpretation", Journal of Money, Credit and Banking 6:141–167.

Rockoff, H. (1975), The Free Banking Era: A Reconsideration (Arno Press, New York).

Rockoff, H. (1993), "The meaning of money in the Great Depression", Historical Research Paper 52 (National Bureau of Economics).

Rolnick, A., and W. Weber (1982), "Free banking, wildcat banking and shinplasters", Quarterly Review – Fall (Federal Reserve Bank of Minneapolis).

Rolnick, A., and W. Weber (1983), "New evidence on the free banking era", American Economic Review 73(5):1080–1091.

Rolnick, A., and W. Weber (1984), "The causes of free bank failures: a detailed examination", Journal of Monetary Economics 14:267–292.

Rolnick, A., and W. Weber (1988), "Explaining the demand for free bank notes", Journal of Monetary Economics 21:47–72.

Rolnick, A., and W. Weber (1998), "The Suffolk banking system reconsidered", Working Paper 587D (Federal Reserve Bank of Minnesota).

Rolnick, A., B. Smith and W. Weber (1998), "The Suffolk bank and the panic of 1837: how a private bank acted as a lender-of-last-resort", Working Paper 592 (Federal Reserve Bank of Minnesota).

Ronn, E., and A. Verma (1986), "Pricing risk-adjusted deposit insurance: an option-based model", Journal of Finance 41:871–895.

Ruckes, M. (1998), "Competing banks, credit standards, and corporate conservatism", Working Paper (University of Mannheim, Germany).

Rudolph, P., and B. Hamdan (1988), "An analysis of post-regulation Savings and Loan failures", Journal of the American Real Estate and Urban Economics Association 16:17–33.

Sahlman, W. (1990), "The structure and governance of venture-capital organizations", Journal of Financial Economics 27:473–521.

Santos, J. (1998), "Banking and commerce: how does the united states compare to other countries?" Federal Reserve Bank of Cleveland Economic Review 34(4):14–26.

Santos, J. (1999), "Bank capital and equity investment regulations", Journal of Banking and Finance 23:1095–1120.

Sapienza, P. (2002), "The effects of banking mergers on loan contracts", Journal of Finance 57:329–368.

Saunders, A., and I. Walter (1994), Universal Banking in the U.S.? (Oxford University Press, Oxford, UK).

Saunders, A., and B. Wilson (1996), "Contagious bank runs: evidence from the 1929–1933 period", Journal of Financial Intermediation 5:409–423.

Saunders, A., and B. Wilson (1999), "The impact of consolidation and safety-net support on Canadian, US, and UK banks: 1893–1992", Journal of Banking and Finance 23:537–571.

Saunders, A., and B. Wilson (2001), "An analysis of bank charter value and its risk-constraining incentives", Journal of Financial Services Research 19:185–195.

Saunders, A., E. Strock and N.G. Travlos (1990), "Ownership structure, deregulation, and bank risk taking", Journal of Finance 45:643–654.

Schenone, C. (2001), "The effect of lending relations on the firm's cost of equity capital in its IPO", Working Paper (Northwestern University, IL).

Schranz, M. (1993), "Takeovers improve firm performance: evidence from the banking industry", Journal of Political Economy 101:299–326.

Schreft, S., and R. Owens (1991), "Survey evidence of tighter credit conditions: what does it mean?", Federal Reserve Bank of Richmond Economic Review 77:29–34.

Seward, J. (1990), "Corporate financial policy and the theory of financial intermediation", Journal of Finance 45:351–375.

Shaffer, S. (1998), "The winner's curse in banking", Journal of Financial Intermediation 7(4):359–392.

Sharpe, S. (1990), "Asymmetric information, bank lending, and implicit contracts: a stylized model of customer relationships", Journal of Finance 45:1069–1087.

Sharpe, S. (1995), "Bank capitalization, regulation, and the credit crunch: a critical review of the research findings", Finance and Economics Discussion Series Paper 95/20 (Board of Governors of the Federal Reserve System, Washington DC).

Slovin, M., M. Sushka and C. Hudson (1988), "Corporate commercial paper, note issuance facilities, and shareholder wealth", Journal of International Money and Finance 7:289–302.

Slovin, M., S. Johnson and J. Glascock (1992), "Firm size and the information content of bank loan announcements", Journal of Banking and Finance 16:1057–1071.

Slovin, M., M. Sushka and J. Polonchek (1992), "Informational externalities of seasoned equity issues: differences between banks and industrial firms", Journal of Financial Economics 32:87–101.

Slovin, M., M. Sushka and J. Polonchek (1993), "The value of bank durability: borrowers as bank stakeholders", Journal of Finance 48(1):247–266.

Smith, B. (1984), "Private information, deposit insurance rules and the stability of the banking system", Journal of Monetary Economics 14:293–317.

Smith, B. (1991), "Bank panics, suspensions and geography: some notes on the 'contagion of fear' in banking", Economic Inquiry 24:230–248.

Smith, C. (1986), "Investment banking and the capital acquisition process", Journal of Financial Economics 15:3–29.

Smith, C., and J. Warner (1979), "On financial contracting: an analysis of bond covenants", Journal of Financial Economics 7(2):117–161.

Sprague, O.M.W. (1910), History of Crises Under the National Banking System (Government Printing Office, Washington, DC).

Stein, J. (1998), "An adverse-selection model of bank asset and liability management with implications for the transmission of monetary policy", RAND Journal of Economics 29(3):466–486.

Stiglitz, J. (1985), "Credit markets and the control of capital", Journal of Money, Credit, and Banking 17(2):133–152.

Stiglitz, J., and A. Weiss (1981), "Credit rationing in markets with imperfect information", American Economic Review 71:393–409.

Stomper, A. (2001), "A theory of banks' industry expertise, market power, and credit risk", Working Paper (University of Vienna, Austria).

Swary, I. (1986), "Stock market reaction to regulatory action in the Continental Illinois Crisis", Journal of Business 59:451–473.

Temin, P. (1976), Did Monetary Forces Cause the Great Depression? (W.W. Norton, New York).

Temin, P. (1989), Lessons From the Great Depression (MIT Press, Cambridge, MA).

Thakor, A. (1996), "Capital requirements, monetary policy, and aggregate bank lending: theory and empirical evidence", Journal of Finance 51(1):279–324.

Thies, C., and D. Gerlowski (1993), "Bank capital and bank failure, 1921–1932: testing the white hypothesis", Journal of Economic History 53:908–914.

Timberlake, R.H. (1984), "The central banking role of clearinghouse associations", Journal of Money, Credit, and Banking 16:1–15.

Townsend, R. (1979), "Optimal contracts and competitive markets with costly state verification", Journal of Economic Theory 21:265–293.

Van Rijckeghem, C., and B. Weder (1999), "Sources of contagion: finance or trade?", International Monetary Fund Working Paper 99/146 (IMF, Washington, DC).

Van Rijckeghem, C., and B. Weder (2000), "Spillovers through banking centers: a panel data analysis", International Monetary Fund Working Paper 00/88 (IMF, Washington, DC).

von Thadden, E.-L. (1995), "Long-term contracts, short-term investment and monitoring", Review of Economic Studies 62:557–575.

von Thadden, E.-L. (1998), "Intermediated versus direct investment: optimal liquidity provision and dynamic incentive compatibility", Journal of Financial Intermediation 7(2):177–197.

von Thadden, E.-L. (2003), "Asymmetric information, bank lending and implicit contracts: the winner's curse", Journal of Finance, forthcoming.

Wagster, J. (1996), "Impact of the 1988 Basle Accord on international banks", Journal of Finance 51:1321–1346.

Wagster, J. (1999), "The Basle Accord of 1988 and the international credit crunch of 1989–1992", Journal of Financial Services Research 15:123–143.

Wall, L.D., and D.R. Peterson (1990), "The effect of Continental Illinois' failure on the financial performance of other banks", Journal of Monetary Economics 26:77–99.

Wallace, N. (1988), "Another attempt to model an illiquid banking system: the Diamond–Dybvig model with sequential service taken seriously", Federal Reserve Bank of Minneapolis Quarterly Review 12(Fall):3–15.

Wansley, J., and U. Dhillon (1989), "Determinants of valuation effects for security offerings of commercial bank holding companies", Journal of Financial Research 12:217–234.

Watts, G. (1972), "The origins and background of central banking in Canada", Bank of Canada Review (May).

Weinberg, J. (1995), "Cycles in lending standards?", Federal Reserve Bank of Richmond Economic Quarterly 81:1–18.

Weinstein, D., and Y. Yafeh (1998), "On the costs of a bank-centered financial system: evidence from the changing main bank relations in Japan", Journal of Finance 53:635–672.

Wheelock, D. (1992a), "Regulation and bank failures: new evidence from the agricultural collapse of the 1920's", Journal of Economic History 52:806–825.

Wheelock, D. (1992b), "Deposit insurance and bank failures: new evidence from the 1920s", Economic Inquiry 30:530–543.

Wheelock, D. (1995), "Regulation, market structure, and the bank failures of the Great Depression", Federal Reserve Bank of St. Louis Review (March/April).

Wheelock, D., and S. Kumbhakar (1995), "Which banks choose deposit insurance? Evidence of adverse selection and moral hazard in a voluntary insurance system", Journal of Money, Credit and Banking 27:186–201.

Wheelock, D., and P. Wilson (1995), "Explaining bank failures: deposit insurance, regulation, and efficiency", Review of Economics and Statistics 77:689–700.

White, E.N. (1983), The Regulation and Reform of the American Banking System, 1900–1929 (Princeton University Press, NJ).

White, E.N. (1984), "A reinterpretation of the banking crisis of 1930", Journal of Economic History 44:119–138.

White, E.N. (1998), "The legacy of deposit insurance: the growth, spread, and cost of insuring financial intermediaries", in: M. Bordo, C. Goldin and E.N. White, eds., The Defining Moment: The Great Depression and the American Economy in the Twentieth Century (University of Chicago Press, Chicago) Chapter 3.

White, L. (1991), The S & L Debacle (Oxford University Press, New York).

Wicker, E. (1980), "A reconsideration of the causes of the banking panic of 1930", Journal of Economic History 40:571–583.

Wicker, E. (1996), The Banking Panics of the Great Depression (Cambridge University Press, UK).

Wicker, E. (2000), Banking Panics of the Gilded Age (Cambridge University Press, UK).

Williamson, S. (1986), "Costly monitoring, financial intermediation, and equilibrium credit rationing", Journal of Monetary Economics 18:159–179.

Williamson, S. (1988), "Liquidity banking, and bank failures", International Economic Review 29:25–43.

Williamson, S. (1992), "Laissez-faire banking and circulating media of exchange", Journal of Financial Intermediation 2:134–167.

Winton, A. (1995a), "Delegated monitoring and bank structure in a finite economy", Journal of Financial Intermediation 4(2):158–187.

Winton, A. (1995b), "Costly state verification and multiple investors: the role of seniority", Review of Financial Studies 8(1):91–123.

Winton, A. (1997), "Competition among financial intermediaries when diversification matters", Journal of Financial Intermediation 6(4):307–346.

Winton, A. (1999), "Don't put all your eggs in one basket? Diversification and specialization in lending", Working Paper (University of Minnesota, Minneapolis, MN).

Winton, A. (2001), "Institutional liquidity needs and the structure of monitored finance", Working Paper (University of Minnesota, Minneapolis, MN).

Yanelle, M.-O. (1989), "The strategic analysis of intermediation", European Economic Review 33(2–3):294–301.

Yanelle, M.-O. (1997), "Banking competition and market efficiency", Review of Economic Studies 64(2):215–239.

Yasuda, A. (1999), "Relationship capital and competition in the corporate securities underwriting market", Working Paper (Wharton School, PA).

Yosha, O. (1995), "Information disclosure costs and the choice of financing source", Journal of Financial Intermediation 4(1):3–20.

Yosha, O. (1997), "Diversification and competition: financial intermediation in a large Cournot–Walras economy", Journal of Economic Theory 75:64–88.

Chapter 9

MARKET MICROSTRUCTURE

HANS R. STOLL

Owen Graduate School of Management, Vanderbilt University

Contents

Handbook of the Economics of Finance, Edited by G.M. Constantinides, M. Harris and R. Stulz

Abstract

Market microstructure deals with the purest form of financial intermediation – the trading of a financial asset, such as a stock or a bond. In a trading market, assets are not transformed but are simply transferred from one investor to another. The field of market microstructure studies the cost of trading securities and the impact of trading costs on the short-run behavior of securities prices. Costs are reflected in the bid-ask spread (and related measures) and in commissions. The focus of this chapter is on the determinants of the spread rather than on commissions. After an introduction to markets, traders and the trading process, I review the theory of the bid–ask spread in Section 3 and examine the implications of the spread for the short-run behavior of prices in Section 4. In Section 5, the empirical evidence on the magnitude and nature of trading costs is summarized, and inferences are drawn about the importance of various sources of the spread. Price impacts of trading from block trades, from herding or from other sources, are considered in Section 6. Issues in the design of a trading market, such as the functioning of call versus continuous markets and of dealer versus auction markets, are examined in Section 7. Even casual observers of markets have undoubtedly noted the surprising pace at which new trading markets are being established even as others merge. Section 8 briefly surveys recent developments in securities markets in the USA and considers the forces leading to centralization of trading in a single market versus the forces leading to multiple markets. Most of this chapter deals with the microstructure of equities markets. In Section 9, the microstructure of other markets is considered. Section 10 provides a brief discussion of the implications of microstructure for asset pricing. Section 11 concludes.

Keywords

bid–ask spread, price impact, market design, dealer market, auction market, short-run price behavior, market fragmentation

JEL classification: G20, G24, G28, G10, G14

1. Introduction

Market microstructure deals with the purest form of financial intermediation – the trading of a financial asset, such as a stock or a bond. In a trading market, assets are not transformed (as they are, for example, by banks that transform deposits into loans) but are simply transferred from one investor to another. The financial intermediation service provided by a market, first described by Demsetz (1968) is immediacy. An investor who wishes to trade immediately – a demander of immediacy – does so by placing a market order to trade at the best available price – the bid price if selling or the ask price if buying. Bid and ask prices are established by suppliers of immediacy. Depending on the market design, suppliers of immediacy may be professional dealers that quote bid and ask prices or investors that place limit orders, or some combination.

Investors are involved in three different markets – the market for information, the market for securities and the market for transaction services. Market microstructure deals primarily with the market for transaction services and with the price of those services as reflected in the bid-ask spread and commissions. The market for securities deals with the determination of securities prices. The literature on asset pricing often assumes that markets operate without cost and without friction whereas the essence of market microstructure research is the analysis of trading costs and market frictions. The market for information deals with the supply and demand of information, including the incentives of securities analysts and the adequacy of information. This market, while conceptually separate, is closely linked to the market for transaction services since the difficulty and cost of a trade depends on the information possessed by the participants in the trade.

Elements in a market are the investors who are the ultimate demanders and suppliers of immediacy, the brokers and dealers who facilitate trading, and the market facility within which trading takes place. Investors include individual investors and institutional investors such as pension plans and mutual funds. Brokers are of two types: upstairs brokers, who deal with investors, and downstairs brokers, who help process transactions on a trading floor. Brokers are agents and are paid by a commission. Dealers trade for their own accounts as principals and earn revenues from the difference between their buying and selling prices. Dealers are at the heart of most organized markets. The NYSE (New York Stock Exchange) specialist and the Nasdaq (National Association of Securities Dealers Automated Quotation) market makers are dealers who maintain liquidity by trading with brokers representing public customers. Bond markets and currency markets rely heavily on dealers to post quotes and maintain liquidity.

The basic function of a market – to bring buyers and sellers together – has changed little over time, but the market facility within which trading takes place has been greatly influenced by technology. In 1792, when the New York Stock Exchange was founded by 24 brokers, the market facility was the buttonwood tree under which they stood. Today the market facility, be it the NYSE, Nasdaq or one of the new electronic markets, is a series of high-speed communications links and computers through which the large majority of trades are executed with little or no human intervention. Investors may enter orders on-line, have them routed automatically to a trading location and executed against standing orders entered earlier, and automatically sent for clearing and settlement. Technology is changing the relationship among investors, brokers and dealers and the facility through which they interact.

Traditional exchanges are membership organizations for the participating brokers and dealers. New markets are computer communications and trading systems that have no members and that are for-profit businesses, capable in principal of operating without brokers and dealers. Thus, while the function of markets – to provide liquidity to investors – will become increasingly important as markets around the world develop, the exact way in which markets operate will undoubtedly change.

The field of market microstructure deals with the costs of providing transaction services and with the impact of such costs on the short run behavior of securities prices. Costs are reflected in the bid-ask spread (and related measures) and commissions. The focus of this chapter is on the determinants of the spread rather than on commissions. After an introduction to markets, traders and the trading process, I review the theory of the bid–ask spread in Section 3 and examine the implications of the spread for the short run behavior of prices in Section 4. In Section 5, the empirical evidence on the magnitude and nature of trading costs is summarized, and inferences are drawn about the importance of various sources of the spread. Price impacts of trading from block trades, from herding or from other sources, are considered in Section 6. Issues in the design of a trading market, such as the functioning of call versus continuous markets and of dealer versus auction markets, are examined in Section 7. Even casual observers of markets have undoubtedly noted the surprising pace at which new trading markets are being established even as others merge. Section 8 briefly surveys recent developments in securities markets in the USA and considers the forces leading to centralization of trading in a single market versus the forces leading to multiple markets. Most of this chapter deals with the microstructure of equities markets. In Section 9, the microstructure of other markets is considered. Section 10 provides a brief discussion of the implications of microstructure for asset pricing. Section 11 concludes.[1]

2. Markets, traders and the trading process

2.1. Types of markets

It is useful to distinguish major types of market structures, although most real-world markets are a mixture of market types. An important distinction is between auction and dealer markets. A pure *auction* market is one in which investors (usually represented

[1] For other overviews of the field of market microstructure, see Madhavan (2000), Chapter 17 in this Handbook by Easley and O'Hara, and O'Hara (1995).

by a broker) trade directly with each other without the intervention of dealers. A *call auction* market takes place at specific times when the security is called for trading. In a call auction, investors place orders – prices and quantities – which are traded at a specific time according to specific rules, usually at a single market clearing price. For example, the NYSE opens with a kind of call auction market in which the clearing price is set to maximize the volume of trade at the opening.

While many markets, including the NYSE and the continental European markets, had their start as call auction markets, such markets have become continuous auction markets as volume has increased. In a *continuous auction* market, investors trade against resting orders placed earlier by other investors and against the "crowd" of floor brokers. Continuous auction markets have two-sides: investors, who wish to sell, trade at the bid price established by resting buy orders or at prices in the "crowd", and investors, who wish to buy, trade at the asking price established by resting sell orders or at prices in the "crowd". The NYSE is said to be a continuous auction market with a "crowd". Electronic markets are continuous auction markets without a "crowd".

A pure *dealer* market is one in which dealers post bids and offers at which public investors can trade. The investor cannot trade directly with another investor but must buy at the dealers ask and sell at the dealers bid. Bond markets and currency markets are dealer markets. The Nasdaq Stock Market started as a pure dealer market, although it now has many features of an auction market because investors can enter resting orders that are displayed to other investors.

Dealer markets are physically dispersed and trading is conducted by telephone and computer. By contrast, auction markets have typically convened at a particular location such as the floor of an exchange. With improvements in communications technology, the distinction between auction and dealer markets has lessened. Physical centralization of trading on an exchange floor is no longer necessary. The purest auction market is not the NYSE, but an electronic market (such as Island or the Paris Bourse) that takes place in a computer. The NYSE, in fact is a mixed auction/dealer market because the NYSE specialist trades for his own account to maintain liquidity in his assigned stocks. The Nasdaq Stock market is in fact also a mixed dealer/auction market because public orders are displayed and may be executed against incoming orders.

2.2. Types of orders

The two principal types of orders are a market order and a limit order. A *market order* directs the broker to trade immediately at the best price available. A *limit order* to buy sets a maximum price that will be paid, and a limit order to sell sets a minimum price that will be accepted. In a centralized continuous auction market, the best limit order to buy and the best limit order to sell (the top of the book) establish the market, and the quantities at those prices represent the depth of the market. Trading takes place as incoming market orders trade with the best posted limit orders. In traditional markets, dealers and brokers on the floor may intervene in this process. In electronic markets the process is fully automated.

In a pure dealer market, limit orders are not displayed but are held by the dealer to whom they are sent, and market orders trade at the dealers bid or ask, not with the limit orders. In some cases, such as Nasdaq before the reforms of the mid 1990s, a limit order to buy only executes if the dealer's ask falls to the level of the limit price. For example suppose the dealer's bid and ask are 20 to $20\frac{1}{4}$, and suppose the dealer holds a limit order to buy at $20\frac{1}{8}$. Incoming sell market orders would trade at 20, the dealer bid, not at $20\frac{1}{8}$, the limit order. The limit order to buy would trade only when the ask price fell to $20\frac{1}{8}$. Nasdaq rules have been modified to require that the dealer trade customer limit orders at the same or better price before trading for his own account (Manning Rule), and to require the display of limit orders (the SEC's order handling rules of 1997).

Orders may also be distinguished by size. Small and medium orders usually follow the standard process for executing trades. Large orders, on the other hand, often require special handling. Large orders may be "worked" by a broker over the course of the day. The broker uses discretion when and how to trade segments of the order. Large orders may be traded in blocks. Block trades are often pre-negotiated "upstairs" by a broker who has identified both sides of the trade. The trade is brought to a trading floor, as required by exchange rules and executed at the pre-arranged prices. The exchange specifies the rules for executing resting limit orders.

2.3. Types of traders

Traders in markets may be classified in a variety of ways.

2.3.1. Active versus passive

Some traders are active (and normally employ market orders), while others are passive (and normally employ limit orders). Active traders demand immediacy and push prices in the direction of their trading, whereas passive traders supply immediacy and stabilize prices. Dealers are typically passive traders. Passive traders tend to earn profits from active traders.

2.3.2. Liquidity versus informed

Liquidity traders trade to smooth consumption or to adjust the risk-return profiles of their portfolios. They buy stocks if they have excess cash or have become more risk tolerant, and they sell stocks if they need cash or have become less risk tolerant. Informed traders trade on private information about an asset's value. Liquidity traders tend to trade portfolios, whereas informed traders tend to trade the specific asset in which they have private information. Liquidity traders lose if they trade with informed traders. Consequently they seek to identify the counterparty. Informed traders, on the other hand, seek to hide their identity. Many models of market microstructure involve the interaction of informed and liquidity traders.

2.3.3. Individual versus institutional

Institutional investors – pension funds, mutual funds, foundations and endowments – are the dominant actors in stock and bond markets. They hold and manage the majority of assets and account for the bulk of share volume. They tend to trade in larger quantities and face special problems in minimizing trading costs and in benefiting from any private information. Individual investors trade in smaller amounts and account for the bulk of trades. The structure of markets must accommodate these very different players. Institutions may wish to cross a block of 100 000 shares into a market where the typical trade is for 3000 shares. Markets must develop efficient ways to handle the large flow of relatively small orders while at the same time accommodating the needs of large investors to negotiate large transactions.

2.3.4. Public versus professional

Public traders trade by placing an order with a broker. Professional traders trade for their own accounts as market makers or floor traders and in that process provide liquidity. Computers and high speed communications technology have changed the relative position of public and professional traders. Public traders can often trade as quickly from upstairs terminals (supplied to them by brokers) as professional traders can trade from their terminals located in offices or on an exchange floor. Regulators have drawn a distinction between professional and public traders and have imposed obligations on professional traders. Market makers have an affirmative obligation to maintain fair and orderly markets, and they are obligated to post firm quotes. However, as the distinction between a day trader trading from an upstairs terminal and a floor trader becomes less clear, the appropriate regulatory policy becomes more difficult.

2.4. Rules of precedence

Markets specify the order in which resting limit orders and/or dealer quotes execute against incoming market orders. A typical rule is to give first priority to orders with the best price and secondary priority to the order posted first at a given price. Most markets adhere to price priority, but many modify secondary priority rules to accommodate large transactions. Suppose there are two resting orders at a bid price of $40. Order one is for 2000 shares and has time priority over order two, which is for 10 000 shares. A market may choose to allow an incoming market order for 10 000 shares to trade with resting order two rather than break up the order into multiple trades. Even price priority is sometimes difficult to maintain, particularly when different markets are involved. Suppose the seller of the 10 000 shares can only find a buyer for the entire amount at $39.90, and trades at that price. Such a trade would "trade-through" the $40 price of order one for 2000 shares. Within a given market, such trade-throughs are normally prohibited – the resting limit order at $40 must trade before the trade at $39.90. In a dealer market, like Nasdaq, where each dealer can be viewed as a separate market, a dealer may not trade through the price of any limit order he holds, but he may trade through the price of a limit order held by another dealer. When there are many competing markets each with its own rules of precedence, there is no requirement that rules of precedence apply across markets. Price priority will tend to rule because market orders will seek out the best price, but time priority at each price need not be satisfied across markets.

The working of rules of precedence is closely tied to the tick size, the minimum allowable price variation. As Harris (1991) first pointed out, time priority is meaningless if the tick size is very small. Suppose an investor places a limit order to buy 1000 shares at $40. If the tick size is $0.01, a dealer or another trader can step in front with a bid of $40.01 – a total cost of only $10. On the other hand, the limit order faces the danger of being "picked off" should new information warrant a lower price. If the tick size were $0.10, the cost of stepping in front of the investor's limit order would be greater ($100). The investor trades off the price of buying immediately at the current ask price, say $40.20, against giving up immediacy in the hope of getting a better price with the limit order at $40. By placing a limit order the investor supplies liquidity to the market. The smaller tick size reduces the incentive to place limit orders and hence adversely affects liquidity.

Price matching and payment for order flow are other features of today's markets related to rules of precedence. Price matching occurs when market makers in a satellite market promise to match the best price in the central market for orders sent to them rather than to the central market. The retail broker usually decides which market maker receives the order flow. Not only is the broker not charged a fee, he typically receives a payment (of one to two cents a share) from the market maker. Price matching and payment for order flow are usually bilateral arrangements between a market making firm and a retail brokerage firm. Price matching violates time priority: When orders are sent to a price matching dealer, they are not sent to the market that first posted the best price. Consequently the incentive to post limit orders is reduced because the limit order may be stranded. Similarly, the incentive of dealers to post good quotes is eliminated if price matching is pervasive: A dealer who quotes a better price is unable to attract additional orders because orders are preferenced to other dealers who match the price.

2.5. The trading process

The elements of the trading process may be divided into four components – information, order routing, execution, and clearing. First, a market provides *information* about past prices and current quotes. Earlier in its history, the NYSE jealously guarded ownership of its prices, making data available only to its members or licensed recipients. But today transaction prices and quotes are disseminated in real-time over a consolidated trade system (CTS) and a consolidated quote system (CQS). Each exchange participating in these systems receives tape revenue for the prices and quotes it disseminates. The real-time dissemination of these prices makes all markets more transparent and allows investors to determine which markets have the best prices, thereby enhancing competition.

Second, a mechanism for *routing orders* is required. Today brokers take orders and route them to an exchange or other market center. For example, the bulk of orders sent to the NYSE are sent via DOT (Designated Turnaround System), an electronic system that sends an order directly to the specialist. Retail brokers establish procedures for routing orders and may route orders in return for payments. Orders may not have the option of being routed to every trading center and may therefore have difficulty in trading at the best price. Central to discussions about a national market system, is the mechanism for routing orders among different market centers, and the rules, if any, that regulators should establish.

The third phase of the trading process is *execution.* In today's automated world this seems a simple matter of matching an incoming market order with a resting quote. However this step is surprisingly complex and contentious. Dealers are reluctant to execute orders automatically because they fear being "picked off" by speedy and informed traders, who have better information. Instead, they prefer to delay execution, if even for only 15 seconds, to determine if any information or additional trades arrive. Automated execution systems have been exploited by speedy customers to the disadvantage of dealers. Indeed, as trading becomes automated the distinction between dealers and customers decreases because customers can get nearly as close to "the action" as dealers.

A less controversial but no less important phase of the trading process is *clearing and settlement.* Clearing involves the comparison of transactions between buying and selling brokers. These comparisons are made daily. Settlement in equities markets in the USA takes place on day $t + 3$, and is done electronically by book entry transfer of ownership of securities and cash payment of net amounts to the clearing entity.

3. Microstructure theory – determinants of the bid–ask spread

Continuous markets are characterized by the bid and ask prices at which trades can take place. The bid–ask spread reflects the difference between what active buyers must pay and what active sellers receive. It is an indicator of the cost of trading and the illiquidity of a market. Alternatively, illiquidity could be measured by the time it takes optimally to trade a given quantity of an asset [Lippman and McCall (1986)]. The two approaches converge because the bid-ask spread can be viewed as the amount paid to someone else (i.e. the dealer) to take on the unwanted position and dispose of it optimally. Our focus is on the bid–ask spread. Bid–ask spreads vary widely. In inactive markets – for example, the real estate market – the spread can be wide. A house could be offered at $500 000 with the highest bid at $450 000. On the other hand the spread for an actively traded stock is today often less than 10 cents per share. A central issue in the field of microstructure is what determines the bid–ask spread and its variation across securities.

Several factors determine the bid–ask spread in a security. First, suppliers of liquidity, such as the dealers who maintain continuity of markets, incur *order handling costs* for which they must be compensated. These costs include the costs of labor and capital needed to provide quote information, order routing, execution, and clearing. In a market without dealers, where limit orders make the spread, order handling costs are likely to be smaller than in a market where professional dealers earn a living. Second, the spread may reflect *non-competitive pricing.* For example, market makers may have agreements to raise spreads or may adopt rules, such as a minimum tick size, to increase spreads. Third, suppliers of immediacy, who buy at the bid or sell at the ask, assume *inventory risk* for which they must be compensated. Fourth, placing a bid or an ask grants an *option* to the rest of the market to trade on the basis of new information before the bid or ask can be changed to reflect the new information. Consequently the bid and ask must deviate from the consensus price to reflect the cost of such an option. A fifth factor has received the most attention in the microstructure literature; namely the effect of *asymmetric information.* If some investors are better informed than others, the person who places a firm quote (bid or ask) loses to investors with superior information.

The factors determining spreads are not mutually exclusive. All may be present at the same time. The three factors related to uncertainty – inventory risk, option effect and asymmetric information – may be distinguished as follows. The inventory effect arises because of possible adverse *public* information *after* the trade in which inventory is acquired. The expected value of such information is zero, but uncertainty imposes inventory risk for which suppliers of immediacy must be compensated. The option effect arises because of adverse *public* information *before* the trade and the inability to adjust the quote. The option effect really results from an inability to monitor and immediately change resting quotes. The adverse selection effect arises because of the presence of *private* information *before* the trade, which is revealed sometime after the trade. The information effect arises because some traders have superior information.

The sources of the bid–ask spread may also be compared in terms of the services provided and the resources used. One view of the spread is that it reflects the cost of the services provided by liquidity suppliers. Liquidity suppliers process orders, bear inventory risk, using up real resources. Another view of the spread is that it is compensation for losses to informed traders. This informational view of the spread implies that informed investors gain from uninformed, but it does not imply that any services are provided or that any real resources are being used.

Let us discuss in more detail the three factors that have received most attention in the microstructure literature – inventory risk, free trading option, and asymmetric information.

3.1. Inventory risk

Suppliers of immediacy that post bid and ask prices stand ready take on inventory and to assume the risk associated with holding inventory. If a dealer buys 5000 shares at the bid, she risks a drop in the price and a loss on the inventory position. An investor posting a limit order to sell 1000 shares at the ask faces the risk that the stock he is trying to sell with the limit order will fall in price before the limit order is executed. In order to take the risk associated with the limit order, the ask price must be above the bid price at which he could immediately sell by enough to offset the inventory risk. Inventory risk was first examined theoretically in Garman (1976), Stoll (1978a), Amihud and Mendelson (1980), Ho and Stoll (1981, 1983). This discussion follows Stoll (1978a).

To model the spread arising from inventory risk, consider the determination of a dealer's bid price. The bid price must be set at a discount below the consensus value of the stock to compensate for inventory risk. Let P be the consensus price, let P^b be the bid price, and let C be the dollar discount on a trade of Q dollars. The proportional discount of the bid price from the consensus stock price, P, is

$$\frac{P - P^b}{P} = \frac{C}{Q} \equiv c.$$

The problem is to derive C or equivalently, c. This can done by solving the dealer's portfolio problem. Let the terminal wealth of the dealer's optimal portfolio in the absence of making markets be $\widetilde{W}$. The dealer's terminal wealth if he stands ready to buy Q dollars of stock at a discount of C dollars is $\widetilde{W} + (1+\tilde{r})Q - (1+r_f)(Q-C)$, where $\tilde{r}$ is the return on the stock purchased and r_f is the cost of borrowing the funds to buy the stock.[2] The minimum discount that the dealer would set is such that the expected utility of the optimal portfolio without buying the stock equals the expected utility of the portfolio with the unwanted inventory:

$$EU[\widetilde{W}] = EU[\widetilde{W} + (1+\tilde{r})Q - (1+r_f)(Q-C)]. \tag{1}$$

Applying a Taylor series expansion to both sides, taking expectations, assuming r_f is small enough to be ignored, and solving for $c = C/Q$, yields

$$c = \tfrac{1}{2}\frac{z}{W_0}\sigma^2 Q, \tag{2}$$

where z is the dealer's coefficient of relative risk aversion, W_0 is the dealer's initial wealth, σ^2 is the variance of return of the stock. The bid price for depth of Q dollars must be below the consensus stock value by the proportion c to compensate the dealer for his inventory costs. These costs arise because the dealer loses diversification and because he assumes a level of risk that is inconsistent with his preferences. The

[2] Q is valued at the consensus price in the absence of a bid–ask spread. The loan is collateralized by the dealer's stock position.

discount of the bid price is greater the greater dealer's risk aversion, the smaller his wealth, the greater the stock's return variance,[3] and the larger the quoted depth.

The proportional discount, c, is affected by the initial inventory of the dealer, which was assumed to be zero in the above derivation. If the dealer enters the period with inventory of I dollars in one or more stocks, the proportional discount for depth of Q can be shown to be

$$c = \frac{z}{W_0}\sigma_{IQ}I + \frac{1}{2}\frac{z}{W_0}\sigma^2 Q, \tag{3}$$

where σ_{IQ} is the covariance between the return on the initial inventory and the return on the stock in which the dealer is bidding. If $I < 0$ and $\sigma_{IQ} > 0$, the dealer may be willing to pay a premium to buy shares because they hedge a short position in the initial inventory. On the other hand, the dealer's asking price will be correspondingly higher with an initial short position because the dealer will be reluctant to sell and add to the short position.

The relation between the bid price and consensus price for depth of Q and initial inventory of I is given by

$$\frac{P - P^b}{P} = \frac{z}{W_0}\sigma_{IQ}I + \frac{1}{2}\frac{z}{W_0}\sigma^2 Q, \tag{4}$$

and the relation between the ask price and the consensus price for depth of Q and initial inventory of I is given by

$$\frac{P^a - P}{P} = -\frac{z}{W_0}\sigma_{IQ}I + \frac{1}{2}\frac{z}{W_0}\sigma^2 Q. \tag{5}$$

Note that the inventory term enters with a negative sign in the ask equation since a positive value of I will lower the price a dealer will ask. (Q is an absolute dollar amount long or short.) The proportional bid–ask spread if inventory costs were the only source of the spread is then given by summing Equations (4) and (5):

$$\frac{P^a - P^b}{P} = 2c = \frac{z}{W_0}\sigma^2 Q, \tag{6}$$

Note that the initial inventory does not appear in the spread expression. Initial inventory affects the placement of the bid and ask but not the difference between the two. The implication for the dynamics of the quotes is that after a sale at the bid, both the bid and the ask price are lowered. The bid is lowered to discourage additional sales to the dealer, and the ask is lowered to encourage purchases from the dealer. Correspondingly, after a purchase at the ask, both bid and ask prices are raised.

---

[3] The variance, not the beta, is relevant because the inventory position is not diversified.

The inventory model can be extended to account for multiple stocks, multiple dealers, and multiple time periods, without altering the essential features underlying the inventory approach.

3.2. Free-trading option

A dealer or limit order placing a bid offers a free put option to the market, a fact first noted by Copeland and Galai (1983). For example, suppose an investor places a limit order to buy 5000 shares at a price of $40 when the last trade was at $40.25. The limit order gives the rest of the market a put option to sell 5000 shares at an exercise price of $40, which will be exercised if new information justifies a price less than $40. Similarly a limit order to sell at $40.50 offers a call option to the rest of the market, which will be exercised if new information justifies a price greater than $40.50. A dealer who places a bid at $40 and an ask at $40.50 is writing a strangle. The value of such options depends on the stock's variability and the maturity of the option. A limit order that is monitored infrequently has greater maturity than a dealer quote that is monitored continuously and is quickly adjusted.

The Black–Scholes model can provide the value of the free-trading option. Suppose the limit order to buy at $40 will not be reviewed for an hour, and suppose the one-hour standard deviation of return is 0.033% (an annualized value of about 200%). The stock price is $40.25 and the exercise price of the put option is $40. The Black–Scholes value of a put option maturing in one hour with a one hour standard deviation of 0.033% is $0.23, approximately the discount of the bid from the quote midpoint. Investors who place limit orders expect to trade at favorable prices that offset the losses when their options end up in the money. The option is free to the person exercising it. The option premium, which is the discount of the bid from the stock's consensus value, is paid by traders who sell at the bid in the absence of new information.

3.3. Adverse selection

Informed investors will sell at the bid if they have information justifying a lower price. They will buy at the ask if they have information justifying a higher price. In an anonymous market, dealers and limit orders must lose to informed traders, for the informed traders are not identified. If this adverse selection problem is too great the market will fail. As Bagehot (1971) first noted, the losses to informed traders must be offset by profits from uninformed traders if dealers are to stay in business and if limit orders are to continue to be posted. Glosten and Milgrom (1985) model the spread in an asymmetric information world. Important theoretical papers building on the adverse-selection sources of the spread include Kyle (1985), Easley and O'Hara (1987) and Admati and Pfleiderer (1988).

The determination of the bid–ask spread in the Glosten/Milgrom world can illustrated in the following simple manner. Assume an asset can take on two possible values – a high value, v^H, and a low value, v^L – with equal probability. Informed investors, who know the correct value, are present with probability π. Assuming risk neutrality, uninformed investors value the asset at $\bar{v} = (v^H + v^L)/2$. The ask price, A, is then the expected value of the asset conditional on a trade at the ask price:

$$A = v^H \pi + \bar{v}(1 - \pi). \tag{7}$$

The bid price is

$$B = v^L \pi + \bar{v}(1 - \pi). \tag{8}$$

Since informed investors trade at the ask (bid) only if they believe the asset value is $v^H(v^L)$, the ask price exceeds the bid price. The bid–ask spread,

$$A - B = \pi(v^H - v^L), \tag{9}$$

depends on the probability of encountering an informed trader and on the degree of asset value uncertainty. Glosten and Milgrom go on to show that prices evolve through time as a martingale, reflecting at each trade the information conveyed by that trade.

4. Short-run price behavior and market microstructure

Market microstructure is the study of market friction. In cross section, assets with greater friction have larger spreads. Friction also affects the short-term time-series behavior of asset prices. Assets with greater friction tend to have greater short-run variability of prices. Garman (1976) first modeled microstructure dynamics under the assumption of Poisson arrival of traders. Many papers have modeled the time series behavior of prices and quotes, including Roll (1984), Hasbrouck (1988, 1991), Huang and Stoll (1994, 1997), Madhavan, Richardson and Roomans (1997).

The evolution of prices through time provides insight as to the sources of trading friction – whether order processing costs, inventory effects, information effects, or monopoly rents.

- If order processing costs were the sole source of the bid–ask spread, transaction prices would simply tend to "bounce" between bid and ask prices. After a trade at the bid, the next price change would be zero or the spread, S. After a trade at the ask, the next price change would be zero or $-S$. Roll (1984) shows that the effect is to induce negative serial correlation in price changes.
- If asymmetric information were the sole source of the spread, transaction prices would reflect the information conveyed by transactions. Sales at the bid would cause a permanent fall in bid and ask prices to reflect the information conveyed by a sale. Conversely purchases at the ask would cause a permanent increase in bid and ask prices to reflect the information conveyed by a purchase. Given the random arrival of traders, price changes and quote changes would be random and unpredictable.

• If inventory costs were the source of the spread, quotes would adjust to induce inventory equilibrating trades. After a sale at the bid, bid and ask prices would fall, not to reflect information as in the asymmetric information case, but to discourage additional sales and to encourage purchases. Correspondingly, after a purchase at the ask, bid and ask prices would rise to discourage additional purchases and to encourage sales. Over time, quotes would return to normal. Trade prices and quotes would exhibit negative serial correlation.

In this section, a model for examining short-run behavior of prices is first presented. The model is then used to analyze the realized spread (what a supplier of immediacy earns) and the serial covariance of price changes. The realized spread and the serial covariance of price changes provide insight into the sources of the quoted spread.

4.1. A model of short-term price behavior

The short-run evolution of prices can be more formally stated. Let the change in the quote midpoint be given as

$$M_t - M_{t-1} = \lambda \frac{S}{2} Q_{t-1} + \varepsilon_t, \tag{10}$$

where M_t = quote midpoint immediately after the trade at time $t-1$; Q_t = trade indicator for the trade at time t (equals 1 if a purchase at the ask and equals -1 if a sale at the bid); S = dollar bid–ask spread; λ = fraction of the half-spread by which quotes respond to a trade at t (the response reflects inventory and asymmetric information factors); ε = serially uncorrelated public information shock. The quote midpoint changes either because there is new public information, ε, or because the last trade, Q_{t-1} induces a change in quotes. A change in the quotes is induced because the trade conveys information and because it distorts inventory.

The trade at price P_t takes place either at the ask (half-spread above the midpoint) or at the bid (half-spread below the midpoint): [4]

$$P_t = M_t + \frac{S}{2} Q_t + \eta_t, \tag{11}$$

where P_t = trade price at time t; η_t = error term reflecting the deviation of the constant half-spread from the observed half-spread, $P_t - M_t$, and reflecting price discreteness.

Combining Equations (10) and (11) gives

$$\Delta P_t = \frac{S}{2} (Q_t - Q_{t-1}) + \lambda \frac{S}{2} Q_{t-1} + e_t, \tag{12}$$

where $e_t = \varepsilon_t + \Delta \eta_t$.

---

[4] It would be a simple matter to model the fact that some trades take place inside the quotes. For example, one could assume that trades are at the quotes with probability ϕ and at the midpoint with probability $(1-\phi)$. Then $P_t = M_t + \phi \frac{S}{2} Q_t + \eta_t$, Madhavan, Richardson and Roomans (1997), for example, make such an adjustment.

4.2. The realized spread

What can a supplier of immediacy expect to realize by buying at the bid and selling his position at a later price (or by selling at the ask and buying to cover the short position at a later price)? The realized half-spread is the price change conditional on a purchase at the bid (or the negative of the price change conditional on a sale at the ask). Since quotes change as a result of trades, the amount earned is less than would be implied if quotes did not change. The difference between the realized and quoted spreads provides evidence about the sources of the spread.

In terms of the model (12), the expected realized half-spread conditional on a purchase at the bid ($Q_{t-1} = -1$) is

$$E\left[\Delta P_t \mid Q_{t-1} = -1\right] = \frac{S}{2}(EQ_t + 1) + \lambda\frac{S}{2}(-1).\tag{13}$$

The expected realized half-spread depends on the expected sign of the next trade, EQ_t, and on λ. Let π be the probability of a reversal – a trade at the ask after a trade at the bid or a trade at the bid after a trade at the ask. Then, conditional on a trade at the bid, $E(Q_t) = \pi(1) + (1 - \pi)(-1)$. If purchases and sales are equally likely, $EQ = 0.0$ (the liquidating transaction will be at midpoint on average). The value of λ depends on the presence of asymmetric information and/or inventory effects. The value of λ associated with alternative sources of the spread and the resulting values of EQ and of the realized spread are given in the following table:

Source of the spread	λ	$E(Q)$	Realized half-spread
Order processing	0	0	$S/2$
Asymmetric information	1	0	0
Inventory	1	$2\pi - 1$	$(2\pi - 1)S/2$

In an order processing world, $\lambda = 0$ because quotes are assumed not to adjust to trades, and $EQ = 0.0$ because purchases and sales are assumed to arrive with equal probability. The implied realized half-spread is $S/2$, that is, the supplier of immediacy earns half the quoted spread. He would earn the spread on a roundtrip trade – buy at the bid and sell at the ask. These earnings defray the order processing costs of providing immediacy.

In an asymmetric information world, quotes adjust to reflect the information in the trade. If adverse information is the sole source of the spread, $\lambda = 1$. A trade at the bid conveys adverse information with value $S/2$, causing quotes to decline by $S/2$. Since quotes reflect all current information, buys and sells continue to be equally likely so that $EQ = 0.0$ at the new quotes. The resulting realized half-spread of zero reflects the fact that, in an asymmetric information world, real resources are not used up to supply immediacy and no earnings result. The spread is simply an amount needed to protect suppliers of immediacy from losses to informed traders.

In an inventory world, quotes also respond to a trade but not because the trade conveys information but because the trade unbalances the inventory of liquidity suppliers. If inventory is the sole source of the spread, $\lambda = 1$. A trade at the bid causes quotes to decline by $S/2$. Since the fundamental value of the stock has not declined (as is the case in the asymmetric information case), the lower bid price makes it more costly to sell, and the lower ask price makes less expensive to buy. As a result, subsequent purchases and sales will not be equally likely. After a trade at the bid, a trade at the ask occurs with probability greater than 0.5, while a trade at the bid occurs with probability less than 0.5. For example if $\pi = 0.7$, $E(Q) = 0.4$, and the realized half-spread would be $0.4S/2$. Given enough trades, quotes would return to their initial level, and the half-spread would be earned, but one is unlikely to observe a complete reversal in one trade.

A direct implication of the inventory world is that *quote changes* are negatively serially correlated, something that is not the case in the order processing world (where successive price changes, but not quote changes, are negatively correlated) or in the asymmetric information world (where neither price changes nor quote changes are serially correlated). The negative serial correlation in quotes tends to be long lived and the mean reversion of inventories tends to be slow, which makes inventory effects difficult to observe.[5] The serial covariance of price changes is examined in greater detail in the next section.

The above discussion has described polar cases. In fact, the sources of the quoted spread are likely to include order processing, asymmetric information, inventory, as well as market power and option effects. The relative importance of asymmetric effects and other effects can be inferred empirically by comparing the quoted half-spread and the realized half-spread. For example if the quoted half-spread were 10 cents, and suppliers of immediacy realized an average of 6 cents by buying at the bid (or selling at the ask) and liquidating their position at a later time, one would infer that the asymmetric portion of the half-spread is 4 cents and the other portions are 6 cents.

4.3. Serial covariance of price changes

Another approach to understanding the implications of market microstructure for price dynamics and the sources of the spread is to calculate the serial covariance of transaction price changes. This can be done by calculating the serial covariance of both sides of Equation (12) under alternative assumption about λ. Consider first the order processing world, where $\lambda = 0$. Assuming in addition that markets are informationally

[5] Madhavan and Smidt (1991, 1993) find that inventories are long lived. Hansch, Naik and Viswanathan (1998) find direct evidence of inventory effects in the London market.

efficient and that the error term is serially uncorrelated and uncorrelated with trades, implies that

$$\text{cov}(\Delta P_t, \Delta P_{t-1}) = \frac{S^2}{4} \, \text{cov}(\Delta Q_t, \Delta Q_{t-1}) = \frac{S^2}{4}(-4\pi^2). \tag{14}$$

Assuming that the probabilities of purchases and sales are equal at $\pi = 0.5$, the serial covariance of price changes is

$$\text{cov}(\Delta P_t, \Delta P_{t-1}) = -\frac{S^2}{4}, \tag{15}$$

a result first derived by Roll (1984). For example, if $S = \$0.20$, the serial covariance is -0.01. Roll pointed out that one could infer the spread from transaction prices as

$$S = 2\sqrt{-\text{cov}(\Delta P_t, \Delta P_{t-1})}. \tag{16}$$

Consider next the pure asymmetric information world or the pure inventory world, where $\lambda = 1$. In either of these cases,[6]

$$\text{cov}(\Delta P_t, \Delta P_{t-1}) = \frac{S^2}{4} \, \text{cov}(Q_t, Q_{t-1}) = \frac{S^2}{4}(1 - 2\pi). \tag{17}$$

In an asymmetric information world, since quotes are "regret free", they induce no serial dependence in trades and $\pi = 0.5$. In that case $(1 - 2\pi) = 0.0$, and $\text{cov}(\Delta P_t, \Delta P_{t-1}) = 0.0$.

In a pure inventory world, quote changes induce negative serial dependence in trading, that is to say $\pi > 0.5$ (but is less than 1). The serial covariance in that case is

$$\text{cov}(\Delta P_t, \Delta P_{t-1}) = \frac{S^2}{4}(1 - 2\pi), \quad \text{where } 0.5 < \pi < 1.0. \tag{18}$$

The serial covariance is negative but not as negative as in the pure order processing world in which $\pi = 0.5$. The serial covariance is attenuated because quotes respond to trades. For example, if $S = 0.20$, $\pi = 0.7$, the serial covariance is -0.004.

If the serial covariance is calculated from actual transaction prices and the Roll transformation applied, the inferred spread is typically less than the quoted spread. This happens for several reasons. First, as noted above, the response of quotes to trades because of information or inventory effects attenuates the bid–ask bounce. The serial covariance is less negative the more important the asymmetric

---

[6] Note that the serial covariance in trade direction is $\text{cov}(Q_t, Q_{t-1}) = (1 - 2\pi)$ whereas the serial covariance in trade direction changes is $\text{cov}(\Delta Q_t, \Delta Q_{t-1}) = -4\pi^2$.

information component of the spread. Second, the negative serial correlation in trades implied by microstructure theory comes from the supply side. However, investors' trading may be positively correlated. For example momentum trading implies $\text{cov}(\Delta P_t, \Delta P_{t-1}) > 0.0$. Positive demand side serial correlation may obscure or lessen negative serial correlation due to microstructure effects. Third, trade reporting procedures and price discreteness can obscure negative serial covariance implied by microstructure factors. For example, an investor's order may not be accomplished in a single trade but may be split into several trades all of the same sign. Breaking up an order in this way induces runs in the direction of trade and makes trade reversals less likely to be observed. Price discreteness can obscure price changes that might otherwise be observed and therefore can obscure serial correlation of price changes.

5. Evidence on the bid–ask spread and its sources

5.1. The spread and its components

Evidence on spreads for a sample of 1706 NYSE stocks in the three months ending in February 1998 is contained in Table 1. The *quoted half-spread* ranges from 8.28 cents per share for small low-priced stocks to 6.49 cents per share for large high-priced stocks, with an overall average of 7.87 cents per share. The higher spreads for small low priced stocks reflect the lesser liquidity of these stocks.

Row 2 of the table presents estimates of the *effective half-spread*. The effective spread is defined as $|P_t - M_t|$, the absolute difference between the trade price and the quote midpoint.[7] If the trade is at the bid or ask, the effective spread equals the quoted spread. However, because it is often possible for an incoming market order to better the quoted price, ("price improvement"), the effective spread may be less than the quoted spread. The process of achieving price improvement is for the dealer to guarantee the current price and seek to better it. Lee (1993) provides evidence on price improvement across different markets. Ready (1999) notes that the dealer has a very short-term option, which is to step ahead of the resting order by bettering the price or to let the incoming market order trade against the resting order. Price improvement can adversely affect resting orders since dealers will likely step ahead if the incoming order is judged to be uninformed and will not step ahead if the incoming order is judged to be informed. The effective half-spread is below the quoted spread in each size category. It averages 5.58 cents over all NYSE stocks.

Both the quoted and effective spreads are measures of total execution cost, inclusive of real costs and of wealth transfers due to asymmetric information. A measure of real

---

[7] This definition poses a number of empirical problems. First, to classify a trade, one must associate the trade price with the correct quotes, which can be problematic if there are differential reporting delays. Second, one must assume that trades above the midpoint are purchases and trades below the midpoint are sales. Lee and Ready (1991) analyze these questions.

Table 1

Spread measures by market value decile, 1706 NYSE stocks[a,b], December 1, 1997 – February 28, 1998

	Market value decile										
	Smallest	2	3	4	5	6	7	8	9	Largest	Overall
Quoted half-spread[c]	8.28	8.56	8.63	8.27	8.55	7.79	7.30	7.90	6.91	6.49	7.87
Effective half-spread[d]	6.09	6.07	6.11	5.79	6.06	5.49	5.09	5.70	4.87	4.57	5.58
Traded half-spread[e]	3.88	3.77	3.83	3.60	3.71	3.42	3.54	3.89	3.73	4.05	3.74
Roll half-spread	4.49	3.68	3.32	3.33	3.28	3.11	3.08	4.17	3.85	5.18	3.81
Stock price[f] ($)	9.33	15.69	22.68	25.20	30.34	32.58	35.58	44.97	50.73	64.45	33.15

[a] Source: Stoll (2000).

[b] In cents per share. The values in the table are averages over 61 days and over the stocks in each category. Measures of statistical significance are not shown. However, all spread measures are significantly different from zero with every *t*–ratio exceeding 10.

[c] The quoted half-spread is half the difference between the ask and the bid, averaged over the day.

[d] The effective half-spread is the absolute value of the trade price less the quote midpoint averaged over the day.

[e] The traded half-spread is half the difference between the average price of trades on the ask side less the average price of trades at the bid side. In calculating the daily average prices, trade prices are weighted by shares traded.

[f] The stock price is the closing price.

cost is the realized spread. Empirically, the realized spread may be estimated simply by calculating the average price change after a trade at the bid or the negative of the average price change after a trade at the ask. The price change is taken from the initial trade price to a subsequent price, where the subsequent price may be the quote midpoint or the trade price of a later trade. Huang and Stoll (1996) calculate realized spreads over 5 and 30 minute intervals. An alternative empirical estimate of the realized spread is to calculate half the average difference between trades at the ask and trades at the bid – what Stoll (2000) has called the traded spread.

The relation between the average realized and traded half-spreads in a given day is as follows: the average *realized half-spread* for m trades taking place at bid prices is

$$\frac{1}{m} \sum_{T=1}^{m} \left(M_{T+1} - P_T^B \right), \tag{19}$$

where M_{T+1} is the quote midpoint at which the trade at time T is assumed to be liquidated, and P_T^B is the bid price at which the trade at time T was initiated. The average realized spread for n trades taking place at ask prices is

$$-\frac{1}{n} \sum_{t=1}^{n} \left(M_{t+1} - P_t^A \right). \tag{20}$$

Note that the time subscripts (t and T) are different to reflect the fact that a trade at the bid and at the ask do not take place at exactly the same time. After each trade, the quotes adjust to reflect the information in the trade and the inventory effects of the trade. Summing Equations (19) and (20) gives

$$\left(\frac{1}{m} \sum_{T=1}^{m} M_{T+1} - \frac{1}{n} \sum_{t=1}^{n} M_{t+1} \right) + \left(\frac{1}{n} \sum_{t=1}^{n} P_t^A - \frac{1}{m} \sum_{T=1}^{m} P_T^B \right). \tag{21}$$

The *traded spread* is defined as

$$\left(\frac{1}{n} \sum_{t=1}^{m} P_t^A - \frac{1}{m} \sum_{T=1}^{m} P_T^B \right), \tag{22}$$

which is the same as Equation (21) under the assumption that the midpoint at which trades are liquidated is the same for trades at the bid and trades at the ask. The traded spread is the average earnings of a supplier of immediacy who buys at the bid and sells at the ask. It is less than the quoted spread because prices tend to move against the supplier of liquidity after each trade.

The traded half-spread data in Row 3 of Table 1 are based on weighted averages of trade prices where the weights are the volume at each price. As expected, the traded half-spread is less than the quoted half-spread, reflecting the fact that suppliers of immediacy earn less than the quoted spread primarily because they lose to informed traders. Over all NYSE stocks, the traded half-spread is 3.74 cents, which implies that losses to informed traders average $5.58 - 3.74 = 1.84$ cents per share. Per share losses to informed traders are less in large stocks than in small stocks, reflecting the fact that there are many more shares traded in the large stocks.

The final measure summarized in Table 1 is the *Roll implied spread,* which is based on the serial covariance of price changes in each stock as given by Equation (16). Like the traded spread, the Roll spread is less than the quoted or effective spread, reflecting the fact that asymmetric information lowers the earnings of suppliers of immediacy relative to the quoted or effective spread.

The comparison of the quoted and effective spreads with the realized spread, as represented by the traded spread or Roll spread, in Table 1 provides clear empirical support for the fact that a significant portion of the spread reflects the real costs of providing immediacy and a portion reflects the losses to informed trading. However the exact composition, and in particular the importance of inventory and asymmetric information effects is uncertain.

A number of authors have analyzed the components of the spread in greater detail and more formally than is possible with the simple comparisons in Table 1. Relevant studies include Glosten and Harris (1988), Stoll (1989), Choi, Salandro and Shastri (1988), George, Kaul and Nimalendran (1991), Lin, Sanger and Booth (1995), Huang and Stoll (1997).

5.2. Cross-section evidence

Whatever the exact sources of the bid–ask spread, research has clearly established that the cross-section variation in spreads can be explained by economic variables. Indeed the relation between the spread of a security and trading characteristics of that security is one of the strongest and most robust relations in finance. The relation has been examined by Demsetz (1968), Stoll (1978b), Benston and Hagerman (1974), Branch and Freed (1977), Tinic (1972), Tinic and West (1974), and many other, more recent papers. Since most of the early empirical work preceded the articulation of the asymmetric information theories of the spread, the explanatory variables were based on inventory and order processing reasons, but in most cases asymmetric information factors can be represented by the same empirical proxies. Important variables include an activity variable like volume of trading, a risk variable like the stock's return variance, variables for company characteristics such as size and stock price that proxy for other aspects of risk, and perhaps other variables such as a variable for trading pressure, and a variable for price discreteness.

Results for the following cross-section relation [taken from Stoll (2000)] are in Table 2:

$$S/P = a_0 + a_1 \log V + a_2 \sigma^2 + a_3 \log \mathrm{MV} + a_4 \log P + a_5 \log N + a_6 \mathrm{Avg}\,|I| + e. \quad (23)$$

The data are averages of daily data for 1706 NYSE/AMSE stocks for the 61 trading days ending February 28, 1998. The variables are as follows: S is the stock's average

Table 2
Cross-section regression of the average proportional half-spread as a function of average stock characteristics in the period[a,b], December 1, 1997 to February 28, 1998

	Dep Mean	Intercept	$\log V$	σ^2	$\log MV$	$\log P$	$\log N$	$\mathrm{Avg}|I|$	Adj R2
S/P	0.389	1.9401	−0.1360	1.5757	0.0400	−0.2126	0.0880	0.0049	0.7974
		21.77	−12.08	18.00	5.75	−18.64	5.45	4.88	

[a] Source: Stoll (2000).
[b] Coefficients are in the first line, and *t*-values are below. Log V is the natural log of the average daily dollar volume; σ^2 is the daily return variance for the prior year; Log MV is the log of the stock's market value at the end of November 1997; Log P is the log of the average closing stock price; Log N is the log of the average number of trades per day; $\mathrm{Avg}|I|$ is the average daily percentage imbalance between the volume at the ask and at the bid. The dependent mean and all coefficients except that on σ^2 are multiplied by 100. There are 1706 observations.

quoted half-spread defined as $\frac{1}{2}$(ask price–bid price); P is the stock's average closing price; V is average daily dollar volume; σ^2 is the daily return variance for the prior year; MV is the stock's market value at the end of November 1997; N is the average number of trades per day; I is the average daily percentage imbalance between volume at the ask and volume at the bid; and e is the error term.[8] Over 79% of the cross-section variation in proportional spreads is explained by stock characteristics. The key results are well known: spreads are lower for stocks with the greater volume, with lower return volatility, with higher price, and with smaller trading imbalances. The positive coefficient on the number of trades is somewhat surprising.

6. Price effects of trading

6.1. Block trading

Models of the bid–ask spread derive the prices at which suppliers of immediacy will buy (at the bid) or sell (at the ask) specified quantities (depth). Orders are assumed to be of a size less than or equal to the posted depth. Orders arrive and are executed at posted quotes, and quotes adjust to reflect information and inventory effects.

Institutional investors, such as mutual funds and pension funds, often must trade quantities that exceed the quoted depth. They are concerned about a price impact over and above that in the spread. An institution interested in selling 50 000 shares of a 40 dollar stock cannot simply place a market order. It has two options. First it can pre-negotiate the sale of the entire block in an upstairs market that is facilitated by major broker dealer firms. Second, it can ask a broker to "work" the order by trading portions of it throughout the day so as to minimize the price impact.

Block trades have been analyzed in a number of papers, including Scholes (1972), Kraus and Stoll (1972b), Holthausen et al. (1987) and others. Markets regulate the interaction of block trades and ongoing trades. Suppose the current price of a stock is 40, and a block sale is negotiated upstairs at a price of 38. In the NYSE, the trade must be brought to the floor, where resting limit orders and floor brokers wishing to buy at 38 or more must be satisfied. Further the block trade must be reported publicly. By contrast, the London Stock Exchange has allowed reporting of the trade to be delayed up to 90 minutes in order to give broker dealers who acquire shares time to dispose of their shares. An alternative to crossing the block at 38 while the last trade took place at 40 is for the broker to trade portions of the block at prices between 40 and 38 until the market price equals the pre-negotiated block price, and then trade the remaining block. The risk of pre-trading portions of the block in this manner is that other traders

---

[8] The above relation is only one of several possible formulations. For example, one could take the dollar spread as the dependent variable. Similarly, the independent variables can be expressed in alternative ways. The fundamental variables – share volume, return variance, price, number of trades and market value – almost always are strongly significant in each formulation.

will become aware of the block and will sell in anticipation, perhaps driving the price down and forcing a lower block price.

The empirical evidence indicates that price impacts of block trading are quite mild. In part this reflects the ability of the broker to pre-trade and minimize the impact of the block. Kraus and Stoll (1972b) find a temporary price impact of 0.70% of the stock price for blocks that are sold and no temporary price impact for blocks that are purchased. The temporary price impact is akin to the bid–ask bounce of ordinary trades. The fact that prices do not bounce back after a block purchase implies that the price increase accompanying such blocks reflects new information. The asymmetry in price impacts between sale and purchase blocks is found in all block studies.

Since block trading is only one technique available to institutions, a natural issue is the overall trading costs of institutional investors. What are the impacts of institutional trading as seen from the perspective of institutions? A number of studies have gained access to institutional trading records in order to answer this question. These include Chan and Lakonishok (1993) and Keim and Madhavan (1997). An interesting feature of institutional trading data is that it is virtually impossible to connect institutional trade records to trades as reported over the tape. This is because institutions receive reports as to the average price of their trades in each stock on each day without a detailed breakdown as to the individual trades. Chan and Lakonishok report that buy programs have a price impact of 0.34% whereas sell programs have a price impact of only −0.04%.

6.2. Herding

Studies of individual institutions' trading do not assess the price impact of aggregate selling or buying pressure by several institutions. It is frequently said that institutions "herd" because they listen to the same analysts and go to the same clubs. In the first study of herding, Kraus and Stoll (1972a), using data collected as part of the Institutional Investor Study,[9] were able to construct monthly trading imbalances for the largest institutional investors in over 400 different stocks. They examine the tendency of institutions to trade in parallel and conclude that parallel trading does not occur more frequently than would be expected by chance. When parallel trading does occur, even though it be by chance, temporary price effects are observed. More recently, Lakonishok, Shleifer and Vishny (1992) analyze herding by pension funds. Wermers (1999) finds that mutual fund herding is related to past, contemporaneous and future returns. Mutual fund buying is more likely when past returns were positive, has a strong contemporaneous positive price effect, and tends to precede future positive returns.

An alternative approach to assessing the price impact of trading imbalances is to infer the imbalance from trade data. For a given day t, sell volume, S_t, is the number of

---

[9] See U.S. SEC (1971), *Institutional Investor Study.* Unlike later studies which rely on end of quarter holdings to infer purchases and sales, the data in the Institutional Investor Study are actual monthly purchases and sales provided by all major institutional investors over a period of 21 months.

shares traded below the quote midpoint, and buy volume, B_t, is the number of shares traded above the quote midpoint. The proportional imbalance on day t is

$$I_t = \frac{B_t - S_t}{B_t + S_t}.$$

One approach to assessing the imbalance in a given stock is to estimate the following regression:

$$\Delta P_t = \lambda_0 + \lambda I_t + \lambda_2 I_{t-1} + e_t, \tag{24}$$

where ΔP_t is the stock's quote midpoint change (net of market) on day t. Use of the midpoint abstracts from the bid–ask bounce. The coefficient, λ, measures the sensitivity of the quote change over a day to the daily imbalance. The coefficient is in the spirit of Kyle (1985). Insofar as the quote change is permanent, λ measures the information content of the day's imbalance. If prices bounce back the next day, one would conclude that the price impact reflects real factors. Stoll (2000) estimates the above regression for 1706 NYSE stocks. Each stocks has 61 days of data. The value of λ is positive and highly significant, indicating that trading pressure affects prices. Easley, Kiefer, O'Hara and Paperman (1996) use data on trading pressures to infer the probability that an information event has occurred. In their model, an excess of sellers over buyers increases the probability that negative private information exists.

6.3. Other studies of the effects of trading

A number of other studies have examined the relation between trading and the pattern of prices over time. French and Roll (1986) find that the variance of overnight returns (close to open) is only 1/5 the variance of daytime returns (open-to-close). While a large portion of the difference is due to the fact that news is not released during the night, they conclude that some of this difference is due to the fact that trading when the market is open causes volatility. Wood, McInish and Ord (1985) find that spreads are greatest in the morning, lowest at midday and increase somewhat at day-end, consistent with the fact that volatility is greatest around the opening. Harris (1989) and Madhavan, Richardson and Roomans (1997) have investigated the pattern of price behavior over the day, and Harris (1986) has investigated the pattern over days of the week. Over all, research on the time series pattern of spreads and volatility suggests that trading affects prices.

7. Market design

Any securities market, be it a traditional membership organization like the NYSE or a new for-profit electronic market, must make some very practical decisions about how trading should be organized. Should the market be a call market or a continuous market? If continuous, how should the market open, and under what circumstances, if any, should trading be halted? Should the market be an order-driven auction market that relies on limit orders to provide immediacy or should it be a quote-driven dealer market that relies on dealer quotes to provide immediacy? What degree of transparency of quotes and trades should be provided? Will traders be able to remain anonymous? How automated should the market be? What should be the minimum tick size at which quotes are made and trades take place? What kinds of orders beyond the standard market and limit orders should be possible?

The answer to these market-design questions ultimately depends on how the sources of trading friction are affected and how well the trading needs of investors are met. Will order-processing costs be reduced? Will risk bearing by dealers and/or limit orders be enhanced? Will the problem of free trading options become greater or less? Will the problem of adverse information become greater or less? Will investors be able to trade quickly? The successful market is one that allows investors to trade when they want to trade, that minimizes real costs of processing orders and of bearing risk, and that deals effectively with the problem of wealth redistribution from informed and speedy traders to uninformed and slow traders.

In this section we first discuss the call-auction process. While most markets offer continuous trading, many open with a call-auction process. Next the issue of dealer versus auction markets is examined, with particular emphasis on the developments in Nasdaq. Finally a number of other issues in market design are considered.

7.1. Call-auction markets

7.1.1. Call-auction process

Most markets began as call-auction markets simply because there was not enough activity to warrant continuous trading. Today most markets are continuous. However, the call-auction mechanism continues to be used to open trading or to restart trading after a halt. [10] In a call-auction market, orders are accumulated and executed at a given time and typically at a single price, p^*, at which supply equals demand. Buy orders at p^* or more buy at p^*. Sell orders at p^* or less sell at p^*. [11]

The benefit of a call market is that it aggregates significant trading interest at particular points in time and limits the free-trading option. The free-trading option is limited for two reasons. First, since all orders will execute at the auction price, aggressive limit orders can be placed without fear of being picked off at those prices. Second, insofar as the auction is transparent and order may be revised, traders can adjust prices as they see other traders place orders and as they see new information.

---

[10] Markets such as the NYSE, the Tokyo Exchange, and the Deutsche Boerse open with an auction procedure. However, Nasdaq allows each trader to start trading at his quotes.

[11] Because of discreteness in order flow, buy volume need not exactly equal sell volume at a given price. Exchanges establish rules on how such volume is allocated.

Adverse information effects may also be reduced in a call auction insofar as investors are able to observe order placement prior to the final price determination. For example, observing a large order to sell will cause potential buyers to adjust their buy orders. Despite the advantages of a call market, most markets are continuous. Investors appear to prefer a continuous market in which they can trade at any time.

It is widely accepted that the most critical and most volatile time in a market's operation is the opening, which typically begins with a call auction. At the opening, information disseminated overnight must be incorporated in securities prices, and orders accumulated overnight must be traded. The final outcome of the opening depends on the net demand of investors and the response of liquidity suppliers.

The working of a call-auction market also depends on the rules of the auction. Important issues are the following:

• What degree of transparency exists? Can investors see all orders and the likely opening price? If they can, better inferences can be made about the presence of informed traders.
• Can orders be canceled and revised on the basis of trial-opening prices or is this a one shot auction?[12] Disclosure of trial-opening prices conveys information and will cause order cancellations and new orders. The ability to cancel orders may also encourage manipulation. One solution is to impose fees for canceling orders and to provide incentives to place orders in a timely fashion.
• Can dealers participate in the auction? On the NYSE, the specialist, and only the specialist, observes the orders and may participate in the auction. This creates a conflict of interest that would not exist if orders were public.

Call-auction price determination in the presence of a single monopolistic informed trader is modeled by Kyle (1985) in one of the most cited papers in the field of microstructure. In the Kyle model, the price is determined in a one-shot auction where uninformed investors and the single informed investor place their orders. Trading by the uninformed investors is exogenous and normally distributed with mean zero and variance σ_u^2. The informed investor knows the distribution of the uninformed order flow (but not its actual value) and takes account of the impact of his order flow on the market clearing price. The auctioneer determines the auction price to reflect the information contained in the aggregate order flow. Let the asset price before the auction be p_0 and let the variance be σ_p^2. Kyle shows that the market clearing price will be

$$\tilde{p} = p_0 + \lambda(\tilde{x} + \tilde{u}), \tag{25}$$

where $\tilde{x}, \tilde{u}$ are the order flow of the informed and the uninformed respectively, and where $\lambda = 2[\sigma_p^2/\sigma_u^2]^{1/2}$. The price impact coefficient, λ, is larger the smaller the variance of the uninformed order flow (because it is more difficult for the informed investor to "hide").

---

[12] An excellent analysis of a one-shot auction is in Ho, Schwartz and Whitcomb (1985).

7.1.2. Evidence on openings

Amihud and Mendelson (1987) implement an interesting approach to assessing the
volatility around the opening while holding constant the amount of public information
released. They calculate daily returns from opening prices, r_0, and from closing
prices, r_c. Both returns span a 24 hour period and thus contain the same amount
of public information and the same variability due to public information. Stoll and
Whaley (1990) apply the Amihud and Mendelson procedure and analyze the sources of
volatility around the opening. Based on a sample of 1374 stocks over a 5-year period,
1982–1986, the average variance ratio is $\mathrm{avg}(\sigma_0^2/\sigma_c^2) = 1.13$. The positive variance
ratio implies that opening prices tend to overshoot and reverse after the opening. The
reversal of opening prices is reflected in negative serial correlation of open-to-open
returns.

Overshooting cannot be ascribed to public or private information arrival because
the amount of public and private information is the same for both returns. A possible
explanation for overshooting at the open is that trading pressures from liquidity shocks
are not completely dampened by liquidity suppliers. Specialists, who are allowed to
trade for their own account, may permit prices to deviate from equilibrium in order
to earn profits. A second explanation is that the opening is a period of intense price
discovery, which requires overnight information to be incorporated in price. The price
of a stock is affected not only by the information in the stock but also by information
in other stocks. Since all stocks do not open at the same time, some prices must be set
in the absence of reliable information as to the value of related stocks. Consequently,
some stocks open too high and others open too low. Prices reverse during the trading
day as opening pricing errors are discovered. Whatever the exact source of opening
volatility, it is an expensive time to trade. Stoll and Whaley compute the Roll implied
spread from the serial covariance of open-to-open returns as 0.898% compared with
an implied spread of 0.097% from the serial covariance of close-to-close returns. On a
40 dollar stock these implied spreads amount to 36 cents and 3.9 cents, respectively.

In a recent paper, Madhavan and Panchapagesan (2000) compare opening prices in
the NYSE opening auction to the opening if the specialist had not intervened. They
conclude that specialist intervention is beneficial in bringing the opening price closer
to the stock's equilibrium price. In contrast to the NYSE, Nasdaq simply starts trading
at posted dealer quotes, which become firm at 9:30 am, the formal start of trading.
Cao, Ghysels and Hatheway (2000) analyze the Nasdaq procedure and argue that it
works fairly well.

Related to the issue of opening trading is the issue of when to halt trading in a
stock or in all stocks. Markets halt trading in individual stocks if news is about to be
disseminated or if order imbalances are large. The purpose of such halts is to give
investors time to digest the news and determine a new price at which demand and
supply are equal. Halts also provide an opportunity for resting limit orders to reset limit
prices. In other words, trading is halted in those occasions when re-opening according
to a call auction appears desirable. Lee, Ready and Sequin (1994) analyze trading halts

in individual stocks. They conclude that halts have certain benefits, but that volume and volatility increase after a halt. After the crash of October 19, 1987, regulatory circuit breakers were adopted that would shut down trading in all stocks. Currently those circuit breakers are set at 10%, 20% and 30% drops in the Dow Jones Index. A 10% drop shuts the market down for one hour; a 20% drop, for two hours; a 30% drop, for the rest of the day.

7.2. Dealer versus auction markets: the Nasdaq controversy

In a continuous dealer market, investors buy at a dealer's ask and sell at a dealer's bid. Most bond and currency markets are dealer markets. In a continuous auction market, investors buy at the ask price established by a previously placed sell-limit order of another investor and sell at the bid price established by a previously placed buy-limit order. Among stock markets, the NYSE is a continuous auction market and Nasdaq is a continuous dealer market, although each has important features of the other. In recent years the Nasdaq Stock Market has come under intense scrutiny and has been required to undergo major changes. While dealer and auction markets have been the subject of theoretical inquiry, [13] little empirical evidence directly contrasting auction and dealer markets existed prior to the now famous study by Christie and Schultz (1994). Christie and Schultz showed that Nasdaq stocks had a tendency to be quoted in even eighths, necessarily bounding the spread from below at $0.25.

   Before presenting some of the evidence on the quality of the Nasdaq and NYSE markets, it would perhaps be useful to contrast the major structural features of these markets:

• The NYSE is a centralized exchange where trading takes place on a physical floor (although most orders now arrive electronically), whereas Nasdaq is a physically disperse set of dealers each of whom posts quotes on the Nasdaq quotation system.
• The NYSE has 1366 members who must buy seats ($2 000 000 in December, 2000) for the right to trade on the exchange. Seat holders are specialists and floor brokers. Nasdaq has over 5000 members of whom about 500 are market makers.
• On the NYSE, each stock is assigned to a specialist who makes markets and oversees the book of limit orders. All limit orders on the NYSE are centralized in the book. The best bid and offer, whether for the book or the specialist, are displayed along with the depth at the quote. On Nasdaq, each stock has at least two market makers quoting markets in the stock. The average number of dealers per stock in March 2001 was 11.8, with the top stocks having more than 40 market makers. Each market maker may hold limit orders sent to him and is obligated to display the best bid and offer, whether from a limit order or his own quote, and the associated depth. Prior to the Order Handling Rules implemented by the SEC in 1997, market makers on Nasdaq were not required to display customer limit orders.

---

[13] See Garbade and Silber (1979), Cohen, Maier, Schwartz and Whitcomb (1981), Ho and Stoll (1983), Madhavan (1992), Pagano and Roell (1992), Biais (1993) and Laux (1995).

- On the NYSE, there has always been a mandated minimum tick size. Until 1997 the minimum increment for quotes and trades was $0.125. On Nasdaq, no increment was mandated, but convention frequently led to trades at increments of even eighths as found by Christie and Schultz (1994). Under SEC urging, the minimum tick size on the NYSE and Nasdaq was reduced to one cent in 2001.
- On the NYSE, orders may be routed electronically over the DOT system directly to the specialist. Execution is not automatic, but occurs only when the specialist accepts the trade. On Nasdaq, orders may be routed to a market maker electronically over SelectNet, which like the DOT system, requires the market maker to accept the trade. Orders may be automatically executed over Nasdaq's SOES (small order execution system) up to the market maker's posted depth.

Christie and Schultz (1994) investigated the spreads of 100 Nasdaq stocks in 1991 in comparison to 100 NYSE stocks. They find a nearly total avoidance of odd eighths quotes for 70 of the 100 Nasdaq stocks and a resulting higher spread on Nasdaq than on the NYSE. They conclude that Nasdaq market makers are implicitly colluding to keep spreads high. Huang and Stoll (1996) compare execution costs for 175 Nasdaq stocks to execution costs for a matched sample of NYSE stocks in 1991. They find that execution costs as measured by the quoted spread, the effective spread (which accounts for trades inside the quotes), the realized spread (which measures revenues of suppliers of immediacy), or the Roll (1984) implied spread, are twice as large for a sample of Nasdaq stocks as they are for a matched sample of NYSE stocks. The results are in Table 3.

Huang and Stoll (1996) conclude that the higher trading costs in Nasdaq are not due to asymmetric information because the asymmetric information component of the spread, measured as the difference between the effective and realized spreads, is the same in the two markets. Partial explanations are provided by differences in the treatment of limit orders and commissions in the two markets. In Nasdaq, limit orders were not displayed (as are limit orders on the NYSE) and consequently, limit orders could not narrow the spread. In Nasdaq institutional investors pay no commissions, although individual investors do. Thus in the case of institutions some of the difference in spreads in the two markets reflects the fact that NYSE spreads can be lower by the amount recovered in commissions. Huang and Stoll also conclude that spread differences are not related to differences in market depth or in the frequency of even eighth quotes, once stock characteristics are held constant.

Two features of Nasdaq contributed to a lack of competition. First, a common feature of multiple dealer markets is that each dealer seeks to capture a certain fraction of the order flow by internalizing trades from a parent broker or by arranging for trades to be preferenced to it. Internalization occurs when a retail broker sends its order flow to its affiliated dealer. Preferencing occurs when a retail broker arranges to send its order flow to chosen dealers, often in return for a payment. The dealer receiving internalized or preferenced order flow promises to trade at the best quote even if he is not currently posting the best quote. When a large fraction of order flow is preferenced or internalized, little incentive exists for any dealer to compete by narrowing the spread

Table 3

Comparison of execution costs in Nasdaq and NYSE for a matched sample of 175 stocks[a,b], based on all transactions in 1991

Execution measure	Nasdaq	NYSE
Quoted half-spread[c]	24.6	12.9
Effective half-spread[d]	18.7	7.9
Realized half spread[e] (5 minutes)		
Trades at bid	15.3	2.7
Trades at ask	13.6	0.8
Roll half-spread[f]	18.3	3.4

[a] Source: Huang and Stoll (1996).
[b] In cents.
[c] The quoted half-spread is half the difference between the quoted ask and quoted bid.
[d] The effective half-spread is the absolute difference between the traded price and the quote midpoint at the time of the trade.
[e] The realized half-spread is the five minute price change after a trade at the bid or the negative of the five minute price change after a trade at the ask.
[f] The Roll half-spread is the square root of the negative of the mean serial covariance of price changes.

because a large fraction of the order flow is already allocated to other dealers. Indeed, narrowing the spread reduces the revenues of all dealers (because they promise to match the best price) and generates considerable pressure from all dealers not to narrow the spread. A second market-structure feature that inhibited competition in Nasdaq was the availability of alternative electronic markets where a dealer could offer better prices to even out inventory without making those prices generally available.[14] Dealers could use Instinet, a proprietary trading system or SelectNet, a Nasdaq system, to trade with other dealers at favorable prices without offering those prices to their retail order flow.

After extended investigations by the Securities and Exchange Commission (SEC) and the Department of Justice, the SEC in 1997 put into effect order handling rules that required limit orders to be displayed and to be given price priority. Strict time priority across dealers and markets is not required. The effect of this rule was to allow limit orders more effectively to compete with dealer quotes. Second, the order handling rules prohibited a dealer from quoting in Nasdaq at a price inferior to the dealer's quote in an electronic communications system (ECN). If the ECN displayed its best quotes in Nasdaq, the dealer obligation to quote the best price in Nasdaq was satisfied. This

---

[14] Preferencing and the use of inter-dealer trading systems are also common on the London Stock Exchange. Papers by Hansch, Naik and Viswanathan (1998) and Reiss and Werner (1998) analyze this market and find that there is some price competition and some response of order flow to prices. Wahal (1997) finds that dealer entry is related to spreads, but entry may simply divide the profits among more players without reducing overall profits.

ECN rule made available to the public the same quotes previously available only on the interdealer market.

The order handling rules had a dramatic effect on quoted spreads, which fell by 30%, as chronicled in Barclay et al. (1999). Effective spreads also fell but not as much. Recent evidence [U.S. SEC (2001)] suggests that effective spreads on Nasdaq continue to exceed those for comparable NYSE stocks.

The benefit of a dealer market arises from the flexible response of dealers to liquidity needs. Dealers are able to respond quickly to changing market conditions. Yet evidence indicates that dealers, left to themselves, raise spreads above those observed when limit orders are also displayed. The benefit of an auction market is that limit orders from the trading public provide liquidity. Fischer Black (1971) predicted that an automated market (much like the new ECNs) would be able to operate without dealers, and that dealers would be driven out of business. It does not appear, however that a pure limit order market is able to provide sufficient liquidity, particularly in less active stocks. Dealer intervention is often needed to bridge gaps in the arrival of limit orders. On the NYSE, for example, the specialist participated on the buy or sell side in 27.5% of the share volume in 2000. [15] The implication is that a mixed dealer/auction market is optimal.

7.3. Other issues in market design

Market centers face a number of other design issues, including the degree of transparency, whether traders remain anonymous, whether trading is fully automated, what minimum price increment should be established, and the kinds of orders that are allowed.

7.3.1. Transparency

Transparency refers to the disclosure of quotes (at which trades can take place) and of transaction prices (at which trades did take place). The NYSE displays only the top of the book, that is the best bid and ask, but not the other orders on the book. The ECNs display the entire book. The benefits of transparency are three-fold. First, transparency speeds price discovery and enhances market efficiency, for with transparent markets all investors see the current quotes and the transaction prices, and no investor trades at the wrong price. Second, transparency helps customers monitor brokers. The public dissemination of quotes and transactions allows a customer to determine that his transaction is in line with others at the same time. Third, transparency enhances competition, for it allows competing dealers to guarantee the best price anywhere, but do it at a lower commission or lower spread. [16] The costs of transparency arise

---

[15] NYSE, *Fact Book, 2000 Data*, p. 18.
[16] Madhavan (1995) analyses the effect of transparency on fragmentation and competition.

from adverse incentive effects. First, traders may be reluctant to place limit orders, particularly if they are large, because the display may convey information that will make the price move against the limit order. Second, display of limit orders may make it easier for traders to exercise the free trading option and thus reduce the incentive to place limit order. If no one knows whether a limit order exists, it is more difficult to pick it off, but if the limit order is displayed, it can be more readily picked off.

7.3.2. Anonymity

Closely related to the issue of transparency is the issue of anonymity. Should the identity of traders be known? Some traders, such as dealers want to be identified because they want to build reputations. Other traders, such as institutions who are likely to be informed, want to be anonymous because disclosure of their identity may cause prices to move against them. If they cannot capitalize on their special information, their incentive to do research is reduced, and information production could be harmed. Admati and Pfleiderer (1991) analyze the idea of sunshine trading by which an uninformed investor creditably reveals himself and thus prevents an adverse price reaction. Several papers, including Benveniste, Marcus and Wilhelm (1992) and Forster and George (1992), analyze the effect of anonymity.

7.3.3. Automation

Automation is an issue because it affects the value of the free-trading option and who has it. When execution is automatic at a dealer's quote, the dealer grants the option. Furthermore, if the dealer is slow to update quotes, several trades might take place before the quote can be changed. The SOES (Small Order Execution System) system of Nasdaq worked in this manner. Upstairs traders sitting at terminals often placed orders more quickly than the reaction time of the dealer. In an order routing system like the NYSE DOT system or the Nasdaq SelectNet system, orders are delivered to the dealer, but the dealer must accept the order within a specified period of time. This gives the dealer some time to react and perhaps change the quote. In effect the dealer now has the option. Before automated routing and execution systems, orders were hand-carried to the floor and some negotiation took place. A completely automated system does not permit negotiation. Hence, a completely automated system is more successful for orders that do not require negotiation, such as most small orders. Large orders, where negotiation is common, are not automated (except in so far as a computer system mimics a negotiation). In an interesting theoretical paper Glosten (1994) shows that an open electronic limit order book would be most efficient and would dominate other exchanges.

7.3.4. Tick size

The tick size is the minimum allowable price variation in a security, usually determined by the exchange on which the security trades. On the NYSE, the tick size before

June 1997 was $1/8^{th}$ dollar by rule. In futures markets, each futures contract has a specified tick size that depends on the value of the futures contract and its variability. For example, the tick size for the S&P 500 futures contract is 0.10 index points or $25 per contract. Mandated tick sizes are not common in dealer markets. For example, Nasdaq has not had a market-wide mandated tick size, although convention led to a minimum tick size of $1/8^{th}$ with a number of stocks trading at wider increments as discussed above. Under SEC pressure, the tick size in equities markets in the USA was reduced to $1/16^{th}$ in the 1997 and to one penny in 2001.

The tick size has several effects. First, the tick size affects incentives to place limit orders, as Harris (1991) first noted, since it represents the cost to getting inside someone else's quote. If the tick size is 12.5 cents, and the standing bid is $20, one must bid at least 20.125 to move ahead of the standing bid. If the tick size is one cent, one must bid only 20.01 to move ahead of the standing bid. Since it is easy to move ahead of a limit order when the tick size is small, fewer limit orders will be placed when the tick size is small, which can have adverse effects on liquidity. A second effect is that a mandated tick size can cause spreads to be artificially large, at least for some trades.[17] When the tick size is 12.5 cents, the minimum spread is 12.5 cents. A 12.5 cent spread may exceed the equilibrium spread for 100 share orders, causing such orders to pay too much.

Currently with a tick size of one cent, many stocks trade at a spread of 5 cents or less, but the depth is less than it would be at a 12.5 cent spread. When the tick size is small and depth at the inside quote is small, it is important that markets display information on the available liquidity at prices away from the inside quote in order to give investors information as to the likely price at which they can trade their orders.

7.3.5. Order types

Another issue in market design is the types of orders that will be allowed. On the one hand a market may wish to restrict certain common order types. For example, electronic markets often forbid straight market orders, requiring instead the use of marketable limit orders. A market order would execute at any price. If the book is thin and another order takes the quantity displayed at the inside, an unsuspecting market order might trade at prices far removed from the equilibrium price. A marketable limit order is an order at the current market price that pays no more (or receives no less) than the current price. On the other hand, automated exchanges offer the possibility of much more complex order types. For example, contingent orders could easily be monitored in a computer. A contingent limit order that adjusts the limit price based on the price of the stock or an index can reduce the free trading option and can alleviate

---

[17] See Harris (1994). Hausman, Lo and MacKinlay (1992) and Ball and Chordia (2001) provide approaches to analyzing true price behavior and true spreads in the presence of artificial price increments imposed by the minimum tick size.

the chance that a limit order is picked off. Opponents of automatic quote updating fear that markets will become computer dueling grounds in which traders program their order submission strategy, turn on the computer, and go back to bed. Nasdaq, to limit pure computer trading, has limited the ability of dealers automatically to update quotes.

8. The market for markets: centralization versus fragmentation of trading

Trading of stocks and related instruments takes place in a variety of different markets. Stocks listed on the NYSE trade there, but also trade on regional exchanges, in the third market, and on some other proprietary systems. Trading of stocks listed on Nasdaq trade there, but also trade on ECN's and on other proprietary systems. Many U.S. stocks trade in foreign markets. Options on stocks trade in five option markets. Futures markets trade stock indexes, and have recently received regulatory approval to trade futures on individual stocks. While the number of markets existing today is greater than ever in the past, many observers argue that markets will merge and consolidate, while others predict increased fragmentation of markets. In this section the evolution of equities markets in the USA and of global equities markets in the last 30 years is reviewed and the forces of centralization and of fragmentation are discussed.

8.1. Evolution of equities markets in the USA

In 1970, the New York Stock Exchange (NYSE) accounted for the overwhelming bulk of trading in stocks, and it faced little or no competition. The American Stock Exchange (AMSE) did not compete because, by agreement, it listed and traded only stocks not listed on the NYSE (accounting for 11% of dollar volume of all listed stocks). The Nasdaq Stock Market did not yet exist, although stocks that were not yet eligible for listing were traded on the OTC market. Stocks listed on the NYSE could be traded on regional stock exchanges under an SEC rule that granted them unlisted trading privileges (UTP). The regional exchanges (Midwest, Pacific, Philadelphia, Boston, Cincinnati) accounted for only 12% of dollar volume of stocks listed on the NYSE. The organization of the NYSE met the classic definition of a cartel:
- limited membership – one must own one of 1366 seats in order to trade on the NYSE;
- fixed prices – commission rates were fixed,
- rules and regulations limiting non-price competition among cartel members – price discounts were prohibited, and Rule 394 prohibited members from trading off the NYSE where they could charge lower commissions.

By 2000, the organization of trading markets had changed in response to technology and regulation. Fixed commissions were abolished in May, 1975. The Nasdaq Stock Market, founded in 1971, now rivals the NYSE with dollar volume exceeding that on the NYSE.[18] With the growth in Nasdaq, the AMSE lost its second place position as a stock market. Instead it has become an index and options market. The regional exchanges (Boston, Cincinnati, Midwest, Pacific, Philadelphia), despite predictions of their imminent demise, have maintained their overall share of NYSE dollar volume, but they continue to be under pressure. A host of new proprietary trading systems that include Instinet, a system aimed at institutional traders, and other electronic communications systems (ECNs) that totally automate trading, now compete for order flow. Some of the major features of changing market organization are outlined here.

8.1.1. Competitive commissions

In 1970, commissions on a 500 share trade of a 40 dollar stock were $270.[19] While institutional investors received a quantity discount, they still paid substantial amounts (for example, 26.2 cents per share on a 5000 share trade). Economic pressures on commissions took two forms. First dealers outside the NYSE offered to trade shares at discounted commissions. The *third market* is the market in NYSE stocks made by brokers and dealers who are not members of the NYSE (and thus exempt from Rule 394). In the 1960s and 1970s, institutional investors used the third market to reduce commissions. Second, while NYSE rules limited rebates of commissions, they did not limit service competition. Consequently brokers rushed to provide services and products in return for lucrative commission business. *Soft dollars* are that portion of the commission over and above the cost of doing the trade. Institutions paid soft dollars for research services, mutual fund sales, phone lines, and a variety of other services. Soft dollars still exist today, but they are limited by regulation to research services, and the amounts are smaller.

In addition to the economic pressures on commission, the Department of Justice and the SEC also attacked fixed commissions. Finally, Congress abolished fixed commissions as part of the Securities Acts Amendments passed on May 1, 1975. Dire consequences were predicted, but the securities industry easily survived the change, as reductions in commissions were more than offset by increased trading volume and more efficient trading procedures.[20] Today the cost of a 500 share trade, handled electronically, is typically less than $25 (despite the inflation since 1970), and institutions typically trade for 5 cents per share.

8.1.2. Rule 394 and the third market

In 1970, NYSE Rule 394 prohibited member firms of the NYSE from trading outside the NYSE either as agent or as principal. Member firms, acting as agents, could not

---

[18] Part of this reflects the trading system of Nasdaq where a dealer tends to be involved as both a buyer and seller, whereas on the NYSE customer to customer trades are more likely.

[19] See Stoll (1979, p. 13).

[20] The effects of the May Day 1975 changes are analyzed in Stoll (1979).

send customer orders to other markets (other than regional exchanges), nor could they trade with customers as principals outside the NYSE. This rule had the beneficial effect of forcing all orders to interact in one market – the NYSE, but it had the harmful effect of limiting competition from new markets. Over time, regulatory pressure weakened Rule 394 and caused it to be abolished in 2001. First, in 1976, the rule was changed to Rule 390, which permitted trades, where the NYSE member acted as agent, to be executed off the NYSE. This modification gave rise to a new third market as member firms sent customer orders to third market makers (such as Madoff and Co.) that promised to match NYSE prices. In addition the third-market-maker paid the broker for the order flow. The new third market specialized in the order flow of small, uninformed, customers in contrast to the third market of the 1970s, which was an institutional market to avoid high commissions.

Second, Rule 390 was weakened by SEC Rule 19c-3 that exempted any stocks listed after April 1979 from application of the rule. Under 19c-3, a NYSE member could trade with customers as a principal and could therefore make in-house market in eligible stocks, but, surprisingly, few members set up in-house markets in listed stocks. Finally, Rule 390 was abolished by the NYSE in 2001 because of SEC pressure and because the rule had become ineffective.

Thus by the year 2001, two of the key features of the NYSE cartel – fixed commissions and the restrictive Rule 394 – had been abolished. The one remaining feature of the cartel – limited direct access for the 1366 members – remains. The privilege of membership continues to have substantial value as NYSE seat prices in 2000 exceeded \$2 million. Members are of three types:[21] specialists (about 450), independent floor brokers (about 525) and floor brokers for retail firms (about 330). Specialists trade for their own accounts as market makers and keep the book of limit orders. Independent floor brokers receive commissions for executing customer orders. Floor brokers that work for retail firms execute the portion of the firms' order flow that is not routed through the electronic DOT system.

8.1.3. National market system

The Securities Acts Amendments of 1975, in addition to abolishing fixed commissions, directs the SEC to facilitate the establishment of a "national market system" that is characterized by the absence of unnecessary regulatory restrictions, fair competition among brokers, dealers and markets, the availability to all of information on transaction prices and dealer price quotations, the linking of markets and the ability to execute orders in the best market. The SEC envisaged a single national market in which orders would be routed to the best market and in which a single CLOB (consolidated limit order book) would contain limit orders and dealer quotes in each stock. A single CLOB has not been implemented, as it would require substantial integration of different markets and would limit competition.

---

[21] See Sofianos and Werner (2000) for a description of the membership.

Certain elements of an NMS have been introduced. These include the consolidated trade system (CTS), the consolidated quote system (CQS), and the intermarket trading system (ITS). CTS and CQS enhance market transparency as they require all exchanges to report centrally their transactions (price and quantity) and quotes, and thereby enable traders in any market to determine if they are trading at the best prices. The CQS and CTS do not provide access for brokers and dealers on one floor to better quotes on another floor. Access is provided through ITS, which links exchange floors and permits traders on one floor to send a "commitment to trade" to another floor. The other floor has a limited time to accept or reject this commitment.

The future of the national market system is cloudy. On the one hand some observers argue that the SEC should impose tighter links among markets and improve ITS. On the other hand, some would let the nature and extent of links be decided by markets and by investors on the basis of available technology. In fact, computer routing systems can quickly send an order to the best market, without the need for a government-sponsored CLOB or ITS.

8.2. Global markets

Equities markets in other parts of the world have changed as much and as rapidly as markets in the USA. In October 1986, the London Stock Exchange (LSE) underwent the "big bang" by which fixed commissions and a restrictive jobber system were eliminated and a dealer trading system similar to Nasdaq was adopted. In the late 1980s, Paris replaced its floor trading system with a computerized limit order book, which is analyzed in Biais, Hillion and Spatt (1995). Toronto was an early adopter of a computerized trading system in 1977. The German markets were late to change but have done so with a vengeance. The Deutsche Boerse is a for-profit business overseeing the automated stock trading platform, Xetra, and several other markets, including the electronic futures market, Eurex. A merger between the LSE and the Deutsche Boerse was attempted but failed. The Paris Bourse has successfully consolidated with Amsterdam and Brussels to form Euronext. As in the USA, private electronic trading systems are also making inroads in Europe. Domowitz (1993) provides a comparison of automated trading systems around the world.

As markets around the world develop, they are in a position to trade securities from any other part of the world. As a matter of technology, the stock of an American company can be traded as easily on the LSE as on the NYSE. However, globalization of markets has not proceeded as rapidly as technology allows. Stocks domiciled in the USA tend to trade primarily when U.S. markets are open and stocks domiciled in Europe tend to trade primarily when European markets are open. There is evidence of some migration of trading from one country to another in the same time zone [Domowitz, Glen and Madhavan (1998)].

Cross-listing of stocks from one country on the exchange of another country is often done in the form of depositary receipts. In the USA, American Depositary Receipts (ADRs) are dollar denominated claims issued by a bank on the underlying shares held by a bank. For example, British Telecom ADR traded on the NYSE is a claim on 10 shares of British Telecom traded in London. Arbitrageurs keep prices of the ADR and UK shares in equilibrium. Nothing in principle prevents stocks from being listed in the USA in terms of their home currency. Traders of such shares in the USA must have the ability to pay or receive a foreign currency. Alternatively, nothing prevents a company from listing its shares in a variety of countries in terms of each local currency.

One of the puzzles in international finance is the slowness with which international diversification has taken place. Investors are said to have a home bias.[22] This phenomenon is reflected in the slowness with which stocks are traded internationally. Stock trading for most companies is concentrated in the company's home country by those investors domiciled in that country.

8.3. Economic forces of centralization and fragmentation

In spite of the weakening of the cartel rules of the NYSE, the NYSE continues to attract most of the order flow in the stocks it lists. At the same time new markets are being founded almost daily both in the USA and abroad. Consequently there is a tension between centralization of trading in a single market and the initiation of new markets that fragment trading. Fragmentation of trading can be said to arise when an order in one market is unable to interact with an order in another market.

The forces of *centralization* are two-fold – one on the supply side and one on the demand side. First, on the supply side, a market reaps economies of scale in processing transactions. The average cost of trading a share of stock declines with the number of shares traded. As a result, the first mover into the trading business has a great advantage because it can process trades at lower cost than a competitor using the same technology. Second, on the demand side, a market generates network externalities. A market is a communications network, and like other networks, its attractiveness depends on the number of others on the network. Traders want to trade where other traders are already trading because the probability of a successful trade is a function of the number of other traders using the market. Consequently, network externalities, like economies of scale, lead to a first mover advantage.

Several factors have made *competition* from satellite markets more effective in recent years and have weakened the centralizing forces of economies of scale and network externalities. First, the transparency of quotes and transaction prices makes it possible for a satellite market to credibly guarantee that the price in the primary market is being matched. For many years, the NYSE jealously guarded its price information and limited the dissemination of its quotes and transaction prices. Without knowledge of where the price is, investors prefer the primary market where price discovery takes

---

[22] For example see Cooper and Kaplanis (1994), Telsar and Werner (1995), Kang and Stulz (1997) and Chapter 16 in this Handbook by Karolyi and Stulz.

place. With transparency, a trader can be assured the price in a satellite market at least matches the price in the primary market.

Second, satellite markets not only match prices, but they also pay for order flow from brokers. A typical payment might be one or two cents per share for market orders from retail investors that are judged to be uninformed. Payment is not made for limit orders or for order flow judged to be informed. Payment for order flow has been criticized because the payment goes to the broker, not to the customer whose order is being routed to the satellite market. While payment for order flow is quite common among satellite exchange, it is not necessarily sufficient to overcome the natural centralizing forces. If the primary market is the low cost producer of transaction services, it can make the same payment. [23]

Third, technological change has made competition more effective. Nimble new exchanges may be able to implement new, low cost, electronic trading systems more quickly than existing markets and thereby attract order flow away from established markets. Communications technology also reduces the switching costs of moving trades from one market center to another. The ease with which orders can be routed to a satellite market has improved.

Fourth, regulatory policy in the USA has fostered competition and fragmentation. The SEC has required greater transparency, which enhances competition from new markets. Second the SEC has required markets to link, which has given satellite markets access to the primary market. Such links enable dealers in the satellite market to lay off inventory in the primary market and provide an opportunity for brokers to route orders to the satellite market.

It is not evident how the conflict between centralization and fragmentation will be resolved in the future. The forces of centralization – economies of scale and network externalities – are strong. While they have been weakened by technology and regulation, they have not been weakened to the extent that markets will necessarily fragment into many separate unconnected market centers. If markets do fragment, the adverse consequences are small because markets are linked by high speed communications systems. The term "fragmentation" has a harmful connotation, but, in fact, fragmentation is just another word for competition. Competition among markets is a good thing because it fosters innovation and efficiency. Separate markets may exist, but when linked by high-speed communications systems they act almost as one.

The cost of fragmentation is that priority rules are difficult to maintain across markets. Price priority can usually be maintained because, with transparency, the investor can send his order to the market with the best price. But even price priority can sometimes be violated, for example, when large orders in one market trade through

---

[23] Battalio, Greene and Jennings (1997) conclude that preferencing arrangements on the Boston and Cincinnati stock exchanges attracted order flow to those exchanges without adversely affecting the quality of markets.

prices in another market. Time priority is likely to be violated as traders prefer to trade in one market over another that may offer the same price.

8.4. The future structure of markets [24]

The evolution of the securities industry will be shaped by technology and by regulation. Technology widens the extent of the market beyond a particular region or a particular country. Communications technology links investors to all markets and hence intensifies competition among existing market centers. Foreign markets can easily trade U.S. stocks, and markets in the USA can easily trade foreign stocks.

Technology changes the nature of exchanges. In the past securities were traded on membership exchanges – mutual organizations organized more like clubs than like businesses. However, the task of trading securities has become a business with private firms taking a larger role. As a consequence some exchanges have de-mutualized in an attempt to organize themselves more effectively and with an eye to raising capital by stock sales.

Technology changes the relative position of customers, retail brokers, exchanges, and market making firms. Retail firms and customers have the ability to create their own markets and put pressure on exchanges to respond to their interests. Large national market making firms are able to trade their order flow on any of a number of markets, thereby put competitive pressure on exchanges. New electronic markets provide low cost trading and put pressure on existing exchanges.

Regulation sets the rules for competition among market centers. The SEC has pushed for links among markets and transparency of prices and quotes. By and large this policy has enhanced competition, but it has limited the flexibility and speed with which markets could act. SEC rules recognize that all market centers are not equal. The SEC rule on alternative trading systems (ATS) distinguishes exchanges and ATS. ATS are electronic trading systems that do not carry out all the functions of an exchange. ATS are regulated as broker dealers with additional requirements depending on their size. An exchange has self-regulatory obligations, has requirements as to governance and board structure, and must participate in market linkages. While exchanges sometimes criticize the SEC for imposing on them the costs of regulating their markets, SRO responsibilities often become a competitive advantage vis a vis non-exchange market centers. In addition, exchanges reap substantial revenues from the sale of quote and price information. As a consequence, several ECNs have applied for exchange status.

9. Other markets

Market microstructure research has focused on equities markets, but other market are clearly important, albeit, less studied.

---

[24] For some thoughtful predictions, see Lee (2002).

9.1. Bond market

The bond market is a dealer market. Dealers display indicative quotes and provide firm quotes in response to customer inquiries. Customers trade directly with dealers, at dealer prices. Dealers can trade anonymously with other dealers through inter-dealer brokers. Inter-dealer brokers display anonymous dealer quotes, usually only to other dealers, and execute inter-dealer transactions.[25] Participants in the bond market are institutional investors – insurance companies, investment companies, banks, etc. – who trade in relatively large amounts. Individual investors are not a major element in bond trading. Secondary market trading of bonds is relatively infrequent as the bonds are often held to maturity.

The microstructure of bond markets has not been studied to the same extent as the microstructure of equities markets, partly because data are not readily available. An early study by Fisher (1959) showed that corporate bond yields varied by marketability. More marketable bonds (measured by number of bonds outstanding) are priced at lower yields to maturity. Grant and Whaley (1978) show that bond spreads depend on risk as measured by duration as well as on quantity outstanding. Hong and Warga (2000) compare transactions data from the NYSE Automated Bond System, where transactions are of small size, and from insurance companies, which trade in large size, and conclude that effective spreads from these two sources are quite similar. Schultz (2001) examines the quoted bid–ask spread of corporate bonds as a function of bond characteristics. He concludes that trading costs are lower for larger trades, which reflects the fact that the bond market is largely an institutional market.

The most active bond market is that for U.S. treasuries, and the most active time is at the initial offering of bonds. Unlike stock issues that occur at a given offering price, bonds have been issued in a sealed bid price discriminatory auction. Jegadeesh (1993) studies Treasury auctions in the period 1986–1991. He finds that the "on the run" bond is typically priced above comparable bonds in the secondary market and that the bid–ask spread is below that in the secondary market. Secondary market trading of government bonds is studied by Elton and Green (1998). They find that most of the cross sectional variation in bid–ask spreads can be explained by factors such as volume and maturity. However they conclude the effect of liquidity on bond prices is small.

9.2. Currency market

The currency market is a dealer market made largely by the same dealers active in the bond market. Currency dealers display indicative quotes, but quotes at which trades may occur are usually made bilaterally. Like the bond market, the currency market has an interdealer market in which dealers can trade anonymously with each other.

---

[25] Exclusive inter-dealer trading also existed in the Nasdaq Stock Market, but was eliminated by the SEC on the grounds that this was a mechanism that contributed to high bid–ask spreads for the public.

Lyons (1995) analyses the behavior of a major currency dealer and concludes that inventory considerations are important determinants of dealer behavior in two senses. First, there is a direct effect from the dealer's desire to have a zero position at day-end. Second, there is an indirect effect from information about other dealers' inventories that influences the dealer's behavior. Other articles examining the microstructure of currency markets include Bessembinder (1994), Bollerslev and Melvin (1994) and Huang and Masulis (1999).

9.3. Futures markets

Organized futures markets are open outcry auction markets. Trading takes place in a pit where traders, representing themselves or customers, signal their desire to trade. In major contracts such as index futures or T-bond futures, hundreds of traders are present, and trading is extremely rapid. Many transactions may occur at nearly the same time. Consequently, unlike the equities market in which all quotes and transaction prices are reported sequentially, in the futures markets not every quote nor every transaction is reported on the ticker tape. Liquidity is provided by scalpers who buy contracts at their bid price and sell contracts at their ask price. Manaster and Mann (1996) analyze floor traders in futures markets. They find evidence of inventory management in that inventories are mean reverting. On the other hand they also find that traders do not pay price concessions in order to manage their inventory.

9.4. Options markets

Active secondary markets in options on common stocks date to the founding of the Chicago Board Options Exchange (CBOE) in 1973. Today equity options are traded on the CBOE, on three other traditional exchanges (American, Philadelphia and Pacific), and on a new electronic exchange, the International Securities Exchange (ISE). The American and Philadelphia exchanges employ a single specialist system whereas the CBOE and Pacific Exchange use a competing market maker system. In recent years the CBOE and Pacific have designated primary market makers and given these firms more responsibility for overseeing the markets in their options. As a practical matter, option trading is more complicated than stock trading simply because the large number of different option contracts for any given stock. For example, IBM stock has over 100 puts and 100 calls with different maturities and strike prices. When the stock price changes, all the option prices must be updated quickly.

The microstructure of options have been analyzed from a number of different perspectives. Vijh (1990) examines option spreads and the price impact of large options trades. He concludes that large options trades are absorbed well by the market. Spreads are as large as those in the underlying stock despite the lower price of the option. A number of papers have investigated whether options prices lead prices of the underlying stocks [Stephan and Whaley (1990), Chan, Chung and Johnson (1993), Easley, O'Hara and Srinivas (1998)]. One would expect such a lead if the informed investors trade in the more leveraged options market rather than in the stock market, but the evidence is mixed.

10. Asset pricing and market microstructure

It seems obvious that microstructure factors ought to affect asset prices. Consider for example a firm raising equity capital for the first time. The price investors would pay for the new shares must undoubtedly depend on the ease with which those shares can be sold in the future. If all investors face a cost of selling the shares that is 20% of the price, the value of the shares will certainly be much lower today than if the disposition cost were 2%. The valuation effect of real friction, such as the cost of processing orders or searching for counterparties, is clearly to reduce an asset's value. The valuation effect of informational friction is less clear. Informational friction arises if one investor is better informed than another. The informed investor with good news will bid up asset prices to the disadvantage of the uninformed investor who sells the shares. Similarly, when disposing of shares, the informational investor receives a better price than the uninformed investor. The presence of informed investors disadvantages uninformed investors and redistributes income from the uninformed to the informed. Informational frictions introduce distributional uncertainty, which may make some investors reluctant to buy an asset, thereby lowering its market price.

A number of studies have examined the relation of microstructure and asset pricing. Stoll and Whaley (1983) show that expected returns are related to transaction costs and they argue that the small firm effect can be explained at least in part by the higher transactions costs of small firms. Amihud and Mendelson (1986) develop and test a model of asset pricing with transaction costs. Brennan and Subrahmanyam (1996) show that required returns are related to the Kyle price impact coefficient. Brennan, Chordia and Subrahmanyam (1998) show that expected returns are negatively related to volume after controlling for other factors such as firm size and book to market ratio, a result they attribute to greater liquidity and lesser trading costs of high volume stocks.

11. Conclusions

In the past twenty years, research on the simple question of what happens when financial assets are bought and sold has grown to the extent that it is now a recognized sub-field within finance – market microstructure. Probably the field has grown so dramatically simply because it is interesting. Microstructure research examines the process of price formation in the presence of risks, costs and asymmetric information, factors that are central to finance. Add to that the availability of large transaction data bases, and one has a recipe for a successful research area.

Microstructure research has also grown because the field deals with important practical issues. Microstructure research influences regulatory policy, such as the regulation of the Nasdaq Stock Market. Microstructure research contributes to institutional trading strategy and the proper measurement and management of trading costs. Microstructure research provides an intellectual framework for designing and operating trading systems.

In this chapter I have tried to convey some of the important institutional features of markets while also presenting the ideas that underpin the scholarly study of market microstructure. Scholarly analysis focuses on the determinants of the bid–ask spread and on the effect of market frictions for short-term behavior of asset prices. If there were no market frictions, bid and ask prices would be equal, and short-term price fluctuations would depend only on information arrival. In fact, market friction, resulting from the costs of processing orders, from inventory risk assumed by suppliers of liquidity, from free options granted by liquidity suppliers, and from asymmetric information, lead to differences in bid and ask prices and to short term price volatility. A desirable market design is one that minimizes the effect of these trading frictions. Evidence suggests that continuous markets are preferred to call markets and that a market that combines features of dealer and auction markets is superior to a pure dealer or auction market.

Markets experience economies of scale and network externalities that could lead to domination by one market, but competition is desirable because it encourages innovation and efficient market design. In recent years, a variety of new markets have challenged established markets with the result that no exchange has achieved a level of dominance that would be implied by economies of scale and network externalities. We can ascribe the competition among markets to the transparency of market price information that enables satellite markets to match prices in the primary markets, to regulatory action, and to innovations by new markets to provide trading technology or appeal to niches of the market not well served by the primary market.

Microstructure remains a fertile field for additional research. The field has focused on relatively narrow questions with little attention to its implications for broader issues such as asset pricing. How precisely and to what degree do measures of liquidity affect asset pricing? To put it another way, the relation between microstructure of financial market and the macrostructure of financial markets deserves further study.

Within the narrower confines of the microstructure sub-field, a variety of issues remain to be resolved. For example, it is not yet clear which – asymmetric information, inventory or order processing costs – are the most important factors in the bid–ask spread. Nor is it clear how these components vary across stocks or how they are affected by regulation, by market design and by stock characteristics. What is the relation between different measures of liquidity? Is the spread of a stock a good predictor of the price impact that might be caused by a trade? These and related questions should keep researchers busy for a while.

References

Admati, A.R., and P. Pfleiderer (1988), "A theory of intraday patterns: volume and price variability", Review of Financial Studies 1:3–40.

Admati, A.R., and P. Pfleiderer (1991), "Sunshine trading and financial market equilibrium", Review of Financial Studies 4(3):443–481.

Amihud, Y., and H. Mendelson (1980), "Dealership market: market making with inventory", Journal of Financial Economics 8:31–53.

Amihud, Y., and H. Mendelson (1986), "Asset pricing and the bid-ask spread", Journal of Financial Economics 17:223–249.

Amihud, Y., and H. Mendelson (1987), "Trading mechanisms and stock returns: an empirical investigation", Journal of Finance 42:533–553.

Bagehot, W. (pseudonym for Jack Treynor) (1971), "The only game in town", Financial Analysts Journal 27:31–53.

Ball, C., and T. Chordia (2001), "True spreads and equilibrium prices", Journal of Finance 56:1801–1835.

Barclay, M., W. Christie, J. Harris, E. Kandel and P. Schultz (1999), "The effects of market reform on the trading costs and depths of Nasdaq stocks", Journal of Finance 54:1–34.

Battalio, R., J. Greene and R. Jennings (1997), "Do competing specialists and preferencing dealers affect market quality?", Review of Financial Studies 10:969–993.

Benston, G., and R. Hagerman (1974), "Determinants of bid-asked spreads in the over-the-counter market", Journal of Financial Economics 1:353–364.

Benveniste, L., A. Marcus and W. Wilhelm (1992), "What's special about the specialist?", Journal of Financial Economics 32(1):61–86.

Bessembinder, H. (1994), "Bid-ask spreads in the interbank foreign exchange markets", Journal of Financial Economics 35:317–348.

Biais, B. (1993), Price formation and the equilibrium liquidity in fragmented and centralized markets, Journal of Finance 48, 157–186.

Biais, B., P. Hillion and C. Spatt (1995), "An empirical analysis of the limit order book and the order flow in the Paris Bourse", Journal of Finance 50:1655–1689.

Black, F. (1971), "Toward a fully automated exchange", Financial Analysts Journal, Part I (July/August); Part II (November/December).

Bollerslev, T., and M. Melvin (1994), "Bid-ask spreads and volatility in the foreign exchange market: an empirical study", Journal of International Economics 36:355–372.

Branch, B., and W. Freed (1977), "Bid-ask spreads on the AMEX and the Big Board", Journal of Finance 32:159–163.

Brennan, M.J., and A. Subrahmanyam (1996), "Market microstructure and asset pricing: on the compensation for illiquidity in stock returns", Journal of Financial Economics 41:441–464.

Brennan, M.J., T. Chordia and A. Subrahmanyam (1998), "Alternative factor specifications, security characteristics, and the cross-section of expected returns", Journal of Financial Economics 49:345–373.

Cao, C., E. Ghysels and F. Hatheway (2000), "Price discovery without trading: evidence from the Nasdaq pre-opening", Journal of Finance 55:1339–1365.

Chan, K., P. Chung and H. Johnson (1993), "Why options prices lag stock prices: a trading-based explanation", Journal of Finance 48:1957–1968.

Chan, L., and J. Lakonishok (1993), "Institutional trades and intraday stock price behavior", Journal of Financial Economics 33:173–199.

Choi, J.Y., D. Salandro and K. Shastri (1988), "On the estimation of bid-ask spreads: theory and evidence", Journal of Financial and Quantitative Analysis 23:219–230.

Christie, W.G., and P.H. Schultz (1994), "Why do NASDAQ market makers avoid odd-eighth quotes?", Journal of Finance 49:1813–1840.

Cohen, K., S. Maier, R. Schwartz and D. Whitcomb (1981), "Transaction costs, order placement strategy, and the existence of the bid-ask spread", Journal of Political Economy 89:287–305.

Cooper, I.A., and E. Kaplanis (1994), "What explains the home bias in portfolio investment?", Review of Financial Studies 7:45–60.

Copeland, T.C., and D. Galai (1983), "Information effects of the bid-ask spread", Journal of Finance 38:1457–1469.

Demsetz, H. (1968), "The cost of transacting", Quarterly Journal of Economics 82:33–53.

Domowitz, I. (1993), "Automating the price discovery process: some international comparisons and regulatory implications", Journal of Financial Services Research 6:305–326.

Domowitz, I., J. Glen and A. Madhavan (1998), "International cross-listing and order flow migration: evidence from an emerging market", Journal of Finance 53:2001–2027.

Easley, D., and M. O'Hara (1987), "Price, trade size, and information in securities markets", Journal of Financial Economics 19:69–90.

Easley, D., N. Kiefer, M. O'Hara and J. Paperman (1996), "Liquidity, information, and infrequently traded stocks", Journal of Finance 51:1405–1436.

Easley, D., M. O'Hara and P.S. Srinivas (1998), "Option volume and stock prices: evidence on where informed traders trade", Journal of Finance 53:431–466.

Elton, E., and C. Green (1998), "Tax and liquidity effects in pricing government bonds", Journal of Finance 53:1533–1562.

Fisher, L. (1959), "Determinants of risk premiums on corporate bonds", Journal of Political Economy 68:217–237.

Forster, M., and T. George (1992), "Anonymity in securities markets", Journal of Financial Intermediation 2:168–206.

French, K., and R. Roll (1986), "Stock return variances: the arrival of information and the reaction of traders", Journal of Financial Economics 17:5–26.

Garbade, K.D., and W.L. Silber (1979), "Structural organization of secondary markets: clearing frequency, dealer activity and liquidity risk", Journal of Finance 34(3):577–593.

Garman, M. (1976), "Market microstructure", Journal of Financial Economics 3:257–275.

George, T.J., G. Kaul and M. Nimalendran (1991), "Estimation of the bid-ask spreads and its components: a new approach", Review of Financial Studies 4:623–656.

Glosten, L.R. (1994), "Is the electronic open limit order book inevitable?", Journal of Finance 49:1127–1161.

Glosten, L.R., and L.E. Harris (1988), "Estimating the components of the bid-ask spread", Journal of Financial Economics 21:123–142.

Glosten, L.R., and P.R. Milgrom (1985), "Bid, ask and transaction prices in a specialist market with heterogeneously informed traders", Journal of Financial Economics 14:71–100.

Grant, D., and R.E. Whaley (1978), "Transaction costs on government bonds: a respecification", Journal of Business 51(1):57–64.

Hansch, O., N.Y. Naik and S. Viswanathan (1998), "Do inventories matter in dealership markets: evidence from the London Stock Exchange", Journal of Finance 53:1623–1656.

Harris, L. (1986), "A transactions data study of weekly and intradaily patterns in stock prices", Journal of Financial Economics 16:99–117.

Harris, L. (1989), "A day-end transaction price anomaly", Journal of Financial and Quantitative Analysis 24:29–45.

Harris, L. (1991), "Stock price clustering and discreteness", Review of Financial Studies 4:389–415.

Harris, L. (1994), "Minimum price variations, discrete bid-ask spreads and quotation sizes", Review of Financial Studies 7:149–178.

Hasbrouck, J. (1988), "Trades, quotes, inventories, and information", Journal of Financial Economics 22:229–252.

Hasbrouck, J. (1991), "Measuring the information content of stock trades", Journal of Finance 46:179–207.

Hausman, J., A.W. Lo and A.C. MacKinlay (1992), "An ordered probit analysis of transaction stock prices", Journal of Financial Economics 31:319–330.

Ho, T., and H.R. Stoll (1981), "Optimal dealer pricing under transactions and return uncertainty", Journal of Financial Economics 9:47–73.

Ho, T., and H.R. Stoll (1983), "The dynamics of dealer markets under competition", Journal of Finance 38:1053–1074.

Ho, T.S.Y., R.A. Schwartz and D.K. Whitcomb (1985), "The trading decision and market clearing under transaction price uncertainty", Journal of Finance 40(1):21–42.

Holthausen, R.W., R.W. Leftwich and D. Mayers (1987), "The effect of large block transactions on security prices: a cross-sectional analysis", Journal of Financial Economics 19:237–267.

Hong, G., and A. Warga (2000), "An empirical study of bond market transactions", Financial Analysts Journal 56(2):32–46.

Huang, R.D., and R. Masulis (1999), "FX spreads and dealer competition across the 24-hour trading day", Review of Financial Studies 12(1):61–93.

Huang, R.D., and H.R. Stoll (1994), "Market microstructure and stock return predictions", Review of Financial Studies 7:179–213.

Huang, R.D., and H.R. Stoll (1996), "Dealer versus auction markets: a paired comparison of execution costs on NASDAQ and the NYSE", Journal of Financial Economics 41:313–357.

Huang, R.D., and H.R. Stoll (1997), "The components of the bid-ask spread: a general approach", Review of Financial Studies 10:995–1034.

Jegadeesh, N. (1993), "Treasury auction bids and the Salomon squeeze", Journal of Finance 48(4): 1403–1419.

Kang, J.-K., and R. Stulz (1997), "Why is there a home bias? An analysis of foreign portfolio equity ownership in Japan", Journal of Financial Economics 46:3–28.

Keim, D., and A. Madhavan (1997), "Transaction costs and investment performance: an inter-exchange analysis of institutional equity trades", Journal of Financial Economics 46:265–292.

Kraus, A., and H.R. Stoll (1972a), "Parallel trading by institutional investors", Journal of Financial and Quantitative Analysis 7:2107–2138.

Kraus, A., and H.R. Stoll (1972b), "Price impacts of block trading on the New York Stock Exchange", Journal of Finance 27:569–588.

Kyle, A.S. (1985), "Continuous auctions and insider trading", Econometrica 53:1315–1335.

Lakonishok, J., A. Shleifer and R. Vishny (1992), "The impact of institutional trading on stock prices", Journal of Financial Economics 32(1):23–43.

Laux, P. (1995), "Dealer market structure, outside competition, and the bid-ask spread", Journal of Economic Dynamics and Control 19:683–710.

Lee, C.M.C. (1993), "Market integration and price execution for NYSE-listed securities", Journal of Finance 48:1009–1038.

Lee, C.M.C., and M.J. Ready (1991), "Inferring trade direction from intraday data", Journal of Finance 46:733–746.

Lee, C.M.C., M.J. Ready and P.J. Sequin (1994), "Volume, volatilty, and NYSE trading halts", Journal of Finance 49:183–214.

Lee, R. (2002), "The future of securities exchanges", in: R. Litan and R. Herring, eds., Brookings-Wharton Papers on Financial Services (Brookings Institution Press, Washington, DC) pp. 1–28.

Lin, J.-C., G. Sanger and G.G. Booth (1995), "Trade size and components of the bid-ask spread", Review of Financial Studies 8:1153–1183.

Lippman, S., and J.J. McCall (1986), "An operational measure of liquidity", The American Economic Review 76:43–55.

Lyons, R. (1995), "Test of microstructural hypotheses in the foreign exchange market", Journal of Financial Economics 39:321–351.

Madhavan, A. (1992), "Trading mechanisms in securities markets", Journal of Finance 47:607–641.

Madhavan, A. (1995), "Consolidation, fragmentation and the disclosure of trading information", The Review of Financial Studies 8:579–603.

Madhavan, A. (2000), "Market microstructure: a survey", Journal of Financial Markets 3(3):205–258.

Madhavan, A., and V. Panchapagesan (2000), "Price discovery in auction markets: a look inside the black box", Review of Financial Studies 13:627–658.

Madhavan, A., and S. Smidt (1991), "A Bayesian model of intraday specialist pricing", Journal of Financial Economics 30:99–134.

Madhavan, A., and S. Smidt (1993), "An analysis of changes in specialist inventories and quotations", Journal of Finance 48:1595–1628.

Madhavan, A., M. Richardson and M. Roomans (1997), "Why do security prices change? A transaction-level analysis of NYSE stocks", Review of Financial Studies 10:1035–1064.

Manaster, S., and S.C. Mann (1996), "Life in the pits: competitive market making and inventory control", Review of Financial Studies 9:953–975.

O'Hara, M. (1995), Market Microstructure Theory (Blackwell, Cambridge, MA).

Pagano, M., and A. Roell (1992), "Auction and dealership markets: what is the difference?", European Economic Review 36:613–623.

Ready, M. (1999), "The specialist's discretion: stopped orders and price improvement", Review of Financial Studies 12:1075–1112.

Reiss, P.C., and I.M. Werner (1998), "Does risk sharing motivate interdealer trading?", The Journal of Finance 53:1657–1703.

Roll, R. (1984), "A simple implicit measure of the effective bid-ask spread in an efficient market", Journal of Finance 39:1127–1139.

Scholes, M. (1972), "The market for securities: substitution versus price pressure and the effects of information on share price", Journal of Business 45:179–211.

Schultz, P. (2001), "Corporate bond trading costs: a peek behind the curtain", Journal of Finance 56:677–698.

Sofianos, G., and I. Werner (2000), "The trades of NYSE floor brokers", The Journal of Financial Markets 3:139–176.

Stephan, J., and R.E. Whaley (1990), "Intraday price changes and trading volume relations in the stock and stock option markets", Journal of Finance 45:191–220.

Stoll, H.R. (1978a), "The supply of dealer services in securities markets", Journal of Finance 33:1133–1151.

Stoll, H.R. (1978b), "The pricing of security dealer services: an empirical study of NASDAQ stocks", Journal of Finance 33:1153–1172.

Stoll, H.R. (1979), "Regulation of securities markets: an examination of the effects of increased competition", Monograph Series in Finance and Economics 2 (New York University, Graduate School of Business) 82 pp.

Stoll, H.R. (1989), "Inferring the components of the bid-ask spread: theory and empirical tests", Journal of Finance 44:115–134.

Stoll, H.R. (2000), "Friction", Journal of Finance 55:1479–1514.

Stoll, H.R., and R.E. Whaley (1983), "Transaction costs and the small firm effect", Journal of Financial Economics 12:57–79.

Stoll, H.R., and R.E. Whaley (1990), "Stock market structure and volatility", The Review of Financial Studies 3:37–71.

Telsar, L., and I.M. Werner (1995), "Home bias and high turnover", Journal of International Money and Finance 14:467–493.

Tinic, S.M. (1972), "The economics of liquidity services", Quarterly Journal of Economics 86:79–93.

Tinic, S.M., and R.R. West (1974), "Marketability of common stocks in Canada and the USA: a comparison of agent vs. dealer dominated markets", Journal of Finance 29:729–746.

U.S. Securities and Exchange Commission (1971), Institutional Investor Study, Report of the Securities and Exchange Commission, 92nd Congress, 1st Session, House Document No. 92-64 (March 12) (GPO, Washington, DC).

U.S. Securities and Exchange Commission (2001), Report on the comparison of order executions across equity market structures, January (GPO, Washington, DC).

Vijh, A. (1990), "Liquidity of the CBOE equity options", Journal of Finance 45:1157–1179.

Wahal, S. (1997), "Entry, exit, market makers and the bid-ask spread", Review of Financial Studies 10:871–901.

Wermers, R. (1999), "Mutual fund herding and the impact on stock prices", Journal of Finance 54(2): 581–622.

Wood, R.L., T.H. McInish and J.K. Ord (1985), "An investigation of transactions data for NYSE stocks", Journal of Finance 40:723–739.

SUBJECT INDEX

habit-formation utility   647, 648
habit-formation utility model   648
Hamilton–Jacobi–Bellman equation   678, 686
Hansen–Jagannathan bounds   768
Hansen–Jagannathan distance measure   773
Hansen–Jagannathan lower bound   910
Hansen–Jagannathan volatility bounds   875
Heath–Jarrow–Morton model   699
hedge funds   958
hedge portfolios   989
hedging demand   848
herding   123, 132, 578
Heston model   707, 709, 711
heterogeneous beliefs   1095
high-contact condition   204
high-order-contact condition   715
highly leveraged companies   226
highly leveraged transactions (HLTs)   229
historical volatility   1181
holding companies   6
holdup problem   37
home bias   977, 997–1004, 1101, 1102
   hedging against inflation risk   1002
home bias puzzle   977
hostile stakes   58
hostile takeover   16
hot hand   1067
hot-issue markets   293
house money effect   1086
household consumption growth   919
housing market   1105
hubris hypothesis   1112
hurdle rate   262

i.o.u.'s   453
Ibbotson Associates Yearbooks   894
idiosyncratic income risk   899
idiosyncratic income shocks   918, 920
idiosyncratic risk   626, 1024
illiquidity   968
imbalance   577, 579
implementation costs   1059
implicit incentives   78
implied binomial tree   1165
implied-tree model   706
implied volatility   1185, 1188
   Black–Scholes   705
   information content   1179–1181
   weighted average   1179, 1181
implied volatility function   705, 1181
Inada conditions   608, 684

incentive compensation   418
incentive-driven theory of capital structure   244
incentive plans   418
income bonds   316
income shocks   918–920, 922
incomplete contracting   119
incomplete contracts   14, 342, 383–386, 492
incomplete markets   172, 314, 329, 651, 686, 911
index funds   322
index inclusions   1063, 1064
individual investors   356
industry risk loadings   182
inefficiencies   53
infinite horizon   921
infinite horizon models   918
inflation-adjusted return   894
inflation illusion   877
information   386, 389, 421
   content of implied volatility   1179–1181
   effects on long-run asset returns   1041
   price adjustment to   1029
information asymmetries   114, 115, 135, 174, 233–235, 313, 315, 316, 339, 342, 377–386, 398, 408, 412, 422, 444–448, 563, 566, 569, 572, 584, 1023, 1029, 1030, 1043
   bank panics   509
information-based theories   1030
information costs   409
information set   353
information/signaling hypothesis   413
informational cascades   289
informational content   387
informationally efficient   126
informationally efficient markets   767
informed investors   581
informed traders   559, 566
infrequent trading issue   1168
initial inventory   565
initial public offerings (IPO)   43, 256–260, 262, 263, 272, 279–299, 355, 356, 403, 946, 959, 1064, 1181
   abnormal returns   295
   allocating and pricing   281, 284
   allocation   960
   as a marketing event   290
   auctions   284
   cycles   960
   Europe   294
   first-day returns   281

HANDBOOKS IN ECONOMICS

1. HANDBOOK OF MATHEMATICAL ECONOMICS (in 4 volumes)
   Volumes 1, 2 and 3 edited by Kenneth J. Arrow and Michael D. Intriligator
   Volume 4 edited by Werner Hildenbrand and Hugo Sonnenschein

2. HANDBOOK OF ECONOMETRICS (in 6 volumes)
   Volumes 1, 2 and 3 edited by Zvi Griliches and Michael D. Intriligator
   Volume 4 edited by Robert F. Engle and Daniel L. McFadden
   Volume 5 edited by James J. Heckman and Edward Leamer
   Volume 6 is in preparation (editors James J. Heckman and Edward Leamer)

3. HANDBOOK OF INTERNATIONAL ECONOMICS (in 3 volumes)
   Volumes 1 and 2 edited by Ronald W. Jones and Peter B. Kenen
   Volume 3 edited by Gene M. Grossman and Kenneth Rogoff

4. HANDBOOK OF PUBLIC ECONOMICS (in 4 volumes)
   Edited by Alan J. Auerbach and Martin Feldstein

5. HANDBOOK OF LABOR ECONOMICS (in 5 volumes)
   Volumes 1 and 2 edited by Orley C. Ashenfelter and Richard Layard
   Volumes 3A, 3B and 3C edited by Orley C. Ashenfelter and David Card

6. HANDBOOK OF NATURAL RESOURCE AND ENERGY ECONOMICS
   (in 3 volumes)
   Edited by Allen V. Kneese and James L. Sweeney

7. HANDBOOK OF REGIONAL AND URBAN ECONOMICS (in 4 volumes)
   Volume 1 edited by Peter Nijkamp
   Volume 2 edited by Edwin S. Mills
   Volume 3 edited by Paul C. Cheshire and Edwin S. Mills
   Volume 4 is in preparation (editors J. Vernon Henderson and Jacques-François Thisse)

FORTHCOMING TITLES

HANDBOOK OF EXPERIMENTAL ECONOMICS RESULTS
Editors Charles Plott and Vernon L. Smith

HANDBOOK ON THE ECONOMICS OF GIVING, RECIPROCITY AND ALTRUISM
Editors Serge-Christophe Kolm and Jean Mercier Ythier

HANDBOOK ON THE ECONOMICS OF ART AND CULTURE
Editors Victor Ginsburgh and David Throsby

HANDBOOK OF ECONOMIC GROWTH
Editors Philippe Aghion and Steven N. Durlauf

HANDBOOK OF LAW AND ECONOMICS
Editors A. Mitchell Polinsky and Steven Shavell

HANDBOOK OF ECONOMIC FORECASTING
Editors Graham Elliott, Clive W.J. Granger and Allan Timmermann

HANDBOOK OF THE ECONOMICS OF EDUCATION
Editors Eric Hanushek and Finis Welch

All published volumes available